TRADITION
& DIVERSITY

Kevin Reilly, Series Editor

THE ALCHEMY OF HAPPINESS
Abu Hamid Muhammad al-Ghazzali
Translated by Claud Field, revised and
annotated by Elton L. Daniel

LIFELINES FROM OUR PAST
A New World History
L. S. Stavrianos

NATIVE AMERICANS
BEFORE 1492
The Moundbuilding Centers of
the Eastern Woodlands
Lynda Norene Shaffer

GERMS, SEEDS, AND ANIMALS
Studies in Ecological History
Alfred W. Crosby

BALKAN WORLDS
The First and Last Europe
Traian Stoianovich

AN ATLAS AND SURVEY OF
SOUTH ASIAN HISTORY
Karl J. Schmidt

THE GOGO
History, Customs, and Traditions
Mathias E. Mnyampala
Translated, introduced, and edited by
Gregory H. Maddox

WOMEN IN WORLD HISTORY:
Volume 1—Readings from
Prehistory to 1500
Volume 2—Readings from 1500
to the Present
Sarah Shaver Hughes and Brady Hughes

MARITIME SOUTHEAST ASIA
TO 1500
Lynda Norene Shaffer

THE COURSE OF HUMAN
HISTORY
Economic Growth, Social Process,
and Civilization
Johan Goudsblom, Eric Jones, and Stephen
Mennell

ON WORLD HISTORY
Johann Gottfried Herder
An Anthology
Edited by Hans Adler and Ernest A. Menze
Translated by Ernest A. Menze with
Michael Palma

TEACHING WORLD HISTORY
A Resource Book
Edited by Heidi Roupp

THE WORLD AND A VERY
SMALL PLACE IN AFRICA
Donald R. Wright

DOUBLE GHOSTS
Oceanian Voyagers on
Euroamerican Ships
David A. Chappell

SHAPING WORLD HISTORY
Breakthroughs in Ecology,
Technology, Science, and Politics
Mary Kilbourne Matossian

TRADITION AND DIVERSITY
Christianity in a World Context
to 1500
Karen Louise Jolly

TRADITION & DIVERSITY

Christianity in a
World Context
to 1500

Karen Louise Jolly

M.E. Sharpe
Armonk, New York
London, England

Library of Congress Cataloging-in-Publication Data

Jolly, Karen Louise.
Tradition and diversity : Christianity in a world context to 1500
/ Karen Louise Jolly.
p.   cm. — (Sources and studies in world history)
Includes bibliographical references and index.
ISBN 1-56324-467-5 (alk. paper). — ISBN 1-56324-468-3 (pbk. : alk. paper)
1. Church history—Primitive and early church, ca. 30–600—Sources.
2. Church history—Middle Ages, 600–1500—Sources.
I. Title.   II. Series.
BR160.A2J65 1997
270—dc21   96-40287
CIP

Printed in the United States of America

The paper used in this publication meets the minimum requirements of
American National Standard for Information Sciences—
Permanence of Paper for Printed Library Materials,
ANSI Z 39.48-1984.

BM (c)   10   9   8   7   6   5   4   3   2   1
BM (p)   10   9

Contents

Abbreviations   xi

Foreword by Kevin Reilly   xiii

Introduction   3

PART 1. ORTHODOXY AND HETERODOXY:
Foundations of Christianity, circa 50–450 C.E.   13

1. Jew and Gentile: Early Origins of Christianity   15
   1.1 Jesus Was Jewish: John's Story of the Samaritan
        Woman at the Well   16
   1.2 The Gospel According to Paul: Jew and Gentile
        in Galatians   19
   1.3 Ritual Practice: The Baptism Ceremony of Hippolytus 22

2. Christian and Roman: Conflict and Assimilation   27
   2.1 Persecution: Dionysius the Wise, Patriarch of Alexandria   28
   2.2 Revelation versus Reason: Tertullian and Clement   34
   2.3 Converting the Empire: Eusebius's Account of Constantine
        and Helen   39
   2.4 Roman versus Christian: The Altar of Victory Dispute 45

3. Heterodoxy and Orthodoxy: Defining Heresy   52
   3.1 Syrian Gnosticism: *Book of Thomas the Contender*   53
   3.2 Origenism: The End of the World   58
   3.3 Arianism: Arius and the Nicene Creed   63
   3.4 Nestorians: Nestorius, Cyril, and Chalcedon   66

4. Life and Death: The Body and Resurrection   73
   4.1 Heroic Martyrdom: Perpetua   74
   4.2 Contemplative Death: Macrina   84
   4.3 Hope of Resurrection: Tomb Inscriptions   96

PART 2. PATTERNS OF ACCOMMODATION IN LATE ANTIQUITY, circa 350–750   99

5.   The Heritage of the Middle Ages   101
5.1   Creating an Authoritative Bible: Jerome   101
5.2   The Two Cities: Augustine of Hippo   105
5.3   Neoplatonic Mysticism: Pseudo-Dionysius the Areopagite   115
5.4   *The Consolation of Philosophy:* Boethius   122

6.   The Power of Christian Saints: Monks, Relics, and Icons   129
6.1   Desert Fathers and Mothers: Abba Anthony and Amma
       Syncletica   130
6.2   The Monastic Exemplar: The Life of Saint Benedict and
       The Rule of Saint Benedict   135
6.3   Relics and Pilgrimage: The Martinellus of Saint Martin
       of Tours   147
6.4   Byzantine Worship: The Debate over Iconoclasm   154

7.   Adaptations of Christianity Outside the Roman World   160
7.1   Saintly Heroes in Ethiopia: *The Book of the Saints of the
       Ethiopian Church*   161
7.2   The Conversion of Nubia: John of Ephesus on Justinian
       and Theodora's Competition   165
7.3   Heroic Martyrs in South Arabia: The Women of Najrân   171
7.4   Nestorian Christians in China: Stele   178

8.   Christian Acculturation in Western Europe   184
8.1   Celtic Christianity and Hermetic Life:
       Saint Columba's Rule   185
8.2   Frankish Christianity: Gregory of Tours on
       Clovis and Clotilda   188
8.3   Anglo-Saxon Christianity: Bede on Edwin and Ethelberga   194
8.4   Saxon Missions: Boniface and Leoba   205

PART 3. CHRISTIAN SOCIETY IN THE EARLY MIDDLE AGES, circa 600–1050   213

9.   Christian Kingship and Society   215
9.1   Theories of Authority and Power: Pope Gelasius I
       and Emperor Justinian   216
9.2   Royal Rituals and Laws: Visigothic Spain   218

9.3 Christian Emperor: Views on the Coronation
     of Charlemagne   227
9.4 Christian King: Alfred the Great   231

10. Christian Education and Theology   238
10.1 The Carolingian Renaissance: Charlemagne and Alcuin   239
10.2 Renaissance Theology: John Scottus Eriugena   243
10.3 Vernacular Learning: Alfred's Program   248

11. Christian Practice and Literature   255
11.1 Sermons: Ælfric of Eynsham   255
11.2 Liturgy: Rites for the Living and the Dead   260
11.3 Christian Poetry: *The Dream of the Rood*   263
11.4 Christian Drama: Hrotsvit of Gandersheim, *Abraham*   269

12. Christian Diversity and Accommodation   283
12.1 Conversion by Treaty: The Vikings   284
12.2 Animism and Accommodation: Charms   288
12.3 Dialogue: *The Dispute of the Church and the Synagogue*   292
12.4 Debate: Patriarch Timothy and Caliph Mahdi   294

PART 4. THE SPIRIT OF ORDER AND PROPHECY,
circa 1050–1200   303

13. Corporate and Individual Reform   305
13.1 The Contest: Gregory VII and Henry IV   307
13.2 Alternatives: Paschal II and Henry V   314
13.3 Holy Places: The Pilgrim's Guide to
     Santiago de Compostela   317
13.4 Holy Women: The Beguine Marie d'Oignies   321

14. Christians, Muslims, and Jews: Views of the Crusades   333
14.1 The European View of the Crusades: Pope Urban II's
     Call to the First Crusade   334
14.2 The Jewish View of the Crusades: Solomon bar Simson
     and Sefer Zekhirah   337
14.3 The Islamic View of the Crusades: Usama ibn Munqidh   346
14.4 Encounter with a Nubian: Robert of Clari on
     the Fourth Crusade   348

15. Ways of Knowing: Faith and Reason   350
15.1 Faith and Reason: Anselm   351
15.2 Dialectics: Abelard   355

15.3 Aristotelianism: Averröes   357
15.4 God and Philosophy: Moses Maimonides   363

16. Individual Diversity: Bernard of Clairvaux and Hildegard of Bingen   **369**
16.1 Hildegard on the Church: To Priests and Popes   370
16.2 Bernard and the Crusades: On Christian Knighthood   372
16.3 Hildegard's Physiology: *Causae et Curae*   373
16.4 Bernard's Way of Knowing: On the Song of Songs   375
16.5 Hildegard's Lyrics: Eucharius   382

PART 5. NEW PATHS OF ORDER AND PROPHECY, circa 1200–1300   **385**

17. Orthodox Reform: Popes, Mendicants, and Scholars   **387**
17.1 Papal Monarchy: Innocent III and the Fourth Lateran Council   388
17.2 Franciscan Spirituality: Francis and Clare   395
17.3 Mendicant Scholarship: Bonaventure   400
17.4 Intellectual Synthesis: Thomas Aquinas   405

18. Over the Line: Heretics, Inquisitors, and Other Radicals   **412**
18.1 Heresy and Inquisition: Waldensians and Albigensians   413
18.2 Spiritual Franciscans: Na Prous Boneta   417
18.3 Political Challenges: Marsilius of Padua   424

19. Popular Religion: Story and Poetry   **430**
19.1 Preacher's Tales: Caesarius of Heisterbach, Jacques de Vitry, Etienne de Bourbon   430
19.2 Monastic Simplicity: "Our Lady's Tumbler"   436
19.3 Popular Saints: The Golden Legend of Thomas Becket   445
19.4 Great Hymns of the Faith: *Veni Sancte Spiritus*   454

20. Cross-Cultural Exchange: Missions and Dialogue   **457**
20.1 Missions to the Mongols: John of Plano-Carpini   457
20.2 Buddhist-Christian Debate: William of Ruysbruck   461
20.3 Missions to India and China: John of Monte Corvino   464
20.4 Dialogue: Ibn Kammûna   468

PART 6. CHANGE AND CONTACT IN THE LATE MIDDLE AGES, circa 1300–1500   475

21. **Dissent and Reform in Late Medieval Christendom**   477
   21.1 Views of the Papacy: Dante and Petrarch   477
   21.2 Papal Schism: The Conciliar Movement   483
   21.3 A Lollard View of the Eucharist: Wickliff's Wicket   487

22. **Diversity in Christianity: Late Medieval Spirituality**   491
   22.1 Contemplative Practice: John of Ruysbroeck   491
   22.2 Anchoress: Julian of Norwich   498
   22.3 Comforting the Condemned: Catherine of Siena   501
   22.4 Divine Wisdom: Saint Gregory Palamas of Byzantium   505

23. **Religious Expression: Ritual, Drama, and Story**   510
   23.1 Ritual: The Seven Sacraments Explained by
        Pope Eugene IV   510
   23.2 Drama: The Chester Cycle, The Last Judgement   515
   23.3 Story: Great John in Russia   526

24. **Cross-Cultural Contact**   531
   24.1 The Black Death and Jews: Jean de Venette
        and Jacob von Königshofen   531
   24.2 Meeting Other Christians: Travels of Quirini in Norway   538
   24.3 The Imagined World: Mandeville's Travels, on
        Prester John   543
   24.4 Classifying the Other: Columbus's Journal   549

Recommended Readings   555

Index   561

Abbreviations

B.C.E.   Before the Common Era.

C.E.   Common Era. Numbers for years match the traditional B.C. and A.D. system.

ANF   *The Ante-Nicene Fathers. Translations of the Writings of the Fathers Down to A.D. 325*, eds. Alexander Roberts and James Donaldson (Buffalo: The Christian Literature Publishing Co.), 1867–87).

Henderson   *Select Historical Documents of the Middle Ages,* ed. Ernest F. Henderson (London: George Bell & Sons, 1896).

NPNF   *A Select Library of Nicene and Post-Nicene Fathers of the Christian Church,* First and Second Series, eds. Philip Schaff and Henry Wace (New York: Christian Literature Company, 1886–99; reprint, Grand Rapids, MI: Wm. B. Eerdmans, 1952–63).

Ogg   *A Source Book of Mediæval History*, ed. Frederic Austin Ogg (New York: American Book Co., 1907).

Robinson   *Readings in European History,* ed. James Harvey Robinson, Vol. 1 (Boston: Ginn and Co., 1904).

Thatcher   *A Source Book for Mediaeval History,* eds. Oliver J. Thatcher and Edgar H. McNeal, (New York: Charles Schribner's Sons, 1907).

TROS   *Translations and Reprints from the Original Sources of European History,* ed. D. C. Munro (Philadelphia: University of Pennsylvania History Dept, 188–; New York: Longmans, 1900).

Foreword

This, the fifteenth title in the series "Sources and Studies in World History," is the first to present essentially European sources. While the study of world history has roots in Christian universalism, it developed in American colleges and universities in recent decades with an almost adolescent suspicion of parental "Western Civilization." This had some justification; it was necessary to develop sources for non-Western history and to insist that world history was not European history. Today, however, the study of world history is mature enough to reclaim Europe, even European Christianity.

Karen Jolly is the ideal person to make that reclamation for this series. As a teacher of world history, as well as Christianity, she brings a global perspective to the history of European Christianity.

This is global history in two senses. First, it is universal in its sweep of European sources: rural and pagan as well as urbane and ordained, heretical and heterodox as well as the official and orthodox. Even within Western Europe we hear the voices of women, Jews, dissidents, and dispossessed as well as the powerful and authoritative. This documentation of all walks of life extends not only throughout Western Europe but includes Byzantine, Nestorian, and Coptic Christians as well.

Even more important, however, is Karen Jolly's ability to place European Christianity in the larger context of world history. She follows the trail of Christians beyond Europe and also admits us to the company of non-Christians, in and outside of Europe, who have firsthand knowledge of Christians and Christianity, and she does this throughout. Part One explores the roots of Christianity in Jewish, Persian, Syrian, Egyptian, Greek, and Roman ideas. Part Two deals with the accommodations of Christian traditions to the cultures of Ethiopia, Nubia, Arabia, and China—as well as pagan Europe. Part Three and Four include Christian dialogues with Jews and with Muslims. Part Five takes us on missions to the Mongols, India, and China. And Part Six concludes with late medieval Christian encounters with new worlds—as imagined and experienced by Mandeville and Columbus.

As her title indicates, Karen Jolly does not ignore tradition, but the special strengths of this collection lie in its rich vein of unusual and unexpected documents. Some of the pieces gathered here will be new to teachers of Christianity, but all of them have been selected with an eye to the student and general reader. Such compelling narratives and vivid personal testaments as these are general affirmations of the power of primary sources as windows on the past. In particular, this collection will vastly expand our understanding of medieval Christianity and help return it to its proper place in world history.

Kevin Reilly

TRADITION & DIVERSITY

Introduction

Imagine that the history of European Christianity is a long tapestry, wider in some places, narrower in others, ragged and unraveling at the edges. This cloth is woven of rich and variegated threads. Amid the riot of colors—some appearing only briefly or for a length, then disappearing off the fringe—certain colors predominate and weave throughout most of the length of the tapestry. Christianity has a long and varied history, consisting of many diverse practices and beliefs, but with a few, core, consistent ideas that travel its length.

This text contains primary sources representing both continuity and change, the traditional and the diverse, in the development of medieval Christianity in Europe. The traditional documents reflect the older historical approach to history and Christianity: the formal pronouncements of the church, the historical accounts by the voices that dominate the surviving records, the cataclysmic events of wars or controversies, the great intellectual achievements of scholars. Many of these documents are about or by famous men, rather than women or ordinary lay people. Significant as these individuals are, a history based on these dominant sources tends to give a false picture of church history as a straight march of progress and development with the winners, the orthodox, inevitably casting aside the inferior views as ignorant or heretical. The other documents in this text provide a broader, heterodox context for these traditional views, in two ways. First, some documents represent diversity within European societies—the writings of the not-so-famous, of women, of people who were not in positions of power, as well as the voices of those who opposed the church or lived outside of it, such as the Jewish populations of Europe. Second, other documents provide diversity by putting Europe in a broader geographical context. These sources reveal Christianity as it developed outside Europe, responses to Christianity from other religions, and cross-cultural interactions between these different religions and societies.

3

What Is Christianity?

Defining Christianity depends on whom you ask, when, and where. Someone in 390 discussing conversion to Christianity might use different terminology and concepts to explain the experience from someone in 1853. A Christian in 1275 might express devotion to Christ by going on a pilgrimage to a saint's shrine, while one in 1972 might go to a Jesus rally. While a thirteenth-century Jewish author argues that Christianity is not truly monotheistic, a contemporary Chinese Buddhist argues that Christianity's monotheism provides a poor explanation for the existence of evil. All of these individuals are discussing the same religion, but the ways in which they express their notions about Christianity reflect their own historical conditions and cultures.

Likewise, the study of Christianity takes different forms. A theological approach might define the religion according to its doctrines and their development. A sociological approach might examine the group behaviors of those who call themselves followers of this religion. A psychological study, on the other hand, might be interested in the emotional experience of the individual in the religion. All of these may be illuminating in different ways.

This book takes a historical approach to the study of Christianity. It looks at Christianity as a historic religion, not as a personal belief system. The purpose of history, according to the philosopher of history R. G. Collingwood, is human self-knowledge through the study of the past. E. H. Carr spoke of history as a dialogue with the past. This text seeks to understand what Christianity is by studying its past and allowing the people of the past to speak for themselves about their perceptions of this religion. The task of the reader-historian is to listen to these voices, try to understand their perspectives, and analyze what they say about Christianity as a living religion over time.

Some Historical Approaches to Christianity

Even within this historical framework, a variety of approaches to the past offer different perspectives. Some approaches focus on the development of the formal church, with its hierarchy of priests, bishops, and popes; others trace the development of Christian ideas by examining the great thinkers, such as Augustine of Hippo and Thomas Aquinas. More recently, cultural historians have complemented these approaches by studying popular religion, the everyday experience of Christianity in ritual and story. This readings book endeavors to present both the formal church and the popular experience. It uses three historical models to do so: the context of world history and cross-cultural studies; the theme of tradition and diversity; and the paradigm of the spirit of order and the spirit of prophecy.

World history is a relatively recent development in the study and teaching of history. Those colleges or schools that offer world history as a basic course usually do so as a substitute for a western civilization survey, in part because they believe students need an understanding of other cultures in an increasingly global environment. The academic study of world history has its own theoretical bases—it is not just studying the world instead of studying Europe or the United States. Rather, world historians choose to study phenomena that cross national, geographic, or linguistic boundaries. In particular, world historians often focus on cross-cultural interaction as a way of understanding historical development. This book draws on world historical ideas about cross-cultural interaction in conjunction with studying the internal development of European Christianity. Consequently, some documents, seemingly the more traditional, reflect European Christian concerns exclusively; however, other documents demonstrate the impact of contact with non-Europeans and non-Christians on this European development.

Because of this dual European and world focus, the theme of tradition and diversity pervades the text. *Tradition* and *diversity* are used with multiple meanings. Tradition reflects the old, and still valuable, approach to the history of Christianity that focuses on the writing of influential individuals (popes, scholars, historians) and the record of great events (conciliar decisions, wars, spectacular conversions); these selections are diversified by including the writings of more ordinary individuals and their more mundane experiences of the religion, whether in vernacular stories, common rituals, or popular dramas. On another level, tradition reflects the dominant orthodoxy of the church, the side that "wins" in the battles against heresy, the voices that dominate the written record; other documents, however, indicate the diversity of voices, some competing with the "official" view and in the process helping shape orthodoxy. Hence, some sections of this text examine acculturation and accommodation as strategies for the survival of Christianity. Tradition also has a geographic focus in its tendency to give greater weight to European views, and northwestern European views in particular (England, France, Germany, and Italy also), while treating other regions as peripheral (Scandinavia, Eastern Europe, the Iberian Peninsula). Some documents in this text were purposely chosen to provide some geographic diversity, both from perspectives outside of Europe proper, and within. Many of these areas—Scandinavia, Iberia, the Eastern Roman Empire, Russia, Ethiopia, and Egypt—deserve separate study outside of a European view, as do of course the Islamic, Chinese, Indian, African, and American peoples with whom Europeans interact. This text uses the cross-cultural aspect of world history to include both a European focus and an awareness of outside forces.

A third theme that appears, particularly in Parts Four and Five, is one drawn from Jeffrey Burton Russell's text *A History of Medieval Christianity: Prophecy and Order*. The subtitle provides a useful paradigm for understanding the creative tension in medieval Christianity. The spirit of order, reflected heavily in the "traditional" documents, seeks to organize the religion and provide continuity through external means—by rituals, laws, customs, and practices shared among all Christians as established by those in authority. The spirit of prophecy, the experiential side of the religion, seeks to provide internal reform and rejuvenation to individual believers, evident in mystics, visionaries, ascetics, and even heretics who challenge the church's authority. Both the spirit of prophecy and the spirit of order want to keep the essential "truth" of Christianity alive, but through different means. Sometimes they work in harmony, each recognizing the value of the other; sometimes they conflict. Medieval Christianity survived and succeeded because of the delicate balancing of these forces, evident in the documents in this text.

Coming to Grips with Medieval Worldviews: Universe A and Universe B

A worldview is the way an individual or a group of people perceive their relationship with the world, each other, and the supernatural or divine. That is, all human beings have a way of understanding their relationship with the physical world or the environment, create systems of categorizing their relationships with other people in the social and political realm, and have some beliefs about the nonphysical world or the spiritual, even if it is to believe in no deities or spiritual agencies at all. These attitudes and beliefs constitute a worldview that may be shared by a larger group of individuals belonging to a culture or religion. Very often, their unconscious behaviors, as well as their conscious actions, reflect these assumptions about the nature of the world, society, and the spiritual dimension.

Worldviews operate under different *modes of rationality*. These different ways of reasoning are all equally consistent within themselves—that is, if you accept their premises. The two different worldviews and modes of rationality that most frequently conflict in modern discussions of medieval Christianity can be designated "Universe A" and "Universe B."[*] The potential for miracles is used as the example to illustrate these two different worldviews.

---

[*]Credit belongs to Dr. Jeffrey Burton Russell of the University of California at Santa Barbara for creating these categories of Universe A and Universe B.

In Universe A, miracles can and do occur. God is active in the world and can intervene to cause something "unnatural" or unusual. Consequently, proof of a miracle is not whether it is possible for it to have happened, but whether or not in a specific instance it did happen. The method in this universe is to demonstrate the consistency of the event with known moral truths (the character of God, Scripture).

In Universe B, miracles cannot happen since the world is governed solely by natural laws and God (if he exists, which cannot be proven) does not intervene to contradict those laws. Consequently, no amount of proof can be mustered to prove a miracle. The method in this universe is that the more unusual something is, the more evidence is needed to prove it, reaching a zero point with miracles (since they are by definition unusual to the point of unique breaches of natural law).

Both universes make certain assumptions about reality that cannot be proved outside of their own system of rationality, thus both develop a logical method of reasoning based on these assumptions. Historians for the most part are not interested in proving the validity of either one. However, the historical study of Christianity does explore the ramifications of Universe A, even though most modern historians operate in Universe B. Negotiating this difference is not easy.

Someone who lives in Universe A and believes in divine intervention in history may struggle with the discipline of history as practiced today because it is a product of Universe B and uses a humanist, secular, and materialist mode of analysis. Someone who lives in Universe B, whose reasoning is based on modern principles of logic, may have trouble making sense of Universe A, common throughout the medieval period.

Some of the documents in this text may seem, from one person's point of view, particularly wrong about the nature of reality or about Christianity; others may seem to represent what another reader thinks is best about the religion. Keep in mind, however, the diversity of views in any given period, and the differences in historical conditions and cultural factors between the modern reader and the medieval subjects reflected in the texts.

This book seeks neither to prove nor to disprove the viability of Christianity as a belief system. Nor does the modern historian have the means to "judge" whether any particular individual or society covered here is "really" Christian or not by some modern notion of what is Christian. Rather, the sources from the past offer the standards of the time—the internal mechanisms they used to determine what they thought was scriptural, true, of God. Readers are encouraged to examine their own perspectives, and then endeavor to get inside the perspective of the person of the time to see his or her point of view. This process is at the heart of the study of history, whose purpose is, after all, human self-knowledge. The pedagogical suggestions below offer some ways of working through this critical thinking process.

Organization

The organization of the text is chronological in the six main parts, with topical chapters within each part. Each chapter has three or four documents exploring an issue, such as popular religion or cross-cultural interactions. Introductions to each part, chapter, and document give some context for the selections and offer some issues and questions to consider. However, this text was designed to be used with a textbook that can give fuller and deeper treatment of these developments and issues. Similarly, this text is limited by size; by no means do these selections represent the breadth of medieval authors and documents available. Rather, the selections here have been chosen to represent specific themes and to create a balance of documents, both traditional and diverse, that offer different points of view on specific subjects.

The Table of Contents lists all of the documents, numbered consecutively by chapter, 1.1, 1.2 . . . 2.1, 2.2, and so on. Each selection therefore has its own unique number that also indicates the chapter to which it belongs. In addition, the index lists documents by topics (e.g., conversion, popular religion, saints). Students may wish to compare selections by theme, or instructors may assign writing assignments based on these issues.

Student Guidelines

Primary sources differ from secondary sources, and this difference affects the reading experience. Primary sources were written by people in the past who were not addressing a modern student sitting in a classroom, but some other audience and for some other purpose. Secondary sources, particularly textbooks, are written by modern historians with the modern student in mind, and they seek to present a predigested view of the past, analyzing the evidence for you. Consulting a textbook in conjunction with this readings book is highly recommended as a way of providing the necessary context and background for the documents included here. The brief introductions in this text give the immediate context and suggest some of the wider issues, but inevitably students find the primary sources baffling simply because they are alien, from a different time and place, written for someone else. Compounding this difficulty is that the documents are excerpts and they are translated from a variety of languages, so something is lost in the process. What follows, then, are some reading guidelines for overcoming these limitations.

First, understand the context. Read the background material in your text-book, read the introductions included here, and even skim through the entire chapter or part to get an idea of the whole picture.

Second, read with a purpose. A student who randomly picks up a primary source on some subject without any preparation will not know what things to notice and which things can safely be ignored. To read intelligently, have a question or two in mind, some things that you want to look for. Some questions are offered for the reader's use before each selection, or students can make up their own based on the subheadings ("What does this document tell me about popular religion?") or the instructor's assignment ("Why are we reading this selection for this subject today?").

Third, test reading comprehension by stopping after each document and writing down an answer to the question(s). This is also a good time to go back and mark or make note of particular quotes that are relevant (rather than highlighting everything interesting while reading). While thinking about the document, start analyzing how it compares or relates to other documents, what its significance is for understanding the period, and what it reveals about the history of Christianity.

Instructor Guidelines

This readings book combines a variety of primary sources, both the standard ones on European church history and some newer, more obscure, and less accessible ones. The aim of this scheme is to allow instructors to provide a variety of reading experiences for their students. The brief introductions prefacing each part, chapter, and document are designed to address the specific events, people, and issues selected in the documents; however, they are meant to be used in conjunction with a textbook. The use of a single reader and one base textbook allows the instructor the freedom to order some more specialized secondary texts on topics of interest, as well as a few well-chosen primary sources to read whole.

The six parts of this text are relatively equal and work well in a six-week summer course, while the twenty-five chapters roughly equal the teaching days of a standard sixteen-week semester. Each of these chapters consists of three or four document excerpts highlighting a theme, and can be assigned for a single class day of discussion. Part One (Chapters 1–4) on the early foundations of Christianity, and Part Six (Chapters 21–24) on the late medieval developments, can be omitted to suit a shorter term or to fit into a sequence of courses on the history of Christianity.

Student writing assignments can be handled in a number of ways. Thought papers can ask students to reflect on one part of the book, or on a theme that runs through several parts, as indicated in the index. An alternative is to allow students to pick one excerpted source and read the whole book (e.g., Augustine's *Confessions* or Bede's *Ecclesiastical History*). Research assignments can use any of these strategies, either a chronological focus, a thematic subject, or in-depth study of an individual document.

Generating and sustaining class discussion of primary sources in a historical context is notoriously difficult, particularly with a religious topic to which students may have a wide variety of personal responses. Following is a three-step process that helps foster critical thinking and historical analysis by getting students to address their own reactions to the readings and then use those reactions to come to an understanding of different perspectives. The three steps are personal response, point of view, and historical analysis.

The personal response allows students to get whatever their gut-level reaction is out on paper and deal with it. Ask students to keep a reading journal and to bring these responses to class. This forms the basis of class discussion: "What did you think of this text, and, most important, why?"

The second level asks students to step outside themselves and consider the point of view of the document or the people at the time who may have read it or experienced the events. This requires some knowledge of the context of the document and events, which can be supplied through textbook reading or lecture. Both in-class writing exercises and small-group discussion are excellent ways for students to experiment with other points of view, even those of their fellow students.

The third step, historical analysis, is the goal of most instructors in the courses they teach. The ability to read a document, understand its context, and explain why it is meaningful does not come instantaneously, but is the product of a variety of learning experiences—reading textbooks and primary sources, listening to lectures, discussing issues with other students. Usually this analytical ability is measured in graded essay exams and take-home papers. The critical thinking skills necessary for writing this kind of analysis can, however, be built up through the first two stages: the writing of personal responses and the discussion of different points of view. Students benefit from seeing their thinking progress through stages and receiving feedback along the way. These three stages can be incorporated into a series of writing and discussion exercises that move them from "I believe" through "They thought" to "I think they thought . . . because . . . ."

The introductions in this text offer some issues and contexts to consider in designing these assignments, and the questions at the head of each document selection give some possible ways of thinking about these sources. On the other hand, the documents or sections can easily be reorganized to suit other course syllabi or thematic issues.

Credits

Choosing, locating, photocopying, scanning, organizing, editing, and sometimes translating primary source documents covering this broad a chronological field is a monumental task. Several individuals and agencies deserve thanks for assisting me in this process. Graduate assistants Julie Clement and Tim Sullivan worked on either end of the project—Julie locating, photocopying, scanning, and editing; Tim proofreading, editing, and advising on selection. At the University of Hawai'i at Mānoa, the Center for Instructional Support generously provided summer funds to hire an assistant, the College of Arts and Humanities provided access to a scanner and OCR software, and the Hamilton Library Interlibrary Loan Department acquired more books than I care to count and thoughtfully extended loan periods without complaint. My thanks also to Paul Hallsall and members of the medieval Internet community who are actively incorporating public domain material into websites for common use, and to members of the Medieval History, Anglo-Saxon, and Medieval Religion discussion lists who answered my queries and pointed me in new directions. And as evident from references in the text, I owe deep thanks to my mentor Jeffrey Burton Russell of the University of California at Santa Barbara.

The resulting text is different from what I originally planned, owing to the constraints of length, obscure languages, out-of-date or incomprehensible translations, and most of all, copyright issues.* Nonetheless, the text adheres to its original purpose of providing a variety of texts on medieval European Christianity from diverse perspectives. Any suggestions, or corrections to the inevitable errors (all my own), are welcome.

---

*In some cases, archaic texts and translations have been modernized.

Part 1
Orthodoxy and Heterodoxy
Foundations of Christianity, circa 50–450 C.E.

The roots of Christian traditions are diverse and complex. Exploring how the religion arose and the forces that influenced. it involves the study of Jewish, Persian, Egyptian, Greek, and Roman ideas, among others. This chapter organizes these diverse forces into two categories, both aspects of Christianity's early origins that establish an important duality in succeeding ages: orthodoxy and heterodoxy, or tradition and diversity. Orthodoxy means the "right teachings" as established by some official group with the authority to decide the true doctrines. The need for an orthodoxy arose over the first five centuries in response to heterodoxy, the condition in which many diverse opinions coexisted and competed. The formation of orthodox opinions involved not only establishing the "truth" but declaring opposing views "heresy." Thus the mainstream traditions of later ages, western Catholicism in Europe and eastern Orthodoxy in Byzantium, were the products of the formation of orthodoxy in the Roman world; both represent a common tradition of Greek- and Roman-influenced Christianity embodied in the canon of New Testament documents, in carefully formulated doctrine, and in codified ritual practices. But this orthodoxy emerged from a dynamic and multicultural environment in which many different versions of Christianity flourished (Gnostic, Arian, and Nestorian, for example) and some established their own churches in regions that were, or became, independent of the Roman domain (Syria, Persia, Egypt, Ethiopia, China, and Europe, the primary focus of this book).

The four chapters of this part follow the development of this orthodoxy amid diversity. The first chapter, "Jew and Gentile," explores the foundation of Christian belief and practice as found in the New Testament documents and early ritual practice; these documents reveal the Jewish and Roman roots of early Christianity as it moved from being a Jewish sect to a world-converting religion. The second chapter examines the issue of conflict between "Christian and Roman" within the empire, with the conversion of the emperor as a turning point for the establishment of orthodoxy. The third chapter, "Heterodoxy and Orthodoxy," explores the formation of heresy by examining several of the alternative interpretations of Christian ideas put forward by Gnostics, Origenists, Arians, and Nestorians. The fourth chapter brings together these themes by exploring one important issue in Christian thought, attitudes toward "life and death."

–1–

Jew and Gentile
Early Origins of Christianity

Christianity arose in the first century C.E. as a Jewish sect in Roman-controlled Palestine, and these two conditions form the predominant elements in the development of early Christianity. These Jewish and Greco-Roman elements are visible in the documents (the New Testament canon) and rituals (baptism, Eucharist) that constitute the basis of orthodox doctrine and practice in the Christianity of the Roman Empire by the end of the fourth century C.E.

The canon of the twenty-seven books found today in the New Testament became the established collection of books orthodox churchmen believed to be "Scripture" or divinely inspired texts by the late fourth century, although earlier lists and collections indicate consensus on most of the books. The formation of the canon of the New Testament and the development of orthodox doctrines proceeded together: doctrines evolved out of these texts (and others), and texts were chosen as Scripture based on their conformity to doctrines. The struggle to define right ideas and texts amid the plethora of documents and interpretations was part of the larger issue of authority within the church, and the development of a hierarchy and a tradition for handing down this authority.

Given the politically charged atmosphere in which these documents evolved after the events they describe, modern scholars debate the authenticity and reliability of the New Testament books as historical sources for the life of Christ and his early disciples. Nonetheless, at the very least these texts represent the ideas and views of a dominant group of Christians in the first few centuries of the religion's development. Christian theologians formulated orthodox doctrines based upon learned interpretations of these New Testament Scriptures (in Greek and later in Latin), and their Jewish predecessors, the Hebrew Bible or Old Testament Scriptures (in Hebrew, and also in Greek, later Latin). The New Testament includes two important categories of writings, the Gos-

15

pels and the Pauline epistles. (The New Testament also includes the historical account of the Acts of Apostles, letters by other authors, and the Revelation of John.) The Four Gospels ("Good News"), credited to Matthew, Mark, Luke, and John, are accounts of the life of Jesus written in the first century C.E. These books illuminate the Jewish ideas associated with Jesus and his immediate followers. Paul, the Jewish-Christian leader who took Christianity to the Gentiles or non-Jews, wrote letters to various churches and individuals explaining Christianity's message and ethics. These letters reveal much about the Romanization of Christianity and the Greek influence on the development of Christian theology. The selections below illustrate these two major areas: the Jewishness of Jesus, and the Romanizing theology of Paul.

At the same time that these books were copied and disseminated within the Roman Empire as sources for Christian belief, the Christian communities also developed ritual practices to express their faith. Rituals were symbolic ways of acting out truths shared by the body of believers as they gathered together; having consistent rituals not only endorsed orthodoxy but ensured continuity and fostered a sense of collegiality or belonging. The third document gives an example of one practice, baptism, the initiation ritual into the religion.

1.1 Jesus Was Jewish:
John's Story of the Samaritan Woman at the Well

According to the Gospel accounts, Jesus was born to a young Jewish woman under humble and yet miraculous circumstances (probably between 6 and 4 B.C.E.); he died some thirty-three years later, under humiliating and tragic circumstances, followed by a miraculous resurrection from the dead. The portrait of Jesus that emerges from these four Gospel accounts, written by followers of Jesus after the events, contains a duality essential to later theology: he was both divine and human, full of power and yet humble, perfectly sinless and yet full of humanity. In the brief time, three or four years, between the beginning of his ministry and his death, Jesus was an itinerant teacher and miracle-worker who gathered around him a group of twelve disciples, as well as a larger group of followers. The teachings of Jesus recorded by the Gospel writers emphasized this same mixture of power from God and humble sympathy for the human condition; similarly, the miracles of healing recorded by the Gospel writers established the power he had from God and the compassion he felt for the weak.

The story of Jesus's encounter with the Samaritan woman excerpted here from John's Gospel, composed circa 90–100 C.E., also displays this mixture of divine power and humble compassion for human frailty. In this story, Jesus and his disciples have crossed into Samaria, a central region of Palestine inhabited after circa 400 B.C.E. by a separate group of Jews who had their own edition of the Scriptures and, for a time, their own temple (destroyed 128 B.C.E.). The person Jesus meets at the well is not only one of these excluded Samaritans and a woman, with whom Jesus as an orthodox man should not be associating, but is also a woman of questionable lifestyle by the moral standards of the day. What does one who claims to be the Messiah (the anticipated savior in Jewish tradition) say to a woman who represents in this society the lowest rungs of humanity?

Questions

1. In what ways is Jesus portrayed as both human and a man of divine power?

2. How does the writer show Jesus crossing social and religious boundaries?

3. According to the author John, what does this Messiah offer to the woman and others like her?

The New Testament, The Gospel According to John

The Pharisees heard that Jesus was gaining and baptizing more disciples than John, although in fact it was not Jesus who baptized, but his disciples. When the Lord learned of this, he left Judea and went back once more to Galilee.

Now he had to go through Samaria. So he came to a town in Samaria called Sychar, near the plot of ground Jacob had given to his son Joseph. Jacob's well was there, and Jesus, tired as he was from the journey, sat down by the well. It was about the sixth hour.

When a Samaritan woman came to draw water, Jesus said to her, "Will you give me a drink?" (His disciples had gone into the town to buy food.)

The Samaritan woman said to him, "You are a Jew and I am a Samaritan woman. How can you ask me for a drink?" (For Jews do not associate with Samaritans.)

Jesus answered her, "If you knew the gift of God and who it is that asks you for a drink, you would have asked him and he would have given you living water."

"Sir," the woman said, "you have nothing to draw with and the well is deep. Where can you get this living water? Are you greater than our father Jacob, who gave us the well and drank from it himself, as did also his sons and his flocks and herds?"

Jesus answered, "Everyone who drinks this water will be thirsty again, but whoever drinks the water I give him will never thirst. Indeed, the water I give him will become in him a spring of water welling up to everlasting life."

The woman said to him, "Sir, give me this water so that I won't get thirsty and have to keep coming here to draw water."

He told her, "Go, call your husband and come back."

"I have no husband," she replied.

Jesus said to her, "You are right when you say you have no husband. The fact is, you have had five husbands, and the man you now have is not your husband. What you have just said is quite true."

"Sir," the woman said, "I can see that you are a prophet. Our fathers worshiped on this mountain, but you Jews claim that the place where we must worship is in Jerusalem."

Jesus declared, "Believe me, woman, a time is coming when you will worship the Father neither on this mountain nor in Jerusalem. You Samaritans worship what you do not know; we worship what we do know, for salvation is from the Jews. Yet a time is coming and has now come when the true worshipers will worship the Father in spirit and truth, for they are the kind of worshipers the Father seeks. God is spirit, and his worshipers must worship in spirit and in truth."

The woman said, "I know that Messiah" (called Christ) "is coming. When he comes, he will explain everything to us."

Then Jesus declared, "I who speak to you am he."

Just then his disciples returned and were surprised to find him talking with a woman. But no one asked, "What do you want?" or "Why are you talking with her?"

Then, leaving her water jar, the woman went back to the town and said to the people, "Come, see a man who told me everything I ever did. Could this be the Christ?" They came out of the town and made their way toward him. . . .

Many of the Samaritans from that town believed in him because of the woman's testimony, "He told me everything I ever did." So when the Samaritans came to him, they urged him to stay with them, and he stayed two days. And because of his words many more became believers.

They said to the woman, "We no longer believe just because of what you said; now we have heard for ourselves, and we know that this man really is the Savior of the world."

John 4:1–30, 39–42. Scripture taken from the HOLY BIBLE, NEW INTERNATIONAL VERSION ®. NIV ®. Copyright © 1973, 1978, 1984 by International Bible Society. Used by permission of Zondervan Publishing House. All rights reserved.

1.2 The Gospel According to Paul: Jew and Gentile in Galatians

According to the account in the New Testament Book of the Acts of the Apostles and his own account in some of his letters, the apostle Paul was an early and zealous persecutor of Christians, who converted to Christianity after the death of Jesus through a miraculous vision. He subsequently became a major leader in the nascent church as a missionary to the Gentiles and as the author of many letters incorporated into the New Testament of the Bible. Thus Paul, in many ways the founder of the religion of Christianity, stands as an anomaly among the early leaders: he did not know Jesus during Jesus's lifetime, but nonetheless he became the major spokesman of ideas that formed the basis of later orthodoxy.

Paul was both a highly educated Jew and a Roman citizen—deeply committed to the Jewish traditions and laws but also a member of the cosmopolitan environment created by Rome, in which many were seeking personal salvation. Consequently, it was Paul who bridged the gap between the Jewish basis of Christianity and the Greco-Roman world by offering conversion to Gentiles free of Jewish restraints, despite considerable opposition from other Jewish-Christian leaders. In Paul's hands, Christianity began to change from a Jewish sect into a world religion. The process by which Paul shaped Jewish-Christian ideas into a meaningful message understandable by non-Jews is exhibited in the following selections from his letter to the believers in Galatia (a province in Asia Minor), written around the middle of the first century. Paul establishes in it a liberating Christian doctrine for Gentiles, as opposed to "Judaizers" who would have the Gentiles become Jews (be circumcised) before converting to Christianity.

Questions

1. How does Paul present himself and his relationships with other leaders in the early church?
2. In Paul's theology, what new message does Christ offer to both Jew and Gentile?
3. What does "freedom" mean for Paul in the context of the constraints of Jewish law and the confines of earthly existence under Roman rule?

The New Testament, Paul's Letter to the Galatians

Fourteen years later I went up again to Jerusalem, this time with Barnabas. I took Titus along also. I went in response to a revelation and set before them the gospel that I preach among the Gentiles. But I did this privately to those who seemed to be leaders, for fear that I was running or had run my race in vain. Yet not even Titus, who was with me, was compelled to be circumcised, even though he was a Greek. This matter arose because some false brothers had infiltrated our ranks to spy on the freedom we have in Christ Jesus and to make us slaves. We did not give in to them for a moment, so that the truth of the gospel might remain with you.

As for those who seemed to be important—whatever they were makes no difference to me; God does not judge by external appearance—those men added nothing to my message. On the contrary, they saw that I had been given the task of preaching the gospel to the Gentiles, just as Peter had been given the task of preaching the gospel to the Jews. For God, who was at work in the ministry of Peter as an apostle to the Jews, was also at work in my ministry as an apostle to the Gentiles. James, Peter and John, those reputed to be pillars, gave me and Barnabas the right hand of fellowship when they recognized the grace given to me. They agreed that we should go to the Gentiles, and they to the Jews. All they asked was that we should continue to remember the poor, the very thing I was eager to do.

When Peter came to Antioch, I opposed him to his face, because he was in the wrong. Before certain men came from James, he used to eat with the Gentiles. But when they arrived, he began to draw back and separate himself from the Gentiles because he was afraid of those who belonged to the circumcision group. The other Jews joined him in his hypocrisy, so that by their hypocrisy even Barnabas was led astray.

When I saw that they were not acting in line with the truth of the gospel, I said to Peter in front of them all, "You are a Jew, yet you live like a Gentile and not like a Jew. How is it, then, that you force Gentiles to follow Jewish customs?

"We who are Jews by birth and not 'Gentile sinners' know that a man is not justified by observing the law, but by faith in Jesus Christ. So we, too, have put our faith in Christ Jesus that we may be justified by faith in Christ and not by observing the law, because by observing the law no one will be justified.

"If, while we seek to be justified in Christ, it becomes evident that we ourselves are sinners, does that mean that Christ promotes sin? Absolutely not! If I rebuild what I destroyed, I prove that I am a lawbreaker. For through the law I died to the law so that I might live for God. I have been crucified with Christ and I no longer live, but Christ lives in me. The life I live in the body, I live by faith in the Son of God, who loved me and gave himself for me. I do not set aside the grace of God, for if righteousness could be gained through the law, Christ died for nothing!"...

Before this faith came, we were held prisoners by the law, locked up until faith should be revealed. So the law was put in charge to lead us to Christ that we might be justified by faith. Now that faith has come, we are no longer under the supervision of the law.

You are all sons of God through faith in Christ Jesus, for all of you who were united with Christ in baptism have been clothed with Christ. There is neither Jew nor Greek, slave nor free, male nor female, for you are all one in Christ Jesus. If you belong to Christ, then you are Abraham's seed, and heirs according to the promise. . . .

You, my brothers, were called to be free. But do not use your freedom to indulge the sinful nature; rather, serve one another in love. The entire law is summed up in a single command: "Love your neighbor as yourself." If you keep on biting and devouring each other, watch out or you will be destroyed by each other.

So I say, live by the Spirit, and you will not gratify the desires of the sinful nature. For the sinful nature desires what is contrary to the Spirit, and the Spirit what is contrary to the sinful nature. They are in conflict with each other, so that you do not do what you want. But if you are led by the Spirit, you are not under law.

The acts of the sinful nature are obvious: sexual immorality, impurity and debauchery; idolatry and witchcraft; hatred, discord, jealousy, fits of rage, selfish ambition, dissensions, factions and envy; drunkenness, orgies, and the like. I warn you, as I did before, that those who live like this will not inherit the kingdom of God.

But the fruit of the Spirit is love, joy, peace, patience, kindness, goodness, faithfulness, gentleness and self-control. Against such things there is no law. Those who belong to Christ Jesus have crucified their sinful nature with its passions and desires. Since we live by the Spirit, let us keep in step with the Spirit. Let us not become conceited, provoking and envying each other.

Brothers, if a man is trapped in some sin, you who are spiritual should restore him gently. But watch yourself, or you also may be tempted. Carry each other's burdens, and in this way you will fulfill the law of Christ. If anyone thinks he is something when he is nothing, he deceives himself. Each man should test his own actions. Then he can take pride in himself, without comparing himself to somebody else, for each man should carry his own load. . . .

Those who want to make a good impression outwardly are trying to compel you to be circumcised. The only reason they do this is to avoid being persecuted for the cross of Christ. Not even those who are circumcised obey the law, yet they want you to be circumcised that they may boast about your flesh. May I never boast except in the cross of our Lord Jesus

Christ, through which the world has been crucified to me, and I to the world. Neither circumcision nor uncircumcision means anything; what counts is a new creation. Peace and mercy to all who follow this rule, even to the Israel of God.

Galatians 2:1–21; 3:26–29; 5:13–6:5; 6:12–16. Scripture taken from the HOLY BIBLE, NEW INTERNATIONAL VERSION ®. NIV ®. Copyright © 1973, 1978, 1984 by International Bible Society. Used by permission of Zondervan Publishing House. All rights reserved.

1.3 Ritual Practice: The Baptism Ceremony of Hippolytus

In the first four centuries, Christian communities adapted two main rituals to express their beliefs: the Eucharist (or "communion") and baptism. The Eucharistic meal of bread and wine, representing the sacrifice of Christ's body and blood for forgiveness of sins, evolved out of Jewish traditions and was practiced on a regular (weekly) basis as part of communal worship. Baptism with water was the once-only initiation into the Christian community. The newly instructed believer, called a catechumen, was plunged beneath water, signifying both death to the old life and washing away of sin; arising from the water, the believer experienced a new, cleansed life. The baptism ceremonies developed in the early church stressed purification through resisting the Devil and spiritual cleansing through ceremonial washing. The events preparatory to the ritual focused on cleansing the believer's life from all demonic influence and testing the convert's sincerity, while the ceremony itself involved an exorcism denying the Devil before making a profession of faith.

The baptism ceremony found in *The Apostolic Tradition of Hippolytus* is a good example of the complexity and seriousness of this ritual. Hippolytus (circa 170–236), whose identity is somewhat uncertain, is a good example of heterodoxy in the early church: a brilliant theologian trained in Greek, he was also a schismatic bishop in Rome, eventually exiled because of his theological position on the nature of Christ and restored to Rome only after his martyrdom. Hippolytus's conflict with other theologians was due also to his more rigorous approach to Christian practice, believing that baptized believers should remain pure, free of serious sins; this approach is reflected in his baptismal ceremony. Scholars have reconstructed the rituals he formulated circa 200 from the Latin, Greek, Coptic, Ethiopic, Syrian, and Arabic texts into which they were incorporated over the next two centuries. This reconstructed document, known as *The Apostolic Tradition of Hippolytus,* gives us some rare insight into early church practice circa 200–400 C.E.

Questions

1. What are the characteristics of a person who is to be baptized?
2. What happens in the ceremony to the baptized convert?
3. What effect do you think this ritual would have on a new believer?

The Apostolic Tradition of Hippolytus Part II

They who are to be set apart for baptism shall be chosen after their lives have been examined: whether they have lived soberly, whether they have honored the widows, whether they have visited the sick, whether they have been active in well-doing. When their sponsors have testified that they have done these things, then let them hear the Gospel. Then from the time that they are separated from the other catechumens, hands shall be laid upon them daily in exorcism and, as the day of their baptism draws near, the bishop himself shall exorcise each one of them that he may be personally assured of their purity. Then, if there is any of them who is not good or pure, he shall be put aside as not having heard the word in faith; for it is never possible for the alien to be concealed.

Then those who are set apart for baptism shall be instructed to bathe and free themselves from impurity and wash themselves on Thursday. If a woman is menstruous, she shall be set aside and baptized on some other day.

They who are to be baptized shall fast on Friday, and on Saturday the bishop shall assemble them and command them to kneel in prayer. And, laying his hand upon them, he shall exorcise all evil spirits to flee away and never to return; when he has done this he shall breathe in their faces, seal their foreheads, ears and noses, and then raise them up. They shall spend all that night in vigil, listening to reading and instruction.

They who are to be baptized shall bring with them no other vessels than the one each will bring for the eucharist; for it is fitting that he who is counted worthy of baptism should bring his offering at that time.

At cockcrow prayer shall be made over the water. The stream shall flow through the baptismal tank or pour into it from above when there is no scarcity of water; but if there is a scarcity, whether constant or sudden, then use whatever water you can find.

They shall remove their clothing. And first baptize the little ones; if they can speak for themselves, they shall do so; if not, their parents or other relatives shall speak for them. Then baptize the men, and last of all the women; they must first loosen their hair and put aside any gold or silver

ornaments that they were wearing: let no one take any alien thing down to
the water with them.

At the hour set for the baptism the bishop shall give thanks over oil and put it
into a vessel: this is called the "oil of thanksgiving." And he shall take other oil
and exorcise it: this is called "the oil of exorcism." [The anointing is performed
by a presbyter.] A deacon shall bring the oil of exorcism, and shall stand at the
presbyter's left hand; and another deacon shall take the oil of thanksgiving, and
shall stand at the presbyter's right hand. Then the presbyter, taking hold of each
of those about to be baptized, shall command him to renounce, saying:

    I renounce thee, Satan, and all thy servants and all thy works.

And when he has renounced all these, the presbyter shall anoint him with
the oil of exorcism, saying:

    Let all spirits depart far from thee.

Then, after these things, let him give him over to the presbyter who baptizes, and let the candidates stand in the water, naked, a deacon going with
them likewise. And when he who is being baptized goes down into the
water, he who baptizes him, putting his hand on him, shall say thus:

    Dost thou believe in God, the Father Almighty?

And he who is being baptized shall say:

    I believe.

  Then

holding his hand placed on his head, he shall baptize him once. And then he
shall say:

> Dost thou believe in Christ Jesus, the Son of God, who was born of
> the Holy Ghost of the Virgin Mary, and was crucified under Pon-
> tius Pilate, and was dead and buried, and rose again the third day,
> alive from the dead, and ascended into heaven, and sat at the right
> hand of the Father, and will come to judge the quick and the dead?

And when he says:

    I believe,

he is baptized again. And again he shall say:

> Dost thou believe in [the] Holy Ghost, and the holy church, and the
> resurrection of the flesh?

He who is being baptized shall say accordingly:

    I believe,

and so he is baptized a third time.

    And afterward, when he has come up [out of the water], he is anointed
by the presbyter with the oil of thanksgiving, the presbyter saying:

    I anoint thee with holy oil in the name of Jesus Christ.

And so each one, after drying himself, is immediately clothed, and then is
brought into the church.

Then the bishop, laying his hand upon them, shall pray, saying:

> O LORD GOD, who hast made them worthy to obtain remission of sins through the laver of regeneration of [the] Holy Spirit, send into them thy grace, that they may serve thee according to thy will; for thine is the glory, to the Father and the Son, with [the] Holy Spirit in the holy church, both now and world without end. Amen.

Then, pouring the oil of thanksgiving from his hand and putting it on his forehead, he shall say:

> I anoint thee with holy oil in the Lord, the Father Almighty and Christ Jesus and [the] Holy Ghost.

And signing them on the forehead he shall say:

> The Lord be with thee;

and he who is signed shall say:

> And with thy spirit.

And so he shall do to each one.

And immediately thereafter they shall join in prayer with all the people, but they shall not pray with the faithful until all these things are completed. And at the close of their prayer they shall give the kiss of peace.

And then the offering is immediately brought by the deacons to the bishop, and by thanksgiving he shall make the bread into an image of the body of Christ, and the cup of wine mixed with water according to the likeness of the blood, which is shed for all who believe in him. And milk and honey mixed together for the fulfillment of the promise to the fathers, which spoke of a land flowing with milk and honey; namely, Christ's flesh which he gave, by which they who believe are nourished like babes, he making sweet the bitter things of the heart by the gentleness of his word. And the water into an offering in a token of the laver, in order that the inner part of man, which is a living soul, may receive the same as the body.

The bishop shall explain the reason of all these things to those who partake. And when he breaks the bread and distributes the fragments he shall say:

> The heavenly bread in Christ Jesus.

And the recipient shall say,

> Amen.

And the presbyters—or if there are not enough presbyters, the deacons—shall hold the cups, and shall stand by with reverence and modesty; first he who holds the water, then the milk, thirdly the wine. And the recipients shall taste of each three times, he who gives the cup saying:

> In God the Father Almighty;

and the recipient shall say,

> Amen.

Then:

> In the Lord Jesus Christ;

[and he shall say,

> Amen.

Then:

> In] [the] Holy Ghost and the holy church;

and he shall say,

> Amen.

So it shall be done to each.

And when these things are completed, let each one hasten to do good works, and to please God and to live aright, devoting himself to the church, practicing the things he has learned, advancing in the service of God.

From *The Apostolic Tradition of Hippolytus,* ed. B. S. Easton (London: Cambridge University Press, 1934; reprint, Archon Books, 1962), pp. 44–49. Reprinted with the permission of Cambridge University Press. Notes omitted.

–2–

Christian and Roman
Conflict and Assimilation

As a consequence of moving out of the domain of Judaism, Christianity created a new sense of identity for its followers beyond the dynamic of Jews and Gentiles: the opposition between Christians and non-Christian Romans or, in the Christians' eyes, pagans.

A Christian was a follower of Christ, either a catechumen or a baptized convert; increasingly these Christians were of non-Jewish or Gentile origin. Whereas in the first century, becoming a Christian for a Jewish convert meant defying the Jewish authorities to join a cult, in the second and third centuries, for a Gentile to become a Christian meant rejecting the Roman world and its syncretic, polytheistic religious traditions to join an obscure, low-class, potentially criminal cult.

Christians generally categorized Roman religions as pagan or heathen. These religions included any number of religious cults or philosophical systems available in the eclectic Roman world. However, whatever their individual belief or group, so-called pagans in the Roman world generally accepted polytheism and the public worship of the emperor. Polytheism—the belief in many gods under one, distant high God—suited the multicultural atmosphere of the Mediterranean world, allowing for a degree of relativism and tolerance for other religions. Most citizens and residents of the Roman Empire recognized the importance of supporting the public cult acknowledging the divine leadership of the Roman Emperor. Christians rejected both of these notions—the polytheism and the patriotic worship of the emperor— consequently they were persecuted by Romans in the first three centuries and were themselves the persecutors of pagan ways once the empire was formally Christian in the fourth century.

The relationship between Christianity and Roman society in these early centuries is thus complex and problematic. Obviously many Romans were attracted enough to the religion to convert, while others opposed it strongly enough to persecute Christians, with a range of attitudes in between. Likewise, some Christians adamantly opposed everything about Roman worldly culture, rejecting family, status, education, even life itself by pursuing martyrdom; other Christians struggled with what degree Greco-Roman culture contained worthwhile elements—ideas, values, practices.

The four documents below illustrate the difficulty of establishing what it meant to be a Christian who believed in otherworldly values while living in the material, temporal world with its corrupting influences. The dilemmas involved in varying Christian responses to persecution—those who were martyred heroically and those who fled—is illustrated in Severus's account of Dionysus, patriarch of Alexandria (2.1). Two early church fathers, Tertullian and Clement (2.2), struggled with the intellectual issues of using Greco-Roman ideas, while Eusebius's *Life of Constantine* (2.3) is concerned with the political and historical implications of a Christian emperor. The debate between the non-Christian Roman Symmachus and the Christian Ambrose (2.4) reflects the political and cultural ramifications of Rome's christianization.

2.1 Persecution: Dionysius the Wise, Patriarch of Alexandria

The persecutions suffered by the Christians in the second and third centuries, combined with their expectation of Christ's imminent return (the *parousia*), caused many of them to reject this world and all it contained in order to imitate Jesus's example of world-renouncing spirituality. Roman persecution of the sect confirmed for Christians the teaching of Jesus that "his kingdom was not of this world." From another point of view, Roman persecution was inevitable given that many Christians purposely set themselves apart from the rest of the Roman world. Heroic martyrs under Roman persecution—sporadic but sometimes severe—became the exemplars to other Christians of the values they believed in and helped them to remain steadfast in a hostile world. Stories of martyrdom, then, are an integral part of the Christian self-identity as told in later church histories, such as the story of the third-century patriarch Dionysius in the *History of the Patriarchs of Alexandria* excerpted here.

The *History of the Patriarchs of Alexandria* is a tenth–twelfth-century compilation in Arabic of earlier biographies and histories tracing the apostolic heritage of the Coptic Church centered in the city of Alexandria. The main author, a Coptic bishop named Severus, lived under Islamic rule several centuries after the Arab conquest of Alexandria in 635. He uses the fourth-century *Ecclesiastical History* of Eusebius and early Coptic biographies to trace the history of the North African church and its leaders, the patriarchs, in their heroic struggles under Roman persecution. Patriarchs were the bishops found in the leading cities of the Mediterranean world: Jerusalem, Rome, Alexandria, Antioch, Constantinople. As central Roman authority crumbled, and political, cultural, and doctrinal issues caused divisions, the Alexandrine patriarchs maintained their own line of authority over Egypt and other parts of Africa that became Christian (see 7.1 and 7.2). Even under Arab Islamic rule, the Coptic Church sought to preserve its identity by keeping alive the stories of the patriarchate.

The story recounted below of Dionysius the Wise, fourteenth patriarch of Alexandria (247–264), demonstrates the difficulties inherent in establishing a solid basis for an otherworldly faith under adverse conditions. Dionysius lived through the violent persecutions under the Emperors Decius (249–251) and Valerian (253–60). In the aftermath of the Decian persecution, the patriarch was faced with an argument over whether those who had "failed" under persecution (apostates) should be denied readmittance to the church, a position advocated by Novatian. This controversy over lenience toward apostates, which simmered for a century after the persecutions, highlighted the central dilemma of being a Christian in a pagan world and forced Christian leaders like Dionysius to formulate a doctrine that maintained the high ideals of imitating Christ's suffering and yet also exemplified the forgiveness offered by Christ, even for the sin of denial.

Questions

1. What do the stories of martyrdom imply about the Christian worldview?
2. Why does the church decide to readmit those who denied Christ?
3. What virtues are exemplified in the patriarch's life?

Dionysius the Wise, the Fourteenth Patriarch of Alexandria
(A.D. 247–264)

Of Dionysius, who was appointed patriarch after Heraclas, somewhat has already been recorded. Churches grew more numerous, and the faithful were multiplied in his days. And the churches were filled with the divine doctrines; and all was done openly, and in public. . . .

After [Emperor] Philip reigned Decius; and there had been between Philip and Decius a great enmity; and therefore the latter inflicted a great persecution upon the Church. The patriarch Fabian was martyred, and Cornelius became patriarch after him. Likewise Alexander, the patriarch of Jerusalem, twice confessed Christ, and showed forth his faith before the misbelievers, and was thrown into prison, and there went to his rest after much suffering. Alexander was endowed by God with a great gift of holiness, patience and courage; and men heard him in the dungeon confessing and glorifying God until he died. After him, a patriarch named Mazabanes sat upon the episcopal throne. The patriarch of Antioch, also, Babylas, confessed Christ, and was imprisoned, and died in the dungeon; and Fabius sat after him. As for the patriarch Dionysius, he says: "I will record what I endured, and call God to be my witness. Decius, the prince of Rome, sought diligently for me, but God concealed me from him, and he could not discover my hiding-place. After four days, God bid me remove from that place; therefore I fled with my disciples and a band of the brethren, and we wandered far. After four days, when the light had waned, and we were approaching Taposiris, the soldiers took us; and this was after four days of concealment. But Timothy, one of my disciples, escaped from our captors; and he returned to the house where we were, after meeting a countryman, who inquired of him what news he had to give him; so he told him what had befallen the patriarch." And that rustic assembled his companions; and when they had rescued the patriarch Dionysius from the soldiers, they made him ride upon a bare-backed ass, as he relates of himself; but his disciples walked on foot.

Dionysius also sent a letter to Fabius, patriarch of Antioch, and narrated to him the history of the martyrs, who suffered under Decius at Alexandria. He related that an old man named Metras was seized; and his captors said to him: "Wilt thou worship the idols?" But he refused; and so they inflicted upon him a painful beating and wounded his face with styli. Then they led him out of the city, and stoned him until he died. Likewise a certain believing woman was led in to offer worship to the idols; but she refused; and they beat her, and stripped her, and bound her feet together and dragged her over the stones so that her flesh was mangled, and her blood ran over the ground in the streets, while she was scourged all the time, until they had drawn her out of the city; and they killed her, and threw her body aside there. Then they returned to the houses of the faithful, and plundered them and wrecked them, and carried off all the gold and silver and furniture that they found in them. At this time Paul of Alexandria was martyred, and received his crown with joy. And none could openly profess the knowledge of God. In those days also a faithful virgin, named Apollonia, received the crown of martyrdom. All her limbs were broken, and she was burnt in the fire while still alive, outside the city, because she would not obey them by giving up her faith and would not deny the Lord Christ. And she looked at the flame of the fire while they burnt her; and it did not terrify her, but she endured it patiently, and gave up her spirit.

And another man was taken, named Serapion, and was severely tortured, and thrown from the third story, so that his bones were broken; thus he suffered martyrdom. And the faithful had neither a place of refuge nor a place of rest to go to, neither by day nor by night; and in this condition they remained for a long time; and this was the work of Decius the prince. And many were martyred whose names were not recorded. And the blessed Julian also was taken; and he was corpulent and stout in body, and was unable to walk, and therefore he had two men with him; so they led them all to the palace; and one of the two men apostatized, but the other confessed the faith together with the aged Julian; so they dragged those two through the city, and burnt them in the fire. And there were many troops prepared for the punishment of the Christians; and they seized another man, who cried aloud, saying: "O Lord take me quickly to thyself!" Then his head was cut off, and he was burnt in the fire. And two others also were martyred with him; besides another man named Alexander, and a number with him, whom they drove to the prison, and afterwards brought forth thence; and they were put to death. And there was a woman who left her children, and was slain. And another believing woman, in the greatness of her zeal for the faith, defied the governor, who therefore put her to death. And a great multitude without number came forward to suffer martyrdom for the name of the Lord Christ with great joy, as a man hastens to his wedding; and likewise many of the inhabitants of the towns and villages.

And a great multitude without number wandered among the mountains, having fled from the unbelievers; and many of them died of hunger and thirst, and from the heat. And an old man, a bishop, from the city called Malij, of the province of Egypt, fled, in company with a woman, who followed him; and these two could not be found, nor were any tidings of them known. And many were captured by the soldiers, who afterwards took a bribe from them, and released them. But many wandered forth at random, and never returned.

"I, Dionysius, the patriarch, have not said all this to no purpose; but I have made known to thy Paternity, my brother Fabius, all the trials which have surrounded us, and what we have endured and encountered. And all those persons that I have mentioned to thee, my brother, merited the kingdom by their suffering and combatings for the name of the Lord Christ. And many of those who apostatized in the persecution have returned to us, and we received them gladly, because we knew the joy of him who desires the repentance of the sinner, and not his death, so that he may be converted and live.

And because I am assured of thy fellowship with me, dear brother, I have expounded to thee what befell us; for we are of one spirit and one faith. And to you also, my brethren and my sons, I wish to relate this, for the sake of my blessed children and their patience; that you may know of the struggles of your faithful brethren for the orthodox faith, and of the happiness to which they have gone, through their endurance for the sake of him who suffered for us and for them, and redeemed us all by his blood. For they were patient for his sake, and would not deny him in the assembly of the unbelievers; and, in their love for him, neither the edge of the sword, nor the plunder of their goods, nor burning in the fire could terrify them. For God showed forth their virtues in this world; and in the next they have a great reward, and a glorious return to him."

Now there was a certain priest, a native of Rome, who said in his pride: "It is not lawful that we should receive any one of those who denied Christ in the time of trouble and persecution, even if he now returns to the Lord; for he fell and did not endure, but was made one of the misbelievers." And this priest used to call those that had been constant, "the Pure"; and he was the head over their community. So a council assembled at Rome, consisting of sixty bishops besides priests and deacons, to try the case of this man and his followers; and they wrote to every place an account of what took place. And there was a man called Novatus, who assisted this priest, out of hatred for the penitents, and helped him to repel from the Church all those that wished to return to her. Accordingly he began to forbid his followers to administer to the people the divine medicine, which consists in repentance and penitence and fasting and watching and weeping and humbly imploring God's forgiveness. So the clergy of Rome wrote to the clergy of Antioch an account of what had passed; and the latter returned an answer to them; and they all agreed that they should receive those that returned to the Church, and absolve them, and help them to repentance, because God himself receives them. Then they excommunicated the proud priest, who despised those penitent apostates; and they sent for the letters of Novatus concerning the conciliation of such men, and learnt what he wrote about them. After that, Novatus, unworthy as he was, usurped the title of bishop and remained in that office for three years, ordaining as priests ignorant men who knew nothing; and he made his followers believe that he was the chief of the bishops, and they honored him accordingly; until the report of his deeds reached Rome, and there was trouble between the two parties in the Church and a great schism.

After that, a synod of bishops assembled, and canceled all that Novatus had done by his lies, and proved to all those that had accepted him that they were simple men without knowledge, and that all his ordinations and other acts were invalid. Then one of those whom Novatus had ordained came forward and confessed his sin, and wept; and so the bishops received and pardoned him. And they wrote about Novatus to the various sees, and warned the Christians not to receive any of his doctrines. And the number of those who published his teaching, and whom he ordained, was as follows: forty-seven priests, and seven deacons, and seven subdeacons, and seven readers and doorkeepers. And he had done many things that were invalid, but which it is unnecessary to relate.

Then the patriarch Dionysius wrote letters to all places, enjoining that those who returned from their apostasy should be received; and he made this a permanent canon for those who should repent of their error. . . .

And the Church remained in tranquility for a short time, until the prince died, and there reigned after him an unbelieving prince named Valerian. And by his command his deputies seized Dionysius, and imprisoned him. And they killed an innumerable number of martyrs; even ripping open the bodies of infants, and taking their intestines, and twisting them round pipes made of reeds which they cast at the devils. Then they tortured Dionysius the patriarch, and demanded that he should worship their idols. So he said to them: "We worship God most high; but you worship what you love. Our worship is offered to the Lord Christ, Creator of heaven and earth, whom we love." Then the governor said to him: "Thou knowest not the measure of the patience of the princes towards thee. For if thou wilt worship our gods, we will honor and promote thee. But if thou wilt not do so, and disobeyest the command, and wilt not worship the gods, then thou shalt see what will happen to thee." And the governor took many of the patriarch's companions, and killed them, after exhorting him at length; and then drove him out, and banished him to a place, called the district of Coluthion, the interpretation of which is Chamberlain. But the inhabitants of that place treated Dionysius and all his companions, who would not worship the idols, hospitably. And after this they brought him back to condemn him to death; and they led him before the governor, who said to him: "We have heard that thou goest to a place apart, and performest the liturgy with thy companions." Dionysius answered: "We never cease to pray, night or day." So the governor exhorted him at length, and then left him; and the patriarch returned to his companions and said to them: "Go to every place, and pray and celebrate the liturgy; and if I am absent from you in the body, yet I am with you in the spirit." Then the patriarch was sent back to the place in which he had been in banishment, and his companions were sad because he was parted from them; but they said: "We know that the Lord Christ is with him in all his ways."

Then an innumerable multitude of the brethren were martyred in those days for the name of the Lord Jesus Christ, because they refused to worship the idols. And Valerian, the prince, made martyrs of many people in every region and every place. Afterwards a multitude of the Barbarians attacked him, and brought great trouble upon him. But he had a son who was very wise, and who remained in possession of the government; and he had been brought up in the days of persecution. And he gave to Dionysius and his companions a letter of release, and commanded that these words should be written in it:"Publius Caesar, the reigning prince, who loves God, writes to Dionysius the patriarch, and Demetrius and the rest of the bishops, and commands that they be kindly treated. Let those that hate them depart from them, and let their churches be opened to them. Let them take courage from our letter; and let no chastisement touch them after this day, nor sadness nor sorrow after this time; so that they may perform their service and their prayers to God; for we have set them free. And I have appointed Aurelius Cyrenius, and commanded him to guard the bishops safely, and treat them kindly. And let them say their prayers and celebrate their liturgies." . . .

At this time Dionysius, patriarch of Alexandria, went to his rest, after remaining in the see for seventeen years; and he died on the 13th day of Barmahat. But in a copy in the Monastery of Father Macarius it is said that he continued upon the episcopal throne seven years. Said, son of Batrik, however, bears witness in the book of the annals that the period was seventeen years; and this agrees with the biography from which the present copy was translated.

From Severus el-Ashmunein, *History of the Patriarchs of the Coptic Church of Alexandria I Saint Mark to Theonas (300)*, ed. and trans. B. T. A. Evetts, in *Patrologia Orientalis Tome 1 Fascicule 2* (Paris: Firmin-Didot, 1907; 1910; 1948), pp. 178–185, 187–191 passim.

2.2 Revelation versus Reason: Tertullian and Clement

One of the central issues confronting early Christians in the Greco-Roman world was whether they should reject the classical traditions of learning and the philosophies bound with those traditions dating back to Plato and Aristotle. As more and more converts emerged from the educated classes, they felt a keen contradiction between the revelatory, otherworldly faith of their religion and the humanistic rationalism of their upbringing. This divide between the Hebrew and the Greek heritages is fundamental to Christian thought, extending down through the ages in debates over faith and reason. As a result of this tension between these two traditions, the rationalism of the Greeks and the revelation of the Bible, early theologians, such as Tertullian and Clement below, debated whether it was appropriate to study and use classical learning to express Christian ideas.

The second-century North African priest and writer Tertullian was born into an educated Roman family and converted to Christianity as an adult. He used his education to write a defense of Christianity (the

Apology) and to define Christian belief in the face of heresy (*On the Prescription Against Heretics*); Tertullian himself later joined a group declared heretical, the Montanists, whose combination of extreme asceticism and ecstatic prophecy was more in line with the Hebrew revelatory tradition than the Greek rationalism of Tertullian's education. Even in the midst of using his classical training in his attacks on heresy, Tertullian reveals his ambivalence about the usability of the pagan philosophies, asking the poignant question in the excerpt below, "What does Jerusalem have to do with Athens?"

Other educated Christians were willing to go further in defending the use of Greek rationalism to discuss issues of truth. Clement of Alexandria (circa 160–215) argued strongly for the similarities and connections between the Greek and the Hebrew traditions, rather than the differences his contemporary Tertullian emphasized. For Clement, the center of all knowledge was the Logos. *Logos* is Greek for "word," used by Christian writers such as John in his Gospel to describe Christ as God Incarnate, God's revealed Word, but also used in philosophy to indicate words as the key to logic or reason. Clement has been both praised for his enlightened attitude and condemned for watering down the Christian revelation. The excerpt below, from his *Stromateis* or *Miscellanies,* discusses the steps to that higher knowledge, one of which is philosophy.

Questions

1. In what ways does Tertullian create an opposition between the Hebrew and Greek traditions of knowledge?

2. How does Clement find similarities and common goals between the two traditions?

3. Do Tertullian and Clement use a similar method of argumentation and evidence? Do you think their positions can be reconciled?

Tertullian, "What Has Jerusalem to Do with Athens?"

Our authorities are the Lord's apostles, and they in turn chose to introduce nothing on their own authority. They faithfully passed on to the nations the teaching which they had received from Christ. So we should anathematize even an angel from heaven if he were to preach a different gospel. . . .

These [heresies] are human and demonic doctrines, engendered for itching ears by the ingenuity of that worldly wisdom which the Lord called foolishness, choosing the foolish things of the world to put philosophy to shame. For worldly wisdom culminates in philosophy with its rash interpretation of God's nature and purpose. It is philosophy that supplies the heresies with their equipment. . . . A plague on Aristotle, who taught them dialectic, the art which destroys as much as it builds, which changes its opinions like a coat, forces its conjectures, is stubborn in argument, works hard at being contentious and is a burden even to itself. For it reconsiders every point to make sure it never finishes a discussion.

From philosophy come those fables and endless genealogies and fruit-less questionings, those "words that creep like as doth a canker." To hold us back from such things, the Apostle testifies expressly in his letter to the Colossians that we should beware of philosophy. "Take heed lest any man circumvent you through philosophy or vain deceit, after the tradi-tion of men," against the providence of the Holy Ghost. He had been at Athens where he had come to grips with the human wisdom which attacks and perverts truth, being itself divided up into its own swarm of heresies by the variety of its mutually antagonistic sects. What has Jeru-salem to do with Athens, the Church with the Academy, the Christian with the heretic? Our principles come from the Porch of Solomon, who had himself taught that the Lord is to be sought in simplicity of heart. I have no use for a Stoic or a Platonic or a dialectic Christianity. After Jesus Christ we have no need of speculation, after the Gospel no need of research. When we come to believe, we have no desire to believe any-thing else; for we begin by believing that there is nothing else which we have to believe. . . .

My first principle is this. Christ laid down one definite system of truth which the world must believe without qualification, and which we must seek precisely in order to believe it when we find it. Now you cannot search indefinitely for a single definite truth. You must seek until you find, and when you find, you must believe. Then you have simply to keep what you have come to believe, since you also believe that there is nothing else to believe, and therefore nothing else to seek, once you have found and be-lieved what he taught who bids you seek nothing beyond what he taught. If you feel any doubt as to what this truth is, I undertake to establish that Christ's teaching is to be found with us. For the moment, my confidence in my proof allows me to anticipate it, and I warn certain people not to seek for anything beyond what they came to believe, for that was all they needed to seek for. They must not interpret, "Seek, and ye shall find," without regard to reasonable methods of exegesis.

From Tertullian, *Prescriptions Against Heretics* in *Early Latin Theology,* ed. and trans. S. L. Greenslade, Library of Christian Classics Series, Vol. 5, pp. 34–38 passim (Philadelphia: The Westminster Press; London: SCM Press, 1956). Used by permission of Westminster John Knox Press and SCM Press Ltd. Notes omitted.

Clement of Alexandria, "In Defense of Greek Culture"

Our book will not shrink from making use of what is best in philosophy and other preparatory instruction. "For not only for the Hebrews and those that are under the law," according to the apostle, "is it right to become a Jew, but also a Greek for the sake of the Greeks, that we may gain all." Also in the Epistle to the Colossians [Paul] writes, "Admonishing every man, and teaching every man in all wisdom, that we may present every man perfect in Christ." . . .

Accordingly, before the advent of the Lord, philosophy was necessary to the Greeks for righteousness. And now it becomes conducive to piety; being a kind of preparatory training to those who attain to faith through demonstration. "For thy foot," it is said, "will not stumble, if thou prefer what is good, whether belonging to the Greeks or to us, to Providence." For God is the cause of all good things; but of some primarily, as of the Old and the New Testament; and of others by consequence, as philosophy. Perchance, too, philosophy was given to the Greeks directly and primarily, till the Lord should call the Greeks. For this was a schoolmaster to bring "the Hellenic mind," as the law, the Hebrews, "to Christ." Philosophy, therefore, was a preparation, paving the way for him who is perfected in Christ.

"Now," says Solomon, "defend wisdom, and it will exalt thee, and it will shield thee with a crown of pleasure." For when thou hast strengthened wisdom with a cope by philosophy, and with right expenditure, thou wilt preserve it unassailable by sophists. The way of truth is therefore one. But into it, as into a perennial river, streams flow from all sides. . . .

The Greek preparatory culture, therefore, with philosophy itself, is shown to have come down from God to men, not with a definite direction, but in the way in which showers fall down on the good land, and on the dunghill, and on the houses. And similarly both the grass and the wheat sprout; and the figs and any other reckless trees grow on sepulchers. And things that grow, appear as a type of truths. For they enjoy the same influence of the rain. But they have not the same grace as those which spring up in rich soil, inasmuch as they are withered or plucked up. And here we are aided by the parable of the sower, which the Lord interpreted. For the husbandman of the soil which is among men is one; He who from the beginning, from the foundation of the world, sowed nutritious seeds; He who in each age rained down the Lord, the Word. But the times and places which received [such gifts], created the differences which exist. Further, the husbandman sows not only wheat (of which there are many varieties), but also other seeds—barley, and beans, and peas, and vetches, and vegetable and flower seeds. And to the same husbandry belongs both planting and the operations necessary in the nurseries, and gardens, and orchards, and the planting and rearing of all sorts of trees.

In like manner, not only the care of sheep, but the care of herds, and breeding of horses, and dogs, and bee-craft, all arts, and to speak comprehensively, the care of flocks and the rearing of animals, differ from each other more or less, but are all useful for life. And philosophy—I do not mean the Stoic, or the Platonic, or the Epicurean, or the Aristotelian, but whatever has been well said by each of those sects, which teach righteousness along with a science pervaded by piety,—this eclectic whole I call philosophy. But such conclusions of human reasonings, as men have cut away and falsified, I would never call divine. . . .

Some, who think themselves naturally gifted, do not wish to touch either philosophy or logic; nay more, they do not wish to learn natural science. They demand bare faith alone, as if they wished, without bestowing any care on the vine, straightway to gather clusters from the first. Now the Lord is figuratively described as the vine, from which, with pains and the art of husbandry, according to the word, the fruit is to be gathered.

We must lop, dig, bind, and perform the other operations. The pruning-knife, I should think, and the pick-axe, and the other agricultural implements, are necessary for the culture of the vine, so that it may produce eatable fruit. And as in husbandry, so also in medicine: he has learned to purpose, who has practiced the various lessons, so as to be able to cultivate and to heal. So also here, I call him truly learned who brings everything to bear on the truth; so that, from geometry, and music, and grammar, and philosophy itself, culling what is useful, he guards the faith against assault. Now, as was said, the athlete is despised who is not furnished for the contest. For instance, too, we praise the experienced helmsman who "has seen the cities of many men," and the physician who has had large experience; thus also some describe the empiric. And he who brings everything to bear on a right life, producing examples from the Greeks and barbarians, this man is an experienced searcher after the truth, and in reality a man of much counsel, like the touch-stone (that is, the Lydian), which is believed to possess the power of distinguishing the spurious from the genuine gold. And our much-knowing gnostic can distinguish sophistry from philosophy, the art of decoration from gymnastics, cookery from physic, and rhetoric from dialectics, and the other sects which are according to the barbarian philosophy, from the truth itself. And how necessary is it for him who desires to be partaker of the power of God, to treat of intellectual subjects by philosophizing! And how serviceable is it to distinguish expressions which are ambiguous, and which in the Testaments are used synonymously!

For the Lord, at the time of His temptation, skillfully matched the devil by an ambiguous expression. And I do not yet, in this connection, see how in the world the inventor of philosophy and dialectics, as some suppose, is seduced through being deceived by the form of speech which consists in ambiguity. And if the prophets and apostles knew not the arts by which the exercises of philosophy are exhibited, yet the mind of the prophetic and instructive spirit, uttered secretly, because all have not an intelligent ear, demands skillful modes of teaching in order to clear exposition. For the prophets and disciples of the Spirit knew infallibly their mind. For they knew it by faith, in a way which others could not easily, as the Spirit has said. But it is not possible for those who have not learned to receive it thus. "Write," it is said, "the commandments doubly, in counsel and knowledge, that thou mayest answer the words of truth to them who send unto thee." What, then, is the knowledge of answering? or what that of asking? It is dialectics. What then? Is not speaking our business, and does not action proceed from the Word? For if we act not for the Word, we shall act against reason. But a rational work is accomplished through God. "And nothing," it is said, "was made without Him"—the Word of God.

From *The Writings of Clement of Alexandria*, trans. William Wilson, in *ANF*, Vol. 2, pp. 306–10.

2.3 Converting the Empire:
Eusebius's Account of Constantine and Helen

The conversion of the emperor of Rome to Christianity would seem to solve all of the early Christians' problems: an end to persecution, freedom to spread their religion, and imperial support to resolve conflicts. However, the miraculous conversion of Constantine, partly through his saintly mother Helen's influence, presents numerous problems, not only for the nascent church but also for contemporary and subsequent church historians trying to explain how God's plan could use such a very human tool as an emperor. For Constantine was not the ideal convert, despite attempts by contemporary writers to shape what was clearly a gradual conversion into a dramatic series of events demonstrating the Christian basis for the emperor's right to rule.

Eusebius of Caesarea (circa 260–339), a close confidant and supporter of the emperor, wrote his *History of the Church* as a means of explaining how Constantine fit into the divine plan of history. He also wrote a biography of Constantine, the *Vita Constantini*, excerpted below, that eulogizes the emperor's role in the fostering of Christianity and exalts his pious mother. The two stories here, one concerning his miraculous victory and conversion at the Battle of Milvian Bridge in 312 and the other about the church foundations he and his mother Helen made in Palestine, represent Eusebius's glorified view of Constantine as both military conqueror and pious builder of churches. While the events undoubtedly occurred in some fashion, Eusebius acts as an interpreter of their meaning for Christian history.

Questions

1. What roles do Constantine's vision, the image of the cross, and the discovery of the Holy Sepulcher play in Eusebius's portrait of the emperor?

2. According to Eusebius, what is Constantine's position in relation to the world and to the church?

3. What picture of Helen does Eusebius paint and what role does she play in the story?

Eusebius, Life of Constantine

While, therefore, he [Constantine] regarded the entire world as one immense body, and perceived that the head of it all, the royal city of the Roman empire, was bowed down by the weight of a tyrannous oppression; at first he had left the task of liberation to those who governed the other divisions of the empire, as being his superiors in point of age. But when none of these proved able to afford relief, and those who had attempted it had experienced a disastrous termination of their enterprise, he said that life was without enjoyment to him as long as he saw the imperial city thus afflicted, and prepared himself for the overthrowal of the tyranny.

Being convinced, however, that he needed some more powerful aid than his military forces could afford him, on account of the wicked and magical enchantments which were so diligently practiced by the tyrant, he sought Divine assistance, deeming the possession of arms and a numerous soldiery of secondary importance, but believing the co-operating power of Deity invincible and not to be shaken. He considered, therefore, on what God he might rely for protection and assistance. While engaged in this enquiry, the thought occurred to him, that, of the many emperors who had preceded him, those who had rested their hopes in a multitude of gods, and served them with sacrifices and offerings, had in the first place been deceived by flattering predictions, and oracles which promised them all prosperity, and at last had met with an unhappy end, while not one of their gods had stood by to warn them of the impending wrath of heaven; while one alone who had pursued an entirely opposite course, who had condemned their error, and honored the one Supreme God during his whole life, had found him to be the Savior and Protector of his empire, and the Giver of every good thing. . . . reviewing, I say, all these considerations, he judged it to be folly indeed to join in the idle worship of those who were no gods, and, after such convincing evidence, to err from the truth; and therefore felt it incumbent on him to honor his father's God alone.

Accordingly he called on him with earnest prayer and supplications that he would reveal to him who he was, and stretch forth his right hand to help him in his present difficulties. And while he was thus praying with fervent entreaty, a most marvelous sign appeared to him from heaven, the account of which it might have been hard to believe had it been related by any other person. But since the victorious emperor himself long afterwards declared it to the writer of this history, when he was honored with his acquaintance and society, and confirmed his statement by an oath, who could hesitate to accredit the relation, especially since the testimony of after-time has established its truth? He said that about noon, when the day was already beginning to decline, he saw with his own eyes the trophy of a cross of light in the heavens, above the sun, and bearing the inscription, CONQUER BY THIS. At this sight he himself was struck with amazement, and his whole army also, which followed him on this expedition, and witnessed the miracle.

He said, moreover, that he doubted within himself what the import of this apparition could be. And while he continued to ponder and reason on its meaning, night suddenly came on; then in his sleep the Christ of God appeared to him with the same sign which he had seen in the heavens, and commanded him to make a likeness of that sign which he had seen in the heavens, and to use it as a safeguard in all engagements with his enemies.

At dawn of day he arose, and communicated the marvel to his friends: and then, calling together the workers in gold and precious stones, he sat in the midst of them, and described to them the figure of the sign he had seen, bidding them represent it in gold and precious stones. And this representation I myself have had an opportunity of seeing.

Now it was made in the following manner. A long spear, overlaid with gold, formed the figure of the cross by means of a transverse bar laid over it. On the top of the whole was fixed a wreath of gold and precious stones; and within this, the symbol of the Savior's name, two letters indicating the name of Christ by means of its initial characters, the letter P being intersected by X in its center: and these letters the emperor was in the habit of wearing on his helmet at a later period. From the cross-bar of the spear was suspended a cloth, a royal piece, covered with a profuse embroidery of most brilliant precious stones; and which, being also richly interlaced with gold, presented an indescribable degree of beauty to the beholder. This banner was of a square form, and the upright staff, whose lower section was of great length, bore a golden half-length portrait of the pious emperor and his children on its upper part, beneath the trophy of the cross, and immediately above the embroidered banner.

The emperor constantly made use of this sign of salvation as a safeguard against every adverse and hostile power, and commanded that others similar to it should be carried at the head of all his armies.

These things were done shortly afterwards. But at the time above specified, being struck with amazement at the extraordinary vision, and resolving to worship no other God save Him who had appeared to him, he sent for those who were acquainted with the mysteries of His doctrines, and inquired who that God was, and what was intended by the sign of the vision he had seen.

They affirmed that He was God, the only begotten Son of the one and only God: that the sign which had appeared was the symbol of immortality, and the trophy of that victory over death which He had gained in time past when sojourning on earth. They taught him also the causes of His advent, and explained to him the true account of His incarnation. Thus he was instructed in these matters, and was impressed with wonder at the divine manifestation which had been presented to his sight. Comparing, therefore, the heavenly vision with the interpretation given, he found his judgment confirmed; and, in the persuasion that the knowledge of these things had been imparted to him by Divine teaching, he determined thenceforth to devote himself to the reading of the Inspired writings.

Moreover, he made the priests of God his counselors, and deemed it incumbent on him to honor the God who had appeared to him with all devotion. And after this, being fortified by well-grounded hopes in Him, he hastened to quench the threatening fire of tyranny. . . .

Moreover, by loud proclamation and monumental inscriptions he made known to all men the salutary symbol, setting up this great trophy of victory over his enemies in the midst of the imperial city, and expressly causing it to be engraven in indelible characters, that the salutary symbol was the safeguard of the Roman government and of the entire empire. Accordingly, he immediately ordered a lofty spear in the figure of a cross to be placed beneath the hand of a statue representing himself, in the most frequented part of Rome, and the following inscription to be engraved on it in the Latin language: BY VIRTUE OF THIS SALUTARY SIGN, WHICH IS THE TRUE TEST OF VALOR, I HAVE PRESERVED AND LIBERATED YOUR CITY FROM THE YOKE OF TYRANNY. I HAVE ALSO SET AT LIBERTY THE ROMAN SENATE AND PEOPLE, AND RESTORED THEM TO THEIR ANCIENT DISTINCTION AND SPLENDOR. . . .

After these things, the pious emperor addressed himself to another work truly worthy of record, in the province of Palestine. What then was this work? He judged it incumbent on him to render the blessed locality of our Savior's resurrection an object of attraction and veneration to all. He issued immediate injunctions, therefore, for the erection in that spot of a house of prayer: and this he did, not on the mere natural impulse of his own mind, but being moved in spirit by the Savior himself. . . .

This temple, then, the emperor erected as a conspicuous monument of the Savior's resurrection, and embellished it throughout on an imperial scale of magnificence. He further enriched it with numberless offerings of inexpressible beauty and various materials—gold, silver, and precious stones, the skillful and elaborate arrangement of which, in regard to their magnitude, number, and variety, we have not leisure at present to describe particularly.

In the same country he discovered other places, venerable as being the localities of two sacred caves: and these also he adorned with lavish magnificence. In the one case, he rendered due honor to that which had been the scene of the first manifestation of our Savior's divine presence, when he submitted to be born in mortal flesh; while in the case of the second cavern he hallowed the remembrance of his ascension to heaven from the mountain top. And while he thus nobly testified his reverence for these places, he at the same time eternized the memory of his mother [Helen], who had been the instrument of conferring so valuable a benefit on mankind.

For she [Helen], having resolved to discharge the duties of pious devotion to the God, the King of kings, and feeling it incumbent on her to render thanksgivings with prayers on behalf both of her own son, now so mighty an emperor, and of his sons, her own grandchildren, the divinely favored Caesars, though now advanced in years, yet gifted with no common degree of wisdom, had hastened with youthful alacrity to survey this venerable land; and at the same time to visit the eastern provinces, cities, and people, with a truly imperial solicitude. As soon, then, as she had rendered due reverence to the ground which the Savior's feet had trodden, according to the prophetic word which says "Let us worship at the place whereon his feet have stood," she immediately bequeathed the fruit of her piety to future generations.

For without delay she dedicated two churches to the God whom she adored, one at the grotto which had been the scene of the Savior's birth; the other on the mount of his ascension. For he who was "God with us" had submitted to be born even in a cave of the earth, and the place of his nativity was called Bethlehem by the Hebrews. Accordingly the pious empress honored with rare memorials the scene of her travail who bore this heavenly child, and beautified the sacred cave with all possible splendor. The emperor himself soon after testified his reverence for the spot by princely offerings, and added to his mother's magnificence by costly presents of silver and gold, and embroidered hangings. And farther, the mother of the emperor raised a stately structure on the Mount of Olives also, in memory of his ascent to heaven who is the Savior of mankind, erecting a sacred church and temple on the very summit of the mount. And indeed authentic history informs us that in this very cave the Savior imparted his secret revelations to his disciples. And here also the emperor testified his reverence for the King of kings, by diverse and costly offerings. Thus did Helena Augusta, the pious mother of a pious emperor, erect over the two mystic caverns these two noble and beautiful monuments of devotion, worthy of everlasting remembrance, to the honor of God her Savior, and as proofs of her holy zeal, receiving from her son the aid of his imperial power. Nor was it long ere this aged woman reaped the due reward of her labors. After passing the whole period of her life, even to declining age, in the greatest prosperity, and exhibiting both in word and deed abundant fruits of obedience to the divine precepts, and having enjoyed in consequence an easy and tranquil existence, with unimpaired powers of body and mind, at length she obtained from God an end befitting her pious course, and a recompense of her good deeds even in this present life.

For on the occasion of a circuit which she made of the eastern provinces, in the splendor of imperial authority, she bestowed abundant proofs of her liberality as well on the inhabitants of the several cities collectively, as on individuals who approached her, at the same time that she scattered largesses among the soldiery with a liberal hand. But especially abundant were the gifts she bestowed on the naked and unprotected poor. To some she gave money, to others an ample supply of clothing: she liberated some from imprisonment, or from the bitter servitude of the mines; others she delivered from unjust oppression, and others again, she restored from exile.

While, however, her character derived luster from such deeds as I have described, she was far from neglecting personal piety toward God. She might be seen continually frequenting his Church, while at the same time she adorned the houses of prayer with splendid offerings, not overlooking the churches of the smallest cities. In short, this admirable woman was to be seen, in simple and modest attire, mingling with the crowd of worshipers, and testifying her devotion to God by a uniform course of pious conduct.

And when at length at the close of a long life, she was called to inherit a happier lot, having arrived at the eightieth year of her age, and being very near the time of her departure, she prepared and executed her last will in favor of her only son, the emperor and sole monarch of the world, and her grandchildren, the Caesars his sons, to whom severally she bequeathed whatever property she possessed in any part of the world. Having thus made her will, this thrice blessed woman died in the presence of her illustrious son, who was in attendance at her side, caring for her and held her hands: so that, to those who rightly discerned the truth, the thrice blessed one seemed not to die, but to experience a real change and transition from an earthly to a heavenly existence, since her soul, remolded as it were into an incorruptible and angelic essence, was received up into her Savior's presence.

From Eusebius, *Life of Constantine,* trans. Arthur Cushman McGiffert, in *NPNF,* Second Series, Vol. 1, pp. 489–91 passim, 493, 526–27, 530–31.

2.4 Roman versus Christian: The Altar of Victory Dispute

Once Christians began to be dominant in the empire, after the conversion of the Emperor Constantine and with the declaration of Christianity as the state religion by Emperor Theodosius in 381, the tension between Roman religious practice and Christianity was reversed. Christian emperors imposed a monotheistic vision by removing the traditional Roman statues and images from the public places of Rome—acts seen as bad luck by many Romans, not just an affront to the gods but a denial of the Roman past and its revered traditions. One such incident in 382, Emperor Gratian's removal of the statue and altar of the winged goddess Victory, produced a debate that reveals much about the changing attitudes and methods of discourse in the christianized Roman Empire, as evidenced in the arguments of Symmachus and Ambrose below.

Quintus Aurelius Symmachus (circa 340–402) was a famed orator and Roman consul. Using the traditional skills of rhetoric essential in Roman governance, Symmachus eloquently addressed the Senate and wrote to the emperor, arguing for the restoration of Victory by appealing to tradition. Ambrose, bishop of Milan from 374 to 397, also came from a high-ranking Roman family, educated in the classical skills of rhetoric and law, and a natural-born leader who even excommunicated an emperor. A dynamic individual, he readily used his rhetorical skills to argue against Symmachus, and won the debate, convincing the emperor, even on later appeals, that the Altar to Victory need not be restored. The following selection records excerpts from Symmachus's address to the Senate and Ambrose's reply.

Questions

1. On what basis does Symmachus defend the Altar of Victory?
2. What techniques does Ambrose use to attack Symmachus's arguments?
3. Whose arguments seem to you to be more forward-looking and reasonable, and why?

The Memorial of Symmachus, Prefect of the City

As soon as the most honorable Senate, always devoted to you, knew that crimes were made amenable to law, and that the reputation of late times was being purified by pious princes, it, following the example of a more favorable time, gave utterance to its long suppressed grief, and bade me be once again the delegate to utter its complaints. But through wicked men audience was refused me by the divine Emperor, otherwise justice would not have been wanting, my lords and emperors, of great renown, Valentinian, Theodosius, and Arcadius, victorious and triumphant, ever august.

In the exercise, therefore, of a twofold office, as your Prefect I attend to public business, and as delegate I recommend to your notice the charge laid on me by the citizens. Here is no disagreement of wills, for men have now ceased to believe that they excel in courtly zeal, if they disagree. To be loved, to be reverenced, to be esteemed is more than imperial sway. Who could endure that private disagreement should injure the state? Rightly does the Senate censure those who have preferred their own power to the reputation of the prince.

But it is our task to watch on behalf of your Graces. For to what is it more suitable that we defend the institutions of our ancestors, and the rights and destiny of our country, than to the glory of these times, which is all the greater when you understand that you may not do anything contrary to the custom of your ancestors? We demand then the restoration of that condition of religious affairs which was so long advantageous to the state. Let the rulers of each sect and of each opinion be counted up; a late one practiced the ceremonies of his ancestors, a later did not put them away. If the religion of old times does not make a precedent, let the connivance of the last do so.

Who is so friendly with the barbarians as not to require an Altar of Victory? We will be careful henceforth, and avoid a show of such things. But at least let that honor be paid to the name which is refused to the goddess—your fame, which will last for ever, owes much and will owe still more to victory. Let those be averse to this power, whom it has never benefited. Do you refuse to desert a patronage which is friendly to your triumphs? That power is wished for by all, let no one deny that what he acknowledges is to be desired should also be venerated.

But even if the avoidance of such an omen were not sufficient, it would at least have been seemly to abstain from injuring the ornaments of the Senate House. Allow us, we beseech you, as old men to leave to posterity what we received as boys. The love of custom is great. Justly did the act of the divine Constantius last but for a short time. All precedents ought to be avoided by you, which you know were soon abolished. We are anxious for the permanence of our glory and your name, that the time to come may find nothing which needs correction.

Where shall we swear to obey your laws and commands? by what religious sanction shall the false mind be terrified, so as not to lie in bearing witness? All things are indeed filled with God, and no place is safe for the perjured, but to be urged in the very presence of religious forms has great power in producing a fear of sinning. That altar preserves the concord of all, that altar appeals to the good faith of each, and nothing gives more authority to our decrees than that the whole of our order issues every decree as it were under the sanction of an oath. So that a place will be opened to perjury, and this will be determined by my illustrious Princes, whose honor is defended by a public oath. . . .

Although he himself [Emperor Constantius] followed another religion, he maintained its own for the empire, for everyone has his own customs, everyone his own rites. The divine Mind has distributed different guardians and different cults to different cities. As souls are separately given to infants as they are born, so to peoples the genius of their destiny. Here comes in the proof from advantage, which most of all vouches to man for the gods. For, since our reason is wholly clouded, whence does the knowledge of the gods more rightly come to us, than from the memory and evidence of prosperity? Now if a long period gives authority to religious customs, we ought to keep faith with so many centuries, and to follow our ancestors, as they happily followed theirs. . . .

We ask, then, for peace for the gods of our fathers and of our country. It is just that all worship should be considered as one. We look on the same stars, the sky is common, the same world surrounds us. What difference does it make by what pains each seeks the truth? We cannot attain to so great a secret by one road; but this discussion is rather for persons at ease, we offer now prayers, not conflict. . . .

And let no one think that I am defending the cause of religion only, for from deeds of this kind have arisen all the misfortunes of the Roman race. The law of our ancestors honored the Vestal Virgins and the ministers of the gods with a moderate maintenance and just privileges. This grant remained unassailed till the time of the degenerate money-changers, who turned the fund for the support of sacred chastity into hire for common porters. A general famine followed upon this, and a poor harvest disappointed the hopes of all the provinces. This was not the fault of the earth, we impute no evil influence to the stars. Mildew did not injure the crops, nor wild oats destroy the corn; the year failed through the sacrilege, for it was necessary that what was refused to religion should be denied to all.

Certainly, if there be any instance of this evil, let us impute such a famine to the power of the season. A deadly wind has been the cause of this barrenness, life is sustained by trees and shrubs, and the need of the country folk has betaken itself once more to the oaks of Dodona. What similar evil did the provinces suffer, so long as the public charge sustained the ministers of religion? When were the oaks shaken for the use of men, when were the roots of plants torn up, when did fertility on all sides forsake the various lands, when supplies were in common for the people and for the sacred virgins? For the support of the priests was a blessing to the produce of the earth, and was rather an insurance than a bounty. Is there any doubt that what was given was for the benefit of all, seeing that the want of all has made this plain? ...

May the unseen guardians of all sects be favorable to your Graces, and may they especially, who in old time assisted your ancestors, defend you and be worshipped by us. We ask for that state of religious matters which preserved the empire for the divine parent of your Highnesses, and furnished that blessed prince with lawful heirs. That venerable father beholds from the starry height the tears of the priests, and considers himself censured by the violation of that custom which he willingly observed.

Reply of St. Ambrose to the Memorial of Symmachus

Ambrose, Bishop, to the most blessed prince and most gracious Emperor Valentianus, the august.

Since the illustrious Symmachus, Prefect of the city, has sent petition to your Grace that the altar, which was taken away from the Senate House of the city of Rome, should be restored to its place; and you, O Emperor, although still young in years and experience, yet a veteran in the power of faith, did not approve the prayer of the heathen, I presented a request the moment I heard of it, in which, though I stated such things as it seemed necessary to suggest, I requested that a copy of the Memorial might be given to me.

So, then, not being in doubt as to your faith, but anxiously considering the risk, and sure of a kindly consideration, I am replying in this document to the assertions of the Memorial, making this sole request, that you will not expect elegance of language but the force of facts. For, as the divine Scripture teaches, the tongue of wise and studious men is golden, which, gifted with glittering words and shining with the brilliancy of splendid utterance as if of some rich color, captivates the eyes of the mind with the appearance of beauty and dazzles with the sight. But this gold, if you consider it carefully, is of value outwardly but within is base metal. Ponder well, I pray you, and examine the sect of the heathen, their utterances, sound weighty and grand, but defend what is without capacity for truth. They speak of God and worship idols. . . .

In his first proposition Rome complains with sad and tearful words, asking, as he says, for the restoration of the rites of her ancient ceremonies. These sacred rites, he says, repulsed Hannibal from the walls, and the Senones from the Capitol. And so at the same time that the power of the sacred rites is proclaimed, their weakness is betrayed. So that Hannibal long insulted the Roman rites, and while the gods were fighting against him, arrived a conqueror at the very walls of the city. Why did they suffer themselves to be besieged, for whom their gods were fighting in arms?

And why should I say anything of the Senones, whose entrance into the inmost Capitol the remnant of the Romans could not have prevented, had not a goose by its frightened cackling betrayed them? See what sort of protectors the Roman temples have. Where was Jupiter at that time? Was he speaking in the goose?

But why should I deny that their sacred rites fought for the Romans? For Hannibal also worshipped the same gods. Let them choose then which they will. If these sacred rites conquered in the Romans, then they were overcome in the Carthaginians: if they triumphed in the Carthaginians, they certainly did not benefit the Romans. . . .

By one road, says he, one cannot attain to so great a secret. What you know not, that we know by the voice of God. And what you seek by fancies, we have found out from the very Wisdom and Truth of God. Your ways, therefore, do not agree with ours. You implore peace for your gods from the Emperors, we ask for peace for the Emperors themselves from Christ. You worship the works of your own hands, we think it an offense that anything which can be made should be esteemed God. God wills not that He should be worshipped in stones. And, in fine, your philosophers themselves have ridiculed these things.

But if you deny Christ to be God, because you believe not that He died (for you are ignorant that that death was of the body not of the Godhead, which has brought it to pass that now no one of those who believe dies), what is more thoughtless than you who honor with insult, and disparage with honor, for you consider a piece of wood to be your god. O worship full of insult! You believe not that Christ could die, O perversity founded on respect! . . .

The last and most important point remains, whether, O Emperors, you ought to restore those helps which have profited you; for he says: 'Let them defend you, and be worshipped by us.' This it is, most faithful princes, which we cannot endure, that they should taunt us that they supplicate their gods in your names, and without your commands, commit an immense sacrilege, interpreting your shutting your eyes as consent. Let them have their guardians to themselves, let these, if they can, protect their worshipers. For, if they are not able to help those by whom they are worshipped, how can they protect you by whom they are not worshipped?

But, he says, the rites of our ancestors ought to be retained. But what, seeing that all things have made progress towards what is better? The world itself, which at first was compacted of the germs of the elements throughout the void, in a yielding sphere, or was dark with the shapeless confusion of the work as yet without order, did it not afterwards receive (the distinction between sky, sea, and earth being established), the forms of things whereby it appears beautiful? The lands freed from the misty darkness wondered at the new sun. The day does not shine in the beginning, but as time proceeds, it is bright with increase of light, and grows warm with increase of heat. . . .

The first age of the year itself, which has tinged us with a likeness to itself as things begin to grow, as it goes on becomes springlike with flowers soon about to fall, and grows up to full age in fruits at the end.

We too, inexperienced in age, have an infancy of our senses, but changing as years go on, lay aside the rudiments of our faculties.

Let them say, then, that all things ought to have remained in their first beginnings, that the world covered with darkness is now displeasing, because it has brightened with the shining of the sun. And how much more pleasant is it to have dispelled the darkness of the mind than that of the body, and that the ray of faith should have shone than that of the sun. So, then, the primeval state of the world as of all things has passed away, that the venerable old age of hoary faith might follow. Let those whom this touches find fault with the harvest, because its abundance comes late; let them find fault with the vintage, because it is at the close of the year; let them find fault with the olive, because it is the latest of fruits.

So, then, our harvest is the faith of souls, the grace of the Church is the vintage of merits, which from the beginning of the world flourished in the Saints, but in the last age has spread itself over the people, that all might notice that the faith of Christ has entered minds which were not rude (for there is no crown of victory without an adversary), but the opinion being exploded which before prevailed, that which was true is rightly preferred. . . .

I have answered those who provoked me as though I had not been provoked, for my object was to refute the Memorial, not to expose superstition. But let their very memorial make you, O Emperor, more careful. For after narrating of former princes, that the earlier of them practiced the ceremonies of their fathers, and the later did not abolish them; and saying in addition that if the religious practice of the older did not make a precedent, the connivance of the later ones did; it plainly showed what you owe, both to your faith, viz., that you should not follow the example of heathen rites, and to your affection, that you should not abolish the decrees of your brother. For if for their own side alone they have praised the connivance of those princes, who, though Christians, yet in no way abolished the heathen decrees, how much more ought you to defer to brotherly love, so that you, who ought to overlook some things even if you did not approve them in order not to detract from your brother's statutes, should now maintain what you judge to be in agreement both with your own faith, and the bond of brotherhood.

From *Letters of St. Ambrose,* trans. H. De Romestin, in *NPNF,* Second Series, Vol. 10, pp. 414–22 passim.

–3–
Heterodoxy and Orthodoxy
Defining Heresy

The authoritative documents and practices examined in the previous chapters eventually became the basis of orthodoxy, but at the time they were produced they were only a small portion of a much larger set of heterodox texts. Some of the documents circulating in this period that did not make it into the western canon show us alternative interpretations of Christian ideas and different cultural adaptations from those found within the Roman Empire.

Far from being peripheral to the tradition, these alternate views had a dynamic relationship with orthodoxy. They not only challenged the early Christian leaders to formulate a coherent orthodox doctrine to counter them but also influenced the main tradition in more subtle ways, sometimes existing in gray areas on the fringe of the acceptable in orthodox tradition. For example, orthodoxy rejected Gnosticism as heresy, but Gnostic ideas contributed to the otherworldly emphasis found among many orthodox ascetics in the early church and later. Likewise, Origen was condemned by orthodoxy two centuries after his death, but his writings influenced many other authors.

The heterodox beliefs that arose in the first few centuries after Jesus mostly revolved around various interpretations of Christ, his nature, his relationship to God the Father, and differing views on the Scriptures. But these theologies were the products of political environments as well, where the motive was not just rightness but also unity and conformity, and where the issue was not just what ideas were true but also who had the authority to define and decide what was true. The mechanisms for establishing true doctrine and uniformity included reasoned debate in church councils, the development of creeds as statements of faith, and the promulgation of laws enforcing one version of truth over another. The persons competing for authority in this decision-making process included theologians, patriarchs, bishops, and emperors, but even ordinary lay people took sides in these debates, creating theological factions.

Consequently, bitter and highly politicized disputes arose between different theologians and bishops in major cities of the empire, such as Antioch and Alexandria; often cities were themselves divided by differing interpretations, sometimes causing civil riots (one imperial edict of the late fourth century, contained in the Theodosian Code, went so far as to forbid religious arguments). These doctrines were taken quite seriously not only as expressions of eternal truths but also as statements of authority within a rapidly changing and highly diverse Roman world. Centrally located bishops of the church, known as patriarchs, ruled from the major Roman cities, and their opinions were respected. Nonetheless, when these men and the bishops and theologians around them could not agree, then they sought to define other sources of authority: councils were convened, and the emperor became an enforcer of conciliar decrees. Dissenting groups, ostracized as heretics, often withdrew to the outer edges of, or beyond, the Roman Empire, founding their own churches and spreading even farther abroad into Asia and sub-Sahara Africa, as examined in Chapter 7.

The following documents explore four of these "heretical" groups who were marginalized within the Roman Empire by conciliar and imperial decisions designed to end divisive conflicts over doctrine by establishing a uniform interpretation. Gnosticism (3.1) as a sect was in some ways short-lived, but had a tremendous influence on orthodox belief. Origen's controversial, yet influential ideas (3.2) received condemnation more for the distortions created by his followers than for his actual views. Arianism (3.3) arose out of an all-too-common conflict between theologians arguing over the precise wording used to denote an indescribable God. Likewise, Nestorians (3.4) argued over the wording to describe the nature of Christ as both divine and human, resulting in their eventual expulsion from the orthodox domains of the empire.

3.1 Syrian Gnosticism
Book of Thomas the Contender

Gnosticism is a difficult set of beliefs to describe because it existed in so many different forms and did not evolve a systematic structure in the way that orthodoxy did. Gnostic ideas arose in the Jewish world simultaneously with Christianity, and converged with it to produce variants that flourished particularly in the second century, although it became marginalized in later centuries as orthodoxy spread. In addition to its predominantly Jewish roots, Gnosticism incorporated into its thought elements of Greek, Syrian, and Egyptian philosophies and mythologies.

In general, Gnostic beliefs emphasized an otherworldliness that denied material reality, setting up a dualism of body as evil versus spirit as good. The Gnostic's goal was the reunion of the soul with the divine. For example, they taught a secret, spiritual knowledge (Greek *gnosis*) that the believer achieved in a mystical revelation rather than grasped through the mind. The illusory and evil nature of the material world extended so far that many Gnostics asserted that the God portrayed in the Old Testament account of Genesis was the Devil, who created material bodies in which to trap spirits. Gnostic stories evolved an entire mythology to explain the genesis of spirit and its entrapment in materiality by evil forces, borrowing, for example, the Egyptian deities Seth and his sister Norea. This dualism of body and spirit also led to the interpretation of Christ as purely spirit and not human at all; his body was merely an illusion.

As a result of this antipathy to the material world, Gnostics attempted to achieve reunion or marriage with the divine spirit through philosophical contemplation or through an extremely ascetic lifestyle, denying the body as a way of demonstrating the utter worthlessness and illusory quality of material reality. Much of the reaction against Gnosticism has to do with its extreme position on the relationship of body and spirit, this world and the other world. Orthodoxy took more of a middle path between the extremes of spiritualized asceticism and worldly materialism, a tension that would continue throughout Christianity's history.

Even though Gnosticism gradually died out as a major belief system after the third century, its influence continued to be felt and its secretive texts survived. A major discovery in the twentieth century was the collection of fifty Coptic (Egyptian) texts known as the Nag Hammadi Library. Some of the books represent the teachings of the second-century Alexandrian Valentinus and his followers, who emphasized the idea of spiritual marriage through ritual reenactments. Others, such as the excerpt below, represent the ascetic tradition originating in Syria and associated with the Gnostic Thomas, a stream of Gnosticism that denied femininity and sexuality.

In the *Book of Thomas the Contender* (composed circa 200–250), the postresurrection Jesus is portrayed in a conversation with his twin brother Judas Thomas, as recorded by someone named Matthew who was walking along with them. The idea of Thomas as a physical human twin of the spiritual Jesus allows for a dialogue within the soul, between the savior/teacher and the seeker who desires self-knowledge. The text echoes passages in the Gospels, but has a decidedly strong emphasis on the dangers of sexuality, as well as the necessity of self-knowledge through some process of interior revelation and realization.

Questions

1. What view of Jesus does the *Book of Thomas the Contender* display?
2. What kind of knowledge is Thomas led to seek, and how?
3. How do you think an orthodox believer would respond to this work?

Book of Thomas the Contender

The secret words that the Savior spoke to Judas Thomas which I, even I Mathaias, wrote down—I was walking, listening to them speak with one another.

The Savior said, "Brother Thomas, while you have time in the world, listen to me and I will reveal to you the things you have pondered in your mind.

"Now since it has been said that you are my twin and true companion, examine yourself that you may understand who you are, in what way you exist, and how you will come to be. Since you are called my brother, it is not fitting that you be ignorant of yourself. And I know that you have understood, because you had already understood that I am the knowledge of the truth. So while you accompany me, although you are uncomprehending, you have (in fact) already come to know, and you will be called 'the one who knows himself.' For he who has not known himself has known nothing, but he who has known himself has at the same time already achieved knowledge about the Depth of the All. So then, you, my brother Thomas, have beheld what is obscure to men, that is, that against which they ignorantly stumble."

Now Thomas said to the Lord, "Therefore I beg you to tell me what I ask before your Ascension, and when I hear from you about the hidden things, then I can speak about them. And it is obvious to me that the truth is difficult to perform before men."

The Savior answered, saying, "If the things that are visible to you are obscure to you, how can you hear about the things that are not visible? If the deeds of the truth that are visible in the world are difficult for you to perform, how indeed, then, shall you perform those that pertain to the exalted height and to the Pleroma [fullness, of the divine reality] which are not visible? And how shall you be called 'Laborers'? In this respect you are apprentices, and have not yet received the height of perfection."

Now Thomas answered and said to the Savior, "Tell us about these things that you say are not visible, [but] are hidden from us."

The Savior said, "[All] bodies [of men and] beasts are begotten [irrational. Surely] it is evident in the way [a creature . . .]. Those, however, that are above [are not visible among] things that are visible, but are visible in their own root, and it is their fruit that nourishes them. But these visible bodies eat of creatures similar to them with the result that the bodies change. Now that which changes will decay and perish, and has no hope of life from then on, since that body is bestial. So just as the body of the beasts perishes, so also will these formations perish. Do they not derive from intercourse like that of the beasts? If (the body) too derives from (intercourse), how will it beget anything different from (beasts)? So, therefore, you are babes until you become perfect."

And Thomas answered, "Therefore I say to you, Lord, that those who speak about things that are invisible and difficult to explain are like those who shoot their arrows at a target at night. To be sure, they shoot their arrows as anyone would—since they shoot at the target—but it is not visible. Yet when the light comes forth and hides the darkness, then the work of each will appear. And you, our light, enlighten, Lord."

Jesus said, "It is in light that light exists."

Thomas spoke, saying, "Lord, why does this visible light that shines on behalf of men rise and set?"

The Savior said, "O blessed Thomas, of course this visible light shone on your behalf—not in order [that] you remain here, but rather that you come forth—and whenever all the elect abandon bestiality, then this light will withdraw up to its essence, and its essence will welcome it since it is a good servant."

Then the Savior continued and said, "O unsearchable love of the light! O bitterness of the fire that burns in the bodies of men and in their marrow, burning in them night and day, burning in the limbs of men and [making] their minds drunk and their souls deranged [and moving] them within males and females [by day and] night and moving them [with] a [movement that moves] secretly and visibly. For the males [move; they move upon the females] and the females upon [the males. Therefore it is] said, 'Everyone who seeks the truth from true wisdom will make himself wings so as to fly, fleeing the lust that scorches the spirits of men.' And he will make himself wings to flee every visible spirit."

And Thomas answered, saying, "Lord, this indeed is what I am asking you about, since I have understood that you are the one who is good for us, as you say."

Again the Savior answered and said, "Therefore it is necessary for us to speak to you, since this is the doctrine for the perfect. If, now, you desire to become perfect, you shall observe these things; if not, your name is 'Ignorant,' since it is impossible for a wise man to dwell with a fool, for the wise man is perfect in all wisdom. To the fool, however, the good and bad are the same—for 'the wise man will be nourished by the truth' and 'will be like a tree growing by the meandering stream'—seeing that there are some who, although having wings, rush upon the visible things, things that are far from the truth. For that which guides them, the fire, will give them an illusion of truth, [and] will shine on them with a [perishable] beauty, and it will imprison them in a dark sweetness and captivate them with fragrant pleasure. And it will blind them with insatiable lust and burn their souls and become for them like a stake stuck in their heart which they can never dislodge. And like a bit in the mouth it leads them according to its own desire.

"It has fettered them with its chains and bound all their limbs with the bitter bond of lust for those visible things that will decay and change and swerve by impulse. They have always been attracted downwards: as they are killed, they are assimilated to all the beasts of the perishable realm."

Thomas answered and said, "It is obvious and has been said, '[Many are the things revealed] to those who do not know [that they will forfeit their] soul.' "

And [the Savior] answered, saying, "[Blessed is] the wise man who [sought after the truth, and] when he found it, he rested upon it forever and was unafraid of those who wanted to disturb him.."..

[A series of "Woe to those who . . ." are omitted here]

"Blessed are you who have prior knowledge of the stumbling blocks and who flee alien things.

"Blessed are you who are reviled and not esteemed on account of the love their Lord has for them.

"Blessed are you who weep and are oppressed by those without hope, for you will be released from every bondage.

"Watch and pray that you not come to be in the flesh, but rather that you come forth from the bondage of the bitterness of this life. And as you pray, you will find rest, for you have left behind the suffering and the disgrace. For when you come forth from the sufferings and passion of the body, you will receive rest from the Good One, and you will reign with the King, you joined with him and he with you, from now on, for ever and ever. Amen."

> The Book of Thomas
> the Contender writing
> to the Perfect.
>
> Remember me also, my brethren,
> [in] your prayers:
> Peace to the Saints
> and the Spiritual.

3.2 Origenism: The End of the World

Probably the most influential, and controversial, early church father is Origen (circa 185–251). Consequently, he illustrates well the dilemma of orthodoxy arising from a heterodox environment. What in his own third-century context was acceptable speculation about unresolved issues became, in the eyes of those after the councils of Nicea and Chalcedon, heresy. His followers in subsequent centuries, known as Origenists, magnified and distorted his arguments about reincarnation, his speculations on the preexistence of the soul, and his discussion of universal salvation; these positions, and Origen unfortunately with them, were condemned by the Emperor Justinian I at the Second Council of Constantinople in 553. Nonetheless, his biblical scholarship left its mark on many early church thinkers such as Gregory of Nyssa (4.2) and later John Scottus Eriugena (10.2).

Origen's vigorous faith and brilliance as a thinker trained in the classics and the Bible appeared at a young age, recognized by both pagans and Christians, some of whom disagreed with his unusual ideas. He also suffered for the faith. His father was a martyr; later in his life Origen himself was jailed, and ultimately died as a result of his torturous experiences in prison under the persecutions of Emperor Decius (249–251).

Origen was preeminently a biblical theologian, focusing his efforts on commentary of the Scriptures and on finding the deeper, spiritual meaning in all things. In some cases, later critics felt that Origen over-spiritualized the text and appeared to deny the literal meaning, while engaging in philosophical speculations using his training in Greek thought. For example, as the excerpts below from his book *On First Principles* indicate, Origen reasoned about the existence of the material world as created by God out of himself, a view known as *emanationism,* as opposed to the main tradition of *creatio ex nihilo*—God creating matter out of nothing. The difficulty with emanationism is the implication that all created things must then return to God in a universal salvation—including sinners and other evil beings—since God could not lose or destroy a part of himself. This reintegration theory was speculative on Origen's part, as he experimented with ideas of God's purifying act at the last judgment. The following excerpts also explain why the resurrection of the body is central to Christian theology, in opposition to the dominant view among non-Christian Roman philosophers of a purely spiritual afterlife and in opposition to Gnostic doctrines of the body as evil.

Questions

1. In Origen's view, what does the resurrection of the body mean?
2. What happens to evil and death at the end of all things, according to Origen?
3. How would these views of the resurrection and the end of the world affect the way Christians lived their lives in the here and now?

Origin, On First Principles: The End of the World

II:10 On the Resurrection

But since the discourse has reminded us of the subjects of a future judgment and of retribution, and of the punishments of sinners, according to the threatenings of holy Scripture and the contents of the Church's teaching—viz., that when the time of judgment comes, everlasting fire, and outer darkness, and a prison, and a furnace, and other punishments of like nature, have been prepared for sinners—let us see what our opinions on these points ought to be. But that these subjects may be arrived at in proper order, it seems to me that we ought first to consider the nature of the resurrection, that we may know what that (body) is which shall come either to punishment, or to rest, or to happiness; which question in other treatises which we have composed regarding the resurrection we have discussed at greater length, and have shown what our opinions were regarding it. But now, also, for the sake of logical order in our treatise, there will be no absurdity in restating a few points from such works, especially since some take offense at the creed of the Church, as if our belief in the resurrection were foolish, and altogether devoid of sense; and these are principally heretics, who, I think, are to be answered in the following manner. If they also admit that there is a resurrection of the dead, let them answer us this, What is that which died? Was it not a body? It is of the body, then, that there will be a resurrection. Let them next tell us if they think that we are to make use of bodies or not. I think that when the Apostle Paul says, that "it is sown a natural body, it will arise a spiritual body," they cannot deny that it is a body which arises, or that in the resurrection we are to make use of bodies. What then? If it is certain that we are to make use of bodies, and if the bodies which have fallen are declared to rise again (for only that which before has fallen can be properly said to rise again), it can be a matter of doubt to no one that they rise again, in order that we may be clothed with them a second time at the resurrection. The one thing is closely connected with the other. For if bodies rise again, they undoubtedly rise to be coverings for us; and if it is necessary for us to be invested with bodies, as it is certainly necessary, we ought to be invested with no other than our own. But if it is true that these rise again, and that they arise "spiritual" bodies, there can be no doubt that they are said to rise from the dead, after casting away corruption and laying aside mortality; otherwise it will appear vain and superfluous for any one to arise from the dead in order to die a second time. And this, finally, may be more distinctly comprehended thus, if one carefully consider what are the qualities of an animal body, which, when sown into the earth, recovers the qualities of a spiritual body. For it is out of the animal body that the very power and grace of the resurrection educe the spiritual body, when it transmutes it from a condition of indignity to one of glory. . . .

We now turn our attention to some of our own (believers), who, either from feebleness of intellect or want of proper instruction, adopt a very low and abject view of the resurrection of the body. We ask these persons in what manner they understand that an animal body is to be changed by the grace of the resurrection, and to become a spiritual one; and how that which is sown in weakness will arise in power; how that which is planted in dishonor will arise in glory; and that which was sown in corruption, will be changed to a state of incorruption. Because if they believe the apostle, that a body which arises in glory, and power, and incorruptibility, has already become spiritual, it appears absurd and contrary to his meaning to say that it can again be entangled with the passions of flesh and blood, seeing the apostle manifestly declares that "flesh and blood shall not inherit the king- dom of God, nor shall corruption inherit incorruption." But how do they understand the declaration of the apostle, "We shall all be changed?" This transformation certainly is to be looked for, according to the order which we have taught above; and in it, undoubtedly, it becomes us to hope for something worthy of divine grace; and this we believe will take place in the order in which the apostle describes the sowing in the ground of a "bare grain of corn [seed of grain], or of any other fruit," to which "God gives a body as it pleases Him," as soon as the grain of corn is dead. For in the same way also our bodies are to be supposed to fall into the earth like a grain; and (that germ being implanted in them which contains the bodily substance) although the bodies die, and become corrupted, and are scattered abroad, yet by the word of God, that very germ which is always safe in the substance of the body, raises them from the earth, and restores and repairs them, as the power which is in the grain of wheat, after its corruption and death, repairs and restores the grain into a body having stalk and ear. And so also to those who shall deserve to obtain an inheritance in the kingdom of heaven, that germ of the body's restoration, which we have before mentioned, by God's command restores out of the earthly and animal body a spiritual one, capable of inhabiting the heavens; while to each one of those who may be of inferior merit, or of more abject condition, or even the lowest in the scale, and altogether thrust aside, there is yet given, in proportion to the dignity of his life and soul, a glory and dignity of body,—nevertheless in such a way, that even the body which rises again of those who are to be destined to everlasting fire or to severe punishments, is by the very change of the resurrection so incorruptible, that it cannot be corrupted and dissolved even by severe punishments. . . .

III:6.3–9 The End

I am of opinion that the expression, by which God is said to be "all in all," means that He is "all" in each individual person. Now He will be "all" in each individual in this way: when all which any rational understanding, cleansed from the dregs of every sort of vice, and with every cloud of wickedness completely swept away, can either feel, or understand, or think, will be wholly God; and when it will no longer behold or retain anything else than God, but when God will be the measure and standard of all its movements; and thus God will be "all," for there will no.longer be any distinction of good and evil seeing evil nowhere exists; for God is all things, and to Him no evil is near: nor will there be any longer a desire to eat from the tree of the knowledge of good and evil, on the part of him who is always in the possession of good, and to whom God is all. So then, when the end has been restored to the beginning, and the termination of things compared with their commencement, that condition of things will be re-established in which rational nature was placed, when it had no need to eat of the tree of the knowledge of good and evil; so that when all feeling of wickedness has been removed, and the individual has been purified and cleansed, He who alone is the one good God becomes to him "all," and that not in the case of a few individuals, or of a considerable number, but He Himself is "all in all . . ."

The last enemy, moreover, who is called death, is said on this account to be destroyed, that there may not be anything left of a mournful kind when death does not exist, nor anything that is adverse when there is no enemy. The destruction of the last enemy, indeed, is to be understood, not as if its substance, which was formed by God, is to perish, but because its mind and hostile will, which came not from God, but from itself, are to be destroyed. Its destruction, therefore, will not be its non-existence, but its ceasing to be an enemy, and (to be) death. For nothing is impossible to the Omnipotent, nor is anything incapable of restoration to its Creator: for He made all things that they might exist, and those things which were made for existence cannot cease to be. For this reason also will they admit of change and variety, so as to be placed, according to their merits, either in a better or worse position; but no destruction of substance can befall those things which were created by God for the purpose of permanent existence. For those things which agreeably to the common opinion are believed to perish, the nature either of our faith or of the truth will not permit us to suppose to be destroyed. Finally, our flesh is supposed by ignorant men and unbelievers to be destroyed after death, in such a degree that it retains no relic at all of its former substance. We, however, who believe in its resurrection, understand that a change only has been produced by death, but that its substance certainly remains; and that by the will of its Creator, and at the time appointed, it will be restored to life; and that a second time a change will take place in it, so that what at first was flesh (formed) out of earthly soil, and was afterwards dissolved by death, and again reduced to dust and ashes ("For dust thou art," it is said, "and to dust shalt thou return"), will be again raised from the earth, and shall after this, according to the merits of the indwelling soul, advance to the glory of a spiritual body.

Into this condition, then, we are to suppose that all this bodily substance of ours will be brought, when all things shall be re-established in a state of unity, and when God shall be all in all. And this result must be understood as being brought about, not suddenly, but slowly and gradually, seeing that the process of amendment and correction will take place imperceptibly in the individual instances during the lapse of countless and unmeasured ages, some outstripping others, and tending by a swifter course towards perfection, while others again follow close at hand, and some again a long way behind; and thus, through the numerous and uncounted orders of progressive beings who are being reconciled to God from a state of enmity, the last enemy is finally reached, who is called death, so that he also may be destroyed, and no longer be an enemy. When, therefore, all rational souls shall have been restored to a condition of this kind, then the nature of this body of ours will undergo a change into the glory of a spiritual body. . . .

The whole of this reasoning, then, amounts to this: that God created two general natures—a visible, i.e., a corporeal nature; and an invisible nature, which is incorporeal. Now these two natures admit of two different permutations. That invisible and rational nature changes in mind and purpose, because it is endowed with freedom of will, and is on this account found sometimes to be engaged in the practice of good, and sometimes in that of the opposite. But this corporeal nature admits of a change in substance; whence also God, the arranger of all things, has the service of this matter at His command in the moulding, or fabrication, or re-touching of whatever He wishes, so that corporeal nature may be transmuted, and transformed into any forms or species whatever, according as the deserts of things may demand; which the prophet evidently has in view when he says, "It is God who makes and transforms all things." . . .

In this way, accordingly, we are to suppose that at the consummation and restoration of all things, those who make a gradual advance, and who ascend (in the scale of improvement), will arrive in due measure and order at that land, and at that training which is contained in it, where they may be prepared for those better institutions to which no addition can be made. For, after His agents and servants, the Lord Christ, who is King of all, will Himself assume the kingdom; i.e., after instruction in the holy virtues, He will Himself instruct those who are capable of receiving Him in respect of His being wisdom, reigning in them until He has subjected them to the Father, who has subdued all things to Himself, i.e., that when they shall have been made capable of receiving God, God may be to them all in all.

From Origen, *De principiis,* in *ANF,* Vol. 4, pp. 293–96, 345–48 passim.

3.3 Arianism:
Arius and the Nicene Creed

Conflicting interpretations of the person of Christ stood at the center of disputes dividing churches and cities. One such conflict with ramifications for Christian theology occurred in the important city of Alexandria, Egypt. Alexandria was a cosmopolitan city, a major center of intellectual life and church authority in the Roman Empire. Debate among Alexandrian churchmen and theologians, trained in classical literature and thought, was often fierce. Arius (circa 260–336), priest and theologian in Alexandria, instigated one such debate over the relationship of Christ as the Son of God to God the Father. This debate between Arius and his opponents broadened to other parts of the empire, and led to the important decisions made at the Council of Nicea (325), called by the newly Christian emperor Constantine to resolve this divisive dispute. Even after this imperial attempt to create and impose a single, unifying doctrine in the form of the Nicene Creed, heterodox views on the nature of Christ and the Trinity continued to exist as alternate doctrines vehemently attacked by later orthodox churchmen. The doctrine of a subordinate Christ, called by Trinitarian opponents *Arianism* after its major spokesperson, survived as a branch of Christianity. For example, many of the Gothic tribes in Europe in the fourth through seventh centuries adopted this form of Christianity, and then had to be unconverted from this "heresy" to orthodox Catholic Christianity as embodied in the Nicene Creed (see 8.2, 9.2).

The documents below display the two positions: the Arian, and what became enforced orthodoxy. Both use philosophical terminology derived from Greek philosophy. Arianism asserts that the Son (Christ) is not eternal or equal to the Father. Opponents of the Arian position argued that the Son must be equal to, and of the same substance as, the Father or risk diminishing the monotheism of Christianity by creating a demigod in Christ. Thus began a long-running dispute that resulted in the pronouncements of the council of Nicea and Arius's expulsion from Alexandria, along with his followers.

Arius, a noted preacher who used Greek logic to argue vigorously for his positions, asserted his position in outright defiance of the teaching of his superior, Alexander, the Bishop of Alexandria (Arius stood up in church and disagreed with the bishop). Arius's published views, as well as other Arian documents, were quoted extensively in the vehement *Orations against Arianism* (after 339) by a later bishop of Alexandria, Athanasius (circa 300–373). The excerpt here from Athanasius's treatise is a passage he quoted from Arius's book, the *Thalia.*

The Nicene Creed was used as a test of orthodoxy by subsequent generations of Catholic and orthodox Christians; as well, it is still used today by a large number of Protestant churches as an affirmation of the essential faith. Nonetheless, this creed was the product of highly politicized circumstances. The emperor Constantine called the council in 325 to resolve what he saw as a divisive debate threatening the unity of the empire. He ordered the bishops at the council to come up with a definitive statement that precluded any other interpretations; this they did, rejecting the Arian view of Christ in favor of arguments propounded by Eusebius of Caesarea (circa 260–339), the emperor's biographer (2.3). The resulting creed went through some later revisions, but the core remained intact as a rebuttal of Arius's view of Christ. The version below is the final formulation of the Nicene Creed from the First Council of Constantinople in 381.

Questions

1. By what logic does Arius make Christ subservient to God the Father?
2. What are the problems of using the logic of Greek thought to propose a rational understanding of God's nature?
3. What points in opposition to Arianism does the Nicene Creed insist on, and why?

Arian Statements Quoted in Athanasius's Orations

From the Thalia *of Arius*

God Himself then, in His own nature, is ineffable by all men. Equal or like Himself He alone has none, or one in glory. And Ingenerate we call Him, because of Him who is generate by nature. We praise Him as without beginning because of Him who has a beginning. And adore Him as everlasting, because of Him who in time has come to be. The Unbegun made the Son a beginning of things originated; and advanced Him as a Son to Himself by adoption. He has nothing proper to God in proper subsistence. For He is not equal, no, nor one in essence with Him. Wise is God, for He is the teacher of Wisdom. There is full proof that God is invisible to all beings; both to things which are through the Son, and to the Son He is invisible. I will say it expressly, how by the Son is seen the Invisible; by that power by which God sees, and in His own measure, the Son endures to see the Father, as is lawful. Thus there is a Triad, not in equal glories. Not intermingling with each other are their subsistences. One more glorious than the other in their glories unto immensity. Foreign from the Son in essence is the Father, for He is without beginning. Understand that the Monad was; but the Dyad was not, before it was in existence. It follows at once that, though the Son was not, the Father was God. Hence the Son, not being (for He existed at the will of the Father), is God Only-begotten, and He is alien from either. Wisdom existed as Wisdom by the will of the Wise God. Hence He is conceived in numberless conceptions: Spirit, Power, Wisdom, God's glory, Truth, Image, and Word. Understand that He is conceived to be Radiance and Light. One equal to the Son, the Superior is able to beget; but one more excellent, or superior, or greater, He is not able. At God's will the Son is what and whatsoever He is. And when and since He was, from that time He has subsisted from God. He, being a strong God, praises in His degree the Superior. To speak in brief, God is ineffable to His Son. For He is to Himself what He is, that is, unspeakable. So that nothing which is called comprehensible does the Son know to speak about; for it is impossible for Him to investigate the Father, who is by Himself. For the Son does not know His own essence, For, being Son, He really existed, at the will of the Father. What argument then allows, that He who is from the Father should know His own parent by comprehension? For it is plain that for that which hath a beginning to conceive how the Unbegun is, or to grasp the idea, is not possible.

From *Select Writings and Letters of Athanasius, Bishop of Alexandria,* trans. Archibald Robertson, in *NPNF,* Second Series, Vol. 4, pp. 457–58.

Nicene Creed, Second Council of Constantinople, A.D. 381

We believe in one God, the FATHER Almighty, Maker of heaven and earth and of all things visible and invisible. And in one Lord JESUS CHRIST, the only-begotten Son of God, begotten of the Father before all worlds [*aeons*] Light of Light, very God of very God, begotten, not made, being of one substance with the Father; by whom all things were made; who for us men, and for our salvation, came down from heaven, and was incarnate by the Holy Ghost of the Virgin Mary, and was made man; he was crucified for us under Pontius Pilate, and suffered, and was buried, and the third day he rose again, according to the Scriptures, and ascended into heaven, and sitteth on the right hand of the Father; from thence he shall come again, with glory, to judge the quick and the dead; whose kingdom shall have no end. And in the HOLY GHOST, the Lord and Giver of life, who precedeth from the Father,* who with the Father and the Son together is worshipped and glorified, who spake by the prophets. In one holy catholic and apostolic church; we acknowledge one baptism for the remission of sins; we look for the resurrection of the dead, and the life of the world to come. Amen.

From *TROS,* Vol. 4, no. 2, p. 11.

3.4 Nestorians: Nestorius, Cyril, and Chalcedon

Another theological debate similar to the Arian dispute occurred between Nestorius and Cyril of Alexandria over the nature of Christ as both human and divine. The incarnation, whereby "God became man," born miraculously of the Virgin Mary, was generally accepted, as evident in the Nicene Creed; but *how* he was both human and divine involved disputes over complex Greek terminology about the nature and essence of being. Nestorius (circa 381–451), trained in the Antioch school and later bishop of Constantinople, argued for a Dyophysite position: Christ has two natures, one human and one divine, and the divine nature entered into a created human form, uniting with it. His opponent Cyril (circa 375–444), who came from the rival school of Alexandria where he became bishop, argued for the Monophysite, or one-nature view of Christ. Understanding the Greek word for nature, *physis,* differently, Monophysites argued that he could logically have only one nature, and that it must be divine, fused eternally with the human.

Dyophysitism saw the divine nature as separate, dwelling within the man Jesus and untouched by the limitations and suffering experienced by the human nature. On the other hand, Monophysites sought to maintain the pure divinity of Christ as the Logos or Divine Word by establishing a single nature for him, and they derided Dyophysites for creating two Christs. However, Nestorius and many of the doctrine's proponents did not believe, as their opponents often claimed, in a

---

*"and from the Son," the filioque clause asserting that the Holy Spirit comes from both the Father and the Son, was added in the Western Church in the eighth century.

Christ completely divided into two persons; Dyophysites used "nature" in a looser sense to describe the two differing qualities of divinity and humanity in the single person of Christ. Nestorius wanted to keep the divine and the human separate enough that he objected to calling the Virgin Mary Theotokos, the "mother of God," as asserted by his adversary Cyril of Alexandria; Nestorius preferred to call her Man-bearer or Christ-bearer to distinguish his human birth from his eternal divine nature, a lesser view of Mary that inflamed the often emotional debate.

Nestorius views were, ironically, quite close to the intermediate proposition established by the council of Chalcedon in 451, excerpted below, that Christ was one person with two natures. However, despite his identification with the Chalcedon decision, Nestorius was labeled a heretic and lived out his life in exile, reflecting on the bitter feelings engendered in the debate with Cyril. Chalcedon also rejected Monophysitism; Monophysites later fled Roman domains under persecution from Chalcedon emperors and churchmen and subsequently formed their own churches.

Below are two documents representing different views in this debate. The first one is from a rare transcription of a Syrian manuscript that is a collection of Nestorian texts (Cambridge MS Oriental 1319). It includes a Nestorian creed, Cyril's condemnation of Dyophysitism, and then a Nestorian rebuttal to Cyril. Against these Nestorian assertions stands the doctrinal decision rendered at Chalcedon in 451, the second excerpt below. Just as the Nicene Creed (3.3) became a test of orthodoxy, so churches divided along Chalcedon: those Dyophysites and Monophysites who rejected Chalcedon became known as non-Chalcedon churches as the Chalcedon creed became orthodoxy for the western churches (see 7.1 and 7.2 for Monophysites in Egypt and Africa and 7.3 for Nestorians in China).

Questions

1. Compare Cyril's and the Nestorian's positions on the incarnation: what are the essential differences?

2. Compare the Nestorian creed and the Chalcedon creed: in what do they agree and where do they disagree?

3. Why is this issue of Christ's nature so important to Christians? What do you think are its ramifications?

Cambridge MS Oriental 1319

The Creed of the Bishops of Persia (Dyophysite)

We believe in one divine nature, everlasting, without beginning, living and quickening all, powerful, creating all powers, wise, imparting all wisdom, simple spirit, infinite, incomprehensible, not compounded and without parts, incorporeal, both invisible and immutable, impassible and immortal; nor is it possible, whether by itself, or by another, or with another, that suffering or change should enter in unto it; but it is perfect in its essence and in everything which belongs to it, nor is it possible for it to receive any addition or subtraction, it being by itself substance, and God over all. . . . and because the Father is impassible and unchangeable, so also is the Son and the Spirit confessed with him (to be) as he is without suffering and change, and just as the Father is believed to be infinite and without parts, so also is confessed Son and Spirit to be without limits and composition; . . . and in order that he might raise our nature to honor, and that he might sow in us the true hope of the resurrection from the dead, and the new and incorruptible life which for ever receives no change, according to his fore-knowledge and his will from everlasting; on this account, for us men, and for our salvation, the Son of God, God the Word, without departing from being with him who begat him, came into the world while he was in the world, and the world came into being through him. And because created natures were not able to behold the glorious nature of his godhead, in an extraordinary manner out of the nature of the house of Adam did he fashion for him a holy temple, a perfect man, from the blessed virgin Mary, who was made perfect in the natural order without (there being) the participation of a husband; and he put him on and united him with himself, and in him he revealed himself to the world and spoke with men, according to the utterance of the holy angel to the mother of our saviour: 'The Holy Spirit shall come, and the power of the most high shall overshadow you; for this reason, he that is born of you is a holy one, and shall be called Son of God.' By the fact of his saying 'He shall be called Son of God', he has taught us concerning the wondrous conjunction of the union, without separation, which from the commencement of his being formed, existed between the human nature that was taken, and God the Word who took it, so that henceforth we know as one prosopon [lit. face; persona] our Lord, Jesus Christ, the Son of God; who is born before the worlds, without beginning, of the Father in the nature of his godhead, and born, in the last times, of the holy virgin, the son of David, in the nature of his manhood, as God had earlier promised to the blessed David: ' Of the fruit of your womb shall I set upon your throne.' And after the issue of these things, the blessed Paul expounded the promise, saying to the Jews concerning David: 'From the seed of this man, God has raised up, as he promised, Jesus, (to be) saviour.' And again, to the Philippians, he wrote thus: 'Think within yourselves that which also Jesus Christ (thought) who, though he was in the form of God, assumed the form of a servant.' For whom else would he be calling 'the form of God' but Christ in his godhead, and whom else again would he be naming 'the form of a servant' but Christ in his manhood? And the former, he said, took, while the latter was taken. Therefore it is not possible to confuse the properties of the natures, for it is impossible that he who took should be he who was taken or that he who was taken should be the taker. For that God the Word should be revealed in the man whom he took, and (that) the human nature which was taken should appear to creation in the order of him who took it and (that) at the same time in his undivided union should be confessed the one Son of God, Christ, this we have learned and do maintain. But that the godhead should be changed into the manhood, and that the manhood should be transmuted into the nature of the godhead is impossible. For the (divine) substance cannot fall under the necessity of change and suffering, because if the godhead underwent change, there would no longer be a revelation but a corruption of godhead, and if again the manhood departed from its nature, there would no longer be salvation, but an extinction of the manhood. And for this reason we believe in our hearts and confess with our lips one Lord Jesus Christ, Son of the living God, whose godhead is not hidden, nor his manhood concealed, but he is perfect God and perfect man. But when we call Christ perfect God we do not name the Trinity, but one of the hypostases [particular individuals] of the Trinity, (namely) God the Word. And when again we give the appellation of man to Christ, we are not naming all men, but that one hypostasis which was manifestly taken for our salvation into the union with God the Word. For this reason our Lord Jesus Christ, who was born in his godhead of his Father everlastingly, is (also) he who, in the last times, was born for us of the virgin in his manhood. And while he remained in his godhead without deficiency and change, in his manhood after his birth, he was also circumcised and grew, in accordance with the witness of the blessed evangelist: 'Jesus grew in stature and in wisdom, and in favour with God and men.' And he observed the law, and was baptized in Jordan by John, and then he began to preach the new covenant. Whilst by the power of his godhead, he was working wonders, the cleansing of lepers, the giving of sight to the blind, the banishment of demons, the raising of the dead, yet in the nature of his manhood, he hungered, and thirsted, and ate, and drank, and was wearied, and slept; and last of all, for our sakes he delivered himself to death, and was crucified and suffered and died without his godhead (either) departing from him, or suffering. And his body was wrapped in a linen cloth, and he was placed in a tomb, and after three days he rose by the power of his godhead, as he had foretold to the Jews: 'Destroy this temple and in three days I will raise it up.' And the evangelist has expounded this utterance, saying: 'For he was speaking of the temple of his body.' And after he arose, he lived on earth with his disciples for forty days, and showed them his hands and his feet, saying: 'Touch me and know that a spirit has not flesh and bones as you have seen that I have', so that by word and by deeds he might assure them of his resurrection, and that by the assurance of his resurrection, he might confirm in us the hope of our resurrection. And after forty days, he ascended into heaven, in the sight of his disciples as they watched him, and a cloud received him, and he was hidden from their eyes according to the testimony of scripture. And we confess that he will come from heaven with the power and glory of his angels in order to effect the resurrection of the whole race of men, and judgement and examination of all rational beings, as the angels said to the apostles at the time of his ascension: 'This Jesus who has been taken up from you into heaven shall so come as you have seen him ascend into heaven.' And by this they have manifestly taught us that even when he was taken up into heaven, the hypostasis of the manhood was not annulled or changed but is preserved in indivisible union with the godhead in that exalted glory in which he will be seen in his final revelation from heaven for the shame of those who crucified him and for the joy and pride of those who believe in him, to whom, with his Father and the Holy Spirit be glory and honour for ever and ever, Amen.

The Monophysite Cyril's Anathema Against Dyophysitism

I. Whoever does not confess that Emmanuel [Jesus, who came into the world] is in truth God, and for this reason the virgin is God-bearer, for she bare after the flesh the Word which is from God the Father when he became flesh—let him be anathema. . . .

V. Whoever says of Christ that he is God-bearing man, and not rather that he is God in truth, as an only Son in nature, in that 'the Word became flesh', and shared like us blood and flesh—let him be anathema.

VI. Whoever says that the Word of God the Father is the God or Lord of Christ, and does not rather confess that he is God and man simultaneously, in that 'the Word became flesh', as it is written—let him be anathema.

VII. Whoever says that Jesus was energized as a man by God the Word, and says that he took the glory of the only begotten on himself as though he was another, apart from him—let him be anathema.

The Theses of Dyophysite Nestorius in Response

1. Whoever does not say of the Holy Trinity that it is equal in substance, and that the everlasting God is one, incorporeal and infinite, wholly impassible and unchangeable, who is the cause and the creator of all, who is known in the three hypostases of Father, Son and Holy Spirit, in which

three hypostatic prosopa [individual persons] and in their peculiarity consists the measure of his eternity and of his substance, and of the fullness of his nature—denies the truth. . . .

4. Whoever says that he, the Son, who is equal to the Father, became not equal, that is: man, and thus suffered, and does not rather say that he took a man, and when he suffered, he was conjoined to him in the union, while he remained impassible—denies the truth. . . .

8. Whoever does not confess of him, who is always, and exists at all times, and did not begin, and cease to be, that he took man for his revelation, but says that he became man, resembling in these matters Apollinarius, and that he was born, and was helped, and that he suffered, and arose, and ascended, and was placed equal with the throne which is on the right hand of God, and that he took away what he had previously given to the holy temple which he had taken through it (*sc.* the temple), also to us, because of whom, and for the salvation of whom, it was taken—denies the truth.

From *A Nestorian Collection of Christological Texts,* ed. and trans. Luise Abramowski and Alan E. Goodman, in *University of Cambridge Oriental Publications No. 19: A Nestorian Collection of Christological Texts,* Vol. 2: Introduction, Translation, Indexes (London: Cambridge University Press, 1972), pp. 88–93, 125–128 passim. Copyright Faculty of Oriental Studies, University of Cambridge, 1972. Reprinted with the permission of Cambridge University Press. Notes omitted.

The Creed of Chalcedon (451)

Following the holy Fathers we teach with one voice that the Son [of God] and our Lord Jesus Christ is to be confessed as one and the same [Person], that he is perfect in Godhead and perfect in manhood, very God and very man, of a reasonable soul and [human] body consisting, consubstantial with the Father as touching his Godhead, and consubstantial with us as touching his manhood; made in all things like unto us, sin only excepted; begotten of his Father before the worlds according to his Godhead; but in these last days for us men and for our salvation born [into the world] of the Virgin Mary, the Mother of God according to his manhood. This one and the same Jesus Christ, the only-begotten Son [of God] must be confessed to be in two natures, unconfusedly, immutably, indivisibly, inseparably [united], and that without the distinction of natures being taken away by such union, but rather the peculiar property of each nature being preserved and being united in one Person and subsistence [prosopon and hypostasis], not separated or divided into two persons, but one and the same Son and only-begotten, God the Word, our Lord Jesus Christ, as the Prophets of old time have spoken concerning him, and as the Lord Jesus Christ hath taught us, and as the

Creed of the Fathers hath delivered to us.

These things, therefore, having been expressed by us with the greatest accuracy and attention, the holy Ecumenical Synod defines that no one shall be suffered to bring forward a different faith, nor to write, nor to put together, nor to excogitate, nor to teach it to others. But such as dare either to put together another faith, or to bring forward or to teach or to deliver a different Creed to as wish to be converted to the knowledge of the truth, from the Gentiles, or Jews or any heresy whatever, if they be Bishops or clerics let them be deposed, the Bishops from the Episcopate, and the clerics from the clergy; but if they be monks or laics [laity]: let them be anathematized.

From *The Seven Ecumenical Councils,* in *NPNF,* Second Series, Vol. 14, pp. 264–65.

-4-

Life and Death

The Body and Resurrection

The duality inherent in Christian thought, between believer and unbeliever, this world and the next, body and spirit, comes out most clearly
in the attitudes and practices surrounding death. Origen's arguments
(3.2) point to considerable discussion among philosophers and theologians about what the resurrection meant. What was it that rose at the
last judgment—The whole body, all the particles miraculously gathered
and reassembled? Or some new spiritual body that God makes, one that
still contains some essence of the person's identity? Identity between
life and the afterlife became a crucial issue, evident in stories of martyrs, the lives of ascetics, and statements on tombstones.

The bodies of martyrs and ascetics are important markers of these
views. The martyr's body was torn and fragmented, sometimes eaten
and digested by wild animals, seemingly losing in the process its
integrity and identity. And yet one of the triumphs of the martyrs'
stories such as Perpetua's (4.1) is her victory over death. The martyr
proclaims over again, like Christ's story, the possibility of resurrection. The ascetic's emaciated body represents likewise the triumph of
the spirit over the body. Macrina's antimaterialism through fasting
and celibacy, as described by her bishop brother (4.2), brings her
closer to the spiritual body she will inherit after death. In both these
cases, the body of the saintly martyr or ascetic becomes an object of
veneration: their bodies remain while their souls have departed, to
be reunited at the last judgment. In the meantime, the two, body and
soul, are still connected in the one person of the saint, hence the
emphasis on tombs and relics of saints in late antiquity (see for
example 6.3).

Perhaps the most revealing marker of death for the Christian, then,
are those things written on their tombstones by loved ones (4.3). Short
inscriptions reveal not only the feelings of the bereaved toward the

73

dead but also some of their beliefs about death and the afterlife. The changes in burial practice in the late Roman Empire are significant, as are the new ways in which Christians express their beliefs in stone.

4.1. Heroic Martyrdom: Perpetua

The story recounted here, primarily of Saint Perpetua but also of her comrade in martyrdom, Saint Felicity, is one of the most poignant and heartrending, purposely so. If Christians were to reject all worldly life and its pleasures in favor of spiritual things, then the most difficult choices involved rejecting one's own family—father, husband, child. That Perpetua and Felicity were willing to make this ultimate sacrifice of leaving their loved ones was testament to the strength of their faith. Moreover, in the context of Late Roman society their feminine identity played a role in this heroism. If persecution meant facing death by dismemberment in an arena filled with wild animals, then nothing was more chilling than seeing the normally noncombatant and defenseless sex face it heroically. A man in the military-minded Roman Empire might be expected to show virile strength in the arena; that a woman should face such a death with calm and even bravado increased the emotional impact of the story and its message of faith.

The emotional power arises not only from the story's graphic descriptions of martyrdom but also from the use of Perpetua's own voice recounting her experiences (framed by the editor's remarks establishing the prophetic context and describing her death). Clearly, Perpetua and those who handed down her story wanted to challenge the listener or reader to consider the validity of Christianity's claims and to exhort the Christian to imitate the virtues acted out in the story. The fundamental value underlying the seemingly suicidal behavior of the martyrs was the belief in an otherworld of greater reality than this illusory and temporal world. What Perpetua sees in her visions is more real to her than this world. Visions of this type offer one more validation to her and to others of the truth of their belief. Like miracles, then, visions were manifestations in this world of the spiritual and eternal realm of God, impinging on and dominating the physical world humans inhabit only temporarily.

Questions

1. How do Perpetua's visions help her to part from her family?

2. In what ways do Perpetua and Felicity behave heroically in their manner of facing death?

3. What impact do you think this story would have on a Christian audience?

The Martyrdom of Saints Perpetua and Felicitas

1. The deeds recounted about the faith in ancient times were a proof of God's favour and achieved the spiritual strengthening of men as well; and they were set forth in writing precisely that honour might be rendered to God and comfort to men by the recollection of the past through the written word. Should not then more recent examples be set down that contribute equally to both ends? For indeed these too will one day become ancient and needful for the ages to come, even though in our own day they may enjoy less prestige because of the prior claim of antiquity.

Let those then who would restrict the power of the one Spirit to times and seasons look to this: the more recent events should be considered the greater, being later than those of old, and this is a consequence of the extraordinary graces promised for the last stage of time. *For in the last days, God declares, I will pour out my Spirit upon all flesh and their sons and daughters shall prophesy and on my manservants and my maidservants I will pour my Spirit, and the young men shall see visions and the old men shall dream dreams.* So too we hold in honour and acknowledge not only new prophecies but new visions as well, according to the promise. And we consider all the other functions of the Holy Spirit as intended for the good of the Church; for the same Spirit has been sent to distribute all his gifts to all, as the Lord apportions to everyone. For this reason we deem it imperative to set them forth and to make them known through the word for the glory of God. Thus no one of weak or despairing faith may think that supernatural grace was present only among men of ancient times, either in the grace of martyrdom or of visions, for God always achieves what he promises, as a witness to the nonbeliever and a blessing to the faithful.

And so, my brethren and little children, *that which we have heard and have touched with our hands we proclaim also to you, so that* those of you that were witnesses may recall the glory of the Lord and those that now learn of it through hearing *may have fellowship* with the holy martyrs and, through them, *with* the Lord *Christ Jesus,* to whom belong splendour and honour for all ages. Amen.

2. A number of young catechumens were arrested, Revocatus and his fellow slave Felicitas, Saturninus and Secundulus, and with them Vibia Perpetua, a newly married woman of good family and upbringing. Her mother and father were still alive and one of her two brothers was a catechumen like herself. She was about twenty-two years old and had an infant son at the breast. (Now from this point on the entire account of her ordeal is her own, according to her own ideas and in the way that she herself wrote it down.)

3. While we were still under arrest (she said) my father out of love for me was trying to persuade me and shake my resolution. 'Father,' said I, 'do you see this vase here, for example, or waterpot or whatever?'

'Yes, I do', said he.

And I told him: 'Could it be called by any other name than what it is?'

And he said: 'No.'

'Well, so too I cannot be called anything other than what I am, a Christian.'

At this my father was so angered by the word 'Christian' that he moved towards me as though he would pluck my eyes out. But he left it at that and departed, vanquished along with his diabolical arguments.

For a few days afterwards I gave thanks to the Lord that I was separated from my father, and I was comforted by his absence. During these few days I was baptized, and I was inspired by the Spirit not to ask for any other favour after the water but simply the perseverance of the flesh. A few days later we were lodged in the prison; and I was terrified, as I had never before been in such a dark hole. What a difficult time it was! With the crowd the heat was stifling; then there was the extortion of the soldiers; and to crown all, I was tortured with worry for my baby there.

Then Tertius and Pomponius, those blessed deacons who tried to take care of us, bribed the soldiers to allow us to go to a better part of the prison to refresh ourselves for a few hours. Everyone then left that dungeon and shifted for himself. I nursed my baby, who was faint from hunger. In my anxiety I spoke to my mother about the child, I tried to comfort my brother, and I gave the child in their charge. I was in pain because I saw them suffering out of pity for me. These were the trials I had to endure for many days. Then I got permission for my baby to stay with me in prison. At once I recovered my health, relieved as I was of my worry and anxiety over the child. My prison had suddenly become a palace, so that I wanted to be there rather than anywhere else.

4. Then my brother said to me: 'Dear sister, you are greatly privileged; surely you might ask for a vision to discover whether you are to be condemned or freed.'

Faithfully I promised that I would, for I knew that I could speak with the Lord, whose great blessings I had come to experience. And so I said: 'I shall tell you tomorrow.' Then I made my request and this was the vision I had.

I saw a ladder of tremendous height made of bronze, reaching all the way to the heavens, but it was so narrow that only one person could climb up at a time. To the sides of the ladder were attached all sorts of metal weapons: there were swords, spears, hooks, daggers, and spikes; so that if anyone tried to climb up carelessly or without paying attention, he would be mangled and his flesh would adhere to the weapons.

At the foot of the ladder lay a dragon of enormous size, and it would attack those who tried to climb up and try to terrify them from doing so. And Saturus was the first to go up, he who was later to give himself up of his own accord. He had been the builder of our strength, although he was not present when we were arrested. And he arrived at the top of the staircase and he looked back and said to me: 'Perpetua, I am waiting for you. But take care; do not let the dragon bite you.'

'He will not harm me,' I said, 'in the name of Christ Jesus.'

Slowly, as though he were afraid of me, the dragon stuck his head out from underneath the ladder. Then, using it as my first step, I trod on his head and went up.

Then I saw an immense garden, and in it a grey-haired man sat in shepherd's garb; tall he was, and milking sheep. And standing around him were many thousands of people clad in white garments. He raised his head, looked at me, and said: 'I am glad you have come, my child.'

He called me over to him and gave me, as it were, a mouthful of the milk he was drawing; and I took it into my cupped hands and consumed it. And all those who stood around said: 'Amen!' At the sound of this word I came to, with the taste of something sweet still in my mouth. I at once told this to my brother, and we realized that we would have to suffer, and that from now on we would no longer have any hope in this life.

5. A few days later there was a rumour that we were going to be given a hearing. My father also arrived from the city, worn with worry, and he came to see me with the idea of persuading me.

'Daughter,' he said, 'have pity on my grey head—have pity on me your father, if I deserve to be called your father, if I have favoured you above all your brothers, if I have raised you to reach this prime of your life. Do not abandon me to be the reproach of men. Think of your brothers, think of your mother and your aunt, think of your child, who will not be able to live once you are gone. Give up your pride! You will destroy all of us! None of us will ever be able to speak freely again if anything happens to you.'

This was the way my father spoke out of love for me, kissing my hands and throwing himself down before me. With tears in his eyes he no longer addressed me as his daughter but as a woman. I was sorry for my father's sake, because he alone of all my kin would be unhappy to see me suffer.

I tried to comfort him saying: 'It will all happen in the prisoner's dock as God wills; for you may be sure that we are not left to ourselves but are all in his power.'

And he left me in great sorrow.

6. One day while we were eating breakfast we were suddenly hurried off for a hearing. We arrived at the forum, and straight away the story went

about the neighbourhood near the forum and a huge crowd gathered. We walked up to the prisoner's dock. All the others when questioned admitted their guilt. Then, when it came my turn, my father appeared with my son, dragged me from the step, and said: 'Perform the sacrifice—have pity on your baby!'

Hilarianus the governor, who had received his judicial powers as the successor of the late proconsul Minucius Timinianus, said to me: 'Have pity on your father's grey head; have pity on your infant son. Offer the sacrifice for the welfare of the emperors.'

'I will not', I retorted.

'Are you a Christian?' said Hilarianus.

And I said: 'Yes, I am.'

When my father persisted in trying to dissuade me, Hilarianus ordered him to be thrown to the ground and beaten with a rod. I felt sorry for father, just as if I myself had been beaten. I felt sorry for his pathetic old age.

Then Hilarianus passed sentence on all of us: we were condemned to the beasts, and we returned to prison in high spirits. But my baby had got used to being nursed at the breast and to staying with me in prison. So I sent the deacon Pomponius straight away to my father to ask for the baby. But father refused to give him over. But as God willed, the baby had no further desire for the breast, nor did I suffer any inflammation; and so I was relieved of any anxiety for my child and of any discomfort in my breasts.

7. Some days later when we were all at prayer, suddenly while praying I spoke out and uttered the name Dinocrates. I was surprised; for the name had never entered my mind until that moment. And I was pained when I recalled what had happened to him. At once I realized that I was privileged to pray for him. I began to pray for him and to sigh deeply for him before the Lord. That very night I had the following vision. I saw Dinocrates coming out of a dark hole, where there were many others with him, very hot and thirsty, pale and dirty. On his face was the wound he had when he died.

Now Dinocrates had been my brother according to the flesh; but he had died horribly of cancer of the face when he was seven years old, and his death was a source of loathing to everyone. Thus it was for him that I made my prayer. There was a great abyss between us: neither could approach the other. Where Dinocrates stood there was a pool full of water; and its rim was higher than the child's height, so that Dinocrates had to stretch himself up to drink. I was sorry that, though the pool had water in it, Dinocrates could not drink because of the height of the rim. Then I woke up, realizing that my brother was suffering. But I was confident that I could help him in his trouble; and I prayed for him every day until we were transferred to the military prison. For we were supposed to fight with the beasts at the military games to be held on the occasion of the emperor Geta's birthday. And I prayed for my brother day and night with tears and sighs that this favour might be granted me.

8. On the day we were kept in chains, I had this vision shown to me. I saw the same spot that I had seen before, but there was Dinocrates all clean, well dressed, and refreshed. I saw a scar where the wound had been; and the pool that I had seen before now had its rim lowered to the level of the child's waist. And Dinocrates kept drinking water from it, and there above the rim was a golden bowl full of water. And Dinocrates drew close and began to drink from it, and yet the bowl remained full. And when he had drunk enough of the water, he began to play as children do. Then I awoke, and I realized that he had been delivered from his suffering.

9. Some days later, an adjutant named Pudens, who was in charge of the prison, began to show us great honour, realizing that we possessed some great power within us. And he began to allow many visitors to see us for our mutual comfort.

Now the day of the contest was approaching, and my father came to see me overwhelmed with sorrow. He started tearing the hairs from his beard and threw them on the ground; he then threw himself on the ground and began to curse his old age and to say such words as would move all creation. I felt sorry for his unhappy old age.

10. The day before we were to fight with the beasts I saw the following vision. Pomponius the deacon came to the prison gates and began to knock violently. I went out and opened the gate for him. He was dressed in an unbelted white tunic, wearing elaborate sandals. And he said to me: 'Perpetua, come; we are waiting for you.'

Then he took my hand and we began to walk through rough and broken country. At last we came to the amphitheater out of breath, and he led me into the center of the arena.

Then he told me: 'Do not be afraid. I am here, struggling with you.' Then he left.

I looked at the enormous crowd who watched in astonishment. I was surprised that no beasts were let loose on me; for I knew that I was condemned to die by the beasts. Then out came an Egyptian against me, of vicious appearance, together with his seconds, to fight with me. There also came up to me some handsome young men to be my seconds and assistants.

My clothes were stripped off, and suddenly I was a man. My seconds began to rub me down with oil (as they are wont to do before a contest). Then I saw the Egyptian on the other side rolling in the dust. Next there came forth a man of marvellous stature, such that he rose above the top of the amphitheater. He was clad in a beltless purple tunic with two stripes (one on either side) running down the middle of his chest. He wore sandals that were wondrously made of gold and silver, and he carried a wand like an athletic trainer and a green branch on which there were golden apples.

And he asked for silence and said: 'If this Egyptian defeats her he will slay her with the sword. But if she defeats him, she will receive this branch.' Then he withdrew.

We drew close to one another and began to let our fists fly. My opponent tried to get hold of my feet, but I kept striking him in the face with the heels of my feet. Then I was raised up into the air and I began to pummel him without as it were touching the ground. Then when I noticed there was a lull, I put my two hands together linking the fingers of one hand with those of the other and thus I got hold of his head. He fell flat on his face and I stepped on his head.

The crowd began to shout and my assistants started to sing psalms. Then I walked up to the trainer and took the branch. He kissed me and said to me: 'Peace be with you, my daughter!' I began to walk in triumph towards the Gate of Life. Then I awoke. I realized that it was not with wild animals that I would fight but with the Devil, but I knew that I would win the victory. So much for what I did up until the eve of the contest. About what happened at the contest itself, let him write of it who will. . . .

[Narrator begins his account of what followed.]

15. As for Felicitas, she too enjoyed the Lord's favour in this wise. She had been pregnant when she was arrested, and was now in her eighth month. As the day of the spectacle drew near she was very distressed that her martyrdom would be postponed because of her pregnancy; for it is against the law for women with child to be executed. Thus she might have to shed her holy, innocent blood afterwards along with others who were common criminals. Her comrades in martyrdom were also saddened; for they were afraid that they would have to leave behind so fine a companion to travel alone on the same road to hope. And so, two days before the contest, they poured forth a prayer to the Lord in one torrent of common grief. And immediately after their prayer the birth pains came upon her. She suffered a good deal in her labour because of the natural difficulty of an eight months' delivery.

Hence one of the assistants of the prison guards said to her: 'You suffer so much now—what will you do when you are tossed to the beasts? Little did you think of them when you refused to sacrifice.'

'What I am suffering now', she replied, 'I suffer by myself. But then another will be inside me who will suffer for me, just as I shall be suffering for him.'

And she gave birth to a girl; and one of the sisters brought her up as her own daughter.

16. Therefore, since the Holy Spirit has permitted the story of this contest to be written down and by so permitting has willed it, we shall carry out the command or, indeed, the commission of the most saintly Perpetua, however unworthy I might be to add anything to this glorious story. At the same time I shall add one example of her perseverance and nobility of soul.

The military tribune had treated them with extraordinary severity because on the information of certain very foolish people he became afraid that they would be spirited out of the prison by magical spells.

Perpetua spoke to him directly. 'Why can you not even allow us to refresh ourselves properly? For we are the most distinguished of the condemned prisoners, seeing that we belong to the emperor; we are to fight on his very birthday. Would it not be to your credit if we were brought forth on the day in a healthier condition?'

The officer became disturbed and grew red. So it was that he gave the order that they were to be more humanely treated; and he allowed her brothers and other persons to visit, so that the prisoners could dine in their company. By this time the adjutant who was head of the gaol was himself a Christian.

17. On the day before, when they had their last meal, which is called the free banquet, they celebrated not a banquet but rather a love feast. They spoke to the mob with the same steadfastness, warned them of God's judgement, stressing the joy they would have in their suffering, and ridiculing the curiosity of those that came to see them. Saturus said: 'Will not tomorrow be enough for you? Why are you so eager to see something that you dislike? Our friends today will be our enemies on the morrow. But take careful note of what we look like so that you will recognize us on the day.' Thus everyone would depart from the prison in amazement, and many of them began to believe.

18. The day of their victory dawned, and they marched from the prison to the amphitheater joyfully as though they were going to heaven, with calm faces, trembling, if at all, with joy rather than fear. Perpetua went along with shining countenance and calm step, as the beloved of God, as a wife of Christ, putting down everyone's stare by her own intense gaze. With them also was Felicitas, glad that she had safely given birth so that now she could fight the beasts, going from one blood bath to another, from the midwife to the gladiator, ready to wash after childbirth in a second baptism.

They were then led up to the gate and the men were forced to put on the robe of priests of Saturn, the women the dress of the priestesses of Ceres. But the noble Perpetua strenuously resisted this to the end.

'We came to this of our own free will, that our freedom should not be violated. We agreed to pledge our lives provided that we would do no such thing. You agreed with us to do this.'

Even injustice recognized justice. The military tribune agreed. They were to be brought into the arena just as they were. Perpetua then began to sing a psalm: she was already treading on the head of the Egyptian. Revocatus, Saturninus, and Saturus began to warn the onlooking mob. Then when they came within sight of Hilarianus, they suggested by their motions and gestures: 'You have condemned us, but God will condemn you' was what they were saying.

At this the crowds became enraged and demanded that they be scourged before a line of gladiators. And they rejoiced at this that they had obtained a share in the Lord's sufferings.

19. But he who said, *Ask and you shall receive,* answered their prayer by giving each one the death he had asked for. For whenever they would discuss among themselves their desire for martyrdom, Saturninus indeed insisted that he wanted to be exposed to all the different beasts, that his crown might be all the more glorious. And so at the outset of the contest he and Revocatus were matched with a leopard, and then while in the stocks they were attacked by a bear. As for Saturus, he dreaded nothing more than a bear, and he counted on being killed by one bite of a leopard. Then he was matched with a wild boar; but the gladiator who had tied him to the animal was gored by the boar and died a few days after the contest, whereas Saturus was only dragged along. Then when he was bound in the stocks awaiting the bear, the animal refused to come out of the cages, so that Saturus was called back once more unhurt.

20. For the young women, however, the Devil had prepared a mad heifer. This was an unusual animal, but it was chosen that their sex might be matched with that of the beast. So they were stripped naked, placed in nets and thus brought out into the arena. Even the crowd was horrified when they saw that one was a delicate young girl and the other was a woman fresh from childbirth with the milk still dripping from her breasts. And so they were brought back again and dressed in unbelted tunics.

First the heifer tossed Perpetua and she fell on her back. Then sitting up she pulled down the tunic that was ripped along the side so that it covered her thighs, thinking more of her modesty than of her pain. Next she asked for a pin to fasten her untidy hair: for it was not right that a martyr should die with her hair in disorder, lest she might seem to be mourning in her hour of triumph.

Then she got up. And seeing that Felicitas had been crushed to the ground, she went over to her, gave her her hand, and lifted her up. Then the two stood side by side. But the cruelty of the mob was by now appeased, and so they were called back through the Gate of Life.

There Perpetua was held up by a man named Rusticus who was at the time a catechumen and kept close to her. She awoke from a kind of sleep (so absorbed had she been in ecstasy in the Spirit) and she began to look about her. Then to the amazement of all she said: 'When are we going to be thrown to that heifer or whatever it is?'

When told that this had already happened, she refused to believe it until she noticed the marks of her rough experience on her person and her dress. Then she called for her brother and spoke to him together with the catechumens and said: 'You must all *stand fast in the faith* and love one another, and do not be weakened by what we have gone through.'

21. At another gate Saturus was earnestly addressing the soldier Pudens. 'It is exactly', he said, 'as I foretold and predicted. So far not one animal has touched me. So now you may believe me with all your heart: I am going in there and I shall be finished off with one bite of the leopard.' And immediately as the contest was coming to a close a leopard was let loose, and after one bite Saturus was so drenched with blood that as he came away the mob roared in witness to his second baptism: 'Well washed! Well washed!' For well washed indeed was one who had been bathed in this manner.

Then he said to the soldier Pudens: 'Goodbye. Remember me, and remember the faith. These things should not disturb you but rather strengthen you.'

And with this he asked Pudens for a ring from his finger, and dipping it into his wound he gave it back to him again as a pledge and as a record of his bloodshed.

Shortly after he was thrown unconscious with the rest in the usual spot to have his throat cut. But the mob asked that their bodies be brought out into the open that their eyes might be the guilty witnesses of the sword that pierced their flesh. And so the martyrs got up and went to the spot of their own accord as the people wanted them to, and kissing one another they sealed their martyrdom with the ritual kiss of peace. The others took the sword in silence and without moving, especially Saturus, who being the first to climb the stairway was the first to die. For once again he was waiting for Perpetua. Perpetua, however, had yet to taste more pain. She screamed as she was struck on the bone; then she took the trembling hand of the young gladiator and guided it to her throat. It was as though so great a woman, feared as she was by the unclean spirit, could not be dispatched unless she herself were willing.

Ah, most valiant and blessed martyrs! Truly are you called and chosen for the glory of Christ Jesus our Lord! And any man who exalts, honours, and worships his glory should read for the consolation of the Church these new deeds of heroism which are no less significant than the tales of old. For these new manifestations of virtue will bear witness to one and the same

Spirit who still operates, and to God the Father almighty, to his Son Jesus Christ our Lord, to whom is splendour and immeasurable power for all the ages. Amen.

4.2. Contemplative Death: Macrina

Ascetic monasticism replaced death by persecution as the new martyrdom in the post-Constantine period. Consequently, the lives—and especially the deaths—of saintly individuals who rejected material life drew attention to Christian otherworldliness and the idea of resurrection. Thus the same repudiation of a normal social life evident in Perpetua's story is manifested in the postpersecution period through the development of monastic enclaves, such as Macrina's below. Less dramatic than death in the arena, the withdrawal from society to live a quiet, secluded life of humility and reflection nonetheless contained the same spirit of renunciation, denying the worth of Roman and Greek values embedded in family, education, and political life. The holiest of these monastics ended their lives in extraordinary ways, with a calm and purity that seemed to foreshadow the afterlife.

"The Life of Saint Macrina" is told by her brother, Saint Gregory of Nyssa (331/40–circa 395). Gregory, and his brother Basil of Caesarea, were both bishops and influential writers in the great renaissance of Christian thinking in Cappadocia (east-central Asia Minor). Gregory attributes to his sister much of the intellectual and spiritual stimulation he and his brother Basil received as young men. He credits her, for example, with turning her brothers away from the much admired classical literature and rhetoric that would have led to political advancement and public fame and directing them toward a Platonic contemplation of divine ideals.

The monastery that Macrina set up on her family's estate in Pontus, Asia Minor, embodied the essential monastic values: humility, in the absence of social rank distinguishing mistress from servant; poverty, in the simple habits of dress and food; chastity, in the rejection of sexual relations and marriage; and discipline, in the regular habit of communal prayers. Yet severe as the physical conditions may have been in Macrina's monastery in her rejection of material comforts, the general level of discourse evident in Gregory's account was still very Roman in its use of classical learning. Gregory wrote the story of his sister's life, excerpted below, as one way of coming to terms with her death, and with the meaning of death for a Christian expecting resurrection. He remembers the ways that she handled the deaths of other family members philosophically; yet he himself struggles with the bodily dissolution of loved ones in the grave. In this story, Gregory wrestles with some of the same issues as Origen, whom Gregory had read, concerning material continuity after death. This philosophical contemplation of the subject of death is personalized through his experience grieving over Macrina.

Questions

1. What Christian values and beliefs does Macrina's life illustrate?
2. What attitudes toward death does Gregory display in his sister's words?
3. What impact do you think this story was supposed to have on its Christian audience?

Saint Gregory of Nyssa, The Life of Saint Macrina

The maiden's name was Macrina. She had been given this name by her parents in memory of a remarkable Macrina earlier in the family, our father's mother, who had distinguished herself in the confession of Christ at the time of the persecutions. This was her official name which her acquaintances used, but she had been given another secretly in connection with a vision which occurred before she came into the light at birth. Her mother was extremely virtuous, following the will of God in all things and embracing an exceptionally pure and spotless way of life, so that she had chosen not to marry. However, since she was an orphan and flowering in the springtime of her beauty, and the fame of her loveliness had attracted many suitors, there was danger that, if she were not joined to someone by choice, she might suffer some unwished-for violence, because some of the suitors maddened by her beauty were preparing to carry her off. For this reason, she chose a man well known and recommended for the dignity of his life, and thus she acquired a guardian for her own life. In her first pregnancy, she became Macrina's mother. When the time came in which she was to be freed from her pain by giving birth to the child, she fell asleep and seemed to be holding in her hands the child still in her womb, and a person of greater than human shape and form appeared to be addressing the infant by the name of Thecla. (There was a Thecla of much fame among virgins.) After doing this and invoking her as a witness three times, he disappeared from sight and gave ease to her pain so that as she awoke from her sleep she saw the dream realized. This, then, was her secret name. It seems to me that the one who appeared was not so much indicating how the child should be named, but foretelling the life of the child and intimating that she would choose a life similar to that of her namesake.

So the child grew, nursed chiefly by her mother although she had a nurse of her own. Upon leaving infancy, she was quick to learn what children learn, and to whatever learning the judgment of her parents directed her, the little one's nature responded brilliantly. Her mother was eager to have the child given instruction, but not in the secular curriculum, which meant, for the most part, teaching the youngsters through poetry. For she thought that it was shameful and altogether unfitting to teach the soft and pliable nature either the passionate themes of tragedy (which are based on the stories of women and give the poets their ideas and plots), or the unseemly antics of comedy, or the shameful activities of the immoral characters in the *Iliad,* defiling the child's nature with the undignified tales about women. Instead of this, whatever of inspired Scripture was adaptable to the early years, this was the child's subject matter, especially the Wisdom of Solomon and beyond this whatever leads us to a moral life. She was especially well versed in the Psalms, going through each part of the Psalter at the proper time; when she got up or did her daily tasks or rested, when she sat down to eat or rose from the table, when she went to bed or rose from it for prayer, she had the Psalter with her at all times, like a good and faithful traveling companion.

Growing up with these and similar pursuits and becoming extraordinarily skilled in the working of wool, she came to her twelfth year in which the flowering of youth begins especially to shine forth. Here, it is worth marveling at how the young girl's beauty did not escape notice, although it had been concealed. Nor did there seem to be anything in all that country comparable to her beauty and her loveliness, so that the hand of the painters could not reproduce its perfection, and the art that devises all things and dares the greatest things, even to the fashioning of planets through imitation, was not powerful enough to imitate the excellence of her form. Consequently, a great stream of suitors for her hand crowded round her parents. Her father (he was wise and considered outstanding in his judgment of what was good) singled out from the rest a young man in the family known for his moderation, who had recently finished school, and he decided to give his daughter to him when she came of age. During this period, the young man showed great promise and brought to the girl's father (as a cherished bridal gift, as it were) his reputation as an orator, displaying his rhetorical skill in lawsuits in defense of the wronged. But envy cut short this bright promise by snatching him from life in his piteous youth.

The girl was not unaware of what her father had decided, and when the young man's death broke off what had been planned for her, she called her father's decision a marriage on the grounds that what had been decided had actually taken place and she determined to spend the rest of her life by herself; and her decision was more firmly fixed than her age would have warranted. When her parents talked of marriage (many men wanted to marry her on account of the reputation of her beauty), she used to say that it was out of place and unlawful not to accept once and for all a marriage determined for her by her father and to be forced to look to another, since marriage is by nature unique, as are birth and death. She insisted that the young man joined to her by her parent's decision was not dead, but living in God because of the hope of the resurrection, merely off on a journey and not a dead body, and it was out of place, she maintained, for a bride not to keep faith with an absent husband. Thrusting aside the arguments of those trying to persuade her, she settled upon a safeguard for her noble decision, namely, a resolve never to be separated for a moment from her mother, so that her mother often used to say to her that the rest of her children she had carried in her womb for a fixed time, but this daughter she always bore, encompassing her in her womb at all times and under all circumstances. Certainly, the companionship of her daughter was not burdensome or disadvantageous for the mother, because the care she received from her daughter surpassed that of many of her maidservants and there was an exchange of kindly offices between them. The older woman cared for the young woman's soul and the daughter for her mother's body, fulfilling in all things every desirable service, often even making bread for her mother with her own hands. Not that this was her principal concern, but when she had anointed her hands with mystic services, thinking that it was in keeping with her way of life, in the remaining time she furnished food for her mother from her own labor, and, in addition, she shared her mother's worries. Her mother had four sons and five daughters. . . .

. . . Macrina was a sharer of her mother's toils, taking on part of her cares and lightening the heaviness of her griefs. In addition, under her mother's direction, she kept her life blameless and witnessed in everything by her, and, at the same time, because of her own life, she provided her mother with an impressive leadership to the same goal; I speak of the goal of philosophy, drawing her on little by little to the immaterial and simpler life. After the mother had skillfully arranged what seemed best for each of Macrina's sisters, her brother, the distinguished Basil, came home from school where he had had practice in rhetoric for a long time. He was excessively puffed up by his rhetorical abilities and disdainful of all great reputations, and considered himself better than the leading men in the district, but Macrina took him over and lured him so quickly to the goal of philosophy that he withdrew from the worldly show and began to look down upon acclaim through oratory and went over to this life full of labors for one's own hand to perform, providing for himself, through his complete poverty, a mode of living that would, without impediment, lead to virtue. But his life and the outstanding activities through which he became famous everywhere under the sun and eclipsed in reputation all those conspicuous in virtue, would make a long treatise and take much time, and my attention must be turned back to the subject at hand. When there was no longer any necessity for them to continue their rather worldly way of life, Macrina persuaded her mother to give up her customary mode of living and her more ostentatious existence and the services of her maids, to which she had long been accustomed, and to put herself on a level with the many by entering into a common life with her maids, making them her sisters and equals rather than her slaves and underlings. . . .

[Gregory describes the noble and ascetic life of his brother Naucratius, who is suddenly killed while hunting for food to give to the poor.] His mother was a three-day journey away from the scene [of her son's death] and someone came to her to report what had taken place. She was perfectly schooled in virtue, but nature won out even over her. She became breathless and speechless on the spot and fainted, reason giving way to passion, and she lay there under the impact of the terrible news like a noble athlete felled by an unforeseen blow.

At this point, the great Macrina's excellence was evident. By setting reason against passion, she kept herself in hand, and, becoming a bulwark of her mother's weakness, she lifted her out of the abyss of grief, and, by her own firmness and unyielding spirit, she trained her mother's soul to be courageous.

Consequently, her mother was not carried away by her misfortune, nor did she react in an ignoble and womanish fashion so as to cry out against the evil or tear her clothes or lament over her suffering or stir up a threnody of mournful melodies. Instead, she conquered her natural impulses and thrust them aside with her own arguments or those suggested by her daughter for the healing of the pain. Then, especially, did the maiden's lofty and exalted soul shine forth because her nature had been subject to the same experience. It had been her brother, and her dearest brother, whom death snatched away in such a manner. Nevertheless, transcending her nature, she lifted her mother up with her own line of reasoning and put her beyond what had happened, directing her by her own example to patience and fortitude. In particular, Macrina's life, always exalted by virtue, did not give the mother an opportunity to grieve for the one who was absent and caused her to rejoice rather in the good that was present. . . .

[Macrina and her mother establish a monastery on their estate, living ascetic lives as equals with the women who joined them, and spending time in contemplating philosophy.]

At this time, our mother, having come to a rich old age, went to God, taking her departure from life in the arms of these two of her children. Worth recording is the blessing she gave to each of her children, suitably remembering each of the absent ones so that none would be without a blessing, and through prayer entrusting especially to God the two who were with her. As they were sitting beside her bed, she touched each of them with her hand and said to God in her last words: 'To you, O Lord, I offer the first and tenth fruit of my pains. The first fruit, my eldest daughter here, and this my tenth, my last-born son. Both have been dedicated to you by law and are your votive offerings. May sanctification, therefore, come to this first and tenth.' And she indicated specifically her daughter and her son. Having finished her blessing, she ended her life, instructing her children to place her body in our father's tomb. These two, having fulfilled her command, attained to a higher level of philosophy, always struggling in their individual lives and eclipsing their early successes by their later ones.

At this time, Basil, distinguished among the holy, was made Bishop of Caesarea. He led his brother to the holy vocation of the priesthood, and consecrated him in the mystical services himself. And through this also, their life progressed to a loftier and higher degree, seeing that their philosophy was enhanced by the consecration. Eight years later, Basil, renowned throughout the entire world, left the world of men and went to God, and his death was a common source of grief for his country and the world. When Macrina heard the report of his distant death, she was greatly disturbed by such a loss. (How could this fail to touch her when even the enemies of truth were affected by it?) But, just as they say gold is tested in many furnaces, that if it gets through the first firing and is tested in the second and, in the last is finally cleansed of all extraneous matter (this is the most accurate proof of true gold if, after all this firing, no impurity remains), something similar happened in her case. When her lofty understanding had been tried by the different attacks of grief, the genuine and undebased quality of her soul was revealed in every way; previously, by the departure of her other brother, then, by the separation from her mother, and, in the third instance, when Basil, the common honor of the family, departed from human life. She remained like an undefeated athlete, in no way overcome by the onslaught of misfortunes.

About nine months after this disaster ... I, Gregory, thought often of visiting Macrina. ... When I had almost finished the journey and was about one day away from my destination, a vision, appearing in my sleep, aroused fearful forebodings about the future. I seemed to be carrying the relics of martyrs in my hand and a light seemed to come from them, as happens when the sun is reflected on a bright mirror so that the eye is dazzled by the brilliance of the beam. That same night, the vision occurred three times. I was not able to interpret its meaning clearly, but I foresaw some grief for my soul and I was waiting for the outcome to clarify the dream. . . .

An attendant led me to the house where the Superior [Macrina, head of the monastery] was and opened the door, and I entered that sacred place. She was already very ill, but she was not resting on a couch or bed, but upon the ground; there was a board covered with a coarse cloth, and another board supported her head, designed to be used instead of a pillow, supporting the sinews of her neck slantwise and conveniently supporting the neck. When she saw me standing at the door, she raised herself on her elbow; her strength was already so wasted by fever that she was not able to come towards me, but she fixed her hands on the floor and, stretching as far forward as she could, she paid me the honor of a bow. I ran to her and, lifting her bowed head, I put her back in her accustomed reclining position. But she stretched out her hand to God and said: 'You have granted me this favor, O God, and have not deprived me of my desire, since you have impelled your servant to visit your handmaid.' And in order not to disturb me, she tried to cover up her groans and to conceal somehow the difficulty she had in breathing, and, through it all, she adjusted herself to the brighter side. She initiated suitable topics of conversation and gave me an opportunity to speak by asking me questions. As we spoke, we recalled the memory of the great Basil and my soul was afflicted and my face fell and tears poured from my eyes. But she was so far from being downcast by our sorrow that she made the mentioning of the saint a starting point towards the higher philosophy. She rehearsed such arguments, explaining the human situation through natural principles and disclosing the divine plan hidden in misfortune, and she spoke of certain aspects of the future life as if she was inspired by the Holy Spirit, so that my soul almost seemed to be lifted up out of its human sphere by what she said and, under the direction of her discourse, take its stand in the heavenly sanctuaries.

. . . Although the fever was burning up all her energy and leading her to death, she was refreshing her body as if by a kind of dew, she kept her mind free in the contemplation of higher things and unimpeded by the disease. If my treatise were not becoming too long, I would put down everything in order: how she was lifted up by her discourse on the soul; how she explained the reason for life in the flesh, why man exists; how he is mortal, whence death comes; and what release there is from death back again into life. In all of this, she went on as if inspired by the power of the Holy Spirit, explaining it all clearly and logically. Her speech flowed with complete ease, just as a stream of water goes down a hill without obstruction. . . .

[Later] As she went on this way, I kept wishing that the day might be lengthened so that we could continue to enjoy the sweetness of her words. But the sound of the choir was calling us to vespers and, having sent me off to the church, the Superior withdrew to God in prayer and the night was devoted to it. When dawn came, it was clear to me that this day was to be the last for her in the life of the flesh, for the fever had consumed all her natural strength. When she saw our concern about her weakness, she tried to rouse us from our downcast hopes by dispersing again with her beautiful words the grief of our souls with her last slight and labored breathing. At this point, especially, my soul was in conflict because of what it was confronted by. My disposition was naturally made gloomy by the anticipation of never again hearing such a voice, but actually I had not yet accepted the idea that she was going to leave this mortal life, and my soul was so exalted by appearances that I secretly thought that she had transcended the common nature. For the fact was that, in her last breath, she experienced nothing strange in the expectation of the change and displayed no cowardice towards the departure from life. Instead, she philosophized with high intelligence on what had been decided upon by her about this life from the beginning up to her last breath, and this made her appear to belong no longer to the world of men. It was as if an angel had by some providence taken on human form, an angel who had no relation with or similarity to the life of the flesh and for whom it was not at all unreasonable to remain detached since the flesh was not part of her experience. For this reason, she seemed to me to be making clear to those present the divine and pure love of the unseen Bridegroom which she had secretly nourished in the depths of her soul, and she seemed to be communicating the disposition in her heart to go to the One she was longing for, so that, once loosed from the chains of the body, she might quickly be with Him. Truly, her race was towards the Beloved and nothing of the pleasure of life diverted her attention.

The day was almost over and the sun was beginning to set, but the zeal in her did not decline. Indeed, as she neared her end and saw the beauty of the Bridegroom more clearly, she rushed with greater impulse towards the One she desired, no longer speaking to those of us who were present, but to that very One toward whom she looked with steadfast eyes. Her couch was turned to the East and, stopping her conversation with us, for the rest of the time she addressed herself to God in prayer, beseeching Him with her hands and speaking in a low soft voice so that we barely heard what she said. This was her prayer and there is no doubt that it made its way to God and that it was heard by Him.

She said: 'O Lord, You have freed us from the fear of death; You have made the end of life here the beginning of a true life for us. For a time, You give rest to our bodies in sleep and You awaken us again with the last trumpet. The dust from which You fashioned us with Your hands You give back to the dust of the earth for safekeeping, and You who have relinquished it will recall it after reshaping with incorruptibility and grace our mortal and graceless substance. You redeemed us from the curse and from sin, having taken both upon Yourself; You crushed the heads of the serpent who had seized us with his jaws in the abyss of disobedience. Breaking down the gates of hell and overcoming the one who had the empire of death, You opened up for us a path to the resurrection. For those who fear You, You gave as a token the sign of the holy cross for the destruction of the Adversary and the salvation of our life. O God everlasting, towards whom I have directed myself from my mother's womb, whom my soul has loved with all its strength, to whom I have dedicated my body and my soul from my infancy up to now, prepare for me a shining angel to lead me to the place of refreshment where is the water of relaxation near the bosom of the holy Fathers. You who broke the flaming sword and compassionately gave Paradise back to the man crucified with You, remember me also in Your kingdom, for I, too, have been crucified with You, having nailed my flesh through fear of You and having feared Your judgments. Let the terrible abyss not separate me from Your chosen ones; let the Slanderer not stand in my way or my sins be discovered before Your eyes if I have fallen and sinned in word or deed or thought because of the weakness of our nature. Do You who have power on earth to forgive sins forgive me so that I may be refreshed and may be found before You once I have put off my body, having no fault in the form of my soul, but blameless and spotless may my soul be taken into Your hands as an offering before Your face.' As she said this, she made the sign of the cross upon her eyes and mouth and heart, and little by little, as the fever dried up her tongue, she was no longer able to speak clearly; her voice gave out and only from the trembling of her lips and the motion of her hands did we know that she was continuing to pray.

Then, evening came on and the lamp was brought in. Macrina directed her eye toward the beam of light and made it clear that she was eager to say the nocturnal prayer and, although her voice failed her, with her heart and the movement of her hands, she fulfilled her desire and moved her lips in keeping with the impulse within her. When she had completed the thanksgiving and indicated that the prayer was over by making the sign of the cross, she breathed a deep breath and with the prayer her life came to an end. From then on, she was without breath and movement, and I recalled an injunction she had given me when I arrived, saying that she wanted my hands to be placed upon her eyes and the customary care of the body to be taken by me. So I placed my hand, deadened by grief, upon her holy face so as not to seem to disregard her request. Actually, her eyes required no attention; it was as if she was asleep with her eyelids becomingly lowered; her lips were set naturally and her hands rested naturally on her breast and the whole position of her body was so spontaneously harmonious that there was no need for any arranging hand.

My soul was disquieted for two reasons, because of what I saw and because I heard the weeping of the virgins. Until now, they had controlled themselves and kept in check the grief in their souls and they had choked down the impulse to cry out for fear of her, as if they were afraid of the reproach of her voice already silent; lest, contrary to her order, a sound should break forth from them and their teacher be troubled by it. But when their suffering could no longer be controlled in silence (their grief was affecting their souls like a consuming fire within them), suddenly, a bitter, unrestrained cry broke forth, so that my reason no longer maintained itself, but, like a mountain stream overflowing, it was overwhelmed below the surface by my suffering and, disregarding the tasks at hand, I gave myself over wholly to lamentation. The cause of the maidens' grief seemed to me to be just and reasonable. They were not bewailing the deprivation of some ordinary bond or carnal attraction or any other such thing for which one mourns. But, as if they were torn away from their hope in God or the salvation of their souls, they cried out and loudly bewailed. . . .

But when I recalled my soul from the depths, gazing intently at the holy head, and, as if I were rebuked for the disorderly conduct of the women, I said: 'Look at her,' shouting at the maidens in a loud voice, 'and be mindful of the instructions she gave you for order and graciousness in everything. Her divine soul sanctioned one moment of tears for us, commanding us to weep at the moment of prayer. This command we can obey by changing the wailing of our lamentation into a united singing of psalms.' I said this with a loud voice to drown out the noise of the wailing. Then, I bade them withdraw a little to their quarters nearby and to leave behind a few of those whose services she accepted during her lifetime. . . .

When this [the burial preparation] was decided upon and it was necessary for the sacred body to be dressed in fine linen, we divided the various tasks among us. I told one of my attendants to bring in the robe. . . .

When the time came to cover the body with the robe, the injunction of the great lady made it necessary for me to perform this function. The woman who was present and sharing the great assignment with us said: 'Do not pass over the greatest of the miracles of the saint.' 'What is that?' I asked. She laid bare a part of the breast and said: 'Do you see this thin, almost imperceptible, scar below the neck?' It was like a mark made by a small needle. At the same time, she brought the lamp nearer to the place she was showing me. 'What is miraculous about that,' I said, 'if the body has a small mark here?' She said: 'This is left on the body as a reminder of the great help of God. At one time, there was a painful sore here and there was the risk that if it was not cut out it would develop into an irremediable illness if it should spread to places near the heart. Her mother begged her to accept the doctor's care and implored her many times saying that the art of medicine was given by God to man for his preservation. But Macrina considered worse than the disease laying bare part of the body to another's eyes, and one evening, after she had finished her usual tasks connected with her mother, she went inside the sanctuary and all night supplicated the God of healing, pouring out a stream from her eyes upon the ground, and she used the mud from her tears as a remedy for the disease. When her mother was earnestly distressed and asking her again to see the doctor, she said that there was a cure for her disease if her mother with her own hand would make the sign of the cross on the place. When the mother put her hand inside to make the sign of the cross on her breast, the sign of the cross worked and the sore disappeared. 'But this,' she said, 'is a small token and was seen then instead of the terrible sore, and remained to the end as a reminder, I suppose, of the divine consideration, a cause and reason for unceasing thanksgiving to God.'

When our work was finished and the body was adorned with what we had, the deaconess spoke again and said that it was not fitting that Macrina should be seen by the maidens dressed as a bride. She said: 'I have a dark mantle of your mother's which I think we should put over her, so that this holy beauty should not be made splendid by the extraneous adornment of the robe.' Her opinion prevailed and the mantle was put over her. But even in the dark, the body glowed, the divine power adding such grace to her body that, as in the vision of my dream, rays seemed to be shining forth from her loveliness.

While we were engaged in these activities and the maidens' psalm-singing, mingled with lamentation, resounded through the place, in some way the report spread about on all sides and all the people of the area began to rush in so that the vestibule was not large enough to hold them. There was an all night vigil with hymn-singing as is the custom in the case of the praise of martyrs, and, when it was finished and day dawned, a crowd of those who had hurried in from the entire countryside, men and women both, broke in on the psalmody with their cries of grief. Although my soul was distressed by my misfortune, I kept thinking, nevertheless, how it should be possible not to leave undone anything suitable for such an occasion. Separating the flow of people according to sex, I put the women with the choir of nuns and the men in the ranks of the monks. I arranged for the singing to come rhythmically and harmoniously from the group, blended well as in choral singing with the common responses of all. But as the day was advancing and the place was overcrowded by the multitude of people, the bishop of the region, whose name was Araxius (he was present with the full company of his priests), ordered the bier to be brought forward immediately, on the grounds that there was quite a distance to be covered and the crowd would prevent the swift movement of the funeral procession. At the same time, he ordered all the priests who were with him to escort the bier themselves.

When this was decided upon and the activity begun, I went to one side of the bier and called him to the other, and two of the others, distinguished in rank, took their position at the opposite end. I led the way slowly, as was fitting, and we proceeded at a moderate rate. The people crowded around the bier and could not get enough of that holy sight, so it was not easy for us to pass. There was a row of deacons and attendants on each side of the funeral train, all holding wax candles; it was a kind of mystical procession, the psalmody continuing from beginning to end harmoniously, as is sung in the hymnody of the three boys. It was a distance of seven or eight stadia from the monastery to the House of the Holy Martyrs, where the bodies of our parents were at rest. We completed the journey with difficulty throughout most of the day, for the accompanying crowd and those who were always being added to our number did not allow us to proceed according to our estimate. When we were inside the gate of the House, we first put down the bier and turned to prayer, but the prayer was the starting point of lamentation for the people. When there was a lull in the psalm-singing and the maidens were looking at the holy face, as the tomb of our parents was being opened in which she was to be placed, one of them cried out saying that no longer would we look upon her divine face. The rest of the maidens joined her in her outburst and confusion drowned out the orderly and sacred singing. Everyone wept in response to the wailing of the maidens. We nodded for silence and the leader guided them to prayer by intoning the usual prayers of the Church and the people came to attention.

When the proper ceremony was finished, the fear of the divine command not to uncover the shamelessness of father and mother came upon me. 'How,' I said, 'shall I ward off such a judgment if I look upon the common shame of human nature in the bodies of our parents, since they have surely fallen apart and disintegrated and been changed into a disgusting and disagreeable formlessness?' As I was considering this, and Noe's anger against his son was rousing fear in me, the story of Noe indicated what ought to be done. Before the bodies came into view when the cover of the tomb was lifted they were covered from one end to the other by a pure linen cloth. When they were covered thus with the linen, the bishop I have mentioned and I lifted that holy body from the bier and placed it beside our mother, fulfilling the common prayer of both of them. For this they had asked from God all through their life, that after death their bodies should be together and that in death they should not be deprived of the comradeship they had had in their lifetime. . . .

Reprinted with permission from Saint Gregory of Nyssa, *Ascetical Works*, trans. Virginia Woods Callahan, in *The Fathers of the Church*, Vol. 58 (Washington, D.C.: Catholic University of America Press, 1967), pp. 164–71, 172–77, 178–83, 184–88.

4.3. Hope of Resurrection: Tomb Inscriptions

Tomb inscriptions are unusual historical documents—artifacts preserved in stone that reveal in formalized ways some very raw human emotions. Brief as they may be, the words incised on stones marking graves can tell us something about changes in belief concerning death and the afterlife. In particular, the death of a child, an untimely death by worldly standards, evoked strong emotions. Selections from both Roman and Christian inscriptions are included below, showing some of the changes in practice and belief in late antiquity (fourth–seventh centuries).

Roman burial practices changed over time, but tended to regard the dead body as something to bury outside the city. Most Roman philosophers believed that only the spirit lived in the afterlife. Thus Roman burial practice focused on the spiritual afterlife, with the body as the discarded husk of the person. In the waning era of the empire, concern for the afterlife and the development of various religious cults led to increased attention to the burial of the dead and perhaps more emotional statements of loss. Nonetheless, it is important to remember that the inscriptions we possess represent only the formalized sentiments that some Romans inscribed on stone—memorials to grief were expressed also in other ways that we cannot recover. Certain frequent formulas were abbreviated on the tombstones. For example, *s.t.t.l.* meant "may the earth be light for you" and *D.M.* committed the person to the spirits of the underworld.

The Christian inscriptions below occurred in this Roman context, but with some additional features peculiar to Christianity. The only way that we can distinguish some memorials as Christian is by the symbols used (for example, crosses) and specifically Christian language referencing the expected resurrection of the body. As noted in Origen's treatise, early Christians believed, unlike most Romans, that the physical body would be resurrected and reunited with the spirit. Consequently, tombs of dead Christians played a different role in the Christian church's consciousness: they often became a place of reflection and worship as Christians contemplated the coming resurrection on the last day. The inscriptions reflect this hope, mixed with the grief of loss over the temporary separation from loved ones. Many of them affirm the baptism of the departed as a marker of their status in the afterlife.

Questions

1. Compare the pagan and Christian inscriptions. In what ways are they similar? different?
2. What emotions about the individual are expressed in these words?
3. What beliefs about the nature of death and the afterlife are evident in these inscriptions?

Tomb Inscriptions

Roman Inscriptions

To the sacred spirits of the underworld. Titus Flavius Trophimus lived nine years. Here he lies. May the earth be light for you.

—Vives 3394, first century, B.C.E.

Faustio, a slave of Deucalion, lived for five years, may your bones rest well for you and your mother.

—Dessau 7981b, probably late second century, C.E.

To the spirits of the underworld: Corellia Optata, aged thirteen. Oh mysterious spirits who dwell in Pluto's Acherusian realms, and whom the meager ashes and the shade, empty semblance of the body, seek, following the brief light of life; sire of an innocent daughter, I, a pitiable victim of unfair hope, bewail her final end. Quintus Corellius Fortis, her father, had this set up.

—CIL 7. 250, first or early second century, C.E.

Christian Inscriptions

For Flavia our most beloved child, who, with a sound mind on the health-bringing day of Easter obtained grace from the glorious fountain and lived beyond after her sacred baptism for five months. She lived three years, ten months, and seven days. Flavianus and Archelais, the parents of their most pious daughter having been laid down on the fifteenth of September.

—Diehl 1523, third century, C.E.

For Julia Florentina, sweetest and most innocent infant, made one of the faithful, her parents placed this. She was born a pagan before it was light on March 6, under Zoilus, Governor of the Province. Eighteen months and twenty-two days later, while dying, she was made one of the faithful, at the eighth hour of the night. She lived another four hours, so that she received communion again, and died at Hyble at the first hour of September 25. When both her parents were weeping for her without ceasing, at night the voice of Divine Majesty was heard, forbidding lamentation for the dead. Her body was buried in its coffin by the presbyter near the Martyrs' tombs on October 9.

—Diehl 1549, fourth century, C.E.

Here rests in peace the servant of Christ Rusticula, a maiden devoted to God, who lived more or less thirteen years. Laid to rest on the sixth day of August.

—Diehl 1716, around fourth or fifth century, C.E.

[Among a row of ring-doves] Marturia, an undefiled maiden, lived thirteen years, five months. Received in peace on the day before the Kalends of January.

—Diehl 1726, fourth century to sixth century, C.E.

[Cross between two stars] Here Iniuriosus rests in peace, who lived four years, nine months, and one day, about to rise up again in Christ. His mother Euladia made this.

—Diehl 3470, fourth century or later, C.E.

Trans. Julie Clement and Karen Jolly, from ed. Hermann Dessau, *Inscriptiones Latinae Selectae*, 3 Vols. (Berlin: Weidmann, 1942); ed. Ernest Diehl, *Inscriptiones Latinae Christianae Veteres*, 4 Vols. (Dublin: Weidmann, 1970); ed. Jose Vives, *Inscriptiones Latinas de la Espana Romana*, 2 Vols. (Barcelona: Universidad de Barcelona, 1951); ed. G. Reimerum Beorlini, *Corpus Inscriptionum Latinarum* (Berlin: Akademie der Wissenschaften, 1863).

Part 2

Patterns of Accommodation in Late Antiquity, circa 350–750

The success of Christianity is due not just to the dominance of an orthodoxy over heterodoxy as discussed in the previous chapters. A second reason for Christianity's survival, not just within the Roman world but also outside it, is found in the accommodations the religion made to the new cultures it encountered. This ability to adapt while still retaining certain core ideas led to the establishment of multiple versions of Christianity—Celtic, Germanic, Ethiopian, even Chinese adaptations. Endlessly fascinating, these variants lead us to question just what the core Christian tradition is, even as we see certain common features shifting and melting into other cultures. The following chapters (5–8) of this second part seek to display this cultural diversity accomplished through accommodation. The first, Chapter 5, "The Heritage of the Middle Ages," acts as a bridge from Part One by exploring the writings of the late antique church fathers who represent the Latin tradition of Christianity and had the greatest impact on the accommodations made in European Christianity. Chapter 6, "The Power of Christian Saints," focuses on the hermits, monks, and saints whose lives, words, and even physical relics became part of the fabric of the medieval heritage. Chapter 7 then examines similar themes of Christian values as "Adaptations Outside the Roman World" that represent cultural accommodations in Africa, Arabia, and China.

The last chapter of this part, Chapter 8, then explores "Christian Acculturation in Western Europe" in the early Middle Ages among the Celtic and Germanic peoples. Too often, the form of Christianity that emerges from

Europe is assumed to be the main or normative version of Christianity, when in fact it is simply one of many cultural adaptations made by the religion as it went to various parts of the world. Nonetheless, among those adaptations, the European ones became the most prominent and dynamic. The symbiotic relationship between nascent European societies and Christianity was so powerful that they became mutually identified: European cultures became "Christian societies," defining what that meant along the way.

In the end, the reader can compare the versions of Christianity, whether in Anglo-Saxon England, China, South Arabia, or Ethiopia, and analyze how religions and cultures interacted. The diversity of accommodations then raises the question of what is essentially "Christian" in all of these cultures: is there something they all have in common? What does it mean, then, to convert to Christianity? Is it to adopt a different culture? If large numbers of people convert, or the ruler converts, does that result in the conversion of the whole culture?

–5–

The Heritage of
the Middle Ages

The late antique Christianity of the Mediterranean world left a lasting legacy in Europe after the decline of the western Roman Empire in the fifth century. The Germanic peoples of Europe inherited classical Greco-Roman culture almost entirely through Christianity; and the Christianity to which most of them eventually converted was Roman, the Latin-speaking Catholic Church centered in the former capital and center of the empire.

Of the many and diverse authors of the first five centuries of Christianity, early medieval literate Christians among the Germanic peoples knew many only by name; mostly the Latin works survived as the knowledge of Greek in the West faded. A handful of Greco-Roman and late antique Christian writings became classics, building the foundation for church doctrine, sermons, and theological treatises. Besides the Scriptures themselves as made available through a Latin edition by Jerome (5.1), significant works heavily copied and imitated by early medieval writers included the extensive works of Augustine (5.2), the mystical, Neoplatonic theology of Pseudo-Dionysius (5.3), and the philosophic contemplation expressed by Boethius (5.4). All of these authors' works are carriers of classical civilization into the Germanic world of Europe.

5.1. Creating an Authoritative Bible: Jerome

The ascetic and scholar Jerome (circa 346–420) serves, along with Augustine of Hippo, as one of the main bridges from the early church to the western, Latin-based Catholic Church. Jerome was a prolific writer of commentaries and often abusive attacks on heretics. Many of his views on asceticism, the Virgin Mary, and saints became the standard in the medieval West. His translation work stands out as one of his major contributions. His rare knowledge of Hebrew, Greek, and Latin allowed him to produce a new Latin edition of the Bible combining variant versions.

Although born in a remote region of the empire, he received both his classical education and his baptism in the city of Rome. From there, he traveled to Antioch and studied Greek, then lived as a hermit in Syria and studied Hebrew; he eventually settled in Bethlehem, where in 386 he founded a double monastery along with a female colleague, Paula. In his monastery, he devoted himself to the ascetic life, contemplation, and intensive study resulting in a voluminous amount of writing; he also participated in a number of the theological controversies of his day. Despite his reputation as a dogmatic, tenacious fighter in the word battles of his day, he had another side to him exhibited in his ascetic life and in his sentimental relationship with Paula and her family (she had five children before entering the monastery). His letters to them, sometimes consoling them for the loss of a loved one or giving advice on rearing a child dedicated to God, reveal a compassionate man with strongly felt principles about the preeminence of the spiritual life.

The three excerpts below are from different prefaces Jerome wrote to various books of the Bible, often for friends or colleagues who requested the work of him. One of them he addressed to the current pope, another to Paula and her daughter Eustochium, who later took over her mother's role as abbess. In these prefaces, Jerome defends his translations and explains his methods of scriptural interpretation, a significant issue throughout Christianity's history. Most theologians used a number of levels of interpretation, examining in turn the literal, the historical, the typological, the metaphorical, and the allegorical meanings. Jerome drew attention to the literal meaning of Scripture. Amid the grammatical differences in the languages he employed, Jerome was most concerned with preserving the divine order of the words.

Questions

1. What is the purpose of Scripture, in Jerome's eyes?
2. In what ways should Scripture be interpreted, and by whom?
3. What views does he try to condemn or seek to avoid, and why?

Jerome, Preface to the Four Gospels
Addressed to Pope Damasus, 383 C.E.

You urge me to revise the old Latin version, and, as it were, to sit in judgment on the copies of the Scriptures which are now scattered throughout the whole world; and, inasmuch as they differ from one another, you would have me decide which of them agree with the Greek original. The labor is one of love, but at the same time both perilous and presumptuous; for in judging others I must be content to be judged by all; and how can I dare to change the language of the world in its hoary old age, and carry it back to the early days of its infancy? Is there a man, learned or unlearned, who will not, when he takes the volume into his hands, and perceives that what he reads does not suit his settled tastes, break out immediately into violent language, and call me a forger and a profane person for having the audacity to add anything to the ancient books, or to make any changes or corrections therein? Now there are two consoling reflections which enable me to bear the odium—in the first place, the command is given by you who are the supreme bishop; and secondly, even on the showing of those who revile us, readings at variance with the early copies cannot be right. For if we are to pin our faith to the Latin tests, it is for our opponents to tell us *which;* for there are almost as many forms of texts as there are copies. If, on the other hand, we are to glean the truth from a comparison of *many,* why not go back to the original Greek and correct the mistakes introduced by inaccurate translators, and the blundering alterations of confident but ignorant critics, and, further, all that has been inserted or changed by copyists more asleep than awake? I am not discussing the Old Testament, which was turned into Greek by the Seventy elders, and has reached us by a descent of three steps. I do not ask what Aquila and Symmachus think, or why Theodotion takes a middle course between the ancients and the moderns. I am willing to let that be the true translation which had apostolic approval. I am now speaking of the New Testament. This was undoubtedly composed in Greek, with the exception of the work of Matthew the Apostle, who was the first to commit to writing the Gospel of Christ, and who published his work in Judaea in Hebrew characters. We must confess that as we have it in our language it is marked by discrepancies, and now that the stream is distributed into different channels we must go back to the fountainhead. I pass over those manuscripts which are associated with the names of Lucian and Hesychius, and the authority of which is perversely maintained by a handful of disputatious persons. It is obvious that these writers could not amend anything in the Old Testament after the labors of the Seventy; and it was useless to correct the New, for versions of Scripture which already exist in the languages of many nations show that their additions are false. I therefore promise in this short Preface the four Gospels only, which are to be taken in the following order, Matthew, Mark, Luke, John, as they have been revised by a comparison of the Greek manuscripts. Only early ones have been used. But to avoid any great divergences from the Latin which we are accustomed to read, I have used my pen with some restraint, and while I have corrected only such passages as seemed to convey a different meaning, I have allowed the rest to remain as they are.

Jerome, Preface to Job, circa 392–393

I am compelled at every step in my treatment of the books of Holy Scripture to reply to the abuse of my opponents, who charge my translation with being a censure of the Seventy. . . . The present translation follows no ancient translator, but will be found to reproduce now the exact words, now the meaning, now both together of the original Hebrew, Arabic, and occasionally the Syriac. For an indirectness and a slipperiness attaches to the whole book, even in the Hebrew; and, as orators say in Greek, it is tricked out with figures of speech, and while it says one thing, it does another; just as if you close your hand to hold an eel or a little muraena [small fish], the more you squeeze it, the sooner it escapes. I remember that in order to understand this volume, I paid a not inconsiderable sum for the services of a teacher, a native of Lydda, who was amongst the Hebrews reckoned to be in the front rank; whether I profited at all by his teaching, I do not know; of this one thing I am sure, that I could translate only that which I previously understood. . . . Wherefore, let my barking critics listen as I tell them that my motive in toiling at this book was not to censure the ancient translation, but that those passages in it which are obscure, or those which have been omitted, or at all events, through the fault of copyists have been corrupted, might have light thrown upon them by our translation; for we have some slight knowledge of Hebrew, and, as regards Latin, my life, almost from the cradle, has been spent in the company of grammarians, rhetoricians, and philosophers. But if, since the version of the Seventy was published, and even now, when the Gospel of Christ is beaming forth, the Jewish Aquila, Symmachus, and Theodotion, judaising heretics, have been welcomed amongst the Greeks—heretics, who, by their deceitful translation, have concealed many mysteries of salvation, and yet, in the Hexapla [Origen's work reconciling the Hebrew and Greek versions of the Old Testament] are found in the Churches and are expounded by churchmen; ought not I, a Christian, born of Christian parents, and who carry the standard of the cross on my brow, and am zealous to recover what is lost, to correct what is corrupt, and to disclose in pure and faithful language the mysteries of the Church, ought not I, let me ask, much more to escape the reprobation of fastidious or malicious readers? Let those who will keep the old books with their gold and silver letters on purple skins, or, to follow the ordinary phrase, in "uncial characters," loads of writing rather than manuscripts, if only they will leave for me and mine, our poor pages and copies which are less remarkable for beauty than for accuracy. I have toiled to translate both the Greek versions of the Seventy, and the Hebrew which is the basis of my own, into Latin. Let every one choose which he likes, and he will find out that what he objects to in me, is the result of sound learning, not of malice.

Jerome, Preface to the Commentary on Ecclesiastes
Addressed to Paula and Eustochium, Bethlehem 388 C.E.

I remember that, about five years ago, when I was still living at Rome, I read Ecclesiastes to the saintly Blesilla, so that I might provoke her to the contempt of this earthly scene, and to count as nothing all that she saw in the world; and that she asked me to throw my remarks upon all the more obscure passages into the form of a short commentary, so that, when I was absent, she might still understand what she read. She was withdrawn from us by her sudden death, while girding herself for our work; we were not counted worthy to have such an one as the partner of our life; and, there- fore, Paula and Eustochium, I kept silence under the stroke of such a wound. But now, living as I do in the smaller community of Bethlehem, I pay what I owe to her memory and to you. I would only point out this, that I have followed no one's authority. I have translated direct from the Hebrew, adapting my words as much as possible to the form of the Septuagint, but only in those places in which they did not diverge far from the Hebrew. I have occasionally referred also to the versions of Aquila, Symmachus, and Theodotion, but so as not to alarm the zealous student by too many novel- ties, nor yet to let my commentary follow the side streams of opinion, turning aside, against my conscientious conviction, from the fountainhead of truth.

From *St. Jerome: Letters and Select Works,* trans. W. H. Fremantle, in *NPNF,* Second Series, Vol. 6, pp. 487–88, 491–92, 487.

5.2 The Two Cities: Augustine of Hippo

Augustine (354–430), bishop of Hippo in North Africa, produced a massive number of influential books that carried the Roman Christian tradition of theology into the Middle Ages and beyond into the Protes- tant Reformation. It is therefore hard to underestimate Augustine's im- pact on the formation of European Christianity, nor is it easy to summarize his numerous works, written over a span of more than forty years through a variety of dramatic changes in the Roman Empire. Sometimes his views on certain issues changed or were contradictory enough to produce controversy among later readers. Nonetheless, his was probably the most brilliant mind at work in the early fifth century attempting to resolve the central dilemmas of the role of Christianity in the world, exhibited in the two excerpts here from the *Confessions* and *The City of God.* Augustine's ability to apply rational arguments to the theological and social controversies of his day is a reflection of his life experience. Augustine's autobiography, *The Confessions*, charts the divine plan of his conversion. Augustine is widely regarded for his intellectual prowess, yet he emphasizes here not just the rational persuasion to become Christian but also the moral condition of his soul; his actual moment of conversion, excerpted below, is entirely revelatory; it also indicates the strong role his Christian mother, Monica, played in his conversion. As a highly educated adult convert, Augustine brought to Christianity his considerable experience in the many philosophies and cults of the eclectic Roman world that he systematically rejected on logical grounds. Consequently he became one of the ablest defenders of orthodox Christianity and the most devastating critic of rival belief systems.

Augustine's most influential work for medieval thought and politics is undoubtedly the multivolume *City of God*, written in response to the sack of the city of Rome in 410. So cataclysmic was this event that many residents of the empire thought the world would end soon; so closely had they identified the empire with Christianity in the post-Constantine period that Roman Christians thought that when one fell, so would the other. Augustine's *City of God* addresses this issue of identifying the Christian Church with the empire: what is the relationship between the eternal kingdom of God and the temporal kingdom of this world? The separation, and yet overlap, Augustine creates between the eternal, spiritual City of God—the true home of all Christians—and the temporal, material City of Man—the temporary journey of life—becomes the basis for innumerable debates over church and state in the Middle Ages. The church as God's representative in the temporal world contains the kingdom of God within the City of Man; and yet a mixture of indistinguishable persons inhabit the church, some members only of the City of Man, some true citizens of God's kingdom. Consequently, given these secular influences and temporal circumstances, the church is frequently in need of reform to keep in mind its spiritual ideals and the Christians' true home. Paradoxically, then, Augustine not only argues for the preeminence of the spiritual City of God but also supports government and an orderly church here on earth in the City of Man, even as it condemns the City of Man as temporal and full of corruption.

Questions

1. What *is* conversion, in Augustine's experience?
2. What is the relationship between the City of God and the City of Man?
3. How can Christians survive in the City of Man?

Augustine, *Confessions*

VIII:6

And how, then, Thou didst deliver me out of the bonds of carnal desire, wherewith I was most firmly fettered, and out of the drudgery of worldly business, will I now declare and confess unto Thy name, "O Lord, my strength and my Redeemer." Amid increasing anxiety, I was transacting my usual affairs, and daily sighing unto Thee. I resorted as frequently to Thy church as the business, under the burden of which I groaned, left me free to do.... [Augustine relates a story of conversion told to him and his friend Alypius by a visitor]

VIII:7

... But Thou, O Lord, whilst he was speaking, didst turn me towards myself, taking me from behind my back, where I had placed myself while unwilling to exercise self-scrutiny; and Thou didst set me face to face with myself, that I might behold how foul I was, and how crooked and sordid, bespotted and ulcerous. And I beheld and loathed myself; and whither to fly from myself I discovered not. And if I sought to turn my gaze away from myself, he continued his narrative, and Thou again opposedst me unto myself, and thrustedst me before my own eyes, that I might discover my iniquity, and hate it. I had known it, but acted as though I knew it not,— winked at it, and forgot it.

But now, the more ardently I loved those whose healthful affections I heard tell of, that they had given up themselves wholly to Thee to be cured, the more did I abhor myself when compared with them. For many of my years (perhaps twelve) had passed away since my nineteenth, when, on the reading of Cicero's *Hortensius,* I was roused to a desire for wisdom; and still I was delaying to reject mere worldly happiness, and to devote myself to search out that whereof not the finding alone, but the bare search, ought to have been preferred before the treasures and kingdoms of this world, though already found, and before the pleasures of the body, though encompassing me at my will. But I, miserable young man, supremely miserable even in the very outset of my youth, had entreated chastity of Thee, and said, "Grant me chastity and continency, but not yet." For I was afraid lest Thou shouldest hear me soon, and soon deliver me from the disease of concupiscence, which I desired to have satisfied rather than extinguished. And I had wandered through perverse ways in a sacrilegious superstition;

not indeed assured thereof, but preferring that to the others, which I did not seek religiously, but opposed maliciously.

And I had thought that I delayed from day to day to reject worldly hopes and follow Thee only, because there did not appear anything certain whereunto to direct my course. And now had the day arrived in which I was to be laid bare to myself, and my conscience was to chide me. "Where art thou, O my tongue? Thou saidst, verily, that for an uncertain truth thou wert not willing to cast off the baggage of vanity. Behold, now it is certain, and yet doth that burden still oppress thee; whereas they who neither have so worn themselves out with searching after it, nor yet have spent ten years and more in thinking thereon, have had their shoulders unburdened, and gotten wings to fly away." Thus was I inwardly consumed and mightily confounded with an horrible shame.... And unto myself, what said I not within myself? With what scourges of rebuke lashed I not my soul to make it follow me, struggling to go after Thee! Yet it drew back; it refused, and exercised not itself. All its arguments were exhausted and confuted. There remained a silent trembling; and it feared, as it would death, to be restrained from the flow of that custom whereby it was wasting away even to death.

VIII:8

In the midst, then, of this great strife of my inner dwelling, which I had strongly raised up against my soul in the chamber of my heart, troubled both in mind and countenance, I seized upon Alypius [his friend], and exclaimed: "What is wrong with us? What is this? What heardest thou? The unlearned start up and 'take' heaven, and we, with our learning, but wanting heart, see where we wallow in flesh and blood! Because others have preceded us, are we ashamed to follow, and not rather ashamed at not following?" Some such words I gave utterance to, and in my excitement flung myself from him, while he gazed upon me in silent astonishment. For I spoke not in my wonted [usual] tone, and my brow, cheeks, eyes, color, tone of voice, all expressed my emotion more than the words. There was a little garden belonging to our lodging, of which we had the use, as of the whole house; for the master, our landlord, did not live there. Thither had the tempest within my breast hurried me, where no one might impede the fiery struggle in which I was engaged with myself, until it came to the issue that Thou knewest, though I did not. But I was mad that I might be whole, and dying that I might have life, knowing what evil thing I was, but not knowing what good thing I was shortly to become. Into the garden, then, I retired, Alypius following my steps. For his presence was no bar to my solitude; or how could he desert me so troubled? We sat down at as great a distance from the house as we could. I was disquieted in spirit, being most impatient with myself that I entered not into Thy will and covenant, O my God, which all my bones cried out unto me to enter, extolling it to the skies. And we enter not therein by ships, or chariots, or feet, no, nor by going so far as I had come from the house to that place where we were sitting. For not to go only, but to enter there, was naught else but to will to go, but to will it resolutely and thoroughly; not to stagger and sway about this way and that, a changeable and half-wounded will, wrestling, with one part falling as another rose.

Finally, in the very fever of my irresolution, I made many of those motions with my body which men sometimes desire to do, but cannot, if either they have not the limbs, or if their limbs be bound with fetters, weakened by disease, or hindered in any other way. Thus, if I tore my hair, struck my forehead, or if, entwining my fingers, I clasped my knee, this I did because I willed it. But I might have willed and not done it, if the power of motion in my limbs had not responded. So many things, then, I did, when to have the will was not to have the power, and I did not that which both with an unequalled desire I longed more to do, and which shortly when I should will I should have the power to do; because shortly when I should will, I should will thoroughly. For in such things the power was one with the will, and to will was to do, and yet was it not done; and more readily did the body obey the slightest wish of the soul in the moving its limbs at the order of the mind, than the soul obeyed itself to accomplish in the will alone this its great will.

VIII:9

Whence is this monstrous thing? And why is it? Let Thy mercy shine on me, that I may inquire, if so be the hiding-places of man's punishment, and the darkest contritions of the sons of Adam, may perhaps answer me. Whence is this monstrous thing? and why is it? The mind commands the body, and it obeys forthwith; the mind commands itself, and is resisted. The mind commands the hand to be moved, and such readiness is there that the command is scarce to be distinguished from the obedience. Yet the mind is mind, and the hand is body. The mind commands the mind to will, and yet, though it be itself, it obeyeth not. Whence this monstrous thing? and why is it? I repeat, it commands itself to will, and would not give the command unless it willed; yet is not that done which it commandeth. But it willeth not entirely; therefore it commandeth not entirely. For so far forth it commandeth, as it willeth; and so far forth is the thing commanded not done, as it willeth not. For the will commandeth that there be a will—not another, but itself. But it doth not command entirely, therefore that is not which it commandeth. For were it entire, it would not even command it to be, because it would already be. It is, therefore, no monstrous thing partly to will, partly to be unwilling, but an infirmity of the mind, that it doth not wholly rise, sustained by truth, pressed down by custom. And so there are two wills, because one of them is not entire; and the one is supplied with what the other needs. . . .

VIII:11

Thus was I sick and tormented, accusing myself far more severely than was my wont, tossing and turning me in my chain till that was utterly broken, whereby I now was but slightly, but still was held. And Thou, O Lord, pressedst upon me in my inward parts by a severe mercy, redoubling the lashes of fear and shame, lest I should again give way, and that same slender remaining tie not being broken off, it should recover strength, and enchain me the faster. For I said mentally, "Lo, let it be done now, let it be done now." And as I spoke, I all but came to a resolve. I all but did it, yet I did it not. Yet fell I not back to my old condition, but took up my position hard by, and drew breath. And I tried again, and wanted but very little of reaching it, and somewhat less, and then all but touched and grasped it; and yet came not at it, nor touched, nor grasped it, hesitating to die unto death, and to live unto life; and the worse, whereto I had been habituated, prevailed more with me than the better, which I had not tried. And the very moment in which I was to become another man, the nearer it approached me, the greater horror did it strike into me; but it did not strike me back, nor turn me aside, but kept me in suspense.

The very toys of toys, and vanities of vanities, my old mistresses, still enthralled me; they shook my fleshly garment, and whispered softly, "Dost thou part with us? And from that moment shall we no more be with thee for ever? And from that moment shall not this or that be lawful for thee for ever?" And what did they suggest to me in the words "this or that?" What is it that they suggested, O my God? Let Thy mercy avert it from the soul of Thy servant. What impurities did they suggest! What shame! And now I far less than half heard them, not openly showing themselves and contradicting me, but muttering, as it were, behind my back, and furtively plucking me as I was departing, to make me look back upon them. Yet they did delay me, so that I hesitated to burst and shake myself free from them, and to leap over whither I was called—an unruly habit saying to me, "Dost thou think thou canst live without them?"

But now it said this very faintly; for on that side towards which I had set my face, and whither I trembled to go, did the chaste dignity of Continence appear unto me, cheerful, but not dissolutely gay, honestly alluring me to come and doubt nothing, and extending her holy hands, full of a multiplicity of good examples, to receive and embrace me. There were there so many young men and maidens, a multitude of youth and every age, grave widows and ancient virgins, and Continence herself in all, not barren, but a fruitful mother of children of joys, by Thee, O Lord, her Husband. And she smiled on me with an encouraging mockery, as if to say, "Canst not thou do what these youths and maidens can? Or can one or other do it of themselves, and not rather in the Lord their God? The Lord their God gave me unto them. Why standest thou in thine own strength, and so standest not? Cast thyself upon Him; fear not, He will not withdraw that thou shouldest fall; cast thyself upon Him without fear, He will receive thee, and heal thee." And I blushed beyond measure, for I still heard the muttering of those toys, and hung in suspense. And she again seemed to say, "Shut up thine ears against those unclean members of thine upon the earth, that they may be mortified. They tell thee of delights, but not as doth the law of the Lord thy God." This controversy in my heart was naught but self against self. But Alypius, sitting close by my side, awaited in silence the result of my unwonted emotion.

VIII:12

But when a profound reflection had, from the secret depths of my soul, drawn together and heaped up all my misery before the sight of my heart, there arose a mighty storm, accompanied by as mighty a shower of tears. Which, that I might pour forth fully, with its natural expressions, I stole away from Alypius; for it suggested itself to me that solitude was fitter for the business of weeping. So I retired to such a distance that even his presence could not be oppressive to me. Thus was it with me at that time, and he perceived it; for something, I believe, I had spoken, wherein the sound of my voice appeared choked with weeping, and in that state had I risen up. He then remained where we had been sitting, most completely astonished. I flung myself down, how, I know not, under a certain fig-tree, giving free course to my tears, and the streams of mine eyes gushed out, an acceptable sacrifice unto Thee. And, not indeed in these words, yet to this effect, spake I much unto Thee—"But Thou, O Lord, how long?" "How long, Lord? Wilt Thou be angry for ever? Oh, remember not against us former iniquities;" for I felt that I was enthralled by them. I sent up these sorrowful cries—"how long, how long? To-morrow, and to-morrow? Why not now? Why is there not this hour an end to my uncleanness?"

I was saying these things and weeping in the most bitter contrition of my heart, when, lo, I heard the voice as of a boy or girl, I know not which, coming from a neighboring house, chanting, and oft repeating, "Take up and read; take up and read." Immediately my countenance was changed, and I began most earnestly to consider whether it was usual for children in any kind of game to sing such words; nor could I remember ever to have heard the like. So, restraining the torrent of my tears, I rose up, interpreting it no other way than as a command to me from Heaven to open the book, and to read the first chapter I should light upon. For I had heard of Antony, that, accidentally coming in whilst the gospel was being read, he received the admonition as if what was read were addressed to him, "Go and sell that thou hast, and give to the poor, and thou shalt have treasure in heaven; and come and follow me." And by such oracle was he forthwith converted unto Thee. So quickly I returned to the place where Alypius was sitting; for there had I put down the volume of the apostles, when I rose thence. I grasped, opened, and in silence read that paragraph on which my eyes first fell,—"Not in rioting and drunkenness, not in chambering and wantonness, not in strife and envying; but put ye on the Lord Jesus Christ, and make not provision for the flesh, to fulfill the lusts thereof." No further would I read, nor did I need; for instantly, as the sentence ended—by a light, as it were, of security infused into my heart—all the gloom of doubt vanished away.

Closing the book, then, and putting either my finger between, or some other mark, I now with a tranquil countenance made it known to Alypius. And he thus disclosed to me what was wrought in him, which I knew not. He asked to look at what I had read. I showed him; and he looked even further than I had read, and I knew not what followed. This it was, verily, "Him that is weak in the faith, receive ye;" which he applied to himself, and discovered to me. By this admonition was he strengthened; and by a good resolution and purpose, very much in accord with his character (wherein, for the better, he was always far different from me), without any restless delay he joined me. Thence we go in to my mother. We make it known to her—she rejoiceth. We relate how it came to pass—she leapeth for joy, and triumpheth, and blesseth Thee, who art "able to do exceeding abundantly above all that we ask or think"; for she perceived Thee to have given her more for me than she used to ask by her pitiful and most doleful groanings. For Thou didst so convert me unto Thyself, that I sought neither a wife, nor any other of this world's hopes—standing in that rule of faith in which Thou, so many years before, had showed me unto her in a vision. And thou didst turn her grief into a gladness, much more plentiful than she had desired, and much dearer and chaster than she used to crave, by having grandchildren of my body.

From Augustine, *Confessions,* in *NPNF,* First Series, Vol. 1, pp. 123–29 passim.

Augustine, The City of God

Book XIV:28

Accordingly, two cities have been formed by two loves: the earthly by the love of self, even to the contempt of God; the heavenly by the love of God, even to the contempt of self. The former, in a word, glories in itself, the latter in the Lord. For the one seeks glory from men; but the greatest glory of the other is God, the witness of conscience. The one lifts up its head in its own glory; the other says to its God, "Thou art my glory, and the lifter up of mine head." In the one, the princes and the nations it subdues are ruled by the love of ruling; in the other, the princes and the subjects serve one another in love, the latter obeying, while the former take thought for all. The one delights in its own strength, represented in the persons of its rulers; the other says to its God, "I will love Thee, O Lord, my strength." And therefore the wise men of the one city, living according to man, have sought for profit to their own bodies or souls, or both, and those who have known God "glorified Him not as God, neither were thankful, but became vain in their imaginations, and their foolish heart was darkened; professing themselves to be wise,"—that is, glorying in their own wisdom, and being possessed by pride,—"they became fools, and changed the glory of the incorruptible God into an image made like to corruptible man, and to birds, and four-footed beasts, and creeping things." For they were either leaders or followers of the people in adoring images, "and worshipped and served the creature more than the Creator, who is blessed for ever." But in the other city there is no human wisdom, but only godliness, which offers due worship to the true God, and looks for its reward in the society of the saints, of holy angels as well as holy men, "that God may be all in all."

Book XIX:17

But the families which do not live by faith seek their peace in the earthly advantages of this life; while the families which live by faith look for those eternal blessings which are promised, and use as pilgrims such advantages of time and of earth as do not fascinate and divert them from God, but rather aid them to endure with greater ease, and to keep down the number of those burdens of the corruptible body which weigh upon the soul. Thus the things necessary for this mortal life are used by both kinds of men and families alike, but each has its own peculiar and widely different aim in using them. The earthly city, which does not live by faith, seeks an earthly peace, and the end it proposes, in the well-ordered concord of civic obedience and rule, is the combination of men's wills to attain the things which are helpful to this life. The heavenly city, or rather the part of it which sojourns on earth and lives by faith, makes use of this peace only because it must, until this mortal condition which necessitates it shall pass away. Consequently, so long as it lives like a captive and a stranger in the earthly city, though it has already received the promise of redemption, and the gift of the Spirit as the earnest of it, it makes no scruple to obey the laws of the earthly city, whereby the things necessary for the maintenance of this mortal life are administered; and thus, as this life is common to both cities, so there is a harmony between them in regard to what belongs to it. But, as the earthly city has had some philosophers whose doctrine is condemned by the divine teaching, and who, being deceived either by their own conjectures or by demons, supposed that many gods must be invited to take an interest in human affairs ... assigned to each a separate function and a separate department ... ; and as the celestial city, on the other hand, knew that one God only was to be worshipped, and that to Him alone was due that service which the Greeks call *latreia* [service, offerings, sacrifice], and which can be given only to a god, it had come to pass that the two cities could not have common laws of religion, and that the heavenly city has been compelled in this matter to dissent, and to become obnoxious to those who think differently, and to stand the brunt of their anger and hatred and persecutions, except in so far as the minds of their enemies have been alarmed by the multitude of the Christians and quelled by the manifest protection of God accorded to them. This heavenly city, then, while it sojourns on earth, calls citizens out of all nations, and gathers together a society of pilgrims of all languages, not scrupling about diversities in the manners, laws, and institutions whereby earthly peace is secured and maintained, but recognizing that, however various these are, they all tend to one and the same end of earthly peace. It therefore is so far from rescinding and abolishing these diversities, that it even preserves and adopts them, so long only as no hindrance to the worship of the one supreme and true God is thus introduced. Even the heavenly city, therefore, while in its state of pilgrimage, avails itself of the peace of earth, and, so far as it can without injuring faith and godliness, desires and maintains a common agreement among men regarding the acquisition of the necessaries of life, and makes this earthly peace bear upon the peace of heaven; for this alone can be truly called and esteemed the peace of the reasonable creatures, consisting as it does in the perfectly ordered and harmonious enjoyment of God and of one another in God. When we shall have reached that peace, this mortal life shall give place to one that is eternal, and our body shall be no more this animal body which by its corruption weighs down the soul, but a spiritual body feeling no want, and in all its members subjected to the will. In its pilgrim state the heavenly city possesses this peace by faith; and by this faith it lives righteously when it refers to the attainment of that peace every good action towards God and man; for the life of the city is a social life.

From Augustine, *The City of God,* in *NPNF,* First Series, Vol. 2, pp. 282–83, 412–13 passim.

5.3 Neoplatonic Mysticism:
Pseudo-Dionysius the Areopagite

The author of these influential treatises on the mystical understanding of God is difficult to identify. Throughout the Middle Ages, readers believed the author was the Dionysius mentioned in the New Testament book of Acts (chapter 17), a Greek convert inspired by the teaching of Paul in the Areopagus, the public center for dialogue in Athens. Later scholarship in the sixteenth through nineteenth centuries demonstrated that an unnamed author around 500 C.E. wrote these works and attributed them to the first-century Dionysius as a way of giving the writings the weight of ancient authority. This false attribution by an author made his work more important, but also allowed him to display humility and deference toward the authorities of the past by making himself invisible.

Regardless of this misattribution, the treatise was immensely popular. The ideas contained in the writings of Pseudo-Dionysius combine Christian mystical belief with Platonic thought in a way that was compelling to medieval thinkers. This Neoplatonism became one of the main currents of thought in early medieval theology, evident also in Boethius (5.4), John Scotus Eriugena (10.2), and many mystics of the high Middle Ages.

Neoplatonism is a late antique version of Plato's philosophical principles about the Ideal realm that lies behind the particular and material reality that humans experience here in this life. The story from Plato's works that best explains his view of Ideals is the allegory of the cave (Book VII of the *Republic*). In the darkened cave Plato describes, people see only shadows dancing on a wall cast by unseen actors passing in front of a fire. All of these viewers' lives are spent observing these two-dimensional images, around which they build elaborate speculations and philosophies. However, one man leaves the cave and encounters the sun (which temporarily blinds him), after which he observes the three-dimensional reality that lies behind the shadows. This transformed philosopher reenters the cave and endeavors to convince the others that he has directly seen the true reality behind the shadows; they only mock him because his eyes are now too accustomed to the sun to be able to distinguish with any clarity the fine nuances of the shadows about which they dispute. Nor do the shadows mean much to this one who has seen the Ideal. In Plato's eyes, this enlightened philosopher's disinterest in the world of men makes him the ideal ruler (Plato's idea of the philosopher-king).

Christian thought, with its heavy emphasis on otherworldly values, easily adapted these Platonic ideas to Christian belief. It was only a small leap to identifying the realm of Ideals with the Mind of God, and to transforming the philosopher into the mystical theologian. The excerpts here from the first chapter of *The Divine Names* and the first two chapters of *The Mystical Theology* demonstrate the philosophical logic that supports this mystical view of life.

Questions

1. What is the "It" referred to throughout *The Divine Names* and how is It known?

2. What does Pseudo-Dionysius propose as the aim and methods of the Christian's contemplation in *The Mystical Theology*?

3. What is the problem that Pseudo-Dionysius is trying to explain in both documents?

The Divine Names, Chapter 1

1. And now, O blessed one, after having considered the *Outlines of Theology*, I shall proceed as far as I am able to the unfolding of the divine names. Let the divine law of the writings now determine us from the beginning of our inquiry: we are to make known the truth of what is said about God "not by trusting the persuasive logoi of human wisdom but by bringing forth the power" of the Spirit which moves the theologians. Hereby, will you be ineffably and unknowingly joined to what is ineffable and unknowable in a far greater union than we can attain through our rational and intellectual powers and activities. . . .

3. When we follow these thearchic bonds [*thearchy:* order or rule of God] which govern the splendid ordering of the super-celestial orders, and both when we honor the thearchic hiddenness beyond intellect and being by non-searching, sacred, and reverent intellects and when we honor what is ineffable by a temperate silence, then we are lifted up to the bright light which wholly illumines us in the sacred writings. They guide us in their light toward the thearchic celebration; we are super-cosmically illuminated by them. Thus, we are formed toward the sacred logos [word] of celebration and toward seeing the thearchic light which is commensurately given to us

by them. Thus do we celebrate the good-giving source of every sacred manifestation of light as it has bestowed itself in the sacred writings:

> It alone is cause, source, being
> and life of all,
> A recalling and resurrecting of those who
> have fallen away from it,
> A renewal and re-formation of those who are
> slipping away toward a destruction of the
> divine form,
> A sacred foundation of those who are tossed about
> in an unholy tempest,
> A security against falling for those who
> stand upright,
> A guiding hand which is stretched out for
> those who are being led back to it,
> An illumination for those who are illumined,
> A source of completion for those
> who are completed,
> A god-source for those who are deified,.
> A simplicity for those who are simplified,
> An unity for those who are unified,
> The source of every source
> beyond-beingly beyond every source,
> And the good gift of what is hidden
> according to the divine law.
> To speak simply:
> It is the life of all that lives and
> the being of all beings,
> The source and cause of every life and being,
> Through its goodness it brings forth and
> conserve beings in *being*.

4. We are initiated into these matters by the sacred writings. You shall find, as it were, that every sacred celebration of the theologians prepares, in a manifesting and celebrating way, the divine names with a view to the good-providing procession of the godhead. For this reason, in nearly all theological matters, we shall see the godhead celebrated as:

—Monad and unity. This is on account of the simplicity and unity of its partlessness which is beyond nature. From this, as a power of unification, we are super-cosmically unified and brought together into a divinely formed monad and divinely imitating unity from the folding together of our divisibility and otherness.

—Trinity. This is the three-person manifestation of the fecundity beyond being. From this all fatherness in heaven and earth both is and is named.

—Cause of beings. For all have been brought forward into *being* through its being-producing goodness.

—Wise and beautiful. For all beings are preserved in what is incorruptible of their own nature and indeed are filled with every divine harmony and sacred good form.

The love of man of the godhead is also excellent. For, in harmony with truth, it has been wholly communicated unto us in one of its three persons so that it recalls and raises human purposes to itself. From this the simple Jesus was ineffably composed; the everlasting received a temporal dimension and came to be equal in our nature with its unchanging and steady founding of those things which are fitting to it. Nevertheless, according to every nature, it exceeds every nature beyond every manner of being.

The hidden traditions of our divinely inspired leaders have given us many other theurgic lights which we have learned in harmony with the writings. Now [in our present life] we analogously learn through the sacred veils of the human love of the writings and of the hierarchic traditions. These hide both what is intelligible in what is sensible and what is beyond being in beings. These bestow form and shape to the formless and shapeless and multiply and break up the unstructured simplicity by a diversity of divisible symbols.

Hereafter, when we have come to be indestructible and immortal and have attained a most blessed and Christ-like lot, "we shall" as the writings say, "be always with the Lord" [1 Thess. 4:17] and shall be filled with his visible theophany in the holy contemplations which shall illumine us with the most brilliant splendors as the disciples were in that most divine transfiguration. We shall share in his intellectual gifts of light with a passionless and pure intellect. We shall share in the unity beyond intellect in the unknown and blessed radiations of the rays that are beyond every light. Thus shall we be a more divine imitation of the super-celestial intellects. For, as the truth of writings say "we shall be equal to the angels and will be sons of God, by being sons of the resurrection." [Luke 20:36]

But now, as far as is attainable by us, we employ the fitting symbols for what is divine; from these we are analogically lifted up to the simple and unified truth of the intellectual visions of God which are beyond our intellection of the divine ideas. Once we cease our intellectual activities, we are thrust upon the ray beyond being as far as the divine law permits. In this ray the limits of all knowledge have pre-subsisted in a more than ineffable way.

It is not possible to conceive, to speak, or in any way to contemplate this ray; for, it is apart from all, beyond unknowing, and at once the completing ends of all essential knowledge and powers. It has anticipated, beyond every manner of being, all in itself and is founded beyond all the super-celestial intellects by its unencompassed powers. For if all knowledge is of beings and has its limits in beings, then that beyond every being is apart from every knowledge. . . .

5. . . . For we have shown that the divinity beyond being is incomprehensible and beyond all names. . . .

Yet since it is cause of all by its *being* (as source of goodness), it is necessary to celebrate the good-source-providence of the godhead in relation to the totality of what is caused. . . .

6. Seeing this, the theologians celebrate it as nameless and in accordance with all names. Thus, they call it nameless when the godhead itself, in one of the mystical sights of the symbolic manifestation of God, rebukes him who says "What is thy name?" by saying "To what end do you ask my name, for it is the most wondrous of all?" [Jud. 13:17–18] and leads him away from a knowledge of the divine names. For is not this truly the most wondrous name: the nameless beyond all names, which is placed beyond "every name which is named either in this age or in the future?" [Eph. 1:21]

Yet they do give it many names and introduce it as: "I am who am," [Exod. 3:14] "life," light," "God," and "truth." Those who are wise of God themselves celebrate the cause of all beings in terms of the totality of what is caused and with many names: "good," "beautiful," "wise," "beloved," "God of gods," "Lord of lords," "Holy of holies," "age," "be-ing," "cause of every age," "leader of life," "wisdom," "intellect," "logos," "knower," "beyond having the treasure of every knowledge," "power," "empowered," "King of those who are ruled," "Ancient of days," "not aging and unchanging," "savior," "justice," "sanctification," "redemption," "surpassing all in greatness," "in the still small breeze." And, further, they say that it is in intellects, in souls, in bodies, in the heaven and in the earth and at one and the same time in itself, in the cosmos, around the cosmos, beyond the cosmos, beyond the heaven, and beyond being. It is named "sun," "air," "fire," "water," "spirit," "dew," "cloud," "a stone itself," and "a rock": all beings, yet nothing among beings.

7. Thus, both nameless and all the names of beings befit the cause of all, be-ing beyond all, precisely so that it would be king of all and all would be about it—being raised to it as cause, source, and limit—and so that it would

be "all in all" [1 Cor. 15:28] as the writings say. Thus, we truly celebrate it to be the support, source of guidance, connection, completion, protection and hearth of ail, and as reverting [all] to itself. [It accomplishes] these in a unified, immeasurable, and excellent way. For it is not only the cause of connection, of life, or of completion such that the goodness beyond name would be named from one or another of its providences. Rather, it has anticipated the all simply and infinitely in itself: the all complete goodness of its one and all causing providence. Thus, it is to be harmoniously celebrated and named in terms of all beings.

Mystical Theology, Chapter 1, The Divine Dark

1.

> O Trinity
> beyond being,
> beyond divinity,
> beyond goodness, and
> guide of Christians in divine wisdom,
> direct us to the mystical summits
> more than unknown and beyond light,
> There the simple, absolved, and
> unchanged mysteries of theology
> lie hidden in the darkness beyond light
> of the hidden mystical silence,
> there, in the greatest darkness,
> that beyond all that is most evident
> exceedingly illuminates the sightless
> intellects.
> there, in the wholly imperceptible and invisible,
> that beyond all that is most evident
> fills to overflowing the sightless intellects
> with the glories beyond all beauty.
> This is my prayer.
> And you, dear Timothy,
> in the earnest exercise of
> mystical contemplation, abandon
> all sensation and all intellectual activities
> all that is sensed and intelligible,
> all non-beings and all beings;
> thus you will unknowingly be elevated,

as far as possible,
to the unity of that beyond being and knowledge.
By the irrepressible and absolving ecstasis
of yourself and of all,
absolved from all, and
going away from all,
you will be purely raised up
to the rays of the divine darkness
beyond being.

2.

Disclose this not to the uninitiated:
not to those, I say, who are
entangled in beings,
imagine nothing to be beyond-beingly
beyond beings, and
claim to know by the knowledge in them
"Him who has made the dark
his hiding place." [Ps. 18:11]

If the divine mystical initiations are beyond these,
what about those yet more profane, who
characterize the cause which lies beyond all
by the last among beings, and
deny it to be preeminent to
their ungodly phantasies and
diverse formations of it.

For while to it,
as cause of all
one must posit and affirm
all the positions of beings,
as beyond be-ing beyond all
one must more properly deny all of these.

Think not that affirmations and denials
are opposed
but rather that, long before, is
that—which is itself beyond all position
and denial—
beyond privation.

Reprinted with permission from *Pseudo-Dionysius Areopagite: The Divine Names and Mystical Theology,* translated by John D. Jones (Milwaukee: Marquette University Press, 1980), pp. 107, 109–116, 211–13. Notes omitted.

5.4 *The Consolation of Philosophy:* Boethius

Boethius's work *The Consolation of Philosophy,* written in 523, was one of the main conduits of classical reasoning to the early Middle Ages, read and translated by scholars and kings. Boethius (b. circa 480) bridged the gap from the Roman world to the Germanic world: born into the senatorial aristocracy, he was educated in the Greek and Latin classics, and then served at the court of the Ostrogothic king Theodoric in Italy. In addition to his public duties as an advisor, Boethius translated important works from Greek and wrote poetry, treatises on logic, and philosophical tracts.

The Consolation of Philosophy stands out among all these works for a number of reasons, most notably its subsequent influence in later ages, its artistry, and its philosophical contemplation. Part of its power derives, however, from the circumstances under which it was written. Boethius was in prison, a victim of the unstable politics of Theodoric's court, and was later to die in disgrace. He had thus fallen from the highest place to the lowest, and felt the sting of injustice. In the *Consolation,* Boethius creates a dialogue with Philosophy, personified as a woman who brings him to enlightenment through her gentle arguments. The *Consolation* is the product of Boethius's reflections on the nature of the world, fortune, God, Good and Evil, and happiness. He brings to bear on these deep subjects all his intellectual experience, to find a way of coping with his circumstances. In some ways, this book is comparable to the life of Macrina that Gregory of Nyssa wrote as a way of coping with his sister's death (4.2). The excerpts below from Book IV address the question of why evil occurs, particularly to the good.

Questions

1. How can evil exist in a worldview that posits the existence of one omnipotent, all-loving deity?

2. What is the relationship of Providence and Fate, according to Boethius?

3. What features would make this work a popular one in succeeding ages?

Boethius, *The Consolation of Philosophy*

Book 4: Prose 1

'Herald of true light,' [Boethius] said . . . this one thing is the chief cause of my grief, namely that, when there exists a good governor of the world, evils should exist at all, or, existing, should go unpunished. I would have you think how strange is this fact alone. But there is an even stranger attached thereto: ill-doing reigns and flourishes, while virtue not only lacks its reward, but is even trampled underfoot by wicked doers, and pays the penalties instead of crime. Who can wonder and complain enough that such things should happen under the rule of One who, while all-knowing and all-powerful, wills good alone?' ...

Book 4: Prose 2

... 'First, then, you must learn that power is never lacking to the good, while the wicked are devoid of all strength. The proofs of these two statements hang upon each other. For good and bad are opposites, and therefore, if it is allowed that good is powerful, the weakness of evil is manifest: if the weakness and uncertainty of evil is made plain, the strength and sureness of good is proved. To gain more full credit for my opinion, I will go on to make my argument sure by first the one, then the other of the two paths, side by side.

'It is allowed that there are two things upon which depend the entire operation of human actions: they are will and power. For if the will be wanting, a man does not even attempt that which he has no desire to perform; if the power be wanting, the will is exercised in vain. Wherefore, if you see a man wish for that which he will in no wise gain, you cannot doubt that he lacks the power to attain that which he wishes.' ...

'Do you remember that happiness is the absolute good, and that the good is desired of all, when in that manner happiness is sought?'

'I need not recall that,' I said, 'since it is present fixedly in my memory.'

'Then all men, good and bad alike, seek to arrive at the good by no different instincts?'

'Yes, that follows necessarily.'

'But it is certain that the good become so by the attainment of good?'

'Yes.'

'Then the good attain that which they wish?'

'Yes,' said I, 'it seems so.'

'But if evil men attain the good they seek, they cannot be evil?'

'No.'

'Since, then, both classes seek the good, which the good attain, but the evil attain not, it is plain that the good are powerful, while the evil are weak?'

'If any doubt that, he cannot judge by the nature of the world, nor by the sequence of arguments.'

Again she said, 'If there are two persons before whom the same object is put by natural instinct, and one person carries his object through, working by his natural functions, but the other cannot put his natural instinct into practice, but using some function unsuitable to nature he can imitate the successful person, but not fulfill his original purpose, in this case, which of the two do you decide to be the more capable?' [Obviously the good] . . .

'But in the case of the highest good,' she said, 'it is equally the purpose set before good and bad men; good men seek it by the natural functions of virtue, while bad men seek to attain the same through their cupidity, which is not a natural function for the attainment of good. Think you not so?'

'I do indeed,' said I; 'this is plain, as also is the deduction which follows. For it must be, from what I have already allowed, that the good are powerful, the wicked weak.' . . .

'See how great is the weakness of these wicked men who cannot even attain that to which their natural instinct leads them, nay, almost drives them. And further, how if they are deprived of this great, this almost invincible, aid of a natural instinct to follow? Think what a powerlessness possesses these men. They are no light objects which they seek; they seek no objects in sport, objects which it is impossible that they should achieve. They fail in the very highest of all things, the crown of all, and in this they find none of the success for which they labor day and night in wretchedness. But herein the strength of good men is conspicuous. If a man could advance on foot till he arrived at an utmost point beyond which there was no path for further advance, you would think him most capable of walking: equally so, if a man grasps the very end and aim of his search, you must think him most capable. Wherefore also the contrary is true; that evil men are similarly deprived of all strength. . . . But they lose thus not only power, but existence all together. For those who abandon the common end of all who exist, must equally cease to exist. And this may seem strange, that we should say that evil men, though the majority of mankind, do not exist at all; but it is so. For while I do not deny that evil men are evil, I do deny that they "are," in the sense of absolute existence. You may say, for instance, that a corpse is a dead man, but you cannot call it a man. In a like manner, though I grant that wicked men are bad, I cannot allow that they are men at all, as regards absolute being. A thing exists which keeps its proper place and preserves its nature; but when anything falls away from its nature, its existence too ceases, for that lies in its nature. You will say, "Evil men are capable of evil": and that I would not deny. But this very power of theirs comes not from strength, but from weakness. They are capable of evil; but this evil would have no efficacy if it could have stayed under the operation of good men. And this very power of ill shews the more plainly that their power is naught. For if, as we have agreed, evil is nothing, then, since they are only capable of evil, they are capable of nothing.'. . .

. . . Therefore the power of doing evil is no power at all. For all these reasons the power of good men and the weakness of evil men is apparent. So Plato's opinion is plain that "the wise alone are able to do what they desire, but unscrupulous men can only labor at what they like, they cannot fulfill their real desires." They do what they like so long as they think that they will gain through their pleasures the good which they desire; but they do not gain it, since nothing evil ever reaches happiness.

Book 4: Prose 3

'Do you see then in what a slough crimes are involved, and with what glory honesty shines forth? It is plain from this that reward is never lacking to good deeds, nor punishment to crime. We may justly say that the reward of every act which is performed is the object for which it is performed. For instance, on the racecourse the crown for which the runner strives is his reward. But we have shewn that happiness is the identical good for the sake of which all actions are performed. Therefore the absolute good is the reward put before all human actions. But good men cannot be deprived of this. And further, a man who lacks good cannot justly be described as a good man; wherefore we may say that good habits never miss their rewards. Let the wicked rage never so wildly, the wise man's crown shall never fail nor wither. And the wickedness of bad men can never take away from good men the glory which belongs to them. Whereas if a good man rejoiced in a glory which he received from outside, then could another, or even he, may be, who granted it, carry it away. But since honesty grants to every good man its own rewards, he will only lack his reward when he ceases to be good. And lastly, since every reward is sought for the reason that it is held to be good, who shall say that the man, who possesses goodness, does not receive his reward? And what reward is this? Surely the fairest and greatest of all. Remember that corollary which I emphasized when speaking to you a little while ago; and reason thus therefrom. While happiness is the absolute good, it is plain that all good men become good by virtue of the very fact that they are good. But we agreed that happy men are as gods. Therefore this is the reward of the good, which no time can wear out, no power can lessen, no wickedness can darken; they become divine. In this case, then, no wise man can doubt of the inevitable punishment of the wicked as well. For good and evil are so set, differing from each other just as reward and punishment are in opposition to each other: hence the rewards, which we see fall to the good, must correspond precisely to the punishments of the evil on the other side. . . .

'Then, from the other point of view of the good, see what a punishment ever goes with the wicked. You have learnt a little while past that all that exists is one, and that the good itself is one; it follows therefrom that all that exists must appear to be good. In this way, therefore, all that falls away from the good, ceases also to exist, wherefore evil men cease to be what they were. The form of their human bodies still proves that they have been men; wherefore they must have lost their human nature when they turned to evil-doing. But as goodness alone can lead men forward beyond their humanity, so evil of necessity will thrust down below the honorable estate of humanity those whom it casts down from their first position. The result is that you cannot hold him to be a man who has been, so to say, transformed by his vices [into various beasts]. . . . Thus then a man who loses his goodness, ceases to be a man, and since he cannot change his condition for that of a god, he turns into a beast.

Book 4: Prose 6

. . . 'For herein lie the questions of the directness of Providence, the course of Fate, chances which cannot be foreseen, knowledge, divine predestination, and freedom of judgment. . . .

'The engendering of all things, the whole advance of all changing natures, and every motion and progress in the world, draw their causes, their order, and their forms from the allotment of the unchanging mind of God, which lays manifold restrictions on all action from the calm fortress of its own directness. Such restrictions are called Providence when they can be seen to lie in the very simplicity of divine understanding; but they were called Fate in old times when they were viewed with reference to the objects which they moved or arranged. It will easily be understood that these two are very different if the mind examines the force of each. For Providence is the very divine reason which arranges all things, and rests with the supreme disposer of all; while Fate is that ordering which is a part of all changeable things, and by means of which Providence binds all things together in their own order. Providence embraces all things equally, however different they may be, even however infinite: when they are assigned to their own places, forms, and times, Fate sets them in an orderly motion; so that this development of the temporal order, unified in the intelligence of the mind of God, is Providence. The working of this unified development in time is called Fate. These are different, but the one hangs upon the other. For this order, which is ruled by Fate, emanates from the directness of Providence. Just as when a craftsman perceives in his mind the form of the object he would make, he sets his working power in motion, and brings through the order of time that which he had seen directly and ready present to his mind. So by Providence does God dispose all that is to be done, each thing by itself and unchangeably; while these same things which Providence has arranged are worked out by Fate in many ways and in time. Whether, therefore, Fate works by the aid of the divine spirits which serve Providence, or whether it works by the aid of the soul, or of all nature, or the motions of the stars in heaven, or the powers of angels, or the manifold skill of other spirits, whether the course of Fate is bound together by any or all of these, one thing is certain, namely that Providence is the one unchangeable direct power which gives form to all things which are to come to pass, while Fate is the changing bond, the temporal order of those things which are arranged to come to pass by the direct disposition of God. Wherefore everything which is subject to Fate is also subject to Providence, to which Fate is itself subject. But there are things which, though beneath Providence, are above the course of Fate. Those things are they which are immovably set nearest the primary divinity, and are there beyond the course of the movement of Fate. As in the case of spheres moving round the same axis, that which is nearest the center approaches most nearly the simple motion of the center, and is itself, as it were, an axis around which turn those which are set outside it. That sphere which is outside all turns through a greater circuit, and fulfills a longer course in proportion as it is farther from the central axis; and if it be joined or connect itself with that center, it is drawn into the direct motion thereof, and no longer strays or strives to turn away. In like manner, that which goes farther from the primary intelligence, is bound the more by the ties of Fate, and the nearer it approaches the axis of all, the more free it is from Fate. But that which clings without movement to the firm intellect above, surpasses altogether the bond of Fate. As, therefore, reasoning is to understanding; as that which becomes is to that which is; as time is to eternity; as the circumference is to the center: so is the changing course of Fate to the immovable directness of Providence. . . . Wherefore in disposing the universe this limitation directs all for good, though to you who are not strong enough to comprehend the whole order, all seems confusion and disorder. Naught is there that comes to pass for the sake of evil, or due to wicked men, of whom it has been abundantly shewn that they seek the good, but misleading error turns them from the right course; for never does the true order, which comes forth from the center of the highest good, turn any man aside from the right beginning.' . . .

'. . . God looks forth from the high watchtower of His Providence, He sees what suits each man, and applies to him that which suits him. Hence then comes that conspicuous cause of wonder in the order of Fate, when a wise man does that which amazes the ignorant. For, to glance at the depth of God's works with so few words as human reason is capable of comprehending, I say that what you think to be most fair and most conducive to justice's preservation, that appears different to an all-seeing Providence. Has not our fellow-philosopher Lucan told us how "the conquering cause did please the gods, but the conquered, Cato?"

What then surprises you when done on this earth, is the true-guided order of things; it is your opinion which is perverted and confused. . . . To some, Providence grants a mingled store of good and bad, according to the nature of their minds. Some she treats bitterly, lest they grow too exuberant with long-continued good fortune; others she allows to be harassed by hardships that the virtues of their minds should be strengthened by the habit and exercise of patience. Some have too great a fear of sufferings which they can bear; others have too great contempt for those which they cannot bear: these she leads on by troubles to make trial of themselves. Some have brought a name to be honored for all time at the price of a glorious death. Some by shewing themselves undefeated by punishment, have left a proof to others that virtue may be invincible by evil. What doubt can there be of how rightly such things are disposed, and that they are for the good of those whom we see them befall? The other point too arises from like causes, that sometimes sorrows, sometimes the fulfilment of their desires, falls to the wicked. As concerns the sorrows, no one is surprised, because all agree that they deserve ill. Their punishments serve both to deter others from crime by fear, and also to amend the lives of those who undergo them; their happiness, on the other hand, serves as a proof to good men of how they should regard good fortune of this nature, which they see often attends upon the dishonest. . . . For a definite order embraces all things, so that even when some subject leaves the true place assigned to it in the order, it returns to an order, though another, it may be, lest aught in the realm of Providence be left to random chance. But "hard is it for me to set forth all these matters as a god," [Homer, *Iliad*, xii. 176] nor is it right for a man to try to comprehend with his mind all the means of divine working, or to explain them in words. Let it be enough that we have seen that God, the Creator of all nature, directs and disposes all things for good. And while He urges all, that He has made manifest, to keep His own likeness, He drives out by the course of Fate all evil from the bounds of His state. Wherefore if you look to the disposition of Providence, you will reckon naught as bad of all the evils which are held to abound upon earth.

From *The Consolation of Philosophy*, trans. W. V. Cooper, in *The Temple Classics*, ed. Israel Golancz (London: J.M. Dent, 1902), pp. 102, 104–10, 111–14, 125–34, passim.

–6–

The Power of Christian Saints

Monks, Relics, and Icons

One of the most powerful forces for conversion in the early ages of Christianity was the example set by saints, whose stories were repeated down through succeeding generations. These biographies present these holy ones as the embodiments of the ideal virtues of the religion and as examples of Christianity's otherworldly power. The lives of these men and women, the hardships they endured, their triumphs over evil forces in the world, and their miracles testified to a power transcending all worldly conditions. Christian saints, like the Hebrew prophets of the Old Testament and Plato's philosopher-king, stood outside the social-political order and thus could reveal otherworldly truths or ideals by speaking freely against the wayward lifestyles of their cultures.

Three major kinds of heroic saints emerged in the first six centuries of Christianity: the martyr, the hermit, and the monk. All manifested the same otherworldly values, denying life in the here and now in favor of the spiritual life with God in eternity, as evident in the earlier stories of martyrs (2.1, 4.1). In manifesting this Christian rejection of temporal life, the ascetic life of hermits and monks readily stood in place of the martyr once the days of persecution had passed and Christianity dominated the religious life of the Roman Empire and later Europe.

Ascetics were individuals who lived frugal lives, eschewing sex, eating the bare minimum to stay alive, dressing poorly, and often living in harsh environments. In many cases, though, their behavior attracted more attention than they wanted: followers came to them, begging to learn their wisdom, desiring to become disciples, as shown in the lives and sayings of the desert fathers and mothers (6.1). Out of this popularity of hermit saints came monasticism: the setting up of orderly houses in which groups of monks could live ascetic lives. In turn, these monasteries gave birth to other saints—noteworthy monks or nuns whose lives stood out among their brethren. Inevitably, this grass-roots movement of monasticism became systematized as part of the order of the church.

Monasticism was an appealing option for many in the disturbing times of late antiquity, particularly in the western portions of the Roman Empire as the government's authority crumbled. Increasingly, the peoples of the western lands looked elsewhere for stability and identity—to the new Germanic kingdoms emerging and to religion. The monastic life was one option for those who valued peace and learning, an escape from political turmoil, economic uncertainty, and endemic warfare. The Life and Rule of Saint Benedict (6.2) demonstrate these monastic values.

Both the eastern and western churches venerated holy men and women for their virtuous lives. In the West, the focus of devotion was the relic, a part of the saint's worldly existence left behind (bones, various body parts, clothing, perhaps items they touched) reverently encased in bejeweled reliquaries; these remnants represented the hope and the power of resurrection. In the East, icons, or images of the holy person, became the focus of devotional practice, as well as a source of controversy. In both cases, relics and icons, the saint became a channel of divine power between this world and the otherworld where the saint's soul now resided with God. Having denied the importance of worldly life through ascetic practice, their earthly remnants or images left a connection open to the spiritual world. Thus many European pilgrims sought out the churches holding such relics, making a physical and spiritual journey to this locus of power, as evident in Saint Martin's shrine (6.3). In the Byzantine church, monasteries produced highly symbolic, reflective icons of the saints for believers to use a focus for meditation, a gateway for contemplating the heavenly realm, as John of Damascus explains (6.4).

In all of these stories and practices, the sense of the interconnection between material experience and otherworldly meaning comes through. Precisely because they rejected power and prestige in this world and embraced poverty and humility, saints had tremendous spiritual potency over the natural world, a strength that transcended even their own lifetimes, a power that lingered on in their earthly remains.

6.1 Desert Fathers and Mothers:
Abba Anthony and Amma Syncletica

Hermits—individuals who hide from society—were, ironically, prominent leaders in the Mediterranean world of the third through sixth centuries. These recluses desired to imitate the life of Christ and rejected the life of the material world as a way of putting spiritual values first in their lives. Consequently, they withdrew from active urban life by re-treating to the deserts, relying on precedents in the Old and New Testa-ments as models, such as Moses leading the children of Israel through the wilderness for forty years or Jesus retreating into the desert where he was tempted by the Devil for forty days. In the desert, hermits eschewed food, sex, and other material comforts, and battled the demonic tempta-tions of gluttony, lust, and greed. Through prayer, fasting, and contem-plation they achieved miraculous victory over both body and soul. Because these hermits had arrived at a state of self-abegnation, of utter indifference to the world, followers called them "abba" (father) or "amma" (mother) and came to treasure their words.

Many of the outstanding examples of hermit life that later influenced the development of monasticism come from Egypt, from the lives of ascetic hermits of the third through fifth centuries who withdrew into deserts around the Nile Valley. The Coptic Church of Egypt placed a great deal of emphasis on the role of holy men and women, and mo-nasticism was central to church life. The "Sayings of the Desert Fathers" is one of a number of collections in the fifth and sixth centuries that portray the lives of these saintly hermits and their words of wisdom. These anecdotes and short sayings inspired many later Christians. They are often short, pithy statements meant to cause reflection. Moreover, their meaning cannot be separated from the example of the individuals who lived these truths. The values espoused by the hermits could not be taught in sayings alone—this was a life to be imitated.

The two stories here show the range of hermit examples. Abba Ant-ony was a third-century hermit known popularly as the Father of Monks because both the eastern and western traditions of monasticism spring from his example, as told by his biographer the bishop Athanasius. Like many hermits, Antony came from a poor background, the son of peas-ants; his wisdom comes, then, not so much from erudition as from experience. Amma Syncletica is an example of a desert mother; fewer in number, women hermits also taught disciples the great truths they learned through endurance and faith. Little else is known about Syn-cletica, but the sayings attributed to her are typical of the gems of wisdom these spiritual teachers gave to those who came to ask "Give me a word, Amma."

Questions

1. What views of life in this world do hermits such as Antony and Syncletica have?
2. How do these two teachers convey their lessons to seekers?
3. What social, spiritual, and emotional values do the hermits teach?

Sayings of the Desert Fathers

Abba Anthony

1. When the holy Abba Anthony lived in the desert he was beset by *accidie* [spiritual apathy], and attacked by many sinful thoughts. He said to God, 'Lord, I want to be saved but these thoughts do not leave me alone; what shall I do in my affliction? How can I be saved?' A short while afterwards, when he got up to go out, Anthony saw a man like himself sitting at his work, getting up from his work to pray, then sitting down and plaiting a rope, then getting up again to pray. It was an angel of the Lord sent to correct and reassure him. He heard the angel saying to him, 'Do this and you will be saved.' At these words, Anthony was filled with joy and courage. He did this, and he was saved.

2. When the same Abba Anthony thought about the depth of the judgements of God, he asked, 'Lord, how is it that some die when they are young, while others drag on to extreme old age? Why are there those who are poor and those who are rich? Why do wicked men prosper and why are the just in need?' He heard a voice answering him, 'Anthony, keep your attention on yourself; these things are according to the judgement of God, and it is not to your advantage to know anything about them.'

3. Someone asked Abba Anthony, 'What must one do in order to please God?' The old man replied, 'Pay attention to what I tell you: whoever you may be, always have God before your eyes; whatever you do, do it according to the testimony of the holy Scriptures; in whatever place you live, do not easily leave it. Keep these three precepts and you will be saved.'

4. Abba Anthony said to Abba Poemen, 'This is the great work of a man: always to take the blame for his own sins before God and to expect temptation to his last breath.'

5. He also said, 'Whoever has not experienced temptation cannot enter into the Kingdom of Heaven.' He even added, 'Without temptations no one can be saved.'

6. Abba Pambo asked Abba Anthony, 'What ought I to do?' and the old man said to him, 'Do not trust in your own righteousness, do not worry about the past, but control your tongue and your stomach.'

7. Abba Anthony said, 'I saw the snares that the enemy spreads out over the world and I said groaning, "What can get through from such snares?" Then I heard a voice saying to me, "Humility." ' . . .

17. One day some old men came to see Abba Anthony. In the midst of them was Abba Joseph. Wanting to test them, the old man suggested a text from the Scriptures, and, beginning with the youngest, he asked them what

it meant. Each gave his opinion as he was able. But to each one the old man said, 'You have not understood it.' Last of all he said to Abba Joseph, 'How would you explain this saying?' and he replied, 'I do not know.' Then Abba Anthony said, 'Indeed, Abba Joseph has found the way, for he has said: "I do not know."' . . .

19. The brethren came to the Abba Anthony and said to him, 'Speak a word; how are we to be saved?' The old man said to them, 'You have heard the Scriptures. That should teach you how.' But they said, 'We want to hear from you too, Father.' Then the old man said to them, 'The Gospel says, "if anyone strikes you on one cheek, turn to him the other also."' (Matt. 5:39) They said, 'We cannot do that.' The old man said, 'If you cannot offer the other cheek, at least allow one cheek to be struck.' 'We cannot do that either,' they said. So he said, 'If you are not able to do that, do not return evil for evil,' and they said, 'We cannot do that either.' Then the old man said to his disciple, 'Prepare a little brew of corn [grain] for these invalids. If you cannot do this, or that, what can I do for you? What you need is prayers.'

Amma Syncletica

1. Amma Syncletica said, 'In the beginning there are a great many battles and a good deal of suffering for those who are advancing towards God and afterwards, ineffable joy. It is like those who wish to light a fire; at first they are choked by the smoke and cry, and by this means obtain what they seek (as it is said: "Our God is a consuming fire" [Heb. 1 2:24]): so we also must kindle the divine fire in ourselves through tears and hard work.'

2. She also said, 'We who have chosen this way of life must obtain perfect temperance. It is true that among seculars, also, temperance has the freedom of the city, but intemperance cohabits with it, because they sin with all the other senses. Their gaze is shameless and they laugh immoderately.' . . .

5. Blessed Syncletica was asked if poverty is a perfect good. She said, 'For those who are capable of it, it is a perfect good. Those who can sustain it receive suffering in the body but rest in the soul, for just as one washes coarse clothes by trampling them underfoot and turning them about in all directions, even so the strong soul becomes much more stable thanks to voluntary poverty.' . . .

9. She also said, 'When you have to fast, do not pretend illness. For those who do not fast often fall into real sicknesses. If you have begun to act well, do not turn back through constraint of the enemy, for through your endurance, the enemy is destroyed. Those who put out to sea at first sail with a favourable wind; then the sails spread, but later the winds become

adverse. Then the ship is tossed by the waves and is no longer controlled by the rudder. But when in a little while there is a calm, and the tempest dies down, then the ship sails on again. So it is with us, when we are driven by the spirits who are against us, we hold to the cross as our sail and so we can set a safe course.'

10. She also said, 'Those who have endured the labours and dangers of the sea and then amass material riches, even when they have gained much desire to gain yet more and they consider what they have at present as nothing and reach out for what they have not got. We, who have nothing of that which we desire, wish to acquire everything through the fear of God.'

11. She also said, 'Imitate the publican, and you will not be condemned with the Pharisee. Choose the meekness of Moses and you will find your heart which is a rock changed into a spring of water.' ...

15. She also said, 'There is an asceticism which is determined by the enemy and his disciples practice it. So how are we to distinguish between the divine and royal asceticism and the demonic tyranny? Clearly through its quality of balance. Always use a single rule of fasting. Do not fast four or five days and break it the following day with any amount of food. In truth lack of proportion always corrupts. While you are young and healthy, fast, for old age with its weakness will come. As long as you can, lay up treasure, so that when you cannot, you will be at peace.'

16. She also said, 'As long as we are in the monastery, obedience is preferable to asceticism. The one teaches pride, the other humility.

17. She also said, 'We must direct our souls with discernment. As long as we are in the monastery, we must not seek our own will, nor follow our personal opinion but obey our fathers in the faith.' ...

19. Amma Syncletica said, 'There are many who live in the mountains and behave as if they were in the town, and they are wasting their time. It is possible to be a solitary in one's mind while living in a crowd, and it is possible for one who is a solitary to live in the crowd of his own thoughts.' ...

21. She also said, 'just as a treasure that is exposed loses its value, so a virtue which is known vanishes; just as wax melts when it is near fire, so the soul is destroyed by praise and loses all the results of its labour.'

22. She also said, 'Just as it is impossible to be at the same moment both a plant and a seed, so it is impossible for us to be surrounded by worldly honour and at the same time to bear heavenly fruit.' ...

24. She also said, 'We must arm ourselves in every way against the demons. For they attack us from outside, and they also stir us up from within; and the soul is then like a ship when great waves break over it, and at the same time it sinks because the hold is too full. We are just like that: we lose as much by the exterior faults we commit as by the thoughts inside

us. So we must watch for the attacks of men that come from outside us, and also repel the interior onslaughts of our thoughts.'

25. She also said, 'Here below we are not exempt from temptations. For Scripture says, "Let him who thinks that he stands take heed lest he fall." (I Cor. 10:12) We sail on in darkness. The psalmist calls our life a sea and the sea is either full of rocks, or very rough, or else it is calm. We are like those who sail on a calm sea, and seculars are like those on a rough sea. We always set our course by the sun of justice, but it can often happen that the secular is saved in tempest and darkness, for he keeps watch as he ought, while we go to the bottom through negligence, although we are on a calm sea, because we have let go of the guidance of justice.'

26. She also said, 'Just as one cannot build a ship unless one has some nails, so it is impossible to be saved without humility.'

Reprinted with permission from *The Desert Christian: Sayings of the Desert Fathers, The Alphabetical Collection,* trans. Benedicta Ward, S.L.G. (New York: Macmillan, 1975), pp. 1–2, 4–5, 230–35 passim. Notes omitted.

6.2 The Monastic Exemplar:
The Life of Saint Benedict and The Rule of Saint Benedict

Monasteries—communities of ascetics living according to a rule—sprang up not only in Egypt but also in Syria, Byzantium, and Europe. The impulse to retreat into a hermetic existence, exemplified in Antony and Syncletica, paradoxically produced an outpouring of interest from prospective disciples. Some hermits therefore established communities and wrote manuals for holy living. For example, Pachomius (292–346) built on Anthony's model and created the first communal monastic life in Egypt. In western Europe, amid a proliferation of rules for monasteries, one emerged as the standard: Saint Benedict and the Benedictine Rule.

Consequently, western monasticism is rooted in Saint Benedict and his Rule. Although scholars cannot definitively trace the later Benedictine Rule to the great fifth-century saint, he is, nonetheless, the legendary founder of this major branch of monasticism named after him. In part, this attribution is due to the patronage of Pope Gregory I (590–604), who wrote Saint Benedict's Life and who fostered Benedictine monasticism in Europe. Gregory the Great's Life of Saint Benedict is one of four parts in the pope's influential and much read treatise *The Dialogues of Saint Gregory,* stories set in a discussion format with a disciple named Peter.

The following two selections, one from the Life of Saint Benedict by Gregory, the other from the Benedictine Rule, reveal the principles of communal life and the centrality of the saintly abbot in the community.

Benedict's life set the preeminent model of the ideal abbot, while the Rule sought to codify this monastic relationship of abbot to monk, in many ways the key to monastic life. Portions of the Rule were (and still are) read aloud each day over meals in Benedictine monasteries such that the whole Rule is read through three times a year. The three dates at the beginning of each chapter indicate the day assigned for that passage.

Questions

1. What does Gregory's Life of Benedict reveal about the saint's relationships with other people, such as his nurse, his monks, and his sister?
2. What are the aims and goals of the Rule?
3. In both texts, what do you learn about the communal life of the brethren and the role of the abbot?

The Dialogues of Saint Gregory Book II:
The Life of Saint Benedict

Preface

There was a man of venerable life, blessed by grace, and blessed in name, for he was called *Benedictus* or Benedict:* who, from his younger years, carried always the mind of an old man; for his age was inferior to his virtue: all vain pleasure he condemned, and though he were in the world, and might freely have enjoyed such commodities as it yieldeth, yet did he nothing esteem it, nor the vanities thereof. He was born in the province of Nursia, of honourable parentage, and brought up at Rome in the study of humanity. But for as much as he saw many by reason of such learning to fall to dissolute and lewd life, he drew back his foot, which he had as it were now set forth into the world, lest, entering too far in acquaintance therewith, he likewise might have fallen into that dangerous and godless gulf: wherefore, giving over his book, and forsaking his father's house and wealth, with a resolute mind only to serve God, he sought for some place, where he might attain to the desire of his holy purpose: and in this sort he departed, instructed with learned ignorance, and furnished with unlearned wisdom. All the notable things and acts of his life I could not learn; but those few, which I mind now to report, I had by the relation of four of his disciples. . . .

Chapter 1: How He Made a Broken Sieve Whole and Sound

Benedict having now given over the school, with a resolute mind to lead his life in the wilderness: his nurse alone, which did tenderly love him, would not by any means give him over. Coming, therefore, to a place called

[*Throughout this reading, the original source translates *Benedictus* as "Bennet."]

Enside and remaining there in the church of Saint Peter, in the company of other virtuous men, which for charity lived in that place, it fell so out that his nurse borrowed of the neighbours a sieve to make clean wheat, which being left negligently upon the table, by chance it was broken in two pieces: whereupon she fell pitifully a weeping, because she had borrowed it. The devout and religious youth Benedict, seeing his nurse so lamenting, moved with compassion, took away with him both the pieces of the sieve, and with tears fell to his prayers; and after he had done, rising up he found it so whole, that the place could not be seen where before it was broken; and coming straight to his nurse, and comforting her with good words, he delivered her the sieve safe and sound: which miracle was known to all the inhabitants thereabout, and so much admired, that the townsmen, for a perpetual memory, did hang it up at the church door, to the end that not only men then living but also their posterity might understand, how greatly God's grace did work with him upon his first renouncing of the world. The sieve continued there many years after, even to these very troubles of the Lombards, where it did hang over the church door.

But Benedict, desiring rather the miseries of the world than the praises of men: rather to be wearied with labour for God's sake, than to be exalted with transitory commendation: fled privily from his nurse, and went into a desert place called Sublacum, distant almost forty miles from Rome, in which there was a fountain springing forth cool and clear water; the abundance whereof doth first in a broad place make a lake, and afterward running forward, cometh to be a river. As he was travelling to this place, a certain monk called Romanus met him, and demanded whither he went, and understanding his purpose, he both kept it close, furthered him what he might, vested him with the habit of holy conversation, and as he could, did minister and serve him.

The man of God, Benedict, coming to this foresaid place, lived there in a strait cave, where he continued three years unknown to all men, except to Romanus, who lived not far off, under the rule of Abbot Theodacus, and very virtuously did steal certain hours, and likewise sometime a loaf given for his own provision, which he did carry to Benedict. And because from Romanus' cell to that cave there was not any way, by reason of an high rock which did hang over it, Romanus, from the top thereof, upon a long rope, did let down the loaf, upon which also with a band he tied a little bell, that by the ringing thereof the man of God might know when he came with his bread, and so be ready to take it. But the old enemy of mankind, envying at the charity of the one and the refection of the other, seeing a loaf upon a certain day let down, threw a stone and brake the bell; but yet, for all that, Romanus gave not over to serve him by all the possible means he could. . . .

Chapter 2: How He Overcame a Great Temptation of the Flesh

Upon a certain day being alone, the tempter was at hand: for a little black bird, commonly called a merle or an ousel, began to fly about his face, and that so near as the holy man, if he would, might have taken it with his hand: but after he had blessed himself with the sign of the cross, the bird flew away; and forthwith the holy man was assaulted with such a terrible temptation of the flesh, as he never felt the like in all his life. A certain woman there was which some time he had seen, the memory of which the wicked spirit put into his mind, and by the representation of her did so mightly inflame with concupiscence the soul of God's servant, which did so increase that, almost overcome with pleasure, he was of mind to have forsaken the wilderness. But, suddenly assisted with God's grace, he came to himself; and seeing many thick briers and nettle-bushes to grow hard by, off he cast his apparel, and threw himself into the midst of them, and there wallowed so long that, when he rose up, all his flesh was pitifully torn: and so by the wounds of his body, he cured the wounds of his soul, in that he turned pleasure into pain, and by the outward burning of extreme smart, quenched that fire which, being nourished before with the fuel of carnal cogitations, did inwardly burn in his soul: and by this means he overcame the sin, because he made a change of the fire. From which time forward, as himself did afterward report unto his disciples, he found all temptation of pleasure so subdued, that he never felt any such thing. Many after this began to abandon the world, and to become his scholars. For being now freed from the vice of temptation, worthily and with great reason is he made a master of virtue. . . .

Chapter 9: How Venerable Benedict, by His Prayer
Removed a Huge Stone

Upon a certain day, when the monks were building up the cells of the same Abbey, there lay a stone which they meant to employ about that business: and when two or three were not able to remove it, they called for more company, but all in vain, for it remained so immovable as though it had grown to the very earth: whereby they plainly perceived that the devil himself did sit upon it, seeing so many men's hands could not so much as once move it: wherefore, finding that their own labours could do nothing, they sent for the man of God, to help them with his prayers against the devil, who hindered the removing of that stone. The holy man came, and after some praying, he gave it his blessing, and then they carried it away so quickly, as though it had been of no weight at all.

Chapter 10: Of the Fantastical Fire, Which Burnt the Kitchen

Then the man of God thought good that they should presently before his departure dig up the ground in the same place; which being done, and a deephole made, the monks found there an idol of brass, which being for a little while by chance cast into the kitchen, they beheld fire suddenly to come from it, which to all their sight seemed to set the whole kitchen on fire; for the quenching whereof, the monks by casting on of water made such a noise, that the man of God, hearing it, came to see what the matter was: and himself beholding not any fire at all, which they said that they did, he bowed down his head forthwith to his prayers, and then he perceived that they were deluded with fantastical fire, and therefore bad them bless their eyes, that they might behold the kitchen safe and sound, and not those fantastical flames, which the devil had falsely devised. . . .

Chapter 20: How Holy Benedict Knew the Proud Thought of One of His Monks

Upon a time, whiles the venerable Father was at supper, one of his monks, who was the son of a great man, held the candle: and as he was standing there, and the other at his meat, he began to entertain a proud cogitation in his mind, and to speak thus within himself: "Who is he, that I thus wait upon at supper, and hold him the candle? and who am I, that I should do him any such service?" Upon which thought straightways the holy man turned himself, and with severe reprehension spake thus unto him: "Sign your heart, brother, for what is it that you say? Sign your heart": and forthwith he called another of the monks, and [ordered] him [to] take the candle out of his hands, and commanded him to give over his waiting, and to repose himself: who being demanded of the monks, what it was that he thought, told them, how inwardly he swelled with pride, and what he spake against the man of God, secretly in his own heart. Then they all saw very well that nothing could be hidden from venerable Benedict, seeing the very sound of men's inward thoughts came unto his ears. . . .

Chapter 33: Of a Miracle Wrought by His Sister Scholastica

What man is there, Peter, in this world, that is in greater favour with God than Saint Paul was: who yet three times desired our Lord to be delivered from the prick of the flesh, and obtained not his petition? Concerning which point also I must needs tell you, how there was one thing which the venerable father Benedict would have done, and yet he could not. For his sister called Scholastica, dedicated from her infancy to our Lord, used once a year to come and visit her brother. To whom the man of God went not far from the gate, to a place that did belong to the Abbey, there to give her entertainment. And she coming thither on a time according to her custom, her venerable brother with his monks went to meet her, where they spent the whole day in the praises of God and spiritual talk: and when it was almost night they supped together, and as they were yet sitting at the table, talking of devout matters, and darkness came on, the holy Nun his sister entreated him to stay there all night, that they might spend it in discoursing of the joys of heaven. But by no persuasion would he agree unto that, saying that he might not by any means tarry all night out of his Abbey. At that time, the sky was so clear that no cloud was to be seen. The Nun, receiving this denial of her brother, joining her hands together, laid them upon the table: and so, bowing down her head upon them, she made her prayers to almighty God: and lifting her head from the table, there fell suddenly such a tempest of lightning and thundering, and such abundance of rain, that neither venerable Benedict, nor his monks that were with him, could put their head out of door: for the holy Nun, resting her head upon her hands, poured forth such a flood of tears upon the table, that she drew the clear air to a watery sky, so that after the end of her devotions, that storm of rain followed: and her prayer and the rain did so meet together, that as she lifted up her head from the table, the thunder began, so that in one and the very same instant, she lifted up her head and brought down the rain. The man of God, seeing that he could not by reason of such thunder and lightning and great abundance of rain, return back to his Abbey, began to be heavy and to complain of his sister, saying: "God forgive you, what have you done?" to whom she answered: "I desired you to stay, and you would not hear me, I have desired our good Lord, and he hath vouchsafed to grant my petition: wherefore if you can now depart, in God's name return to your monastery, and leave me here alone." But the good father, being not able to go forth, tarried there against his will, where willingly before he would not stay. And so by that means they watched all night, and with spiritual and heavenly talk did mutually comfort one another: and therefore by this we see, as I said before, that he would have had that thing, which yet he could not: for if we respect the venerable man's mind, no question but he would have had the same fair weather to have continued as it was, when he set forth, but he found that a miracle did prevent his desire, which, by the power of almighty God, a woman's prayers had wrought. And it is not a thing to be marvelled at, that a woman which of long time had not seen her brother, might do more at that time than he could, seeing, according to the saying of Saint John, *God is charity* and therefore of right she did more which loved more. . . .

Chapter 36: How Holy Benedict Wrote a Rule for His Monks

Desirous I am, Peter, to tell you many things of this venerable father, but some of purpose I let pass, because I make haste to entreat also of the acts of other holy men: yet I would not have you to be ignorant, but that the man of God amongst so many miracles, for which he was so famous in the world, was also sufficiently learned in divinity for he wrote a rule for his monks, both excellent for discretion and also eloquent for the style. Of whose life and conversation, if any be curious to know further, he may in the institution of that rule understand all his manner of life and discipline: for the holy man could not otherwise teach, than himself lived.

Chapter 37: How Venerable Benedict Did Prophesy to His Monks, the Time of His Own Death

The same year in which he departed this life, he told the day of his holy death to his monks, some of which did live daily with him, and some dwelt far off, willing those that were present to keep it secret, and telling them that were absent by what token they should know that he was dead. Six days before he left this world, he gave order to have his sepulchre opened, and forthwith falling into an ague, he began with burning heat to wax faint, and when as the sickness daily increased, upon the sixth day he commanded his monks to carry him into the oratory, where he did arm himself with receiving the body and blood of our Saviour Christ; and having his weak body holden up betwixt the hands of his disciples, he stood with his own lifted up to heaven, and as he was in that manner praying, he gave up the ghost. Upon which day two monks, one being in his cell, and the other far distant, had concerning him one and the self-same vision: for they saw all the way from the holy man's cell, towards the east even up to heaven, hung and adorned with tapestry, and shining with an infinite number of lamps, at the top whereof a man, reverently attired, stood and demanded if they knew who passed that way, to whom they answered saying, that they knew not. Then he spake thus unto them: "This is the way," quoth he, "by which the beloved servant of God, Benedict, is ascended up to heaven." And by this means, as his monks that were present knew of the death of the holy man, so likewise they which were absent, by the token which he foretold them, had intelligence of the same thing. Buried he was in the oratory of Saint John Baptist which himself built, when he overthrew the altar of Apollo; who also in that cave in which he first dwelled, even to this very time, worketh miracles, if the faith of them that pray requireth the same.

From *The Dialogues of Saint Gregory,* ed. Edmund G. Gardner (London: Philip Lee Warner, 1911), pp. 51–53, 55, 69–70, 80–81, 94–95, 99–100.

The Rule of Saint Benedict

Prologue

[January 1, May 2, September 1]

Listen, oh son, to your teacher's commands, and turn the ear of your heart: welcome willingly and fulfill effectively the admonition of your loving Father: that through labor of obedience you may return to Him, from whom you had retreated through idleness of disobedience. To you therefore, my discourse is aimed, whoever you may be who are renouncing your own free-will to be a soldier for the Lord Christ, the true King, and are assuming strong, noble weapons of obedience. Among the first, whatever good you begin to do, request of Him with most earnest prayer to accomplish it: that He who now has deemed us worthy to count among his sons should not at any time be grieved on account of our evil actions. For we must always so yield to Him on account of the good thing He has given us, that not only will He never as an angry Father disinherit His children, nor as a fearful Lord exasperated by our evil deeds, surrender us as wicked servants to perpetual punishment, who were unwilling to follow Him to glory.

[January 2, May 3, September 2]

Let us rise up, therefore, at last, for the Scripture arouses us moreover saying: "Now is the hour for us to arise from slumber." And let us open our eyes to the sacred light, let us hear with attentive ears, the warning which the divine voice declares daily to us, saying: "Today if you hear His voice, harden not your hearts." And again: "He who has ears listen, let him hear what Scripture says to the Church." And what does He say?: "Come, my children, listen to me, I will teach you the fear of the Lord. Run quickly while you have the light of life, lest the darkness of death capture you."

[January 3, May 4, September 3]

And the Lord, seeking his worker in the multitude of people to whom He cries aloud, says again: "Who is the man who wishes life, and longs to see good days?" And if hearing Him you reply, I am he, God says to you: "If you will have true and eternal life, keep your tongue from evil, and your lips so that they do not speak malice. Turn away from evil, and do good: seek peace and pursue it. And when you have done these things, my eyes will be on you, and my ears open to your prayers; and before you call upon men, I will say to you: Behold, I am present." What can be sweeter to us than the voice of the Lord inviting us, dearest brothers? Behold, the Lord demonstrates to us in his kindness the way of life.

[January 4, May 5, September 4]

Having girded up our loins, therefore, with faith and observance of good deeds, let us walk in His path by the guidance of the Gospel, that we may earn to see Him who has called us into His kingdom. If we wish to reside in the tent of the kingdom, we must hasten to it with good deeds or we shall arrive not at all. But let us ask the Lord, with the Prophet, saying to Him: "Lord, who shall reside in Your tent, or who shall rest on Your sacred mountain?" After this question, brother, let us listen to the Lord as He responds and shows us the way to His tent, saying: "He who walks without stain and practice justice, he who speaks the truth from his heart, he who has not used his tongue for malice, he who has done no evil to neighbor, he who has given no place to slander against his neighbor." It is he who, under any tempting from the wicked devil, has led him to nothing by refusing him and his temptation from the sight of his heart, and who held his young thoughts, and dashed them against Christ. It is they who, fearing the Lord, do not elevate themselves on their good observances; but considered that good which is in them is not possible from themselves, but must be from the Lord, glorying the work of the Lord in them, using the words of the prophet: "Not to us, Lord, not to us, but to Your name give the glory." Just as also the Apostle Paul ascribed nothing of the praise of his teaching to himself saying: "By the grace of God I am what I am." And again he says: "He who glories, let him glory in God."

[January 5, May 6, September 5]

And hence the Lord says in the Gospel: "Whoever listens to these words of mine and acts on them, I will liken him to a wise man who built his house on rock. The floods came, the winds blew and beat against that house, and it did not fall, because it was founded on rock." Having given us these words, the Lord is waiting daily for us to respond by our deeds to His sacred admonitions. The days of this life are stretched and a truce granted to us for this reason, that we may amend our evil ways. The Apostle says: "Do you not know that God's patience is inviting you to repent?" For the merciful Lord says: "I desire not the death of the sinner, but that he should be converted and live."

[January 6, May 7, September 6]

So therefore, brothers, we have questioned the Lord who is to reside in His tent, and we have heard His orders to those who would dwell there: but it remains for us to fulfill the duties. Therefore we must prepare our hearts and our bodies to do battle by the sacred obedience of His orders; and let us ask the Lord that He be happy to minister the help of His grace to us which our nature finds hardly possible. And if we want to flee the sufferings of hell and we wish to attain eternal life, while as yet there is time, and we are in this body, and there is time to fulfill all these things through the light of life, we must hasten to do now what will free us for eternity.

[January 7, May 8, September 7]

And so, we are about to found, therefore, a school for the Lord's service; in the organization of which we trust that we shall ordain nothing severe and nothing burdensome. But even if, the demands of justice dictating it, something a little irksome shall be the result, for the purpose of amending vices or preserving charity—thou shalt not therefore, struck by fear, flee the way of salvation, which cannot be entered upon except through a narrow entrance. But as one's way of life and one's faith progresses, the heart becomes broadened, and, with the unutterable sweetness of love, the way of the mandates of the Lord is traversed. Thus, never departing from His guidance, continuing in the monastery in His teaching until death, through patience we are made partakers in Christ's passion, in order that we may merit to be companions in His kingdom.

Chapter 2: What the Abbot Should Be Like

[January 9, May 10, September 9]

An abbot who is worthy to preside over a monastery ought always to remember what he is called, and carry out with his deeds the name of a Superior. For he is believed to be Christ's representative, since he is called by His name, the apostle saying: "Ye have received the spirit of adoption of sons whereby we call Abba, Father." And so the abbot should not—grant that he may not—teach, or decree, or order any thing apart from the precept of the Lord; but his order or teaching should be sprinkled with the ferment of divine justice in the minds of his disciples. . . .

Chapter 3: About Calling in the Brethren to Take Council

[January 16, May 17, September 16]

As often as anything especial is to be done in the monastery, the abbot shall call together the whole congregation, and shall himself explain the question at issue. And, having heard the advice of the brethren, he shall think it over by himself, and shall do what he considers most advantageous. And for this reason, moreover, we have said that all ought to be called to take counsel: because often it is to a younger person that God reveals what is best. The brethren, moreover, with all subjection of humility, ought so to give their advice, that they do not presume boldly to defend what seems good to them; but it should rather depend on the judgment of the abbot; so that whatever he decides to be the more salutary, they should all agree to it. But even as it behoves the disciples to obey the master, so it is fitting that he should providently and justly arrange all matters.

[January 17, May 18, September 17]

In all things, indeed, let all follow the Rule as their guide; and let no one rashly deviate from it. Let no one in the monastery follow the inclination of his own heart; and let no one boldly presume to dispute with his abbot, within or without the monastery. But, if he should so presume, let him be subject to the discipline of the Rule. The abbot, on the other hand, shall do all things fearing the Lord and observing the Rule; knowing that he, without a doubt, shall have to render account to God as to a most impartial judge, for all his decisions. But if any lesser matters for the good of the monastery are to be decided upon, he shall employ the counsel of the elder members alone, since it is written: "Do all things with counsel, and after it is done thou wilt not repent."...

Chapter 5: Concerning Obedience

[January 22, May 23, September 22]

The first grade of humility is obedience without delay. This becomes those who, on account of the holy service which they have professed, or on account of the fear of hell or the glory of eternal life consider nothing dearer to them than Christ: so that, so soon as anything is commanded by their superior, they may not know how to suffer delay in doing it, even as if it were a divine command. Concerning whom the Lord said: "As soon as he heard of me he obeyed me." And again he said to the learned men: "He who heareth you heareth me." Therefore let all such, straightway leaving their own affairs and giving up their own will, with unoccupied hands and leaving incomplete what they were doing—the foot of obedience being foremost—follow with their deeds the voice of him who orders. And, as it were, in the same moment, let the aforesaid command of the master and the perfected work of the disciple—both together in the swiftness of the fear of God—be called into being by those who are possessed with a desire of advancing to eternal life. And therefore let them seize the narrow way of which the Lord says: "Narrow is the way which leadeth unto life." Thus, not living according to their own judgment nor obeying their own desires and pleasures, but walking under another's judgment and command, passing their time in monasteries, let them desire an abbot to rule over them. Without doubt all such live up to that precept of the Lord in which he says: "I am not come to do my own will but the will of him that sent me." . . .

Chapter 73. Concerning the Fact that
Not Every Just Observance Is Decreed in This Rule

[May 1, August 31, December 31]

We have written out this Rule, indeed, that we may show those observing it in the monasteries how to have some honesty of character, or beginning of conversion. But for those who hasten to the perfection of living, there are the teachings of the holy Fathers: the observance of which leads a man to the heights of perfection. For what page, or what discourse, of Divine authority of the Old or the New Testament is not a most perfect rule for human life? Or what book of the holy Catholic Fathers does not trumpet forth how by the right path we shall come to our Creator? Also the reading aloud of the Fathers, and their decrees, and their lives; also the Rule of our holy Father Basil—what else are they except instruments of virtue for well-living and obedient monks? We, moreover, blush with confusion for the idle, and the evilly living and the negligent. Thou, therefore, whoever doth hasten to the celestial fatherland, perform with Christ's aid this Rule written out as the least of beginnings: and then at length, under God's protection, thou wilt come to the greater things that we have mentioned; to the summits of learning and virtue.

Prologue: January 1–6 translated by Julie Clement and Karen Louise Jolly from the Latin in J. P. Migne, *Patrologia Latina* 66: 216–18 (checked against the *Regula Sancti Benedicti*, Order of Saint Benedict, http:www.hu/regula/l_regula); balance of material from *Select Historical Documents of the Middle Ages,* trans. and ed. Ernest F. Henderson (London: George Bell; New York: AMS, 1892), pp. 274, 275, 278–79, 313–14.

6.3 Relics and Pilgrimage:
The Martinellus of Saint Martin of Tours

Saint Martin of Tours was a fourth-century former soldier turned monk, a dynamic bishop, and a martyr—a classic candidate for heroic sainthood. His popularity in the Middle Ages as a saint was fostered by the writings of Sulpicius Severus and Gregory of Tours, both of whom wrote about his saintly life and miracles. Gregory in particular favored the patron saint of his bishopric not only in his biography of the saint and in accounts of his miracles but also in his writing of a nationalist history of the Franks, the Germanic people who came to dominate the region of Gaul (8.2). Saint Martin became a rallying point in the conversion of the Frankish peoples.

As a consequence of this promotion of Saint Martin, the sites where his relics lay, or where he lived and performed miracles, were venerated as pilgrimage destinations—people would travel from afar to come to these places to experience physical and spiritual healing through his intercession. They came to pray, meditate, and listen to preaching; they also gave gifts to support the church and monastery.

The text of *The Martinellus,* excerpted below, is a collective title for ninth-century manuscripts about Saint Martin. A series of these documents record poems from murals or inscriptions placed around the church and relics at different stations where people could stop to reflect and pray. The first set of four come from Martin's cell at the monastery of Marmoutier; the rest are from the church of Saint Martin at Tours. Each poem below is prefaced with a brief description of the inscription's placement.

Questions

1. What do the inscriptions exhort the pilgrim to do and why?

2. In what ways does moving around the various sites constitute a spiritual journey or progression for the pilgrim?

3. What do these poems reveal to us about late antique or early medieval spirituality in Gaul?

The Martinellus

Marmoutier

. . . . . .

"The verses begin at the entrance to the first cell of St. Martin."

Behold, we come here; alas, no one shouts out.
Behold, we come here, but the weapons of the cross
    are silent.

Truly the warrior of the Lord is asleep; alas, would that he
   might shout out!
The warrior sleeps, a man who must be missed.
But let us enter and with our weeping and our prayers
   beseech
the Lord of the saints, the God of Martin.
Let us kneel at the place that the saint moistened with his
   weeping: his spirit will be our assistance.
The warrior sleeps; but you, Christ, protect us.
You who do not sleep, protect Israel.

. . . . . .

"Next in another cell."

Here lived the man who kissed the feet of the Lord;
here lived the man who carried the weapons of the cross;
here lived the bishop who was holy and pure;
here lived the man who was chaste in body and in heart;
here lived the man whose holy faith was a shield,
the defender of the cross who was brilliantly distinguished
for his eloquence;
here lived the fortunate recluse in a cave;
here lived the man who [now] lives in Paradise.

. . . . . .

"Next inside the cell."

Holy God, have pity on the place that you have always
   loved.
Cherish, enhance, protect, always love [it],
when at the completion of his life you have transferred
   our shepherd to those bright, holy, and
   wonderful places.
Holy [God], in the shelter of your wings
protect, preserve, cherish, and always love us too.
We make our request as suppliants; may you give
   generously and grant
that the saint himself might simultaneously assist us.

. . . . . .

"Next there over the location of his bed."

We see here what sorts of weapons the warrior often uses
[even] when it happened that the man was absent;
note the black coals, each of them horrifying,
and the clouds of dust, all most foul.
A cloak, a stone beneath his head, and a pile of cinders,
you were considered a bed here for his weary limbs.
A small stool was his resting place during the silent night;
during the day this stool [served] him in place of a chair
    or a throne.

The Church of Saint Martin and Other Shrines at Tours

. . . . . .

"The verses of the church begin; first [those] on the east
side [of the bell tower]."

As you enter the church, lift your eyes upward;
a deep faith recognizes the lofty entrances.
Be humble in your conscience, but in hope follow the one
    who calls you;
Martin opens the door that you venerate.
This tower is protection for the timid and an obstacle to
    the proud;
it excludes the arrogant and defends the meek in heart.
More lofty still is that [tower or dome] that has taken
    Martin to the citadel of heaven
and that rises through the starry roads.
From there he summons the people, he who as a guide
    to Christ's rewards
has traveled on and sanctified that journey through
    the stars.

. . . . . .

"On another side [of the bell tower]."

As you are about to enter the nave, as you venerate the
    threshold of Christ,
dispel the concerns of this world from your entire heart
and free your spirit from wicked desires.
The man who offers just prayers returns with his vows
    fulfilled.

[another inscription] . . .

You who are about to seek the temple of God with a calm
    mind
. . . .
[and] who are entering to request forgiveness for your
    recent sins,
in your spirit you should not falter in your faith.
You obtain what you seek if you ask with a pure heart.
As he said, faith will be your salvation.

. . . . . .

"At the entrance on the west side [of the church], a
painted representation of the widow mentioned in a
Gospel."

Let whoever comes to renew his vows to the highest God
learn to confess Christ according to the account in a Gospel.
Although he trembles in his heart and prays as a suppliant
    stooping on his knees,
if he ceases his good works, his faith is certainly
    meaningless.
Rich and poor are alike liable to this law;
he who lacks wealth will demonstrate his good works by
    his intentions.
Nor do meager and limited resources excuse anyone;
the merit is determined by the intent, not by the value.
He who has bestowed whatever is necessary presents
    very much;
although he will have given little, he wishes [to present]
    all the greatest gifts.
Among these piles of wealth and the gifts of the powerful
    we know that the faith of the poor widow was
    preferred.
As she purchased the kingdoms of heaven for two mites,
The just father took her upward among the stars.
Not she who gave much, but she who left nothing for
    herself
has deserved to be praised by the mouth of the judge God.

. . . . . .

"Over the door on the side of [the church facing] the
Loire River."

The disciples were sailing on the lake at the command of
the Lord. As the winds were blowing and the waves were
being tossed up, the Lord walked on his feet on the lake.
He also extended his hand to Saint Peter who was sinking;
and that man was saved from danger.

. . . . . .

"Next."

[Here is] the most holy church of Christ which is the
mother of all churches, which the apostles founded, and in
which the Holy Spirit descended upon the apostles in the
form of tongues of fire. In it are located the throne of the
apostle James and the pillar on which Christ was whipped.

. . . . . .

["Next."]

You who have knelt on the ground, lowered your face to
    the dust,
and pressed your moist eyes to the compacted ground,
lift your eyes, and with a trembling gaze look at the
    miracles
and entrust your cause to the distinguished patron.
No page can embrace such miracles.
Even though the very blocks and stones are engraved with
    these inscriptions,
a terrestrial building does not enclose what the royal
    palace of heaven acknowledges and what the stars
    inscribe in glittering jewels.
If you seek Martin's assistance, rise beyond the stars
and touch the heavens after having encountered the
    chorus of angels in the upper air.
There look for the patron who is joined to the Lord
and who always follows the footsteps of the eternal king.
If you doubt, look at the miracles that are heaped before
    your eyes

and by means of which the true Savior honors the merit of
    his servant.
You come as an eyewitness among so many thousands of
    others
when you carefully observe what must be narrated and
    repeat what you have seen.
Whatever a page in the holy books has recorded,
he renews through the restoration of God. [Many] rejoice
    in his gift:
the blind, the lame, the poor, the possessed, the distressed,
    the sick,
the disabled, the oppressed, the imprisoned, the grieving,
    the needy.
Every remedy rejoices in the marvels of the apostles.
Whoever has come in tears, leaves in happiness. All
    clouds vanish.
A medicine soothes whatever guilt disturbs.
Seek his protection; you do not knock at these doors in
    vain.
Such lavish generosity extends into the entire world.

. . . . . .

"On the arch of the apse above the altar."

How awesome is this place! Truly it is the temple of God
    and the gateway to heaven.

. . . . . .

"On one side of the tomb."

Here is buried Bishop Martin of sacred memory, whose
soul is in the hand of God. But he is wholly present here,
made manifest to everyone by the goodwill of his
miracles.

. . . . . .

"Next on the other side [of the tomb]."

He has fought the good fight, he has completed the race,
he has preserved the faith. And so there is reserved for
him a crown of righteousness that the Lord, the just judge,
will restore to him on that day.

. . . . . .

"Next on the top [of the tomb]."

Confessor by his merits, martyr by his suffering, apostle
        by his actions,
Martin presides from heaven here at this tomb.
May he be mindful [of us], and by cleansing the sins of
        our wretched life
may he conceal our crimes with his merits.

. . . . . .

"Next in the apse."

The body of Martin that is venerable for the entire world
and in which honor lives [even] after the years of his life
was at first covered here by a chapel with ordinary
        decoration
that was not appropriate for its own confessor.
The citizens never ceased being burdened with shame
from the great reputation of the man and the trivial
        renown of the place.
Perpetuus, who is the sixth bishop in succession,
eliminated the long-standing disgrace
by removing the inner sanctuary of the small chapel
and constructing an impressive edifice on a larger
        building.
With the assistance of the powerful patron the church grew
in size, and simultaneously the builder grew in merit.
The church is capable of rivaling the temple of Solomon,
a building that was the seventh wonder of the world.
For if that temple glittered with jewels, gold, and silver,
this church surpasses all precious metals through faith.
Ravenous envy, be gone; let our ancestors be forgiven, and
let our babbling descendants neither alter nor add
        anything.
Until the coming of Christ who revives all people,
may the walls of Perpetuus endure perpetually.

"In the shrine [of the holy relics? of the holy saints?]."

This residence contains the crowns of five blessed [saints].
If you read the inscription carefully, you will also learn
     their names
that remain and always will remain recorded in heaven.
Here Saint John the Baptist rejoices from the womb.
Here [are] pious Felix and Victor; gracious Gervasius
and holy Protasius are here as witnesses throughout the
     ages
who have demonstrated the true faith by their suffering,
their blood, and their deaths.
Joined together, these five fingers from the body of Christ
fashion with their great struggle a lofty palm
that the ornament with perpetual blossoms worthy of God.

. . . . . .

"Next, the verses there."

If your faith is holy, and if your mind is devoted to Christ
and steady under the weight of the merits of the sacred
     bishop,
here, diligent reader, you can learn about Martin's
birth, military service, baptism, deeds, parents,
teaching, habits, proclamations, wars, triumphs,
sufferings, homeland, dangers, sayings, labors,
distinctions, miracles, lifetime, proclamations, and
     commendations.

6.4 Byzantine Worship: The Debate over Iconoclasm

The cultural divide between Europe and Byzantium, between western Catholicism and eastern Orthodoxy, deepened in the eighth century. One symptom of this breach is the controversy over iconoclasm—the breaking of images. Byzantine religious practice used icons, or pictures of saints, as a focus for worship. In the West, veneration of saints focused more on relics, body parts of saints encased in reliquaries.

When certain Byzantine leaders sought to do away with icons, Christian leaders in Europe did not fully grasp the implications and took sides, asserting authority in a matter that was in some ways beyond them. Eventually, the veneration of icons became orthodoxy for Byzantium, as explained by John of Damascus in the document excerpted here.

The controversy in Byzantium began in the eighth century, when Emperor Leo III the Isaurian, an iconoclast, banned icons and ordered his army to destroy them as well as to persecute the monks who made them and defended their use. This struggle was more than a doctrinal one: it pitted the supremacy of the emperor as a religious leader against the formidable influence of the independent-minded monasteries that produced icons and fostered their use. Thus icons became one of the main cultural evidences of Byzantium's unique brand of Christianity, something very different from western practice. John of Damascus's defense of divine images makes powerful philosophical arguments for the use of icons as a means of worship.

John of Damascus (circa 650–749) was a monk, priest, and a scholar literate in both Greek and Arabic. He wrote poetry, sermons, and treatises defending orthodoxy against various heretical groups, in addition to an influential compendium of Greek philosophical and theological arguments called *The Fount of Knowledge*. John opposed the iconoclasts in the following excerpt from *On the Divine Images,* and consequently faced the anathema of the Emperor Leo; however, as a resident in Muslim lands at his monastery and in Jerusalem, he wrote freely outside of the emperor's reach.

Questions

1. In John's arguments, how are icons—painted pictures—a central and meaningful part of Christian worship and spiritual life?
2. What methods of argument does John employ to make his point?
3. Why do you think this position favoring icons became orthodoxy? What is its appeal?

John of Damascus, On the Divine Images

Chapter XV: Concerning the Honor Due to the Saints and Their Remains

To the saints honor must be paid as friends of Christ, as sons and heirs of God: in the words of John the theologian and evangelist, *As many as received Him, to them gave He power to become sons of God. So that they are no longer servants, but sons: and if sons, also heirs, heirs of God and joint heirs with Christ:* and the Lord in the holy Gospels says to His apostles, *Ye are My friends. Henceforth I call you not servants, for the servant knoweth not what his lord doeth.* And further, if the Creator and Lord of all things is called also King of Kings and Lord of Lords and God of Gods, surely also the saints are gods and lords and kings. For of these God is and is called God and Lord and King. *For I am the God of Abraham,* He said to Moses, *the God of Isaac and the God of Jacob.* And God made Moses a god to Pharaoh. Now I mean gods and kings and lords not in nature, but as rulers and masters of their passions, and as preserving a truthful likeness to the divine image according to which they were made (for the image of a king is also called king), and as being united to God of their own free-will and receiving Him as an indweller and becoming by grace through participation with Him what He is Himself by nature. Surely, then, the worshipers and friends and sons of God are to be held in honor? For the honor shewn to the most thoughtful of fellow-servants is a proof of good feeling towards the common Master.

These are made treasuries and pure habitations of God: *For I will dwell in them,* said God, *and walk in them, and I will be their God.* The divine Scripture likewise saith that the souls of the just are in God's hand and death cannot lay hold of them. For death is rather the sleep of the saints than their death. *For they travailed in this life and shall to the end,* and *Precious in the sight of the Lord is the death of His saints.* What, then, is more precious than to be in the hand of God? For God is Life and Light, and those who are in God's hand are in life and light.

Further, that God dwelt even in their bodies in spiritual wise, the Apostle tells us, saying, *Know ye not that your bodies are the temples of the Holy Spirit dwelling in you?,* and *The Lord is that Spirit,* and *If any one destroy the temple of God, him will God destroy.* Surely, then, we must ascribe honor to the living temples of God, the living tabernacles of God. These while they lived stood with confidence before God.

The Master Christ made the remains of the saints to be fountains of salvation to us, pouring forth manifold blessings and abounding in oil of sweet fragrance: and let no one disbelieve this. For if water burst in the desert from the steep and solid rock at God's will and from the jawbone of an ass to quench Samson's thirst, is it incredible that fragrant oil should burst forth from the martyrs' remains? By no means, at least to those who know the power of God and the honor which He accords His saints.

In the law every one who toucheth a dead body was considered impure, but these are not dead. For from the time when He that is Himself life and the Author of life was reckoned among the dead, we do not call those dead who have fallen asleep in the hope of the resurrection and in faith on Him. For how could a dead body work miracles? How, therefore, are demons driven off by them, diseases dispelled, sick persons made well, the blind restored to sight, lepers purified, temptations and troubles overcome, and how does every good gift from the Father of lights come down through them to those who pray with sure faith? How much labor would you not undergo to find a patron to introduce you to a mortal king and speak to him on your behalf? Are not those, then, worthy of honor who are the patrons of the whole race, and make intercession to God for us? Yea, verily, we ought to give honor to them by raising temples to God in their name, bringing them fruit offerings, honoring their memories and taking spiritual delight in them, in order that the joy of those who call on us may be ours, that in our attempts at worship we may not on the contrary cause them offense. For those who worship God will take pleasure in those things whereby God is worshipped, while His shield-bearers will be wroth at those things wherewith God is wroth. In psalms and hymns and spiritual songs, in contrition and in pity for the needy, let us believers worship the saints, as God also is most worshipped in such wise. Let us raise monuments to them and visible images, and let us ourselves become, through imitation of their virtues, living monuments and images of them. Let us give honor to her who bore God as being strictly and truly the Mother of God. Let us honor also the prophet John as forerunner and baptist, as apostle and martyr, *For among them that are born of women there hath not risen a greater than John the Baptist,* as saith the Lord, and he became the first to proclaim the Kingdom. Let us honor the apostles as the Lord's brothers, who saw Him face to face and ministered to His passion, *for whom God the Father did foreknow He also did predestinate to be conformed to the image of His Son, first apostles, second prophets, third pastors and teachers.* Let us also honor the martyrs of the Lord chosen out of every class, as soldiers of Christ who have drunk His cup and were then baptized with the baptism of His life-bringing death, to be partakers of His passion and glory: of whom the leader is Stephen, the first deacon of Christ and apostle and first martyr. Also let us honor our holy fathers, the God-possessed ascetics, whose struggle was the longer and more toilsome one of the conscience: *who wandered about in sheepskins and goatskins, being destitute, afflicted, tormented; they wandered in deserts and in mountains and in dens and caves of the earth, of whom the world was not worthy.* Let us honor those who were prophets before grace, the patriarchs and just men who foretold the Lord's coming. Let us carefully review the life of these men, and let us emulate their faith and love and hope and zeal and way of life, and endurance of sufferings and patience even to blood, in order that we may be sharers with them in their crowns of glory.

Chapter XVI: Concerning Images

But since some find fault with us for worshiping and honoring the image of our Savior and that of our Lady, and those, too, of the rest of the saints and servants of Christ, let them remember that in the beginning God created man after His own image. On what grounds, then, do we show reverence to each other unless because we are made after God's image? For as Basil, that much-versed expounder of divine things, says, the honor given to the image passes over to the prototype. Now a prototype is that which is imaged, from which the derivative is obtained. Why was it that the Mosaic people honored on all hands the tabernacle which bore an image and type of heavenly things, or rather of the whole creation? God indeed said to Moses, *Look that thou make them after their pattern which was shewed thee in the mount.* The Cherubim, too, which o'ershadow the mercy seat, are they not the work of men's hands? What, further, is the celebrated temple at Jerusalem? Is it not hand-made and fashioned by the skill of men?

Moreover the divine Scripture blames those who worship graven images, but also those who sacrifice to demons. The Greeks sacrificed and the Jews also sacrificed: but the Greeks to demons and the Jews to God. And the sacrifice of the Greeks was rejected and condemned, but the sacrifice of the just was very acceptable to God. For Noah sacrificed, and God *smelled a sweet savour,* receiving the fragrance of the right choice and good-will towards Him. And so the graven images of the Greeks since they were images of deities, were rejected and forbidden.

But besides this who can make an imitation of the invisible, incorporeal, uncircumscribed, formless God? Therefore to give form to the Deity is the height of folly and impiety. And hence it is that in the Old Testament the use of images was not common. But after God in His bowels of pity became in truth man for our salvation, not as He was seen by Abraham in the semblance of a man, nor as He was seen by the prophets, but in being truly man, and after He lived upon the earth and dwelt among men, worked miracles, suffered, was crucified, rose again and was taken back to Heaven, since all these things actually took place and were seen by men, they were written for the remembrance and instruction of us who were not alive at that time in order that though we saw not, we may still, hearing and believing, obtain the blessing of the Lord. But seeing that not every one has a knowledge of letters nor time for reading, the Fathers gave their sanction to depicting these events on images as being acts of great heroism, in order that they should form a concise memorial of them. Often doubtless, when we have not the Lord's passion in mind and see the image of Christ's crucifixion, His saving passion is brought back to remembrance, and we fall down and worship not the material but that which is imaged: just as we do not worship the material of which the Gospels are made, nor the material of the Cross, but that which these typify. For wherein does the cross, that typifies the Lord, differ from a cross that does not do so? It is just the same also in the case of the Mother of the Lord. For the honor which we give to her is referred to Him Who was made of her incarnate. And similarly also the brave acts of holy men stir us up to be brave and to emulate and imitate their valor and to glorify God. For as we said, the honor that is given to the best of fellow-servants is a proof of good-will towards our common Lady, and the honor rendered to the image passes over to the prototype. But this is an unwritten tradition, just as is also the worshiping towards the East and the worship of the Cross, and very many other similar things.

A certain tale, too, is told, how that when Augarus was king over the city of the Edessenes, he sent a portrait painter to paint a likeness of the Lord, and when the painter could not paint because of the brightness that shone from His countenance, the Lord Himself put a garment over His own divine and life-giving face and impressed on it an image of Himself and sent this to Augarus, to satisfy thus his desire.

Moreover that the Apostles handed down much that was unwritten, Paul, the Apostle of the Gentiles, tells us in these words: *Therefore, brethren, stand fast and hold the traditions which ye have been taught of us, whether by word or by epistle.* And to the Corinthians he writes, *Now I praise you, brethren, that ye remember me in all things, and keep the traditions as I have delivered them to you.*

From John of Damascus, *Exposition of the Orthodox Faith,* in *NPNF,* Second Series, Vol. 9, pp. 86–88.

–7–

Adaptations of Christianity Outside the Roman World

Christianity has come to be so completely identified with so-called western culture that it is often forgotten that it spread from its origins in Palestine south and east, into Africa, Arabia, China, and India, as well as westward and northward into Europe. The similarities and differences between the various cultural adaptations of Christianity raise many questions about what is essential to Christianity and what is cultural addition. This chapter examines the adaptations occurring outside Europe, before turning in the next chapter to the acculturation of Christianity within the various Germanic cultures of Europe. The aim of these two chapters is to recognize the variety of ways that Christianity's basic ideas expressed themselves in different cultural forms. Examining the areas outside western Europe first allows us to view the acculturation process without assuming a European form of Christianity, and helps us recognize how much western Christianity was another cultural adaptation—a highly successful one.

Usually the western world focuses on the Roman and Eastern Orthodox churches because these two churches became dominant forces in Roman, Greek, and European cultures; and so the cultural adaptations made there are often taken as essential to Christianity—the institutions, creeds, rituals, and popular practices of European Christianity, for example, are inextricably both Christian and European. But as we have seen in the first chapter, some Christians, oftentimes followers of heterodox doctrines rejected as heresy by the Roman and Byzantine churches, spread to areas outside the Roman Empire's domain, where they established themselves as minority groups within other cultures.

The Mediterranean world of the Roman Empire in the fourth through sixth centuries was not, as we sometimes think, isolated from or ignorant of Africa, Arabia, or Asia. Egypt and Byzantium competed with the

Persians for influence in the trade-rich zone around the Red Sea and leading to the Indian Ocean, the east coast of Africa encompassing the Nubian and Ethiopian kingdoms and on the other side, South Arabia (Yemen). Likewise, through Syria and on into China, trade routes connected East and West. More than material goods flowed along these routes; missionaries, books, and ideas also were exchanged. The first three selections below examine the spread southward from the Coptic Church in Egypt and the Byzantine Christian influence from the eastern Roman Empire into Ethiopia (7.1), Nubia (7.2), and South Arabia (7.3) in the fourth through sixth centuries. The Axumite kingdom of Ethiopia, converted to Monophysite Christianity, exerted the greatest influence over the other two areas. In all three regions, stories of conversion and of heroic martyrdom echo some of the same themes evident in the spread of Christianity in the Mediterranean areas, but reflect their own local cultures. The fourth selection (7.4) examines the Nestorian faith that took root in China in the seventh through ninth centuries, and as a consequence of Taoist, Confucianist, and Buddhist influence, took on a particularly Chinese flavor.

7.1 Saintly Heroes in Ethiopia:
The Book of the Saints of the Ethiopian Church

A quick glance at Ethiopia's long and rich history reveals a strong Christian tradition with its own saints and heroes comparable to the examples in the documents of Chapter 6. Because of its position on the northeastern edge of the African continent, on the Blue Nile and abutting the Red Sea, the Axumite kingdom in Ethiopia during the third through eighth centuries was a major cultural crossroads for the complex interactions of peoples in both the Mediterranean and Indian Ocean worlds. Religious affiliation was often linked to political alliances—Axum became closely tied to Egypt as opposed to Rome or Byzantium, for example. Consequently, the legendary events, often dramatic, of Christian conversion need to be placed in the context of a broad exposure to monotheistic traditions and ideas from a number of cultures such that the eventual dominance of Christianity occurred gradually and as part of competing political interests.

According to the stories in church histories, Christianity officially came to Ethiopia in two waves of missionaries in the fourth and fifth centuries, the first to the court, the second more to the general population. In the first wave, according to Rufinus's *Ecclesiastical History,* two young, shipwrecked brothers, Aedesius and Frumentius, introduced the Ethiopian court to Christian ideas, partly through acting as advisors during the regency of the underage king, Ezana I (reigned circa 330 to after 356). Frumentius later journeyed to Egypt, where he was consecrated bishop (*Abun*) of Ethiopia by the Patriarch of Alexandria, the Monophysite Athanasius (circa 300–373). Subsequent attempts by an Arian Roman Emperor (Constantius II) to invalidate Frumentius's appointment, recorded in Athanasius's *Apology to the Emperor Constantius,* were fruitless, demonstrating both the independence of the Ethiopian ruler from Roman control and the strength of Ethiopia's connection to Egypt. The Ethiopian Church, after the definitive decision at Chalcedon in 451, remained Monophysite, in line with the Alexandrine bishops.

The second wave of conversion involved Monophysite monks fleeing persecution from orthodox church leaders after 451 (Council of Chalcedon, 3.4). The most famous were the Syrian "Nine Saints," who built monasteries throughout Ethiopia and assisted in the translation of the Bible into classical Ethiopic as well as collecting other, mostly Monophysite, writings. These efforts effectively took Christianity into the general culture of Ethiopia, whereas the previous wave was limited to the Axumite court. The power of the ascetic values of these monks is clearly evident in the later stories of these saints' lives, written to commemorate their feastdays.

Below are several of these brief sketches of the lives of the founding saints of Ethiopian Christianity. First is the brief account of Abba Salama, the name given to Frumentius as the first bishop. Then three of the Nine Saints are given: Pantaleon, Aragawi, and Garima.

Questions

1. What view of conversion is presented in these stories?

2. What role do holy men play in the establishment of Christian values?

3. Do you see any cultural or theological differences between these stories from the Ethiopian Monophysite church and the orthodox stories of saints from the Roman world?

The Book of the Saints of the Ethiopian Church

[Salama]

And on this day also died Abba Salama, the Revealer of the Light, the Bishop of Ethiopia; now his history is as follows: A certain man from the country of the Greeks, a master of learning, whose name was Merpes (Meropius?), came wishing to see the country of Ethiopia, and he had with him two youths of his family, and the name of one was "Fere Menatos (Frumentius)," and that of the other was "Adesyos (Aedesius)"; now there are some who call him "Sidrakos." And he arrived in a ship at the shore of the Sea of Ethiopia, and he saw all the beautiful things which his heart desired, and as he was wishing to return to his country, enemies rose up against him and killed him, and all those who were with him. And these two youths were left [alive], and the men of the city made them captives, and taught them the work of war, and took them as a present to the King of Aksum whose name was "Alameda." And the king made Adyos (sic) director of his household, and Fere Menatos keeper of the Laws and Archives of Aksum; and after a few days the king died, and left a little son with his mother, and the Azgaga reigned with him. And Adesyos and Fere Menatos brought up the children, and taught them little by little the Faith of Christ, and they built for them a place of prayer, and they gathered together to it the children and they taught them psalms and hymns. And when they had brought the boy to the stage of early manhood, they asked him to dismiss them to their native country; and Adyoses (sic) departed to the country of Tyre to see his kinsfolk, and Fere Menatos departed to Alexandria, to the Archbishop Athanasius, and he found that he had been restored to his office. And he related everything which had happened unto him because of their Faith in the country of Ethiopia, and how the people believed on Christ, but had neither bishops nor priests. And then Abba Athanasius appointed Fere Menatos Bishop of the country of Ethiopia, and sent him away with great honour. And he arrived in the country of Ethiopia during the reign of Abreha and Asbeha, and he preached the peace of Christ in all the regions thereof, and because of this he was called "Abba Salama." And after he had saluted the men of Ethiopia he died in peace. Salutation, salutation, I say, with joyful voice to Abba Salama.

[Pantaleon]

And on this day died Saint Abba Pantaleon of the cell. This holy man was the son of noble folk, who were among the great ones of Rome, and who sat on the right hand of the emperor. When his mother had weaned him she took him to a monastery where he grew up in wisdom and exhortation, and fasting and prayer. Then he travelled to the country of Ethiopia with Nine Saints in the days of 'Al'Ameda the king, the son of Sal Adab the king, and they lived in Bet Katin. Then they separated, and Abba Pantaleon went up to the top of a little mountain, and he made himself a cell which was five cubits long, and two cubits wide, and three cubits deep; its roof was a single stone, and it had no door, but only a small opening. And he stood on his feet for a period of five and forty years, without sitting down, and without lying down to sleep. He ate and drank so little that his skin cleaved to his bones, and his eyelashes were worn away by his tears. And he continued to work innumerable miracles in healing the sick and in opening the eyes of the blind. One day he planted a tree at dawn and by the time the evening came it had grown very tall, and had dried up, and his disciple had prepared (?) it and burned it, and tied up the charcoal in his garment and taken it for the censer. When Kaleb was going forth to wage war against another king, he came to Abba Pantaleon and embraced his cell, and told him his trouble. And Abba Pantaleon said, "Go in peace, for God is able to do all things, and He shall give thee victory over thy enemy"; and to return safely and in peace. When Kaleb the king had come to the country of Saba, he made war on the people thereof, and he slew them all and conquered them, and there were not left any who were not scattered like leaves. And all those who saw Saint Abba Pantaleon testified concerning him, saying, "We saw Abba Pantaleon standing with us in the battle, and he was overthrowing our enemies." When Kaleb the king returned, having conquered the King of Judah, he forsook his kingdom, and became a monk with Pantaleon. When Saint Abba Pantaleon had finished his strife, our Lord Jesus Christ came to him and made a covenant with him concerning him that should call upon his name, and celebrate his commemoration, and write an account of his contending; and He said unto him, "It is now sufficient for thee; go to thy rest." And straightway his bones broke and he died in peace and was buried in his cell.

Salutation to Pantaleon as the perfect man.

Salutation, twofold, to Pantaleon who caused the death of 5050 warriors in the battle.

Salutation to Pantaleon in his cell.

[Aragawi]

And on this day also is commemorated our holy Father Aragawi, who is surnamed Za-Mikael. This holy man became a guide to the servants of God on the road. And he went up to the holy Dabra Damo holding the tail of a serpent, and there he fought countless noble fights. And God graciously made a covenant with him concerning the man who should call upon his name, and the man who should celebrate his commemoration, and then he was hidden from the face of death by the grace of God. He established among his children the Rules for the Monastic Life, which he had learned in the house of his father Pachomius. Salutation to Za-Mikael who was surnamed "Aragawi."

[Garima]

And on this day also is celebrated the commemoration of the blessed Saint Abba Garima. The father of this saint was Emperor of Rome, and his name was Masfeyanos; the name of his mother was Sefengeya, and she was barren. And having besought our holy Lady, the Virgin Mary, the God-bearer, she gave her this son; and she called his name "Isaac" [later renamed Garima]. When he had grown up she taught him the Books of the Church, and then Isaac was appointed deacon. And the men of Rome having made him emperor, he sat and judged justly and righteously for seven years. And when Saint Abba Pantaleon of the cell heard [of him], he sent to him, saying, "O my son Isaac, let the dead bury their dead, and do thou come and seek the kingdom of my Lord Jesus Christ"; and Abba Garima, having heard him, forsook the kingdom, and went forth by night. Then the angel Saint Gabriel appeared, and he carried him on his shining wing and at the third hour brought him into the hand of Abba Pantaleon. Now the length of the road was a journey of ten months and four days. The King of Ethiopia at that time was Alameda. When Abba Pantaleon saw Saint Isaac he embraced him, and kissed him, and then he arrayed him in the garb of the monk; and the saint fasted and prayed so strenuously that his flesh congealed on his bones. Then he went to a place [in] Madra (?) and he lived there for three and twenty years, working countless signs and wonders, and casting out devils, and healing the sick. One day he sowed wheat at dawn, and reaped it in the evening, and some of it he offered as an offering; and on the following day he took the remainder up to the threshing floor, and he trod out the sheaves of wheat, and obtained therefrom seventy-seven measures of grain. And he also planted a vine shoot on a rock, and it took root, and put forth leaves and bore fruit immediately. And once when he was writing a letter, and the sun was about to set, he adjured the sun to stand still and it did so until he had finished his letter. And the spittle which he spat out remaineth unto this day, and is a means for healing the sick; and once when a reed fell from his hand, it took root that very day.... And having finished his good course, our Redeemer appeared unto him, and promised him that [He would forgive the sins of] him that should call upon his name, and celebrate his commemoration. And straightway he was caught up in a shining cloud and disappeared. Salutation to Abba Garima.

From *The Book of the Saints of the Ethiopian Church,* ed. E. A. W. Budge, 4 Vols. (London: Cambridge University Press, 1928), Vol. IV: 1164–65; Vol. I: 116–18, 155; Vol. IV: 1009–10. Reprinted with the permission of Cambridge University Press. Spellings of proper names have been simplified.

7.2 The Conversion of Nubia:
John of Ephesus on Justinian and Theodora's Competition

Between the mid-sixth and the mid-fifteenth century, a Christian culture also flourished in the territory of Nubia, between Egypt and Ethiopia along the Red Sea on the northeast coast of Africa. The orthodox Christian doctrine of all of this region was the non-Chalcedon Monophysite position, evident in the Coptic Church in Egypt, and the Monophysite Ethiopian Church. Nubia's conversion to Monophysite Christianity as told by church historians of the time reveals much about the intertwining political and religious dimensions of conversion. It is a complicated story involving Byzantine rulers, Monophysite bishops, and esoteric heresies.

Legendary evidence suggests that Christian influence reached Nubia in the third and fourth centuries from Byzantine, Egyptian, and Ethiopian contacts. The main conversion events, however, took place in the sixth century as recorded in Severus el-Ashmunein's *History of the Patriarchs* (2.1) and John of Ephesus's *Ecclesiastical History* (excerpted below). Both writers tell the dramatic story of how Monophysite missionaries won the race to Nubia from the Byzantine court, sent by the Monophysite Empress Theodora in a competition with her husband, the Chalcedon-supporting Emperor Justinian.

The account given here by John of Ephesus (circa 507–89), a Monophysite monk and bishop, gives insight into both the Byzantine Empire and church. He records the mission of Julian, sent by Theodora, and Julian's success as bishop. The excerpt also includes an account of Longinus, the bishop ordained after Julian, who went as a missionary from Nubia to the "Alodaei" (Alwa) in 581, a story that reveals much about the political dimensions of the region. Alwa was a kingdom southwest of Nubia and within the Axumite (Ethiopian) kingdom's sphere of influence. Longinus's success in converting the Alodaei under Nubian sponsorship effectively distances Alwa from Axumite political domination. In a competition to convert their neighbors to the orthodox belief of Monophysite Christianity, Nubia is now one up on Axum.

Questions

1. What approach did these missionaries use in successfully converting new peoples?

2. How do political and religious elements intertwine in the spread of Christianity?

3. What seem to be the chief elements these Christians value as essential to their faith?

John of Ephesus, Ecclesiastical History

Chapter 6: About the Barbarous People of the Nobades, and About the Cause of Their Conversion to Christianity

Among the clergy in attendance upon pope Theodosius, was a presbyter named Julianus, an old man of great worth, who conceived an earnest spiritual desire to christianize the wandering people who dwell on the eastern borders of the Thebais beyond Egypt, and who are not only not subject to the authority of the Roman empire, but even receive a subsidy on condition that they do not enter nor pillage Egypt. The blessed Julianus, therefore being full of anxiety for these people, went and spoke about them to the late queen Theodore (d. 547), in the hope of awakening in her a similar desire for their conversion; and as the queen was fervent in zeal for God, she received the proposal with joy and promised to do everything in her power for the conversion of these tribes from the errors of idolatry.

The king, however, hearing that she was sending somebody from that Synod which was opposed to him, did not like the thing, and arranged that a letter be dispatched to his bishops in the Thebaid district ordering them to enter the territory and instruct the people avoiding to mention that Synod. Hence he was himself with zeal and sent immediately some ambassadors with gold and baptismal garments and gifts destined to the king of that people and letters to the governor of Thebaid to take care of the ambassadors and forward them to that people. Therefore, as soon as the queen was informed of this, she wrote a letter, cunningly worded, to the governor of Thebaid, which was brought by an official. The letter was to this effect: "In as much as both his majesty and myself have purposed to send an embassy to the people of the Nobadae, and I am now dispatching a blessed man named Julian; and further my will is, that my ambassador should arrive at the aforesaid people before his majesty's; be warned, that, if you permit his ambassador to arrive there before mine, and do not hinder him by various pretexts until mine shall have reached you, and have passed through your province, and arrived at his destination, your life shall answer for it; for I will immediately send and take off your head."

When the governor of Thebaid read this and the king's ambassador reached him, he played him off saying: "Be patient, while we look for and prepare the camels and the men who know the road of the desert: then you shall have them and enter that country." So he dismissed him and awaited till the ambassadors of the gentle queen arrived: they found the camels ready with the men and, the same day, without delay, they pretended to seize violently the camels and left first. The governor then sent a messenger to the king's ambassador: "Lo! when I had made my preparation, and was desirous of sending you onward, ambassadors from the queen arrived, and fell upon me with violence, and took away the beasts of burden I had got ready, and have passed onward. And I am too well acquainted with the fear in which the queen is held, to venture to oppose them. But abide still with me, until I can make fresh preparations for you, and then you shall also go in peace." The king's ambassador, hearing this, rent his garments, threatening and insulting (the governor). After a few days he could proceed, too, and finally left, without detecting the trick played against him.

Chapter 7: Julian's and His Companions' Arrival in the Country of the Nobades; How They Were Received and the Other Things They Did with God's Help

As Julian and his fellow-ambassadors reached the country and sent information to the king and his princes, a whole army was sent to meet them; they received Julian's expedition with joy and introduced them to their king, and the latter also received them gladly. Then (Julian) produced the letters of the queen; they were read and their content was understood; they accepted also the great gifts and the numerous baptismal garments, everything in plenty. They soon offered themselves gladly to be instructed, renouncing the errors of their forefathers and confessing the God of the Christians, saying: "This is the one true God, and there is no other beside Him."

After having instructed and prepared them thoroughly, Julian's group informed them also 'that certain disputes had arisen among Christians about some point of faith and that, therefore, even blessed Theodosius had been removed by the king from his see having refused to obey; that the queen, however, had supported him valiantly, and added: she herself has sent us to you with this faith, that you may follow the patriarch Theodosius and may receive baptism in his faith and may keep his truth. But the king also has sent his ambassadors who are already coming after us'. Then they taught the Nobades how to receive them and what to answer to them.

They had been just instructed firmly in all these things, when the king's ambassador arrived; he also gave the king the letters and presents, and began to inform and tell him, according to his instructions, as follows: "The king of the Romans has sent us to you, that in case of your becoming Christians, you may cleave to the church and those who govern it, and not be led astray after those who have been expelled from it." And when the king of the Nobadae and his princes heard these things, they answered them, saying: "The honorable present which the king of the Romans has sent us we accept, and will also ourselves send him a present. But his faith we will not accept: for if we consent to become Christians, we shall walk after the example (of pope Theodosius) who, because he was not willing to accept the wicked faith of the king, was driven away by him and expelled from his church. If, therefore, we abandon our heathenism and errors, we cannot consent to fall into the wicked faith professed by the king." Then they dismissed the ambassadors, putting such things into writing.

Blessed Julian remained two years with them bearing the great heat; he told later that he used to [sit] from the third to the tenth hour in caves full of water with the whole people of the region, naked or, better, wearing only a cloth, while he could perspire only with the help of water. He persevered, however, and instructed and baptized the king and his noblemen and a lot of people with them, arranging also to have with him a certain bishop from the Thebaid, an old man by name Theodore. After having taught them and having organized the community, he entrusted them to that bishop, then left them and came to Constantinople. I was present when the queen received him with great honor and he used to tell many wonderful things about that great people, which things I omit because they are too many, being content with the few I relate.

Chapter 8: How the Pious (Pope) Theodosius on His Death Bed Remembered This People (Nabados) and Ordered that Longinus Immediately Be Sent as Their Bishop. How Longinus Went There to Replace Julianus, Who, Having Passed Away, was Lost to Them.

Pope Theodosius, on the day he died, remembered this people; more so, because the pious Julian, who had instructed them, had passed away and his loss was felt deeply. Queen Theodore, too, had died. Therefore, Theodosius gave orders that pious Longinus should take the place of Julian, for Longinus was a man fired with zeal and capable of completing the conversion of the Nabados and strengthening them in the Christian religion. Immediately after the death of the pope, Longinus was ordained bishop of those countries and made preparations for the journey. When he arrived in that country he was received with great rejoicing. He instructed all the people again in the Christian religion, preaching and enlightening them. He also built a church and established the clergy, organized the liturgy and set up all the church institutions. . . .

Chapter 51: The Narrative of Longinus's Entering the Alodian Country and How He Converted Them with Gladness and Baptized Them

When the king of the Alodaei sent the delegation to the king of the Nobades, asking that bishop Longinus be sent to them to instruct his people and baptize them, it was clear that the good disposition of that people towards conversion had been produced in a certain miraculous way by God. Then 'God moved the spirit' of Longinus to depart and come to them; the king and nobles and chiefs (of the Nobades), though sorry that he should leave them, allowed him to go, in the company of some people who [knew] the desert. On the road he got sick and so also some of his companions; as he writes in his letter, besides other animals, seventeen camels died in the desert because of the heat. Moreover, another people, called Macuritae, was midway between the two kingdoms; their king, informed that Longinus was on the way, was moved by satanic envy to place watchmen on all the borders of his kingdom, on all roads, mountains and plains up to the Suph [=Red] Sea, to hold Longinus and hamper the salvation of that great people of the Alodaei. God, however, hid him and blinded the eyes of those who wanted to hold him and 'he passed through them' without being seen by them.

When he reached the borders of the kingdom to which he was directed, the king, soon informed, sent one of his noblest men, by name Itiqya, as he says in his letter, who received him with great attention and introduced him into the country with great honours. And when he reached (the capital), the king himself moved to meet him and received him with great joy. And having settled among them and spoken the Word of God to the king and to all his nobles, they received it with open heart; within a few days they were instructed and the king was baptized together with all his nobles and a great part of the population. That king, therefore, full of joy and gladness, sent the following letter of gratitude to the king of the Nobades.

Chapter 52: The Letter of the King of the Alodaei
to the King of the Nobades

"Thy love is remembered by us, my lord, our brother Orfiulo, because thou hast now shown thyself my true kinsman, and that not only in the body, but also in the spirit, in having sent hither our common spiritual father, who has shown me the way of truth, and of the true light of Christ our God, and has baptized me, and my nobles, and all my family. And in everything the work of Christ is multiplied, and I have hope in the holy God, and am desirous moreover of doing thy pleasure, and driving thy enemies from thy land. For he is not thy enemy alone, but also mine: for thy land is my land, and thy people my people. Let not their courage therefore fail, but be manful and take courage: for it is impossible for me to be careless of thee and thy land, especially now that I have become a Christian, by the help of my father, the holy father Longinus. As we have need, however, of church furniture, get some ready for us: for I feel certain that thou wilt send me these things with carefulness, and I will make thee an answer: but on the day on which I was keeping festival I did not wish to write, lest my letters should fail. Be not anxious then, but encourage thyself, and play the man: for Christ is with us."

From *Oriental Sources Concerning Nubia*, ed. G. Vantini (Heidelberg: Heidelberger Akademie der Wissenschafted, and Warsaw: Polish Academy of Sciences, 1975), pp. 6–12, 17–23; reprinted from R. Payne-Smith, *Ecclesiastical History*, Book IV (Oxford 1860).

7.3 Heroic Martyrs in South Arabia: The Women of Najrân

The intertwining of the political, religious, and cultural dimensions in late antiquity could be explosive: as political and religious identities intermixed, changes in rule could mean religious persecution for those caught on the wrong side. New dynasties or new alliances could shift the balance of power to another religion; frequently these local political shifts were perceived as spiritual battles between right and wrong beliefs, creating a whole new group of martyrs. The complex dynamics of Christian, Jewish, and other belief systems in South Arabia (Yemen), fueled by outside powers competing for hegemony in the region, erupted in the early sixth century and resulted in some widely read stories of horrific martyrdom—stories that inflamed partisan sentiments even more.

In the early sixth century, conflict broke out in South Arabia that brought severe persecution to Himyarite Christians, who were identified by virtue of their religion as pro-Axumite and pro-Byzantine. Yusuf Dhu-Nuwas, a convert to Judaism, took power in Himyar in 517 and sought to eliminate Byzantine and Axumite influence in favor of a Persian orientation. The bloody political takeover thus took on religious dimensions. Christians of Najarân, a Himyarite city, sent their bishop to Axum to ask for help, quickly supplied by the Ethiopians, who did not want to lose this vital trading link. The occupying Ethiopian troops met with resistance from non-Christian groups, and even from the small Persian Nestorian Christian population living there. Dhu-Nuwas was successful in tricking the Ethiopians out of the capital city of Zaras (slaughtering most of them), but still met with resistance from three predominantly Christian cities that were subdued only through great bloodshed. One of these cities was Najarân, where a massive slaughter of over 700 Christians took place. The negative reactions from neighboring empires, especially the Byzantines, isolated Dhu-Nuwas and disrupted Himyarite trade. In 525, a coalition of Ethiopian, Byzantine, and rebel Himyarites overthrew Dhu-Nuwas and put in place a Christian ruler under Axumite influence. The stories of the Najarân deaths spread quickly to other Christian realms, where they were recounted in terms of heroic martyrdom for the cause of Christ. The stories appear in numerous accounts in Greek, Syriac, Arabic, Ethiopic, and other languages. The following excerpts are from a Syriac source, Simeon of Beth Arsham, and describe the deaths of aristocratic women, their children, and their servants.

Questions

1. How does martyrdom function as both a religious and a political statement?
2. What Christian values are exhibited in these stories?
3. Compare these martyrdoms to the story of Perpetua and Felicitas (4.1).

Simeon of Beth Arsham, The Martyrs of Najrân

The Burning of the Church and the Martyrs

And the Jews thus brought all their (bones) [the martyred Christian leaders] together into the church and heaped them in the center of the church; and they brought in the presbyters, the deacons, the subdeacons, the readers, the sons of the covenant and the daughters of the covenant, and the laity, both men and women, some of whose names we intend to write at the end of our letter; and they filled the whole church from one side to the other, [with the Christians], all of whom came to about two thousand, as those who came from Najrân have said. And they brought wood and surrounded the church from the outside and threw fire into it and burnt it together with all that was found in it.

And when the other women who had not been seized with their companions saw the church and the priests and the sons of the covenant burning in the fire, they hastened to the church crying to one another: "Come, companions! Let us enjoy the scent of the priests." And thus they hastened and entered the fire and were burnt. . . .

Ruhayma

Among them, however, there was one whose name was RHWM [Ruhayma], daughter of AZM' [Azma'], from the family called JW [Jaw], who was a relative of the victorious HRTH BR-KNB [Hârith, son of Ka'b]. Because of her high position, her lineage, and her beauty, the king ordered that she not be killed, thinking that he would be able to persuade her to deny Christ and the Cross. And thus she entered the city grieving that she had not died.

The Handmaids

And he ordered the handmaids to be brought [before him] and said to them, too: "Behold! You have seen your masters and mistresses and your relatives dying an evil death because they did not wish to deny Christ and the Cross. But you, do now spare yourselves and listen to me, and deny Christ and the Cross, and you shall be free women and you will be given in marriage to free-born men." But these [women] said to him: "Far be it from us that we should deny Christ and the Cross; and far be it from us that we should survive our masters and relatives. Rather, with them and like them, we shall die for the sake of Christ; and far be it from us that we should consent to [what] you [say] or accept your promise." And when the king saw that they would not be persuaded to make their denial, he ordered them taken to LWDYÂ, that is, to the valley, and killed there; and [his men] did this to them, and they were all crowned by the sword.

Mâhyâ

And on the very same day, after the handmaids had been killed, a handmaid of the victorious HRTH BR-KNB [Hârith, son of Ka'b], whose name was MÂHYÂ, was hiding in a house. She had led a wicked life, was loud-tongued ... and insolent, and she was hated by everyone because of her wickedness; throughout her life she was masculine in all her deeds, and even her masters used to fear her because of her wickedness. When she heard that her masters, her kinsfolk and her relatives had been killed, she made haste and went out to the market-place, bound herself with a girdle round the loins as a man would, and ran in the streets of the city, crying and saying: "Christian men and women! This is the moment for you to render to Christ what you owe Him. Go out and die for the sake of Christ, just as He died for your sake. He who does not go out today to Christ, he does not belong to Him; he who does not respond to Christ today will not be summoned tomorrow. This is the moment of combat. Go out and give succor to your master, Christ, because tomorrow the door will be closed by Him and you will not be able to enter into His presence. I know that you hate me; but, by Christ, from this day onward, I shall not be your adversary; no, by Christ, I shall no longer utter insolent words against you. Look at me and see that there is no evil [coming] out of me; follow me, lest I should go alone and lest the Jews should flee before me as they used to, and [so] would not kill me." And she was crying in this manner until she came and stood before the king.

And when those Jews who had known her saw her, they said to their king: "Behold! Here is the satan of the Christians, there is no evil spirit that does not reside in her." As for her she said to the king: "To you, O Jew, butcher of the Christians, I say: 'Come and slaughter me, too, because I am a Christian. I am the handmaid of HRTH BR-KNB [Hârith, son of Ka'b], whom you killed yesterday. Do not think that you have overcome my master! Nay, it is my master who has overcome you; for you have been overcome because you lied in the name of your God, while my master has overcome you because he lied not and denied not Christ'. And lo! . . . I say to you: 'If you had come against my master with a legion [of soldiers], and if he had ordered me, I myself would have come out against you with a spear and a sword and I would have kicked you with my feet, but if my master had so willed, he would surely have trampled you as [he would] a fly'."

And the king ordered her stripped naked and when they disrobed her she said to the king: "It is to your shame and the shame of all the Jews, your companions, that you have done (this). As for me, I am not ashamed of this, because I have done this of my own accord many a time, and I disrobed before men and women and was not ashamed because I am a woman, just as I was created by God. But as for you, all the Himyarites know the unseemliness with which that (robber) merchant from the Hîra of Nu'mân conducted himself towards you, for having saved you from death [at the hands] of the Cushites (during) the war."

This robber was present in the land of the Himyarites at the time when the Cushites came out and massacred the Himyarites and apprehended this Jew (wanting to kill him); but this robber stood up [for him] (and) swore in his behalf by the Holy Gospel that he was a Christian, and it was in this way that this Jew was delivered from death. But now after he had become king and had massacred the Christians, he sent [some] of the loot of the Christians to this robber in the Hîra of Nu'mân, together with a letter of thanks. And it was owing to this that all the Christians hated this robber and because of him that the blessed one reviled the king, as has been written above.

And the king ordered an ox and a donkey to be brought and they threw ropes round her legs and tied one leg to the ox and the other to the donkey and the sons of the Jews took up rods and beat the ox and the donkey. And in this way they dragged her round the wall of the city three times and (thus) she gave up her spirit (as a martyr) for the sake of Christ. [And] after (that) . . . they brought her in front of the northern gate of the city, opposite the courtyard of her master, HRTH [Hârith], where there was a big tree called ATHÂLH, that is, the tamarisk. And they hung her on it from head downwards until the evening, and the Jews would come and throw stones and [shoot] arrows at her. And in the evening they took her down from the tree, dragged her, and threw her in LWDYÂ [the valley].

Ruhayma Again; Her Grand-Daughter, Ruhayma; and Her Daughter, Umma

On Sunday, three days after the free-born women and the handmaids had been killed, the king sent to RHWM [Ruhayma], the daughter of AZM'

[Azmaʻ], that if she denied Christ she would live but if she did not deny, she would die. When she received the word, she made haste and went out to the market in the middle of the city, she, the woman whose face no one had ever seen outside the door of her house and who had never walked during the day in the city until that day when she stood before the whole city, with her head uncovered, crying and saying: "O women of Najrân, my Christian, Jewish, and Pagan companions, hearken. You know that I am a Christian, and you know my lineage and family and who I am; and that I have gold and silver and slaves and handmaids and field produce and that I lack nothing. And now that my husband has been killed for the sake of Christ, if I desired to marry another, I should not be lacking a husband. And here I am saying to you that on this very day I am in possession of forty thousand *denarii,* sealed and placed in my treasury apart from the treasury of my husband, and jewelry and pearls and jacinths; and there are among you women who, together with their daughters, have seen these in my house. And you know, my (companions), that a woman (has no days) of joy comparable to the days (of her wedding); and from the wedding (onward it is all grief and) groans: when she gives birth (to children) she (does so) with anguish and wailing; (when she is) deprived of them she is (in pain and) distress . . . and when she buries her children, she does so with weeping and lamentation. But from this day onward, I am free from all these [cares], continuing to rejoice in the days of my first wedding. And here are my three virgin daughters, since they are not betrothed to men, I have adorned them for Christ. Look at me, for twice have you seen my face: at my first wedding, and now at this second one also; with unveiled face before all of you I went over to my first spouse, and now [again] with unveiled face I am going to Christ, my Lord and my God, and the Lord and God of my daughters, just as He himself came to us. Look at me and at my daughters, for I am not less beautiful than you are, and here in my beauty I am going to Christ, my Lord, uncorrupted by the infidelity of the Jews. And this, my beauty, will be a witness for me before my Lord that it was unable to lead me astray into the sin of denying Christ, my Lord. My gold, my silver and all the jewelry of my adornment, my slaves and handmaids and all I possess will be a testimony for me that I did not, for the love of them, deny Christ. And now the king has sent [word] to me to deny Christ and [so] live, but I sent [word] back to him that if I denied Christ, I should die, but if I did not deny Christ, I should live. Far be it from me, my companions, far be it from me that I should deny Christ, my God, Him in whom I believed, in whose name I was baptized and had my daughters also baptized, whose Cross I adore, and for whose sake I shall die, I and my daughters, as He died for us. Behold! The gold of the earth is abandoned to the earth. Whosoever wishes to take my gold, let him take it; whosoever wishes to take my silver and my jewelry, let him take it, for I have abandoned everything of my own free will, in order to go and receive from my Lord a recompense. Blessed are you, my companions, if you listen to my words. (Blessed are you, my companions), if (you know the truth for which) . . . I and my daughters are dying. Blessed are you, my companions, if you love Christ. Blessed am I and my daughters because we are journeying to such blessedness. From now onward, peace and tranquility will [reign] among the people of Christ, and the blood of my brothers and sisters who have been killed for Christ will be a wall to this city, if it abides [faithfully] by Christ, my Lord. Behold how with unveiled face I am going out of your city in which I have lived as if in a temporary dwelling, so that I may journey, I and my daughters, to the other city, because it is to that place that I have betrothed them. Pray for me, my companions, so that Christ, my Lord, may receive and may forgive me for having remained alive three days after the father of my daughters [had been killed]."

When the blessed RHWM [Ruhayma] said these [words], a lamentation was [raised] by all the women of the city, so that the wicked king was perturbed together with those who were with him outside the city. And when the men he had sent to fetch the blessed one came and told him all that the victorious one had said and that the women had raised the lamentation on account of her, he wanted to kill them for having let her make all this speech and lead the city astray by her sorceries. After this she went out of the city, head uncovered, with her daughters, and came and stood before the king with her face unveiled, unabashed, and holding with her hand her daughters who were adorned as though for a wedding. And she loosed the braids of her hair and wound them in her hand and bared her neck and stretched her throat and bowed her head before the king crying: "A Christian am I, and so are my daughters, and for the sake of Christ we are going to die; cut off our heads so that we may go and join our brethren and the father of my daughters." And after this (the king) again coaxed her with these words: "Say only (that He is a man), that Christ whom they hung on the Cross, and go home, you and your daughters."

But a daughter of the blessed Ruhayma . . . who was nine years old, when she heard the king tell her mother to deny Christ and to spit at the Cross, filled her mouth with spittle and spat at the king.

And at this point the free-born men who have just now arrived from Najrân have added that this girl who insulted the king was not the daughter of the blessed RHWM [Ruhayma], but her granddaughter, and her name was RHWM [Ruhayma] after her grandmother; her mother had been killed with those women who had been killed the day before.

This girl said to the king: "May you be spat at, you who are not ashamed to tell my grandmother to deny Christ and to spit at the Cross. May you be abjured, [you] and all the Jews, your companions; and may all those be abjured, who, like you, deny Christ and his Cross. Christ knows that my grandmother is better than your mother, and my lineage is better than your lineage, and [yet] you had the audacity to tell my grandmother to spit at the Cross and to deny Christ; may your mouth be shut, O Jew, the killer of his Lord." And when the girl said these [words] to the king, he ordered her grandmother thrown on the ground. And in order to frighten all the Christians, he ordered that this girl be slain, and her blood be poured into her grandmother's mouth.

And after this, the daughter of the blessed one, whose name was AWMH [Umma], was also slain and her blood was also poured into the mouth of her mother. And after this the king ordered her raised from the ground and asked her: "How did the blood of your daughters taste to you?" She said: "Like a pure sacrificial offering without blemish, thus it tasted to me both in my mouth and in my soul." And he gave his orders immediately and her head was cut off.

And at this point those who came from Najrân have added these [words] and related as follows: that after the (blessed) RHWM [Ruhayma] had been killed, the chieftains approached the king and said to him: ... "This (woman) has done many good deeds to everyone, to the king, to the notables, and to the poor; and in like manner she formerly treated M'DWKRM [Ma'dî-karib, who before you has been king in this land. For he was in difficulty and borrowed from her twelve thousand *denarii*, and finally, when she saw that he was in difficulty, she renounced claim to the debt, [both the sum] and the interest. She has also made many people prosperous in every way. But we entreat you to grant us and do for us this one favor, namely, that this woman be buried because of her many good deeds towards everyone; for in every way she was a doer of good deeds, apart from this—[her] Christianity." And the king ordered that she be buried; and they shrouded her with worn-out linen and buried her at the edge of LWDYÂ that is, the valley, where her companions had been killed.

And those who came from Najrân said also that the victorious HRTH BR-KNB [Hârith, son of Ka'b], because of the intercession of the chieftains, was buried near the wall of the city, opposite the gate of his courtyard.

The blessed RHWM [Ruhayma], daughter of AZM' [Azma'], and her daughter, whose name was AWMH [Umma], and her grand-daughter, whose name was RHWM [Ruhayma], were [all] crowned on Sunday, on the twentieth of the Latter Tishrin [November].

Reprinted with permission from *The Martyrs of Najrân: New Documents*, ed. and trans. Irfan Shahîd, Subsidia Hagiographica 49 (Brussells: Société des Bollandistes, 1971), pp. 46–47, 54–59. The spellings of proper names have been modernized.

7.4 Nestorian Christians in China: Stele

From the eastern churches in Syria and Persia, Dyophysite Christianity or Nestorianism (3.4) spread farther east along the Central Asian trade routes, particularly into China, where it flourished during the seventh to the ninth centuries. The China of this period (T'ang Dynasty, 618–907) had its own strong traditions in Confucianism, Taoism, and ancestor worship that each influenced the formation of a Chinese Christianity. In contrast to these indigenous belief systems, the experiences of Buddhism and Christianity in China make an interesting comparison, as both are foreign religions with adherents attempting to adapt the religion to Chinese culture.

Buddhism has a strong monastic tradition, as did the Nestorian Christian tradition that entered China, so that Nestorian monks represented a recognizable and respected tradition. Nestorian Christianity, although smaller and shorter lived in China than Buddhism, did flourish for a while because it also learned to assimilate Chinese ideas, showing in particular deep respect for the Chinese emperor and the values that supported imperial rule. Some of the key ideas that appear in the document below emphasize the Chinese values of harmony and balance. The *T'ao (Dao)*, loosely translated "the Way," indicates the Order of the Universe. *T'ien (Tian)*, or "Heaven," should not be understood exclusively in the Christian sense of a spiritual home where God resides; rather, it is a Chinese concept for the impersonal Force or Will that directs the cosmos. Likewise, the emphasis on the concept of balance usually expressed as *Yin* and *Yang*, although those terms do not appear here, should not be confused with the Christian tension between good and evil. Yin and Yang were opposite, but necessary forces for balance in the universe, expressed often as male and female (or as in the analogy of positive and negative poles of electricity). "The Way" or "The Luminous Religion," as Christianity is called in this document, establishes a language for discussing Christian belief that reflects Buddhist, Taoist, and Confucian ideas.

The document below is a transcription from a late eighth-century *stele* or monument inscribed with a long text eulogizing not only the history of Christianity but also the Chinese rulers who sponsored the religion. The 1623 discovery of the stele was surprising enough to evoke disbelief until other documents confirmed the existence of this early Chinese Christianity. The stele is dated 781, but relates the events of 635 when Emperor T'ai-tsung (Taizong) received the Nestorian mission. The opening and closing passages are given here, with the middle section of glorified imperial support omitted. At the end of the document, excluded here, are witnessing statements in both Chinese and Syriac. The carvings on the top of the stele, like the text, integrate

Chinese themes and beliefs with Christian symbols. A traditional Chinese icon of a pearl rests between two mythical creatures of Buddhist origin. Inscribed below are a cross (obviously Christian) and a lotus flower (a Buddhist symbol). Altogether, the monument is testimony to a vital, dynamic Chinese Nestorian Christianity—one that was still present when thirteenth-century Europeans visited the Mongol court in China (20.3).

Questions

1. What evidence of Dyophysite views of Christ appear here?
2. In what ways are Chinese ideas mixed with Christian ones?
3. How do you think an orthodox Christian of Europe or Byzantium would respond to this adaptation?

Ta-ch'in Ching-chiao Liu-hsing Chung-kuo pei Stele, circa 781

(Eulogy on a Monument Commemorating the Propagation of the Luminous Religion in the Middle Kingdom, with a Preface to the Same, Composed by Ching-ching, a Priest of the Ta-ch'in Monastery. [In Syriac], Adam, Priest and Chorepiscopus, and Papash' of Chinastan. . . .)

Behold! there is One who is true and firm, who, being Uncreated, is the Origin of the Origins; who is ever Incomprehensible and Invisible, yet ever mysteriously existing to the last of the lasts; who, holding the Secret Source of Origin, created all things, and who, surpassing all the Holy ones, is the only unoriginated Lord of the Universe,—is not this our [Eloha], the Triune, mysterious Person, the unbegotten and true Lord?

Dividing the Cross, He determined the four cardinal points. Setting in motion the primordial spirit (wind), He produced the two principles of Nature. The dark void was changed, and Heaven and Earth appeared. The sun and moon revolved, and day and night began. Having designed and fashioned all things, He then created the first man and bestowed on him an excellent disposition, superior to all others, and gave him to have dominion over the Ocean of created things.

The original nature of Man was pure, and void of all selfishness, unstained and unostentatious, his mind was free from inordinate lust and passion. When, however, Satan employed his evil devices on him, Man's pure and stainless (nature) was deteriorated; what is just and noble was eliminated from that which is called right on the one hand (lit., in this place), and what is fundamentally identical (with wickedness) was abstracted from that which is named wrong on the other (lit., in that place).

In consequence of this, three hundred and sixty-five (spiritual beings) with different seeds (of error) arose in quick succession and left deep furrows behind. They strove to weave nets of the laws wherewith to ensnare the innocent. Some pointing to natural objects pretended that they were the right objects to worship; others got hold of (the idea that) non-existence (lit., Emptiness) and existence (are alike, after all). Some sought to call down blessings (happiness or success) by means of prayers and sacrifices; others again boasted of their own goodness, and held their fellows in contempt. (Thus) the intellect and the thoughts of Men fell into hopeless confusion; and their mind and affections began to toil incessantly; but all their travail was in vain. The heat of their distress became a scorching flame; and self-blinded, they increased the darkness still more; and losing their path for a long while they went astray and became unable to return home again.

Whereupon one Person of our Trinity, the Messiah, who is the Luminous Lord of the Universe, folding up Himself and concealing His true Majesty, appeared upon earth as a man. Angels proclaimed the Glad Tidings. A virgin gave birth to the Holy One in Ta-ch'in. A bright Star announced the blessed event. Persians saw the splendour and came forth with their tribute.

Fulfilling the old Law as it was declared by the twenty-four Sages, He (the Messiah) taught how to rule both families and kingdoms according to His own great Plan. Establishing His New Teaching of Non-assertion which operates silently through the Holy Spirit, another Person of the Trinity, He formed in man the capacity for well-doing through the Right Faith. Setting up the standard of the eight cardinal virtues, He purged away the dust from human nature and perfected a true character. Widely opening the Three Constant Gates, He brought Life to light and abolished Death. Hanging up the bright Sun, He swept away the abodes of darkness. All the evil devices of the devil were thereupon defeated and destroyed. He then took an oar in the Vessel of Mercy and ascended to the Palace of Light. Thereby all rational beings were conveyed across the Gulf. His mighty work being thus completed, He returned at noon to His original position (in Heaven). The twenty-seven standard works of His Sutras were preserved. The Great means of Conversion (or leavening, i.e., transformation) were widely extended, and the sealed Gate of the Blessed Life was unlocked. His Law is to bathe with water and with the Spirit, and thus to cleanse from all vain delusions and to purify men until they regain the whiteness of their nature.

(His ministers) carry the Cross with them as a Sign. They travel about wherever the sun shines, and try to re-unite those that are beyond the pale (i. e., those that are lost). Striking the wood, they proclaim the Glad Tidings (lit., joyful sounds) of Love and Charity. They turn ceremoniously to the East, and hasten in the Path of Life and Glory. They preserve the beard to show that they have outward works to do, whilst they shave the crown (tonsure) to remind themselves that they have no private selfish desires. They keep neither male nor female slaves. Putting all men on an equality, they make no distinction between the noble and the mean. They neither accumulate property nor wealth; but giving all they possess, they set a good example to others. They observe fasting in order that they may subdue "the knowledge" (which defiles the mind). They keep the vigil of silence and watchfulness so that they may observe "the Precepts." Seven times a day they meet for worship and praise, and earnestly they offer prayers for the living as well as for the dead. Once in seven days, they have "a sacrifice without the animal" (i. e., a bloodless sacrifice). Thus cleansing their hearts, they regain their purity. This ever True and Unchanging *Way* is mysterious, and is almost impossible to name. But its meritorious operations are so brilliantly manifested that we make an effort and call it by the name of "The Luminous Religion." . . .

To the glory of God for all these eminent and meritorious events (above described), we engrave the following Eulogy in a form of poetical composition on this great Monument.

> It is the true Lord who was Uncreated,
> And was ever profoundly firm and unchangeable.
> He created the Universe after His own plan,
> And raised the Earth and framed the Heaven.
> Dividing His God-head, He took human form
> And through Him, Salvation was made free to all.
> The Sun arising, the Darkness was ended.
> All these facts prove that He is the True Mystery.
>
> The most Glorious and Accomplished Sovereign
> Surpassed all His predecessors in upholding "The *Way*."
> Taking Time at its flood, He so settled all disorders
> That Heaven was expanded and Earth widened.
> The brightest and most brilliant of all teachings—
> The teaching of the Luminous Religion—
> Took root deep and firm in our Land of T'ang.
> With the translation of the Scriptures
> And the building of convents,
> We see the living and the dead all sailing in one Ship of
>   Mercy;
> All manner of blessings arose, and peace and plenty
>   abounded.

Kao-tsung succeeded to the Throne of his Fathers;
He re-built the edifices for Holy use.
Palaces of Peace and Concord stood resplendent far and
  near;
The rays shining from them filled every part of the
  Empire.
The truths of "The *Way*" were made clear to all men.
Setting up a new institution, he created "the Lord
  Spiritual";
And every man enjoyed most blessed peace and joy,
Whilst the land saw neither pain nor grief.

When Hsüan-tsung commenced his glorious career,
With might and main, he pursued the Way of Truth.
The temple-names written by the Emperor shone forth;
The tablets of the celestial hand-writing reflected
  gloriously.
The Imperial Domain was embellished and studded with
  gems,
While the least and the remotest places attained the
  highest virtue.

All sorts of works undertaken by the people flourished
  throughout the land;
And each man enjoyed his own prosperity.

When Su-tsung finally was restored to the Throne,
The Celestial Dignity guided the Imperial vehicle;
At length the sacred Sun sent forth its crystal rays;
Felicitous winds blew, and the Darkness fled;
Thus the precious Throne was made secure
To the Imperial family of the great T'ang.
The causes of calamity took flight—never to return;
Tumults were settled and men's passions subdued;
The ideals of the Middle Kingdom were at last realised.
Tai-tsung was filial to his parents and just to all.
His virtues united with the great Plans of the Universe.
By his unselfish benevolence, he helped all mankind,
Whilst the greatest blessings were realised in the
  abundance of wealth and prosperity.
By burning fragrant incense, he showed his gratitude;

With benevolence he distributed his gifts to the people.
The Empire became so enlightened as though the glory of
    the Rising Sun in the Eastern Valley
And the full Moon in her secret cave were brought
    together as one.

When our present Emperor ascended the Throne,
He took the reins of government and named the
    "Chien-chung" (Period).
He devoted himself to the cultivation of the Luminous
    Virtue.
His military sway quelled the tumults of the Dark Sea in
    the Four Quarters,
Whilst his Peaceful rule of Enlightenment purified every
    part of the world.
As the light from a candle shines forth, so doth his glory
    penetrate the secrets of men.
As the mirror reflects all things, so nothing is hid from his
    observant eye.
The whole Universe gets life and light because of him.
And even many of the rudest tribes outside the Empire
    take pattern by his government.
How vast and extensive is the True *Way:*
Yet how minute and mysterious it is.
Making a great effort to name it,
We declared it to be "Three-in-one"!
O Lord nothing is impossible for Thee!
Help Thy servants that they may preach!
Hereby we raise this noble Monument,
And we praise Thee for Thy great blessings upon us!

Erected in the Second year of the Chien-chung Period (781 A.D.) of the
Great T'ang (Dynasty), the year Star being in Tso-o, on the seventh day of
the First month (the day being), the great "Yao-sên-wên" day; when the
Spiritual Lord, the Priest Ning-shu (i.e., "mercy and peace"), was entrusted
with the care of the Luminous Communities of the East.

Reprinted with permission from *The Nestorian Documents and Relics in China,* ed. and trans.
Yoshiro Saeki (1st ed. London, Society for Promoting Christian Knowledge, 1916; 2nd ed.
Tokyo, Maruzen, 1951), pp. 53–56, 64–68. Notes omitted.

–8–

Christian Acculturation in Western Europe

The conversion to Christianity by the various Celtic and Germanic peoples of Europe during the third through eighth centuries was a significant aspect in the formation of western culture. In particular, royal conversions to the Roman form of Christianity demonstrate the increasing hegemony of the Roman Church as linked to the rising monarchies of Europe. While many Germanic kings—particularly among the Gothic tribes—had adopted Arian theology, the Roman bishops who followed the Trinitarian views of Nicea used their influence to convert these kings and still non-Christian kings to their "Catholic" or Roman version of Christianity in adherence to the Nicene Creed. The resulting synthesis of Christian, Roman, and Celtic/Germanic traits produced unique Christian societies in the British Isles and on the continent of Europe, generating regional versions of the religion that nonetheless shared some common traditions of conversion.

Christianity flourished among the Celtic inhabitants in the British Isles in the third through sixth centuries, and then survived in Wales, Ireland, and parts of northern England after the sixth-century Anglo-Saxon invasions. Anglo-Saxon Christianity developed among these new migrants to the British Isles after several royal conversions to Roman Christianity in the seventh century. Frankish Christianity was rooted in an earlier royal conversion to Roman Christianity in the fifth century that helped define and solidify the Franks, the ancestors of the French. The Anglo-Saxon conversion was so successful that, within a generation, they sent missionaries back to the continent, aided by the Franks, to convert the Saxons of northern Germany. The narrative histories of these conversions, excerpted in this chapter, were written after the events to create a sense of national identity, and so they emphasize the divinely sponsored dominance of Roman Christianity, as opposed to Celtic or Arian versions of Christianity.

The reason this synthesis between Roman Christianity and European cultures was so dynamic was that Christianity came in during the settlement phase, when Germanic migrants were in the process of establishing their nascent kingdoms. Christian bishops, churches, and rituals played a key role in the creation of many of the successful kingdoms in these areas. Consequently, it is hard to separate the strands of political and cultural identity from religious affiliations, and difficult to isolate conversion to Christianity from the general social and political forces at work in this period.

Just as Christianity gradually became an integral part of the Roman Empire after the conversion of Constantine, so too the Frankish and Anglo-Saxon kings made the Christian religion part of their rallying cry for unifying their realms, and found the literate clergy excellent advisors, thinkers, and writers in fostering royal administration. On an even wider scale than just the conversion of royalty and the establishment of Christian kingdoms is the general conversion of culture through the gradual influence of the church in society, and vice-versa, the acculturation of Christianity to Germanic cultures. In the same way that Roman Christianity represents a particular cultural adaptation of the religion within the Roman Empire, so also the European churches found ways to accommodate local folklore and tradition within the Christian cosmology, rituals, and literature. In this way, not only were the Germanic peoples Christianized but the Christian religion in Europe was "Germanicized."

The first selection from Irish hermit life (8.1) delineates an early phase of this acculturation process among the Celtic inhabitants of the British Isles during and after the Roman occupation, circa 200–600. The second and third selections explore the creation of "national" identities through conversion in the histories of the Franks (8.2) and the Anglo-Saxons (8.3). The fourth selection examines the eighth-century mission from the dynamic Anglo-Saxon church back to the continent, to the Saxons of northern Germany (8.4). All four selections reveal different aspects of conversion and the acculturation processes that accompany this transformation.

8.1 Celtic Christianity and Hermetic Life:
Saint Columba's Rule

Christianity was introduced to the Celtic peoples of the British Isles in the third through fifth centuries. The conversion stories of this period were (and are) enormously popular—for example, the familiar story of Saint Patrick (circa 389–461), missionary to Ireland. The retreat of the Roman Empire and the subsequent arrival of Anglo-Saxon invaders in the sixth and seventh centuries isolated Celtic Christians from the continental form of Christianity centered in Rome. It is possible, then, to speak of Celtic Christianity as a distinctive set of adaptations of the religion to the culture of Celtic peoples, who maintained their own traditions in Ireland and Wales even after the dominance of the Anglo-Saxons over much of the rest of Britain in the seventh and eighth centuries. Celtic traditions remained an influential force in territories conquered by the Anglo-Saxons, who were eventually converted by Roman missionaries (8.3).

Celtic practice of Christianity is distinctive especially for its emphasis on two aspects of Christianity: monastic asceticism, influenced by the Egyptian monastic tradition (6.1); and a strongly antihierarchical individualism reminiscent of Perpetua (4.1). Both of these elements of Christianity flourished precisely because they resonated with Celtic cultures.

The selection below from the Rule of Saint Columba reflects these ascetic and individualistic ideals as practiced by Irish hermits. Saint Columba or "Columcille" (521–97) fostered ascetic monasticism and scholarship at his monasteries in Ireland and Britain, particularly the famous and influential monastery on the island of Iona. Both travel and living on an island were common metaphors for the spiritual journey through asceticism. His Rule and the brief, anonymous poem on hermetic life given below make use of these metaphors.

Questions

1. In what ways does the Rule of Saint Columba reflect the values of the desert hermits (6.1) and the monastic Rule of Benedict (6.2)?

2. In what ways is Columba's Rule different from hermetic and monastic practice elsewhere?

3. What view do these documents have of being "alone?"

Rule of Saint Columba

Be alone in a separate place near a chief city, if thy conscience is not prepared to be in common with the crowd.

Be always naked in imitation of Christ and the Evangelists.

Whatsoever little or much thou possessest of anything, whether clothing, or food, or drink, let it be at the command of the senior and at his disposal, for it is not befitting a religious to have any distinction of property with his own free brother.

Let a fast place, with one door, enclose thee.

A few religious men to converse with thee of God and his Testament; to visit thee on days of solemnity; to strengthen thee in the Testaments of God, and the narratives of the Scriptures.

A person too who would talk with thee in idle words, or of the world; or who murmurs at what he cannot remedy or prevent, but who would distress thee more should he be a tattler between friends and foes, thou shalt not admit him to thee, but at once give him thy benediction should he deserve it.

Let thy servant be a discreet, religious, not tale-telling man, who is to attend continually on thee, with moderate labour of course, but always ready.

Yield submission to every rule that is of devotion.

A mind prepared for red martyrdom.

A mind fortified and steadfast for white martyrdom.

Forgiveness from the heart to every one.

Constant prayers for those who trouble thee.

Fervor in singing the office for the dead, as if every faithful dead was a particular friend of thine.

Hymns for souls *to be sung* standing.

Let thy vigils be constant from eve to eve, under the direction of another person.

Three labors in the day, viz., prayers, work, and reading.

The work to be divided into three parts, viz., thine own work, and the work of thy place, as regards its real wants; secondly, thy share of the brethren's [work]; lastly, to help the neighbours, viz. by instruction or writing, or sewing garments, or whatever labour they may be in want of, ut Dominus ait, "Non apparebis ante Me vacuus" [as the Lord says, "You shall not come before me empty handed"].

Everything in its proper order; Nemo enim coronabitur nisi qui legitime certaverit [For no one will receive a crown except the one who contends the right way].

Follow alms-giving before all things.

Take not of food till thou art hungry.

Sleep not till thou feelest desire.

Speak not except on business.

Every increase which comes to thee in lawful meals, or in wearing apparel, give it for pity to the brethren that want it, or to the poor in like manner.

The love of God with all thy heart and all thy strength;

The love of thy neighbour as thyself.

Abide in the Testaments of God throughout all times.

Thy measure of prayer shall be until thy tears come;

Or thy measure of work of labor till thy tears come;

Or thy measure of thy work of labor, or of thy genuflexions, until thy perspiration often comes, if thy tears are not free.

The Rule of S. Columba, from *Councils and Ecclesiastical Documents Relating to Great Britain and Ireland,* eds. Arthur West Haddan and William Stubbs (Oxford: Clarendon Press, 1873, 1878; reissued as one vol. 1964), Vol II, Part I, 119–21.

The Hermit

Alone in my little hut without a human being in my company, dear has been the pilgrimage before going to meet death.

A remote hidden little cabin, for forgiveness of my sins; a conscience upright and spotless before holy Heaven. . . .

A cold anxious bed, like the lying-down of the doomed, a brief apprehensive sleep, invocations frequent and early. . . .

Treading the paths of the Gospel, singing psalms every Hour; an end of talking and long stories; constant bending of the knees.

My Creator to visit me, my Lord, my King, my spirit to seek Him in the eternal kingdom where He is. . . .

Alone in my little hut, all alone so, alone I came into the world, alone I shall go from it.

Excerpted from *A Celtic Miscellany: Translations from the Celtic Literatures,* trans. Kenneth Hurlstone Jackson (Harmondsworth, UK: 1971), pp. 281, 282. First published in 1951 by Routledge & Kegan Paul. Copyright © Kenneth Hurlstone Jackson, 1951, 1971. Used by permission of Routledge.

8.2 Frankish Christianity:
Gregory of Tours on Clovis and Clotilda

Conversion linked to stable kingship is a dominant theme in the ecclesiastical and national histories written in the early Middle Ages by such influential writers as Gregory of Tours for the Franks and Bede for the Anglo-Saxons (8.3). Both authors, as influential churchmen, created national identities rooted not just in ethnicity but also in religious principle.

The Franks founded one of the most successful Germanic kingdoms. This kingdom eventually grew into an empire, briefly, under Charlemagne and his successors (9.3, 10.1), and became the basis of modern France. According to the *History of the Franks* by Gregory of Tours (538–93), this success is due in part to divine favor linked to the dominance of Roman Christianity in the region. The linchpin of this national church history is found in the person of the king: when the king converts, then the kingdom is led toward truth and stability. Writing a century after Clovis, Gregory of Tours overtly copies the model of Constantine (2.3) to foster an image of Clovis as a divinely appointed agent to fulfill the Franks' destiny as a Catholic Christian kingdom.

In the case of young Clovis (reigned 480–511), Christian influence came from several directions, but especially from his Christian wife, Clotilda, and from local bishops eager to advise him and steer him away from the Arian Christianity of neighboring kings, such as the Visigothic ruler in Spain, the current Burgundian king, and the powerful Theodoric in Italy. "Arian" churches (named after Arius) did not accept the Trinitarian position adopted at the Council of Nicea (3.3) that formed the basis of the "Catholic" church centered Rome. Arian theology had successfully converted a number of Germanic rulers in the Iberian Peninsula, North Africa, Gaul, and Italy. Local and neighboring Catholic bishops sought to influence Clovis to choose their Roman Christianity as a counterpoint to these Arian rulers. Gregory of Tours goes out of his way to paint the Arians as evil, recounting the tortures of Catholic Christians at the hands of Arian rulers, and to demonstrate that Arian kingdoms were doomed to fail while Catholic ones, such as the Franks under Clovis, were destined by God to rule. Clovis's conversion is thus set in the context of military expansion: his need to dominate the neighboring rulers (coincidentally many of them Arian) and his need for divine aid in battle work together in his conversion to Roman Catholic Christianity. Clovis's aggressiveness as a militaristic, and sometimes ruthless, king may seem at odds with the pacifist elements and otherworldly values of Christianity evident in monasticism, asceticism, and martyrdom. Thus this excerpt from Bishop Gregory of Tours's *History* raises many questions about conversion and the idea of a Christian government.

Questions

1. What factors does Gregory of Tours highlight as influences on Clovis's decision to convert to Roman Christianity? What role do women like Clotilda play in these conversion efforts?

2. What view of Arians does Gregory of Tours display here?

3. Compare Clovis to Constantine (2.3): what are the characteristics of a Christian ruler?

Gregory of Tours, Clovis and Clotilda

27. After these events Childeric died and Clovis his son reigned in his stead. . . . At that time many churches were despoiled by Clovis's army,

since he was as yet involved in heathen error. Now the army had taken from a certain church a vase of wonderful size and beauty, along with the remainder of the utensils for the service of the church. And the bishop of the church sent messengers to the king asking that the vase at least be returned, if he could not get back any more of the sacred dishes. On hearing this the king said to the messenger: "Follow us as far as Soissons, because all that has been taken is to be divided there and when the lot assigns me that dish I will do what the father asks." Then when he came to Soissons and all the booty was set in their midst, the king said: "I ask of you, brave warriors, not to refuse to grant me in addition to my share, yonder dish," that is, he was speaking of the vase just mentioned. In answer to the speech of the king those of more sense replied: "Glorious king, all that we see is yours, and we ourselves are subject to your rule. Now do what seems well-pleasing to you; for no one is able to resist your power." When they said this a foolish, envious and excitable fellow lifted his battle-ax and struck the vase, and cried in a loud voice: "You shall get nothing here except what the lot fairly bestows on you." At this all were stupefied, but the king endured the insult with the gentleness of patience, and taking the vase he handed it over to the messenger of the church, nursing the wound deep in his heart. And at the end of the year he ordered the whole army to come with their equipment of armor, to show the brightness of their arms on the field of March. And when he was reviewing them all carefully, he came to the man who struck the vase, and said to him: "No one has brought armor so carelessly kept as you; for neither your spear nor sword nor ax is in serviceable condition." And seizing his ax he cast it to the earth, and when the other had bent over somewhat to pick it up, the king raised his hands and drove his own ax into the man's head. "This," said he, "is what you did at Soissons to the vase." Upon the death of this man, he ordered the rest to depart, raising great dread of himself by this action. He made many wars and gained many victories. In the tenth year of his reign he made war on the Thuringi and brought them under his dominion.

28. Now the king of the Burgundians was Gundevech, of the family of king Athanaric the persecutor, whom we have mentioned before. He had four sons; Gundobad, Godegisel, Chilperic and Godomar. Gundobad killed his brother Chilperic with the sword, and sank his wife in water with a stone tied to her neck. His two daughters he condemned to exile; the older of these, who became a nun, was called Chrona, and the younger Clotilda. And as Clovis often sent embassies to Burgundy, the maiden Clotilda was found by his envoys. And when they saw that she was of good bearing and wise, and learned that she was of the family of the king, they reported this to King Clovis, and he sent an embassy to Gundobad without delay asking her in

marriage. And Gundobad was afraid to refuse, and surrendered her to the men, and they took the girl and brought her swiftly to the king. The king was very glad when he saw her, and married her, having already by a concubine a son named Theodoric.

29. He had a first-born son by queen Clotilda, and as his wife wished to consecrate him in baptism, she tried unceasingly to persuade her husband, saying: "The gods you worship are nothing, and they will be unable to help themselves or any one else. For they are graven out of stone or wood or some metal. And the names you have given them are names of men and not of gods, as Saturn, who is declared to have fled in fear of being banished from his kingdom by his son; as Jove himself, the foul perpetrator of all shameful crimes, committing incest with men, mocking at his kinswomen, not able to refrain from intercourse with his own sister as she herself says. . . . What could Mars or Mercury do? They are endowed rather with the magic arts than with the power of the divine name. But he ought rather to be worshipped who created by his word heaven and earth, the sea and all that in them is out of a state of nothingness, who made the sun shine, and adorned the heavens with stars, who filled the waters with creeping things, the earth with living things and the air with creatures that fly, at whose nod the earth is decked with growing crops, the trees with fruit, the vines with grapes, by whose hand mankind was created, by whose generosity all that creation serves and helps man whom he created as his own." But though the queen said this the spirit of the king was by no means moved to belief, and he said: "It was at the command of our gods that all things were created and came forth, and it is plain that your God has no power and, what is more, he is proven not to belong to the family of the gods." Meantime the faithful queen made her son ready for baptism; she gave command to adorn the church with hangings and curtains, in order that he who could not be moved by persuasion might be urged to belief by this mystery. The boy, whom they named Ingomer, died after being baptized, still wearing the white garments in which he became regenerate. At this the king was violently angry, and reproached the queen harshly, saying: "If the boy had been dedicated in the name of my gods he would certainly have lived; but as it is, since he was baptized in the name of your God, he could not live at all." To this the queen said: "I give thanks to the omnipotent God, creator of all, who has judged me not wholly unworthy, that he should deign to take to his kingdom one born from my womb. My soul is not stricken with grief for his sake, because I know that, summoned from this world as he was in his baptismal garments, he will be fed by the vision of God."

After this she bore another son, whom she named Chlodomer at baptism; and when he fell sick, the king said: "It is impossible that anything else should happen to him than happened to his brother, namely, that being baptized in the name of your Christ, he should die at once." But through the prayers of his mother, and the Lord's command, he became well.

30. The queen did not cease to urge him to recognize the true God and cease worshiping idols. But he could not be influenced in any way to this belief, until at last a war arose with the Alamanni, in which he was driven by necessity to confess what before he had of his free will denied. It came about that as the two armies were fighting fiercely, there was much slaughter, and Clovis's army began to be in danger of destruction. He saw it and raised his eyes to heaven, and with remorse in his heart he burst into tears and cried: "Jesus Christ, whom Clotilda asserts to be the son of the living God, who art said to give aid to those in distress, and to bestow victory on those who hope in thee, I beseech the glory of thy aid, with the vow that if thou wilt grant me victory over these enemies, and I shall know that power which she says that people dedicated in thy name have had from thee, I will believe in thee and be baptized in thy name. For I have invoked my own gods, but, as I find, they have withdrawn from aiding me; and therefore I believe that they possess no power, since they do not help those who obey them. I now call upon thee, I desire to believe thee, only let me be rescued from my adversaries." And when he said this, the Alamanni turned their backs, and began to disperse in flight. And when they saw that their king was killed, they submitted to the dominion of Clovis, saying: "Let not the people perish further, we pray; we are yours now." And he stopped the fighting, and after encouraging his men, retired in peace and told the queen how he had had merit to win the victory by calling on the name of Christ. This happened in the fifteenth year of his reign.

31. Then the queen asked saint Remi, bishop of Rheims, to summon Clovis secretly, urging him to introduce the king to the word of salvation. And the bishop sent for him secretly and began to urge him to believe in the true God, maker of heaven and earth, and to cease worshiping idols, which could help neither themselves nor any one else. But the king said: "I gladly hear you, most holy father; but there remains one thing: the people who follow me cannot endure to abandon their gods; but I shall go and speak to them according to your words." He met with his followers, but before he could speak the power of God anticipated him, and all the people cried out together: "O pious king, we reject our mortal gods, and we are ready to follow the immortal God whom Remi preaches." This was reported to the bishop, who was greatly rejoiced, and bade them get ready the baptismal font. The squares were shaded with tapestried canopies, the churches adorned with white curtains, the baptistery set in order, the aroma of incense spread, candles of fragrant odor burned brightly, and the whole shrine

of the baptistery was filled with a divine fragrance: and the Lord gave such grace to those who stood by that they thought they were placed amid the odors of paradise. And the king was the first to ask to be baptized by the bishop. Another Constantine advanced to the baptismal font, to terminate the disease of ancient leprosy and wash away with fresh water the foul spots that had long been borne. And when he entered to be baptized, the saint of God began with ready speech: "Gently bend your neck, Sigamber; worship what you burned; burn what you worshipped." . . . And so the king confessed all-powerful God in the Trinity, and was baptized in the name of the Father, Son and holy Spirit, and was anointed with the holy ointment with the sign of the cross of Christ. And of his army more than 3000 were baptized. His sister also, Albofled, was baptized, who not long after passed to the Lord. . . . Another sister also was converted, Lanthechild by name, who had fallen into the heresy of the Arians, and she confessed that the Son and the holy Spirit were equal to the Father, and was anointed. . . .

37. Now Clovis the king said to his people: "I take it very hard that these Arians hold part of the Gauls. Let us go with God's help and conquer them and bring the land under our control." Since these words pleased all, he set his army in motion and made for Poitiers where Alaric was at that time. But since part of the host was passing through Touraine, he issued an edict out of respect to the blessed Martin that no one should take anything from that country except grass for fodder, and water. But one from the army found a poor man's hay and said: "Did not the king order grass only to be taken, nothing else? And this," said he, "is grass. We shall not be transgressing his command if we take it." And when he had done violence to the poor man and taken his hay by force, the deed came to the king. And quicker than speech the offender was slain by the sword, and the king said: "And where shall our hope of victory be if we offend the blessed Martin? It would be better for the army to take nothing else from this country." . . .

38. Clovis received an appointment to the consulship from the emperor Anastasius, and in the church of the blessed Martin he clad himself in the purple tunic and chlamys, and placed a diadem on his head. Then he mounted his horse, and in the most generous manner he gave gold and silver as he passed along the way which is between the gate of the entrance [of the church of Saint Martin] and the church of the city, scattering it among the people who were there with his own hand, and from that day he was called *consul* or *Augustus*. Leaving Tours he went to Paris and there he established the seat of his kingdom.

From Gregory of Tours, *History of the Franks,* trans. Ernest Brehaut (New York: Columbia, 1916), pp. 36–41, 47–8 passim.

8.3 Anglo-Saxon Christianity:
Bede on Edwin and Ethelberga

The Venerable Bede was an eighth-century monk and prolific author in Northumbria, England. From his vantage point in the northern monasteries of Wearmouth and Jarrow, with access to books and contemporary sources, he wrote an *Ecclesiastical History of the English People* that helped shape the idea of a shared historical identity for "English" people. Like Gregory of Tours for the Franks, Bede created a Christian identity for his people, the Anglo-Saxons who had settled in Britain. Ironically, these so-called Anglo-Saxons—sixth-century migrants and invaders who pushed out the local Celts—were actually a mixture of different Germanic groups only gradually coalescing into distinct kingdoms linked by a common set of interests. What Bede recounts in his story is the conversion of the roughly eight newly formed Anglo-Saxon kingdoms of England in the sixth through eighth centuries, and their rise and fall in fortunes, which he links to their faithfulness to Christianity.

Bede (673–735) begins his history with a description of the British Isles, the Roman occupation, and the earliest Christian inhabitants and saints, but quickly moves to the great Roman mission sent in 596 by Pope Gregory I (author of the famous *Dialogues* and life of St. Benedict, 6.2). The pope commissioned a group of monks, led by Augustine of Canterbury (not Hippo), to approach the pagan Anglo-Saxon kings of England, who were already developing ties through marriage to continental Christian dynasties. In Bede's history, the successful conversion of these key rulers was the foundation of strong kingdoms. The pope continued to advise the missionaries on the best strategies, as indicated in the first excerpt below, a letter from Pope Gregory to one of the bishops and in letters the pope wrote to kings and queens in England.

The main story excerpted here from Bede is of one of those royal conversions, that of the king of Northumbria, Edwin (reigned 616–33). As with the Frankish King Clovis, many factors influenced Edwin's decision to convert, and the decision had far-reaching consequences for his kingdom and its governance. In the account, the pope addresses Ethelburga, Edwin's Christian wife, whose marriage, like Clothilde's to King Clovis, was part of a strategy to solidify alliances and a means of introducing the new religion.

Questions

1. According to Bede, what convinces Edwin to convert to Christianity, and why? What role does Ethelburga play in his conversion?

2. From his various letters, what do you gather is Pope Gregory's approach to converting these Anglo-Saxon peoples?

3. Compare Bede and Gregory of Tours's views of Edwin and Clovis as Christian kings: in what ways are their conversions similar as well as different?

Bede, Edwin and Ethelburga

I:30 The Letter of Pope Gregory to Bishop Mellitus

. . . . . .

"To his most beloved son, the Abbot Mellitus; Gregory, the servant of the servants of God. We have been much concerned, since the departure of our congregation that is with you, because we have received no account of the success of your journey. When, therefore, Almighty God shall bring you to the most reverend Bishop Augustine, our brother, tell him what I have, upon mature deliberation on the affair of the English, determined upon, viz., that the temples of the idols in that nation ought not to be destroyed; but let the idols that are in them be destroyed; let holy water be made and sprinkled in the said temples, let altars be erected, and relics placed. For if those temples are well built, it is requisite that they be converted from the worship of devils to the service of the true God; that the nation, seeing that their temples are not destroyed, may remove error from their hearts, and knowing and adoring the true God, may the more familiarly resort to the places to which they have been accustomed. And because they have been used to slaughter many oxen in the sacrifices to devils, some solemnity must be exchanged for them on this account, as that on the day of the dedication, or the nativities of the holy martyrs, whose relics are there deposited, they may build themselves huts of the boughs of trees, about those churches which have been turned to that use from temples, and celebrate the solemnity with religious feasting, and no more offer beasts to the Devil, but kill cattle to the praise of God in their eating, and return thanks to the Giver of all things for their sustenance; to the end that, whilst some gratifications are outwardly permitted them, they may the more easily consent to the inward consolations of the grace of God. For there is no doubt that it is impossible to efface every thing at once from their obdurate minds; because he who endeavours to ascend to the highest place, rises by degrees or steps, and not by leaps. Thus the Lord made Himself known to the people of Israel in Egypt; and yet He allowed them the use of the sacrifices which they were wont to offer to the Devil, in his own worship; so as to command them in his sacrifice to kill beasts, to the end that, changing their hearts, they might lay aside one part of the sacrifice, whilst they retained another; that whilst they offered the same beasts which they were wont to offer, they should offer them to God, and not to idols; and thus they would no longer be the same sacrifices. This it behoves your affection to communicate to our aforesaid brother, that he, being there present, may consider how he is to order all things. God preserve you in safety, most beloved son.

"Given the 17th of June, in the nineteenth year of the reign of our lord, the most pious emperor, Mauritius Tiberius, the eighteenth year after the consulship of our said lord. The fourth indiction."

II:9

. . . . . .

At this time the nation of the Northumbrians, that is, the nation of the Angles that live on the north side of the river Humber, with their king, Edwin, received the faith through the preaching of Paulinus, above mentioned. This Edwin, as a reward of his receiving the faith, and as an earnest of his share in the heavenly kingdom, received an increase of that which he enjoyed on earth, for he reduced under his dominion all the borders of Britain that were provinces either of the aforesaid nation, or of the Britons, a thing which no British king had ever done before; and he in like manner subjected to the English the Mevanian islands, as has been said above. The first whereof, which is to the southward, is the largest in extent, and most fruitful, containing nine hundred and sixty families, according to the English computation; the other above three hundred.

The occasion of this nation's embracing the faith was, their aforesaid king, being allied to the kings of Kent, having taken to wife Ethelberga, otherwise called Tate, daughter to King Ethelbert. He having by his ambassadors asked her in marriage of her brother Eadbald, who then reigned in Kent, was answered, "That it was not lawful to marry a Christian virgin to a pagan husband, lest the faith and the mysteries of the heavenly King should be profaned by her cohabiting with a king that was altogether a stranger to the worship of the true God." This answer being brought to Edwin by his messengers, he promised in no manner to act in opposition to the Christian faith, which the virgin professed; but would give leave to her, and all that went with her, men or women, priests or ministers, to follow their faith and worship after the custom of the Christians. Nor did he deny, but that he would embrace the same religion, if, being examined by wise persons, it should be found more holy and more worthy of God.

Hereupon the virgin was promised, and sent to Edwin, and pursuant to what had been agreed on, Paulinus, a man beloved of God, was ordained bishop, to go with her, and by daily exhortations, and celebrating the heavenly mysteries, to confirm her and her company, lest they should be corrupted by the company of the pagans. Paulinus was ordained bishop by the Archbishop Justus, on the 21st day of July, in the year of our Lord 625, and so he came to King Edwin with the aforesaid virgin as a companion of their union in the flesh. But his mind was wholly bent upon reducing the nation to which he was sent to the knowledge of truth; according to the words of the apostle, "To espouse her to one husband, that he might present her as a chaste virgin to Christ." Being come into that province, he laboured much, not only to retain those that went with him, by the help of God, that they should not revolt from the faith, but, if he could, to convert some of the pagans to a state of grace by his preaching. But, as the apostle says, though he laboured long in the word, "The god of this world blinded the minds of them that believed not, lest the light of the glorious Gospel of Christ should shine unto them." . . .

On that same holy night of Easter Sunday, the queen had brought forth to the king a daughter, called Eanfled. The king, in the presence of Bishop Paulinus, gave thanks to his gods for the birth of his daughter; and the bishop, on the other hand, returned thanks to Christ, and endeavoured to persuade the king, that by his prayers to Him he had obtained that the queen should bring forth the child in safety, and without much pain. The king, delighted with his words, promised, that in case God would grant him life and victory over the king by whom the assassin had been sent, he would cast off his idols, and serve Christ; and as a pledge that he would perform his promise, he delivered up that same daughter to Paulinus, to be consecrated to Christ. She was the first baptized of the nation of the Northumbrians, on Whitsunday, with twelve others of her family. . . . Returning thus victorious unto his own country, he would not immediately and unadvisedly embrace the mysteries of the Christian faith, though he no longer worshipped idols, ever since he made the promise that he would serve Christ; but thought fit first at leisure to be instructed, by the venerable Paulinus, in the knowledge of faith, and to confer with such as he knew to be the wisest of his prime men, to advise what they thought was fittest to be done in that case. And being a man of extraordinary sagacity, he often sat alone by himself a long time, silent as to his tongue, but deliberating in his heart how he should proceed, and which religion he should adhere to.

II: 10

. . . . . .

At this time he received letters from Pope Boniface IV exhorting him to embrace the faith, which were as follows—

Copy of the letter of the Holy and Apostolic Pope of the Church of Rome, Boniface, to the glorious Edwin, King of the English.

"*To the illustrious Edwin, king of the English, Bishop Boniface, the servant of the servants of God.* Although the power of the Supreme Deity cannot be expressed by human speech, as consisting in its own greatness, and in invisible and unsearchable eternity, so that no sharpness of wit can comprehend or express it; yet in regard that the goodness of God, to give some notion of itself, having opened the doors of the heart, has mercifully, by secret inspiration, infused into the minds of men such things as He is willing shall be declared concerning Himself, we have thought fit to extend our priestly care to make known to you the fulness of the Christian faith; to the end that, informing you of the Gospel of Christ, which our Saviour commanded should be preached to all nations, they might offer to you the cup of life and salvation.

"Thus the goodness of the Supreme Majesty, which, by the word of his command, made and created all things, the heaven, the earth, the sea, and all that is in them, disposing the order by which they should subsist, hath, with the counsel of his co-eternal Word, and the unity of the Holy Spirit, formed man after his own likeness, out of the slime of the earth; and granted him such super-eminent prerogative, as to place him above all others; so that, observing the command which was given him, his continuance should be to eternity. This God, Father, Son, and Holy Ghost, which is an undivided Trinity, mankind, from the east unto the west, by confession of faith to the saving of their souls, do worship and adore, as the Creator of all things, and their own Maker; to whom also the heights of empire, and the powers of the world, are subject, because the bestowal of all kingdoms is granted by his disposition. It hath pleased Him, therefore, of his great mercy, and for the greater benefit of all his creatures, by his Holy Spirit wonderfully to kindle the cold hearts also of the nations seated at the extremities of the earth in the knowledge of Himself.

"For we suppose your excellency has, from the country lying so near, fully understood what the clemency of our Redeemer has effected in the enlightening of our glorious son, King Eadbald, and the nations under his subjection; we therefore trust, with assured confidence of celestial hope, that his wonderful gift will be also conferred on you; since we understand that your illustrious consort, which is known to be a part of your body, is illuminated with the reward of eternity, through the regeneration of holy baptism. We have, therefore, taken care by these presents, with all possible affection, to exhort your illustrious selves, that, abhorring idols and their worship, and contemning the follies of temples, and the deceitful flatteries of auguries, you believe in God the Father Almighty, and his Son Jesus Christ, and the Holy Ghost, to the end that, being discharged from the bonds of captivity to the Devil, by believing you may, through the co-operating power of the holy and undivided Trinity, be partaker of the eternal life.

"How great guilt they lie under, who adhere to the pernicious superstitions and worship of idolatry, appears by the examples of the perdition of those whom they worship. Wherefore it is said of them by the Psalmist, 'All the gods of the Gentiles are devils, but the Lord made the heavens.' And again, 'they have eyes and do not see, they have ears and do not hear, they have noses and do not smell, they have hands and do not feel, they have feet and do not walk. Therefore they are like those that confide in them.' For how can they have any power to yield assistance, that are made for you out of corruptible matter, by the hands of your inferiors and subjects, to wit, on whom you have by human art bestowed an inanimate similitude of members? Who, unless they be moved by you, will not be able to walk; but, like a stone fixed in one place, being so formed, and having no understanding, but absorbed in insensibility, have no power of doing harm or good. We cannot, therefore, upon mature deliberation, find out how you come to be so deceived as to follow and worship those gods, to whom you yourselves have given the likeness of a body.

"It behooves you, therefore, by taking upon you the sign of the holy cross, by which the human race is redeemed, to root out of your hearts all those arts and cunning of the Devil, who is ever jealous of the works of the Divine goodness, and to lay hold and break in pieces those which you have hitherto made your material gods. For the very destruction and abolition of these, which could never receive life or sense from their makers, may plainly demonstrate to you how worthless they were which you till then had worshipped, when you yourselves, who have received life from the Lord, are certainly better than they, as Almighty God has appointed you to be descended, after many ages and through many generations, from the first man whom He formed. Draw near, then, to the knowledge of Him who created you, who breathed the breath of life into you, who sent his only-begotten Son for your redemption, to cleanse you from original sin, that being delivered from the power of the Devil's wickedness, He might bestow on you a heavenly reward.

"Hear the words of the preachers, and the Gospel of God, which they declare to you, to the end that, believing, as has been said, in God the Father Almighty, and in Jesus Christ his Son, and the Holy Ghost, and the indivisible Trinity, having put to flight the sensualities of devils, and driven from you the suggestions of the venomous and deceitful enemy, and being born again by water and the Holy Ghost, you may, through his assistance and bounty, dwell in the brightness of eternal glory with Him in whom you shall believe. We have, moreover, sent you the blessing of your protector, the blessed Peter, prince of the apostles, that is, a shirt, with one gold ornament, and one garment of Ancyra, which we pray your highness to accept with the same goodwill as it is friendly intended by us."

II:11

. . . . . .

The same pope also wrote to King Edwin's consort, Ethelberga, to this effect—

The copy of the letter of the most blessed and apostolic Boniface, Pope of the city of Rome, to Ethelberga, King Edwin's queen.

"*To the illustrious lady his daughter, Queen Ethelberga, Boniface, bishop, servant of the servants of God:* The goodness of our Redeemer has with much providence offered the means of salvation to the human race, which He rescued, by the shedding of his precious blood, from the bonds of captivity to the Devil; so that making his name known in divers ways to the Gentiles, they might acknowledge their Creator by embracing the mystery of the Christian faith, which thing, the mystical purification of your regeneration plainly shows to have been bestowed upon the mind of your highness by God's bounty. Our mind, therefore, has been much rejoiced in the benefit of our Lord's goodness, for that He has vouchsafed, in your conversion, to kindle a spark of the orthodox religion, by which He might the more easily inflame in his love the understanding, not only of your glorious consort, but also of all the nation that is subject to you.

"For we have been informed by those, who came to acquaint us with the laudable conversion of our illustrious son, King Eadbald, that your highness, also, having received the wonderful sacrament of the Christian faith, continually excels in the performance of works pious and acceptable to God. That you likewise carefully refrain from the worship of idols, and the deceits of temples and auguries, and having changed your devotion, are so wholly taken up with the love of your Redeemer, as never to cease lending your assistance for the propagation of the Christian faith. And our fatherly charity having earnestly inquired concerning your illustrious husband, we were given to understand that he still served abominable idols, and would not yield obedience or give ear to the voice of the preachers. This occasioned us no small grief, for that part of your body still remained a stranger to the knowledge of the supreme and undivided Trinity. Whereupon we, in our fatherly care, did not delay to admonish your Christian highness, exhorting you, that, with the help of the Divine inspiration, you will not defer to do that which, both in season and out of season, is required of us; that with the co-operating power of our Lord and Saviour Jesus Christ, your husband also may be added to the number of Christians; to the end that you may thereby enjoy the rights of marriage in the bond of a holy and unblemished union. For it is written, 'They two shall be in one flesh.' How can it be said, that there is unity between you, if he continues a stranger to the brightness of your faith, by the interposition of dark and detestable error?

"Wherefore, applying yourself continually to prayer, do not cease to beg of the Divine Mercy the benefit of his illumination: to the end, that those whom the union of carnal affection has made in a manner but one body, may, after death, continue in perpetual union, by the bond of faith. Persist, therefore, illustrious daughter, and to the utmost of your power endeavour to soften the hardness of his heart by insinuating the Divine precepts; making him sensible how noble the mystery is which you have received by believing, and how wonderful is the reward which, by the new birth, you have merited to obtain. Inflame the coldness of his heart by the knowledge of the Holy Ghost, that by the abolition of the cold and pernicious worship of paganism, the heat of Divine faith may enlighten his understanding through your frequent exhortations; that the testimony of the holy Scripture may appear the more conspicuous, fulfilled by you, 'The unbelieving husband shall be saved by the believing wife.' For to this effect you have obtained the mercy of our Lord's goodness, that you may return with increase the fruit of faith, and the benefits entrusted in your hands; for through the assistance of his mercy we do not cease with frequent prayers to beg that you may be able to perform the same.

"Having premised thus much, in pursuance of the duty of our fatherly affection, we exhort you, that when the opportunity of a bearer shall offer, you will as soon as possible acquaint us with the success which the Divine Power shall grant by your means in the conversion of your consort, and of the nation subject to you; to the end, that our solicitude, which earnestly expects what appertains to the salvation of you and yours, may, by hearing from you, be set at rest; and that we, discerning more fully the brightness of the Divine propitiation diffused in you, may with a joyful confession abundantly return due thanks to God, the Giver of all good things, and to St. Peter, the prince of apostles. We have, moreover, sent you the blessing of your protector, St. Peter, the prince of the apostles, that is, a silver looking-glass, and a gilt ivory comb, which we entreat your glory will receive with the same kind affection as it is known to be sent by us."

II:12

. . . . . .

Thus the aforesaid Pope Boniface wrote for the salvation of King Edwin and his nation. But a heavenly vision, which the Divine Mercy was pleased once to reveal to this king, when he was in banishment at the court of Redwald, king of the Angles, was of no little use in urging him to embrace and understand the doctrines of salvation. Paulinus, therefore, perceiving that it was a very difficult task to incline the king's lofty mind to the humility of the way of salvation, and to embrace the mystery of the cross of life, and at the same time using both exhortation with men, and prayer to God, for his and his subjects' salvation; at length, as we may suppose, it was shown him in spirit what was the vision that had been formerly revealed to the king. Nor did he lose any time, but immediately admonished the king to perform the vow which he made, when he received the oracle, promising to put the same in execution, if he was delivered from the trouble he was at that time under, and should be advanced to the throne.

The vision was this . . . the person [in the vision] that talked to him laid his hand on his head saying, "When this sign shall be given you, remember this present discourse that has passed between us, and do not delay the performance of what you now promise." Having uttered these words, he is said to have immediately vanished, that the king might understand it was not a man, but a spirit, that had appeared to him. . . .

King Edwin, therefore, delaying to receive the word of God at the preaching of Paulinus, and using for some time, as has been said, to sit several hours alone, and seriously to ponder with himself what he was to do, and what religion he was to follow, the man of God came to him, laid his right hand on his head, and asked, "Whether he knew that sign?" The king in a trembling condition, was ready to fall down at his feet, but he raised him up, and in a familiar manner said to him, "Behold, by the help of God you have escaped the hands of the enemies whom you feared. Behold you have of his gift obtained the kingdom which you desired. Take heed not to delay that which you promised to perform; embrace the faith, and keep the precepts of Him who, delivering you from temporal adversity, has raised you to the honour of a temporal kingdom; and if, from this time forward, you shall be obedient to his will, which through me He signifies to you, He will not only deliver you from the everlasting torments of the wicked, but also make you partaker with Him of his eternal kingdom in heaven."

II:13

. . . . . .

The king, hearing these words, answered, that he was both willing and bound to receive the faith which he taught; but that he would confer about it with his principal friends and counsellors, to the end that if they also were of his opinion, they might all together be cleansed in Christ the Fountain of Life. Paulinus consenting, the king did as he said; for, holding a council with the wise men, he asked of every one in particular what he thought of the new doctrine, and the new worship that was preached? To which the chief of his own priests, Coifi, immediately answered, "O king, consider what this is which is now preached to us; for I verily declare to you, that the religion which we have hitherto professed has, as far as I can learn, no virtue in it. For none of your people has applied himself more diligently to the worship of our gods than I; and yet there are many who receive greater favours from you, and are more preferred than I, and are more prosperous in all their undertakings. Now if the gods were good for any thing, they would rather forward me, who have been more careful to serve them. It remains, therefore, that if upon examination you find those new doctrines, which are now preached to us, better and more efficacious, we immediately receive them without any delay."

Another of the king's chief men, approving of his words and exhortations, presently added: "The present life of man, O king, seems to me, in comparison of that time which is unknown to us, like to the swift flight of a sparrow through the room wherein you sit at supper in winter, with your commanders and ministers, and a good fire in the midst, whilst the storms of rain and snow prevail abroad; the sparrow, I say, flying in at one door, and immediately out at another, whilst he is within, is safe from the wintry storm; but after a short space of fair weather, he immediately vanishes out of your sight, into the dark winter from which he had emerged. So this life of man appears for a short space, but of what went before, or what is to follow, we are utterly ignorant. If, therefore, this new doctrine contains something more certain, it seems justly to deserve to be followed." The other elders and king's counsellors, by Divine inspiration, spoke to the same effect.

But Coifi added, that he wished more attentively to hear Paulinus discourse concerning the God whom he preached; which he having by the king's command performed, Coifi, hearing his words, cried out, "I have long since been sensible that there was nothing in that which we worshipped; because the more diligently I sought after truth in that worship, the less I found it. But now I freely confess, that such truth evidently appears in this preaching as can confer on us the gifts of life, of salvation, and of eternal happiness. For which reason I advise, O king, that we instantly abjure and set fire to those temples and altars which we have consecrated without reaping any benefit from them." In short, the king publicly gave his licence to Paulinus to preach the Gospel, and renouncing idolatry, declared that he received the faith of Christ: and when he inquired of the high priest who should first profane the altars and temples of their idols, with the enclosures that were about them, he answered, "I; for who can more properly than myself destroy those things which I worshipped through ignorance, for an example to all others, through the wisdom which has been given me by the true God?" Then immediately, in contempt of his former superstitions, he desired the king to furnish him with arms and a stallion; and mounting the same, he set out to destroy the idols; for it was not lawful before for the high priest either to carry arms, or to ride on any but a mare. Having, therefore, girt a sword about him, with a spear in his hand, he mounted the king's stallion and proceeded to the idols. The multitude, beholding it, concluded he was distracted; but he lost no time, for as soon as he drew near the temple he profaned the same, casting into it the spear which he held; and rejoicing in the knowledge of the worship of the true God, he commanded his companions to destroy the temple, with all its enclosures, by fire. This place where the idols were is still shown, not far from York, to the eastward, beyond the river Derwent, and is now called Godmundingham, where the high priest, by the inspiration of the true God, profaned and destroyed the altars which he had himself consecrated.

II:14

. . . . . .

King Edwin, therefore, with all the nobility of the nation, and a large number of the common sort, received the faith, and the washing of regeneration, in the eleventh year of his reign, which is the year of the incarnation of our Lord 627, and about one hundred and eighty after the coming of the English into Britain. He was baptized at York, on the holy day of Easter, being the 12th of April, in the church of St. Peter the Apostle, which he himself had built of timber, whilst he was catechising and instructing in order to receive baptism. In that city also he appointed the see of the bishopric of his instructor and bishop, Paulinus. But as soon as he was baptized, he took care by the direction of the same Paulinus, to build in the same place a larger and nobler church of stone, in the midst whereof that same oratory which he had first erected should be enclosed. Having therefore laid the foundation, he began to build the church square, encompassing the former oratory. . . .

Reprinted with permission from *Bede's Ecclesiastical History of the English Nation*, trans. J. Stevens (1723), rev. 1847 J. A. Giles (London: J.M. Dent, 1910; reprint 1963), pp. 52–53; 79–93 passim.

8.4 Saxon Missions: Boniface and Leoba

Northumbria, as evidenced by the conversion of Edwin and the writings of Bede above, produced a dynamic Christian culture in the late eighth century. Before its glorious monasteries, Jarrow, Lindisfarne, and Wearmouth, were destroyed by Viking invasions in the ninth century, they sent out their own missionaries, back to the continent to convert Saxon tribes in northern Germany. These missions were not spectacularly successful in terms of converting numbers of Saxons, who were a highly resistant group eventually convinced only by the strong military arm of Charlemagne.

But the activities of the most famous, and fiery missionary, Boniface (d. 754), and the foundation of monasteries by his colleague Leoba, left an indelible mark. Stories of Boniface's heroic attempts to convert the "cruel pagans" were handed down for generations, and set precedents for conversion techniques. Working together with the pope and the Franks, Boniface established bishoprics throughout Germany, assisted in the reform of the Frankish church, and supported the new Carolingian dynasty by crowning Pepin the Short as king. Boniface was also supported by a number of English disciples and benefactors, particularly religious women. Some of these women, abbesses and nuns, supplied him with books and altar cloths and received advice from him in the administration of their monasteries. His colleague Leoba (circa 700–79), a nun at Wimborne in Dorset, England, joined Boniface in Germany as abbess of Tauberbischofsheim. This monastery, along with the Fulda monastery founded by Boniface, became centers for demonstrating the Christian values embodied in the monastic lifestyle to a population of rough-and-tumble Saxons.

The ideals and activities of these two missionaries, Boniface and Leoba, are known through biographies and letters. The following excerpts are from (1) a letter Boniface's mentor, Bishop Daniel of Winchester (in England), wrote to him in 723 or 724, advising him on conversion techniques; (2) the *Life of Boniface* by Willibald, one of Boniface's English pupils, written between 754 and 768; and (3) the *Life of Leoba* by Rudolph of Fulda, a German monk, written circa 835.

Questions

1. How does Bishop Daniel's advice on converting pagans compare to Boniface's approach to converting the Hessians?

2. What role do religious women such as Leoba play in this missionary effort?

3. Compare these missionary strategies to the English and Frankish efforts in the two previous sections (8.2 and 8.3): in what different ways can conversion be accomplished?

Letter of Bishop Daniel of Winchester to Boniface (723–724)

To Boniface, honoured and beloved leader, Daniel, servant of the people of God.

Great is my joy, brother and colleague in the episcopate, that your good work has received its reward. Supported by your deep faith and great courage, you have embarked upon the conversion of heathens whose hearts have hitherto been stony and barren; and with the Gospel as your ploughshare you have laboured tirelessly day after day to transform them into harvest-bearing fields. Well may the words of the prophet be applied to you: "A voice of one crying in the wilderness, etc."

Yet not less deserving of reward are they who give what help they can to such a good and deserving work by relieving the poverty of the labourers, so that they may pursue unhampered the task of preaching and begetting children to Christ. And so, moved by affection and good will, I am taking the liberty of making a few suggestions, in order to show you how, in my opinion, you may overcome with the least possible trouble the resistance of this barbarous people.

Do not begin by arguing with them about the genealogies of their false gods. Accept their statement that they were begotten by other gods through the intercourse of male and female and then you will be able to prove that, as these gods and goddesses did not exist before, and were born like men, they must be men and not gods. When they have been forced to admit that their gods had a beginning, since they were begotten by others, they should be asked whether the world had a beginning or was always in existence. There is no doubt that before the universe was created there was no place in which these created gods could have subsisted or dwelt. And by "universe" I mean not merely heaven and earth which we see with our eyes but the whole extent of space which even the heathens can grasp in their imagination. If they maintain that the universe had no beginning, try to refute their arguments and bring forward convincing proofs; and if they persist in arguing, ask them, Who ruled it? How did the gods bring under their sway a universe that existed before them? Whence or by whom or when was the first god or goddess begotten? Do they believe that gods and goddesses still beget other gods and goddesses? If they do not, when did they cease and why? If they do, the number of gods must be infinite. In such a case, who is the most powerful among these different gods? Surely no mortal man can know. Yet man must take care not to offend this god who is more powerful than the rest. Do they think the gods should be worshipped for the sake of temporal and transitory benefits or for eternal and future reward? If for temporal benefit let them say in what respect the heathens are better off than the Christians. What do the heathen gods gain from the sacrifices if they already possess everything? Or why do the gods leave it to the whim of their subjects to decide what kind of tribute shall be paid? If they need such sacrifices, why do they not choose more suitable ones? If they do not need them, then the people are wrong in thinking that they can placate the gods with such offerings and victims.

These and similar questions, and many others that it would be tedious to mention, should be put to them, not in an offensive and irritating way but calmly and with great moderation. From time to time their superstitions should be compared with our Christian dogmas and touched upon indirectly, so that the heathens, more out of confusion than exasperation, may be ashamed of their absurd opinions and may recognize that their disgusting rites and legends have not escaped our notice.

This conclusion also must be drawn: If the gods are omnipotent, beneficent and just, they must reward their devotees and punish those who despise them. Why then, if they act thus in temporal affairs, do they spare the Christians who cast down their idols and turn away from their worship the inhabitants of practically the entire globe? And whilst the Christians are allowed to possess the countries that are rich in oil and wine and other commodities, why have they left to the heathens the frozen lands of the north, where the gods, banished from the rest of the world, are falsely supposed to dwell?

The heathens are frequently to be reminded of the supremacy of the Christian world and of the fact that they who still cling to outworn beliefs are in a very small minority.

If they boast that the gods have held undisputed sway over these people from the beginning, point out to them that formerly the whole world was given over to the worship of idols until, by the grace of Christ and through the knowledge of one God, its Almighty Creator and Ruler, it was enlightened, vivified and reconciled to God. For what does the baptizing of the children of Christian parents signify if not the purification of each one from the uncleanness of the guilt of heathenism in which the entire human race was involved?

It has given me great pleasure, brother, for the love I bear you, to bring these matters to your notice. Afflicted though I am with bodily infirmities, I may well say with the psalmist: "I know, O Lord, that thy judgment is just and that in truth thou hast afflicted me." For this reason, I earnestly entreat Your Reverence and those with you who serve Christ in the spirit to pray for me that the Lord who made me taste of the wine of compunction may quickly aid me unto mercy, that as He has punished me justly, so He may graciously pardon and mercifully enable me to sing in gratitude the words of the prophet: "According to the number of my sorrows, thy consolations have comforted my soul."

I pray for your welfare in Christ, my very dear colleague, and beg you to remember me.

Willibald, Life of St. Boniface (Chapter 6)

Now many of the Hessians who at that time had acknowledged the Catholic faith were confirmed by the grace of the Holy Spirit and received the laying-on of hands. But others, not yet strong in the spirit, refused to accept the pure teachings of the Church in their entirety. Moreover, some continued secretly, others openly, to offer sacrifices to trees and springs, to inspect the entrails of victims; some practised divination, legerdemain [sleight-of-hand] and incantations; some turned their attention to auguries, auspices and other sacrificial rites; whilst others, of a more reasonable character, forsook all the profane practices of heathenism and committed none of these crimes. With the counsel and advice of the latter persons, Boniface in their presence attempted to cut down, at a place called Gaesmere, . . . a certain oak of extraordinary size called by the pagans of olden times the Oak of Jupiter. Taking his courage in his hands (for a great crowd of pagans stood by watching and bitterly cursing in their hearts the enemy of the gods), he cut the first notch. But when he had made a superficial cut, suddenly the oak's vast bulk, shaken by a mighty blast of wind from above, crashed to the ground shivering its topmost branches into fragments in its fall. As if by the express will of God (for the brethren present had done nothing to cause it) the oak burst asunder into four parts, each part having a trunk of equal length. At the sight of this extraordinary spectacle the heathens who had been cursing ceased to revile and began, on the contrary, to believe and bless the Lord. Thereupon the holy bishop took counsel with the brethren, built an oratory from the timber of the oak and dedicated it to St. Peter the Apostle. He then set out on a journey to Thuringia, having accomplished by the help of God all the things we have already mentioned. Arrived there, he addressed the elders and the chiefs of the people, calling on them to put aside their blind ignorance and to return to the Christian religion which they had formerly embraced. . . .

Rudolf of Fulda, Life of St. Leoba

At the time when the blessed virgin Leoba was pursuing her quest for perfection in the monastery the holy martyr Boniface was being ordained by Gregory, Bishop of Rome and successor to Constantine, in the Apostolic

See. His mission was to preach the Word of God to the people in Germany. When Boniface found that the people were ready to receive the faith and that, though the harvest was great, the labourers who worked with him were few, he sent messengers and letters to England, his native land, summoning from different ranks of the clergy many who were learned in the divine law and fitted both by their character and good works to preach the Word of God. With their assistance he zealously carried out the mission with which he was charged, and by sound doctrine and miracles converted a large part of Germany to the faith. As the days went by, multitudes of people were instructed in the mysteries of the faith and the Gospel was preached not only in the churches but also in the towns and villages. Thus the Catholics were strengthened in their belief by constant exhortation, the wicked submitted to correction, and the heathen, enlightened by the Gospel, flocked to receive the grace of Baptism. When the blessed man saw that the Church of God was increasing and that the desire of perfection was firmly rooted he established two means by which religious progress should be ensured. He began to build monasteries, so that the people would be attracted to the church not only by the beauty of its religion but also by the communities of monks and nuns. And as he wished the observance in both cases to be kept according to the Holy Rule, he endeavoured to obtain suitable superiors for both houses. For this purpose he sent his disciple Sturm, a man of noble family and sterling character, to Monte Cassino, so that he could study the regular discipline, the observance and the monastic customs which had been established there by St. Benedict. As the future superior, he wished him to become a novice and in this way learn in humble submission how to rule over others. Likewise, he sent messengers with letters to the abbess Tetta, of whom we have already spoken, asking her to send Leoba to accompany him on this journey and to take part in this embassy: for Leoba's reputation for learning and holiness had spread far and wide and her praise was on everyone's lips. The abbess Tetta was exceedingly displeased at her departure, but because she could not gainsay the dispositions of divine providence she agreed to his request and sent Leoba to the blessed man. Thus it was that the interpretation of the dream which she had previously received was fulfilled. When she came, the man of God received her with the deepest reverence, holding her in great affection, not so much because she was related to him on his mother's side as because he knew that by her holiness and wisdom she would confer many benefits by her word and example.

In furtherance of his aims he appointed persons in authority over the monasteries and established the observance of the Rule: he placed Sturm as abbot over the monks and Leoba as abbess over the nuns. He gave her the monastery at a place called Bischofsheim, where there was a large community of nuns. These were trained according to her principles in the discipline of monastic life and made such progress in her teaching that many of them afterwards became superiors of others, so that there was hardly a convent of nuns in that part which had not one of her disciples as abbess. She was a woman of great virtue and was so strongly attached to the way of life she had vowed that she never gave thought to her native country or her relatives. She expended all her energies on the work she had undertaken in order to appear blameless before God and to become a pattern of perfection to those who obeyed her in word and action. She was ever on her guard not to teach others what she did not carry out herself. In her conduct there was no arrogance or pride; she was no distinguisher of persons, but showed herself affable and kindly to all. In appearance she was angelic, in word pleasant, clear in mind, great in prudence, Catholic in faith, most patient in hope, universal in her charity. But though she was always cheerful, she never broke out into laughter through excessive hilarity. No one ever heard a bad word from her lips; the sun never went down upon her anger. In the matter of food and drink she always showed the utmost understanding for others but was most sparing in her own use of them. She had a small cup from which she used to drink and which, because of the meagre quantity it would hold, was called by the sisters "the Beloved's little one." So great was her zeal for reading that she discontinued it only for prayer or for the refreshment of her body with food or sleep: the Scriptures were never out of her hands. For, since she had been trained from infancy in the rudiments of grammar and the study of the other liberal arts, she tried by constant reflection to attain a perfect knowledge of divine things so that through the combination of her reading with her quick intelligence, by natural gifts and hard work, she became extremely learned. She read with attention all the books of the Old and New Testaments and learned by heart all the commandments of God. To these she added by way of completion the writings of the church Fathers, the decrees of the Councils and the whole of ecclesiastical law. She observed great moderation in all her acts and arrangements and always kept the practical end in view, so that she would never have to repent of her actions through having been guided by impulse. She was deeply aware of the necessity for concentration of mind in prayer and study, and for this reason took care not to go to excess either in watching or in other spiritual exercises. Throughout the summer both she and all the sisters under her rule went to rest after the midday meal, and she would never give permission to any of them to stay up late, for she said that lack of sleep dulled the mind, especially for study. When she lay down to rest, whether at night or in the afternoon, she used to have the Sacred Scriptures read out at her bedside, a duty which the younger nuns carried out in turn without grumbling. It seems difficult to believe, but even when she seemed to be asleep they could not skip over any word or syllable whilst they were reading without her immediately correcting them. Those on whom this duty fell used afterwards to confess that often when they saw her becoming drowsy they made a mistake on purpose to see if she noticed it, but they were never able to escape undetected. Yet it is not surprising that she could not be deceived even in her sleep, since He who keeps watch over Israel and neither slumbers nor sleeps possessed her heart, and she was able to say with the spouse in the Song of Songs; "I sleep, but my heart watcheth."

She preserved the virtue of humility with such care that, though she had been appointed to govern others because of her holiness and wisdom, she believed in her heart that she was the least of all. This she showed both in her speech and behaviour. She was extremely hospitable. She kept open house for all without exception, and even when she was fasting gave banquets and washed the feet of the guests with her own hands, at once the guardian and the minister of the practice instituted by our Lord. . . .

The people's faith was stimulated by such tokens of holiness [a miracle of healing], and as religious feeling increased so did contempt of the world. Many nobles and influential men gave their daughters to God to live in the monastery in perpetual chastity; many widows also forsook their homes, made vows of chastity and took the veil in the cloister. To all of these the holy virgin pointed out both by word and example how to reach the heights of perfection.

In the meantime, blessed Boniface, the archbishop, was preparing to go to Frisia, having decided to preach the Gospel to this people riddled with superstition and unbelief. He summoned . . . Leoba to him and exhorted her not to abandon the country of her adoption and not to grow weary of the life she had undertaken, but rather to extend the scope of the good work she had begun. He said that no consideration should be paid to her weakness and that she must not count the long years that lay ahead of her; she must not count the spiritual life to be hard nor the end difficult to attain, for the years of this life are short compared to eternity, and the sufferings of this world are as nothing in comparison with the glory that will be made manifest in the saints. He commended her to Lull and to the senior monks of the monastery who were present, admonishing them to care for her with reverence and respect and reaffirming his wish that after his death her bones should be placed next to his in the tomb, so that they who had served God during their lifetime with equal sincerity and zeal should await together the day of resurrection.

After these words he gave her his cowl and begged and pleaded with her not to leave her adopted land. And so, when all necessary preparations had been made for the journey, he set out for Frisia, where he won over a multitude of people to the faith of Christ and ended his labours with a glorious martyrdom. His remains were transported to Fulda and there, according to his previous wishes, he was laid to rest with worthy tokens of respect.

The blessed virgin, however, persevered unwaveringly in the work of God. She had no desire to gain earthly possessions but only those of heaven, and she spent all her energies on fulfilling her vows. Her wonderful reputation spread abroad and the fragrance of her holiness and wisdom drew to her the affections of all. She was held in veneration by all who knew her, even by kings. Pippin, King of the Franks, and his sons Charles and Carloman treated her with profound respect, particularly Charles, who, after the death of his father and brother, with whom he had shared the throne for some years, took over the reins of government. He was a man of truly Christian life, worthy of the power he wielded and by far the bravest and wisest king that the Franks had produced. His love for the Catholic faith was so sincere that, though he governed all, he treated the servants and handmaids of God with touching humility. Many times he summoned the holy virgin to his court, received her with every mark of respect and loaded her with gifts suitable to her station. Queen Hiltigard also revered her with a chaste affection and loved her as her own soul. She would have liked her to remain continually at her side so that she might progress in the spiritual life and profit by her words and example. But Leoba detested the life at court like poison. The princes loved her, the nobles received her, the bishops welcomed her with joy. And because of her wide knowledge of the Scriptures and her prudence in counsel they often discussed spiritual matters and ecclesiastical discipline with her. But her deepest concern was the work she had set on foot. She visited the various convents of nuns and, like a mistress of novices, stimulated them to vie with one another in reaching perfection.

Sometimes she came to the Monastery of Fulda to say her prayers, a privilege never granted to any woman either before or since, because from the day that monks began to dwell there entrance was always forbidden to women. Permission was only granted to her, for the simple reason that the holy martyr St. Boniface had commended her to the seniors of the monastery and because he had ordered her remains to be buried there. . . .

Reprinted with permission from *The Anglo-Saxon Missionaries in Germany,* trans. C. H. Talbot (London: Sheed and Ward, 1954), pp. 75–78; 45–46; 213–16, 221–23 passim.

Part 3

Christian Society in the Early Middle Ages,
circa 600–1050

The first two parts demonstrated how Christianity varied according to cultural context (Jewish, Roman, African, Chinese) and how individuals converted to Christianity for a variety of reasons related to their cultural heritage (Roman, Celtic, or Germanic). These variations in conversion raise the question addressed in this chapter: what is the relationship between culture and Christianity? In other words, how did the incoming religion interact with the beliefs, values, and behaviors of the converted?

This question becomes an important issue in the study of the early Middle Ages when converted kings (such as Clovis and Edwin, 8.2 and 8.3) attempted to mix the adopted religion into their societies. At this stage, between 600 and 1050, the focus of conversion in the historical accounts increasingly shifts from the individual to a *social* conversion process. In some ways the same dynamics we saw at work in the conversion of individuals also takes place in the conversion of societies: just as an individual's conversion was a complex affair in which his or her own background and interests interacted with the new religion, so too on the social level, conversion to Christianity changed the culture and the culture brought change to Christianity. The results of this accommodation and assimilation gave rise to new forms of Christianity—for example, Anglo-Saxon Christianity or Frankish Christianity—and a new concept of society, "Christian society."

This social assimilation process between religion and culture is demonstrated in four ways in this part. The first chapter, Chapter 9, illustrates the religious and political merger evident in the ideal of "Christian Kingship and Society" in the laws, histories, and biographies written by churchmen. Chapter 10, "Christian Education and Theology," explores the intellectual re-

fostered by royal interest in literature and learning as a basis for stable kingdoms. Chapter 11, "Christian Practice and Literature," reveals the range of European Christian values evident in sermons, penitentials, liturgy, drama, and poetry. Chapter 12, "Christian Diversity and Accommodation," demonstrates that, despite this ideal of a unified Christian society under a king, conversion was often a contentious process as European Christianity struggled with accommodating local cultures and with defining itself in relation to other religions.

The larger question to ask as you examine these documents is: what does it really mean to call a whole society Christian? Some related questions to consider are: how and why was this label, "Christian society," used? In what ways can we call early medieval society Christian? By whose definition of what is Christian?

–9–

Christian Kingship
and Society

The overlap between spiritual and secular affairs evident in the idea of Christian kingship appears to defy the idea of a separation between church and state as we have come to think of it today. Yet the idea of a separation of spiritual and secular is fundamental to medieval thought, particularly in medieval Europe.

The close relationship of these two hierarchies was evident in Constantine's involvement in the Council of Nicea in 325 (3.3), and was a subject of controversy in Augustine's *Two Cities* (5.2). The concept of two governing centers was further defined by Pope Gelasius I in the fifth century (9.1). And yet, after the split between the eastern and western halves of the Roman Empire in the fifth century, the eastern or Byzantine Empire maintained a strong emperor directing church affairs in the tradition of Constantine, evident in Justinian's code of law (9.1).

However, in the former western Roman Empire, now broken into tribal kingdoms, church and state interacted on more equal terms. Christian conversion occurred at a pivotal moment in the settlement of Europe, just when strong leaders, such as Clovis and Edwin in the previous chapter, emerged from these tribal groups and founded kingdoms. Roman Church leaders—bishops, abbots, monastic missionaries—worked with Christian rulers to unify their newly emerging kingdoms through a common ideology, Catholic Christianity. One of the primary ways to support this notion of a Christian society was to sanctify kingship as a divinely sponsored idea: a Christian king, leading a Christian people, under God, and with the aid of church leaders. This view of the kingdom as a divinely ordained hierarchy can be seen, for example, in the rituals surrounding the Visigothic king (9.2).

The sacralizing of kingship is potent, but is still limited by the parallel church hierarchy with its claim to divine authority. Because of the existence of this spiritual hierarchy of priests and bishops by their side, early medieval kings who converted to Christianity and incorporated

215

the influence of churchmen into their courts *could not* claim to be a god or be God's sole representative. Instead, kings and bishops created separate but overlapping hierarchies and together fostered a Christian society over which they jointly presided. The tensions in this relationship are evident in the differing accounts of Charlemagne's coronation as emperor by the pope (9.3). Overall, however, the early medieval kingdoms established a precedent of close working relationships between royal leadership and episcopal leadership. Kings incorporated high-ranking churchmen (themselves members of the aristocracy) into the royal council of advisors, where their learning and literacy was highly prized in the development of royal administration. According to the surviving documents, authored or influenced almost exclusively by churchmen, the ideal Christian king surrounded himself with able men and issued laws reflecting Christian principles. In this way, a stable kingdom was unified partly through religious identity and values. The biography and laws of King Alfred the Great in Anglo-Saxon England (9.4) exemplify these ideals.

9.1 Theories of Authority and Power:
Pope Gelasius I and Emperor Justinian

The conversion of the Roman emperor Constantine, and the subsequent foundation of Christianity as the state religion of the empire by Emperor Theodosius, left a troubling legacy for the kings and churchmen of medieval Europe: what is the relationship between the secular and spiritual hierarchies of governance, between king or emperor and bishop or pope? Pope Gelasius I in 494 established a theoretical basis for the existence of two separate hierarchies, the secular *power* of royal governance and the spiritual *authority* of the church; this document, excerpted below, was quoted innumerable times by both sides throughout the medieval debates over the relationship of church and state.

In the eastern Roman Empire (Byzantium), the strong imperial governance of religious affairs found in the reign of Constantine continued. The patriarch of Constantinople governed the eastern church, nonetheless emperors continued to involve themselves in theological controversies as part of their political policies. Emperor Justinian I (482–565, reigned 527–565) is a excellent example of a dynamic ruler fully engaged in theological disputes.

Justinian is famous on a number of grounds: for his attempts to reconquer and control the western portion of the Roman Empire, for his wife's formidable influence (see 7.2), and for his law codes. The excerpt below from one of Justinian's law codes, the *Novellae* (535) or new laws, establishes the emperor's view of imperial authority in relationship to the church.

Questions

1. What is the difference between *power* and *authority* in Pope Gelasius's view of the sacred and royal functions?

2. What is Justinian's view of the relationship between the sacred and the imperial "gifts" from God to mankind?

3. Compare Gelasius's and Justinian's treatments of the two centers of governance: which do you think each would put higher than, or above, the other?

Pope Gelasius I, Two Swords Theory (494)

There are two powers, august Emperor, by which this world is chiefly ruled, namely, the sacred authority [*auctoritas*] of the priests and the royal power [*potestas*]. Of these that of the priests is the more weighty, since they have to render an account for even the kings of men in the divine judgment. You are also aware, dear son, that while you are permitted honorably to rule over human kind, yet in things divine you bow your head humbly before the leaders of the clergy and await from their hands the means of your salvation. In the reception and proper disposition of the heavenly mysteries you recognize that you should be subordinate rather than superior to the religious order, and that in these matters you depend on their judgment rather than wish to force them to follow your will.

If the ministers of religion, recognizing the supremacy granted you from heaven in matters affecting the public order, obey your laws, lest otherwise they might obstruct the course of secular affairs by irrelevant considerations, with what readiness should you not yield them obedience to whom is assigned the dispensing of the sacred mysteries of religion. Accordingly, just as there is no slight danger in the case of the priests if they refrain from speaking when the service of the divinity requires, so there is no little risk for those who disdain —which God forbid—when they should obey. And if it is fitting that the hearts of the faithful should submit to all priests in general who properly administer divine affairs, how much the more is obedience due to the bishop of that see which the Most High ordained to be above all others, and which is consequently dutifully honored by the devotion of the whole Church.

From Robinson, pp. 72–73.

Justinian, The Civil Law, Novella VI

The priesthood [*sacerdotium*] and the Empire [*imperium*] are the two greatest gifts which God, in His infinite clemency, has bestowed upon mortals; the former has reference to Divine matters, the latter presides over and directs human affairs, and both, proceeding from the same principle, adorn the life of mankind; hence nothing should be such a source of care to the emperors as the honor of the priests who constantly pray to God for their salvation. For if the priesthood is everywhere free from blame, and the Empire full of confidence in God is administered equitably and judiciously, general good will result, and whatever is beneficial will be bestowed upon the human race. Therefore We have the greatest solicitude for the observance of the divine rules and the preservation of the honor of the priesthood, which, if they are maintained will result in the greatest advantages that can be conferred upon us by God, as well as in the confirmation of those which We already enjoy, and whatever We have not yet obtained We shall hereafter acquire. For all things terminate happily where the beginning is proper and agreeable to God. We think that this will take place if the sacred rules of the Church which the just, praiseworthy, and adorable Apostles, the inspectors and ministers of the Word of God, and the Holy Fathers have explained and preserved for Us, are obeyed.

From *The Civil Law*, trans. S. P. Scott (Philadelphia: The Jefferson Medical College of Philadelphia, 1932), Vol. 16, p. 30.

9.2 Royal Rituals and Laws: Visigothic Spain

The Iberian Peninsula (modern Spain and Portugal) has a rich and varied religious and cultural history that includes not only Roman and Gothic influence but also Muslim, Jewish, and Christian traditions interacting and conflicting. Amid this historic diversity, various rulers attempted at one time or another to bring unity through religious uniformity. For example, Visigothic Spain circa 400–700 C.E. demonstrates the ideals of Christian kingship and the overlap of secular and spiritual interests in royal courts. The royal impetus for strong hierarchical leadership bolstered by religious rituals and for a clear orthodox belief system enforced through law evident in the two documents excerpted here needs to be seen against the backdrop of a complex cultural and religious heritage.

Roman presence and control of Spain dates back to the third century B.C.E. and the spread of the Pax Romana. Christian missions reached the peninsula within the first generation of Christians, reputedly through the apostle Paul, but Christianity seems to have been established mostly in the fourth century, strengthened by the Christianizing of the Roman Empire under Constantine and Theodosius. In the fifth century, Germanic groups disrupted the Roman peace; by the end of the century, one of the Arian Gothic tribes, the Visigoths (or West Goths) dominated the Iberian Peninsula, establishing a monarchy that lasted until the Arab Islamic conquest in 711. These Arian Visigoths ruled over a largely Roman Catholic local population; however, in the late sixth century the Visigothic King Recared (586–601), in a move designed to solidify his rule, converted to the Roman church and rigidly maintained that orthodoxy. The first excerpt below is from a seventh-century liturgical ritual performed in the church by churchmen to bless and sanctify the king before he went to war (the *Ordo quando rex cum exercitu ad prelium egreditur;* the Ritual when the king goes out to battle with his army). The second set of excerpts is from the *Lex Visigothorum* or Visigothic law codes, a compilation of laws from a series of Visigothic kings covering everything from criminal behavior (theft, poisoning) to social or religious issues such as abortion and sexual practices. The excerpts below from this massive compilation explain the principles of law and legislate against Jews and other heretics, and hence reveal the royal notion of what a Christian society meant.

Questions

1. Why was it important for the church to bless the king before he went to battle? What does this ritual show about the relationship between church and king?

2. What is the function of law in Christian society?

3. Why do you think the Visigothic kings found it necessary to legislate religious behavior and to restrict Judaism in particular?

Ordo quando rex cum exercitu ad prelium egreditur
(Ritual when the king goes out to battle with his army)

When the king arrives at the door of the church two deacons clothed in albs offer him incense. All the clergy, in albs, remain in the choir, except for those who will precede the king with the cross. When the king enters the church, and has prostrated himself in prayer, when he rises up the verse shall be sung:

"May God be in your journey and His angel accompany you."

Then this prayer is said:

"O Lord of Hosts, the strength of virtues and virtue of the strong, the champion against the enemy, the victory of the humble, the achiever of victories, the height of kings, the ruler of kingdoms, be present to our religious prince, with the peoples subject to him, as leader of the saving way, the way of peace, the inspirer of right decision. May the king have, by Thy Grace, O Lord, strong armies, faithful generals, minds in concord, by which he may overcome the adversary and defend his own. Give him, O Lord, of Thy Spirit, to think of what are needful and to perform them, so that, fortified by Thy Protection, marching with his subject people and going out from this present church of Thy Apostles Peter and Paul with angel guardians, he may valiantly carry out the acts of war, so that, always adhering to Thee, he may triumph over his enemies and, returning, restore to us who beseech Thee the height of saving joy."

Blessing:

"May the Spirit of the Good God lead us by the ineffable grace of Divinity into the right road. Amen.

May He be your guide on the way who willed to be our way of salvation. Amen.

So that you who have vowed your conscience to God may, protected by His aid, unroll the way of your saving journey. With the aid of the mercy of our God. . . ."

The deacon goes to the altar and raises the golden cross, in which wood of the Holy Cross is enclosed, which always goes with the king in the army, and bears it to the bishop. Then the bishop, having washed his hands, hands it to the king, and the king to the priest, who will bear it before him. As the cross is placed in the king's hand, the bishop begins this antiphon, which is chanted with these verses:

"Accept from the Hand of the Lord certain judgment as a helmet, and may God's creature be armed for the punishment of thy enemies. Take up the inexpugnable shield of equity. For the punishment [of thy enemies]."

For power is given you from the Lord and virtue from the Most High. For the punishment [of thy enemies]."

After the second verse all shall go up and receive their standards from the priest behind the altar and shall go forth immediately, the clergy in the choir chanting the same antiphon, with these verses:

"Blessed be Israel! Who is like unto thee, O People saved by the Lord? The shield of thy aid, the sword of thy glory. For the punishment. . . .

Thy enemies shall deny thee and thou shalt break their necks. For the punishment. . . .

Thy foot shalt not be moved nor shall He slumber who guards thee. For the punishment. . . .

Behold He shall not slumber nor sleep who guards Israel. For the punishment. . . .

The Lord shall protect thee, the Lord is thy protection upon thy right hand. For the punishment. . . .

By day the sun shall not burn thee nor the moon by night. For the punishment. . . .

The Lord shall guard thee from all evil: the Lord shall guard thy soul. For the punishment. . . ."

After all raise their standards and go outside the door of the church at once "Glory to the Father" shall be sung. . . . Then the deacon saying: "Humble yourselves for the blessing," this blessing shall be said by the bishop:

"The Saving Sign of Wood and Nail, which thou, Sacred Prince, hast received with pious hands, may it be for thy salvation and an increase of perpetual blessing. May thy egress be in peace and may the Cross of Christ always be present on the way to your armies. May it give you religious counsel and prepare strong means for your expedition. May this Wood, by which Christ despoiled Principalities and Powers, triumphing over them in Himself, become the means of your gaining singular glory in victory. Amen. So that, by the victory of the Holy Cross, you may complete your journey, begun here, happily, and bring back to us flourishing titles of your triumphs. Amen. As we bid you farewell with the kiss of peace we shall receive you on your happier return here with praises of victory. Amen. By the Grace of Our Lord Jesus Christ."

After this blessing the deacon says: "In the Name of Our Lord Jesus Christ, go in peace." "Thanks be to God."

And so the king bids farewell to the bishop and at once this antiphon [is begun] by those who march before the king with the Cross:

"O Lord God, the strength of my salvation, cover my head in the day of battle."

And they sing before the king until he has gone outside the door of the church. But the priest or deacon who has taken the Cross from the king shall always go before him until he has mounted. And so they begin the journey.

Reprinted from *Christianity and Paganism, 350–750,* ed. J. N. Hillgarth (Philadelphia: University of Pennsylvania Press, 1986), pp. 93–95 and translated from *Le Liber Ordinum,* ed. M. Férotin, Monumenta ecclesiae liturgica, V (Paris: Firmin-Didot, 1904), col. 149–53.

Visigothic Law Codes

Book I, Title II: The Law

I. What the Lawmaker Should Observe in Framing the Laws

In all legislation the law should be fully and explicitly set forth, that perfection, and not partiality, may be secured. For, in the formation of the laws, not the sophisms of argument, but the virtue of justice should ever prevail. And here is required not what may be prompted by controversy, but what energy and vigor demand; for the violation of morals is not to be coerced by the forms of speech, but restrained by the moderation of virtue.

II. What the Law Is

The law is the rival of divinity; the oracle of religion; the source of instruction; the artificer of right; the guardian and promoter of good morals; the rudder of the state; the messenger of justice; the mistress of life; the soul of the body politic.

III. What the Law Does

The law rules every order of the state, and every condition of man; it governs wives and husbands; youth and age; the learned and the ignorant; the polished and the rude. It aims to provide the highest degree of safety for both prince and people, and, in renown and excellence, it is as conspicuous as the noon-day sun.

IV. What the Law Should Be

The law should be plain, and not lead any citizen to commit error or fraud. It should be suitable to the place and the time, according to the character and custom of the state; prescribing justice and equity; consistent, honorable, worthy, useful, and necessary; and it should be carefully noted whether its provisions are framed rather for the convenience, than for the injury, of the public; so that it may be determined whether it sufficiently provides for the administration of justice; whether or not it appears to be contrary to religion, and whether it defends the right, and may be observed without detriment to any one.

V. Why the Law Is Made

Laws are made for these reasons: that human wickedness may be restrained through fear of their execution; that the lives of innocent men may be safe among criminals; and that the temptation to commit wrong may be restrained by the fear of punishment.

VI. How the Law Should Triumph over Enemies

Domestic peace having been once established and the plague of contention having been entirely removed from prince, citizen, and the populace, expeditions then may be made safely against the enemy and he may be attacked confidently and vigorously, in the certain hope of victory; when nothing is to be anticipated or feared from dissensions at home. The entire body of the people being prosperous and secure, through the influence of peace and order, they can set forth boldly against the enemy and become invincible, where salutary arts are aided by just laws. For men are better armed with equity than with weapons; and the prince should rather employ justice against an enemy than the soldier his javelin; and the success of the prince will be more conspicuous when a reputation for justice accompanies him, and soldiers who are well governed at home will be all the more formidable to a foe. It is a matter of common experience, that justice, which has protected the citizen, overwhelms the enemy; and that those prevail in foreign contests who enjoy domestic peace; and while the moderation of the prince insures temperance in the enforcement of the law, so the united support of the citizens promotes victory over the enemy. For the administration of the law is regulated by the disposition and character of the king; from the administration of the law proceeds the institution of morals; from the institution of morals, the concord of the citizens; from the concord of the citizens, the triumph over the enemy. So a good prince ruling well his kingdom, and making foreign conquests, maintaining peace at home, and overwhelming his foreign adversaries, is famed both as the ruler of his state and a victor over his enemies, and shall have for the future eternal renown; after terrestrial wealth, a celestial kingdom; after the diadem and the purple, a crown of glory; nor shall he then cease to be king; for when he relinquished his earthly kingdom, and conquered a celestial one, he did not diminish, but rather increased his glory.

Book XII, Title II: Concerning the Eradication of the Errors of All Heretics and Jews

The Glorious Flavius Recesvintus, King

I. Laws Having Been Given to True Believers, it is Now Necessary to Place Restraints upon Infidels

Hitherto, we have directed our steps cautiously through the arduous paths which traverse the iniquities of the Jews; and have used moderation in the restraint of human crimes and infirmities. For it has been our manifest purpose and task, both to remove ill-founded opinions, and to prohibit what is evil, as well as to abolish what has been wrongfully done, and is abhorrent to decency and honor. As the law penetrates the secret recesses of minds conscious of guilt, so its censure corrects the depravity of morals, and prevents the perpetration of crime. And, indeed, we do not attempt to bring about this purity of soul for any other purpose than for the sake of the

Church of the living God, which has invested so many different nations and peoples with the robe of immortality, and has united them to herself with the bonds of one holy religion. For the excellence of our strength and earthly glory are derived from the virtues of God, and his influence, sometimes acting through compassion, sometimes through fear of the sword of justice, prevents the commission of sin; and on one occasion diminishes crime by the practice of moderation, on another, extirpates it by an exhibition of severity. Following, not only the example of noble and illustrious races who restrained the illegal excesses of the people by leniency and rational laws, but also copying the rules and imitating the example of the Holy Fathers throughout the entire globe of the earth, we shall endeavor, as far as lies in our power, to reduce to action the precepts which we have received from them. For this reason, our relatives and subjects will know that our decrees are suitable, and dictated by honesty of purpose, in that they forbid the commission of crime, and are not opposed to the opinions of the Holy Fathers heretofore promulgated. And we are confident that we shall receive two rewards from the generosity of God: one, that we will be permitted to remain in the enjoyment of peace with our neighbors, as we are now; and the other, that, when our rule is ended, we shall receive a due acknowledgment from heaven. Thus, when, by means of the laws directed to our faithful people, this salutary remedy shall have been administered to the adherents of the Holy Faith, (as medicine is absorbed by the members of the body), and peace and charity shall everywhere prevail; confiding in the virtue of God, we shall attack his enemies, pursue his rivals, and conquer his adversaries; contending manfully, and constantly persevering; dispersing and overcoming those enemies, as dust is driven by the wind, or as mud is dried up in the fields, we shall acquire the reward of Faith; and when we shall include all people as true believers in our holy religion, and shall bring all infidels to belief in its truths, our glory shall increase, and our kingdom shall be exalted.

Flavius Recesvintus, King

II. Concerning the Renunciation of the Errors of all Heresies

The eternal counsel of Almighty wisdom and Divine piety, as we understand it, and revealed to us in former ages, for the benefit of our own times, dissipated the errors of perfidious heretics, as well as abolished the false maxims of impious doctrines. Nevertheless, that such a time may not come during our lives, as that of which the representative of Divine Grace formerly said: "A time will come when persons will not desire sound doctrine, but with eager ears, and according to their desires, will seek masters for themselves; and who will not listen to the truth, but will turn to false doctrines; and, as it is proper that whatever remains in the light of the Faith should be defended, by legal edicts, from the efforts of all who seek to contradict it; and that whatever ideas have arisen through the influence of error, be removed by legal proceedings; therefore, we decree that no man of whatever race or lineage, either native or foreigner, proselyte or old in faith, visitor or resident, shall openly or silently, impugn the unity of the Catholic faith; or take part in any injurious disputes affecting the truth of said faith; or countenance the same by remaining silent." No one shall attack the decrees of the Gospel, or criticize the institutions of the Church, or call in question the sacred institutions established by the ancient Fathers; no one shall treat with contempt discussions concerning points of doctrine which arise in modern assemblies; no one shall entertain any thoughts against the holy edicts or the true religion, or shall utter any words in depreciation of the same; or perfidiously cause a controversy to arise with an obstinate unbeliever; or engage in a quarrel on account of the contempt of honor exhibited by a listener. Any person who violates any of the provisions aforesaid shall be arrested; and should he be an ecclesiastic, or belong to any religious order, he shall lose his rank and dignity; shall be regarded forever as a criminal; and shall be punished by the loss of all his property. If he should belong to the laity, he shall be deprived of honor and position, and stripped of all his possessions. Every violator of this law shall be condemned to perpetual exile, unless he should be converted from his errors by the interposition of Divine mercy, when he may be suffered to remain and live in accordance with the commands of God.

Flavius Recesvintus, King

III. Concerning the Laws Promulgated on Account of the Wickedness of the Jews

The execrable errors of heretics in general, having been already prohibited and disposed of, it now becomes our duty to make special provision for some that exist in our days, and of which we are, at present, well aware. For while the virtue of God, by the sword of his Word, extirpated all other heresies, root and branch, we have to lament that the soil of our kingdom is still only defiled by the infamy of the Jews. Therefore, to the end that we may establish peace in our realm, by the spirit of God (which, indeed, seems folly to pagans and scandal to the Jews themselves), we, who believe in the virtues of Christ, and the wisdom of God, for the sake of whose commiseration we attempt, with pious intentions, to put an end to ancient errors, that others may not arise in future ages; decree by this law, which shall be forever observed, and by the mandate of the Holy Scriptures, that our edicts, as well as those promulgated by our royal predecessors against the perfidy and persons of the Jews, shall be forever inviolate, and shall be obeyed for all time. And if anyone should violate said laws, he shall be liable for the damages provided by them, and to the punishments especially prescribed for their infraction.

Flavius Recesvintus, King

IV. Concerning the Extirpation of the Errors of the Jews in General

No Jew who has received the sacred rite of baptism shall renounce the faith of the holy Christian religion, or blaspheme said faith, in any way. No Jew shall impugn its precepts by deed or word; or speak insultingly of it either secretly or openly. No Jew shall flee to avoid being received into the Church, or conceal himself for such a purpose, after having taken to flight. No Jew shall entertain the hope of resuming his errors, or of performing the ceremonies of his infamous belief. No Jew shall entertain in his heart any perfidy against the Christian religion, and in favor of his own sect, or exhibit such perfidy by word or deed. No Jew shall attempt to infringe, or oppose, any regulations or laws of the Christians which have been published. No one shall venture to conceal a Jew who is aware of the existence of these offences which have been prohibited, or who has committed them. No one shall delay to denounce a fugitive Jew when he is found, or to reveal his hiding place. Any person who violates the provisions of the aforesaid law, shall be subjected to the punishment prescribed for the same.

[some titles of restrictions:]

V. Jews Shall not Celebrate the Passover According to Their Custom. . . .

VI. Jews Shall Not Contract Marriage According to Their Custom. . . .

VII. Jews Shall Not Perform the Rite of Circumcision. . . .

VIII. Jews Shall Not Divide their Food into Clean and Unclean, According to their Custom. . . .

XVII. Concerning Judaizing Christians

As the crime of hypocrisy should be deplored by all Christians; for the same reason it should be evident, that no person, under any circumstances, is deserving of pardon, who is proved to have renounced a good religion for a bad one. Therefore, because a cruel and astounding act of presumption should be expiated by a still more cruel punishment, we declare, by the following edict: that, whenever it has been proved that a Christian, of either sex, and especially one born of Christian parents, has practiced circumcision, or any other Jewish rite, or anything else forbidden by God, he shall be put to an ignominious death by the zeal and co-operation of Catholics, under the most ingenious and excruciating tortures that can be inflicted; that he may learn how horrible and detestable that offense is, which he has so infamously perpetrated. All the property of such a person shall be confiscated for the benefit of the royal treasury, in order that his heirs and relatives may not, through consenting to his errors, be contaminated by them.

From *The Visigothic Code (Forum Judicum)*, trans. S. P. Scott (Boston: The Boston Book Co., 1910), pp. 5–7, 363–67 passim, 376–77.

9.3 Christian Emperor: Views on the Coronation of Charlemagne

The Franks after Clovis (8.2) achieved a remarkable synthesis of Germanic, Christian, and Roman traditions that combined to produce a dynamic civilization. The Frankish kingdom reached its peak in the Carolingian empire established under Charles the Great, or "Charlemagne." His coronation as "emperor" in the Roman tradition reveals the strengths, and the weaknesses, of this synthesis of traditions, as a Frankish Christian king is anointed Roman emperor by the pope.

The alliance of Roman Christian interests and Frankish concerns, evident in Gregory of Tours's *History of the Franks* and the story of King Clovis, came together in the mid-eighth century in a famous series of events over three years that historians call the "Franco-Papal Alliance." Because of the weakness of the Merovingian dynasty of kings, the Frankish kingdom was actually run by a powerful family holding the "right-hand man" position in the kingdom, called the mayor of the palace. Also by this time, the papacy in Rome was vulnerable to a number of forces, including Roman political factions, invading Lombards, and ineffectual but high-handed treatment from the Byzantine Empire.

These Frankish and papal needs and interests intersected in an alliance. In 749, the then-mayor of the palace, Pepin, unhappy with his situation, sought the advice of the pope on whether it was appropriate for him to usurp the kingship from the powerless King Childeric and begin a new dynasty. Pope Zachary's reply acknowledged that the one who actually ran the kingdom ought to be called king, and thus he implicitly gave Pepin permission to seize the kingship, which Pepin did. In 753, Pepin came to the defense of the papacy against the invading Lombards, after which, in 756, Pepin granted land in Italy to the Roman see—that is, to the pope. These events lay the groundwork for a reciprocal relationship between the papacy in Rome and the Frankish government. Increasingly, the papacy turned to the Franks as their best allies and defenders.

The problematic nature of this reciprocal relationship whereby the Franks provided the secular sword of defense for the papacy, while the papacy lent spiritual authority to the Frankish kings, came to the fore in the reign of Charlemagne (768–814), in many ways the quintessential Christian king, extolled as a great conqueror and a great Christian leader simultaneously. In particular, his coronation as emperor by the pope on Christmas Day 800, after Charlemagne had gone to Rome to rescue Pope Leo from political adversaries, is a symbolic event in the relationship between Church and kingship.

The incident itself is a rich source of insight for historians because we have different accounts of what happened. These multiple views of the same event allow us to explore the various ways Christian leadership in Europe was portrayed from different angles, using different analogies or models. The following short excerpts from five documents offer diverse perspectives (Frankish, Papal, Byzantine), a variety of interpretations (political, theoretical), and some widely divergent views of the relationship between the pope and the emperor.

Questions

1. Is there any consensus about what happened on Christmas Day 800? Where do these views diverge, and why?

2. What total picture do we get of the relationship between emperor and pope?

3. What do you think are the implications of this event and its various interpretations for the future?

From Einhard's Life of Charlemagne

XXVII. He was very forward in succoring the poor, and in that gratuitous generosity which the Greeks call alms, so much so that he not only made a point of giving in his own country and his own kingdom, but when he discovered that there were Christians living in poverty in Syria, Egypt, and Africa, at Jerusalem, Alexandria, and Carthage, he had compassion on their wants, and used to send money over the seas to them. The reason that he zealously strove to make friends with the kings beyond seas was that he might get help and relief to the Christians living under their rule. He cherished the Church of St. Peter the Apostle at Rome above all other holy and sacred places, and heaped its treasury with a vast wealth of gold, silver, and precious stones. He sent great and countless gifts to the popes; and throughout his whole reign the wish that he had nearest at heart was to re-establish the ancient authority of the city of Rome under his care and by his influence, and to defend and protect the Church of St. Peter, and to beautify and enrich it out of his own store above all other churches. Although he held it in such veneration, he only repaired to Rome to pay his vows and make his supplications four times during the whole forty-seven years that he reigned.

XXVIII. When he made his last journey thither, he had also other ends in view. The Romans had inflicted many injuries upon the Pontiff Leo, tearing out his eyes and cutting out his tongue, so that he had been compelled to call upon the King for help. Charles accordingly went to Rome, to set in order the affairs of the Church, which were in great confusion, and passed the whole winter there. It was then that he received the titles of Emperor and Augustus, to which he at first had such an aversion that he declared that he would not have set foot in the Church the day that they were conferred, although it was a great feast-day, if he could have foreseen the design of the Pope. He bore very patiently with the jealousy which the Roman emperors showed upon his assuming these titles, for they took this step very ill; and by dint of frequent embassies and letters, in which he addressed them as brothers, he made their haughtiness yield to his magnanimity, a quality in which he was unquestionably much their superior.

From Einhard, *Life of Charlemagne,* trans. Samuel Epes Turner (New York: American Book Company, 1880), pp. 64–66.

The Frankish Royal Annals (801)

On the most holy day of the nativity of the Lord when the king rose from praying at Mass before the tomb of blessed Peter the apostle, Pope Leo placed a crown on his head and all the Roman people cried out, "To Charles Augustus, crowned by God, great and peace-giving emperor of the Romans, life and victory." And after the laudation he was adored by the pope in the manner of the ancient princes and, the title of Patrician being set aside, he was called emperor and Augustus.

From *The Crisis of Church and State 1050–1300,* trans. Brian Tierney (Toronto: Medieval Academy Reprints and Translations, 1988), p. 23.

From the Life of Pope Leo III

After these things, on the day of the birth of our Lord Jesus Christ, when all the people were assembled in the Church of the blessed St. Peter, the venerable and gracious Pope with his own hands crowned him [Charlemagne] with an exceedingly precious crown. Then all the faithful Romans, beholding the choice of such a friend and defender of the holy Roman Church, and of the pontiff, did by the will of God and of the blessed Peter, the key-bearer of the heavenly kingdom, cry with a loud voice, "To Charles, the most pious Augustus, crowned of God, the great and peace-giving Emperor, be life and victory." While he, before the altar of the church, was calling upon many of the saints, it was proclaimed three times, and by the common voice of all he was chosen to be emperor of the Romans. Then the most holy high priest and pontiff anointed Charles with holy oil, and also his most excellent son to be king, upon the very day of the birth of our Lord Jesus Christ.

From Ogg, pp. 133–4.

From the Annals of the Monastery of Lorsch

And because the name of emperor had now ceased among the Greeks, and their empire was possessed by a woman [Irene], it seemed both to Leo the pope himself, and to all the holy fathers who were present in the self-same council, as well as to the rest of the Christian people, that they ought to take to be emperor Charles, king of the Franks, who held Rome herself, where the Caesars had always been wont to sit, and all the other regions which he ruled through Italy and Gaul and Germany; and inasmuch as God had given all these lands into his hand, it seemed right that with the help of God, and at the prayer of the whole Christian people, he should have the name of emperor also. [The Pope's] petition King Charles willed not to refuse, but submitting himself with all humility to God, and at the prayer of the priests, and of the whole Christian people, on the day of the nativity of our Lord Jesus Christ, he took on himself the name of emperor, being consecrated by the Pope Leo. . . . For this also was done by the will of God . . . that the heathen might not mock the Christians if the name of emperor should have ceased among them.

From Ogg, p. 132.

Theophanes's Chronicle (Byzantine)

Annus Mundi 6293 (September 1, 800–August 31, 801)

In this year—the ninth indiction—on December 25 Charles the king of the Franks was crowned by pope Leo. He wished to marshal an expedition against Sicily, but desisted, wanting instead to marry Irene. In the following year—the tenth indiction—he dispatched ambassadors to gain that end.

In March of the ninth indiction the pious Irene forgave the Byzantines the city taxes, and lightened the "commercia" at Abydos and Hieron. These and many other benefactions earned her great thanks.

Reprinted with permission from *The Chronicle of Theophanes: An English Translation of Anni Mundi 6095–6305 (*A.D. 602–813), ed. Harry Turtledove (Philadelphia: University of Pennsylvania Press, 1982), p. 157. Note omitted.

9.4 Christian King: Alfred the Great

As with the Franks, the creation of a stable kingdom in Anglo-Saxon England was linked to the establishment of a stable religion (and vice-versa, a solid, growing church depended on a peaceful, supportive kingdom). Alfred, like Charlemagne, has been lauded as a great king for accomplishing this synthesis, at least in theory. What we see in both their reigns is the creation of an *idea* of Christian kingship, promoted in the Christian literature of the time and looked back to afterward as a major turning point in the history of a people.

In many ways, the term *Anglo-Saxon England* is a fiction for the period before the early tenth century, since England was not united under any central government. Despite tribal and regional divisions, Bede's eighth-century *Ecclesiastical History* (8.3) proposed a sense of national "English" identity through the common bond of Roman Christianity. But throughout the seventh, eighth, and ninth centuries, the British Isles were inhabited by a conglomeration of Celts, Angles, Saxons, Picts, and Scandinavian newcomers (Vikings), among others. Eight Anglo-Saxon kingdoms emerged and competed with one another for hegemony in these centuries, but it was only after the devastation wreaked by the Viking invaders-turned-settlers in the ninth century that one kingdom, by default, emerged as a major royal center: Wessex, under the fearless leadership of King Alfred (871–899). Alfred barely held off a complete takeover by the Vikings, and managed to establish an uneasy equilibrium between Viking-held and Anglo-Saxon territories. He secured this peace by formulating a conversion and peace treaty with the Scandinavians, or "Danes," by granting them a large portion of eastern England later known as "the Danelaw" (12.1).

Like Einhard's biography of Charlemagne (9.3), the biography of Alfred by Asser, bishop of Sherborne (d. circa 909), seeks to put together an account of his life that emphasizes the integral role his faith and the church played in his success as a king, in conjunction with his prowess as a great military leader. The following selection shov.'s some of the traits Asser deemed important for a Christian king.

Questions

1. In Asser's mind, what qualities make a king great?
2. What significance does book learning have for the king? Why?
3. How does Alfred rule over a "Christian society"?

Asser's Life of King Alfred

22. . . . He was extraordinarily beloved by both his father and mother, and indeed by all the people, beyond all his brothers; in inseparable companionship with them he was reared at the royal court. As he advanced through the years of infancy and youth, he appeared more comely in person than his brothers, as in countenance, speech, and manners he was more pleasing than they. His noble birth and noble nature implanted in him from his cradle a love of wisdom above all things, even amid all the occupations of this present life; but—with shame be it spoken!—by the unworthy neglect of his parents and governors he remained illiterate till he was twelve years old or more, though by day and night he was an attentive listener to the Saxon poems which he often heard recited, and, being apt at learning, kept them in his memory. He was a zealous practicer of hunting in all its branches, and followed the chase with great assiduity and success; for his skill and good fortune in this art, and in all the other gifts of God, were beyond those of every one else, as I have often witnessed.

23. . . . Now on a certain day his mother was showing him and his brothers a book of Saxon poetry, which she held in her hand, and finally said: 'Whichever of you can soonest learn this volume, to him will I give it.' Stimulated by these words, or rather by divine inspiration, and allured by the beautifully illuminated letter at the beginning of the volume, Alfred spoke before all his brothers, who, though his seniors in age, were not so in grace, and answered his mother: 'Will you really give that book to that one of us who can first understand and repeat it to you?' At this his mother smiled with satisfaction, and confirmed what she had before said: 'Yes,' said she, 'that I will.' Upon this the boy took the book out of her hand, and went to his master and learned it by heart, whereupon he brought it back to his mother and recited it.

24. . . . After this he learned the daily course, that is, the celebration of the hours, and afterwards certain Psalms, and many prayers, contained in a book which he kept day and night in his bosom, as I myself have seen, and always carried about with him, for the sake of prayer, through all the bustle and business of this present life. But, sad to relate, he could not gratify his ardent wish to acquire liberal art, because, as he was wont to say, there were at that time no good teachers in all the kingdom of the West Saxons. . . .

41. . . . That same year [871], after Easter, the aforesaid King Aethelred, having bravely, honorably, and with good repute governed his kingdom five years through many tribulations, went the way of all flesh, and was buried in Wimborne Minster, where he awaits the coming of the Lord and the first resurrection with the just.

42. . . . That same year the aforesaid Alfred, who had been up to that time, during the lifetime of his brothers, only of secondary rank, now, on the death of his brother, by God's permission undertook the government of the whole kingdom, amid the acclamations of all the people; and indeed, if he had chosen, he might easily have done so with the general consent whilst his brother above named was still alive, since in wisdom and every other good quality he surpassed all his brothers, and especially because he was brave and victorious in nearly every battle. . . . Let no one be surprised that the Christians had but a small number of men, for the Saxons as a people had been all but worn out by eight battles in this selfsame year against the heathen, in which there died one king, nine chieftains, and innumerable troops of soldiers, not to speak of countless skirmishes both by night and by day, in which the oft-named King Alfred, and all the leaders of that people, with their men, and many of the king's thanes, had been engaged in unwearied strife against the heathen. How many thousand heathen fell in these numberless skirmishes God alone knows, over and above those who were slain in the eight battles above mentioned.

43. . . . In that same year the Saxons made peace with the heathen, on condition that they should take their departure; and this they did. . . .

76. . . . In the meantime, the king, during the wars and frequent trammels of this present life, the invasions of the heathen, and his own daily infirmities of body, continued to carry on the government, and to practice hunting in all its branches; to teach his goldsmiths and all his artificers, his falconers, hawkers, and dog-keepers; to build houses, majestic and rich beyond all custom of his predecessors, after his own new designs; to recite the Saxon books, and especially to learn by heart Saxon poems, and to make others learn them, he alone never ceasing from studying most diligently to the best of his ability. He daily attended mass and the other services of religion; recited certain psalms, together with prayers, and the daily and nightly

hour-service; and frequented the churches at night, as I have said, that he might pray in secret, apart from others. He bestowed alms and largesses both on natives and on foreigners of all countries; was most affable and agreeable to all; and was skillful in the investigation of things unknown. Many Franks, Frisians, Gauls, heathen, Welsh, Irish, and Bretons, noble and simple, submitted voluntarily to his dominion; and all of them, according to their worthiness, he ruled, loved, honored, and enriched with money and power, as if they had been his own people. Moreover, he was sedulous and zealous in the habit of hearing the divine Scriptures read by his own countrymen, or if, by any chance it so happened that any one arrived from abroad, to hear prayers in company with foreigners. His bishops, too, and all the clergy, his ealdormen and nobles, his personal attendants and friends, he loved with wonderful affection. Their sons, too, who were bred up in the royal household, were no less dear to him than his own; he never ceased to instruct them in all kinds of good morals, and, among other things, himself to teach them literature night and day. But as if he had no consolation in all these things, and suffered no other annoyance either from within or without, he was so harassed by daily and nightly sadness that he complained and made moan to the Lord, and to all who were admitted to his familiarity and affection, that Almighty God had made him ignorant of divine wisdom and of the liberal arts; in this emulating the pious, famous, and wealthy Solomon, King of the Hebrews, who at the outset, despising all present glory and riches, asked wisdom of God, and yet found both, namely, wisdom and present glory; as it is written, 'Seek first the kingdom of God and his righteousness, and all these things shall be added unto you.' But God, who is always the observer of the thoughts of the inward mind, the instigator of meditations and of all good purposes, and a plentiful aider in the formation of good desires—for He would never inspire a man to aim at the good unless He also amply supplied that which the man justly and properly wished to have—stirred up the king's mind from within, not from without; as it is written, 'I will hearken what the Lord God will say concerning me.' He would avail himself of every opportunity to procure assistants in his good designs, to aid him in his strivings after wisdom, that he might attain to what he aimed at; and, like a prudent bee, which, rising in summer at early morning from her beloved cells, steers her course with rapid flight along the uncertain paths of the air, and descends on the manifold and varied flowers of grasses, herbs, and shrubs, essaying that which most pleases her, and bearing it home, he directed the eyes of his mind afar, and sought that without which he had not within, that is, in his own kingdom. . . .

91. . . . Now the king was pierced with many nails of tribulation, though established in the royal sway; for from the twentieth year of his age to the

present year, which is his forty-fifth, he has been constantly afflicted with most severe attacks of an unknown disease, so that there is not a single hour in which he is not either suffering from that malady, or nigh to despair by reason of the gloom which is occasioned by his fear of it. Moreover the constant invasions of foreign nations, by which he was continually harassed by land and sea, without any interval of quiet, constituted a sufficient cause of disturbance.

What shall I say of his repeated expeditions against the heathen, his wars, and the incessant occupations of government? ... For we have seen and read letters, accompanied with presents, which were sent to him from Jerusalem by the patriarch Elias. What shall I say of his restoration of cities and towns, and of others which he built where none had been before? of golden and silver buildings, built in incomparable style under his direction? of the royal halls and chambers, wonderfully erected of stone and wood at his command? of the royal vills constructed of stones removed from their old site, and finely rebuilt by the king's command in more fitting places?

Not to speak of the disease above mentioned, he was disturbed by the quarrels of his subjects, who would of their own choice endure little or no toil for the common need of the kingdom. He alone, sustained by the divine aid, once he had assumed the helm of government, strove in every way, like a skillful pilot, to steer his ship, laden with much wealth, into the safe and longed-for harbor of his country, though almost all his crew were weary, suffering them not to faint or hesitate, even amid the waves and manifold whirlpools of this present life. Thus his bishops, earls, nobles, favorite thanes, and prefects, who, next to God and the king, had the whole government of the kingdom, as was fitting, continually received from him instruction, compliment, exhortation, and command; nay, at last, if they were disobedient, and his long patience was exhausted, he would reprove them severely, and censure in every way their vulgar folly and obstinacy; and thus he wisely gained and bound them to his own wishes and the common interests of the whole kingdom. But if, owing to the sluggishness of the people, these admonitions of the king were either not fulfilled, or were begun late at the moment of necessity, and so, because they were not carried through, did not redound to the advantage of those who put them in execution—take as an example the fortresses which he ordered, but which are not yet begun or, begun late, have not yet been completely finished—when hostile forces have made invasions by sea, or land, or both, then those who had set themselves against the imperial orders have been put to shame and overwhelmed with vain repentance. I speak of vain repentance on the authority of Scripture, whereby numberless persons have had cause for sorrow when they have been smitten by great harm through the perpetration of deceit. But though by this means, sad to say, they may be bitterly af-flicted, and roused to grief by the loss of fathers, wives, children, thanes, man servants, maid servants, products, and all their household stuff, what is the use of hateful repentance when their kinsmen are dead, and they cannot aid them, or redeem from dire captivity those who are captive? for they cannot even help themselves when they have escaped, since they have not wherewithal to sustain their own lives. Sorely exhausted by a tardy repen-tance, they grieve over their carelessness in despising the king's commands; they unite in praising his wisdom, promising to fulfil with all their might what before they had declined to do, namely, in the construction of fortresses, and other things useful to the whole kingdom. . . .

102. . . . But the second part of all his revenues, which came yearly into his possession, and was included in the receipts of the exchequer, as I mentioned just above, he with full devotion dedicated to God, ordering his officers to divide it carefully into four equal parts with the provision that the first part should be discreetly bestowed on the poor of every nation who came to him; on this subject he said that, as far as human discretion could guarantee, the remark of Pope Gregory on the proper division of alms should be followed, 'Give not little to whom you should give much, nor much to whom little, nor nothing to whom something, nor something to whom nothing.' The second share to the two monasteries which he had built, and to those who were serving God in them, as I have described more at length above. The third to the school which he had studiously formed from many of the nobility of his own nation, but also from boys of mean condition. The fourth to the neighboring monasteries in all Wessex and Mercia, and also during some years, in turn, to the churches and servants of God dwelling in Wales, Cornwall, Gaul, Brittany, Northumbria, and some-times, too, in Ireland; according to his means, he either distributed to them beforehand, or agreed to contribute afterwards, if life and prosperity did not fail him. . . .

106. . . . He strove also, in his judgments, for the benefit of both his nobles and commons, who often quarreled fiercely among themselves at the meetings of the ealdormen and sheriffs, so that hardly one of them admitted the justice of what had been decided by these ealdormen and sheriffs. In consequence of this pertinacious and obstinate dissension, all felt con-strained to give sureties to abide by the decision of the king, and both parties hastened to carry out their engagements. But if any one was con-scious of injustice on his side in the suit, though by law and agreement he was compelled, however reluctant, to come for judgment before a judge like this, yet with his own good will he never would consent to come. For he knew that in that place no part of his evil practice would remain hidden; and

no wonder, for the king was a most acute investigator in executing his judgments, as he was in all other things. He inquired into almost all the judgments which were given in his absence, throughout all his dominion, whether they were just or unjust. If he perceived there was iniquity in those judgments, he would, of his own accord, mildly ask those judges, either in his own person, or through others who were in trust with him, why they had judged so unjustly, whether through ignorance or malevolence—that is, whether for the love or fear of any one, the hatred of another, or the desire of some one's money. At length, if the judges acknowledged they had given such judgment because they knew no better, he discreetly and moderately reproved their inexperience and folly in such terms as these: 'I greatly wonder at your assurance, that whereas, by God's favor and mine, you have taken upon you the rank and office of the wise, you have neglected the studies and labors of the wise. Either, therefore, at once give up the administration of the earthly powers which you possess, or endeavor more zealously to study the lessons of wisdom. Such are my commands.' At these words the ealdormen and sheriffs would be filled with terror at being thus severely corrected, and would endeavor to turn with all their might to the study of justice, so that, wonderful to say, almost all his ealdormen, sheriffs, and officers, though unlearned from childhood, gave themselves up to the study of letters, choosing rather to acquire laboriously an unfamiliar discipline than to resign their functions. But if any one, from old age or the sluggishness of an untrained mind, was unable to make progress in literary studies, he would order his son, if he had one, or one of his kinsmen, or, if he had no one else, his own freedman or servant, whom he had long before advanced to the office of reading, to read Saxon books before him night and day, whenever he had any leisure. And then they would lament with deep sighs from their inmost souls that in their youth they had never attended to such studies. They counted happy the youth of the present day, who could be delightfully instructed in the liberal arts, while they considered themselves wretched in that they had neither learned these things in their youth, nor, now they were old, were able to do so. This skill of young and old in acquiring letters, I have set forth as a means of characterizing the aforesaid king.

From *Asser's Life of Alfred,* trans. Albert S. Cook (Boston: Ginn & Company, 1906), pp. 13–15, 22–24, 37–40 passim, 51–54, 60–61, 63–65.

–10–

Christian Education and Theology

Conversion to Christianity in the early Middle Ages was more than just a religious act on the part of an individual or a group of people. As we have seen with Christian kings, conversion was a political act with broad social implications for these nascent Germanic societies as they sought to define themselves according to ethnic and religious markers. Nor did Christianity come only as a belief system to these converting Germanic peoples; rather, the religion came via Rome and the acculturation found in Roman Christianity. The Germanic kingdoms that converted to Roman Christianity also acquired aspects of Roman civilization and culture maintained by the church. In particular, the literature and learning fostered by religious leaders was highly prized at the courts of Charlemagne, Alfred, and other European kings who sought to create centralized administrations and cultural homogeneity in their diverse kingdoms. In recruiting scholars to their courts, sponsoring book production, mandating uniform curriculum for priests, and establishing schools for clergy, these kings inadvertently began "renaissances" in literature and learning.

However, it is wise to keep in mind the context in which these outpourings of literary production occurred. These kings were interested in unity through uniformity and in the preservation of knowledge for social and political stability. Driven by this need for a stable body of literature, a great many works were saved from destruction through massive copying efforts. Nonetheless, the primary agenda behind royal sponsorship of education was political and cultural consolidation, not necessarily a new movement in thought or aesthetics.

The following documents demonstrate the connection of political and pedagogical goals on the part of kings and churchmen. The writings of Charlemagne and his court scholar Alcuin (10.1) illustrates the ideals behind their program of scholarship that resulted in a "Carolingian renaissance." One product of that renaissance was the learned John Scottus Eriugena (10.2), one of a small class of highly trained scholars. In England, Alfred imitated Charlemagne and sought to revive Latin learning, partly through sponsoring translations into the vernacular language of Anglo-Saxon such classic authors as Boethius and Gregory the Great (10.3).

10.1 The Carolingian Renaissance: Charlemagne and Alcuin

The following three, short excerpts from the court of Charlemagne demonstrate both the hunger for learning and the type of intellectual food that nourished it. At the center of the Carolingian revival of learning was the religious scholar Alcuin (735–804), a product of the same Northumbrian monastic environment that produced Bede (8.3) and Boniface (8.4). Alcuin was the librarian at the cathedral school in York when Charlemagne called him to his capital Aix-la-Chapelle (Aachen), where he founded the palace school; in his later years Alcuin became abbot of the monastery of Saint Martin at Tours (6.3). Alcuin not only taught classical educational skills but also wrote hundreds of letters and produced a revised copy of the Latin Bible to replace the badly copied and inaccurate versions then circulating. This latter work shows how important it was to Charlemagne that the church and the kingdom have certain uniform standards and texts in common. In many ways Alcuin fulfilled Charlemagne's ideals for education and learning in his realm; and he left a lasting mark on subsequent scholarship.

The Carolingian drive for learning is evident in the letter of Charlemagne to the abbot of the monastery at Fulda. It shows Charlemagne's view of the monasteries and their function within his kingdom, and why he thinks education is important to the total health of his realm.

The second and third selections reveal something of the content of Alcuin's educational program and his pedagogy as he sought to educate young sons of the aristocracy, as well as a mixed group of pupils destined to become priests or monks. His dialogue on grammar, conducted between a Frankish and Saxon pupil, and his dialogue with the young Prince Pepin, both show how grammar is the beginning of philosophy and wisdom. The dialogue format was a favorite literary device, and was apparently the method of instruction in the classroom. In modern educational parlance, these early medieval teachers taught reading as more than decoding words on a page; rather, learning to read meant contemplating philosophical issues of language and truth involving a kind of Socratic dialogue that might be classified today as critical thinking skills.

Questions

1. Why does Charlemagne want to promote literacy at the court and among the clergy?
2. What is Alcuin endeavoring to teach these pupils, and why?
3. In what ways are these documents evidence of a renaissance, or rebirth, in literature and learning in the eighth and ninth centuries?

Letter of Charlemagne to the Abbot of Fulda

Charles, by the grace of God, King of the Franks and Lombards and Patrician of the Romans, to Abbot Baugulf and to all the congregation, also to the faithful committed to you, we have directed a loving greeting by our ambassadors in the name of omnipotent God.

Be it known, therefore, to your devotion pleasing to God, that we together with our faithful, have considered it to be useful that the bishoprics and monasteries entrusted by the favor of Christ to our control, in addition, to the order of monastic life and the intercourse of holy religion, in the culture of letters also ought to be zealous in teaching those who by the gift of God are able to learn, according to the capacity of each individual, so that just as the observance of the rule imparts order and grace to honesty of morals, so also zeal in teaching and learning may do the same for sentences, so that those who desire to please God by living rightly should not neglect to please him also by speaking correctly. For it is written: "Either from thy words thou shalt be justified or from thy words thou shalt be condemned." For although correct conduct may be better than knowledge, nevertheless knowledge precedes conduct. Therefore, each one ought to study what he desires to accomplish, so that so much the more fully the mind may know what ought to be done, as the tongue hastens in the praises of omnipotent God without the hindrances of errors. For since errors should be shunned by all men, so much the more ought they to be avoided as far as possible by those who are chosen for this very purpose alone, so that they ought to be the especial servants of truth. For when in the years just passed letters were often written to us from several monasteries in which it was stated that the brethren who dwelt there offered up in our behalf sacred and pious prayers, we have recognized in most of these letters both correct thoughts and uncouth expressions; because what pious devotion dictated faithfully to the mind, the tongue, uneducated on account of the neglect of study, was not able to express in the letter without error. Whence it happened that we began to fear lest perchance, as the skill in writing was less, so also the wisdom for understanding the Holy Scriptures might be much less than it rightly ought to be. And we all know well that, although errors of speech are dangerous, far more dangerous are errors of the understanding. Therefore, we exhort you not only not to neglect the study of letters, but also with most humble mind, pleasing to God, to study earnestly in order that you may be able more easily and more correctly to penetrate the mysteries of the divine Scriptures. Since, moreover, images, tropes and similar figures are found in the sacred pages, no one doubts that each one in reading these will understand the spiritual sense more quickly if previously he shall have been fully instructed in the mastery of letters. Such men truly are to be chosen for this work as have both the will and the ability to learn and a desire to instruct others. And may this be done with a zeal as great as the earnestness with which we command it. For we desire you to be, as it is fitting that soldiers of the church should be, devout in mind, learned in discourse, chaste in conduct and eloquent in speech, so that whosoever shall seek to see you out of reverence of God, or on account of your reputation for holy conduct, just as he is edified by your appearance, may also be instructed by your wisdom, which he has learned from your reading or singing, and may go away joyfully giving thanks to omnipotent God. Do not neglect, therefore, if you wish to have our favor, to send copies of this letter to all your suffragans and fellow-bishops and to all the monasteries.

From *TROS,* Vol. 6, No. 5, pp. 12–14.

Alcuin on Grammar and Education

In Albinus's [Alcuin's] school, there were two boys, one a Frank, the other a Saxon; they had recently mastered the first rudiments of grammar. Therefore they decided to rehearse their few scraps of literary knowledge by asking each other questions to test their memory.

First the Frank said to the Saxon:

"Well, my Saxon friend; you answer my questions because you are older. I am fourteen; you are fifteen, I think."

The Saxon replied:

"Yes, I will do this: but on the condition that we may consult the Master if any question should arise which is beyond our understanding, or which requires a knowledge of philosophy."

"All right boys," said the Master, "this is a sound suggestion, and I willingly agree. But first of all, tell me: which do you think is the best point for starting your debate?"

PUPIL: The letters [of the alphabet] of course, Sir.

MASTER: This answer would be right if you had not just brought up the subject of philosophy. As it is, you must start your debate with a definition of words for the sake of which letters have been invented. Better still, we should first ask ourselves: What are the different aspects of a debate?

PUPIL: Sir, we humbly beg you to explain this to us; we must admit that we do not know the aspects of a debate.

MASTER: Every sentence and argument consists of three parts: things, intellect and words. A thing is what we are first aware of; then we learn to understand its nature by the operation of our intellect; finally we express it by words: and for the sake of words letters have been invented.." . .

FRANK: How can I know which gender any word is?

SAXON: There are definite rules about various endings of words which indicate the gender a word might be—but to go through these rules would take a long time and be rather tedious in a debate between boys such as this.

FRANK: But I have already told you.

SAXON: So what?

FRANK: So what? You are only envious because I know more.

SAXON: Certainly not, brother: but I wanted to check your greed for showing off.

FRANK: So you want to check my greed—but what about your own stubbornness?

SAXON: Well carry on: I shall stick to your plan.

Reprinted with permission from *The Era of Charlemagne: Frankish State and Society,* ed. and trans. Stewart C. Easton and Helene Wieruszowski (Huntington, NY: Krieger, 1961; reprint 1979), pp. 176–77. Excerpt translated by H.F. Orton from *Alcuin Opera,* Migne, *Patr. Lat.* CI, cols. 854, 862–863.

From a Brief Dialogue Entitled "The Dispute of the Most Noble Young Prince Pepin with his Master Alcuin"

P. What is a letter?
A. The guardian of history.

P. What is a word?
A. The mind's betrayer.

P. What created a word?
A. The tongue.

P. What is the tongue?
A. Something that whips the air.

P. What is the air?
A. The protection of life.

P. What is life?
A. The joy of the blessed, the sorrow of sinners, the expectation of death.

P. What is death?
A. An unavoidable occurrence, an uncertain journey, the tears of the living, the confirmation of the testament, the thief of man.

P. What is man?
A. The slave of death, a passing wayfarer, the guest of a place.

P. To what is man like?
A. A fruit [homo—pomo; the Latin play of words cannot be rendered].

P. Where is he situated?
A. Within six walls.

P. Which?
A. Above, below, before, behind, right and left.

P. In how many ways does he vary?
A. In hunger and satiety, repose and labour, in wakeful hours and sleep.

P. What is sleep?
A. The image of death.

[This dialogue continues in this vein, covering knowledge of both natural and spiritual issues].

Reprinted with permission from *The Era of Charlemagne: Frankish State and Society,* ed. and trans. Stewart C. Easton and Helene Wieruszowski (Huntington, NY: Krieger, 1961; reprint 1979), pp. 177–78. Note omitted.

10.2 Renaissance Theology: John Scottus Eriugena

The purpose of Charlemagne's plan for educating clergy was to maintain consistency and uniformity in Frankish society and not necessarily to foster creativity or intellectual innovation. Nonetheless, the preservation of literature and learning that his agenda entailed and the foundation of religious schools did produce in the next generation a rebirth in thought, often called the Carolingian renaissance. One stellar example of this new creativity in learning is the ninth-century theologian and philosopher John Scottus Eriugena. His original and speculative writings demonstrate a revitalized interest in the classics of Christian philosophy.

John Scottus Eriugena (circa 810–877) was an Irish scholar serving at the court of Charles the Bald (King of France 840–877); he may have later returned to the British Isles and participated in Alfred's revival of learning there. Unlike the vast majority of his educated colleagues, Eriugena read Greek in addition to Latin. This meant that he could read Pseudo-Dionysius the Areopagite (5.3) and Gregory of Nyssa (4.2) in addition to Augustine of Hippo (5.2) and Boethius (5.4) in his investigations of Neoplatonic philosophy. Eriugena's *De Divisione Naturae* is a systematic exploration of the fourfold nature of the world as it is held together by a transcendent God. This work is not only derivative of earlier works but innovative in creating new metaphysical understandings of the world.

Thus Eriugena serves as evidence not only of a brilliant mind but also of the environment in the ninth century that allowed such a mind to flourish. The following excerpts from the dialogue of master and disciple in his *De Divisione Naturae* discuss the nature of creation, human beings, the human mind, and knowledge.

Questions

1. In Eriugena's Neoplatonic system, which is greater, the idea of something or the thing itself? That is, which is higher, thought or material existence? Why?

2. What is Eriugena's view of man (humanity)?

3. Compare his writings to those of Pseudo-Dionysius and Boethius: in what ways is Eriugena part of the same tradition of thought?

John Scottus Eriugena, *De Divisione Naturae*

Master. You demand a very lofty physical theory of human creation, and you compel us to draw out our discussion to much greater length. It would suffice for me to answer you briefly when you ask why God should have created man, whom he proposed to make in his own image, in the genus of animals, that he wished so to fashion him that there would be a certain animal in which he manifested his own express image. But whoever asks why he wished that, asks the causes of the divine will, to ask which is too presumptuous and arrogant. *"For who hath known the sense of the Lord?"* Yet, if I say this, you will perhaps be silent ungratefully, and you will think that we can conclude nothing with respect to the pure and the perfect. I shall not, therefore, say why he willed, because that is beyond all understanding, but I shall say, as he himself has permitted, what he has willed to do. He has made all creation, visible and invisible, in man since the whole spread of created nature is understood to be in him. For although it is still unknown how much the first Creation of man after the transgression is in defect of the eternal light, nevertheless there is nothing naturally present in the celestial essences which does not subsist essentially in man. For there is understanding and reason, and there is naturally implanted the ground reason [ratio] of possessing a celestial and angelic body, which after the resurrection will appear more clearly than light both in the good and the evil. For it will be common to all human nature to rise again in eternal and incorruptible spiritual bodies. *"It is sown,"* he says, *"an animal body; it is raised a spiritual body."* All this sensible world is fashioned in man. There is no part of it to be found, whether corporeal or incorporeal, which does not subsist created in man, which does not perceive, which does not live, which is not incorporated in him. Do not think of the corporeal size in man; consider rather the natural power, especially since you see even in the human body the pupil of the eye, which subsists with the greatest power although it is the most minute in quantity of all the members. If, therefore, God did not create man in the genus of animals, or certainly, if he did not place the whole nature of all animals in man, how would all creation, visible and invisible, be comprehended in him? And we can therefore say rationally that God wished to place man in the genus of animals for this reason, that he wished to create every creature in him. But, if you ask me why he wished to create every creature in him, I answer that he wished to make him in his image and likeness, so that, as the principal example surpasses all by the excellence of essence, so his image would excel all things of creation in dignity and grace. I confess however that I ignore completely why he wished to make man especially in his image before other creatures visible and invisible. . . .

Mast[er]. Do you think that everything which is known by the understanding and reason or which is imagined by the bodily sense, can in a certain manner be created and produced in him who understands and perceives?

Disc[iple]. It seems to me that it can. Indeed I think that the species of sensible things and the quantities and qualities which I attain by corporeal sense are in a certain way created in me; for, when I imprint the phantasies of them in memory, and when I treat of them within myself, divide, compare, and, as it were, collect them into a kind of unity, I perceive a certain knowledge of things which are outside me being produced in me. In the same way I understand that there arise and are made in me, when I seek them out earnestly, certain ideas like intelligible species, of the intelligibles within, which I contemplate with the mind alone, as, for example, the ideas of the liberal disciplines. But what there is between the knowledge and the things themselves, of which the knowledge is, I do not see clearly.

Mast[er]. What does it seem to you? Are things and the ideas of things, which are made in the soul, of the same nature or different?

Disc[iple]. Of different natures. For how can the corporeal species, of, for example, a certain animal, or herb, or tree, and the idea of it which is produced in an incorporeal nature be of one single nature? For the same reason how can the intelligible species of any discipline and the idea of it be made of one single nature?

Mast[er]. If, then, they are of different genera or natures, and not of the same, tell me, I ask, which of them do you judge must be set down as the more excellent of them; are things of a more exalted nature than their own ideas; or are ideas themselves more exalted than things?

Disc[iple]. I should have said that visible species are of a better nature than their ideas, if Saint Augustine did not state the following opinion in the ninth book *on the Trinity* in the eleventh chapter:

> Since, he says, we learn bodies through the sense of the body, some likeness of bodies is made in our mind; this is phantasy in memory. For bodies themselves are not at all in the mind when we reflect on them, but only their likenesses. Nevertheless the imagination of the body in the mind is better than the species of the body, inasmuch as it is in a better nature, that is, in vital substance, such as the mind. However I do not dare to say that intelligible things are better than their idea which is in the soul.

Reason teaches, to be sure, that that which understands is better than that which is understood. For, if the knowledge of all things subsists in the divine wisdom, I should pronounce this knowledge of all things, not rashly, to be incomparably better than all things of which it is the knowledge. And if that is so, such an order, I believe, proceeds from the divine providence through all creation, that not only every nature which comprehends the idea of the thing following it, is better and superior, but also, because of the dignity of the nature in which it is, the idea itself excels greatly that of which it is the idea. And by this fact I should say more easily that the idea of intelligible things is more ancient than the intelligible things themselves.

Mast[er]. You would perhaps be right in saying that if what is formed is more excellent than what forms.

Disc[iple]. Why do you oppose that?

Mast[er]. Because the idea of the arts which is in the soul seems to be formed from the arts themselves. But if you established by very sure reason that the idea was not formed from the arts, but the arts from the idea, your reasoning would perhaps start out rightly. . . .

Mast[er]. Do you think the human mind is one thing and the idea of it in the mind of the one forming it and knowing it another?

Disc[iple]. That can not be. For I understand the substance of the entire man to be no other than his idea in the mind of the artificer who knew all things in himself before they were made; and that very knowledge is the true and only substance of those things which are known, since they subsist formed most perfectly in it eternally and immutably.

Mast[er]. We can then define man thus: Man is a certain intellectual idea formed eternally in the divine mind.

Disc[iple]. That is an extremely true and a very well tested definition of man; and not only of man but also of all things which are formed in the divine wisdom. Nor do I fear them who define man, not as he is understood to be, but by those things which are understood about him, saying that man is a rational mortal animal capable of sense and discipline; and what is more wonderful, they call this definition substantial [*usiadis*] whilst it is not substantial but taken extrinsically about substance from those things which are accidental to substance through generation. But the idea of man in the divine mind is nothing of these. There indeed it is simple, nor can it be called this or that, standing above all definition and collection of parts, for only that it is predicated of it, but not what it is. For that alone is indeed a true substantial [*usiadis*] definition, which affirms only that it is but negates that it is anything in particular [*quid esse*]. . . .

Mast[er]. . . . True knowledge of all of these is implanted in human nature, although its presence is as yet concealed from the soul itself until it is restored to its pristine integrity, in which it will understand very purely the magnitude and beauty of the image fashioned in it, and nothing will shut it off from the things which are fashioned in it, encompassed as it will be by divine light and turned to God, in whom it will contemplate all things perspicuously. Or did the magnificent Boethius mean something else to be understood when he says?

> Wisdom is the comprehension of the truth of things which are and which draw as by lot their immutable substance. But we say that those things are which do not grow by any increase, and are not diminished by any withdrawing, nor changed by any variations, but with the endeavor and resources of their own nature preserve themselves always in their own power. These are qualities, quantities, forms, magnitudes, smallnesses, equalities, conditions, acts, dispositions, places, times, and whatever is in any way found joined to bodies: they are themselves incorporeal in nature and thrive by reason of the immutable substance, but they are changed through participation of the body and pass into changeable inconstancy through contact with the variable thing.

And where do you understand these things to subsist except in their ideas in the mind of the wise man? For where they are understood, there they are, and as a matter of fact they are nothing more than their being understood.

Reprinted with the permission of Scribner, a division of Simon & Schuster Inc., from *Selections from Medieval Philosophers*, Vol. 1 translated by Richard McKeon. Copyright 1929 Charles Scribner's Sons; copyright renewed (c) 1957 Richard McKeon, pp. 108–20 passim. Notes omitted.

10.3 Vernacular Learning: Alfred's Program

Alfred, king of England 871–899, had educational goals similar to Charlemagne's, but under different, post-Viking invasion conditions. Alfred's kingdom was forged out of adversity rather than prosperity. The rise of Alfred's Wessex as the leader of the Anglo-Saxon kingdoms was partly by default as the other kingdoms collapsed under the pressure of Viking invasions. Hence, Alfred's policies are for the most part defensive: hold back the Vikings, maintain a peace, restore some of what was lost. His campaign to increase literacy and foster education was a positive step to restore the level of learning evident in Bede's Northumbria in the eighth century, but it is tinged with regret at the intellectual decline in his own times, as described for example in Asser's biography (9.4).

As king, Alfred bemoans the loss of Latin literacy and supports endeavors to increase the knowledge of the language among the clergy, at the same that he sponsors numerous translation projects to bring Latin learning into the Anglo-Saxon language. Ironically, this stop-gap translation effort contributes to a renaissance of sorts in Anglo-Saxon literature as numerous works in the vernacular are copied or written for an audience able to read Anglo-Saxon but not Latin. From Alfred's prefaces to these translated works and other letters, we can learn much about his aims.

The two excerpts below reflect Alfred's concerns for scholarship and reveal something of Alfred's overall educational goals. The first excerpt is from Alfred's introduction to his translation of the *Pastoral Charge* (or *Pastoral Care*), a book written by Pope Gregory the Great as an instruction manual for bishops. Alfred's choice of this book shows his deep concern for reforming the clergy and his reverence for Pope Gregory, who was instrumental in the conversion of England and in the formation of Benedictine monasticism (6.2). Alfred's introduction to the *Pastoral Charge* vividly portrays the king's view of the state of learning in England, what he thinks has been lost, and how he hopes to recover this lost knowledge.

The second excerpt, the Letter of Fulk, archbishop of Rheims in Frankish lands, is in response to Alfred's request for scholars to come to

England; similar to Charlemagne who requested learned men from all over Europe, including England, Alfred seeks teachers from the centers of learning on the continent. Fulk's letter illustrates both the religious quality of this learning and how that learning meets the needs of Alfred's kingdom.

Questions

1. What hopes does Alfred have for his kingdom, as indicated in the introduction to Gregory's *Pastoral Charge*?

2. In his letter Fulk indicates that Alfred paid for the scholarly services he requested by sending a gift of expensive dogs. What does Fulk think that Alfred is getting in return for this material gift?

3. Compare these two excerpts with those from Asser's life of Alfred (9.4): what picture of this king do you see?

Alfred's Introduction to the *Pastoral Charge*

King Alfred bids greet Bishop Waerferth with loving words and with friendship; and I let it be known to thee that it has very often come into my mind what wise men there formerly were throughout England, both of sacred and secular orders; and what happy times there were then; and how the kings who had power over the nation in those days obeyed God and his ministers; how they preserved peace, morality, and order at home, and, at the same time enlarged their territory abroad; and how they prospered both in war and in wisdom; and also the sacred orders, how zealous they were both in teaching and learning, and in all the services they owed to God; and how foreigners came to this land in search of wisdom and instruction, the which we should now have to get from abroad if we were to have them.

So general became the decay of learning in England that there were very few on this side of the Humber who could understand the rituals in English, or translate a letter from Latin into English; and I believe that there were not many beyond the Humber. There were so few, in fact, that I cannot remember a single person south of the Thames when I came to the throne. Thanks be to God Almighty that we now have some teachers among us. And therefore I command thee to disengage thyself, as I believe thou art willing, from worldly matters as often as thou art able, that thou mayest apply the wisdom which God has given thee wherever thou canst. Consider what punishments would come upon us if we neither loved wisdom ourselves nor suffered other men to obtain it: we should love the name only of Christian, and very few of the Christian virtues.

When I thought of all this I remembered also how I saw the country before it had been all ravaged and burned; how the churches throughout the whole of England stood filled with treasures and books. There was also a great multitude of God's servants, but they had very little knowledge of the books, for they could not understand anything of them because they were not written in their own language. As if they had said: "Our forefathers, who formerly held these places, loved wisdom, and through it they obtained wealth and bequeathed it to us. In this we can still see their traces, but we cannot follow them, and therefore we have lost both the wealth and the wisdom, because we would not incline our hearts after their example."

When I remembered all this, I wondered extremely that the good and wise men who were formerly all over England, and had learned perfectly all the books, did not wish to translate them into their own language. But again I soon answered myself and said, "Their own desire for learning was so great that they did not suppose that men would ever be so careless, and that learning would so decay; and they wished, moreover, that the wisdom in this land might increase with our knowledge of languages." Then I remembered how the law was first known in Hebrew, and when the Greeks had learned it how they translated the whole of it into their own language, and all other books besides. And again the Romans, when they had learned it, translated the whole of it, through learned interpreters, into their own language. And also all other Christian nations translated a part of it into their own language.

Therefore it seems better to me, if you agree, for us also to translate some of the books which are most needful for all men to know into the language which we can all understand; and for you to see to it, as can easily be done if we have tranquility enough, that all the free-born youth now in England, who are rich enough to be able to devote themselves to it, be set to learn as long as they are not fit for any other occupation, until that they are well able to read English writing; and let those afterwards be taught more in the Latin language who are to continue learning, and be promoted to a higher rank.

When I remembered how the knowledge of Latin had decayed throughout England, and yet that many could read English writing, I began, among other various and manifold troubles of this kingdom, to translate into English the book which is called in Latin *Pastoralis,* and in English *Shepherd's Book* sometimes word by word, and sometimes according to the sense, as I had learned it from Plegmund, my archbishop, and Asser, my bishop, and Grimbold, my mass-priest, and John, my mass-priest. And when I had learned it, as I could best understand it and most clearly interpret it, I translated it into English.

I will send a copy of this to every bishopric in my kingdom; and on each copy there shall be a clasp worth fifty mancuses. And I command, in God's name, that no man take the clasp from the book, or the book from the minster. It is uncertain how long there may be such learned bishops, as thanks be to God there now are nearly everywhere; therefore I wish these copies always to remain in their places, unless the bishop wish to take them with him, or they be lent out anywhere, or any one wish to make a copy of them.

From Robinson, pp. 222–24.

The Letter of Fulk to King Alfred

To the most glorious and Christian king of the English, Alfred, Fulk, by the grace of God archbishop of Reims and servant of the servants of God, wishes ever victorious rule of a temporal kingdom and eternal joy of celestial dominion.

First, truly, we give thanks to the Lord our God, "the Father of lights" and the Author of all good things, from whom is "every best gift and every perfect gift"; who has not only wished the light of his knowledge to shine in your heart through the grace of the Holy Spirit, but has also deigned to kindle the fire of his love; that illumined and likewise kindled by this, you administer strenuously the profit of the kingdom committed to you from above, both by striving for and defending its peace with warlike weapons, with the divine assistance, and by earnestly desiring with a religious heart to raise the dignity of the ecclesiastical order with spiritual weapons. Hence we beseech the heavenly clemency with unwearied prayers, that he who has directed and kindled your heart to this, may cause you to have that wish by satisfying your desire with good things; in order that peace may increase for your kingdom and your people in your days, and also that the ecclesiastical order which, as you say, has fallen in ruins in many respects, whether by the frequent invasion and attack of pagans, whether by the great passage of time or the carelessness of prelates or the ignorance of those subject to them may be reformed, improved and extended by your diligence and zeal as quickly as possible.

Since you desire that it may chiefly be done through our help, and on this account seek counsel and support from our see, over which the blessed Remigius, truly the Apostle of the Franks, presides, we believe that this is not done without divine prompting; that, just as once the people of the Franks deserved to be freed by the same blessed Remigius from manifold error and to know the worship of the one true God, so the people of the English may beg to receive such a man from his see and teaching, through whom it may learn how to guard against superstitions, to cut off superfluities, and to extirpate any things harmful, springing from ancient use and barbarian custom; and, walking through the Lord's field, may learn to pluck the flowers and avoid the snake.

Certainly Saint Augustine, the first bishop of your people, sent to you by the blessed Gregory, your Apostle, neither could demonstrate in a short time all the decrees of the apostolic ordinances, nor wished suddenly to burden a rude and barbarous race with new and unknown laws; for he knew how to have regard to their weakness, and to say with the Apostle, as it were to little ones in Christ: "I gave you milk to drink, not meat." And just as Peter and James "who seemed to be pillars," with Barnabas and Paul and the rest of the assembled elders, did not wish to burden with a heavy yoke the primitive Church flocking from the nations to the faith of Christ, except to enjoin them to "abstain from things sacrificed to idols, from fornication, from things strangled and from blood"; thus also we know was done with you in the beginning.

But indeed, the rearing from barbaric and savage beginnings to the divine knowledge required this alone; and faithful and wise servants, set over the Lord's family, knew well to give to their fellow servants their measure of wheat in due season, that is, for the capture of hearers. As time passed and the Christian religion grew, Holy Church would not and had no right to be content with these things, but only with the model received from those Apostles, their masters and founders, who after the propagation and diffusion of the evangelical teaching by the celestial master himself, accounted it not superfluous and useless, but necessary and beneficial, to establish the faithful more perfectly with the frequent admonitions of their letters, and to strengthen them more firmly in the true faith, and to deliver to them more abundantly a way of living and a pattern of religion.

Nevertheless, whether disturbed by adversities or nourished by good fortune, the church has never ceased to seek the advantage of its sons whom daily it begets to Christ, and to further their progress either in private or in public, inflamed by the fire of the Holy Spirit. Hence councils were assembled not only from neighbouring cities and provinces, but just as often from regions across the sea; hence synodal decrees were often issued; hence sacred canons were often established and consecrated by the Holy Spirit, by which the catholic faith is greatly strengthened and the unity of the peace of the church kept inviolate, and also its order befittingly arranged. Indeed, as it is not allowed to any Christian to transgress these canons, for clerics and priests not to know them is especially and utterly abominable. Since for the reasons mentioned above the salutary observance of these canons and of the religious and ever to be honoured tradition either never became fully known among your people, or else has now for the most part grown cold, it seemed right and pleasing to your authority and royal prudence, with the best—and, we believe, divinely inspired—counsel, to consult our insignificance on this matter and to seek the see of the blessed Remigius, by whose merits and teaching that same see, the church over all the churches of the Gauls, from his times ever flourished and excelled with all religion and doctrine.

And since, when about to seek and beg such things from us, you did not choose to appear illiberal and with an empty hand, your royal lordship deigned to honour us with a very great gift, very necessary and timely, and sufficiently suited to the matter in question; on which account we have both given praises, admiring greatly the heavenly providence, and also have returned no small thanks to your royal generosity.

You indeed have sent us dogs, of noble stock and excellent, nevertheless corporeal and mortal, for driving away the fury of visible wolves, with which our country, among other scourges inflicted on us by the just judgment of God, greatly abounds; yourself also seeking from us dogs, not corporeal, but spiritual, not such, to wit, as the prophet upbraids, saying; : "Dumb dogs, not able to bark," but such as the psalmist speaks of: "The tongue of thy dogs may be red with the same [blood] of thy enemies"; who surely shall know how and be fit to bark loudly for their master, and continually guard his flock with the most vigilant and sagacious watch, and keep afar off the blood-thirsty wolves of the unclean spirits, who are the betrayers and devourers of souls. Of this number you ask us for one in particular, by name Grimbald, priest and monk, to be chosen for this office and appointed to the charge of pastoral authority; to whom truly the universal Church, which nourished him from an early age in true faith and holy religion, and which advanced him by ecclesiastical custom through the various grades to the priestly dignity, testi-fies, proclaiming him to be most worthy of pontifical honour and capable also of teaching others. But as we wished rather that this should be done in our kingdom, and planned at one time to perform it with Christ's consent at an opportune season, so that we might have him, whom we had as a faithful son, also as a colleague in our ministry and a most trusty helper in every ecclesiastical service, it is not without immense grief—as we might say—that we suffer him to be torn from us, and to be separated from our sight by such a distance of land and sea.

But, on the other hand, because love counts no cost, nor faith any loss, and no distance between lands separates those whom the chain of true love binds, we have most willingly granted the request of you to whom we can deny nothing, nor do we grudge him to you, at whose advancement we rejoice as at our own, and whose gains we consider ours. For we know that in every place the same God is served, and that the Catholic and Apostolic

Church is one, whether Roman or across the sea. Therefore it is for us to concede him to you canonically, but for you to receive him honourably; he is to be sent to you on conditions and terms which are both for the glory of your kingdom and for the honour of our church and episcopate, with his electors, and with some of the magnates and chief men of your kingdom, that is, both bishops, priests and deacons, and also religious laymen. They shall by word of mouth avow and promise in the presence of all our church that they will hold him in due honour all the time of his life; and also that they will observe inviolably all their days the canonical decrees and the ecclesiastical injunctions handed down by the Apostles and the apostolic men of the church, which they can then hear and see from us, and afterwards learn from this their pastor and teacher according to the form handed on by us. When they have done this with divine benediction, receiving him duly consecrated according to ecclesiastical custom by the authority of the blessed Remigius through our ministry and the laying on of hands, and most fully instructed in all things, they are to escort him with due honour to his own see, eager and glad that they will always enjoy his support and be constantly instructed by his teaching and example.

Because truly "the members have care one for another, and either rejoice if one member rejoice, or if one member suffer all the members suffer with it," we commend him more carefully and particularly to your royal highness and most far-seeing clemency, that he may always teach with free authority without opposition from anyone, and put into effect whatever he can find consonant with the integrity of the church and the instruction of your people, and useful according to canonical authority and the custom of our church; lest perchance, which God forbid, anyone led by diabolical prompting shall set on foot controversy or stir up sedition against him with the zeal of malice and ill-will.

Thus it will be your care to foresee this and restrain in every way with the royal censure such persons if by chance they should appear, and to subdue barbaric ferocity with the bridle of your governance; but it will be his care to consult always with pastoral skill the welfare of those committed to him and rather to draw all to him with love than to drive them with fear.

May your most noble dignity, your most holy piety, and also most unconquered fortitude, ever rejoice and flourish in Christ the King of Kings and Lord of Lords.

Reprinted with permission from *English Historical Documents c. 500–1042*, ed. Dorothy Whitelock (London: Eyre & Spottiswoode, 1955; Routledge, 1979), pp. 221–224. This letter was edited by Francis Wise, *Annales rerum gestarum Alfredi Magni auctore Asserio Menevensi* (Oxford, 1722), pp. 123–129. Notes omitted.

-11-

Christian Practice and Literature

Christianity as a religious system was not restricted to philosophers and the ruling elite. Christian rituals also penetrated into, and were modified by, everyday experience; and Christian beliefs transformed, and were transformed by, popular literature and culture. However, because the primary evidence left to us, written documents, were produced exclusively by the literate minority of religious scholars, we have to read between the lines sometimes to understand how Christian ideas reached into everyday life—and vice-versa, how pre-existing ideas in Germanic cultures altered Christian practices. Thus the relationship between the "formal" religion of the bishops, priests, monks, and religious scholars and the "popular" religion of the vast majority of Christians in early medieval Europe is reciprocal—each influenced the other, and both were integral parts of medieval Christianity in Europe.

The four excerpts in this section focus on a variety of types of documents in order to examine the more practical aspects of Christian living and to see how Germanic concepts merged with Christian ones to produce a dynamic body of literature. The first two selections, from sermons (11.1) and the liturgy (11.2), reveal Christian practice as taught to the laity by the church itself. The last two selections examine Christian poetry (11.3) and drama (11.4) that reflect Germanic themes and ideas.

All of these documents emanate from religious centers of learning and therefore reflect the formal religion. However, these documents also address the needs and concerns of the larger Christian community and therefore give us a glimpse of popular religion in the early Middle Ages.

11.1 Sermons: Ælfric of Eynsham

The late tenth–early eleventh century in Anglo-Saxon England was a dynamic period of change and growth. The Scandinavian newcomers

were settling into eastern England, not without conflict with their English neighbors. Burgeoning lay piety caused dramatic growth in the
numbers of local churches built in villages and on manors. Church
leaders were faced with a need to both convert the remaining "heathens" (non-Christians) and reform the existing as well as new churches,
some of which had lapsed into ignorance or bad habits. Ælfric, abbot of
Eynsham (circa 955–1010), a product of an earlier monastic reform
movement, worked with the royal administration and other churchmen
to bring reform to the late Anglo-Saxon secular clergy (priests).

As part of their reform agenda, Ælfric and his colleagues sought to
change the priests' lives by setting a high standard of conduct for them,
including celibacy. Ælfric wanted the clergy to be able to teach and
preach to their congregations, so he produced sermon collections in the
Anglo-Saxon language for them as models of good preaching. The example below, Ælfric's sermon for Midlent, is typical of the kind of
biblical interpretation Ælfric and other sermon writers used to draw a
lesson out of the Scriptures. He reads the Bible story of Jesus feeding the
5000 first on the literal level, then reads it for the typological and
allegorical meaning as a sign of Christ and a metaphor for the believer,
and finally applies the moral of the story to his audience.

Questions

1. What is Ælfric's method of teaching the Bible?
2. What different kinds of meanings and lessons does he draw from
Scripture?
3. What overall worldview emerges from this sermon?

Ælfric, Sermon at Midlent

"Jesus went over the sea of Galilee, which is called of Tiberias, and a great
multitude followed him, because they had seen the miracles which he had
wrought on the diseased men. Then Jesus went up into a mountain, and
there sat with his disciples, and the holy Easter-tide was then very nigh.
Jesus then looked up, and saw that there was a great multitude coming, and
said to one of his disciples, who was called Philip, With what can we buy
bread for this people? This he said to prove the disciple: himself knew what
he would do. Then Philip answered, Though two hundred pennyworth of
bread were bought, yet could not every one of them get a morsel. Then said
one of his disciples, who was called Andrew, Peter's brother, Here beareth
a lad five barley loaves, and two fishes, but what is that for so great a
multitude? Then said Jesus, Make the people sit. And there was much grass
on the place pleasant to sit on: and they then all sat, about five thousand men.

Then Jesus took the five loaves, and blessed, and brake, and divided them among those sitting: in like manner also he divided the fishes; and they all had enough. When they all were full, Jesus said to his disciples, Gather the remainder, and let it not be lost. And they gathered the fragments, and filled twelve baskets with the remainder. The people, who saw this miracle, said that Christ was the true prophet who was to come to this world."

The sea which Jesus passed over betokeneth this present world, which Christ came to and passed over; that is he came to this world in human nature, and passed over this life; he came to death, and from death arose; and went up on a mountain, and there sat with his disciples, for he ascended to heaven, and there sits now with his saints. Rightly is the sea compared to this world, for it is sometimes serene and pleasant to navigate on, sometimes also very rough and terrible to be on. So is this world; sometimes it is desirable and pleasant to dwell in, sometimes also it is very rugged, and mingled with divers things, so that it is too often very unpleasant to inhabit. Sometimes we are hale, sometimes sick; now joyful, and again in great affliction; therefore is this life, as we before said, compared to the sea.

When Jesus was sitting on the mountain, he lifted up his eyes, and saw that there was a great multitude coming. All those who come to him, that is those who incline to the right faith, Jesus sees, and on them he has pity, and enlightens their understanding with his grace, that they may come to him without error, and to these he gives ghostly food, that they may not faint by the way. When he asked Philip, whence they could buy bread for the people, he showed Philip's ignorance. Well Christ knew what he would do, and he knew that Philip knew not. Then said Andrew, that a lad there bare five barley loaves and two fishes. Then said Jesus, "Make the people sit," and so on, as we have before repeated it to you. Jesus saw the hungry people, and he compassionately fed them, both by his goodness and by his might. What could his goodness alone have done, unless there had been might with that goodness? His disciples would also have fed the people, but they had not wherewithal. Jesus had the good will to nourish them, and the power to execute it.

God hath wrought many miracles and daily works; but those miracles are much weakened in the sight of men, because they are very usual. A greater miracle it is that God Almighty every day feeds all the world, and directs the good, than that miracle was, that he filled five thousand men with five loaves: but men wondered at this, not because it was a greater miracle, but because it was unusual. Who now gives fruit to our fields, and multiplies the harvest from a few grains of corn, but he who multiplied the five loaves? The might was there in Christ's hands, and the five loaves were, as it were, seed, not sown in the earth, but multiplied by him who created the earth.

This miracle is very great, and deep in its significations. Often some one sees fair characters written, then praises he the writer and the characters, but knows not what they mean. He who understands the art of writing praises their fairness, and reads the characters, and comprehends their meaning. In one way we look at a picture, and in another at characters. Nothing more is necessary for a picture than that you see and praise it: but it is not enough to look at characters without, at the same time, reading them, and understanding their signification. So also it is with regard to the miracle which God wrought with the five loaves: it is not enough that we wonder at the miracle, or praise God on account of it, without also understanding its spiritual sense.

The five loaves which the lad bare, betoken the five books which the leader Moses appointed in the old law. The lad who bare them, and tasted not of them, was the Jewish people, who read the five books, and knew therein no spiritual signification, before Christ came, and opened the books, and disclosed their spiritual sense to his disciples, and they afterwards to all christian people. We cannot now enumerate to you all the five books, but we will tell you that God himself dictated them, and that Moses wrote them, for the guidance and instruction of the ancient people of Israel, and of us also in a spiritual sense. These books were written concerning Christ, but the spiritual sense was hidden from the people, until Christ came himself to men, and opened the secrets of the books, according to the spiritual sense. . . .

He brake the five loaves and gave to his disciples, and bade them bear them to the people; for he taught them the heavenly lore: and they went throughout all the world, and preached, as Christ himself had taught. When he had broken the loaves then were they multiplied, and grew in his hands; for the five books were spiritually devised, and wise doctors expounded them, and founded on those books many other books; and we with the doctrine of those books are daily spiritually fed.

The loaves were of barley. Barley is very difficult to prepare, and, nevertheless, feeds a man when it is prepared. So was the old law very difficult and obscure to understand; but, nevertheless, when we come to the flour, that is to the signification, then it feeds and strengthens our mind with the hidden lore. There were five loaves, and there were five thousand men fed; because the Jewish people was subject to God's law, which stood written in five books. When Christ asked Philip, and proved him, as we before read, by that asking he betokened the people's ignorance, who were under that law, and knew not the spiritual sense which was concealed in that law.

The two fishes betokened the Psalms and the sayings of the prophets. The one of these announced and proclaimed Christ's advent with psalm-singing, and the other with prophecy, as if they were meat to the five barley loaves, that is, to the five legal books. The people, who were there fed, sat on the grass. The grass betokened fleshly desire, as the prophet said, "Every flesh is grass, and the glory of the flesh is as the blossom of plants." Now should everyone who will sit at God's refection, and partake of spiritual instruction, tread and press down the grass, that is, he should overpower his fleshly lusts, and ever dispose his body to the service of God.

There were counted at that refection five thousand males; because those men who belong to the spiritual refection should be manfully made, as the apostle said; he said, "Be watchful, and stand on faith, and undertake manfully, and be bold." Though if a woman be manly by nature, and strong to God's will, she will be counted among the men who sit at the table of God. Thousand is a perfect number, and no number extends beyond it. With that number is betokened the perfection of those men who nourish their souls with God's precepts.

"Jesus then bade the remainder to be gathered, that it might not be lost; and they filled twelve baskets with the fragments." The remainder of the refection, that is the depth of the doctrine, which secular men may not understand, that should our teachers gather, that it may not be lost, and preserve in their scrips, that is, in their hearts, and have ever ready to draw forth the wisdom and doctrine both of the old law and of the new. They gathered then twelve baskets full of the fragments. The twelvefold number betokened the twelve apostles; because they received the mysteries of the doctrine, which the lay folk could not understand.

"The people, who saw that miracle, said of Christ, that he was the true prophet who was to come." In one sense they said the truth: he was a prophet, for he knew all future things, and also prophesied many things which will, without doubt, be fulfilled. He is a prophet, and he is the prophecy of all prophets, for all the prophets have prophesied of him, and Christ has fulfilled the prophecies of them all. The people saw the miracle, and they greatly wondered at it. That miracle is recorded, and we have heard it. What their eyes did in them, that does our faith in us. They saw it, and we believe it, who saw it not; and we are therefore accounted the better, as Jesus, in another place, said of us, "Blessed are they who see me not, and, nevertheless, believe in me, and celebrate my miracles."

The people said of Christ, that he was a true prophet. Now we say of Christ, that he is Son of the Living God, who was to come to redeem the whole world from the power of the devil, and from hell-torment. The people knew not of those benefits, that they might have said that he was God, but they said that he was a prophet. We say now, with full belief, that Christ is a true prophet, and Prophet of all prophets, and that he is truly Son of the Almighty God, as mighty as his Father, with whom he liveth and reigneth in unity of the Holy Ghost, ever without end to eternity. Amen.

From *The Homilies of the Anglo-Saxon Church: The Homilies of Ælfric,* Vol. 1, ed. Benjamin Thorpe (London: Ælfric Society, 1844; Reprint, New York: Johnson, 1971), pp. 181–93 passim.

11.2 Liturgy: Rites for the Living and the Dead

Birth and death, the two markers of life, are often surrounded by rituals that give them meaning in the community. Christianity provided special observances for both that gave a Christian interpretation to them. Birth had a double meaning: physical birth and spiritual birth witnessed in baptism, as seen for example in the Baptismal Ritual of Hippolytus (1.3). Death also had two meanings: the end of the physical life of the body and the transformation of the spiritual life through death. Illness—with the possibility of dying—also had a spiritual dimension. Since body and soul were deemed interdependent, the threat of separation was a spiritual issue as well as a medical one. Someone might become gravely ill through unknown causes—attack by evil spiritual forces, through sin, or by God's will. In any case, all health must be sought from God who made all things. Consequently, priests often performed healing rituals designed to address both the physical illness and its potential spiritual cause, or at least to call on the Great Healer to intervene. These rituals for the sick are found in the same liturgical manuals with baptisms, the mass, and other blessings.

Christian rituals at the death bed were designed to see the individual and his family members through this transition from death to life by protecting and nurturing the spiritual life. The *Sacramentary of Gellone* (circa 760), excerpted below, gives one example of a prayer said by the priest over the dying individual. It expresses the hopes of both the living and the dying and relies on certain basic Christian doctrines to provide reassurance. Rituals for the sick are closely related to those for the dying. The priest likewise is called upon to invoke spiritual aid for the soul and the body of the suffering individual. The examples below from the *Leofric Missal* include Latin prayers for the sick that can be added to the mass at appropriate times and a blessing in Latin of various body parts, asking God to "exorcise" ills from each. Curiously, very similar blessings naming body parts are found in medical manuscripts from the early Middle Ages (see 12.2). The line between spiritual liturgy and physical medicine is not entirely clear.

Questions

1. Who is invoked in the sacrament for the dying, and why? What power do these beings have in the journey of the soul?

2. Why do you think the Latin exorcism for the sick names every body part?

3. What does the prayer of the priest in both documents accomplish for the patient and for the family?

Sacrament for the Dying: Sacramentary of Gellone (circa 760)

Go forth, O soul, from this world, in the Name of God the Father Almighty who created you, in the Name of Jesus Christ, the Son of the Living God, who suffered for you, in the Name of the Holy Spirit, who was poured out on you, in the name of angels and archangels, of thrones and dominions, of principalities and powers and of all the heavenly virtues, of Cherubim and Seraphim, of the whole human race which has been taken up by God, of the Patriarchs and Prophets, Apostles and Martyrs, Confessors and Bishops, priests and deacons and of every rank in the Catholic Church, of monks and hermits, virgins and faithful widows. Today your servant's place is established in peace and his dwelling in Jerusalem on high. Receive your servant, Lord.

Free, O Lord, the soul of your servant from all the perils of hell and from the snares of sin and from all tribulations. Free, O Lord, this soul as you freed Noah from the flood, as you freed Enoch and Elijah from the common death of the world. Free him as you freed Job from his sufferings and Moses from the hand of Pharaoh, the king of the Egyptians. Free his soul as you freed Daniel from the lion's den and the three boys from the fiery furnace and the hands of the wicked ruler. Free him as you freed Jonah from the whale's belly and Susanna from false witnesses. Free him as you freed David from the hand of King Saul and from Goliath and from all his dangers. Free your servant as you freed Peter and Paul from prisons and torment. So deign to free the soul of this man and allow him to dwell with you in heaven. Through Jesus Christ.

O God, before whose sight all who are born are brought, as you are the giver of life be merciful in punishment. We ask that you grant your servant a place with your saints and an inheritance with your elect. Through. . . .

God, with whom all those dying are alive (for in dying our bodies do not perish but are changed for the better), we humbly ask that you dispose that the soul of your servant be taken by the hands of the holy angels to the bosom of your friend, the Patriarch Abraham, to be raised again on the last great Judgment Day. Mercifully cleanse and forgive whatever evil by the devil's wiles he may have contracted in this mortal region. Through. . . .

O Lord, grant us your aid. Of your mercy receive the spirit of your servant, beloved by us, freed from the bonds of the body, in the peace of your saints, that, escaping the place of punishment and the flames of Gehenna, he may attain the region of the living. Who reigns.

[Then there are recited the following prayers: "The just shall be in everlasting remembrance" (Psalm 111); "Do not give the soul trusting in you, O Lord, to beasts" (Psalm 73:19); "Let the just rejoice in the sight of God" (Psalm 67:4); "Precious in the sight of the Lord is the death of his saints" (Psalm 115:15); "The saints will rejoice in glory" (Psalm 149:5).]

Receive, O Lord, the soul of your servant, returning to you; clothe him with a heavenly garment and wash him in the holy spring of eternal life, that he may rejoice among those who rejoice, and be wise with those who are wise, that he may take his place among the Martyrs, and go forth among the Patriarchs and Prophets, and that he may seek to follow Christ with the Apostles, and behold God's Glory with angels and archangels, and joy among the golden jewels of Paradise, and come to knowledge of mysteries, and find God among the Cherubim and Seraphim, and hear the song of songs among the twenty-four elders (Apocalypse 4), and wash his garments among those washing their stoles in the source of light (Apocalypse 7:14), and, among those knocking, may he find the doors of the Heavenly Jerusalem lie open (Apocalypse 3:20), and may he be with those who see God face to face, and sing the new song (Apocalypse 5:9) with the singers and hear heavenly sounds with those who hear them. Through Our Lord Jesus Christ your son.

Reprinted with permission from *Christianity and Paganism, 350–750,* ed. J. N. Hillgarth (Philadelphia: University of Pennsylvania Press, 1986), pp. 193–95 and translated from *Corpus Christianorum Series Latina,* ed. A. Dumas, 159 (Turnhout: Brepols, 1981), pp. 460–62.

Leofric Missal

Mass for the Infirm

Omnipotent everlasting God, eternal health of believers, hear us on behalf of Your servant(s) X for whom we implore the aid of Your mercy, that, with health restored to him/them, they may return thanks unto You in Your church. Through Christ our Lord.

Secret Prayers

O God, at whose commands the motions of our life run, accept the prayers and sacrifices of Your manservants and maidservants; for those/he who are ailing we implore Your mercy, so that, as we have feared for their/his danger, so may we rejoice in their/his health. For ever and ever, Amen.

The Preface to the Canon

. . . Eternal God, who therefore scourges Your servants physically so that they may progress in mind, powerfully declaring what may be the excellent salvation of Your faithful, while You show that this infirmity might therefore work health for us. Through Christ our Lord.

At the Conclusion

O God who alone presides over human infirmity, show the virtue of Your aid over our sick so that, by the strength of Your mercy the helpers/helper of Your holy church might merit being restored. Through Christ our Lord.

Alternate Conclusion

Omnipotent everlasting God who drives out illnesses of soul and body, show the power of Your aid over our sick, that by the strength of Your mercy to all of the faithful they/he may be returned to service.

Exorcism

Lord, holy Father, omnipotent eternal God, through the imposition of this scripture and taste of this water expel the devil from this man, from the head, from the hair, from the crown, from the brain, from the forehead, from the eyes, from the ears, from the nostrils, from the mouth, from the tongue, from the epiglottis, from the throat, from the neck, from the whole body, from all limbs, from the connections of his members, within and without, from the bones, from the veins, from the nerves, from the blood, from the perception, from the thoughts, from all conversation, and may the power of Christ work in you, in him who for you has died, so that you may merit eternal life.

Translated by Karen Louise Jolly from *The Leofric Missal,* ed. F. E. Warren (Oxford, UK: Clarendon Press, 1883), pp. 193, 235. Special thanks to Sarah Larratt Keefer for translation assistance.

11.3 Christian Poetry: *The Dream of the Rood*

Christian belief also expressed itself in traditional forms of poetry in Germanic languages. In some movingly beautiful ways, early medieval Christians portrayed their beliefs using the language, imagery, and values of their Germanic heritage. One example, among many, of early medieval poetry expressing Christian belief in a Germanic form is the Anglo-

Saxon poem *The Dream of the Rood* (or cross). The text of the poem is from one manuscript, the Vercelli Book (circa 960–980), but pieces reminiscent of the poem are also found on two crosses, the eighteen-foot stone Ruthwell Cross (seventh–eighth century) and the eighteen-inch silver-on-wood Brussels Cross (late tenth–early eleventh century). Both of these crosses seem to indicate that the poem had a wider oral history outside of the single complete text we possess in the manuscript.

The poem is multilayered, with a poet-narrator dreaming about a vision of an animate, anthropomorphized cross (rood), who is in turn remembering the event of Christ's death. The cross portrays itself as a great hero, and by extension Christ as a hero who chooses to mount the cross in order to do battle. The poet-dreamer, like the dual image of the cross, experiences a personal transformation through the vision and the reader then experiences the same through the poem. The language of the poem is very Anglo-Saxon in form, with alliteration across the half-lines and metaphorical compounds that cannot be adequately duplicated in translation. For example, the Anglo-Saxon opening reads thus:

> *Hwæt! ic swefna cyst secgan wylle,*
> *hwæt me gemætte to midre nihte,*
> *sythan reordberend reste wunedon.*
> *Thuhte me thæt ic gesawe syllicre treow*
> *on lyft lædan leohte bewunden,*
> *beama beorhtost. Eall thæt beacen wæs*
> *begoten mid golde. . . .*

Notice in line 3 a metaphorical word compound known as a kenning: *reordberend* means "speechbearer"—that is, human beings. In lines 5 and 6, the triple alliteration is particularly clear (*lyft, lædan, leohte; beama, beorhtost, beacen*). These are classic traits of Germanic poetry, here used to express Christian sentiments.

Questions

1. What Christian ideas predominate in the poem?
2. What about the poem seems to reflect Germanic customs and values to you?
3. How do the Christian and Germanic elements combine to produce a unified worldview?

The Dream of the Rood

Lo! I will tell the best of dreams,
what I dreamed in the middle of the night,
when speech-bearers were asleep.

It seemed to me that I saw a wondrous tree
borne aloft, enveloped in light
the brightest of timbers. That beacon was all
covered with gold. Gems stood
fair at the earth's surface; likewise there were five
up on the crossbeam. All the hosts of angels looked
    thereon,
fair through creation. This was certainly no gallows of a
    criminal.
But there looked upon it holy saints,
men on earth, and all of this glorious creation.
Wondrous was the victory-tree, and I guilty with sins,
wounded with transgressions. I saw the tree of glory
adorned with clothes, joyously shining,
decked with gold. Gems had
covered worthily the Ruler's tree.
However I through that gold could perceive
the former agony of wretches, that before it had
bled on the right side. I was all with sorrow troubled,
I was afraid because of the fair vision. I saw that eager
    beacon
change clothes and color; at times it was bedewed with
    moisture,
drenched with flowing blood; at other times with treasure
    adorned.
Yet while lying there a long awhile
I beheld sorrowfully the Savior's tree,
until I heard it speaking.
The best of woods began to speak words:
"It was long ago (I yet remember it),
that I was hewn down at the edge of the woods,
removed from my roots. Strong enemies took me away
    from there,
made then a spectacle, commanded me to bear their
    criminals aloft.
Men carried me there on their shoulders, until they set me
    on a hill.
Enemies enough fastened me there. I saw then the Lord of
    Mankind
eagerly hasten that he would ascend onto me.
Then I dared not there against the Lord's word

bend or break, when I saw tremble
the surface of the earth. I could all
those enemies fell, however I stood fast.
Then the young hero unclothed himself (that was God
    almighty)
strong and resolute. He ascended onto the high gallows,
brave in the sight of many, when he would redeem
    mankind.
I trembled when the hero embraced me. I dared not
    however bend to the earth,
fall to the earth's surface, but I must stand fast.
A cross was I raised up; I lifted up the great king,
heaven's lord; I dared not bow.
They drove through me with dark nails. On me are those
    wounds visible,
open wounds of malice. I dared not injure any of them.
They mocked both of us together. I was all drenched with
    blood,
poured from the man's side, when he had sent forth his
    spirit.
On that hill I had to endure many
cruel fates. I saw the God of hosts
cruelly stretched out. Darkness had
covered with clouds the Ruler's corpse,
bright splendor; a shadow went forth,
black under the clouds. All creation wept,
lamented the king's fall. Christ was on the cross.
Nevertheless there came eager ones from afar
to the prince. I beheld all that.
Grievously I was with sorrow engulfed; I bent however to
    the men's hands,
with great strength of humility. They seized there
    almighty God
lifted him up from that burdensome torment. The warriors
    left me
to stand drenched with blood; I was all wounded with
    arrows.
Then they laid down the limb-weary one, and stood at the
    head of his body.
They beheld there heaven's lord, and he rested himself
    there for awhile,

exhausted after the great battle. They began then to make
    for him a tomb
the warriors in the sight of the slayers. They carved it
    from bright stone.
They set therein the Lord of victory. Then they began to
    sing a sorrow-song for him,
destitute in the eventide, before they departed,
weary, from their glorious lord. He rested there alone.
Yet we weeping there for a good while
stood there, while the voices went up
of warriors. The corpse cooled,
the fair life-building. Then men began to fell us
all to the earth. That was a dreadful fate!
Men buried us in deep pits. Yet the Lord's servants,
friends, discovered me there,
and adorned me with gold and silver.
Now you have been able to hear, my beloved man,
how I survived the work of wicked men
grievous trouble. The time is now come
that they will adore me far and wide—
men around the earth and all this glorious creation
will pray to this beacon. On me the warrior of God
suffered awhile. Therefore I now gloriously
tower under the heavens, and I may heal
everyone who reveres me.
For a time I had become a severe punishment,
loathsome to people, before I opened the right way of life
to them, to speech-bearers.
Lo, the Prince of glory honored me then
over all forest trees, Guardian of heaven-kingdom,
just as he also his mother, Mary herself,
almighty God, before all men
honored over all womankind.
Now I command you, my beloved man,
that you tell these visions to men,
reveal with words that it is a wondrous tree
on which almighty God suffered
for the many sins of mankind
and for Adam's deed of old.
He tasted death there; yet after, the Lord arose
by his great might as a help for men.

Then he ascended into the heavens. Hither again he will
    come
into this middle-earth to seek mankind
on Doomsday, the Lord himself,
Almighty God amid all his angels.
Then he will judge, he who possesses the right to judge
everyone, just as each earned
when they were here in this transitory life.
Nor should anyone be unafraid
of the words which the Lord says;
he asks before the multitude: where is the man
who for the name of the Lord would taste
of bitter death, as he did before on that cross.
But they then will be afraid and few will think
what they can begin to say to Christ.
Anyone there then need not be afraid
who before in his heart bears the best of beacons.
But through the cross must he seek the kingdom
far from the earth-way, each soul
who wishes to dwell with the Ruler."
I prayed myself then to that cross with a joyous heart,
very strongly, there I was alone
all to myself; my spirit was
longing for departure; I endured a great
time of longing. Now for me the joy of life is
that I may seek the victory-sign,
often alone more than other men,
to fully adore it. In me is a desire for that,
great in my mind, and my protection is
directed from the cross. I possess not many rich
friends on the earth. But they forth hence
departed from the joys of the world, they sought the King
    of glory,
and live now in heaven with the High Father,
hope in glory; and I hope myself
every day for when the cross of the Lord,
which I here on earth beheld before,
will fetch me from this transitory life
and then bring me where there is great bliss,
joy in heaven, where there are the people of God,
set at the banquet, where there is single bliss;

and he will then place me where I thereafter may
dwell in glory, fully with the holy ones
enjoying blessing. The Lord is to me a friend,
he who here on earth before suffered
on the gallow-tree for the sins of men:
he redeemed us, and gave us life,
a heavenly home. Hope was restored
with blessing and joy, for those who before suffered burning.
The Son was victorious on the journey,
mighty and successful. When he will come with many,
a host of spirits into the kingdom of God,
the Ruler almighty, to joy amid angels,
and all the saints who went into heaven before
in glory, then their Lord,
almighty God, came to his own realm.

Translated by Karen Louise Jolly from *The Vercelli Book,* ed. George Philip Krapp, *Anglo-Saxon Poetic Records,* Vol. 2 (New York: Columbia University Press, 1932), pp. 61–65, and *The Dream of the Rood,* ed. Bruce Dickins and Alan S. C. Ross (New York: Appleton-Century-Crofts, 1966), pp. 20–35.

11.4 Christian Drama: Hrotsvit of Gandersheim, *Abraham*

The reflective and learned environment of the monastery often produced some of the most beautiful early medieval literature—works that draw on the classical, Christian, and Germanic traditions. Hrotsvit of Gandersheim (circa 932–1000) was a highly educated nun in Germany (from the monastic tradition established there by Boniface and Leoba, 8.4) who wrote poetry and dramas. She took Christian legends and set them in her own language with her own creative genius.

The play here, entitled *Abraham,* is based on a fourth-century legend about the Syrian hermits of the desert. Hrotsvit retells the story in dramatic dialogue using complex classical styles of rhymed rhythmic prose. Hrotsvit developed the characters of the hermit Abraham and his niece Mary, who fails in her initial attempts to follow the hermetic life. Abraham's redemption of Mary is a moving allegory of salvation that plays with notions of sexuality and virginity, sin and spirituality in the relationship of the lover and the beloved. The drama as produced for an audience of nuns or possibly lay people might have had the same cathartic effect as the poem *The Dream of the Rood.*

Questions

1. What is the message that Abraham brings to Mary, and why does he go to such lengths to deliver it?

2. Consider the relationship of Abraham and Mary in light of the medieval layers of interpretation discussed by Ælfric (11.1): what are all the possible meanings or interpretations of their relationship—as a type, as an allegory, as a moral?

3. Compare this play to *The Dream of the Rood* (11.3). How do you think a medieval audience would respond to this drama?

Hrotsvit of Gandersheim, *Abraham*

The fall and repentance of Mary, the hermit Abraham's niece/ who, after she had lived twenty years in anchoretic peace,/ and having lost her virginity,/ returned to the world's vanity,/ and did not even fear to live in a brothel with prostitutes./ But after two years, admonished by the aforementioned Abraham who sought her out disguised as a lover, she returned and purged herself from the stains of her sins for a period twenty years lasting,/ through effusive tears, vigils, prayers and the constant exercise of fasting.

I.I

Abraham: Do you, brother and cohermit Effrem, find it convenient to allow/ that I speak with you now,/ or do you wish for me to wait until you have finished your divine praises?

Effrem: Our conversations should always be in His praise,/ Who promised to be in the midst of those who have gathered in His name.

Abraham: I have come to speak of nothing else except of what I know is in concordance with God's will.

Effrem: Then I shall not keep myself from you another moment but turn/ and give myself entirely to your concern.

Abraham: A certain impending task has upset my mind/ concerning which I hope that you will be inclined to concur with my judgment.

Effrem: As we are to be of one heart and one soul, we ought to want the same/ and not want the same.

Abraham: I have a young niece bereaved of the solace of both parents, for whom I bear great affection, for whom I feel sorry/ and on whose account I tire myself with constant worry.

Effrem: And what are the cares of this world to you, you who have triumphed over the world?

Abraham: This is my care: that the immense radiance of her beauty should wane/ and be dimmed by some pollution's stain.

Effrem: Such concern no blame will earn.

Abraham: I hope that so it'll be.

Effrem: How old is she?

Abraham: When the course of this year is completed, she will have breathed of life for two Olympiades.

Effrem: An immature girl.

Abraham: That's the reason for my concern.

Effrem: Where does she dwell?

Abraham: In my own cell. When, asked by her relatives, I undertook to raise her, but decided to bequeath her wealth to the poor.

Effrem: Contempt for worldly things befits the soul intent on heaven.

Abraham: I desire passionately that to Christ she be espoused and that for His service she be trained.

Effrem: An aim worthy to be praised.

Abraham: I am forced to do so by her name.

Effrem: What is she called?

Abraham: Mary.

Effrem: Is that so? The excellence of such an exalted name/ deserves virginity's garland and acclaim.

Abraham: I am convinced that, if she is kindly urged by our exhortations and aid,/ she will prove easy to persuade.

Effrem: Let us go to her and let us instill in her mind the desirable security of the virginal life.

II.I

Abraham: Oh my adopted daughter, oh, part of my soul, Mary, heed my fatherly admonitions/ and the beneficial instructions/ of my companion Effrem. Strive to imitate in your chastity/ her who is the fount of virginity and whose name you bear.

Effrem: It would be most unfitting, daughter, if you, who are joined to Mary, the mother of God through your name's secret mystery/ and have been, thereby, raised to the axis of the sky among the stars that never set, if you wished to debase yourself in your actions/ and sink to the lowest realms of the world.

Mary: I am ignorant of the secret of my name:/ therefore, I do not grasp the meaning of what you say in such a roundabout way.

Effrem: Mary means *stella maris,* the "star of the sea," around which, as you may learn, the earth is borne and the poles turn.

Mary: Why is it called the "star of the sea"?

Effrem: Because it never sets but is the source/ that guides sailors on the path of the right course.

Mary: But how could it ever happen that I, such a little thing and made of clay,/ could, through my own merits, attain to that glorious place/ where the mysterious symbol of my name resides in grace?

Effrem: Through the unimpaired wholeness of your body and the pure holiness of your mind.

Mary: Great is the honor for a mortal to equal the rays of stars.

Effrem: For if you remain uncorrupt and a virgin, you will become the equal of God's angels; Surrounded by them, when you have cast off the burden of your heavy body, you will traverse the sky,/ rising above the ether high,/ and journey through the circle of the zodiac, not slowing down or delaying your flight/ until you have reached the Virgin's Son's arms' delight,/ and are embraced by Him in the luminous wedding chamber of His mother.

Mary: Whoever undervalues this is an ass. Therefore I renounce the world and deny myself so that I may deserve to be bequeathed the joys of such great felicity.

Effrem: Behold, the child's breast brings forth the mature wisdom of age.

Abraham: It is by the grace of God on High.

Effrem: This no one can deny.

Abraham: Yet even though God's grace has been made manifest, it would not be prudent to leave such a young child to her own counsel.

Effrem: True.

Abraham: Therefore, I shall build her a little cell, narrow of entrance and adjacent to my own dwelling. I will visit her often and through the window/ instruct her in the Psalms and other pages of God's law.

Effrem: Rightly so.

Mary: I commit myself, father Effrem, to your guidance.

Effrem: May the Heavenly Bridegroom, to Whose affections you have pledged yourself at such a tender age/ succour you, daughter, from all the guiles of Satan.

III.I

Abraham: Brother Effrem, whenever anything happens to me;/ either good fortune or misery,/ to you I come, you alone I consult; so do not turn away from the laments I utter/ but help me in the pain I suffer.

Effrem: Abraham, Abraham, what a heart-rending sight./ Why are you more dejected than is meet and is right?/ A hermit should never be perturbed in the manner of men in the world.

Abraham: My distress in incomparable,/ my grief is intolerable.

Effrem: Don't keep me in suspense with your roundabout words,/ but explain what occurred.

Abraham: Mary, my adopted daughter whom for twice ten years, I brought up to the best of my ability, whom I instructed to the best of my skill . . .

Effrem: What happened to her whom you so clearly cherished?

Abraham: Woe is me, she has perished.

Effrem: How?

Abraham: In great wretchedness; then she stole away, secretly.

Effrem: With what tricks did the guile of the ancient serpent beset her?

Abraham: Through the forbidden passion of a certain deceiver/ who, disguised as a monk, often came to see her/ under the pretence of instructive visits,/ until he ignited the undisciplined instincts of her youthful heart to burn in love for him, so much so that she jumped from her window to perform that awful deed.

Effrem: Ah, I shudder to hear it.

Abraham: And when the wretched girl, so beguiled,/ found herself lapsed and defiled,/ she beat her breast,/ lacerated her face and her hands,/ tore her clothes amidst sighs,/ pulled out her hair, and raised her voice in lamentations to the skies.

Effrem: Not without reason, for her ruin must be mourned/ and with great outpouring of tears deplored.

Abraham: She bewailed not to be what she was.

Effrem: Poor girl, alas.

Abraham: She mourned that she had acted against our admonitions.

Effrem: Rightly so.

Abraham: She lamented that she had rendered void the toils of her vigils, prayers and fastings.

Effrem: If she had persevered in such great remorse, she would have been saved.

Abraham: She did not persevere for long/ but added worse to prior wrong.

Effrem: In fear my stomach is turned; my limbs are all unnerved.

Abraham: For after she has punished herself with these laments, defeated by the immenseness of her grief, she was carried headlong, into the lap of desperation.

Effrem: Alas, alas, what grave perdition!

Abraham: And because she despaired of ever attaining forgiveness, she chose to return to the world and to serve its vanities.

Effrem: Well, up until now, the spirits of iniquity had been unaccustomed to gain/ such victory in the abode where hermits stay.

Abraham: But now we are the demons' prey.

Effrem: I wonder how it could have happened that she escaped you unnoticed.

Abraham: For some days I was much troubled by the horror of a revelation,/ a vision, which, if my mind had not been careless, would have foretold me of her perdition.

Effrem: I would like to know the nature of this vision.

Abraham: I thought I stood before the entrance of my cell,/ when, behold, a dragon of miraculous size and of foul smell,/ came, rushing with great speed towards a little white dove near me. He snatched the dove, devoured it and then suddenly vanished.

Effrem: A vision with clear meaning.

Abraham: But, I, when I roused myself from the vision, thought about what I had seen and was gripped with terror/ that a persecution threatened the church which might lead some of the faithful into error.

Effrem: That was to be feared.

Abraham: Therefore, prostrate in prayer, I beseeched Him Who has foreknowledge of future events to unveil for me the meaning of the sight.

Effrem: You did right.

Abraham: Then on the third night,/ when I gave my exhausted body to sleep,/ I thought I saw the very same dragon, wallowing deep,/ crushed under my feet and I saw the same white dove, dart forth unhurt.

Effrem: I am delighted to hear this because without doubt, your daughter Mary will someday return.

Abraham: When I awoke, I smoothed my prior grief with the solace of this new vision, and collected myself to remember my pupil; then I also recalled, not without sadness that I have not heard her recite her customary prayers for the last two days.

Effrem: You remembered too late.

Abraham: I confess it. Then I approached her cell, knocked on her window and repeatedly called my daughter by name.

Effrem: Alas, you called in vain.

Abraham: I did not realize that yet, but asked her why she was neglecting her prayers and to my concern,/ I received not the slightest sound of response in turn.

Effrem: What did you do then?

Abraham: When I understood, at last, that she whom I sought had left I was aghast with fear, my innermost parts trembled,/ and in terror quaked all my members.

Effrem: No wonder! Indeed, even now, listening to you I feel the same sensation.

Abraham: Then I filled the air with doleful sounds wild,/ asking what wolf has snatched away my lamb, what thief has stolen my child?

Effrem: You were right to bewail the loss of her whom you have raised.

Abraham: Then people came who knew for sure/ that what I have now told you is actually true/ and they said that she has given herself over to sin.

Effrem: Where is she gone?

Abraham: It is not known.

Effrem: What will you do next?

Abraham: I have a loyal friend who, without rest, is traveling through the villages and towns and will not stop/ until he finds the very spot/ whereto she is bound.

Effrem: What if she is found?

Abraham: I will change my habit and will go to her disguised as a lover. Perchance, admonished by me after her awful shipwreck, she may return to the safe port of earlier tranquillity.

Effrem: And what will you do if meat to eat and wine to drink is placed before you?

Abraham: I will not refuse so that I won't be recognized.

Effrem: Indeed it is praiseworthy that you should use correct discretion in saving the erring girl for Christ even if it means that you will have to relax the strict rules of our monastic practice.

Abraham: I am all the more eager to undertake this daring deed now that I know that you agree with me.

Effrem: He who knows the secrets of our hearts, and knows the intents that underlie our actions, does not disapprove that one of us relaxes temporarily the rigor of our strict rules and behaves like our weaker brethren, if it is done so that he may all the more efficiently win/ and regain a soul that has strayed into sin.

Abraham: Meanwhile, it will be your task to assist me with prayers so that I will not be impeded by the devil's guiles.

Effrem: May the greatest of all goods, without which no other good may be, bring you intent to good ends.

IV

Abraham: Is this my friend whom I sent out two years ago to find Mary? It is he, indeed!

Friend: Greetings, venerable father.

Abraham: Greetings, dear friend. Long I have waited/ and I even abated/ and lost hope for your return.

Friend: The reason I took so long was that I did not wish to agitate you with unconfirmed news; but when I could investigate and the truth learn,/ I promptly hurried to return.

Abraham: Did you see Mary?

Friend: I have.

Abraham: Where?

Friend: In a city, close by.

Abraham: With whom does she reside,/ on whom does she rely?

Friend: It hurts me to reply.

Abraham: Why?

Friend: It is too awful to say.

Abraham: But tell me, I pray.

Friend: She has chosen as her abode the house of a certain procurer who treats her with tender love. And not without profit I may say, for every day he receives large sums of money from her lovers.

Abraham: From Mary's lovers?

Friend: Yes, from them.

Abraham: Who are her lovers?

Friend: There are many.

Abraham: Woe is me. Oh, good Jesus, what misfortune is this I hear, that she, whom I raised to be Your bride,/ has strange lovers at her side?

Friend: This has been the custom of whores in all ages/ that they delight in the love of strangers.

Abraham: Bring me a soldier's clothes and a good steed/ so that, after I lay aside my religious habit, disguised as a lover to her I may speed.

Friend: Here is all you need.

Abraham: Give me a hat, too, that which to cover my tonsure I pray.

Friend: This too is very necessary so as not to give your identity away.

Abraham: Should I take this coin I have to pay the innkeeper?

Friend: Otherwise you won't be able to meet with Mary.

V

Abraham: Greetings good host!

Innkeeper: Who is it that calls? Greetings!

Abraham: Do you have a nice place for a traveler to stay overnight?

Innkeeper: Indeed we do; our hospitality is for all who alight.

Abraham: Good!

Innkeeper: Come in, so that dinner can be prepared for you.

Abraham: I owe you much for this merry welcome, but I ask for even more from you.

Innkeeper: Tell me what you desire,/ so that I can attain to what you aspire.

Abraham: Here, take this little gold that I brought and arrange that that most beautiful girl who, as I hear, stays with you, shares our meal.

Innkeeper: Why do you wish to see her?

Abraham: I would delight in getting to know her whose beauty I have heard praised by so many and so often.

Innkeeper: Whoever praised her beauty, did not tell a lie, for in the loveliness of her face she outshines all other women.

Abraham: That is why I burn/ and for her love so yearn.

Innkeeper: I wonder that in your decrepit old age you aspire/ and the love of a young woman desire.

Abraham: For sure, I come for no other purposes but to see her.

VI

Innkeeper: Come, Mary, come along. Show your beauty to our newcomer.

Mary: Here I come.

Abraham: What boldness, what constancy of mind I must muster as I see her whom I raised in my hidden hermitage decked out in a harlot's garb./ But this is not the time to show in my face what is in my heart;/ I must be on guard:/ like a man I will bravely suppress my tears gushing forth. With feigned cheerfulness of countenance I will veil the bitterness of my internal grief.

Innkeeper: Lucky Mary, be merry; because now not only men your age flock to you, as before, but even men ripe of age seek your favors.

Mary: Those who seek me in love, receive equal love from me in return.

Abraham: Come on Mary, give me a kiss.

Mary: I will not only give you a taste of sweet kisses/ but will caress your ancient neck with close embraces.

Abraham: That is what I am after.

Mary: What is it I feel? What is this spell?/ What is this rare and wonderful odor I smell?/ Oh, the smell of this fragrance reminds me of the fragrance of chastity I once practiced.

Abraham: Now, now I must pretend, now I must persist and be lustful in the manner of lewd young men and play the game/ so that I am not recognized by my seriousness or else she might leave and hide for shame.

Mary: Woe me, wretched woman! How I sunk, how I fell into perdition's ravine!

Abraham: This is not a fit place for complaints, where the band of jolly guests convene.

Innkeeper: Lady Mary, why do you sigh?/ Why do you cry?/ In the two years you have lived here, never such groans and complaints bursting forth did I hear; never such grieving words!

Mary: Oh, I wish I could have died three years ago, then I would not have sunk into such disgrace and woe.

Abraham: I didn't come all this way/ to join you in lamenting your sins but to be joined to you making love and being gay.

Mary: I was moved by a slight regret to utter such words; but let us now dine and be merry because, as you admonished me,/ this is certainly not the time to bewail one's sins.

Abraham: Abundantly we have wined [drunk],/ abundantly we have dined and are now tipsy, good host, with the generous portions you served. Give us now leave to rise from the table/ so that I might be able/ to lay down and refresh my weary body by sweet rest.

Innkeeper: I'm at your behest.

Mary: Rise, my lord, rise up. I shall accompany you to your bedroom.

Abraham: That pleases me. In fact, I could not have been forced to go, were I not to go with you.

VII

Mary: Here is a bedroom for us to stay in. Here is the bed, decked with rich and lovely covers. Sit down, so that I may take off your shoes so you won't have to tire yourself removing them.

Abraham: First, lock the door so no one may enter.

Mary: Don't worry on that account,/ I will make sure that the bolt is secure/ and that no one finds easy access to disturb us.

Abraham: Now the time has come to remove my hat and reveal who I am. Oh my adoptive daughter, oh part of my soul, Mary,/ don't you recognize me,/ the old man who raised you like a father and who pledged you with a ring/ to the only begotten Son of the Heavenly King?

Mary: Woe is me! It is my father and teacher Abraham who speaks!

Abraham: What happened to you, daughter?

Mary: Tremendous misery.

Abraham: Who deceived you? Who seduced you?

Mary: He who overthrew our first parents.

Abraham: Where is the angelic life that already here on earth you led?

Mary: Destroyed, it fled.

Abraham: Where is the modesty of your virginity? Where your admirable continence?

Mary: Lost and gone from hence.

Abraham: What reward for the efforts of your fasting, prayers, and vigils can you hope for unless you return to your senses, you who fell,/ from the height of heaven and have sunk in the depth of hell?

Mary: Woe is me, alas!

Abraham: Why did you disdain me?/ Why did you desert me?/ Why did you not tell me of your wretched sin; so that I and my beloved friend Effrem could perform worthy penance for you?

Mary: After I first sinned, and sunk into perfidy/ I did not dare, polluted as I was, to even approach your sanctity.

Abraham: Who ever has lived free from sin/ except for the Son of the virgin?

Mary: No one.

Abraham: It is human to err but evil to persist in sin; he who fell suddenly is not the one to be blamed/ but he who fails to rise promptly again.

Mary: Woe is me, wretched woman.

Abraham: Why do you fall down?/ Why do you stay unmoving, lying on the ground? Arise and hear what I have to say!

Mary: I fell, shaken with fear because I could not bear the force of your fatherly admonitions.

Abraham: Consider my love for you and put aside your fears.

Mary: I cannot.

Abraham: Did I not relinquish my accustomed hermitage on your behalf/ and did I not leave aside/ all observance of our regular rule,/ so much so, that I who am an old hermit, have turned into a pleasure-seeking lewd fool,/ and I who for so long practiced silence, made jokes and spoke merry words so that I wouldn't be recognized? Why do you still stare at the ground with lowered face? Why do you refuse to speak with me?

Mary: I am troubled by my grave offence; this is why I don't dare to presume to lift my eyes to heaven or have the confidence to speak with you.

Abraham: Don't lose faith, my daughter, don't despair,/ but from the abyss of dejection repair/ and place your hope in God.

Mary: The enormity of my sins has cast me into the depth of despair.

Abraham: Your sins are grave, I admit,/ but heavenly pity is greater than anything we can commit./ Therefore cast off your despair/ and beware/ to leave unused this short time given to you for penitence because of laziness, that divine grace abounds even where the abomination of sins prevails.

Mary: If I had any hope of receiving forgiveness, my eagerness to do penance would burst forth.

Abraham: Have mercy on my exhaustion which I had to bear on your account, and cast off this dangerous and sinful despair which we know to be a graver offense then all other sins. For whoever despairs,/ thinking that God forbears/ to come to the aid of sinners, that person sins irremediably. Because just as the spark from a flintstone cannot set the sea on fire,/ so the bitter taste of our sins cannot likewise aspire/ to change the sweetness of divine goodwill.

Mary: It is not the magnificence of heavenly grace which I doubt,/ but when I consider my own sin, so profound,/ then I fear that the performance of even a worthy penance will not suffice.

Abraham: I take your sins upon myself; Only come back to the place which you deserted/ and take up again the life which you subverted.

Mary: I will never go against any of your wishes but will embrace obediently all your commandments.

Abraham: Now I believe, you are my child whom I raised, indeed; now I feel you are the one to be loved above all others.

Mary: I possess some clothes and a little gold;/ I wait to be told/ how to dispose of them.

Abraham: What you acquired through sin,/ must be cast off together with the sins.

Mary: I thought, perhaps, they could be given to the poor or offered to the sacred altars.

Abraham: It is neither sanctioned nor acceptable that gifts be given to God which were acquired through sin.

Mary: Beyond this, I have no concern.

Abraham: Dawn arrives; the day breaks. Let us return!

Mary: You, beloved father, must lead the way/ as the good shepherd leads the sheep gone astray;/ and I, advancing in your footsteps, will follow your lead.

Abraham: Not so; on foot I will proceed/ but on my horse you will have a seat/ so that the sharp rocks of the road will not harm your tender little feet.

Mary: What shall I say? How shall I ever compensate for your kindness? You do not force me, miserable wretch, with threats, but exhort me to do penance with kind benevolence.

Abraham: I ask nothing of you, except that you remain intent upon spending the rest of your life in God's service.

Mary: Out of my own free will I shall remain contrite,/ I shall persist in my penance with all my might,/ and even if I lose the ability to perform the act,/ the will, though, shall never lack.

Abraham: It is important that you serve the divine will as eagerly/ as you served the worldly vanities.

Mary: The will of the Lord be done in me, because of your merits.

Abraham: Let us return and hurry our way.

Mary: Let us hurry, I am weary of delay.

VIII

Mary: With what speed we have traveled over this difficult and rugged road.

Abraham: Whatever is done with devotion, is accomplished with ease. Behold, here is your deserted little cell.

Mary: Woe me, this cell is witness to my sin,/ therefore I fear to go in.

Abraham: And understandably. Any place where the ancient enemy has won a triumph is to be avoided.

Mary: And where do you intend me to devote myself to my penance?

Abraham: Go into the small interior room/ so that the ancient serpent will not find the opportunity to deceive you anew.

Mary: I will not contradict you but embrace eagerly what you command.

Abraham: I shall go to Effrem, my friend, so that he who alone mourned with me over your loss may rejoice with me over your return.

Mary: A worthy concern!

IX

Effrem: Are you bringing me joyous news?

Abraham: Most joyous news.

Effrem: I am glad. Doubtless you have found Mary.

Abraham: Indeed I found her and led her back, rejoicing, to the fold.

Effrem: I believe this was done by the grace of God.

Abraham: I doubt it not.

Effrem: I would like to know how from this day on she will conduct her life and her penance fulfill?

Abraham: Entirely according to my will.

Effrem: That will be a great advantage to her.

Abraham: Whatever I have suggested for her to do, however difficult, however harsh, she has not refused to perform.

Effrem: Very praiseworthy.

Abraham: She put on a hair shirt and is weakened by the constant exercise of vigils and fastings, but still she forces her tender body to follow her soul's mandate/ and observes the strictest rules, bearing penance's weight.

Effrem: It is only right that the filth of her sinful delight/ be purged by the bitter severity of her plight.

Abraham: Whoever hears her lamentations is wounded in his heart by its force;/ whoever feels the pangs of her remorse, himself feels remorse.

Effrem: It usually happens so.

Abraham: She works with all her strength to become an example of conversion/ for those for whom she was the cause of perdition.

Effrem: That is proper.

Abraham: She strives, to appear as brightly radiant as she was once foul.

Effrem: I rejoice in hearing this; I am happy with heartfelt joy.

Abraham: And justifiably, for even the angelic choirs rejoice and praise the Lord when a sinner repents.

Effrem: No wonder, for the steadfast perseverance of the just man delights Him no more than the penance of a sinner.

Abraham: So that He should be all the more praised for this gain,/ as there was no hope for her to become herself again.

Effrem: Rejoicing let us praise and by praising let us glorify the only begotten Son of God, honored, kind and cherished,/ who does not wish that those whom he redeemed with his precious blood should ever perish.

Abraham: His be all honor, and glory, praise and jubilation, for time everlasting, Amen.

Reprinted with permission from *The Dramas of Hrotsvit of Gandersheim,* trans. Katharina M. Wilson (Saskatoon and Toronto: Peregrina Press, 1985), pp. 77–90. Notes omitted.

–12–

Christian Diversity and Accommodation

The story of conversion and the rise of Christian kingdoms in the early Middle Ages is presented by Christian authors as a synthetic narrative, a progression of events directed by divine will. Within this historical vision, the forces of good and evil are clearly evident: Christian kings should lead their societies under a banner of Christian values, aided by church leaders. However, hidden within this narrative of progress toward greater Christian unity are stories of diversity—both cultural diversity within Europe in the different patterns of conversion and diversity in cross-cultural interaction. This last section examines some of the evidence of this diversity.

The three excerpts in 12.1 look at how Viking settlers converted in England, France, and Normandy. In all three negotiations, under Charlemagne, Alfred, and Charles the Simple, the conversion of these Vikings involves more than just a change in religion. A second type of internal accommodation and diversity is evident in the production of medical remedies, copied in monastic manuscripts, that incorporate both Christian ritual and Germanic charm formulas (12.2). These popular remedies are comparable to the formal remedies found in the liturgy (11.2), but contain more evidence of Germanic folklore and how it was transformed by Christianity.

Christian Europe did not evolve in isolation from other religious traditions, either: Judaism, Eastern Orthodoxy centered in Byzantium, and Islam provided the opportunity for both dialogues and conflicts that helped European Christians define who they are and what they are not. The "Dialogue between the Church and the Synagogue" (12.3) indicates that relations between Jews and Christians in Anglo-Saxon England might have been more than academic, more than a mere intellectual exercise in debate—defining Jewish difference was a necessary step for many in defining Christian identity.

Finally, it is wise to remember that other versions of Christianity flourished outside Europe and even Byzantium, and engaged in dialogue with other religious traditions. The dialogue of Patriarch Timothy with the Caliph Mahdi (12.4) shows a Nestorian church leader debating with a Muslim ruler over the differences in their faiths.

All of these dialogues or debates—between Christians, Jews, and Muslims—and the treaties of conversion between different cultural groups—Franks, Anglo-Saxons, and Scandinavians—serve as examples of how cultural identity is formed through opposition, through defining the other. And yet at the same time, as the treaties, dialogues, and most especially the medical charms reveal, Christian identity is the product of cultural accommodation and assimilation.

12.1 Conversion by Treaty: The Vikings

The image of Vikings in popular literature as violent, barbaric raiders, whose fierce ship prows came swiftly over the seas to the coasts of Europe and down the rivers into the heartlands, is partly the product of the Christian narrators of history who dominate the evidence left to us. The Vikings were also fearless explorers who sailed off to new lands to the west (Greenland, Iceland, and Vinland in North America), and astute traders plying the routes around the North Sea, the Baltic, and in the Mediterranean.

Most of all, the Vikings are also distant cousins of the settled peoples of England and continent, among whom they found a new home and a new multicultural identity. Viking settlers in the Danelaw of England made peace with King Alfred and eventually contributed to an Anglo-Scandinavian mixture evident in the reign of King Cnut (1016–1035). Viking invaders in northern France negotiated a peace with the French king and created a new place and a new identity: Normandy and the Normans, maintaining their own Viking-French hybrid identity for centuries.

The three excerpts here reveal the negotiations that took place to incorporate Viking newcomers into the existing scheme. In part, these efforts succeeded because of certain shared cultural characteristics between the Scandinavian Vikings and the Anglo-Saxons or the Franks. But just as many misunderstandings and confusions took place that indicate the problematic nature of these cross-cultural encounters. In all three cases, conversion occurs within a larger context of political negotiation and peace making. The first, from the reign of Charlemagne, is the account by a monk of Saint Gall of the baptisms of "Northmen" or Viking visitors performed annually at the court—and some of the mixed motives involved in this ritual, at least according to the monastic author. The second, from Asser's Life of Alfred, shows how the king negotiated a peace treaty with the Viking leader Guthrum that involved conversion and oath taking. In the third, from a later Norman legend about the founding of Normandy under Rollo in 911 or 912, the Normans recall their rough-and-tumble Viking roots in contrast to the courtly French, who negotiated this peace treaty with the Vikings using homage and fealty, conversion, and marriage.

Questions

1. Why do the Vikings in these stories want to convert to Christianity?
2. What else accompanies their conversion, and why? What does this say about conversion in the early Middle Ages?
3. What Viking characteristics appear in all of these stories?

Monk of Saint Gall, Deeds of Charles the Great

Speaking of the Northmen, I will illustrate their esteem for the faith, and for baptism, by telling an anecdote of the days of our grandfathers. This terrible people, who had stood in awe of the great Emperor Charles and paid him tribute, continued after his death to exhibit to his son Louis [the Pious] the respect they had shown his father. After a time the pious emperor had compassion upon their ambassadors, and asked them whether they would accept the Christian faith. They answered that they were ready to obey him in all things, always and everywhere. He then commanded that they be baptized in his name of whom the learned Augustine said: "If there were no Trinity, the Truth itself would not have said, 'Go ye therefore, and teach all nations, baptizing them in the name of the Father, and of the Son, and of the Holy Ghost.' "

The Northmen were treated like adopted sons by the chief lords of the court. They received from the king's closet the white baptismal robe, and from their sponsors the Frankish dress—costly garments, and weapons, and ornaments.

This custom was followed for a long time. The Northmen came year after year in even greater numbers, not for Christ's sake, but for worldly gain. They did not come now as ambassadors; but as submissive vassals they hastened at the holy Eastertide to do homage to the emperor. Finally one year they came fifty strong. The emperor asked them whether they would be baptized. They assented, and he commanded that they be straightway sprinkled with holy water. There were not enough linen robes, so the emperor had more garments cut out and sewed up roughly like a bag or towel.

One of these robes was suddenly put upon one of the oldest of the Northmen. He looked at it awhile with critical eyes, and grew not a little angry. Then he said to the emperor: "I have been baptized here twenty times before, and every time I was clad in the best and whitest garments; and now you give me a sack which befits a swineherd rather than a warrior. I have given up my own garments and would be ashamed of my nakedness if I cast aside this one also, else I would leave thy robe to thee and thy Christ."

From Robinson, pp. 151–52.

Asser, Life of Alfred

The same year, after Easter, king Alfred, with a few followers, made for himself a stronghold in a place called Athelney, and from thence sallied with his vassals and the nobles of Somersetshire, to make frequent assaults upon the pagans. Also, in the seventh week after Easter, he rode to the stone of Egbert, which is in the eastern part of the wood which is called Selwood, which means in Latin Silva Magna, the Great Wood, but in British Coit-mawr. Here he was met by all the neighboring folk of Somersetshire, and Wiltshire and Hampshire, who had not, for fear of the pagans, fled beyond the sea; and when they saw the king alive after such great tribulation, they received him, as he deserved, with joy and acclamations, and encamped there for one night. When the following day dawned, the king struck his camp, and went to Okely, where he encamped for one night. The next morning he removed to Edington, and there fought bravely and per-severingly against all the army of the pagans, whom, with the divine help, he defeated with great slaughter, and pursued them flying to their fortifica-tion. Immediately he slew all the men, and carried off all the booty that he could find without the fortress, which he immediately laid siege to with all his army; and when he had been there fourteen days, the pagans, driven by famine, cold, fear, and last of all by despair, asked for peace, on the condi-tion that they should give the king as many hostages as he pleased, but should receive none of him in return, in which form they had never before made a treaty with any one. The king, hearing that, took pity on them, and received such hostages as he chose; after which the pagans swore, more-over, that they would immediately leave the kingdom; and their king, [Guthrum], promised to embrace Christianity, and receive baptism at king Alfred's hands. All of which articles he and his men fulfilled as they had promised. For after seven weeks [Guthrum], king of the pagans, with thirty men chosen from the army, came to Alfred at a place called Aller, near Athelney, and there king Alfred, receiving him as his son by adoption, raised him up from the holy laver of baptism on the eighth day, at a royal villa named Wedmore, where the holy chrism was poured upon him. After his baptism he remained twelve nights with the king, who, with all his nobles, gave him many fine houses.

From *Source-Book of English History,* ed. Guy Carleton Lee (New York: Henry Holt and Co, 1906), pp. 97–99.

Founding of the Duchy of Normandy

The king [the West Frankish King Charles the Simple] had at first wished to give to Rollo the province of Flanders, but the Norman rejected it as being too marshy. Rollo refused to kiss the foot of Charles when he received from him the duchy of Normandy. "He who receives such a gift," said the bishops to him, "ought to kiss the foot of the king." "Never," replied he, "will I bend the knee to any one, or kiss anybody's foot." Nevertheless, impelled by the entreaties of the Franks, he ordered one of his warriors to perform the act in his stead. This man seized the foot of the king and lifted it to his lips, kissing it without bending and so causing the king to tumble over backwards. At that there was a loud burst of laughter and a great commotion in the crowd of onlookers. King Charles, Robert, Duke of the Franks, the counts and magnates, and the bishops and abbots, bound themselves by the oath of the Catholic faith to Rollo, swearing by their lives and their bodies and by the honor of all the kingdom, that he might hold the land and transmit it to his heirs from generation to generation throughout all time to come. When these things had been satisfactorily performed, the king returned in good spirits into his dominion, and Rollo with Duke Robert set out for Rouen.

In the year of our Lord 912 Rollo was baptized in holy water in the name of the sacred Trinity by Franco, archbishop of Rouen. Duke Robert, who was his godfather, gave to him his name. Rollo devotedly honored God and the Holy Church with his gifts. . . . The pagans, seeing that their chieftain had become a Christian, abandoned their idols, received the name of Christ, and with one accord desired to be baptized. Meanwhile the Norman duke made ready for a splendid wedding and married the daughter of the king [Gisela] according to Christian rites.

Rollo gave assurance of security to all those who wished to dwell in his country. The land he divided among his followers, and, as it had been a long time unused, he improved it by the construction of new buildings. It was peopled by the Norman warriors and by immigrants from outside regions. The duke established for his subjects certain inviolable rights and laws, confirmed and published by the will of the leading men, and he compelled all his people to live peaceably together. He rebuilt the churches, which had been entirely ruined; he restored the temples, which had been destroyed by the ravages of the pagans; he repaired and added to the walls and fortifications of the cities; he subdued the Britons who rebelled against him; and with the provisions obtained from them he supplied all the country that had been granted to him.

"De Moribus et Actis Primorum Normanniae Ducum" in Ogg, pp. 171–73.

12.2 Animism and Accommodation: Charms

Germanic culture did not disappear with the advent of Christianity, as we have seen in the literature of the early Middle Ages. Christianity, as an incoming religion, brought with it certain cultural characteristics from its earlier merger with Roman culture. When this Roman Christianity encountered Germanic culture, it not only displaced Germanic pagan religious beliefs but also incorporated Germanic folk ideas. In the process, Christianity itself was transformed by local cultures. The Anglo-Saxon medical remedies excerpted here demonstrate on a practical level how this accommodation took place. The combination of Christian liturgy and Germanic folk charms, Christian doctrines of the Trinity sitting side by side with Germanic animistic beings, may seem odd on the surface. But their combination relies on certain similarities between the new religion and the old culture.

First of all, both Germanic cultures and Christian doctrine believed in invisible spiritual agencies, whether invisible elves of Germanic lore whose venomous shots need purging or demons to be exorcised as in the Christian cosmology. The demonization of elves is evident in the remedies below. Second, both the Germanic and Christian traditions accepted the notion that natural ingredients such as herbs contained virtues or powers that could be activated for healing (evident, for example, in the use of the herb *ælfthone* for *elf* afflictions). In the pagan system, this might have been accomplished with specific rituals and chants appealing to animistic spirits. In the Christian view, these herbs were made potent by appeals to God. The two approaches in Anglo-Saxon and Latin merge in the remedies below.

Third, in both traditions words have power to transform natural objects. Germanic charms, words chanted by an experienced practitioner, commanded or invoked the invisible powers in nature for the purpose of healing. The words of the priest in the mass transform bread and wine into body and blood. It is not surprising, then, that so many remedies prescribe masses said over herbs to invoke their natural potency to cure illnesses that may have an invisible (hence spiritual) cause. Note, for example, the similarity between the exorcism of body parts in [4b] on page 291 and the Leofric Missal excerpt (11.2).

The remedies below come from a tenth-century Anglo-Saxon manu-script, *The Leechbook,* produced in a monastic setting. The remedies are for various ailments caused by elves—invisible, amoral creatures who shoot animals and humans—and they use other traditional Ger-manic traits, such as the number 9. However, these remedies are mixed with other spiritual ills—temptation, nightmares, madness—and they use Christian liturgy in combination with Germanic elements to combat these mind-altering afflictions.

Questions

1. What kinds of needs would these remedies meet?
2. Why do these afflictions require appeals to spiritual agencies to make the remedies work?
3. Are these remedies in your view Christian or not?

The Leechbook

III:lxi

Work a salve against elfkind and nightgoers, . . . and the people with whom the Devil has intercourse. Take eowohumelan, wormwood, bishopwort, lupin, ashthroat, henbane, harewort, haransprecel, heathberry plants, cropleek, garlic, hedgerife grains, githrife, fennel. Put these herbs into one cup, set under the altar, sing over them nine masses; boil in butter and in sheep's grease, add much holy salt, strain through a cloth; throw the herbs in running water. If any evil temptation, or an elf or nightgoers, happen to a man, smear his forehead with this salve, and put on his eyes, and where his body is sore, and cense him [with incense], and sign [the cross] often. His condition will soon be better.

III:lxii

[1] Against elf disease. . . . Take bishopwort, fennel, lupin, the lower part of *ælfthone,* and lichen from the holy sign of Christ [cross], and incense; a handful of each. Bind all the herbs in a cloth, dip in hallowed font water thrice. Let three masses be sung over it, one "Omnibus sanctis [For all the saints]," a second "Contra tribulationem [Against tribulation]," a third "Pro infirmis [For the sick]." Put then coals in a coal pan, and lay the herbs on it. Smoke the man with the herbs before . . . [9 A.M.] and at night; and sing a litany, the Creed [Nicene], and the Pater noster [Our Father]; and write on him Christ's mark on each limb. And take a little handful of the same kind of herbs, similarly sanctified, and boil in milk; drip holy water in it thrice. And let him sip it before his meal. It will soon be well with him.

[2] For the same. . . . Go on Thursday evening when the sun is setting to where you know helenium . . . stands. Sing then the Benedicite [Blessed be . . .], the Pater noster, and a litany. And stick your knife into the plant; leave it sticking therein and go away. Go again, when day and night first divide [dawn]; at that same dawn, go first to church, and cross yourself and offer yourself to God. Go then silently; and though you meet on the way some fearful thing coming or a man, you should not speak to him any word, until you come to the plant that you marked on the evening before. Sing then the Benedicite, and the Pater noster and a litany. Dig up the plant; leave the knife sticking in it. Go again as quick as you can to church, and lay it under the altar with the knife. Let it lie until the sun is up. Wash it then; make it into a drink: with bishopwort and lichen from Christ's sign, boil thrice in [different kinds of] milk; and pour holy water thrice on it. And sing on it the Pater noster, and the Creed and the Gloria in excelsis deo [Glory to God in the highest]; and sing on it a litany. And also write a cross around it with a sword on [each of] four halves. And then let [the patient] drink the drink. It will soon be well with him.

[3] Again for that. Lay under the altar these herbs, let nine masses be sung over them: incense, holy salt, three heads of cropleek, *ælfthone's* lower part, and helenium. Take in the morning a cup full of milk; drip thrice some holy water in it. Let him sip it as hot as he can. Eat with it three bits of *ælfthone*. When he wants to rest, have coals there inside. Lay incense and *ælfthone* on the coals, and smoke him with that until he sweats; and smoke the house throughout; and eagerly sign the man. And when he goes to rest, let him eat three bits of helenium, and three of cropleek, and three of salt. And let him have a cup full of ale and drip thrice holy water in it. Let him eat each bit; then let him rest. Do this for nine mornings and nine nights. It will soon be well with him.

[4a] If he has elf-heartburn, . . . his eyes are yellow where they should be red. If you want to cure this person, consider his bearing, and know of which sex he is. If it is a male, . . . and he looks up when you first see him, and his appearance is yellow black, then that man you may cure completely, if he has not been therein too long. If it is a woman . . . and she looks down when you first see her, and her appearance is dark red, this you might also cure. If it is on him a day's space longer than twelve months, and his visage be such, then you might better him for awhile, but may not however completely cure him.

[4b] Write this writing: . . . "It is written, king of kings and lord of lords. Veronica, Veronica. Lurlure? Yahweh? Holy, holy, holy. . . . Lord, God of Hosts. Amen, Alleluia."

Sing this over the drink and the writing: . . . "God Almighty, father of our lord Jesus Christ, through the imposition of this writing expel from your servant, (name), all attacks of muses/fairies . . . from the head, from the hair, from the brain, from the forehead, from the tongue, from the epiglottis, from the throat, from the pharynx, from the teeth, from the eyes, from the nostrils, from the ears, from the hands, from the neck, from the arms, from the heart, from the breath, from the knees, from the hips, from the feet, from the connections of all body members within and without. Amen."

[4c] Work then a drink: font water, rue, sage, hassock, dragonzan, of the smooth waybread the lower part, feverfue, a head of dill, three cloves of garlic, fennel, wormwood, lovage, lupin; an equal amount of each. Write thrice a cross with oil of unction . . . and say . . . "Peace be with you." Take then the writing, write a cross with it over the drink, and sing this there over it [Latin]: . . . "God Almighty, father of our lord Jesus Christ, through the imposition of this writing and through this medicine expel the Devil from your servant, (name)" and the Creed and the Pater noster. Wet the writing in the drink, write a cross with it on each limb, and say . . . "May the sign of the cross of Christ conserve you in life eternal, Amen." If you prefer not, tell [the patient] himself or whatever relative he has nearest related to him, and sign as best he can. This craft is mighty against every temptation of the fiend.

III:lxiii

If a man is in the water elf disease, . . . then the nails of his hand are dark and the eyes teary, and he will look down. Give him this as medicine: . . . everthroat, hassock, the lower part of fane, yewberry, lupin, helenium, marshmallow head, fen mint, dill, lily, attorlathe, pulegium, marrubium, dock, elder, fel terre, wormwood, strawberry leaves, consolde. Soak with ale; add holy water to it. Sing this [charm] over it thrice:

I have bound on the wounds the best of war bandages, so the wounds neither burn nor burst, nor go further, nor spread, nor jump, nor the wounds increase, . . . nor sores deepen. But may he himself keep in a healthy way. . . . May it not ache you more than it aches earth in ear. . . .

Sing this many times, "May earth bear on you with all her might and main." These [charms] a man may sing over a wound.

III:lxiv

Against the Devil and against madness, . . . a strong drink. Put in ale hassock, lupin roots, fennel, ontre, betony, hind heolothe, marche, rue, wormwood, nepeta (catmint), helenium, *ælfthone,* wolfs comb. Sing twelve masses over the drink; and let him drink. It will soon be well with him.

A drink against the Devil's temptations: thefanthorn, cropleek, lupin, ontre, bishopwort, fennel, hassock, betony. Sanctify these herbs; put into ale holy water. And let the drink be there in where the sick man is. And continually before he drinks sing thrice over the drink, . . . "God, in your name make me whole (save me)."

Translated by Karen Louise Jolly, *Popular Religion in Late Saxon England: Elf Charms in Context* (Chapel Hill: University of North Carolina Press, 1996), pp. 159–67 passim. Used by permission of the publisher.

12.3 Dialogue: *The Dispute of the Church and the Synagogue*

Christian conceptions of Judaism and attitudes toward Jews form one part of the emerging Christian identity in the early Middle Ages; the ways in which medieval Christians perceived and categorized Jews reflects these Christians' views of themselves. Anti-Judaism—the rejection of the religion of Judaism—dates back to the roots of Christianity itself: as increasingly the Church, after Paul's missions, was made up of Gentile converts, the Jews became the people who had the truth but rejected it, the ones who "killed Christ." Out of this anti-Judaism, popular waves of anti-Semitism often arose—hatred and persecution of Jews as an ethnic group (Semites). By contrast, Jews outside of Europe often enjoyed greater tolerance under Islam and frequently resided as scholars and doctors at the courts of Islamic rulers.

In the early Middle Ages throughout much of Europe, Jews were a small minority group whose separate cultural and religious life revolved around the synagogue in contrast to the ideal of a Christian society centered on the church. Virulent anti-Semitism was not yet apparent, but anti-Judaism was inherent in Christian teachings. The following treatise, *The Dispute of the Church and the Synagogue,* is dated into the middle of the tenth century and was probably written in England. It uses the classical formula of a dialogue to explore the issue of belief, in this instance personifying Christianity as the voice of the Church and Judaism as the voice of the Synagogue. The dialogue is framed as a fair exchange of views between two sides, treating the Jewish position sympathetically in a way that shows that the Christians writing it must have had some exposure to Jewish thought. Nonetheless, it is designed to show the difference between the two religions from a Christian point of view.

Questions

1. What do the two sides in this debate have in common with each other that forms the basis for dialogue? What are the main differences between the two sides?

2. Of what use is this dialogue for any Christian who read it in the early Middle Ages?

3. How do you think an early medieval Jew would respond to this document?

The Dispute of the Church and the Synagogue

The Voice of the Church: You, O Synagogue, who once were the chosen and beloved of the great king, but afterwards you were repudiated and cast out— deservedly, because of your sins—I address you. Your arrogance, which prompts you not to blush, compels me to assert you just, even though you are full of all manner of crimes; and the abominable blasphemies and detractions with which you provoked my Lord and myself, now his servant, compel me to refute your fatuities and calumnies with an account of the truth. . . .

The Synagogue: Since you say I am repudiated and cast out and you delight in being taken into my place, and since you bear witness to my degeneration from the faith and nobility of my fathers, you compel me to answer your objections and assertions. Tell me first, then, how you claim that I have degenerated from the birthright of my fathers. For I have taken pains always to preserve uncontaminated that birthright which I accepted from them, nor have I mixed my people with ignoble or alien peoples in marriage, except with those who have passed over to embrace my race and my law. . . . I hold the glory of the faith which you know was so eminent in my fathers and from which you, boldly and wickedly, recently declared me relapsed; I hold the glory which I knew the reverend fathers had from God; and I believe in and worship one God, creator of all and, because I trust that he can never fail, I look for [the fulfillment of] those promises which he foretold by means of his prophets of our race. . . .

The Church: When I carefully search into and diligently study the things foretold about the coming of Christ by the holy prophets—both the hidden and the visible signs, the weak and the strong, the gentle and the terrible—I see that he, who was foretold, was to have come, a man hidden and in the open, weak and strong, gentle and terrible, to be judged and to judge. You, indeed, who reflect upon those signs which witness to his visible work and power; why do you not recall those which witness to his hidden works and weakness? . . . Thus Isaiah says: we saw him and there was no beauty in him nor comeliness and his face was as if hidden away and contemptible. So we did not recognize him. . . .

The Synagogue: It seems inconsistent that one and the same [man] should undergo agony and slanderous affronts, and yet be lifted up amid glory, as is written of him; for the same man to be condemned to death and yet to be given dominion over the whole world: rather, if it all was necessary, one man should be understood to have sustained the affronts, and another one altogether deserves to reign eternally. If, indeed, as you try to assert, he must be understood to be God's own son, it should seem much more of an indignity, when they say that he could endure so much.

Reprinted with permission from *The Records of Medieval Europe*, ed. Carolly Erickson (New York: Anchor Books/Doubleday, 1971), pp. 212–14. Excerpt translated from " 'Altercatio Aecclesie contra Sinagogam,' Texte inédit du Xe siècle, *"Revue du moyen-âge Latin*, X, 1–2 (January–June, 1954), 53–56, 110, 112.

12.4 Debate: Patriarch Timothy and Caliph Mahdi

As evident in the residence of Jewish and Christian scholars in Muslim lands, such as John of Damascus (6.4), the Islamic courts were centers of scholarly enterprise and cross-cultural religious dialogue. Discussions between scholars of these three traditions—Muslim, Christian, and Jewish—relied on certain commonalities: monotheism, the Jewish biblical texts, and the inheritance of classical philosophy. In addition, the Middle East maintained a diverse set of cultural influences from Persia, India, and the Far East, as well as Byzantium, that fostered intellectual speculation.

One such religious dialogue occurred in 781, when Timothy, the patriarch of the East Syrian Church (Nestorian in doctrine), spent two days in debate with Mahdi, the Abassid Caliph in Baghdad. The document is Timothy's record in Syriac of the discussion, which took place in Arabic. Consequently, the bulk of the arguments are the ones that the patriarch was making to the "king," the Caliph Mahdi, who acted more as a questioner and critic. Both men were well read enough to use each other's texts in their arguments, and both relied on a common system of logical discourse to make their points. The excerpts below show their arguments on Mohammed, the Trinity, and the true religion. This latter section also discusses the superiority of the Nestorian or Dyophysite (two-nature) doctrine of Christ compared to the other churches in the east, the Monophysite Jacobites and the orthodox Melkites (see reading 3.4).

Questions

1. Why can the patriarch Timothy and the Caliph Mahdi have this discussion?

2. On what do these two men agree? Where do their differences lie?

3. How can either one establish what is true about God?

The Apology of Timothy the Patriarch before the Caliph Mahdi

Our God-loving King ended the above subject here, and embarked on another theme and said to me: "How is it that you accept Christ and the Gospel from the testimony of the Torah and of the prophets, and you do not accept Muhammad from the testimony of Christ and the Gospel?" And I replied to his Majesty: "O our King, we have received concerning Christ numerous and distinct testimonies from the Torah and the prophets. All of the latter prophesied in one accord and harmony in one place about His mother: "Behold a virgin shall conceive and bear a son," and taught us that He shall be conceived and born without marital intercourse like the Word of God. It is indeed fit that the One who was born of the Father without a mother should have been born in the flesh from a virgin mother without a father, in order that His second birth may be a witness to His first birth. In another place they reveal to us His name: "And His name shall be called Emmanuel, Wonderful, Counsellor, and Mighty God of the worlds."

"In another place the prophets reveal to us the miracles that He will work at His coming in saying, 'Behold your God will come. . . . He will come and save you. Then the eyes of the blind shall be opened, and the ears of the deaf shall hear. Then shall the lame man leap as an hart, and the tongue of the dumb shall be loosened.' Yet in another place they disclose to us His passion and His death, 'He shall be killed for our transgressions, and humbled for our iniquities.' Sometimes they speak to us about His resurrection, 'For Thou hast not left my soul in Sheol, nor hast Thou suffered Thy Holy One to see corruption,' and 'The Lord hath said unto me, Thou art my Son; this day have I begotten Thee.' Some other times they teach us concerning His Ascension to Heaven, 'Thou hast ascended on high, Thou hast led captivity captive, and Thou hast made gifts to men,' and 'God went up in glory, and the Lord with the sound of a trumpet.'

"Some other times they reveal to us His coming down from heaven in saying, 'I am one like the son of men coming on the clouds of heaven, and they brought Him near before the Ancient of days, and there was given Him dominion, and glory and a kingdom that all peoples of the earth should serve Him and worship Him. His dominion is an everlasting dominion, and His kingdom shall not pass away nor be destroyed.' These and scores of other passages of the prophets show us Jesus Christ in a clear mirror and point to Him. So far as Muhammad is concerned I have not received a single testimony either from Jesus Christ or from the Gospel which would refer to his name or to his works."

And our benevolent and gracious King made a sign to mean that he was not convinced, then he repeated twice to me the question: "Have you not received any?"—And I replied to him: "No, O God-loving King, I have not received any."—And the King asked me: Who is then the Paraclete?"— And I answered: The Spirit of God."—And the King asked: "What is the Spirit of God?"—And I replied: "God, by nature; and one who proceeds, by attribute; as Jesus Christ taught about Him."—And our glorious King said:

"And what did Jesus Christ teach about Him?"—And I answered: "He spoke to His disciples as follows: 'When I go away to Heaven, I will send unto you the Spirit-Paraclete who proceedeth from the Father, whom the world cannot receive, who dwelleth with you and is among you, who searcheth all things, even the deep things of God, who will bring to your remembrance all the truth that I have said unto you, and who will take of mine and show unto you.' "

And our King said to me: "All these refer to Muhammad."—And I replied to him: "If Muhammad were the Paraclete, since the Paraclete is the Spirit of god, Muhammad, would, therefore, be the Spirit of God; and the Spirit of God being uncircumscribed like God, Muhammad would also be uncircumscribed like God; and he who is uncircumscribed being invisible, Muhammad would also be invisible and without a human body; and he who is without a body being uncomposed, Muhammad would also be un-composed. Indeed he who is a spirit has no body, and he who has no body is also invisible, and he who is invisible is also uncircumscribed; but he who is circumscribed is not the Spirit of God, and he who is not the Spirit of God is not the Paraclete. It follows from all this that Muhammad is not the Paraclete. The Paraclete is from heaven and of the nature of the Father, and Muhammad is from the earth and of the nature of Adam. Since heaven is not the same thing as earth, nor is God the Father identical with Adam, the Paraclete is not, therefore, Muhammad.

"Further, the Paraclete searches the deep things of God, but Muhammad owns that he does not know what might befall him and those who accept him. He who searches all things even the deep things of God is not identical with the one who does not know what might happen to him and to those who acknowledge him. Muhammad is therefore not the Paraclete. Again, the Paraclete, as Jesus told His disciples, was with them and among them while He was speaking to them, and since Muhammad was not with them and among them, he cannot, therefore, have been the Paraclete. Finally, the Paraclete descended on the disciples ten days after the ascension of Jesus to heaven, while Muhammad was born more than six hundred years later, and this impedes Muhammad from being the Paraclete. And Jesus taught the disciples that the Paraclete is one God in three persons, and since Muham-mad does not believe in the doctrine of three persons in one Godhead, he cannot be the Paraclete. And the Paraclete wrought all sorts of prodigies and miracles through the disciples, and since Muhammad did not work a single miracle through his followers and his disciples, he is not the Paraclete.

"That the Spirit-Paraclete is consubstantial with the Father and the Son is borne out by the fact that He is the maker of the heavenly powers and of everything, and since he who is the maker and creator of everything is God, the Spirit-Paraclete is therefore God; but the world is not able to receive God, as Jesus Christ said, because God is uncircumscribed. Now if Muhammad were the Paraclete, since this same Paraclete is the Spirit of God, Muhammad would therefore be the Spirit of God. Further, since David said, 'By the Spirit of God all the powers have been created,' celestial and terrestrial, Muhammad would be the creator of the celestial and terrestrial beings. Now since Muhammad is not the creator of heaven and earth, and since he who is not creator is not the Spirit of God, Muhammad is, therefore, not the Spirit of God; and since the one who is not the Spirit of God is by inference not the Paraclete, Muhammad is not the Paraclete.

"If he were mentioned in the Gospel, this mention would have been marked by a distinct portraiture characterising his coming, his name, his mother, and his people as the true portraiture of the coming of Jesus Christ is found in the Torah and in the prophets. Since nothing resembling this is found in the Gospel concerning Muhammad, it is evident that there is no mention of him in it at all, and that is the reason why I have not received a single testimony from the Gospel about him."

And the God-loving King said to me: "As the Jews behaved towards Jesus whom they did not accept, so the Christians behaved towards Muhammad whom they did not accept."—And I replied to his Majesty: "The Jews did not accept Jesus in spite of the fact that the Torah and the prophets were full of testimonies about Him, and this renders them worthy of condemnation. As to us we have not accepted Muhammad because we have not a single testimony about him in our Books."—And our King said: "There were many testimonies but the Books have been corrupted, and you have removed them."—And I replied to him thus: "Where is it known, O King, that the Books have been corrupted by us, and where is that uncorrupted Book from which you have learned that the Books which we use have been corrupted? If there is such a book let it be placed in the middle in order that we may learn from it which is the corrupted Gospel and hold to that which is not corrupted. If there is no such a Gospel, how do you know that the Gospel of which we make use is corrupted?

"What possible gain could we have gathered from corrupting the Gospel? Even if there was mention of Muhammad made in the Gospel, we would not have deleted his name from it; we would have simply said that Muhammad has not come yet, and that he was not the one whom you follow, and that he was going to come in the future. Take the example of the Jews: they cannot delete the name of Jesus from the Torah and the Prophets, they only contend against Him in saying openly that He was going to come in the future, and that He has not come yet into the world. They resemble a blind man without eyes who stands in plain daylight and contends that the sun has not yet risen. We also would have done likewise; we would not have dared to remove the name of Muhammad from our Book if it were found anywhere in it; we would have simply quibbled concerning his right name and person like the Jews do in the case of Jesus. To tell the truth, if I had found in the Gospel a prophecy concerning the coming of Muhammad, I would have left the Gospel for the Kur'an, as I have left the Torah and the Prophets for the Gospel."

And our King said to me: "Do you not believe that our Book was given by God?"—And I replied to him: "It is not my business to decide whether it is from God or not. But I will say something of which your Majesty is well aware, and that is all the words of God found in the Torah and in the Prophets, and those of them found in the Gospel and in the writings of the Apostles, have been confirmed by signs and miracles; as to the words of your Book they have not been corroborated by a single sign or miracle. It is imperative that signs and miracles should be annulled by other signs and miracles. When God wished to abrogate the Mosaic law, He confirmed by the signs and miracles wrought by the Christ and the Apostles that the words of the Gospel were from God, and by this He abrogated the words of the Torah and the first miracles. Similarly, as He abrogated the first signs and miracles by second ones, He ought to have abrogated the second signs and miracles by third ones. If God had wished to abrogate the Gospel and introduce another Book in its place He would have done this, because signs and miracles are witnesses of His will; but your Book has not been confirmed by a single sign and miracle. Since signs and miracles are proofs of the will of God, the conclusion drawn from their absence in your Book is well known to your Majesty. . . ."

And our gracious and wise King said to me: "What do you say about Muhammad?"—And I replied to his Majesty: "Muhammad is worthy of all praise, by all reasonable people, O my Sovereign. He walked in the path of the prophets, and trod in the track of the lovers of God. All the prophets taught the doctrine of one God, and since Muhammad taught the doctrine of the unity of God, he walked, therefore, in the path of the prophets. Further, all the prophets drove men away from bad works, and brought them nearer to good works, and since Muhammad drove his people away from bad works and brought them nearer to the good ones, he walked, therefore, in the path of the prophets. Again, all the prophets separated men from idolatry and polytheism, and attached them to God and to His cult, and since Muhammad separated his people from idolatry and polytheism, and attached them to the cult and the knowledge of one God, beside whom there is no other God, it is obvious that he walked in the path of the prophets. Finally Muhammad taught about God, His Word and His Spirit, and since all the prophets had prophesied about God, His Word and His Spirit, Muhammad walked, therefore, in the path of all the prophets.

"Who will not praise, honor and exalt the one who not only fought for God in words, but showed also his zeal for Him in the sword? As Moses did with the Children of Israel when he saw that they had fashioned a golden calf which they worshipped, and killed all of those who were worshipping it, so also Muhammad evinced an ardent zeal towards God, and loved and honoured Him more than his own soul, his people and his relatives. He praised, honoured and exalted those who worshipped God with him, and promised them kingdom, praise and honour from God, both in this world and in the world to come in the Garden. But those who worshipped idols and not God he fought and opposed, and showed to them the torments of hell and of the fire which is never quenched and in which all evildoers burn eternally.

"And what Abraham, that friend and beloved of God, did in turning his face from idols and from his kinsmen, and looking only towards one God and becoming the preacher of one God to other peoples, this also Muhammad did. He turned his face from idols and their worshippers, whether those idols were those of his own kinsmen or of strangers, and he honoured and worshipped only one God. Because of this God honoured him exceedingly and brought low before his feet two powerful kingdoms which roared in the world like a lion and made the voice of their authority heard in all the earth that is below heaven like thunder, viz: the Kingdom of the Persians and that of the Romans. The former kingdom, that is to say the Kingdom of the Persians, worshipped the creatures instead of the Creator, and the latter, that is to say the Kingdom of the Romans, attributed suffering and death in the flesh to the one who cannot suffer and die in any way and through any process. He further extended the power of his authority through the Commander of the Faithful and his children from east to west, and from north to south. Who will not praise, O our victorious King, the one whom God has praised, and will not weave a crown of glory and majesty to the one whom God has glorified and exalted? These and similar things I and all God-lovers utter about Muhammad, O my sovereign."

And our King said to me: "You should, therefore, accept the words of the Prophet."—And I replied to his gracious Majesty: "Which words of his our victorious King believes that I must accept?"—And our King said to me: "That God is one and that there is no other one besides Him."—And I replied: "This belief in one God O my Sovereign, I have learned from the Torah, from the Prophets and from the Gospel. I stand by it and shall die in it."—And our victorious King said to me: "You believe in one God, as you said but one in three."—And I answered his sentence: "I do not deny that I believe in one God in three, and three in one, but not in three different

Godheads, however, but in the persons of God's Word and His Spirit. I believe that these three constitute one God, not in their person but in their nature. I have shown how in my previous words." . . .

And our victorious King asked: "And who are those who say that God suffered and died in the flesh."—And I answered: "The Jacobites and Melchites say that God suffered and died in the flesh, as to us we not only do not assert that God suffered and died in our nature, but that He even removed the possibility of our human nature that He put on from Mary by His impassibility, and its mortality by His immortality, and He made it to resemble divinity, to the extent that a created being is capable of resembling his Creator. A created being cannot make himself resemble his Creator, but the Creator is able to bring His creature to His own resemblance. It is not the picture that makes the painter paint a picture in its own resemblance, but it is the painter that paints the picture to his own resemblance; it is not the wood that works and fashions a carpenter in its resemblance, but it is the carpenter that fashions the wood in his resemblance. In this same way it is not the mortal and passible nature that renders God passible and mortal like itself, but it is by necessity God that renders the passible and mortal human nature impassible and immortal like Himself. On the one hand, this is what the Jacobites and Melchites say, and, on the other, this is what we say. It behoves your Majesty to decide who are those who believe rightly and those who believe wrongly."

And our victorious King said: "In this matter you believe more rightly than the others. Who dares to assert that God dies? I think that even demons do not say such a thing. In what, however, you say concerning one Word and Son of God, all of you are wrong."—And I replied to his Majesty: "O our victorious King, in this world we are all of us as in a dark house in the middle of the night. If at night and in a dark house a precious pearl happens to fall in the midst of people, and all become aware of its existence, every one would strive to pick up the pearl, which will not fall to the lot of all but to the lot of one only, while one will get hold of the pearl itself, another one of a piece of glass, a third one of a stone or of a bit of earth, but every one will be happy and proud that he is the real possessor of the pearl. When, however, night and darkness disappear, and light and day arise, then every one of those men who had believed that they had the pearl, would extend and stretch his hand towards the light, which alone can show what every one has in hand. He who possesses the pearl will rejoice and be happy and pleased with it, while those who had in hand pieces of glass and bits of stone only will weep and be sad, and will sigh and shed tears.

"In this same way we children of men are in this perishable world as in darkness. The pearl of the true faith fell in the midst of all of us, and it is undoubtedly in the hand of one of us, while all of us believe that we possess the precious object. In the world to come, however, the darkness of mortality passes, and the fog of ignorance dissolves since it is the true and the real light to which the fog of ignorance is absolutely foreign. In it the possessors of the pearl will rejoice, be happy and pleased, and the possessors of mere pieces of stone will weep, sigh, and shed tears, as we said above."

And our victorious King said: "The possessors of the pearl are not known in this world, O Catholicos."—And I answered: "They are partially known, O our victorious King."—And our victorious and very wise King said: "What do you mean by partially known, and by what are they known as such?"—And I answered: "By good works, O our victorious King, and pious deeds, and by the wonders and miracles that God performs through those who possess the true faith. As the lustre of a pearl is somewhat visible even in the darkness of the night, so also the rays of the true faith shine to some extent even in the darkness and the fog of the present world. God indeed has not left the pure pearl of the faith completely without testimony and evidence, first in the prophets and then in the Gospel. He first confirmed the true faith in Him through Moses, once by means of the prodigies and miracles that He wrought in Egypt, and another time then He divided the waters of the Red Sea into two and allowed the Israelites to cross it safely, but drowned the Egyptians in its depths. He also split and divided the Jordan into two through Joshua, son of Nun, and allowed the Israelites to cross it without any harm to themselves, and tied the sun and the moon to their own places until the Jewish people were well avenged upon their enemies. He acted in the same way through the prophets who rose in different generations, viz.: through David, Elijah, and Elisha.

"Afterwards He confirmed the faith through Christ our Lord by the miracles and prodigies which He wrought for the help of the children of men. In this way the Disciples performed miracles greater even than those wrought by Christ. These signs, miracles, and prodigies wrought in the name of Jesus Christ are the bright rays and the shining lustre of the precious pearl of the faith, and it is by the brightness of such rays that the possessors of this pearl which is so full of lustre and so precious that it outways all the world in the balance, are known.

And our victorious King said: "We have hope in God that we are the possessors of this pearl, and that we hold it in our hands."—And I replied: "Amen, O King. But may God grant us that we too may share it with you, and rejoice in the shining and beaming lustre of the pearl! God has placed the pearl of His faith before all of us like the shining rays of the sun, and every one who wishes can enjoy the light of the sun.

"We pray God, who is King of Kings, and Lord of Lords, to preserve the crown of the kingdom and the throne of the Commander of the Faithful for multitudinous days and numerous years! May He also raise after him Musa and Harun and 'Ali to the throne of his kingdom for ever and ever! May He subjugate before them and before their descendants after them all the barbarous nations, and may all the kings and governors of the world serve our Sovereign and his sons after him till the day in which the Kingdom of Heaven is revealed from heaven to earth!"

And our victorious King said: "Miracles have been and are sometimes performed even by unbelievers."—And I replied to his Majesty: "These, O our victorious King, are not miracles but deceptive similitudes of the demons, and are performed not by the prophets of God and by holy men, but by idolaters and wicked men. This is the reason why I said that good works and miracles are the lustre of the pearl of the faith. Indeed, Moses performed miracles in Egypt and the sorcerers Jannes and Jambres performed them also there, but Moses performed them by the power of God, and the sorcerers through the deceptions of the demons. The power of God, however, prevailed, and that of the demons was defeated.

"In Rome also Simon Cephas and Simon Magus performed miracles, but the former performed them by the power of God, and the latter by the power of the demons, and for this reason Simon Cephas was honoured and Simon Magus was laughed at and despised by every one, and his deception was exposed before the eyes of all celestial and terrestrial beings."

At this our victorious King rose up and entered his audience chamber, and I left him and returned in peace to my patriarch residence.

Here ends the controversy of the Patriarch Mar Timothy with Mahdi, the Caliph of the Muslims. May eternal praise be to God!

From "The Apology of Timothy the Patriarch before the Caliph Mahdi," trans. A. Mingana, in *Bulletin of the John Rylands Library* 12 (1928): 168–73, 197–98, 223–26. Reproduced by courtesy of the Director and University Librarian, the John Rylands University Library of Manchester. Notes omitted.

Part 4

The Spirit of Order and Prophecy, circa 1050–1200

The rising Gothic churches, with their seemingly effortless upward sweep of pillars, pointed arches, and flying buttresses, with vast airy reaches illuminated by jewel-like stained glass, symbolize the spirit of high medieval religiosity. Built by booming towns in the new market economy of the eleventh century and by monasteries and cathedrals profiting from the pilgrim traffic, the cathedrals express not only economic prosperity but also spiritual fervor. Agricultural abundance contributed to urbanization, new wealth, and a growing urban class of laity seeking spiritual meaning in the midst of an increasingly materialistic social environment. The cathedrals are a visual expression of the desire to reach toward God with church spires pointing toward the heavens, to be illumined by the light of God's love, and to be dazzled by his omnipotence. The monumental changes in the eleventh and twelfth centuries in lifestyle and belief at all levels of European society are also visible in the texts excerpted below concerning church reform, popular piety, the Crusades, and scholasticism.

These diverse texts illustrate the tension in medieval Christianity between what historian Jeffrey Russell calls prophecy and order in his book by that name. The "spirit of prophecy" endeavors to bring about interior reform through spiritual exercises, while the "spirit of order" works to reform the corporate body of the church outwardly to get rid of corrupting secular influences. While the spirit of prophecy, evident in mysticism, pilgrimage, and monastic zeal, encourages individual spirituality, the spirit of order as evidenced in laws and decrees is concerned with conformity. Sometimes these two forces conflicted, as in the church condemnation of some prophetic individuals as heretics when they rejected church authority;

303

often prophecy and order balanced each other, as when lay piety and monastic revival contributed to the reform of church leadership back to its spiritual ideals.

The four chapters in this part highlight this theme of prophecy and order in the context of the changes in European Christianity. The first, Chapter 13, addresses the issue of reform through both the spirit of order and the spirit of prophecy. Orderly reform of the corporate institution expressed itself in the Gregorian reform movement that sought to establish independent ecclesiastical authority free of secular intrusion. Prophetic reform expressed itself in the search for individual holiness and personal salvation, whether through an ascetic lifestyle or by journeying in the world as a pilgrim. Chapter 14 combines the prophetic and orderly elements by examining Christian, Muslim, and Jewish perspectives of the Crusades; the crusading movement was an expression of both spiritual desire and material greed, and filled both a religious need for pilgrimage and a need for order and control within Christendom. Chapter 15 looks at the intellectual reform known as scholasticism; it examines the interaction of Islamic, Jewish, and Christian thinkers by focusing on the issue of faith and reason as ways of knowing. The last chapter of this part, Chapter 16, is a little different: it reveals the diversity of twelfth-century life and thought by looking at two influential individuals, Bernard of Clairvaux and Hildegarde of Bingen. In their varied writings we see both the spirit of prophecy and the spirit of order at work.

–13–

Corporate and Individual Reform

Reform movements reflect an effort to reintroduce earlier spiritual ideals that have suffered from the corruption of worldly influence. Reform springs both from a desire to reorder society and from individual spiritual renewal, and these two often overlap. Lay piety, for example, contributed to monastic reform, and monastic reform contributed to papal reform. In reform, then, the spirit of order and the spirit of prophecy can work hand-in-hand to bring revival to Christian experience on both the corporate and the individual level. The documents in this chapter look first at corporate reform, centered in the papacy, and second at individual spirituality in the practices of asceticism and pilgrimage.

The orderly reform efforts begun in the eleventh century responded to deteriorating conditions produced in the preceding two centuries, when secular control of the church contributed to a lowering of spiritual standards. For example "lay proprietorship" of churches meant that lords who "owned" the churches or monasteries they built saw the priest or abbot as their vassal. Frequently, then, these ecclesiastical positions were bought and sold within the network of medieval aristocratic connections, a practice known as *simony*. Likewise, kings perceived their bishops and archbishops as court officials whose appointment should be directed by royal interests of state as well as spiritual concerns. The papacy itself also fell under the negative influence of local lay aristocratic control, with popes put into power by rival factions in Rome.

Ironically, laymen initiated the reform of the church leadership to get rid of these secular influences. Aristocrats wanted churches and priests on their manors for their spiritual well-being, and kings wanted to govern "Christian societies" with the help of high-born, well-trained bishops. For example, one of the first sparks of reform was Duke William's foundation of Cluny in 910 as an independent monastery, electing its own abbot and answering to no one except the pope (and even the pope could not alienate Cluny's land). A number of subsequent church reformers emerged out of Cluniac monasteries. On the papal level, imperial intervention initiated reform when King Henry III of Germany deposed three rival popes, putting in place his own reform-minded candidate, Leo IX (1049–1054).

It is in this context of an imperial-initiated reform papacy that the classic investiture contest between emperor and pope took place in the eleventh and twelfth centuries over who has the right to appoint bishops and "invest" them with the regalia of office. The investiture contest symbolizes the central dilemma of medieval governance: defining and negotiating the relationship between spiritual authority and secular temporal power. Two conditions underlay this tension between church and state. One was the existence of two separate hierarchies, "two swords," the church with its spiritual authority over European Christians, and the divinely granted temporal power of the king (9.1). The second condition was the overlap whereby bishops ruled their flocks under the jurisdiction of both "swords," as endowed with ecclesiastical authority through their spiritual office, and as landowning court officials of the king with temporal jurisdiction. Bishops as vassals of the king received church lands and symbols of their control over that jurisdiction; bishops as ministers of the church received regalia signifying their authority over a spiritual jurisdiction, the bishopric. As a consequence, the papacy "competed" with kings and emperors to exert authority over the bishops in the investiture contest, as Gregory VII does in his battles with Emperor Henry IV (13.1). Alternatives to these struggles for power and authority are few, such as Pope Paschal's divestment plan (13.2) and are not pursued, leaving the church in a centuries-long battle with political authorities.

The focused debate on the reform of the church evident in these high-level power plays, if taken alone, gives a picture of the medieval Christian church as an institution obsessed with obtaining power and status in the temporal world in order to fulfill its duties as spiritual leader of Christendom. And yet medieval Christianity also encompassed a strong prophetic voice concerned with individual spirituality.

The urban environment of the high Middle Ages produced changes in social class, lifestyle, and religious expression that encouraged personal and emotional expressions of piety. In the previous centuries, those who wanted to live a life devoted to God joined a monastery, imitating Christ by withdrawing from the world into a wilderness retreat where they could focus on prayer, meditation, and good works. With the increase in material prosperity evident in towns, many lay people sought new avenues for developing their spiritual lives, or at least rebalancing spirituality in relation to their temporal lives. In the examples below, some individuals chose a radical lifestyle compared to their contemporaries. Some expressed their desire for holiness by traveling temporarily on pilgrimage (13.3). Others adopted a permanent itinerant, and ascetic, lifestyle as religious philanthropists dedicated to charitable works, like the Beguines (13.4). The institutional church fostered pilgrimage as one avenue for attracting the laity; the Beguines, much more in the spirit of prophecy, operated outside the formal church, taking spiritual sustenance out to the most needy.

In all of these texts and examples, a common theme appears: the desire for holiness. Many people felt that material prosperity was damaging to the soul, that the urban life catered to the sins of greed and gluttony. They sought to purify their lives by withdrawing from that lifestyle, either temporarily on pilgrimage or permanently through religious vows. These practices indicate the duality of the medieval Christian worldview between body and soul, this world and the next, temporality and spirituality. In many ways, this cultural phenomenon mirrors the political dilemma manifested in the investiture contest: what is the relationship between the material and the spiritual? How should a Christian live in this world?

13.1 The Contest: Gregory VII and Henry IV

Pope Gregory VII (1073–1085) brought both vision and conflict to papal reform and governance. His vigorous leadership evidences the classic medieval dichotomy of looking both forward and backward: Gregory's vision for reform relied on traditional church texts for support (including the work of his mentor Pope Leo IX), yet his methods of implementing reform were innovative and had far-reaching implications for church-state relations. For example, the *Dictatus Papae* or Dictates of the Pope (1075), apparently chapter headings for a treatise of arguments never written, included such assertions as: (12) the pope has the power to depose emperors, and (19) the pope can be judged by no one.

The investiture contest between Pope Gregory VII and "Emperor" Henry IV, king of Germany, was precipitated both by Gregory's reform vision and Henry's own need to establish his authority in Germany. In the same way that the pope saw control over the appointment of bishops as central to his agenda for papal-led church reform, the emperor saw this right to control bishops as essential to his own ability to effectively unite and control the independent-minded duchies of Germany. Clear evidence of this divisiveness is the fact that, while the emperor called on the German bishops to support his imperial position, the pope called on the rebellious German princes to back papal claims. The dispute over who can appoint bishops took on heightened significance when emperor and pope each claimed that his authority came directly from God and not through the agency of the other and each contended that he could appoint or depose the other. Instead of two separate hierarchies, each asserted some kind of divinely granted over-lordship over the other.

Two incidents highlight this struggle for authority. The first occurred after Gregory's excommunication of Henry in 1076 over the appoint-ment of the bishop of Milan. Henry broke the deadlock dramatically by appearing before the pope as a penitent begging for forgiveness, stand-ing barefoot in the snow outside the gates of the castle of Canossa where the pope was staying. As spiritual leader, Gregory was obligated to absolve the repentant sinner; however, he had no way to force the emperor to make any concessions regarding investiture.

In many ways, Henry succeeded in making clear the fundamental dilemma of overlapping spiritual and secular authority: the pope cannot always act in both roles simultaneously. In the second incident, in 1080, Gregory excommunicated Henry and supported a rival king in a bloody civil war in Germany; then Henry deposed Gregory, elected his own pope, and besieged Rome for three years (1081–1084) before breaking into the city. Only then did the pope's "allies," the Normans in southern Italy, come to his rescue, scaring off the imperial troops. But the Normans then savaged the city of Rome, and left taking the pope southward with them, where he died in 1085.

The issue left unresolved in this dispute was that of authority: can an emperor depose and appoint popes, or can a pope depose and appoint emperors? Gregory's claims to authority after his second deposition of Henry are laid out in the following letter to Bishop Hermann of Metz in March 1081.

Questions

1. What does Gregory believe to be the main differences between the emperorship and the papacy?
2. What kinds of evidence does Gregory use to support his point of view?
3. What does Gregory believe is the role of the church in European society?

Letter of Gregory VII to Bishop Hermann of Metz, March 15, 1081

Bishop Gregory, servant of the servants of God to his beloved brother in Christ, Hermann bishop of Metz greeting and apostolic benediction. It is doubtless owing to a dispensation of God that, as we learn, thou art ready to bear labors and dangers in defense of the truth. . . . we wish, beloved, with the voice of exhortation, to impress this upon thee: thou should'st the more delight to stand in the army of the Christian faith among the first, the more thou art convinced that they are the most worthy and the nearest to God the victors. Thy demand, indeed, to be aided, as it were, by our writings and fortified against the madness of those who babble forth with unhallowed mouth that the authority of the holy and apostolic see had no right to excommunicate Henry—a man who despises the Christian law; a destroyer, namely, of the churches and of the empire; a favorer of heretics and a partaker with them—or to absolve any one from the oath of fealty to him, does not seem to us to be altogether necessary when so many and such absolutely certain proofs are to be found in the pages of Holy Scripture. . . .

For, to cite a few passages from among many, who does not know the words of our Lord and Savior Jesus Christ who says in the gospel: "Thou art Peter and upon this rock will I build my church, and the gates of hell shall not prevail against it; and I will give unto thee the keys of the kingdom of Heaven; and whatsoever thou shalt bind upon earth shall be bound also in Heaven, and whatsoever thou shalt loose upon earth shall be loosed also in Heaven"? Are kings excepted here, or do they not belong to the sheep which the son of God committed to Saint Peter? Who, I ask, in this universal concession of the power of binding and loosing, can think that he is withdrawn from the authority of Saint Peter, unless, perhaps, that unfortunate man who is unwilling to bear the yoke of the Lord and subjects himself to the burden of the devil, refusing to be among the number of Christ's sheep? It will help him little to his wretched liberty, indeed, that he shake from his proud neck the divinely granted power of Peter. For the more any one, through pride, refuses to bear it, the more heavily shall it press upon him unto damnation at the judgment.

The holy fathers, indeed, as well in general councils as otherwise in their writings and doings, have called the holy Roman church the universal mother, accepting and serving with great veneration this institution founded by the divine will, this pledge of a dispensation to the church, this privilege handed over in the beginning and confirmed to Saint Peter the chief of the apostles. And even as they accepted its proofs in confirmation of their faith and of the doctrines of holy religion, so also they received its judgments—consenting in this, and agreeing as it were with one spirit and one voice: that all greater matters and exceptional cases, and judgments over all churches, ought to be referred to it as to a mother and a head; that from it there was no appeal; that no one should or could retract or refute its decisions. Wherefore the blessed pope Gelasius, armed with the divine authority, when writing to the emperor Anastasius how and what he should think concerning the primacy of the holy and apostolic see, instructed him as follows: "Although," he said, "before all priests in common who duly exercise divine functions it is right that the necks of the faithful should be bowed, by how much more should the bishop of the Roman see be obeyed, whom both the supreme deity has willed to predominate over all priests and the subsequent piety of the whole church in common has honored? From which thy prudence clearly sees that, with him whom the voice of Christ placed over all, and whom a venerable church has always professed and devoutly holds as its primate, no one can, by any human device whatever, gain an equal privilege and be equally acknowledged." Likewise pope Julius, when writing to the oriental bishops concerning the power of that same holy and apostolic see, said: "It would have become ye, brethren, to choose your words and not to speak ironically against the holy Roman and apostolic church, since our Lord Jesus Christ, addressing it as was fitting, said: 'Thou art Peter, and upon this rock will I build any church, and the gates of hell shall not prevail against it; and I will give unto thee the keys of the kingdom of Heaven.' For it has the power, granted to it by a special privilege, of opening and closing for whom it will the gates of the kingdom of Heaven." Is it not lawful, then, for him to whom the power of opening and closing Heaven is granted to exercise judgment upon earth? God forbid that it should not be! Remember what the most blessed apostle Paul says: 'Know ye not that we shall judge angels? How much more the things of earth!" The blessed pope Gregory also decreed that those kings should fall from their dignity who should dare to violate the statutes of the apostolic see, writing to a certain abbot, Senator, as follows: "But if any king, priest, judge or secular person, disregarding this the page of our decree, shall attempt to act counter to it he shall lose the dignity of his power and honor and shall know that he, in the sight of God, is guilty of committing a crime. And unless he restore the things which have been wrongfully removed by him, or unless he atone by fitting penance for his unlawful acts, he shall be kept away from the most sacred body and blood of our Lord and Savior Jesus Christ and shall undergo a stern vengeance at the eternal judgment."

But if the blessed Gregory, the most gentle of teachers, decreed that kings who should violate his decrees in the matter of a single hospice should not only be deposed but also excommunicated and, at the last judgment, condemned: who, save one like to them, will blame us for having deposed and excommunicated Henry, who is not alone a scorner of the apostolic judgments but also, as far as in him lies, a treader under foot of holy mother church herself and a most shameless robber and atrocious destroyer of the whole realm and of the churches. . . .

But to return to the matter in hand. Is not a dignity like this, founded by laymen—even by those who do not know God—subject to that dignity which the providence of God Almighty has, in His own honor, founded and given to the world? For His Son, even as He is undoubtingly believed to be

God and man, so is He considered the highest priest, the head of all priests, sitting on the right hand of the Father and always interceding for us. And He despised a secular kingdom, which makes the sons of this world swell with pride, and came of his own will to the priesthood of the cross. Who does not know that kings and leaders are sprung from those who—ignorant of God—by pride, plunder, perfidy, murders—in a word by almost every crime, the devil, who is the prince of this world, urging them on as it were—have striven with blind cupidity and intolerable presumption to dominate over their equals; namely, over men? To whom, indeed, can we better compare them, when they seek to make the priests of God bend to their footprints, than to him who is head over all the sons of pride and who, tempting the Highest Pontiff Himself, the Head of priests, the Son of the Most High, and promising to Him all the kingdoms of the world, said: All these I will give unto Thee if Thou wilt fall down and worship me?" who can doubt but that the priests of Christ are to be considered the fathers and masters of kings and princes and of all the faithful? Is it not considered miserable madness for a son to attempt to subject to himself his father, a pupil his master; and for one to bring into his power and bind with iniquitous bonds him by whom he believes that he himself can be bound and loosed not only on earth but also in Heaven? This the emperor Constantine the Great, lord of all the kings and princes of nearly the whole world evidently understood—as the blessed Gregory reminds us in a letter to the emperor Mauritius—when, sitting last after all the bishops in the holy council of Nicea, he presumed to give no sentence of judgment over them, but, even calling them gods, decreed that they should not be subject to his judgment but that he should be dependent upon their will. Also the aforementioned pope Gelasius, persuading the said emperor Anastasius not to take offense at the truth which had been made clear to his senses, added this remark: "For, indeed, O august emperor, there are two things by which this world is chiefly ruled—the sacred authority of the pontiffs and the royal power; whereby the burden of the priests is by so much the heavier according as they, at the divine judgment of men, are about to render account for the kings themselves." And a little further on he says: Thou dost know, therefore, that in these matters thou art dependent on their judgment and that thou art not to wish to reduce them to do thy will."

Very many of the pontiffs, accordingly, armed with such decrees and with such authorities, have excommunicated—some of them kings; some, emperors. For, if any special example of the persons of such princes is needed,—the blessed pope Innocent excommunicated the emperor Arcadius for consenting that Saint John Chrysostom should be expelled from his see. Likewise another Roman pontiff—Zacchary, namely—deposed a king of the Franks, not so much for his iniquities as for the reason that he was not fitted to exercise so great power. And he substituted Pipin, father of the emperor Charles the Great, in his place—loosing all the Franks from the oath of fealty which they had sworn him. . . . And the blessed Ambrose—who, although a saint, was not, indeed, bishop over the whole church—excommunicated and excluded from the church the emperor Theodosius the Great for a fault which, by other priests, was not regarded as very grave. He shows, too, in his writings that, not by so much is gold more precious than lead, as the priestly dignity is more lofty than the royal power; speaking thus towards the beginning of his pastoral letter: "The honor and sublimity of bishops, brethren, is beyond all comparison. If one should compare them to resplendent kings and diademed princes it would be far less worthy than if one compared the base metal lead to gleaming gold. For, indeed, one can see how the necks of kings and princes are bowed before the knees of priests; and how, having kissed their right hands, they believe themselves to be fortified by their prayers." And, after a little: "Ye should know, brethren, that we have thus mentioned all these things in order to show that nothing in this life can be found more lofty than priests or more sublime than bishops." . . .

Furthermore every Christian king, when he comes to die, seeks as a miserable suppliant the aid of a priest to the end that he may evade hell's prison, that he may pass from the shadows to the light, that, at the last judgment, he may appear absolved from the bonds of his sins. But what man—a layman even, not to speak of priests—has ever implored the aid of an earthly king for the salvation of his soul when his last hour was near? And what king or emperor is able, by reason of the office imposed upon him, to snatch any Christian from the power of the devil through holy baptism, to number him among the sons of God and to fortify him with the divine unction? And who of them—which is the greatest thing in the Christian religion—can with his own lips make the body and blood of our Lord? Or who of them possesses the power of binding and loosing in Heaven and on earth? From which things it is clearly seen how greatly priests excel in power and dignity. Or who of them can ordain any one as clerk in the holy church—much less depose him for any fault? For in the matter of ecclesiastical grades a greater power is needed to depose than to ordain. For bishops may ordain other bishops, but by no means depose them without the authority of the apostolic see. Who, therefore, that is even moderately intelligent can doubt that priests are to be preferred to kings? But if kings are to be judged by priests for their sins, by whom should they be judged with more right than by the Roman pontiff? Finally, any good Christians whatever have much more right to be considered kings than have bad princes. For the former, seeking the glory of God, strenuously rule themselves; but the latter, enemies unto themselves, seeking the things which are their own and not the things which are God's, are tyrannical oppressors of others. The former are the body of the true king, Christ; the latter, of the devil. The former restrain themselves to the end that they may eternally reign with the supreme emperor; but the sway of the latter brings about this—that they shall perish in eternal damnation with the prince of darkness who is king over all the sons of pride. . . .

We refer to kings and emperors who, too much swollen by worldly glory, rule not for God but for themselves. . . . Wherefore to kings and emperors especially it is of advantage, when their mind tends to exalt itself and to delight in its own particular glory, to find out a means of humbling themselves and to be brought to realize that what they have been rejoicing in is the thing most to be feared. Let them, therefore, diligently consider how dangerous and how much to be feared the royal or imperial dignity is. For in it the fewest are saved; and those who, through the mercy of God, do come to salvation are not glorified in the holy church and in the judgment of the Holy Spirit to the same extent as many poor people. For, from the beginning of the world until these our own times, in the whole of authentic history we do not find seven emperors or kings whose lives were as distinguished for religion and as beautified by significant portents as those of an innumerable multitude who despised the world—although we believe many of them to have found mercy in the presence of God Almighty. For what emperor or king was ever honored by miracles as were Saint Martin, Saint Antony and Saint Benedict—not to mention the apostles and martyrs? And what emperor or king raised the dead, cleansed lepers, or healed the blind? See how the holy church praises and venerates the emperor Constantine of blessed memory, Theodosius and Honorius, Charles and Louis as lovers of justice, promoters of the Christian religion, defenders of the churches: it does not, however, declare them to have been resplendent with so great a glory of miracles. . . . Moreover, if the judgment of the holy church severely punishes a sinner for the slaying of one man, what will become of those who, for the sake of worldly glory, hand over many thousands to death? . . . And, so long as they do not repent with their whole heart and are unwilling to let go what has been acquired or retained through shedding of blood, their penitence before God will remain without the worthy fruit of penitence. Surely, therefore, they ought greatly to fear. And it should frequently be recalled to their memory that, as we have said, in the different kingdoms of the earth, from the beginning of the world, very few of the innumerable multitude of kings are found to have been holy: whereas in one see alone—the Roman one, namely—almost a hundred of the successive pontiffs since the time of Saint Peter the apostle are counted among the most holy. Why, then, is this—except that the kings and princes of the earth, enticed by vain glory, prefer, as has been said, the things that are their own to the things that are spiritual; but the pontiffs of the church, despising vain glory, prefer to carnal things the things that are of God? The former readily punish those who sin against themselves and are indifferent to those who sin against God; the latter quickly pardon those who sin against themselves and do not lightly spare those who sin against God. The former, too much bent on earthly deeds, think slightingly of spiritual ones; the latter, sedulously meditating on heavenly things, despise the things which are of earth. . . .

Therefore let those whom holy church, of its own will and after proper counsel, not for transitory glory but for the salvation of many, calls to have rule or dominion, humbly obey. . . . Let them also carefully retain what God says in the gospel: "I do not seek my glory"; and, "He who wishes to be the first among you shall be the servant of all." Let them always prefer the honor of God to their own; let them cherish and guard justice by observing the rights of every man; let them not walk in the counsel of the ungodly but, with an assenting heart, always consort with good men. Let them not seek to subject to themselves or to subjugate the holy church as a handmaid; but chiefly let them strive, by recognizing the teachers and fathers, to honor in due form her eyes—namely the priests of God. . . . And so by humbly doing these things, and by observing the love of God and of their neighbor as they ought, they may hope for the mercy of Him who said: "Learn of Me, for I am meek and lowly of heart." If they shall have humbly imitated Him they shall pass from this servile and transitory kingdom to a true kingdom of liberty and eternity.

From Henderson, pp. 394–405 passim.

13.2 Alternatives: Paschal II and Henry V

The events of the investiture contest escalated the tensions between secular and spiritual leadership, from efforts to reform the church to rid it of secular interference, to struggles between pope and emperor concerning their respective jurisdiction over bishops, to a battle between the two leaders to determine who had authority over the other. Amid these events, church leaders, scholars, and court officials carried on extensive theoretical debates concerning the relationship of church and state, laying the basis for medieval and later political theory.

Several theorists, and one pope, put forward the radical proposal that the church *give up* its temporal holdings in order to retain independence in its spiritual domain. Instead of increasing papal power over kings and emperors in order to wrest control of the bishops from them, this theory suggested that bishops and churches be removed from royal and imperial oversight by divesting them of any secular significance or material worth. Bishops could then concentrate on their spiritual duties without having to worry about administering vast landholdings. They could be supported by the tithes and gifts of their congregations.

Pope Paschal II (1099–1118), in the documents below, suggested this simple solution to Emperor Henry V (d. 1125) when they met in 1111 to resolve the imperial-papal conflict. While the emperor was quite happy to accept this generous proposal, he rightly suspected that it would never be accepted. Both the Roman cardinals and the German bishops revolted against it, effectively blocking Paschal from pursuing this plan. Henry then captured the hapless pope and forced him to sign over investiture rights to the emperor, a concession rejected by the cardinals and other reformers, and revoked by Paschal himself after Henry let him go.

In hindsight, Paschal's original proposal appears brilliant, but was in its own time unrealistic. However, the argument that he makes for divestment highlights the critical issue for the church: as the spiritual leader in the temporal world, what should be the church's relationship to property? In an environment of increasing wealth and materialism, the attitude toward worldly goods becomes a central issue for the spirit of prophecy. In the coming centuries, pious lay people, mendicant reformers, and heretics will challenge the church hierarchy's authority on these grounds.

The document below is Paschal's offer in February 1111 to Henry V, renouncing church property.

Questions

1. What are the pros and cons of Paschal's proposal?
2. On what basis does he make this argument?
3. Do you think the church needs to be stronger or weaker in order to function as spiritual leader?

Paschal's Privilege of the First Convention, Feb. 12, 1111

Bishop Paschal, servant of the servants of God. To his beloved son Henry and his successors, forever. It is both decreed against by the institutions of the divine law, and interdicted by the sacred canons, that priests should busy themselves with secular cases, or should go to the public court except to rescue the condemned, or for the sake of others who suffer injury. Wherefore also the apostle Paul says: "If ye have secular judgments constitute as judges those who are of low degree in the church." Moreover in portions of your kingdom bishops and abbots are so occupied by secular cares that they are compelled assiduously to frequent the court, and to perform military service. Which things, indeed, are scarcely if at all carried on without plunder, sacrilege, arson. For ministers of the altar are made ministers of the king's court; inasmuch as they receive cities, duchies, margravates, monies and other things which belong to the service of the king. Whence also the custom has grown up—intolerably for the church—that elected bishops should by no means receive consecration unless they had first been invested through the hand of the king. From which cause both the wickedness of simoniacal heresy and, at times, so great an ambition has prevailed that the episcopal sees were invaded without any previous election. At times, even, they have been invested while the bishops were alive. Aroused by these and very many other evils which had happened for the most part through investitures, our predecessors the pontiffs Gregory VII and Urban II of blessed memory, frequently calling together episcopal councils did condemn those investitures of the lay hand, and did decree that those who should have obtained churches through them should be deposed, and the donors also be deprived of communion—according to that chapter of the apostolic canons which runs thus: "If any bishop, employing the powers of the world, do through them obtain a church: he shall be deposed and isolated, as well as all who communicate with him." Following in the traces of which (canons), we also, in an episcopal council, have confirmed their sentence. And so, most beloved son, king Henry,—now through our office, by the grace of God, emperor of the Romans,—we decree that those royal appurtenances are to be given back to thee and to thy kingdom which manifestly belonged to that kingdom in the time of Charles, Louis, and of thy other predecessors. We forbid, and under sentence of anathema prohibit, that any bishop or abbot, present or future, invade these same royal appurtenances. In which are included the cities, duchies, margravates, counties, monies, toll, market, advowsons [right to appoint vacant clerical positions] of the kingdom, rights of the judges of the hundred courts, and the courts which manifestly belonged to the king together with what pertained to them, the military posts and camps of the kingdom. Nor shall they henceforth, unless by favor of the king, concern themselves with those royal appurtenances. But neither shall it be allowed our successors, who shall follow us in the apostolic chair, to disturb thee or thy kingdom in this matter. Furthermore, we decree that the churches, with the offerings and hereditary possessions which manifestly did not belong to the kingdom, shall remain free; as, on the day of thy coronation, in the sight of the whole church, thou didst promise that they should be. For it is fitting that the bishops, freed from secular cares, should take care of their people, and not any longer be absent from their churches. For, according to the apostle Paul, let them watch, being about to render account, as it were, for the souls of these (their people).

From Henderson, pp. 405–407.

13.3 Holy Places: The Pilgrim's Guide to Santiago de Compostela

Many pious laity, zealous for individual reform, sought a spiritual reprieve from the materialism of everyday life by making a pilgrimage. These trips to famous religious sites such as Jerusalem or Rome and to various churches with saint's relics served as spiritual journeys for the soul (see Martin of Tours, 6.3). Some pilgrims went as a penance assigned by a priest during confession. Others went to saints' shrines seeking physical healing or spiritual rejuvenation. Many undoubtedly went for a mixture of reasons, perhaps partly for escape from normal life evident, for example, in Chaucer's *Canterbury Tales.*

One of the most famous European tours for pilgrims, stopping at shrines along the way, was the pilgrimage culminating in the terminus at the shrine of Saint James (Saint Iago, or Santiago) in Compostela, Spain. Saint James was one of the three closest disciples of Jesus. According to later legends, James is credited with the evangelization of Spain. Sometime after his martyrdom, beheaded by Herod in Jerusalem, his body was returned to Spain and buried. In the early ninth century, his tomb was "rediscovered" and became the basis of the cult of Saint James, strengthened by Carolingian support and the ideological aims of the French in the reconquista of Spain from the hands of the Muslims. Consequently, the four main routes to Santiago begin in France.

So many pilgrims traveled these roads from France into Spain to Compostela that a guidebook was written for the pilgrims (circa 1139–1173). The four brief excerpts below from this guide illustrate the significance of this pilgrimage. The first is a general description of the major pilgrimages to the most holy "hospices" in the Christian world—hospices here indicates that these sites were seen as spiritual resting places for the cure of the soul. The second excerpt tells the story of one of the holy sites along the route to Compostela, that of Saint Giles. The last two excerpts describe the pilgrim's experience at the shrine of Saint James.

Questions

1. What in the guide would attract a pilgrim to these sites?
2. What kinds of things might a pilgrim expect to experience along the way?
3. What are the spiritual aspirations that such a journey would fulfill?

The Pilgrim's Guide to Santiago de Compostela

Chapter IV: The Three Hospices of the World

God has, in a most particular fashion, instituted in this world three columns greatly necessary for the support of his poor, that is to say, the hospice of Jerusalem, the hospice of Mount-Joux, and the hospice of Santa Cristina on the Somport Pass. These hospices, established in places they were very much needed, are holy sites, the house of God for the restoring of saintly pilgrims, the resting of the needy, the consolation of the sick, the salvation of the dead, and the assistance lent to the living. Therefore, he who had built those holy places, no matter who he may be, will partake, without any doubt, of the kingdom of God. . . .

Saint Giles

Likewise, one must pay a visit with particular attentiveness to the most dignified remains of the most pious and Blessed Giles, confessor and abbot. Because the most Blessed Giles, extraordinarily famous in all latitudes of the world, must indeed be venerated by all, celebrated with dignity by all, by all esteemed, invoked and beseeched. After the prophets and the apostles, nobody among the other saints is more worthy, nobody more holy, nobody more glorious, nobody more prompt to lend help. In effect, it is he who, ahead of all other saints, is accustomed to come most rapidly to the assistance of the needy, the afflicted and the anguished who invoke him. Oh, what a beautiful and valuable labor it is to visit his tomb! The very day that one invokes him with all one's heart, no doubt one will be happily assisted.

I myself have verified what I am saying. I have once seen somebody in the town of the saint who, the day he had invoked him, escaped, under the protection of the blessed confessor, from the house of a certain shoemaker Peyrot; this house, old and decrepit, soon after collapsed. Who, then, shall look at his dwelling the longest? Who shall worship God in his most sacred basilica? Who shall embrace most fervently his sarcophagus? Who shall kiss his altar ever to be venerated, or who shall tell the story of his most pious life?

Thus, a sick man wears his tunic and is restored to health; another man is bitten by a snake and, by his inexhaustible virtue, is healed; still another one, deranged in his mind, is delivered from the devil; a storm in the sea abates; the daughter of Theocritus is returned to her father restored to long-desired health; a sick man, wanting health in his whole body, regains his long-wished-for sanity; a hind, previously untamed, is domesticated by his command and becomes his servant; the monastic order, under the patronage of this abbot, flourishes; a possessed is delivered from the devil; a sin of Charles, revealed to him by an angel, is remitted to the king; a dead man is returned to life; a crippled man is restored to health; and furthermore, two door leaves of cypress engraved with the images of the princes of the apostles make their journey on the waves of the sea from the city of Rome as far as the port of the Rhône with no other guidance but his sovereign power.

I regret, indeed, having to die before being able to report all his feats worthy of veneration: these are truly so many and so great. This most brilliant Greek star, having illuminated with his rays the people of Provence, reclined magnificently among them without ever declining but increasing, without letting his light go but offering it, redoubled, to everybody, without descending towards the abyss but ascending to the summit of Olympus. While setting, his light did not darken but, through his starry signs, it became only more brilliant than the other holy stars in the four parts of the earth.

It was at midnight, a Sunday, the first of September, that this star declined, that a choir of angels set him in their midst on an elevated throne, and that the Gothic people together with a monastic order offered him hospitality with an honorable tomb on their free territory, that is to say, between the city of Nimes and the river Rhône. . . .

[Description of the golden casket, engravings, and sculpture]

Such is then the tomb of the Blessed Giles the confessor, in which his venerated body honorably rests. May therefore the Hungarians who aim to possess his body blush; may those of Chamalières, who vainly imagine having the whole of his body, be thrown into confusion; may those of Saint-Seine, who pride themselves in having his head, waste away; may the Normans of Cotentin, who boast of having the whole of his body, stand likewise in fear, because in no way could his most sacred bones, as this was proven by many, be removed from his place. Some people have in effect tried once to snatch away quite fraudulently the venerable arm of the blessed confessor and to carry it out of the country of Giles towards faraway shores, but in no manner could they get off with it.

There are four bodies of saints which, as it is told and as it has been proven by many, could never be removed by anybody and by any means from their sarcophagi: namely, those of the Blessed James the Zebedee, of the Blessed Martin of Tours, of Saint Leonard of Limoges, and of the Blessed Giles the confessor of Christ. It is told that Philip, king of France, attempted once to carry off their bodies to France, but he could in no way remove them from their sarcophagi. . . .

Chapter X: The Distribution of the Offerings
at the Altar of Saint James

Seventy-two canons, corresponding to the number of the seventy-two Disciples of Christ, are attached to this church; they follow the rule of the Blessed Doctor Isidore of Spain. They divide among themselves, by successive weeks, the oblations of the altar of Saint James. To the first canon correspond the oblations of the first week; to the second, those of the second; to the third, those of the third; and so they share the oblations to the last one.

Each Sunday, tradition dictates that the oblations be shared out in three parts: the first is assigned to the hebdomadary to whom it corresponds; the other two are first drawn together and are then divided in their turn into three parts; one of these is given to the canons for their communal meal; another, to the fabric of the basilica; and the third one, to the archbishop of the church. But the oblations of the week which goes from Palm to Easter must be given, according to accepted custom, to the poor pilgrims of Saint James lodged in the hospice. Furthermore, were the justice of God appropriately observed, one would be the justice of God appropriately observed, one would be obliged to give at all times the tenth part of the oblations of the altar of Saint James to the poor who drop in at the hospice.

Indeed, all poor pilgrims must, the first night that follows the day of their arrival to the altar of the Blessed James, receive at the hospice, for the love of God and the Apostle, full hospitality. Those who are sick, to be sure, must be charitably taken care of there either until their death or until their complete recovery. So it is done at Saint-Léonard: no matter how many poor pilgrims make it there, all receive subsistence. Furthermore, custom dictates that the leprous of the city be given the oblations that reach the altar each Sunday, from the beginning of the morning until the hour of terce. And if a prelate of the same basilica committed fraud in this matter or changed in some way the destiny of the oblations, as we have just described it, may his sin stand between God and him.

Chapter XI: The Proper Welcoming of the Pilgrims
of Saint James

Pilgrims, whether poor or rich, who return from or proceed to Santiago, must be received charitably and respectfully by all. For he who welcomes them and provides them diligently with lodging will have as his guest not merely the Blessed James, but the Lord himself, who in His Gospels said: "He who welcomes you, welcomes me." Many are those who in the past brought upon themselves the wrath of God because they refused to receive the pilgrims of Saint James or the indigent.

In Nantua, which is a city between Genève and Lyon, a weaver refused to hand out some bread to a pilgrim who had asked for it: all of a sudden some linen of his dropped to the ground torn in its middle. In Villeneuve, a woman kept some bread under hot ashes. A needy pilgrim of Saint James asked her for alms by the love of God and the Blessed James. When she answered that she had no bread, the pilgrim exclaimed: "May the bread you have turn into stone!" And when the pilgrim left her house and was already at a considerable distance, this vicious woman turned to the ashes with the idea of retrieving her bread, but found only a round stone instead. With contrite heart she set out to look for the pilgrim, but could not find him anymore.

Two valiant Frenchmen, returning one day from Santiago destitute of all, kept asking for lodging, by the love of God and Saint James, all about the city of Poitiers from the house of Jean Gautier and as far as Saint-Porchaire—and they could find none. And having finally been put up by some poor man in the last house of that street next to the basilica of Saint-Porchaire, by the effects of divine vengeance, a violent fire burned to the ground that very night the entire street, starting from the house where they first asked for lodging and up to the one which had welcomed them. And these were about one thousand houses in all. But the one in which the servants of God had been put up remained, by divine grace, untouched.

That is the reason why it should be known that the pilgrims of Saint James, whether poor or rich, have the right to hospitality and to diligent respect.

> Here ends the fourth book of Saint James the Apostle;
> Glory to him who wrote it and glory to him who reads it.

This book has first been diligently received by the Church of Rome; it was written in various places, that is to say, in Rome, in the lands of Jerusalem, in France, in Italy, in Germany, in Frisia and mainly in Cluny.

13.4 Holy Women: The Beguine Marie d'Oignies

Marie d'Oignies (1173–1213) is considered the first Beguine, and her biographer Jacques de Vitry (circa 1170–1240) is credited with spreading the ideas behind this new and controversial religious order. The female Beguines, and their male counterparts the Beghards, expressed their holiness through public charitable works, seeking out and caring for the outcasts of society, in particular lepers and the poor. The Beguines were not content to live as nuns in an enclosure, but preferred to serve out in the world. The movement began in the French city of Liège with Marie and a group of women followers, but spread rapidly in France and Germany. The formal church eyed them with suspicion, fearful that they were associated with the heretical Albigensians, and never sanctioned the order. Its aims and spirit were similar to, and influenced the development of, the Franciscan order (18.2).

Jacques de Vitry's biography of Marie is written in the style of a saint's life, probably with the aim of recommending her for canonization. Although the officials of the church refused to recognize her or the movement, it is clear that de Vitry was not alone in admiring the piety of these women. While their behavior may have seemed too independent and assertive for the church hierarchy, they obviously played a major role in medieval European Christian society.

The excerpts below illustrate something of her early life and rejection of the urban lifestyle for an ascetic one, her visions and scriptural insights, and her holy death. Marie's life as told by Jacques de Vitry is a good example of the kind of mysticism and piety that arose out of the urban environment of late twelfth-century Europe.

Questions

1. What aspects of Marie's life does Jacques de Vitry admire, and why?
2. Why would church officials be wary of women like Marie?
3. How do her visions and deeds reflect the pious concerns of the wealthy urban class?

The Life of Marie d'Oignies

Book I Her Childhood

There was in the diocese of Liège in a town called Nivelles a certain young woman whose name was Marie, as gracious in life as in name. Her parents were not of common stock but even though they abounded in riches and many temporal goods yet, even from her early childhood, her inclination was never attracted by transitory goods. Cast in this way upon the Lord (cf. 1 Pt 5:7) almost from the womb, she never or rarely mixed with those who were playing as is the custom of small girls nor "did she make herself partaker with them that walked in lightness" (Tb 3:17). Rather she kept her soul from the concupiscence and vanity of them all and foreshadowed in her youth what, through a divine sign, she would be in the future in her old age. Wherefore when she was still young, she would frequently kneel before her bed at night and offer up certain prayers which she had learned to the Lord as the first fruits of her life (cf. Ex 22:29).

Thus mercy and righteousness grew in her from her infancy and she loved the ascetic life as with a natural affection. Once, for example, it happened that when some Cistercian brothers were passing in front of her father's house, she glanced up at them and, admiring their religious habit, she followed them stealthily. When she could do no more, she put her own feet in the footprints of those lay brothers or monks from her great desire.

And when her parents, as is the custom of worldly people, wished to adorn her in delicate and refined clothing, she was saddened and rejected them as if what she had read had impressed itself naturally in her spiritual consciousness, that is to say those things which Peter the apostle had said concerning women: "Do not dress up for show: doing up your hair, wearing gold bracelets and fine clothes" (1 Pt 3:3), and what Paul the apostle had said: "Without braided hair or gold and jewellry or expensive clothes" (1 Tm 2:9). When her parents saw this kind of behaviour, they mocked their little girl and said, "What kind of person is our daughter going to be?"

Her Marriage

Her parents were indignant when they saw these auspicious deeds and when she was fourteen years old they joined her in marriage to a certain youth. Living apart from her parents, she was now set on fire with such an ecstasy of ardour and punished her body with such warfare that she enslaved it to such a degree that it frequently happened that after she had toiled for a large part of the night with her own hands; she would pray for a lengthy period after she had finished her work. As often as was licit for her, she passed a very short part of the night in sleep on planks which she had concealed at the foot of her bed. And because she clearly did not have power over her own body, she secretly wore a very rough cord under her clothing which she bound with great force.

I do not say these things to commend the excess but so that I might show her fervour. In these and in many other things wherein the privilege of grace operated, let the discreet reader pay attention that what is a privilege for a few does not make a common law. Let us imitate her virtues but we cannot imitate the works of her virtues without individual privilege. Although the body be forced to serve the spirit (cf. Rm 7:25) and although we ought "to carry the wounds of the Lord Jesus Christ in our body" (Gal 6:17), yet we know that "the honour of the King loves justice" (Ps 98:4) and sacrifice from the robbery of the poor is not pleasing to the Lord (cf. Is 61:8). Necessary things are not to be taken from the poverty of the flesh, although vices are to be checked. Therefore, admire rather than imitate what we have read about the things certain saints have done through the familiar counsel of the Holy Spirit.

The Conversion of Her Husband and Their Chaste Life

And after she had lived in marriage in this fashion for a short time with her husband, whose name was John, the Lord looked on the humility of his handmaid and hearkened to the tears of the suppliant and John, who previously had had Marie as a wife, was inspired to entrust her to the protection of God. The Lord entrusted a chaste woman to a chaste man; he left her a faithful provider so that she might be comforted by the presence of a protector and thereby serve the Lord more freely. And John, who formerly had acted with a certain natural sweetness of spirit, did not oppose the holy plan of his wife (as is the custom of other men) but he suffered with her and bore with her labours good-naturedly enough. He was visited by the Lord and he not only promised to live a celibate and truly angelic life in continence, but also promised to imitate his companion in her holy plan and in her holy ascetic life by giving up everything to the poor for Christ.

The further he [John] was separated from her in carnal love, so much the more closely was he joined to her by the knot of spiritual matrimony through natural love. For this reason the Lord later appeared to his handmaid in a vision and promised that he would repay her in heaven in reparation for the marriage and for her partner who, through love of chastity, had withdrawn himself from carnal commerce on earth.

Let the unhappy men blush and tremble who befoul themselves outside marriage with illicit comminglings, when these two blessed young people abstained from licit embraces for the Lord and overcame the intensity of fervid adolescence with the fervour of an ascetic life. They extinguished fire with fire and deserved triumphal crowns. The Lord gave them a place in his house, within his walls and a name better than sons and daughters while, like the blessed martyrs, they pierced their flesh with the nails of the fear of the Lord. They did not burn in the fire but immolated their self-will while near an abundance of sexual delights. Although near a river, they thirsted and in the midst of banquets, they hungered. Indeed, they utterly degraded themselves for the Lord, when they, for a time, laboured in a place called Willambrouk near Nivelles for the sake of the Lord.

The Contempt and Persecution of Her Relatives

Demons looked at them and regarded them with malice. Worldly people, as well as their own relatives, looked at them and gnashed their teeth against the persons whom they had honoured before when they were wealthy. The persons made poor for Christ's sake were now condemned and mocked. They were accounted vile and degraded for the Lord's sake and "the reproaches of their accusers fell" (Ps 68:10) on them for the sake of the Lord.

Do not fear, O handmaid of Christ, to put aside worldly joy and honour, to approach the persecutions of the cross with your Christ, your Bridegroom. It is good for you "to be abject in the house of the Lord, better than to dwell in the tabernacles of sinners" (Ps 83:11). You have lost the favour of relatives, but you have found the favour of Christ. Indeed, you did not lose the favour of relatives since they loved only your goods and never loved you. For as flies follow honey and wolves follow carrion, so did this crowd follow its prey which is not a man.

Her Compunction and Tears

. . . One day, already chosen by you, she was visited by you and she considered the benefits which you had generously shown forth in the flesh to humanity. She found such grace of compunction therein that a great abundance of tears was pressed out by the wine-press of your cross in the passion and her tears flowed so copiously on the floor that the ground in the church became muddy with her footprints. Wherefore for a long time after this visitation she could neither gaze at an image of the cross, nor speak, nor hear other people speaking about the passion of Christ, without falling into ecstasy through a defect of the heart. Therefore she sometimes moderated her sorrow and restrained the flood of her tears and, disregarding Christ's humanity, would raise her consciousness to his divinity and majesty so that she might therein find consolation in his impassibility. But when she tried to restrain the intensity of the flowing river, then a greater intensity wondrously sprang forth. When she directed her attention to how great he was who had endured such degradation for us, her sorrow was renewed and new tears were revived in her soul through her sweet compunction.

One day, just before Good Friday, when the passion of Christ was approaching, she began to offer herself as a sacrifice with the Lord in even greater showers of tears and with sighs and gasps. One of the priests of the church softly but firmly exhorted her to pray in silence and to restrain her tears. She was always timid and, with the simplicity of a dove, tried to obey in all things but, conscious of the impossibility of this thing, she slipped out of the church unknown to him and hid herself in a secret place which was removed from everyone. There she tearfully implored the Lord that he show this priest that it is not in man's power to restrain the intensity of tears when the waters flow with the vehemence of the blowing spirit (cf. Ps 147:18; Ex 14:21).

Once when the priest celebrated Mass, "the Lord opened and none shut" (Is 22:22) and "he sent forth waters and they overturned the earth" (Jb 12:15). The spirit [of the priest] was drowned in such a flood of tears that he almost suffocated, and as much as he tried to repress its intensity, by that much the more was he drenched with his tears and the book and the altar cloths were dripping as well. What could he do, he who had been so thoughtless, he who had rebuked the handmaid of Christ? To his chagrin, he learned through experience what he previously had not wanted to know through [a lack of] humility and compassion. After many sobs and with many faltering and disordered stammerings, he barely escaped disaster. One who saw this and who knew the priest personally bears witness to this. A long time after Mass had ended, the handmaid of Christ returned and, in a wondrous manner as if she had been present, reproachfully told the priest what had happened. "Now," she said, "You have learned from experience that it is not in man's power to restrain the intensity of the spirit when the south wind blows."

Both day and night her eyes continuously brought forth outpourings of the waters, not only on her cheeks but also on the church floor, and lest her tears make the ground all muddy, she caught them in the veil with which she covered her head. She used up so many veils in this manner that she often had to change her wet veil for a dry one. . . .

Thus since her spirit had partaken of food, she considered all delights of the flesh to be foolish. One day she brought back to her memory a time when she had been forced to eat meat and had to drink a little watered wine because she had had a very serious illness. Then from a kind of horror at her previous delight, she did not have rest in her spirit and by wondrously torturing her flesh, she afflicted herself until she had made recompense for those delights she had had before. From the fervour of her spirit and as if inebriated, she began to loathe her flesh when she compared it with the sweetness of the paschal Lamb and she needlessly cut out a large piece of her flesh with a knife which she then buried in the earth from a sense of reticence. She had been so inflamed by an overwhelming fire of love that she had risen above the pain of her wound and, in this ecstasy of mind, she had seen one of the seraphim standing close by her. After she had died, the women who were washing her corpse were amazed when they found the places of the wounds, but those who had known of this event through confession understood what the scars were. Why do those who show amazement at the worms which swarmed from the wounds of Simeon and at the fire with which Antony burnt his feet not astonished at such fortitude in the frail sex of a woman who, wounded by charity and invigorated by the wounds of Christ, neglected the wounds of her own body? . . .

Sometimes she would gently rest with the Lord in a sweet and blessed silence for thirty-five days and she never ate any corporeal food and could utter no word except this alone: "I want the Body of Our Lord Jesus Christ." When she had received it, she would remain with the Lord in silence for whole days at a time. On those days she had the feeling that her spirit was separated, as it were, from her body or as if it were lying in a vessel of clay or, again, as if her body were enveloped in garments of clay and her spirit clothed in them, so abstracted was she from sensible things and rapt above herself in some kind of ecstasy. Nevertheless after five weeks she returned to herself and opened her mouth and received corporeal food and she spoke to those who had been standing around her and who had been struck with wonder.

A long time after this, it happened that she could not in any way endure the smells of meats or of any fried food or even the smell of wine except in the ablution after she had taken wine at the sacrament of the Body of Christ. Then she was able to endure both the smell and the taste without any difficulty. When she was passing through various towns, she used to go to the bishop of the town or to someone else so that she could receive a strengthening of her faith through the sacrament and the smells did not bother her which previously she had not been able to endure. . . .

Her Clothing and Appearance

She who was clothed in the fleece of the spotless Lamb, she who was inwardly adorned with wedding garments, had "put on Christ" (Rm 13:14) from within and did not worry about her outward adornment. Yet she wore ordinary clothes because she was not at all pleased by affected filth nor meticulous cleanliness. She fled both ornamentation and filth equally because the one smelled of delights and the other of vainglory. She knew that the blessed John the Baptist had been commended by the Lord for the harshness of his clothing and that Truth had spoken these words: "Those who are clothed in soft garments are in the houses of the king" (Mt. 11:8). She did not wear a linen shirt against her skin but a rough hair shirt which is called "estamine" in the vernacular. For a covering, she had a white woolen tunic and a cloak of the same simple colour without the addition of any fur or any puffery. She knew that after the fall of our first parents, the Lord did not cover their nakedness with precious but unnatural clothing or with coloured fabrics.

She was content with the simplicity of these clothes and did not fear the external cold at all because she was burning inwardly. Sometimes did not even need material fire to ward off the winter cold and once, in a wondrous manner when the winter was even more bitter than usual and the icy waters froze over from the cold, her outer body became hot while she was praying in conformity to the way she was glowing in the spirit, and sometimes her aromatic sweat even made her clothing smell sweet. Frequently when she offered her prayers to God from the thurible of her heart, the odour of her garments was like the odour of incense.

What do you say to this, you extravagant and ostentatious women, you who adorn your cadavers in many different ways and put tails on your clothing, you who manifest degenerate bestiality while you array yourselves as though you were temples? Your garments will be eaten by worms (cf. Prv 25:20] and will stink while, on the other hand, the clothes of this holy woman have been kept as relics because they smell sweetly. They are precious garments because no matter how thin they were, she was never conquered by cold. They have been sanctified because of the cold and, precisely because of this sanctification, they have been kept carefully after her death by the devout and are honoured with a pious love. . . .

Although she was taught inwardly by the unction of the Holy Spirit and by divine revelations, yet externally she most gladly listened to the testimonies of the scriptures which were entirely in accord with the Holy Spirit. Although the Lord could have illumined his disciples inwardly without verbally instructing them, yet he taught them exteriorly through the office of the voice, and expounded the scriptures to them when he said, "Now you are clean because of the word which I have spoken to you" (Jn 15:3]. Therefore every day she was more and more washed clean with the words of holy scripture and was edified by exhortations to virtue. She was illumined by faith, if indeed that could be called faith for she perceived with the eyes of faith the invisible things which God had revealed to her as if they were visible. Once when she was present at the door of the church in the village of Itère near Nivelles and a boy was being prepared for baptism, she saw an unclean spirit coming out of the boy in great confusion and when they lifted the boy out of the holy font, her eyes were opened and she saw the holy Spirit descending into the soul of the boy and a multitude of the holy angels around the reborn child.

Frequently when the priest was raising the host she saw between the hands of the priest the outward appearance of a beautiful boy and an army of the heavenly spirits descending with a great light. When the priest received the host after the *Confiteor,* she saw the Lord in the spirit who remained in the soul of the priest and filled him with a wondrous brightness. If, on the other hand, he received it unworthily, she saw the Lord withdrawing with indignation and the soul of the wretched man remaining empty and shadowy. Even when she was not present in the church but, as was her habit, was praying in her cell with her eyes covered with a white veil, when Christ descended to the altar and when the holy words were being said, then she was marvellously transformed and was sensible of his coming. When the sick received the sacrament of Extreme Unction and she was with them, she sensed the presence of Christ with a multitude of the saints mercifully strengthening the sick, expelling demons, and purging the soul. It was as if he were transfusing himself in light through the entire body of the sick person as the various parts of the body were being anointed. . . .

She not only had patience for resisting those who were opposed to her with the spirit of fortitude but she was also patient in her abstinence from all carnal allurements. Thus she chastised her body and placed it in servitude so that it obeyed the bidding of the spirit and did not contradict it nor did she ever excuse herself with any pretence. She did not grumble against the Lord but by imitating the fortitude of the Lord, she never became careless through sloth and never or rarely did her body fail through hard work. Thus did that youthful drummer as it were dry out her body by stretching it between two crosses so that she did not feel even the first stirrings of lust rise against her for many years. And from the great trust which she had towards men, from the abundance of her innocence and pure simplicity she thought them all to be like her. For this reason when one of her close friends clasped her hand from an excess of spiritual affection because he was very close to her—although in his chaste mind he thought no evil—he felt the first masculine stirrings rising in him. She knew nothing about this and when she heard a voice from above saying "Do not touch me" (Jn 20:7), she did not understand what it meant. Truly the God of mercy has compassion on our weaknesses and he did not want to discompose the man in front of the holy woman but, as though he were jealous, he wished to guard the chastity of his friend and therefore warned the man of the danger which was looming. Therefore when she said to him "I just now heard a voice saying 'Do not touch me' but I do not know what it means," he understood what it was and the more carefully guarded himself against other such occasions and gave thanks that his weakness had not been discovered and went away. . . .

Sometimes it seemed to her that she held him [Jesus] tightly between her breasts like a clinging baby for three or more days and she would hide him there lest he be seen by others and at other times she would kiss him as if he were an infant. Sometimes the holy Son of the Virgin showed himself to her in the form of a gentle lamb beside her skirts. On other occasions the holy Son of the Virgin appeared to her in the form of a dove for the consolation of his daughter, and sometimes he would walk around the church as if he were the zodiacal ram with a bright star in the middle of his forehead and, as it seemed to her, would visit his faithful ones. And just as the Lord showed himself to his doubting disciples in the form of a pilgrim (Lk 24:15–31) and took the shape of a merchant when he sent St. Thomas to the Indies, just so he deigned to manifest himself to his friends in the form of a friend. St. Jerome testified that when St. Paula came to Bethlehem, she saw him in the form of a baby lying in a crib, thus showing himself in a form suitable to the feast that was being celebrated. When, at the Nativity, he appeared as a baby sucking at the breasts of the Virgin Mary or crying in his cradle, she was drawn to him in love just as if he had been her own baby. In this way the various feasts took on a new interest according to how he manifested himself and each produced a different state of affective love. At the feast of the Purification, she saw the Blessed Virgin offering her Son in the temple and Simeon receiving him in his arms. In this vision she exulted no less from joy than if she had been present herself at this event in the temple. It sometimes happened during this same feast that after she had been walking in procession for a long time with her candle snuffed out, it suddenly burned with a most brilliant light which no one except God had kindled. Sometimes the Lord appeared to her on the cross during Passiontide, but this only happened rarely because she could scarcely endure it. Often when a great solemnity was approaching, she would feel joy for the entire octave before the feast. Thus was she transformed throughout the course of a whole year in different ways and was wondrously filled with love. . . .

Her Death

When her last hour was approaching, the Lord showed to his daughter among the brothers the portion of her inheritance (cf. Lk 15:12) and she saw the place in heaven which the Lord had prepared for her. She saw and rejoiced. We could in some way estimate the height of the place and the magnitude of its glory if we could remember the precious stones and the virtues of gems which she herself wondrously described; if, that is, we could remember the names of the stones which the Lord had named when he showed them to her. We cannot understand but, because it is written "Eye has not seen, O God, those things which you have prepared for those who love you" (Is 64:1) we can understand only with what glory she was worthy to be adorned. She who served the Lord so devoutly, who loved Christ so ardently, is the one whom the Lord singularly honoured with so many privileges on earth. When we were with her on the Thursday before her death and were helping her at Vespers, she could neither speak to us nor turn her eyes towards us. She was lying outside her cell in the open air and her eyes were fixed immovably towards heaven and her countenance began to brighten with a certain peacefulness. Then it was as though she were smiling and from her joy she began to sing I know not what in a low voice for a very long time, for at that time she could not raise her voice. When I approached closer, I could understand only this little bit of her song: "How beautiful you are Lord, our King." After she had sung and smiled and occasionally clapped her hands and had remained for a long time in such joy, she returned to herself and it was as if she once again felt how sick she was, and she began to groan a little. When we asked her what she had seen and if she was able or wished to tell us a little, she said "I could tell marvels if I dared." On the Saturday at Vespers, when her wedding day was close at hand, the handmaid of Christ (who had eaten nothing now for fifty-two days) began to sing the Alleluia in a sweet voice, that is to say on that day of rejoicing and exultation, that day which the Lord had made, that day which the Lord had foreordained and promised for his handmaid, that day of the Lord, that day of the Resurrection, that day of the Vigil of St. John the Baptist when, it is said, the apostle John left this world although the Church is accustomed to celebrate his feast at another time. For almost the whole night she was as joyful and exultant as if she had been invited to a banquet.

Satan appeared to her on Sunday, "lying in wait at her heel" (Gn 3:17). He disturbed her greatly and she began to fear for a little time and asked for help from those who were standing around her. She, however, took confidence again from the Lord and with strength "broke the head of the worm" (Ps 73:14) and, making the sign of the cross, she said "Get behind me filth and foulness." When he had departed, she began again to sing the Alleluia and to give thanks to God. When, on the day of the feast of St. John the Baptist, the time of holy Vespers was drawing near and at about the hour when the Lord sent out his spirit on the cross (that is to say, about the ninth hour), she also migrated to the Lord. Neither the gladness of her countenance nor the exultation of her face was changed by any of the pain of death. I do not ever remember that her face had more serenity even when she was healthy, nor had it ever shone with a greater expression of joy. Her face did not appear pallid or blue after death, as is usual. She brought many to devotion in and after her death by her angelic dove-like face, bright and clear in its simplicity and expression. Many were sweetly moistened with an abundant flood of tears at her death and they understood that they had been visited by the Lord through her merits in exactly the way that a certain holy woman had foreseen through the Holy Spirit when she had predicted that those who were present at her passing would receive much consolation from the Lord. When her tiny holy body was washed after death, it was found to be so small and shrivelled by her illness and fasting that her spine touched her belly and the bones of her back seemed to lie under the skin of her stomach as if under a thin linen cloth.

Reprinted with permission from *The Life of Marie d'Oignies,* by Jacques de Vitry, trans. Margot King (Toronto: Peregrina Publishing Co., 1993), pp. 46–49, 50–52, 54, 56–57, 67–68, 98–99, 101, 112–13, 129–31. Notes omitted.

–14–

Christians, Muslims, and Jews

Views of the Crusades

The Crusades in many ways embody some of the fundamental features of medieval European civilization. This religious-military movement reflects economic, political, social, and religious forces and trends in the Middle Ages. The Crusades are also significant for our comprehension of medieval history because they brought Europeans into contact with other civilizations that subsequently influenced European history and thought. This section endeavors to present the diversity of motives behind the Crusades, as well as different perspectives on their impact as seen through the eyes of Christians, Muslims, and Jews whose lives were affected by the crusading phenomenon.

The term "Crusades" refers to the military expeditions undertaken by Christian knights and troops to recover and protect the "Holy Land." The First Crusade, called in 1095 by Pope Urban II, was a response to the recent conquest of Palestine by Turkish Muslims, who, according to accounts received in Europe, attacked innocent pilgrims traveling in the Holy Land. Subsequent Crusades had a variety of aims related to asserting Christian European control over Palestine under this general humanitarian aim of protecting victims of heathen aggression and establishing Christian oversight in a land deemed holy by Jews, Muslims, and Christians. The amount of violence involved in this task, repeated in the five major Crusades throughout the twelfth and thirteenth centuries, seems to contradict the ostensibly defensive and religious aims of the Crusaders.

Historically, many other factors intertwined with these high religious ideals motivating the Crusades, as indicated in Pope Urban II's speech calling the First Crusade (14.1). God, greed, and glory worked often inseparably in the minds of young military men who sought their spiritual and material fortunes abroad. The failure of the Crusaders to live up

333

to the Crusading ideals is unsurprising: human behavior and motives are always complex, particularly in a broad movement that involved mobilizing hundreds of men from all ranks and a variety of regions to band together (not always harmoniously) on an aggressive mission of peace.

Idealistic as the original task may have been, the Crusades as a form of cross-cultural contact had both negative and positive long-term consequences for Christians, Muslims, and Jews in the Mediterranean region, evident in the selections from Jewish and Muslim chroniclers (14.2 and 14.3) and in the encounter with a Nubian Christian (14.4). As European Christian military groups traveled, they encountered along the way, more forcefully than before, the otherness of non-Christian Europeans such as Jews, non-European Christians in Byzantium, and non-Christians outside Europe. These encounters contributed to a growing sense of a separate European Christian cultural identity.

14.1 The European View of the Crusades:
Pope Urban II's Call to the First Crusade

The First Crusade was called in 1095 by Pope Urban II (1088–99) at a council held in Clermont, France. However, the ideas behind the Crusade have their origins in a variety of conditions in eleventh-century Europe. One was the peace movement (the Peace of God and the Truce of God) designed to curb the endemic warfare among a restless warrior class, and the need to redirect warrior energy into appropriate channels. A second factor was a growing awareness of Christian European identity as both "European" and "Christian," visible for example in the "reconquest" of Spain from Muslim hands. A third element in this Christian sense of identity and brotherhood appears in the practice of pilgrimage to sites outside of Europe, such as Jerusalem, that Europeans now took a proprietary interest in protecting.

Young warrior aristocrats were a likely audience for this message calling for a righteous militarism, as Urban's speech to a group of primarily Frankish warriors indicates. Robert the Monk, in his *History of the Crusade to Jerusalem,* was one of several authors who incorporated Urban's speech at Clermont into his account of the First Crusade. These versions all differ from one another, but nonetheless still reflect the Crusade ideas that became essential to the men who heeded the call.

Questions

1. What are all the motives for going on Crusade, as revealed in this document?

2. What elements galvanize these often bickering warriors into a single fighting group?

3. In what ways is the Crusade a just cause for war, from a medieval Christian perspective?

Robert the Monk, Pope Urban II's Call to the 1st Crusade

In the year of our Lord's Incarnation one thousand and ninety-five, a great council was convened within the bounds of Gaul, in Auvergne, in the city which is called Clermont. Over this Pope Urban II presided, with the Roman bishops and cardinals. This council was a famous one on account of the concourse of both French and German bishops, and of princes as well. Having arranged the matters relating to the Church, the lord Pope went forth into a certain spacious plain, for no building was large enough to hold all the people. The Pope then, with sweet and persuasive eloquence, addressed those present in words something like the following, saying:

"Oh, race of Franks, race beyond the mountains [the Alps], race beloved and chosen by God (as is clear from many of your works), set apart from all other nations by the situation of your country, as well as by your Catholic faith and the honor you render to the holy Church: to you our discourse is addressed, and for you our exhortations are intended. We wish you to know what a serious matter has led us to your country, for it is the imminent peril threatening you and all the faithful that has brought us hither.

"From the confines of Jerusalem and from the city of Constantinople a grievous report has gone forth and has been brought repeatedly to our ears; namely, that a race from the kingdom of the Persians, an accursed race, a race wholly alienated from God, 'a generation that set not their heart aright, and whose spirit was not steadfast with God' [Ps., lxxviii. 8], has violently invaded the lands of those Christians and has depopulated them by pillage and fire. They have led away a part of the captives into their own country, and a part they have killed by cruel tortures. They have either destroyed the churches of God or appropriated them for the rites of their own religion. They destroy the altars, after having defiled them with their uncleanness. . . . The kingdom of the Greeks [the Eastern Empire] is now dismembered by them and has been deprived of territory so vast in extent that it could not be traversed in two months' time.

"On whom, therefore, rests the labor of avenging these wrongs and of recovering this territory, if not upon you—you, upon whom, above all other nations, God has conferred remarkable glory in arms, great courage, bodily activity, and strength to humble the heads of those who resist you? Let the deeds of your ancestors encourage you and incite your minds to manly achievements—the glory and greatness of King Charlemagne and of his son

Louis [the Pious], and of your other monarchs, who have destroyed the kingdoms of the Turks and have extended the sway of the holy Church over lands previously pagan. Let the holy sepulcher of our Lord and Saviour, which is possessed by the unclean nations especially arouse you, and the holy places which are now treated with ignominy and irreverently polluted with the filth of the unclean. Oh most valiant soldiers and descendants of invincible ancestors, do not degenerate, but recall the valor of your ancestors.

"But if you are hindered by love of children, parents, or wife, remember what the Lord says in the Gospel, 'He that loveth father or mother more than me is not worthy of me' [Matt., x. 37]. 'Every one that hath forsaken houses, or brethren, or sisters, or father, or mother, or wife, or children, or lands, for my name's sake, shall receive an hundred-fold, and shall inherit everlasting life' [Matt., xix. 29]. Let none of your possessions restrain you, nor anxiety for your family affairs. For this land which you inhabit, shut in on all sides by the seas and surrounded by the mountain peaks, is too narrow for your large population; nor does it abound in wealth; and it furnishes scarcely food enough for its cultivators. Hence it is that you murder and devour one another, that you wage war, and that very many among you perish in civil strife.

"Let hatred, therefore, depart from among you; let your quarrels end; let wars cease; and let all dissensions and controversies slumber. Enter upon the road of the Holy Sepulcher; wrest that land from the wicked race, and subject it to yourselves. That land which, as the Scripture says, 'floweth with milk and honey' [Num., xiii. 27] was given by God into the power of the children of Israel. Jerusalem center of the earth; the land is fruitful above all others, like another paradise of delights. This spot the Redeemer of mankind has made illustrious by His advent, has beautified by His sojourn, has consecrated by His passion, has redeemed by His death, has glorified by His burial.

"This royal city, however, situated at the center of the earth, is now held captive by the enemies of Christ and is subjected, by those who do not know God, to the worship of the heathen. She seeks, therefore, and desires to be liberated, and ceases not to implore you to come to her aid. From you especially she asks succor, because, as we have already said, God has conferred upon you, above all other nations, great glory in arms. Accordingly, undertake this journey eagerly for the remission of your sins, with the assurance of the reward of imperishable glory in the kingdom of heaven."

When Pope Urban had skillfully said these and very many similar things, he so centered in one purpose the desires of all who were present that all cried out, "It is the will of God! It is the will of God!" When the venerable Roman pontiff heard that, with eyes uplifted to heaven, he gave thanks to

God and, commanding silence with his hand, said:

"Most beloved brethren, today is manifest in you what the Lord says in the Gospel, 'Where two or three are gathered together in my name, there am I in the midst of them' [Matt., xviii. 20]. For unless God had been present in your spirits, all of you would not have uttered the same cry; since, although the cry issued from numerous mouths, yet the origin of the cry was one. Therefore I say to you that God, who implanted this in your breasts, has drawn it forth from you. Let that, then, be your war cry in battle, because it is given to you by God. When an armed attack is made upon the enemy, let this one cry be raised by all the soldiers of God: 'It is the will of God! It is the will of God!'

"And we neither command nor advise that the old or feeble, or those incapable of bearing arms, undertake this journey. Nor ought women to set out at all without their husbands, or brothers, or legal guardians. For such are more of a hindrance than aid, more of a burden than an advantage. Let the rich aid the needy; and according to their wealth let them take with them experienced soldiers. The priests and other clerks [clergy], whether secular or regular, are not to go without the consent of their bishop; for this journey would profit them nothing if they went without permission. Also, it is not fitting that laymen should enter upon the pilgrimage without the blessing of their priests.

"Whoever, therefore, shall decide upon this holy pilgrimage, and shall make his vow to God to that effect, and shall offer himself to Him for sacrifice, as a living victim, holy and acceptable to God, shall wear the sign of the cross of the Lord on his forehead or on his breast. When he shall return from his journey, having fulfilled his vow, let him place the cross on his back between his shoulders. Thus shall ye, indeed, by this twofold action, fulfill the precept of the Lord, as He commands in the Gospel, 'He that taketh not his cross, and followeth after me, is not worthy of me' " [Luke xiv. 27].

From Ogg, pp. 284–88.

14.2 The Jewish View of the Crusades: Solomon bar Simson and Sefer Zekhirah

Jewish residents of Europe, especially those along the overland routes to the east, offer us a different perspective of the Crusade movement, from the point of view of collateral victims. While Jews were not the target of the Crusader's pilgrimage, the religious fervor and militaristic zeal of the Crusaders spilled over into violent anti-Semitism. The *Chronicle of Solomon bar Simson* and the *Sefer Zekhirah* record the horrific experiences of Jews during the First and Second Crusades.

The *Chronicle of Solomon bar Simson* (circa 1140) is a historical narrative of the First Crusade (1096) written partly in the first person by Solomon bar Simson, who is known only through this chronicle. It is one of the most complete Hebrew chronicles for this Crusade, and thus is an invaluable source about the persecutions of Jews and the destruction of Jewish communities that occurred in German cities, especially Mainz, and in Hungary as the waves of Crusaders passed through on their way to Palestine. The selection below details the origins of the First Crusade and the violence in Mainz, as well as the Jewish response.

The *Sefer Zekhirah* or *Book of Remembrance* by Rabbi Ephraim of Bonn (1133–circa 1196) is a Hebrew chronicle of the Second Crusade (1147–1148). This Second Crusade, led by the kings of France and Germany, was called to recover the Crusader lands that had been recaptured by Muslims, and was sponsored by the famous preacher Bernard of Clairvaux. Bernard preached against harm to Jews or other noncombatants, but his message failed to prevent many atrocities during the Second Crusade. Rabbi Ephraim, a liturgist and poet as well as chronicler, portrays both the better efforts of Christians to behave civilly and the worst sorts of persecution of Jews. What makes his account particularly compelling is his use of liturgical poetry, in the form of lamentations over the suffering of his people.

Questions

1. What is Solomon's explanation for the reasons behind the First Crusade?

2. What is Rabbi Ephraim's view of Christian behavior as compared to Jewish behavior?

3. How do both authors explain the existence of such evil within the context of their own belief in God?

Chronicle of Solomon bar Simson

I will now recount the event of this persecution in other martyred communities as well—the extent to which they clung to the Lord, God of their fathers, bearing witness to His Oneness to their last breath.

In the year four thousand eight hundred and fifty-six, the year one thousand twenty-eight of our exile, in the eleventh year of the cycle Ranu, the year in which we anticipated salvation and solace, in accordance with the prophecy of Jeremiah: "Sing with gladness for Jacob, and shout at the head of the nations," etc.—this year turned instead to sorrow and groaning, weeping and outcry. Inflicted upon the Jewish People were the many evils related in all the admonitions; those enumerated in Scripture as well as those unwritten were visited upon us.

At this time arrogant people, a people of strange speech, a nation bitter and impetuous, Frenchmen and Germans, set out for the Holy City, which had been desecrated by barbaric nations, there to seek their house of idolatry and banish the Ishmaelites [Muslims] and other denizens of the land and conquer the land for themselves. They decorated themselves prominently with their signs, placing a profane symbol—a horizontal line over a vertical one—on the vestments of every man and woman whose heart yearned to go on the stray path to the grave of their Messiah. Their ranks swelled until the number of men, women, and children exceeded a locust horde covering the earth; of them it was said: "The locusts have no king yet go they forth all of them by bands." Now it came to pass that as they passed through the towns where Jews dwelled, they said to one another: "Look now, we are going a long way to seek out the profane shrine and to avenge ourselves on the Ishmaelites, when here, in our very midst, are the Jews—they whose forefathers murdered and crucified him for no reason. Let us first avenge ourselves on them and exterminate them from among the nations so that the name of Israel will no longer be remembered, or let them adopt our faith and acknowledge the offspring of promiscuity."

When the Jewish communities became aware of their intentions, they resorted to the custom of our ancestors, repentance, prayer, and charity. The hands of the Holy Nation turned faint at this time, their hearts melted, and their strength flagged. They hid in their innermost rooms to escape the swirling sword. They subjected themselves to great endurance, abstaining from food and drink for three consecutive days and nights, and then fasting many days from sunrise to sunset, until their skin was shriveled and dry as wood upon their bones. And they cried out loudly and bitterly to God.

But their Father did not answer them; He obstructed their prayers, concealing Himself in a cloud through which their prayers could not pass, and He abhorred their tent, and He removed them out of His sight—all of this having been decreed by Him to take place "in the day when I visit"; and this was the generation that had been chosen by Him to be His portion, for they had the strength and the fortitude to stand in His Sanctuary, and fulfill His word, and sanctify His Great Name in His world. It is of such as these that King David said: "Bless the Lord, ye angels of His, ye almighty in strength, that fulfill His word," etc. . . .

The leaders of the Jews gathered together and discussed various ways of saving themselves. They said: "Let us elect elders so that we may know how to act, for we are consumed by this great evil." The elders decided to ransom the community by generously giving of their money and bribing the various princes and deputies and bishops and governors. Then, the community leaders who were respected by the local bishop approached him and his officers and servants to negotiate this matter. They asked: "What shall we do about the news we have received regarding the slaughter of our brethren in Speyer and Worms?" They [the Gentiles] replied: "Heed our advice and bring all your money into our treasury. You, your wives, and your children, and all your belongings shall come into the courtyard of the bishop until the hordes have passed by. Thus will you be saved from the errant ones."

Actually, they gave this advice so as to herd us together and hold us like fish that are caught in an evil net, and then to turn us over to the enemy, while taking our money. This is what actually happened in the end, and "the outcome is proof of the intentions." The bishop assembled his ministers and courtiers—mighty ministers, the noblest in the land—for the purpose of helping us; for at first it had been his desire to save us with all his might, since we had given him and his ministers and servants a large bribe in return for their promise to help us. Ultimately, however, all the bribes and entreaties were of no avail to protect us on the day of wrath and misfortune.

It was at this time that Duke Godfrey [of Bouillon], may his bones be ground to dust, arose in the hardness of his spirit, driven by a spirit of wantonness to go with those journeying to the profane shrine, vowing to go on this journey only after avenging the blood of the crucified one by shedding Jewish blood and completely eradicating any trace of those bearing the name "Jew," thus assuaging his own burning wrath. To be sure, there arose someone to repair the breach—a God-fearing man who had been bound to the most holy of altars—called Rabbi Kalonymos, the *Parnass* of the community of Mainz. He dispatched a messenger to King Henry in the kingdom of Pula, where the king had been dwelling during the past nine years, and related all that had happened.

The king was enraged and dispatched letters to all the ministers, bishops, and governors of all the provinces of his realm, as well as to Duke Godfrey, containing words of greeting and commanding them to do no bodily harm to the Jews and to provide them with help and refuge. The evil duke then swore that he had never intended to do them harm. The Jews of Cologne nevertheless bribed him with five hundred *zekukim* of silver, as did the Jews of Mainz. The duke assured them of his support and promised them peace.

However, God, the maker of peace, turned aside and averted His eyes from His people, and consigned them to the sword. No prophet, seer, or man of wise heart was able to comprehend how the sin of the people infinite in number was deemed so great as to cause the destruction of so many lives in the various Jewish communities. The martyrs endured the extreme penalty normally inflicted only upon one guilty of murder. Yet, it must be stated with certainty that God is a righteous judge, and we are to blame.

Then the evil waters prevailed. The enemy unjustly accused them of evil acts they did not do, declaring: "You are the children of those who killed our object of veneration, hanging him on a tree; and he himself had said: 'There will yet come a day when my children will come and avenge my blood.' We are his children and it is therefore obligatory for us to avenge him since you are the ones who rebel and disbelieve in him. Your God has never been at peace with you. Although He intended to deal kindly with you, you have conducted yourselves improperly before Him. God has forgotten you and is no longer desirous of you since you are a stubborn nation. Instead, He has departed from you and has taken us for His portion, casting His radiance upon us."

When we heard these words, our hearts trembled and moved out of their places. We were dumb with silence, abiding in darkness, like those long dead, waiting for the Lord to look forth and behold from heaven.

And Satan—the Pope of evil Rome—also came and proclaimed to all the nations believing in that stock of adultery—these are the stock of Seir—that they should assemble and ascend to Jerusalem so as to conquer the city, and journey to the tomb of the superstition whom they call their god. Satan came and mingled with the nations, and they gathered as one man to fulfill the command, coming in great numbers like the grains of sand upon the seashore, the noise of them clamorous as a whirlwind and a storm. When the drops of the bucket had assembled, they took evil counsel against the people of the Lord and said: "Why should we concern ourselves with going to war against the Ishmaelites dwelling about Jerusalem, when in our midst is a people who disrespect our god—indeed, their ancestors are those who crucified him. Why should we let them live and tolerate their dwelling among us? Let us commence by using our swords against them and then proceed upon our stray path."

The heart of the people of our God grew faint and their spirit flagged, for many sore injuries had been inflicted upon them and they had been smitten repeatedly. They now came supplicating to God and fasting, and their hearts melted within them. But the Lord did as He declared, for we had sinned before Him, and He forsook the sanctuary of Shiloh—the Temple-in-Miniature—which He had placed among His people who dwelt in the midst of alien nations. His wrath was kindled and He drew the sword against them, until they remained but as the flagstaff upon the mountaintop and as the ensign on the hill, and He gave over His nation into captivity and trampled them underfoot. See, O Lord, and consider to whom Thou hast done thus: to Israel, a nation despised and pillaged, Your chosen portion! Why have You uplifted the shield of its enemies, and why have they gained in strength? Let all hear, for I cry out in anguish; the ears of all that hear me shall be seared:

How has the staff of might been broken, the rod of glory—the sainted community comparable to fine gold, the community of Mainz! It was caused by the Lord to test those that fear Him, to have them endure the yoke of His pure fear.

Rabbi Ephraim, *Book of Remembrance*

Hearken to me, and I shall recount the matter of the decree:

> I shall write a book of remembrance, relating the incidents
>   of the decree,
> Regarding the evil and adversity which occurred to the
>   remnant who survived
> The first bitter decree.
> "Blessed be the Lord," we declare,
> For having kept us alive to recount these events. In His
>   mercy may He speedily avenge us
> Upon those who have shed and profaned our blood. And
>   may He rebuild the Temple in the city of Zion.

Let this be recorded for later generations to praise and magnify Almighty God. For Satan came to Ashdod to pillage Israel and Judah; the enemy traveled in large groups and camped in Haradah. This occurred in the year 4906 [1146], when our adversaries came and oppressed Israel. For Radulf was wicked and he treacherously persecuted the Jews. Radulf, the priest of idolatry, arose against the nation of God to destroy, slay, and annihilate them just as wicked Haman had attempted to do. He set forth from France and traveled across the entire land of Germany—may God spare the Jewish community there, Amen!—to seek out and to contaminate the Christians with the horizontal-vertical sign. He went along barking and was named "barker," summoning all in the name of Christ to go to Jerusalem to war against Ishmael. Wherever he went, he spoke evil of the Jews of the land and incited the snake and the dogs against us, saying: "Avenge the crucified one upon his enemies who stand before you; then go to war against the Ishmaelites."

. Upon hearing this, our hearts melted and our spirit failed us, because of the fury of the oppressor who intended to destroy us. We cried out to our God, saying: "Alas, Lord, God, not even fifty years, the number of years of a jubilee, have passed since our blood was shed in witness to the Oneness of Your Revered Name on the day of the great slaughter. Will You forsake us eternally, O Lord? Will You extend Your anger to all generations? Do not permit this suffering to recur."

The Lord heard our outcry, and He turned to us and had mercy upon us. In His great mercy and grace, He sent a decent priest, one honored and respected by all the clergy in France, named Abbé Bernard of Clairvaux, to deal with this evil person. Bernard, too, spoke raucously, as is their manner; and this is what he said to them: "It is good that you go against the Ishmaelites. But whosoever touches a Jew to take his life, is like one who harms Jesus himself. My disciple Radulf, who has spoken about annihilating the Jews, has spoken in error, for in the Book of Psalms it is written of them: 'Slay them not, lest my people forget.' "

All the Gentiles regarded this priest as one of their saints, and we have not inquired whether he was receiving payment for speaking on behalf of Israel. When our enemies heard his words, many of them ceased plotting to kill us. We also gave our wealth as ransom for our lives. The Lord, being merciful to us, permitted a remnant to survive on the earth and enabled us to remain alive. Whatever they asked of us, either silver or gold, we did not withhold from them. Were it not for the mercy of our Creator in sending the aforementioned Abbé and his later epistles, no remnant or vestige would have remained of Israel. Blessed be the Redeemer and Saviour, blessed be His Name!

In the month of Elul, at the time when Radulf the priest—may God hound and smite him—arrived at Cologne, Simon the Pious, of the city of Trier, returned from England where he had spent some time. When Simon came to Cologne, he boarded the vessel to return to Trier. As he set out from Cologne to board the ship, he encountered worthless persons who had been defiled by the abominable profanation. They entreated him to profane himself [i.e., to become baptized] and deny the Living God. He refused, remaining steadfast in loving and cleaving to his God. Then came persons of brazen face who severed his head from his body by placing it in a winepress and then cast away his pure corpse.

When the Jews of the city heard of this, they grieved, their hearts went out, and they became fearful, and they said: "Behold the days of reckoning have come, the end has arrived, the plague has begun, our days are completed, for our end is here. We declare: 'We have been cut off!' " The people wept exceedingly for the precious soul that had perished and been cut off from the land of the living because of the transgressions of my people. The leaders of the community went and spoke to the burghers requesting the return of the saint's head and body. After receiving a bribe, the burghers returned the corpse, and the righteous man was brought to Jewish burial. May his soul rest in goodness, and his seed inherit the earth.

A Jewish woman named Mistress Mina of Speyer left the city, and they seized her and cut off her ears and the thumbs of her hands; thus did she suffer for the sanctification of her Creator. Happy is the people whose lot is thus; happy is the people whose God is the Lord. . . .

As a result [of unfounded accusations against the Jews who had fled for safety to the fortress of Wurzburg], the errant ones and the poorer segment of the population, those who derive joy from things of no consequence, arose and smote the Jews. A saintly person named Rabbi Isaac, son of our Rabbi Eliakim, a modest and humble man, venerable and pleasant, was slain over his book; and there were twenty-one others with him. One of them was a Hebrew lad, an accomplished student, by the name of Simon, son of Isaac, who suffered twenty wounds and then survived for fully a year. They took his sister to their place of idolatry so as to profane her, but she sanctified the Name and spat upon the abomination. They then struck her with stone and fist, for they do not bring swords into the disgusting house. She did not die, but lay prostrate upon the ground feigning death. They bruised, struck, and burnt her repeatedly to determine whether or not she had truly died. They then placed her on a marble slab, but she did not awaken or make the slightest motion with her hand or foot. Thus did she deceive them till nightfall. Finally a Gentile laundress came and bore her to her home, where she concealed her and saved her life. The remaining Jews took refuge in the courtyard of their neighbors. On the following day, they fled to Fort Stuhlbach. Blessed is He Who granted them rescue.

> Alas, my melancholy soul yearns as does the hart,
> For the slain of Wurzburg, a community like a vine
>   intertwined.
> How is it suddenly slaughtered, and sunken to the
>   lowest level?
> Therefore I weep in sorrow, my spirit and soul are melted,
> I shall not grant myself respite. She that was adorned with
>   the commandments as with a wreath,
> How is she now set forth naked, and has drawn back
>   in shame!
> Henceforth their portion in life shall be to abide in the
>   Garden of Eden, arrayed in a circle,
> Standing there in a ring, transcending temporal life,
> In eternal existence, constant ascent, abounding in
>   strength and exultation.

On the following day, the bishop ordered that all the slaughtered saints be collected on wagons—all the choice severed limbs: hips and shoulders, thumbs of hands and feet, sanctified with holy oil, together with everything else that remained of their bodies and limbs—and buried in his garden. Hezekiah, son of our Master Rabbi Eliakim, and Mistress Judith, his wife, purchased this Garden of Eden from the bishop and consecrated it as an eternal burial ground. "May the generous one be blessed for his bountifulness, for having given." . . .

May the jealous and vengeful God reveal to us His vengeance against both Edom and Ishmael, as He did against Pharaoh and all of Egypt; as the fox declared in song to the animals after the repast.

May the blood of our pious ones that was spilt like water seethe His purple garment, as His son Rabbi Meir declared: "When a man is pained, what does the Divine Presence say? 'My head is heavy upon me, my arm is heavy upon me.' And if God suffers such anguish for the spilt blood of the wicked, how much more is His mercy aroused for the spilt blood of the righteous?" For Israel has been compared to the dove, as it is written: "Thine eyes are [as] doves." Whereas all other birds struggle and quiver upon being slaughtered, and the dove does not, but rather stretches out its neck, so do none except Israel offer their lives for the Blessed Holy One, as it is written: "For Thy sake are we killed all the day, etc."

And the Holy Torah which they tore and trampled will cry out in anguish and protest before its Creator, and He will topple them and cast them down into the dust.

The reward of pious persons who were slain bearing witness to the Oneness of the Name is homiletically expounded in the Midrash *Lekah Tov* and *Shohar Tov* on the passage "How Great is Your Goodness!" to the effect that each martyr possesses eight vestments, like a High Priest, and two crowns. Moreover, their glory surpasses that of the High Priest, for the High Priest sprinkled the blood of sacrifices, whereas they sprinkled their own blood and the blood of their precious children; they bound 'Akedot, erected altars, and prepared sacrifices. May God remember them to the good, and may their righteousness stand the entire congregation of Israel in good stead forever and ever.

> May the Rock Who is white and ruddy overturn Edom as
>   He did Sodom.
> "So that my glory may sing praise to Thee, and not be
>   silent."
> And may He inflict upon the accursed nation of Ishmael
>   the upheaval of Gomorrah.

May He lead back the stray lamb as in former times, to its
   abode,
May He erect the chosen Edifice in splendor and in
   majesty,
And make the crown resplendent as before. Restore unto
   us complete Sovereignty
Over the entire domain once entrusted unto us. And give
   over the entire Land [of Israel] into our hands.
As of yet, we suffer great privation, for, while copper may
   be replaced with gold,
What recompense can be made for Rabbi Akiba and his
   colleagues? But no! We cannot question the ways
Of Him Who is fearful and awesome. We must always
   declare His righteousness.
It is we who have sinned; what can we then say? May His
   strength be aroused
And his mercies awakened upon us, amen. May it thus
   speedily
Occur upon the completion of the Book of Remembrance.

Completed is the Book of Remembrance, annal of events.
Blessed be the Rock of Perfection,
The Lord abounding in mercy.
And may I, Ephraim the youth, be amongst those who shall be granted
The full measure of solace assured in the Torah.
Amen, amen.

Reprinted from *The Jews and the Crusaders: The Hebrew Chronicles of the First and Second Crusades,* ed and trans. Shlomo Eidelberg (Madison: The University of Wisconsin Press, 1977), pp. 21–22; 121–23, 127–28, 132–33. Reprinted by permission of the University of Wisconsin Press. Notes omitted.

14.3 The Islamic View of the Crusades: Usama ibn Munqidh

Arab historians of the warfare between European Christian and Islamic troops make clear the strength and organization of Islamic government and military operations compared to their Christian counterparts. Perhaps one of the most interesting cultural accounts of the Crusaders, however, is from the autobiography of Usama ibn Munqidh (twelfth century), amir of Shaizar. Usama delights in recounting short vignettes of Frankish-Muslim encounters, both positive and negative. In the eyes of this cultured Muslim, the "Franks" (Europeans) often appear as boorish, unsophisticated louts. In other passages, Usama describes Frankish military prowess and chivalric qualities, as well as compliments some Franks who became more civilized (that is, learned to live like Muslims). The brief excerpt below describes an intriguing cross-cultural encounter between Usama, a newly arrived Frank, and some resident Templars (the order of Knights established by Bernard of Clairvaux as a monastic group charged with protecting pilgrims in Palestine).

Questions

1. What causes misunderstanding in the situation Usama describes?
2. What does Usama think of Europeans in general?
3. What does this story indicate about the acculturation of Europeans who traveled to the Holy Land?

Usama ibn Munqidh, *The Book of Reflections*

This is an example of Frankish barbarism, God damn them! When I was in Jerusalem I used to go to the Masjid al-Aqsa, beside which is a small oratory which the Franks have made into a church. Whenever I went into the mosque, which was in the hands of Templars who were friends of mine, they would put the little oratory at my disposal, so that I could say my prayers there. One day I had gone in, said the *Allah akhbar* and risen to begin my prayers, when a Frank threw himself on me from behind, lifted me up and turned me so that I was facing east. 'That is the way to pray!' he said. Some Templars at once intervened, seized the man and took him out of my way, while I resumed my prayer. But the moment they stopped watching him he seized me again and forced me to face east, repeating that this was the way to pray. Again the Templars intervened and took him away. They apologized to me and said: 'He is a foreigner who has just arrived today from his homeland in the north, and he has never seen anyone pray facing any other direction than east.' 'I have finished my prayers,' I said, and left, stupefied by the fanatic who had been so perturbed and upset to see someone praying facing the *qibla* [sacred site in Mecca]!

I was present myself when one of them came up to the amir Mu'in ad-Din—God have mercy on him—in the Dome of the Rock, and said to him: 'Would you like to see God as a baby?' The amir said that he would, and the fellow proceeded to show us a picture of Mary with the infant Messiah on her lap. 'This,' he said, 'is God as a baby.' Almighty God is greater than the infidels' concept of him!

Reprinted with permission from *Arab Historians of the Crusades*, Francesco Gabrieli (Italian translation), trans. E. J. Costello (Berkeley: University of California Press, 1969), pp. 79–80. Notes omitted.

14.4 Encounter with a Nubian:
Robert of Clari on the Fourth Crusade

Travel to the Holy Land produced cross-cultural fertilization, reconnecting Christian regions previously cut off from one another. The Fourth Crusade (1201–1204) is a good example both of the potential for reunifying Christians and some of the disastrous results when western and eastern Christianity briefly merged through this Crusade. In the midst of the Crusader conquest of Constantinople en route to the Holy Land, one foot soldier, Robert of Clari, recorded an encounter with a Nubian pilgrim who was on his way to Rome and Compostela. This episode highlights the multicultural nature of the Christian religion.

Robert was a foot soldier from Picardy who went on the Fourth Crusade and afterward wrote an account entitled *The Conquest of Constantinople*. His record provides an interesting view of the city and the Crusaders from the perspective of an ordinary person. The following excerpt describes an encounter in 1203. The Crusaders were in the Byzantine court endeavoring to establish their claimant on the throne. A visiting Nubian king comes in. The three-way interaction between the Greek, the Latin, and the Nubian Christian says a great deal about the cultural dynamics among Christians.

Questions

1. What seems to surprise the Europeans about this Nubian? Why?
2. In what ways does the Nubian demonstrate an awareness of different versions of Christianity?
3. What does this incident reveal about the relationships between different Christian cultures?

Robert of Clari, The Conquest of Constantinople

Afterwards it happened that the barons went one day for diversion to the palace to see Isaac and the emperor his son. And while the barons were there at the palace, a king came there whose skin was all black, and he had a cross in the middle of his forehead that had been made with a hot iron. This king was living in a very rich abbey in the city, in which the former emperor Alexius had commanded that he should be lodged and of which he was to be lord and owner as long as he wanted to stay there. When the emperor saw him coming, he rose to meet him and did great honor to him. And the emperor asked the barons: "Do you know," said he, "who this man is?" "Not at all, sire," said the barons. "I'faith," said the emperor, "this is the king of Nubia, who is come on pilgrimage to this city." Then they had an interpreter talk to him and ask him where his land was, and he answered the interpreter in his own language that his land was a hundred days' journey still beyond Jerusalem, and he had come from there to Jerusalem on pilgrimage. And he said that when he set out from his land he had fully sixty of his countrymen with him, and when he came to Jerusalem there were only ten of them alive, and when he came from Jerusalem to Constantinople there were only two of them alive. And he said that he wanted to go on pilgrimage to Rome and from Rome to St. James, and then come back to Jerusalem, if he should live so long, and then die there. And he said that all the people of his land were Christians and that when a child was born and baptized they made a cross in the middle of his forehead with a hot iron, like the one he had. And the barons gazed at this king with great wonder.

From *The Conquest of Constantinople* by Robert of Clari, trans. Edgar Holmes McNeal. Copyright © 1936 by Columbia University Press (New York: Columbia University Press, 1936; reprint New York: Octagon Books, 1966), pp. 79–80. Reprinted with permission of the publisher. Notes omitted.

–15–

Ways of Knowing
Faith and Reason

In addition to geographic expansion and cross-cultural interchange, the twelfth century witnessed an explosion in intellectual endeavors. Two main factors contributed to this growth in scholarship and writing: first, the rise of urban schools with an increase in literacy laid the groundwork for rational inquiry; and second, the subsequent reintroduction of classical literature (specifically Aristotle), transmitted through Islamic and Jewish texts, invigorated speculative philosophy and theology in these medieval universities. Out of these new institutions of learning, a new "school of thought," scholasticism, arose that began to use Aristotelian models to categorize knowledge in new ways. One of the central issues for scholasticism and its opponents was the "faith versus reason" debate—particularly evident in discussions of human knowledge of God's existence. All of the documents in this section reflect on the problem of epistemology (how we know what we know) and demonstrate the importance of Islamic and Jewish scholarship in the formulation of this debate.

The rediscovery of Aristotle in the context of the burgeoning universities of Europe sparked philosophical debate over the whole question of knowledge and how to categorize it. Scholasticism sought new ways of understanding the relationship between faith (knowledge gained from God's revelation), and reason, (knowledge acquired through human exploration and interpretation). For example, while all scholastics believed in God, they were interested in explaining with rational philosophical proofs how it is that this truth is knowable to the human mind—that is, how belief in God is also logical. Opponents of scholasticism—for example, Bernard of Clairvaux (17.4)—understood that the knowledge of God was at heart an experience of faith beyond the intellect, and feared that excessive emphasis on the power of reason would diminish the direct knowledge of God.

The following four document selections illustrate the beginnings of these changes in ways of thinking about knowledge in the eleventh and twelfth centuries. The first (15.1), the *Proslogion* of Anselm, lays the groundwork for scholasticism, even before the reintroduction of Aristotle, by experimenting with logical proofs for God's existence. With the second excerpt (15.2), from Abelard, the debate over faith and reason erupts. Abelard was a philosopher trained in logic who began to address theological issues with that training, stressing the processes of reason in a way that, in the eyes of many churchmen, threatened faith because human reason could only give a limited comprehension of God. The extreme position emphasizing reason, radical Aristotelianism, is evident in the third selection (15.3), from the Islamic Spanish scholar Averroës, whose views when translated into Latin only served to heighten the divide between the new reasoners and the old. The fourth selection (15.4), from the renowned Jewish scholar Moses Maimonides, works out some of the issues of the relationship between philosophy and the knowledge of God. All of these works continued to have a dramatic impact on European scholarship in the next century, as explored in Part Five.

15.1 Faith and Reason: Anselm

Many scholars consider the reasoned discourses of Anselm on the Incarnation and on the existence of God the beginning of the scholastic movement. He established a clear relationship between faith and reason in his statement that "I believe in order that I might understand," an approach evident in the excerpts below from his proofs of the existence of God.

St. Anselm (1033–1109) was an international scholar and influential political figure. Born in Lombardy (northern Italy), he became abbot of Bec in Normandy and later archbishop of Canterbury in England. As archbishop, he was involved in the investiture controversy in England; as a consequence of disputes with the king, he spent some time in exile, which he used profitably by writing theology.

The *Proslogion* is written as a dialogue between Anselm and a "straw man" opponent named Gaunilon, whose questions and reactions allow Anselm to respond to counterarguments (only Anselm's opening arguments are given here). This debate is *not* about whether or not God exists. It is about how the human mind can logically understand the existence of God. All disputants in such debates *believed* in God and in some way *knew* that he existed. The question for the intellectuals engaged in the debate was whether God's existence could be demonstrated using the philosophical tools inherited from antiquity and developed by the medieval mind. In that sense, these are intellectual exercises for a small group of philosophers reveling in the God-given gift of reason.

Questions

1. According to Anselm, in what different ways can a human being know God?

2. What kind of argument is Anselm using when he asserts that God is "that which nothing greater can be conceived?"

3. What do Anselm's arguments tell us about the intellectual climate in the early twelfth century?

Anselm, *Proslogion*

Chapter 1: Exciting the Mind to Contemplate God

Come now, little man, flee for a little your occupations, escape for a bit from your tumultuous thoughts. Set aside now your burdensome cares, and postpone your laborious occupations. Free yourself for a little for God, and rest for a little while in him. 'Enter into the inner chamber' of your mind, exclude all things except God and whatever helps you while seeking him, and 'locking the door,' seek Him [Matt. 6:6] Speak now, [with] all my heart, speak now to God: 'I seek your face; your face, O Lord, I desire.' [Ps 26:8]

Come now then, you, My Lord God, teach my heart where and how to seek you, where and how to find you. Lord, if you are not here, where shall I find you who are absent? If however you are everywhere, why do I not see you present? But certainly you inhabit 'light inaccessible' [1 Tim. 6:16]. And where is this light inaccessible? Or how may I approach that light inaccessible? Or who will take and lead me into it, that I may see you in it? And then by what signs, in what appearance, shall I seek you? I have never seen you, my Lord God, I do not know your face. What shall he do, most high Lord, this exiled one who is far away? What shall your servant do, anxious with love for you and yet cast a long way 'from your face'? [Ps. 1:13] He longs to see you, and [yet] your face is too far from him. He desires to draw close to you, and [yet] your habitation is inaccessible. He wishes to find you, and [yet] he does not know the place where you are. He strives to seek you, and [yet] does not know what you look like. Lord, you are my God, and you are my Lord, and [yet] I have never seen you. You have made me and restored me, and you have granted to me every good thing that I have, and still I do not know you. Finally, I was made in order to see you, and yet I have not done what I was made for. . . .

. . . Allow me to look upon your light, whether from afar or from the depths. Teach me to seek you, and show yourself to this one seeking; because I can neither seek you unless you teach, nor find you unless you show yourself. May I in desiring you, seek you, and in seeking desire [you]. May I in loving find [you], and in finding, love [you].

I acknowledge, Lord, and give thanks, that you created in me your image, so that I remember you, think on you, love you. But this [image] is ruined, being worn down by vices; it is obscured by the fumes of sin, so that it cannot do what it was made for, unless you renew and reform it. I do not try, Lord, to penetrate your great height, because my understanding is not equal to it at all; but I desire to understand somewhat of your truth, which my heart believes and loves. For I do not seek to understand so that I may believe, but I believe so that I may understand. For this also I believe: that 'unless I believe, I shall not understand.' [Is. 7:9]

Chapter 2: That Truly God Exists

Therefore, Lord, who gives understanding to faith, give to me what understanding you know to be appropriate, because you exist just as we believe, and you are what we believe [you to be]. And certainly we believe you to be *that beyond which nothing greater can be thought.* Or is there nothing of that nature, since 'the fool says in his heart, there is no God'? [Ps 13:1, 52:1] But certainly this same fool, when he hears what I am saying, *'that beyond which nothing greater can be thought'*, he understands what he hears; and what he understands is in his understanding, even if he does not understand that it exists. For it is one thing for a thing to be in the mind, and another to understand that the thing exists. For when a painter thinks about what he will make, he has something in his mind, but he does not yet know it to exist because he has not made it yet. When he truly paints it, then he has it both in his mind and knows that it exists because he made it. Therefore even the fool must agree that *that beyond which nothing greater can be thought* exists because when he hears he understands, and whatever is understood is in the mind. And certainly *that beyond which nothing greater can be thought* cannot be only in the mind. If it exists only in the mind, it can be thought to be in reality, which is greater. If therefore *that beyond which nothing greater can be thought* is only in the mind, then the thought itself of *that beyond which nothing greater can be thought* is *that beyond which nothing greater can be thought.* But certainly this cannot be. Therefore without any doubt something *beyond which nothing greater can be thought* exists, both in the mind and in reality.

Chapter 3: That [God] Cannot Be Thought Not to Exist

It therefore exists so truly that it cannot be thought not to exist. For something can be thought to exist that cannot be thought not to exist; this is greater than what can be thought not to exist. Thus if *that beyond which nothing greater can be thought,* can be thought not to exist, then *that beyond which nothing greater can be thought* is not the *that beyond which nothing greater can be thought,* which cannot be agreed. So therefore the something *beyond which nothing greater can be thought* exists so truly that it cannot be thought not to exist.

And you are it, Lord our God. So truly you are, lord my God, that you cannot be thought not to exist. And deservedly. For if some mind could think of something greater than you, the creature would ascend above the creator, and would judge the creator; that would be absurd. And whatever exists other than you alone, can be thought not to exist. Therefore you alone of all things most truly exist, and have existence to the maximum; and whatever else there is exists not as truly, and has lesser existence. Why then 'said the fool in his heart, there is no God,' when it is so obvious to rational minds that you exist the most of all things? Why, unless because he is stupid and a fool?

Chapter 4: How the Fool Said in His Heart What Cannot Be Thought

Truly how did he say in his heart what he could not think? Or how could he not think what he said in his heart, when it means the same to 'say in the heart' and 'to think?' What if truly, he really did both (since he apparently did): he thought because he said in his heart, and he did not say in his heart because he could not think. There must not be only one way for something to be said in the heart or thought. For in one way a thing is thought when the word signifying it is thought; while in another way, when that same thing is understood. In the first way, God can be thought not to exist, but not in the second way. No one who understands what God is can think that God does not exist; even though he may say those words in his heart, he either says them without any meaning or with some other meaning attached to them. For God is *that beyond which nothing greater can be thought.* Whoever understands this well, also understand that he exists so much so that he cannot be thought not to exist.

I thank you, good Lord, I give you thanks, because what I believed before through your gift I now understand through your illumination, so that even if I did not believe you to exist, I would be unable to not understand it.

Translated by Karen Louise Jolly, from St. Anselm's *Proslogion,* reproduced in *St. Anselm's Proslogion,* ed. M. J. Charlesworth (Notre Dame: University of Notre Dame Press, © 1965, 1979), pp. 110–20 (Latin), even pages.

15.2 Dialectics: Abelard

Abelard (1079–1142) is one of the most celebrated and controversial figures of the twelfth century, both for his love affair with Heloise (circa 1100–1163) and for his intellectual brilliance. More so than any other figure in his time, Abelard brings to the fore some of the essential issues of medieval scholarship. The experiences of his life and work raise questions about both the social place of the scholar and the role of philosophy in theology. The excerpt from the writings of Abelard below shows his philosophical approach to theology, an approach that was one of the causes of his troubles. As a philosopher, Abelard was influenced by the influx of Aristotelian thought to use dialectics to reason about philosophical issues, such as questions of being and essence, or the existence of universals. However, when he began applying this same form of logical discourse to the revealed truths studied by theology—a subject he was not trained in—many theologians objected to both his methods and his results. The preface of Abelard's controversial work *Sic et Non* (Yes and No) excerpted below clearly lays out his philosophy of knowledge and his dialectic method.

Questions

1. How does Abelard view Scripture and the traditions of the church fathers?
2. What is the dialectical method that he employs? Why would this method provoke controversy when applied to some of the theological questions that he lists?
3. What role does Abelard think that reason plays in relationship to faith? How does that compare to Anselm's view?

Abelard, Sic et Non

There are many seeming contradictions and even obscurities in the innumerable writings of the church fathers. Our respect for their authority should not stand in the way of an effort on our part to come at the truth. The obscurity and contradictions in ancient writings may be explained upon many grounds, and may be discussed without impugning the good faith and insight of the fathers. A writer may use different terms to mean the same thing, in order to avoid a monotonous repetition of the same word. Common, vague words may be employed in order that the common people may understand; and sometimes a writer sacrifices perfect accuracy in the interest of a clear general statement. Poetical, figurative language is often obscure and vague.

Not infrequently apocryphal works are attributed to the saints. Then, even the best authors often introduce the erroneous views of others and leave the reader to distinguish between the true and the false. Sometimes, as Augustine confesses in his own case, the fathers ventured to rely upon the opinions of others.

Doubtless the fathers might err; even Peter, the prince of the apostles, fell into error; what wonder that the saints do not always show themselves inspired? The fathers did not themselves believe that they, or their companions, were always right. Augustine found himself mistaken in some cases and did not hesitate to retract his errors. He warns his admirers not to look upon his letters as they would upon the Scriptures, but to accept only those things which, upon examination, they find to be true.

All writings belonging to this class are to be read with full freedom to criticize, and with no obligation to accept unquestioningly; otherwise the way would be blocked to all discussion, and posterity be deprived of the excellent intellectual exercise of debating difficult questions of language and presentation. But an explicit exception must be made in the case of the Old and New Testaments. In the Scriptures, when anything strikes us as absurd, we may not say that the writer erred, but that the scribe made a blunder in copying the manuscripts, or that there is an error in interpretation, or that the passage is not understood. The fathers make a very careful distinction between the Scriptures and later works. They advocate a discriminating, not to say suspicious, use of the writings of their own contemporaries.

In view of these considerations, I have ventured to bring together various dicta of the holy fathers, as they came to mind, and to formulate certain questions which were suggested by the seeming contradictions in the statements. These questions ought to serve to excite tender readers to a zealous inquiry into truth and so sharpen their wits. The master key of knowledge is, indeed, a persistent and frequent questioning. Aristotle, the most clear-sighted of all the philosophers, was desirous above all things else to arouse this questioning spirit, for in his *Categories* he exhorts a student as follows: "It may well be difficult to reach a positive conclusion in these matters unless they be frequently discussed. It is by no means fruitless to be doubtful on particular points." By doubting we come to examine, and by examining we reach the truth.

[Abelard supplies one hundred and fifty-eight problems, carefully balancing the authorities pro and con, and leaves the student to solve each problem as best he may. This doubtless shocked many of his contemporaries. Later scholastic lecturers did not hesitate to muster all possible objections to a particular position, but they always had a solution of their own to propose and defend.

The following will serve as examples of the questions Abelard raised . . .]

> Should human faith be based upon reason, or no?
> Is God one, or no?
> Is God a substance, or no?
> Does the first Psalm refer to Christ, or no?
> Is sin pleasing to God, or no?
> Is God the author of evil, or no?
> Is God all-powerful, or no?
> Can God be resisted, or no?
> Has God free will, or no?
> Was the first man persuaded to sin by the devil, or no?
> Was Adam saved, or no?
> Did all the apostles have wives except John, or no?
> Are the flesh and blood of Christ in very truth and essence
>   present in the sacrament of the altar, or no?
> Do we sometimes sin unwillingly, or no?
> Does God punish the same sin both here and in the future,
>   or no?
> Is it worse to sin openly than secretly, or no?

From Robinson, pp. 450–51.

15.3 Aristotelianism: Averroës

The writings of the twelfth-century Islamic philosopher Averroës sparked great controversy when translated and used by some European Christian thinkers in the thirteenth century. Averroës's view of the relationship of faith and reason as adapted by some of these followers, known as Averroists, represents the extreme end in the debates raging among scholars about systems of knowledge. Averroists were willing to make reason preeminent, even at the expense of beliefs handed down by tradition and accepted by faith, to the great consternation of many church leaders. This excerpt from Averroës himself provides one context for understanding this debate that will be addressed by Thomas Aquinas in the next century (18.5).

Ibn Rushd, Abū al-Walīd Muhammad (1126–1198), known in Europe as Averroës, was a scholar at the Islamic court in Cordoba, Spain, one of the great centers of intellectual activity in the Islamic world. Like many Jewish and Muslim scholars in Islamic courts, he studied and wrote about medicine, philosophy, and theology. His greatest impact on European scholars came about through the Latin translations of his commentaries on Aristotle. Averröes's work "On the Harmony of Religion and Philosophy" seeks to justify, as did Clement in the second century (2.2), the use of classical philosophy to discuss theological or revealed truths, at least for a small elite group of well-trained intellectuals. Moreover, he rejected any encroachments by theology into the territory of philosophy. This isolation of the rationalist logic of philosophy from revealed truth contained in theology caused the greatest uproar when it was used by followers of Averröes in Europe.

The following excerpts from the openings of the first three chapters of Averröes's "On the Harmony of Religion and Philosophy" address both the issue of the consistency of philosophy and theology and the limitations of this rational method.

Questions

1. Where does Averröes place philosophy in relation to religion—higher or lower?

2. How does he distinguish between different kinds of knowledge, and different kinds of knowers?

3. Compare Averröes to Anselm and Abelard in their use of philosophical reasoning.

Averröes, On the Harmony of Religion and Philosophy

[What is the attitude of the Law to philosophy?]

Thus spoke the lawyer, imām, judge, and unique scholar, Abul Walid Muhammad Ibn Ahmad Ibn Rushd:
Praise be to God with all due praise, and a prayer for Muhammad His chosen servant and apostle. The purpose of this treatise is to examine, from the standpoint of the study of the Law, whether the study of philosophy and logic is allowed by the Law, or prohibited, or commanded—either by way of recommendation or as obligatory.

Chapter One: The Law Makes Philosophic Studies Obligatory

[If teleological study of the world is philosophy, and if the Law commands such a study, then the Law commands philosophy.]

We say: If the activity of 'philosophy' is nothing more than study of existing beings and reflection on them as indications of the Artisan, i.e. inasmuch as they are products of art (for beings only indicate the Artisan through our knowledge of the art in them, and the more perfect this knowledge is, the more perfect the knowledge of the Artisan becomes), and if the Law has encouraged and urged reflection on beings, then it is clear that what this name signifies is either obligatory or recommended by the Law. . . .

Chapter Two: Philosophy Contains Nothing Opposed to Islam

[Demonstrative truth and scriptural truth cannot conflict.]

Now since this religion is true and summons to the study which leads to knowledge of the Truth, we the Muslim community know definitely that demonstrative study does not lead to [conclusions] conflicting with what Scripture has given us; for truth does not oppose truth but accords with it and bears witness to it.

[If the apparent meaning of Scripture conflicts with demonstrative conclusions it must be interpreted allegorically, i.e. metaphorically.]

This being so, whenever demonstrative study leads to any manner of knowledge about any being, that being is inevitably either unmentioned or mentioned in Scripture. If it is unmentioned there is no contradiction, and it is in the same case as an act whose category is unmentioned, so that the lawyer has to infer it by reasoning from Scripture. If Scripture speaks about it, the apparent meaning of the words inevitably either accords or conflicts with the conclusions or demonstration about it. If this [apparent meaning] accords there is no argument. If it conflicts there is a call for allegorical interpretation of it. The meaning of 'allegorical interpretation' is: extension of the significance of an expression from real to metaphorical significance, without forsaking therein the standard metaphorical practices of Arabic, such as calling a thing by the name of something resembling it or a cause or consequence or accompaniment of it, or other things such as are enumerated in accounts of the kinds of metaphorical speech. . . .

Chapter Three: Philosophical Interpretations of Scripture
Should Not Be Taught to the Majority.
The Law Provides Other Methods of Instructing Them

[The purpose of Scripture is to teach true theoretical and practical science and right practice and attitudes.]

You ought to know that the purpose of Scripture is simply to teach true science and right practice. True science is knowledge of God, Blessed and

Exalted, and the other beings as they really are, and especially of noble beings, and knowledge of happiness and misery in the next life. Right practice consists in performing the acts which bring happiness and avoiding the acts which bring misery; and it is knowledge of these acts that is called 'practical science'. They fall into two divisions: (1) outward bodily acts; the science of these is called 'jurisprudence'; and (2) acts of the soul such as gratitude, patience and other moral attitudes which the Law enjoins or forbids; the science of these is called 'asceticism' or 'the sciences of the future life'. . . .

[Scripture teaches concepts both directly and by symbols, and uses demonstrative, dialectical and rhetorical arguments. Dialectical and rhetorical arguments are prevalent because the main aim of Scripture is to teach the majority. In these arguments concepts are indicated directly or by symbols, in various combinations in premises and conclusion.]

We say: The purpose of Scripture is to teach true science and right practice; and teaching is of two classes, [of] concepts and [of] judgements, as the logicians have shown. Now the methods available to men of [arriving at] judgements are three: demonstrative, dialectical and rhetorical; and the methods of forming concepts are two: either [conceiving] the object itself or [conceiving] a symbol of it. But not everyone has the natural ability to take in demonstrations, or [even] dialectical arguments, let alone demonstrative arguments which are so hard to learn and need so much time [even] for those who are qualified to learn them. Therefore, since it is the purpose of Scripture simply to teach everyone, Scripture has to contain every method of [bringing about] judgements of assent and every method of forming concepts.

Now some of the methods of assent comprehend the majority of people, i.e. the occurrence of assent as a result of them [is comprehensive]: these are the rhetorical and the dialectical [methods]—and the rhetorical is more comprehensive than the dialectical. Another method is peculiar to a smaller number of people: this is the demonstrative. Therefore, since the primary purpose of Scripture is to take care of the majority (without neglecting to arouse the élite), the prevailing methods of expression in religion are the common methods by which the majority comes to form concepts and judgements.

These [common] methods in religion are of four classes:

One of them occurs where the method is common, yet specialized in two respects: i.e. where it is certain in its concepts and judgements, in spite of being rhetorical or dialectical. These syllogisms are those whose premises, in spite of being based on accepted ideas or on opinions, are accidentally certain, and whose conclusions are accidentally to be taken in their direct meaning without symbolization. Scriptural texts of this class have no allegorical interpretations, and anyone who denies them or interprets them allegorically is an unbeliever.

The second class occurs where the premises, in spite of being based on accepted ideas or on opinions, are certain, and where the conclusions are symbols for the things which it was intended to conclude. [Texts of] this [class], i.e. their conclusions, admit of allegorical interpretation.

The third is the reverse of this: it occurs where the conclusions are the very things which it was intended to conclude, while the premises are based on accepted ideas or on opinions without being accidentally certain. [Texts of] this [class] also, i.e. their conclusions, do not admit of allegorical interpretation, but their premises may do so.

The fourth [class] occurs where the premises are based on accepted ideas or opinions, without being accidentally certain, and where the conclusions are symbols for what it was intended to conclude. In these cases the duty of the élite is to interpret them allegorically, while the duty of the masses is to take them in their apparent meaning.

[Where symbols are used, each class of men, demonstrative, dialectical and rhetorical, must try to understand the inner meaning symbolized or rest content with the apparent meaning, according to their capacities.]

In general, everything in these [texts] which admits of allegorical interpretation can only be understood by demonstration. The duty of the élite here is to apply such interpretation; while the duty of the masses is to take them in their apparent meaning in both respects, i.e. in concept and judgement, since their natural capacity does not allow more than that.

But there may occur to students of Scripture allegorical interpretations due to the superiority of one of the common methods over another in [bringing about] assent, i.e. when the indication contained in the allegorical interpretation is more persuasive than the indication contained in the apparent meaning. Such interpretations are popular; and [the making of them] is possibly a duty for those whose powers of theoretical understanding have attained the dialectical level. To this sort belong some of the interpretations of the Ash'arites and Mu'tazilites—though the Mu'tazilites are generally sounder in their statements. The masses on the other hand, who are incapable of more than rhetorical arguments, have the duty of taking these [texts] in their apparent meaning, and they are not permitted to know such interpretations at all.

Thus people in relation to Scripture fall into three classes:

One class is those who are not people of interpretation at all: these are the rhetorical class. They are the overwhelming mass, for no man of sound intellect is exempted from this kind of assent.

Another class is the people of dialectical interpretation: these are the dialecticians, either by nature alone or by nature and habit.

Another class is the people of certain interpretation: these are the demonstrative class, by nature and training, i.e. in the art of philosophy. This interpretation ought not to be expressed to the dialectical class, let alone to the masses.

[To explain the inner meaning to people unable to understand it is to destroy their belief in the apparent meaning without putting anything in its place. The result is unbelief in learners and teachers. It is best for the learned to profess ignorance, quoting the *Qur'ān* on the limitations of man's understanding.]

When something of these allegorical interpretations is expressed to anyone unfit to receive them—especially demonstrative interpretations because of their remoteness from common knowledge—both he who expresses it and he to whom it is expressed are led into unbelief. The reason for that [in the case of the latter] is that allegorical interpretation comprises two things, rejection of the apparent meaning and affirmation of the allegorical one; so that if the apparent meaning is rejected in the mind of someone who can only grasp apparent meanings, without the allegorical meaning being affirmed in his mind, the result is unbelief, if it [the text in question] concerns the principles of religion.

Allegorical interpretations, then, ought not to be expressed to the masses nor set down in rhetorical or dialectical books, i.e. books containing arguments of these two sorts, as was done by Abū Hāmid. They should not be expressed to this class; and with regard to an apparent text, when there is a self-evident doubt whether it is apparent to everyone and whether knowledge of its interpretation is impossible for them, they should be told that it is ambiguous and [its meaning] known by no one except God; and that the stop should be put here in the sentence of the Exalted, 'And no one knows the interpretation thereof except God.' The same kind of answer should also be given to a question about abstruse matters, which there is no way for the masses to understand; just as the Exalted has answered in His saying, 'And they will ask you about the Spirit. Say, "The Spirit is by the command of my Lord; you have been given only a little knowledge'."

Reprinted with permission from *Averroes on the Harmony of Religion and Philosophy*, trans. and ed. George F. Hourani. Printed for The Trustees of the "E. J. W. Gibb Memorial" (London: Luzac, 1961), pp. 44, 50, 63–66. Notes omitted.

15.4 God and Philosophy: Moses Maimonides

The writings of the renowned Jewish scholar Moses Maimonides influenced European Christian thought by imparting more of Aristotle's philosophy as applied to theology. Like his contemporary Averroës, Maimonides was a highly trained thinker and doctor working within the international community of scholars in the Islamic world. Similarly, he is also an excellent example of the brilliant scholarship outside of Christendom that, once read within European universities, strengthened scholastic and rationalist arguments.

Moses Maimonides (1135–1204) fled from his homeland of Spain during persecution of Jews there and went to Cairo, where he served as a leader in the Egyptian Jewish community as a doctor, a theologian, and a philosopher. His extensive writings included a work of systematic theology explaining Jewish Law (*Mishneh Torah*, 1180) that had a lasting impact on rabbinic theology. The influential *Guide of the Perplexed* (1190), excerpted below, synthesizes Neoplatonic and Aristotelian thought and offers a way to integrate faith and reason. The following selection from the second part of the book lays out twenty-five premises for demonstrating the existence of God, citing Aristotle's logic as a basis for these statements.

Questions

1. How would you describe the kind of logic Maimonides uses? Does it make sense to you? Why or why not?
2. Compare Maimonides's system of reasoning with that of Abelard (15.2) and Averroës (15.3): in what ways are they similar in their use of Aristotle?
3. Compare Maimonides's proofs for the existence of God with Anselm's (15.1): how are they different?

Moses Maimonides, *The Guide of the Perplexed*

In the name of the Lord, God of the World

[Introduction to the Second Part]

The premises needed for establishing the existence of the deity, may He be exalted, and for the demonstration that He is neither a body nor a force in a body and that He, may His name be sublime, is one, are twenty-five—all of which are demonstrated without there being a doubt as to any point concerning them. For Aristotle and the Peripatetics after him have come forward with a demonstration for every one of them. There is one premise that we will grant them, for through it the objects of our quest will be demonstrated, as I shall make clear; this premise is the eternity of the world.

1] The first premise: The existence of any infinite magnitude is impossible.

2] The second premise: The existence of magnitudes of which the number is infinite is impossible—that is, if they exist together.

3] The third premise: The existence of causes and effects of which the number is infinite is impossible, even if they are not endowed with magnitude. For instance, the assumption that one particular intellect, for example, has as its cause a second intellect, and that the cause of this second intellect is a third one, and that of the third a fourth, and so on to infinity, is likewise clearly impossible.

4] The fourth premise: Change exists in four categories: it exists in the category of substance, the changes occurring in a substance being generation and corruption. It exists in the category of quantity, namely, as growth and decrease. It exists in the category of quality, namely, as alteration. It exists in the category of place, namely, as the motion of translation. It is this change in the category of place that is more especially called motion.

5] The fifth premise: Every motion is a change and transition from potentiality to actuality.

6] The sixth premise: Of motions, some are essential and some accidental, some are violent and some are motions of a part—this being a species of accidental motion. Now essential motion is, for example, the translation of a body from one place to another. Accidental motion is, for example, when a blackness existing in this particular body is said to be translated from one place to another. Violent motion is, for example, the motion of a stone upwards through the action of something constraining it to that. Motion of a part is, for example, the motion of a nail in a ship; for when the ship is in motion, we say that the nail is likewise in motion. Similarly when any compound is in motion as a whole, its parts are likewise said to be in motion.

7] The seventh premise: Everything changeable is divisible. Hence everything movable is divisible and is necessarily a body. But everything that is indivisible is not movable; hence it will not be a body at all.

8] The eighth premise: Everything that is moved owing to accident must of necessity come to rest, inasmuch as its motion is not in virtue of its essence. Hence it cannot be moved forever in that accidental motion.

9] The ninth premise: Every body that moves another body moves the latter only through being itself in motion when moving the other body.

10] The tenth premise: Everything that is said to be in a body is divided into two classes: either it subsists through the body, as do the accidents, or the body subsists through it, as in the case of the natural form. Both classes are to be considered as a force in the body.

11] The eleventh premise: Some of the things that subsist through body are sometimes divided through the division of the body and hence are divisible according to accident, as for instance the colors and the other forces that are distributed through the whole of the body. In a like manner some of the things that constitute a body are not divisible in any way, as for instance the soul and the intellect.

12] The twelfth premise: Every force that is found distributed through a body is finite because the body is finite.

13] The thirteenth premise: It is impossible that one of the species of motion be continuous, except local motion, and of this only that which is circular.

14] The fourteenth premise: Local motion is the primary and the first by nature among all motions; for generation and corruption are preceded by alteration, and alteration is preceded by the approach of that which alters to that which is to be altered; and there is no growth and diminution except when they are preceded by generation and corruption.

15] The fifteenth premise: Time is an accident consequent upon motion and is necessarily attached to it. Neither of them exists without the other. Motion does not exist except in time, and time cannot be conceived by the intellect except together with motion. And all that with regard to which no motion can be found, does not fall under time.

16] The sixteenth premise: In whatsoever is not a body, multiplicity cannot be cognized by the intellect, unless the thing in question is a force in a body, for then the multiplicity of the individual forces would subsist in virtue of the multiplicity of the matters or substances in which these forces are to be found. Hence no multiplicity at all can be cognized by the intellect in the separate things, which are neither a body nor a force in a body, except when they are causes and effects.

17] The seventeenth premise: Everything that is in motion has of necessity a mover; and the mover either may be outside the moved object, as in the case of a stone moved by a hand, or the mover may be in the body in motion, as in the case of the body of a living being, for the latter is composed of a mover and of that which is moved. It is for this reason that when a living being dies and the mover—namely, the soul—is lacking from it, that which is moved—namely, the organic body—remains at the moment in its former state, except that it is not moved with that motion. However, inasmuch as the mover that exists in that which is moved is hidden and does not appear to the senses, it is thought of living beings that they are in motion without having a mover. Everything moved that has a mover within itself is said to be moved by itself—the meaning being that the force moving that which, in the object moved, is moving according to essence, exists in the whole of that object.

18] The eighteenth premise: Everything that passes from potentiality to actuality has something other than itself that causes it to pass, and this cause is of necessity outside that thing. For if that cause were that thing and there were no obstacle to prevent this passage, the thing would not have been for a certain time *in potentia* [potentiality] but would have always been *in actu* [actuality]. If, however, the cause of the passage from potentiality to actuality subsisted in the thing, and if there was at the same time an obstacle to it, which was subsequently removed, there is no doubt that the factor that put an end to the obstacle is the one that caused that potentiality to pass into actuality. Understand this.

19] The nineteenth premise: Everything that has a cause for its existence is only possible with regard to existence in respect to its own essence. For it exists if its causes are present. If, however, they are not present, or if they become nonexistent, or if their relation that entails the existence of the thing in question has changed, that thing does not exist.

20] The twentieth premise: Everything that is necessarily existent in respect to its own essence has no cause for its existence in any way whatever or under any condition.

21] The twenty-first premise: Everything that is composed of two notions has necessarily that composition as the cause of its existence as it really is, and consequently is not necessarily existent in respect to its own essence, for it exists in virtue of the existence of its two parts and of their composition.

22] The twenty-second premise: Every body is necessarily composed of two things and is necessarily accompanied by accidents. The two things constituting it are its matter and its form and the accidents accompanying it are quantity, shape, and position.

23] The twenty-third premise: It is possible for whatsoever is in potentia and in whose essence there is a certain possibility, not to exist in actu at a certain time.

24] The twenty-fourth premise: Whatsoever is something in potentia is necessarily endowed with matter, for possibility is always in matter.

25] The twenty-fifth premise: The principles of an individual compound substance are matter and form. And there is no doubt about the necessity of there being an agent, I mean to say a mover that moves the substratum so as to predispose it to receive the form. That is the proximate mover, which predisposes the matter of a certain individual. At this point it is necessary to engage in speculation with regard to motion, the mover, and the moved. However, with regard to all this, everything that it was necessary to explain has already been explained. The text of the words of Aristotle is: Matter does not move itself. This therefore is the capital premise calling for an inquiry concerning the existence of the Prime Mover.

Of the twenty-five premises that I have put before you in the form of a preface, some become manifest with very little reflection and are demonstrative premises and first intelligibles or notions approaching the latter, as may be seen in the epitome we have made of their orderly exposition. Others require a number of demonstrations and premises leading up to them. However, all of them have been given demonstrations as to which no doubt is possible. With regard to some of them, this has been done in the Book of "Akroasis" and its commentaries; with regard to others, in the Book of "Metaphysics" and its commentary. I have already made it known to you that the purpose of this Treatise is not to transcribe the books of the philosophers and to explain the most remote of the premises, but to mention the proximate premises that are required for our purpose.

I shall add to the premises mentioned before, one further premise that affirms as necessary the eternity of the world. Aristotle deemed it to be correct and the most fitting to be believed. We shall grant him this premise by way of a hypothesis in order that the clarification of that which we intended to make clear should be achieved. This premise, which among them is the twenty-sixth, consists in Aristotle's statement that time and movement are eternal, perpetual, existing in actu. Hence it follows of necessity, in his opinion, that there is a body, moving with an eternal movement, existing in actu; and this is the fifth body. For this reason, he says that the heaven is not subject to generation and corruption. For according to him, movement is not subject to generation and corruption; for he says that every movement is necessarily preceded by another movement either of the same species as itself or of other species, and that what is thought with regard to living beings—namely, that their local movement is not preceded at all by another movement—is not correct. For the cause of their movement after rest goes back finally to things calling for this local movement; these things being either an alteration of temperament necessitating a desire to seek what agrees with the living being or to flee from what disagrees with it, or an imagination, or an opinion occurring to it. Accordingly, any one of these three factors sets the living being in motion, and every one of them is necessitated by other movements. Similarly he says that in the case of everything that comes about in time, the possibility of its coming-about precedes in time its coming-about. From this there follow necessarily several points liable to validate his premise. According to this premise, a finite moving object moves upon a finite distance an infinite number of times, going back over the same distance in a circle. Now this is impossible except in circular movement, as is demonstrated in the thirteenth of these premises. According to this premise, that which is infinite must necessarily exist as a succession and not simultaneously.

This is the premise that Aristotle constantly wishes to establish as true. Now to me it seems that he does not affirm categorically that the arguments he puts forward in its favor constitute a demonstration. The premise in question is rather, in his opinion, the most fitting and the most probable. However, his followers and the commentators of his books claim that the premise is necessary and not merely possible and that it has already been demonstrated. On the other hand, every Mutakallim desires to establish that it is impossible. They say that there can be no mental representation of the coming-about in succession of an infinite number of things occurring in time. The strength of their argument is that it constitutes, in their opinion, a first intelligible. But to me it seems that the premise in question is possible—that is, neither necessary, as is affirmed by the commentators of the writings of Aristotle, nor impossible, as is claimed by the Mutakallimun. It is not the purpose now to explain the arguments of Aristotle, or to raise our doubts concerning him, or to explain my opinion concerning the creation of the world in time. But the purpose at this point is to circumscribe the premises that we need for our three problems; after first having set forth these premises and having agreed to take them as granted, I shall set out explaining what necessarily follows from them.

Reprinted with permission from Moses Maimonides, *The Guide of the Perplexed,* Part II, trans. Shlomo Pines (Chicago: University of Chicago Press, 1963), pp. 235–41. Notes omitted.

–16–

Individual Diversity
Bernard of Clairvaux and Hildegard of Bingen

One way to capture the diversity of twelfth-century Christianity is to look at the lives and writings of influential individuals who reflect medieval beliefs and values in this critical century. The tensions of twelfth-century society exhibited in this chapter—between prophecy and order, church and state, faith and reason, mystical contemplation and active military crusading—appear in the writings of two figures prominent in different ways: Bernard of Clairvaux and Hildegard of Bingen. Both were monastics, both influenced church reform, and both could be classified as mystics, but here the similarities end and their personalities diverge. Bernard was active in European affairs at every level, exerting his influence and rendering his opinion on church-state affairs, the Crusades, heresy, Abelard, and church building, as well as preaching sermons on the mystical understanding of God. Hildegard's immediate influence was limited to her monastery and some correspondence with a few notable individuals, yet her writings, covering everything from philosophy to medicine to music, in many ways embody twelfth-century female spirituality and have an enduring quality that transcends her own century.

St. Bernard (1090–1154) was a Cistercian monk and founder of the Abbey of Clairvaux, where he was abbot. The Cistercian order was a reformed monastic order, self-consciously stricter than the Cluniac monasteries. They preferred isolated locations, silence, and a minimum of distractions; consequently, Bernard in his writings condemned the excesses of ceremony and decoration in the new Gothic cathedrals. Bernard preached the Second Crusade in 1146, and designed the monastic order of the Knights Templar, Crusaders who took vows to fight for God. He also was a vigilant opponent of heresy, writing condemnations of various suspicious teachers, including Abelard. His persecution of Abelard for applying philosophy to theology highlights the different modes of rationality between the two men: Bernard clearly saw the danger of using reason as the primary way of knowing God, and sought instead to emphasize a more mysterious knowledge of God through contemplation. This exalted view of the believer's relationship to God is evident in his sermons.

St. Hildegard (1098–1179) was abbess of a Benedictine house near Bingen in Germany. She entered a hermitage (later a monastery) at the young age of eight, dedicated by her aristocratic parents, and took vows as a teenager; thus her life was shaped by the monastic discipline and the scholarly studies she enjoyed there. She apparently had visionary and prophetic experiences in childhood, but only realized her gift after she became abbess, when she began writing about her visions (she even sought confirmation from Bernard of Clairvaux). Because of her fame and popularity, she founded a new monastery at Rupertsberg, near Bingen. Her writings include an account of her visions, a scientific encyclopedia (mostly of medicine), poetry, music, and voluminous correspondence with popes, emperors, fellow monastics, priests, and lay people. Hildegard was highly regarded in her own time as a wise seer, and her exhortations and other writings continued to be influential in subsequent generations.

The following selections from these two influential writers address some of the issues covered in the previous chapters: church reform, the Crusades, scholarship, and spirituality.

16.1 Hildegard on the Church: To Priests and Popes

Both Hildegard and Bernard took on a prophetic role within the church, Hildegard speaking out from her monastery to rebuke errant clergy by holding up to them the standards set by God. The following is an example from a sermon she preached.

Questions

1. What is Hildegard's solution for corruption among the clergy?
2. What role does she see monasticism playing in society?

To Priests and Popes

After Justice has brought her accusation before the Supreme Judge, hearing her cries of complaint, he will, by his just judgement, allow his vengeance to rage against the transgressors of righteousness; and the enemies of God and Justice will have their tyranny turned upon themselves, while God and

Justice say in turn: 'How long will we suffer and endure these ravening wolves, who ought to be physicians and are not?'

But because they have the power of preaching, imposing penance and granting absolution, for that reason, they hold us in their grasp like ferocious beasts. Their crimes fall upon us and through them the whole Church withers, because they do not proclaim what is just; and they destroy the law like wolves devouring sheep. They are voracious in their drunkenness and they commit copious adulteries, and because of such sins, they judge us without mercy.

For they are also plunderers of their congregations, through their avarice, devouring whatever they can; and with their offices they reduce us to poverty and indigence, contaminating both themselves and us. For this reason, let us judge and single them out in a fair trial, because they lead us astray rather than teaching us what is right. We should do this so that we are not destroyed, since if they persevere in this way, they will throw the whole land into confusion by bringing it under their sway. But now, let us tell them to fulfill the obligations of their priestly habit and office according to true religion, as the ancient Fathers established them, or depart from us and leave us what they have.

Spurred on by the divine decree, the people will angrily propose to them these and similar things, and overwhelming them will say, 'We do not want them to rule over us along with the estates and fields and other secular concerns over which we have been established as princes.'

And how can it be right that the shaven-headed with their robes and chasubles should have more soldiers and more weapons than we do? Surely too, it is inappropriate for a cleric to be a soldier or a soldier a cleric? So let us take away from them what is not fairly but unjustly theirs. But we should give careful consideration to what was offered up with great discernment for the souls of the departed, and leave that to them since it does not constitute plunder.

For the Almighty Father has rightly divided all things—heaven for heavenly things, earth for earthly things. In this way there is a just division among the sons of men, that the religious have those things which relate to them, while the laity have their own portion, so that neither party should oppress the other through acts of plundering. God indeed has not decreed that the tunic and cloak should be given to one son while the other remains naked, but has ordered that the cloak should be given to one, the tunic to the other. And so let the laity have the cloak, because of the bulk of their worldly concerns and on account of their offspring who are always growing and multiplying. But let the tunic be given to the religious population, so that they lack neither food nor clothing, but do not possess more than they need.

16.2 Bernard and the Crusades: On Christian Knighthood

Bernard was instrumental in the calling of the Second Crusade and actively involved in the effort to keep the Crusades morally responsible, just missions to assist pilgrims and contain the violent Turks. He was appalled by some of the uncontrolled violence and immoral behavior of the warriors in the First Crusade and warriors in general. For example, he strenuously objected to the attacks on Jews by marauding crusaders and mobs (see Sefer Zekhirah's comments in 14.2), although he wrote against Jewish belief and thought in a strongly anti-Judaic vein that must have encouraged outright anti-Semitism.

As a way of limiting warrior violence in the pursuit of just Christian warfare, Bernard wrote a code of conduct for "Christian knighthood," excerpted below, and founded the semi-monastic order of the Knights Templar (see Usama's remarks about the Templars in 14.3). In this excerpt, Bernard contrasts the ideal Christian knight with the self-serving temporal warrior.

Questions

1. What view does Bernard have of the ordinary behavior of the warrior class? How does he seek to change them?

2. How does this vision of knighthood fulfill some of Pope Urban's goals as stated in his call to the First Crusade (14.1)?

On Christian Knighthood

A new kind of knighthood is now heard of in the land; it has arisen in that region once visited by the Rising Star from on high, and from whence he drove out the princes of darkness with the strength of his hand—where even now with the hands of his worthies he is crushing their minions, sons of disloyalty, and driving them out, and is accomplishing the redemption of his people, raising again the trumpet of our salvation in the house of his son David. . . .

He is a fearless knight, in truth, and secure on all sides, who, as he has girded his body with iron, so has girded his soul with the shield of faith. Surely, fortified with both these weapons, he fears neither demon nor man. Nor does he who desires to die fear death. For what should he fear in living or in dying, for whom to live is Christ, to die is gain? To be sure, he stands faithfully and willingly for Christ; but he desires even more to be dissolved and be with Christ, for this is better. . . .

What end and reward therefore does it have, this worldly—I do not say knighthood [*militia*] but roguery [*malitia*]—if as a murderer a man sins mortally and when killed, perishes eternally. . . . You [worldly knights] cover your horses with silks; you have I know not what little cloths hanging from your cuirasses; you paint your lances, shields and saddles; you encrust your reins and spurs with gold, silver and gems; and in this splendor, with shameful fury, impudently oblivious, you race on to your death. Are these the trappings of a military man, or are they rather womanly ornaments? . . .

The knight of Christ, I say, is safe in slaying, safer if he is slain. He is accountable to himself when he is slain, to Christ when he slays. "For he beareth not the sword in vain: for he is the minister of God, a revenger to execute wrath upon him that doeth evil, to praise him that doeth good." For when he kills a malefactor, he does not commit homicide but, I might say, malicide, and is clearly reputed to be the vindicator of Christ, bringing punishment to evildoers, and praise in truth to good men. Moreover, when he is himself killed, it is known that he does not perish, but triumphs. The death he inflicts is Christ's gain; the death he dies, his own. The Christian is glorified in the death of a pagan, because thereby Christ is glorified; in the death of a Christian, the liberality of the King is shown, when the knight is led to his reward. . . .

Reprinted with permission from *The Records of Medieval Europe,* ed. Carolly Erickson (New York: Anchor Books, 1971), pp. 184–86 passim. Translated from Bernard of Clairvaux, *Liber ad Milites Templi De Laude Novae Militiae, Sancti Bernardi Opera,* ed. J. Leclercq, III, 214, 216–17. Notes omitted.

16.3 Hildegard's Physiology: *Causae et Curae*

Hildegard also wrote scientific works, particularly medicinal in focus. Her encyclopedic compendium *Nine Books on the Subtleties of Different Kinds of Creatures,* often called the *Book of Simple Medicine* or *Physica,* contained an herbal (listing of herbs and their functions), a bestiary (a similar list of animal and animal parts), and a lapidary (stones useful for various purposes). These sorts of books are similar to modern reference works, useful for looking up particular ingredients. Hildegard also produced a book of remedies, called the *Book of Compound Medicine* or *Causes and Cures,* organized according to illnesses. The following brief selection from this work explains the theoretical basis of medicinal practice inherited from the Greeks, the four "humors" or elements that make up human (and cosmic) physiology, and then explains gender differences according to this scheme.

Questions

1. What distinguishes woman from man?
2. What attitude toward sexuality does Hildegard, a celibate nun, seem to have?

Hildegard's Physiology

The Four Elements

That there are only four elements: There cannot be more than four, or fewer. They consist of two kinds: upper and lower. The upper are celestial, the lower terrestrial. The things that live in the upper ones are impalpable and are made of fire and air; those that move in the lower are palpable, formed bodies, and consist of water and mud.

For spirits are fiery and airy, but man is watery and muddy. When God created man, the mud from which he was formed was stuck together with water, and God put a fiery and airy breath of life into that form. . . .

Adam and Eve

When God created Adam, Adam experienced a sense of great love in the sleep that God instilled in him. And God gave a form to that love of the man, and so woman is the man's love. And as soon as woman was formed God gave man the power of creating, that through his love—which is woman—he might procreate children. When Adam gazed at Eve, he was entirely filled with wisdom, for he saw in her the mother of the children to come. And when she gazed at Adam, it was as if she were gazing into heaven, or as the human soul strives upwards, longing for heavenly things—for her hope was fixed in him. And so there will be and must be one and the same love in man and woman, and no other.

The man's love, compared with the woman's, is a heat of ardour like a fire on blazing mountains, which can hardly be put out, whilst hers is a wood-fire that is easily quenched; but the woman's love, compared with the man's, is like a sweet warmth proceeding from the sun, which brings forth fruits.

But the great love that was in Adam when Eve came forth from him, and the sweetness of the sleep with which he then slept, were turned in his transgression into a contrary mode of sweetness. And so, because a man still feels this great sweetness in himself, and is like a stag thirsting for the fountain, he races swiftly to the woman and she to him—she like a threshing floor pounded by his many strokes and brought to heat when the grains are threshed inside her.

Reprinted with permission from *Hildegard of Bingen: An Anthology,* eds. Fiona Bowie and Oliver Davies, trans. Robert Carver (London: SPCK, 1990), pp. 108–109 passim.

16.4 Bernard's Way of Knowing: On the Song of Songs

Bernard could be a harsh, unyielding, and aggressive political opponent, and he is clearly an active player in temporal affairs. However, what drives Bernard is a strong idealism rooted in his practice of contemplating God. For example, in his treatise *On Consideration,* Bernard exhorts the pope (the newly elected Eugenius III) to dedicate himself to a contemplative life and to eschew all the worldly pursuits associated with the papal quest for power. He calls on the pope to act the role of the Old Testament prophets to the Hebrew kings: "Learn that thou hast more need of a hoe than of a scepter for fulfilling the functions of a prophet." He also shows no reticence in reminding the pope of his human nature: "Whenever you remember your dignity as Sovereign Pontiff, reflect also that not only were you once, but that you are still nothing better than the vilest slime of the earth." He criticizes the pomp surrounding the papacy as unscriptural and dangerous:

> Now we nowhere find that Peter ever appeared in public adorned with silk and jewels, covered with cloth of gold, riding on a white horse, surrounded by a military escort, and a throng of clamorous attendants. And nevertheless it seemed to him that even without such aids he could accomplish sufficiently well the task enjoined him in the words, "If thou lovest Me, feed My sheep" (John xxi. 17). In all that belongs to earthy magnificence thou has succeeded not Peter, but Constantine. However, I would counsel thee to tolerate this pomp and this splendor at least for a time, yet not to desire them as if they were essential to thy state.*

Clearly, Bernard believed that a contemplative life was the key to right leadership in the temporal world.

Bernard's concern for both individual spirituality and right order in the church is also exhibited in his reaction to the new school of thought known as scholasticism, found in the universities (Chapter 15). Bernard's preeminent goal was knowing the unknowable God, as exhibited in his mystical writings, so he was disturbed by the increasing emphasis placed on human reason as a way of comprehending divine truths. And because of his concern for right teaching in the church, he

---

*From *St. Bernard's Treatise on Consideration,* trans. Priest of Mount Melleray (Dublin: Browne and Nolan, 1921), pp. 118–19.

prosecuted any teacher who might be leading others astray with potentially wrong doctrine. He was a master of rhetoric, delivering inspiring sermons, as well as scathing invective against Jewish thought, heretics, and errant scholars (he called Jewish intelligence "coarse, dense, and bovine"). The most famous example is Bernard's persecution of Abelard (16.2), whom he accused of producing heretical doctrine on the Holy Spirit using these new methods of reasoning. His lack of appreciation for the scholastic method probably caused him to misread Abelard's arguments, as many others found nothing heretical in his books. Nonetheless, Bernard hounded Abelard into retirement and cautious teaching.

Much of Bernard's writing is concerned with this prophetic or mystical side of the Christian experience. One of his most famous treatises is a group of monastic sermons commenting on the Old Testament book *The Song of Songs*, essentially a love poem. Christian theologians read this book allegorically, as a love relationship between the believer and Christ, the bridegroom. In the first excerpt below from this treatise, Bernard offers an allegorical explication of "the kiss" between the two lovers. It is a powerful evocation of this mystical relationship.

The second excerpt below from *The Song of Songs* sermons illustrates Bernard's thinking regarding the uses of this secular literature. His arguments outlining what is spiritually profitable and unprofitable in such studies are comparable to the discussions of Clement and Tertullian (2.2).

Questions

1. What do you think Bernard wanted his hearers to learn or understand from his sermon on this passage of Scripture?
2. What is Bernard's attitude toward human knowledge?
3. How does his approach compare with that of the scholastics in Chapter 15?

Song of Songs, Sermon 2: On the Kiss

When I reflect, as I often do, on the ardour with which the patriarchs longed for the incarnation of Christ, I am pierced with sorrow and shame. And now I can scarcely contain my tears, so ashamed am I of the lukewarmness and lethargy of the present times. For which of us is filled with joy at the realization of this grace as the holy men of old were moved to desire by the promise of it?

Soon now we shall be rejoicing at the celebration of his birth (Lk 1:14). But would that it were really for his birth! How I pray that that burning desire and longing in the hearts of these holy men of old may be aroused in me by these words: "Let him kiss me with the kiss of his mouth" (Sg 1:1).

In those days a spiritual man could sense in the Spirit how great would be the grace released by the touch of those lips (Ps 44:3). For that reason, speaking in the desire prompted by the Spirit (Is 26:8), he said, "Let him kiss me with the kiss of his mouth," desiring with all his heart that he would not be deprived of a share in that sweetness.

The good men of those days could say, "Of what use to me are the words the prophets have uttered? Rather, let him who is beautiful beyond the children of men (Ps 44:3) kiss me with the kiss of his mouth. I am no longer content with what Moses says, for he sounds to me like someone who cannot speak well" (Ex 4:10). Isaiah is "a man of unclean lips" (Is 6:5). Jeremiah is a child who does not know how to speak (Jn 1:6). All the prophets are empty to me.

But he, he of whom they speak, let *him* speak to me. Let him kiss me with the kiss of his mouth. Let him not speak to me in them or through them, for they are "a watery darkness, a dense cloud" (Ps 17:12). But let him kiss me with the kiss of his mouth, whose gracious presence and eloquence of wonderful teaching causes a "spring of living water" to well up in me to eternal life (Jn 4:14). Shall I not find that a richer grace is poured out upon me from him whom the Father has anointed with the oil of gladness more than all his companions, if he will deign to kiss me with the kiss of his mouth (Ps 44:8)? His living and effective word (Heb 4:12) is a kiss; not a meeting of lips, which can sometimes be deceptive about the state of the heart, but a full infusion of joys, a revelation of secrets, a wonderful and inseparable mingling of the light from above and the mind on which it is shed, which, when it is joined with God, is one spirit with him (I Cor 6:17).

It is with good reason, then, that I have nothing to do with dreams and visions, reject figures and mysteries, and even the beauty of angels seems tedious to me. For my Jesus outshines them so far in his beauty and loveli-ness (Ps 44:5). That is why I ask him, not any other, angel or man, to kiss me with the kiss of his mouth.

I do not presume to think that I shall be kissed by his mouth. That is the unique felicity and singular prerogative of the humanity he assumed. But, more humbly, I ask to be kissed by the kiss of his mouth, which is shared by many, those who can say, "Indeed from his fullness we have all re-ceived" (Jn 1:16).

Listen carefully here. The mouth which kisses signifies the Word who assumes human nature; the flesh which is assumed is the recipient of the kiss; the kiss, which is of both giver and receiver, is the Person which is of both, the Mediator between God and man, the Man Christ Jesus (I Tm 2:5).

For this reason, none of the saints presumed to say, "Let him kiss me with his mouth," but, "with the kiss of his mouth," thus acknowledging that prerogative of him on whom uniquely once and for all the Mouth of the Word was pressed, when the whole fullness of the divinity gave itself to him in the body (Col 2:9).

O happy kiss, and wonder of amazing self-humbling which is not a mere meeting of lips, but the union of God with man. The touch of lips signifies the bringing together of souls. But this conjoining of natures unites the human with the divine and makes peace between earth and heaven (Col 1:20). "For he himself is our peace, who made the two one" (Eph 2:14). This was the kiss for which the holy men of old longed, the more so because they foresaw the joy and exultation (Sir 15:6) of finding their treasure in him, and discovering all the treasures of wisdom and knowledge in him (Col 2:3), and they longed to receive of his fullness (Jn 1:16).

I think that what I have said pleases you. But listen to another meaning. . . .

Here we must add that he who makes himself our Mediator with God is the Son of God and he is himself God. What is man that he should take notice of him, or the son of man, that he should think of him? (Ps 143:3). Where am I to find the faith to dare to trust in such majesty? How, I say, shall I, who am dust and ashes, presume to think that God cares about me (Sir 10:9)? He loves his Father. He does not need me, nor my possessions (Ps 15:2). How then shall I be sure that he will never fail me?

If it is true, as you prophets say, that God has the intention of showing mercy, and thinks to make himself manifest for our reassurance (Ps 76:8), let him make a covenant of peace (Sir 45:30), an everlasting covenant with me (Is 61:8) by the kiss of his mouth.

If he is not going to go back on what he has said (Ps 88:35), let him empty himself, humble himself (Phil 2:7), bend low and "kiss me with the kiss of his mouth." If the Mediator is to be acceptable to both sides, let God the Son of God become man; let him become the son of man, and make me sure of him with the kiss of his mouth. When I know that the Mediator who is the Son of God is mine, then I shall accept him trustingly. . . .

O Root of Jesse, who stand as a sign to the peoples (Is 11:10), how many kings and prophets wanted to see you and did not (Lk 10:24)? Simeon is the happiest of them all because by God's mercy he was still bearing fruit in old age. For he rejoiced to think that he would see the sign so long desired. He saw it and was glad (Jn 8:56). When he had received the kiss of peace he departed in peace, but first he proclaimed aloud that Jesus was born, a sign that would be rejected (Lk 2:25–34).

And so it was. The sign of peace arose and was rejected, by those who hate peace (Ps 119:7). For what is peace to men of goodwill (Lk 2:14) is a stone to make men stumble, a rock for the wicked to fall over (I Pt 2:8).

"Herod was troubled, and all Jerusalem with him" (Mt 2:3). He came to his own and his own did not receive him (Jn 1: 11). Happy those shepherds keeping watch at night who were found worthy to be shown the sign of this vision (Lk 23:8). For even at that time he was hiding himself from the wise and prudent and revealing himself to the simple (Mt 11:25; Lk 10:21). Herod wanted to see him (Lk 23:8), but because he did not want to see him out of goodwill, he did not deserve to see him.

The sign of peace was given only to men of goodwill; the only sign which was given to Herod and his like is the sign of Jonah and the prophet (Mt 12:39). The angel said to the shepherds, "This is a sign for you" (Lk 2:12), you who are humble, you who are obedient, you who are not haughty (Rom 12:16), you who are keeping vigil and meditating on God's law day and night (Ps 1:2). "This is a sign for you," he said.

What is this sign? The sign the angels promised, the sign the people asked for, the sign the prophets foretold, the Lord Jesus has now made, and he shows it to you; the sign in which unbelievers receive the faith, the faint-hearted hope, the perfect security. This is your sign.

What is it a sign of? Indulgence, grace, peace, the peace which will have no end (Is 9:7). It is this sign: "You will find a baby wrapped in swaddling clothes and lying in a manger" (Lk 2:12). But this baby is God himself, reconciling the world to himself in him (2 Cor 5:19). He will die for your sins and rise again to make you just (Rom 4:25), so that, made just by faith, you may be at peace with God (Rom 5:1).

This was the sign of faith that the prophet once asked Achaz the king to ask of the Lord his God, either from the heavens or from the depths of hell (Is 7:11). But the wicked king refused, not believing, wretched man, that in this sign the heights would be joined to the depths in peace. This came to pass when the Lord descended even to hell, and greeted those who dwell there with a holy kiss (I Cor 16:20), so that even they received the sign of peace, and then he returned to heaven and made it possible for the spirits there to share the same sign in everlasting joy.

We must come to the end of this sermon. But let me sum up briefly what I have said. It seems clear that this holy kiss was given to the world for two reasons: to give the weak faith and to satisfy the desire of the perfect. This kiss is no other than the Mediator between God and men, the man Christ Jesus (I Tm 2:5), who with the Father and the Holy Spirit lives and reigns world without end, Amen.

From *Bernard of Clairvaux* by G. R. Evans, © 1987 by Gillian R. Evans (New York: Paulist Press, 1987), pp. 215–20. Used by permission of Paulist Press. Notes omitted.

On Knowledge

The knowledge of literature is good for our instruction, but the knowledge of our own infirmity is more useful to salvation. . . .

I may seem to you, perhaps, to speak too severely of knowledge; to blame, as it were, the learned, and to forbid the study of literature. But I would by no means do this. I am not ignorant how great are the services that have been rendered to the Church, and are rendered to her continually, by her learned sons, whether in repulsing the attacks of her enemies or in instructing the simple. Besides, I have read the words of the Prophet: *Because thou hast rejected knowledge I will also reject thee, and thou shalt be no priest to Me* (Hosea iv.6); and also: *They that be wise shall shine as the brightness of the firmament, and they that turn many to righteousness as the stars for ever and ever* (Dan. xii.3). But I know also where I have read: *Knowledge puffeth up* (I Cor. viii.1); and again: *He that increaseth knowledge increaseth sorrow* (Eccles. i.18). You see that there is a difference between these [kinds of knowledge], for one kind renders [the possessor] vain, and another renders him sad. Now, I would ask you whether of the two is the more conducive to salvation, that which puffs up or that which saddens? But I doubt not that you would prefer the latter, since pain is a means to health, of which tumor and swelling is but a semblance. But he who entreats for salvation is near to gain it, for he *that asketh receiveth* (Luke xi.10). . . .

. . . For there are those who wish to learn merely in order that they may know, and such curiosity is blamable. There are others who wish to learn for no other reason than that they may be looked upon as learned, which is a ridiculous vanity; and these will not escape the censure which a satiric poet levels against them when he says: 'To know a thing is nothing in your eyes, unless some other person is aware of your knowledge.' (Persius, *Satire I.,* 27) And others, again, desire to learn only that they may make merchandise of their knowledge, for example, in order to gain money or honours; and such trafficking is ignoble. But there are those who desire to learn that they may edify others; that is charity. And, lastly, there are some who wish to learn that they may be themselves edified; and that is prudence.

Of all these the two last are the only learners who do not fall into an abuse of knowledge; since they wish to know only that they may do good. Says the Psalmist: *A good understanding have all they that do His commandments* (Ps. cxi.10). But let all the others note what is said by the Apostle: *To him that knoweth to do good, and doeth it not, to him it is sin* (James iv. I7); as if he had said by a metaphor: 'To take food, and not to digest it, is injurious to the health. For food badly cooked and ill-digested generates unhealthy humors, and injures the body instead of nourishing it. So also much knowledge stuffed into the memory, which is, as it were, the stomach of the soul, if it is not digested by the fire of charity, and transfused into the limbs, that is, into the actions and habits, so that it is made the means of good actions through the good that is known, shall not that knowledge be counted for sin, like food turned into bad and injurious humors?' Is not sin, in fact, as a bad humor in the soul? and are not bad tendencies and habits as depraved humors? He who knows the good, and does it not, will his conscience not suffer from inflammations and torturing pains? ...

Do you observe with what emphatic truth the Apostle asserts that *knowledge puffeth up?* I wish, then, that the soul should first of all commence by acquiring a knowledge of itself, as is required both by natural order and by that of usefulness. The natural order, because we are to ourselves the first and nearest fact; but also that of usefulness, since the knowledge of ourselves does not puff us up, but rather humbles us, and prepares us for edification. For certainly the spiritual edifice cannot stand except on the firm foundation of humility. ... For how can it be otherwise than humbled, in obtaining this true knowledge of itself, when it beholds itself laden with sins, heavily burdened with its mortal body, involved in earthly cares, infected with the corruption of carnal desires, blind, bent earthwards, weak, entangled with many errors, exposed to a thousand perils, trembling with a thousand fears, struggling with a thousand difficulties, the subject of a thousand suspicions and a thousand distressing necessities, prone to vices, but to virtues slow and backward? How, after that revelation of himself to himself, can he lift up his eyes and walk with head erect? Will he not rather be converted at the sight of so many miseries, at the sharp pang of the 'thorn which is fastened' [into it]? (Ps. xxxi. 4, Vulg.). He will be converted, I say, to tears, to sighs and groans; he will be converted to the Lord, and in deep humility will cry to Him: *Heal my soul, for I have sinned against Thee* (Ps. xli.4). And then, when converted unto the Lord, it shall receive consolation, because He is the Father of mercies, and the God of all consolation.

As for me, as long as I look at myself, I see only one subject after another for bitter regret. But if I look up, and lift up my eyes towards the help of the Divine compassion, the joyful sight of God tempers at once the bitter revelation of myself, and I say to Him: *My soul is troubled within me, therefore will I remember Thee* (Ps. xlii. 6). ... Thus, the knowledge of thyself will be a step to the knowledge of God: He will become visible in His image, which is renewed in thee; whilst thou, beholding with confidence as in a glass the glory of the Lord, art changed into the same image from glory to glory, even as by the Spirit of the Lord (2 Cor. iii. 18).

From *Life and Works of Saint Bernard, Abbot of Clairvaux,* ed. John Mabillon, trans. and ed. Samuel J. Eales, Vol IV: Cantica Canticorum, Sermon XXXVI (London: John Hodges, 1896), pp. 233–36 passim.

16.5 Hildegard's Lyrics: Eucharius

One of Hildegard's most outstanding and enduring contributions are her lyric compositions, found in the *Symphonia.* She wrote these lyrics, with musical notation, for devotional use. That is, these lyrics are for the nuns to chant either singly or corporately as a form of worship and meditation. They were not intended for public performance in front of an audience. Nor did Hildegard view them as the means to an ecstatic experience; despite the evocative imagery and sometimes spectacular musical range in these songs, the language and ideas are ordered and controlled.

The lyric below is in honor of Saint Eucharius, first bishop of Trier. Although he is now dated into the late third century, medieval legends counted him as one of the seventy-two disciples of Jesus, and an evangelist sent by Peter to Gaul. Hildegard wrote this tribute for the monks at the St. Eucharius monastery in Trier. This is a narrative poem, in that it relates the story of the saint's life, including his courage while evangelizing Trier and the founding of a church there.

Questions

1. How does Hildegard use imagery to convey a vision of the saint and of God?

2. How does this poem compare with Hildegard's other writings? Is there a common thread tying them together?

Eucharius

Eucharius!
you walked blithely when you stayed
with the Son of God,
touching him, watching
his miracle-working.

You loved him with a perfect love
when terror fell on your friends—
who being human had no
strength to bear the brightness
of the good.

But you—in a blaze of utmost love—
drew him to your heart
when you gathered the sheaves
of his precepts.

Eucharius!
when the Word of God possessed you
in the blaze of the dove,
when the sun rose in your spirit,
you founded a church in your bliss.

Daylight shimmers in your heart
where three tabernacles stand
on a marble pillar
in the city of God.

In your preaching Ecclesia
savors old wine with new—
a chalice twice hallowed.

And in your teaching Ecclesia
argued with such force
that her shout rang over the mountains,
that the hills and the woods might bow
to suck her breasts.

Pray for this company now,
pray with resounding voice
that we forsake not Christ
in his sacred rites,
but become before his altar
a living sacrifice.

From Saint Hildegard of Bingen: *Symphonia: A Critical Edition of the Symphonia Armonie Celestium Revelationum [Symphony of the Harmony of Celestial Revelations].* Ed. and trans. Barbara Newman (Ithaca: Cornell University Press, 1988), pp. 209, 211. Copyright © 1989 by Cornell University. Used by permission of the publisher, Cornell University Press. Discography: *A Feather on the Breath of God: Sequences and Hymns by Abbess Hildegard of Bingen,* Gothic Voices with Emma Kirkby, directed by Christopher Page (London: Hyperion, 1984).

Part 5

New Paths of Order and Prophecy, circa 1200–1300

The thirteenth century was a period of fruition, in which the innovations of the twelfth century in governance, scholarship, and spirituality bore fruit. At the same time, the latent tensions in a dynamic period of economic, social, and political change grew stronger. In particular, the simultaneous growth of centralized church governance and diversifying heretical groups heightened the tension between the prophetic and orderly aspects of medieval Christianity. At the same time that the notion of a Christian society took on a concrete and legal meaning, interactions between Catholic European Christians and those who were not—Muslims, Jews, heretics—increased, contributing to a stronger assertion of Christian identity in the midst of this cross-cultural influence. The chapters of this part examine these diverse forces in four areas. The first two (Chapters 17 and 18) examine the issue of reform by looking at both orthodox and unorthodox movements; the second two (Chapters 19 and 20) look at European Christian experience at home and then abroad in contact with non-Europeans and non-Christians.

Chapter 17 examines orthodox reform efforts in both the spirit of order and the spirit of prophecy by looking at papal activities and the mendicant movements, including scholarship. Then, Chapter 18 examines reform efforts that "went over the line" into heresy or direct challenges to the order of the church, at least in the eyes of some. Documents in this chapter, on heresy, inquisition, and papal monarchy, are comparable to the mainstream reform efforts of Chapter 17. Chapter 19 examines religious expression in popular stories and poetry that reflect thirteenth-century values and beliefs within Europe. Chapter 20 looks at cross-cultural interaction, particularly as European missionaries begin to open dialogue with Muslims.

One thread running through all of these sections is the mendicant movement. In many ways, the Franciscan and Dominican orders act as a touchstone for many of the developments in thirteenth-century Europe, combining both the prophetic and the orderly elements of reform. The mendicant orders were founded at the beginning of the century, and throughout this century and those that followed, their members became reformers, scholars, teachers, and missionaries, and even spawned some heretical groups. As you read through these four chapters, keep in mind the role that the mendicants played in medieval society and in the development of a distinctive Christian identity for Europeans.

–17–

Orthodox Reform

Popes, Mendicants, and Scholars

Within the "order" of the church, the impetus for reform came from law, new urban piety, and scholarship. Papal reform in the thirteenth century turned toward law and administration as the main ways to solidify the church's position in society. Like the secular governments of the period, church governance became increasingly centralized and complex, developing laws and a bureaucracy for administering church affairs. The papacy of Innocent III exemplifies this effort to make the spiritual position of the church a legal reality, as indicated in the Fourth Lateran Council (17.1).

Simultaneously, urban piety produced new religious orders, the mendicants (or "beggars"). The mendicant orders, the Franciscans and Dominicans, differ from the earlier monastic orders in pursuing corporate poverty as well as individual poverty. Mendicants reacted against urban wealth by becoming wandering beggars, dependent on charity; as a result, they reached out to the poor and ignorant in European society. These orders are only one expression of lay piety reacting to urban materialism, evident, for example, in the writings of Francis and Clare (17.2). While the orders of Francis and Dominic became orthodox, other groups—Beguines (13.4), Spiritual Franciscans (18.2), Waldensians and Albigensians (18.1)—were declared heretical.

The Franciscans and Dominicans produced brilliant scholars active in the major universities of Europe. Some of them, such as the Franciscan Bonaventure, emphasized the mystical or spiritual knowledge of God (17.3), while others, such as the Dominican Thomas Aquinas, utilized the scholastic methods of the twelfth century to produce a new and dynamic synthesis of faith and reason (17.4). Other scholars, such as Marsilius of Padua (18.3), used the developments in law and scholasticism to challenge the position of the church in society.

All three of these areas—law, mendicant piety, and scholarship—

constitute reform in the sense of bringing change to keep old ideas alive and viable. The papacy used the new tools of law and bureaucracy to restore order to Christian society. The mendicant movement enlivened Christian society with the spirit of prophecy, while scholars found new ways to express the oldest ideas of Christian belief.

17.1 Papal Monarchy:
Innocent III and the Fourth Lateran Council

Pope Innocent III (1198–1216) has been called by one author "the high noon of the medieval papacy." If the papacy did reach a pinnacle of authority and centrality in Europe, then Innocent's reign represents the best of that effort to create a papal monarchy over European Christian society. Under Innocent III—one of the so-called lawyer popes of the thirteenth century—papal administration flourished, evident in the selections below from the Fourth Lateran Council.

Innocent III is as complex as the papal government of this period. He was a trained lawyer, a consummate politician, extremely pious, and a great preacher. He used his legal training to revamp papal administration; he used his political acumen to manipulate the powerful kings of his era, the French Philip Augustus, King John of England, and the German princes vying for the imperial crown. He called the Fourth Crusade to the Holy Land, and set in motion the Albigensian Crusade against heresy within Europe (18.1). In addition to these administrative and political activities, he produced volumes of beautiful, spiritually insightful sermons, and also authorized the ministry of Saint Francis, whom he recognized as an essential voice of prophecy in the work of the church (17.2).

The best evidence of the sheer force of Innocent's moral and administrative authority in Europe is the Fourth Lateran Council called by Innocent in 1215 to reform and systematize church governance and Christian society. The resulting canons regulate everything from the dress of priests to lay participation in church rituals. This massive amount of legislation was produced in three weeks by the 1,200 churchmen in attendance. The first excerpt below is from one of Innocent's letters calling churchmen to the council, and explains his reasons for reform. The second excerpt from the canons of IV Lateran reveals more of his, and the council's, vision of Christian society in what is expected of Catholics and in the exclusion of Jews and heretics.

Questions

1. Why does the church need reform, according to Innocent's letter of invitation? What problems plague the church and how should they be resolved?

2. What do canons 1, 21, and 22 reveal about the expected lifestyle of an orthodox member of Christian society?

3. Why does the council create legislation about Jews and heretics?

Innocent III, Letter of Invitation to the Fourth Lateran Council

To the archbishop and bishops, to the abbots and priors, of the province of Canterbury.

Beasts of many kinds are attempting to destroy the vineyard of the Lord of Sabaoth, and their onset has so far succeeded against it that over no small area thorns have sprung up instead of vines, and (with grief we report it!) the vines themselves are variously infected and diseased, and instead of the grape they bring forth the wild grape. Therefore we invoke the testimony of Him, who is a faithful witness in the heavens, that of all the desires of our heart we long chiefly for two in this life, namely, that we may work successfully to recover the Holy Land and to reform the Universal Church, both of which call for attention so immediate as to preclude further apathy or delay unless at the risk of great and serious danger. Hence we have often poured forth our tears and supplications before God, humbly beseeching Him that in these matters He would reveal to us His good pleasure, and would inspire affection, kindle desire, and strengthen purpose by granting an opportunity and occasion to achieve these objects with success. Therefore (as concern for so great a purpose required) we have had much careful discussion on these matters with our brethren and other prudent men, and on their advice we have finally decided that to attain these objects one thing must be done, namely, that, since these objects affect the condition of the whole body of the faithful, we should summon a general council according to the ancient custom of the Holy Fathers—this council to be held at a convenient time and to be concerned only with the spiritual good of souls. It will be a council in which (in order to uproot vices and implant virtues, to correct abuses and reform morals, to eliminate heresies and strengthen faith, to allay differences and establish peace, to check persecutions and cherish liberty, to persuade Christian princes and peoples to grant succour and support for the Holy Land from both clergy and laymen, and for other reasons which it would be tedious to enumerate here), whatever, with the council's approval, shall have seemed expedient for the honour and glory of the Divine Name, for the healing and salvation of our souls, and for the good and benefit of Christian people, may be wisely established as decrees of inviolable force affecting prelates and clergy regular and secular.

But because a general council could not be conveniently assembled until two years from now, we have arranged in the meantime for discreet men in the several provinces to investigate fully matters which require the corrective of an apostolic ordinance, and for the sending of suitable agents to organize preparations for a Crusade so that, if in response to necessity the sacred council approves, we personally may take over control and prosecute the business the more effectively. Believing, therefore, that this wholesome proposal cometh down from Him from whom is derived every good and perfect gift, by apostolic letter we charge and command you all to make such preparation as will enable you, within two and a half years from this 1213th year of our Lord's Incarnation and on the 1st November, to present yourselves before us in modesty and prudence; and you will arrange that in your province one or two suffragan bishops should remain to carry on ecclesiastical administration, but so that both they and any others who, being detained for a canonical reason, cannot come in person shall send suitable deputies in their place. You will observe such moderation in your retinue and equipage as has been appointed by the Lateran Council: no one is to bring more than is permitted, anyone may bring less: no one is to incur excessive and ostentatious expenditure, but only such as is essential and moderate: each must prove himself in deed and in bearing to be a true worshipper of Christ, for it is not worldly applause but spiritual advancement that is to be sought in this matter. You, brothers archbishops and bishops, are to command, as from us, all chapters of churches, cathedral and otherwise, to be represented at the council by their provosts or deans or by other suitable persons; for certain matters will be treated at the council which particularly concern the chapters of churches. Meantime, both personally and by discreet agents, you will enquire precisely about all matters which seem to call for energetic correction or reform, and conscientiously writing a report you will deliver it for the scrutiny of the sacred council. As regards the necessary aid for the Holy Land, where God our King of old deigned to work salvation in the midst of the earth, you must earnestly devote to it your help and labour, faithfully and wisely assisting those whom we shall have deputed for the special management of the business.

Wherefore, let no one deceitfully excuse himself and withdraw from the execution of so holy a work, if he would escape canonical punishment. Let no one plead the difficulties caused by dissensions or by the roads; for, since the Lord now shews a token for good, these troubles for the most part are beginning to abate: the greater the dangers that threaten, the stronger the remedies that should be applied. No man will ever cross the ocean if he is always waiting for the sea to cease its turmoil.

The Lateran, the 19th of April, in the sixteenth year of our Pontificate.

Reprinted with permission from C. R. Cheney and W. H. Semple, *Selected Letters of Pope Innocent III Concerning England, 1198–1216* (London: Thomas Nelson & Sons, 1953), pp. 144–47. Notes omitted.

Fourth Lateran Council, Select Canons

Canon 1

We firmly believe and openly confess that there is only one true God, eternal and immense, omnipotent, unchangeable, incomprehensible, and ineffable, Father, Son, and Holy Ghost; three Persons indeed but one essence, substance, or nature absolutely simple; the Father (proceeding) from no one, but the Son from the Father only, and the Holy Ghost equally from both, always without beginning and end. The Father begetting, the Son begotten, and the Holy Ghost proceeding; consubstantial and coequal, co-omnipotent and coeternal, the one principle of the universe, Creator of all things invisible and visible, spiritual and corporeal, who from the beginning of time and by His omnipotent power made from nothing creatures both spiritual and corporeal, angelic, namely, and mundane, and then human, as it were, common, composed of spirit and body. The devil and the other demons were indeed created by God good by nature but they became bad through themselves; man, however, sinned at the suggestion of the devil. This Holy Trinity in its common essence undivided and in personal properties divided, through Moses, the holy prophets, and other servants gave to the human race at the most opportune intervals of time the doctrine of salvation.

And finally, Jesus Christ, the only begotten Son of God made flesh by the entire Trinity, conceived with the co-operation of the Holy Ghost of Mary ever Virgin, made true man, composed of a rational soul and human flesh, one Person in two natures, pointed out more clearly the way of life. Who according to His divinity is immortal and impassable, according to His humanity was made passable and mortal, suffered on the cross for the salvation of the human race, and being dead descended into hell, rose from the dead, and ascended into heaven. But He descended in soul, arose in flesh, and ascended equally in both; He will come at the end of the world to judge the living and the dead and will render to the reprobate and to the elect according to their works. Who all shall rise with their own bodies which they now have that they may receive according to their merits, whether good or bad, the latter eternal punishment with the devil, the former eternal glory with Christ.

There is one Universal Church of the faithful, outside of which there is absolutely no salvation. In which there is the same priest and sacrifice, Jesus Christ, whose body and blood are truly contained in the sacrament of the altar under the forms of bread and wine; the bread being changed (*transsubstantiatis*) by divine power into the body, and the wine into the blood, so that to realize the mystery of unity we may receive of Him what He has received of us. And this sacrament no one can effect except the priest who has been duly ordained in accordance with the keys of the Church, which Jesus Christ Himself gave to the Apostles and their successors.

But the sacrament of baptism, which by the invocation of each Person of the Trinity, namely, of the Father, Son, and Holy Ghost, is effected in water, duly conferred on children and adults in the form prescribed by the Church by anyone whatsoever, leads to salvation. And should anyone after the reception of baptism have fallen into sin, by true repentance he can always be restored. Not only virgins and those practicing chastity, but also those united in marriage, through the right faith and through works pleasing to God, can merit eternal salvation. . . .

Canon 3

We excommunicate and anathematize every heresy that raises itself against the holy, orthodox and Catholic faith which we have above explained; condemning all heretics under whatever names they may be known, for while they have different faces they are nevertheless bound to each other by their tails, since in all of them vanity is a common element. Those condemned, being handed over to the secular rulers or their bailiffs, let them be abandoned, to be punished with due justice, clerics being first degraded from their orders. As to the property of the condemned, if they are laymen, let it be confiscated; if clerics, let it be applied to the churches from which they received revenues. But those who are only suspected, due consideration being given to the nature of the suspicion and the character of the person, unless they prove their innocence by a proper defense, let them be anathematized and avoided by all until they have made suitable satisfaction; but if they have been under excommunication for one year, then let them be condemned as heretics. Secular authorities, whatever office they may hold, shall be admonished and induced and if necessary compelled by ecclesiastical censure, that as they wish to be esteemed and numbered among the faithful, so for the defense of the faith they ought publicly to take an oath that they will strive in good faith and to the best of their ability to exterminate in the territories subject to their jurisdiction all heretics pointed out by the Church; so that whenever anyone shall have assumed authority, whether spiritual or temporal, let him be bound to confirm this decree by oath. . . .

But since some, under "the appearance of godliness, but denying the power thereof," as the Apostle says (II Tim. 3: 5), arrogate to themselves the authority to preach, as the same Apostle says: "How shall they preach unless they be sent?" (Rom. 10: 15), all those prohibited or not sent, who, without the authority of the Apostolic See or of the Catholic bishop of the locality, shall presume to usurp the office of preaching either publicly or privately, shall be excommunicated and unless they amend, and the sooner the better, they shall be visited with a further suitable penalty. We add, moreover, that every archbishop or bishop should himself or through his archdeacon or some other suitable persons, twice or at least once a year make the rounds of his diocese in which report has it that heretics dwell, and there compel three or more men of good character or, if it should be deemed advisable, the entire neighborhood, to swear that if anyone know of the presence there of heretics or others holding secret assemblies, or differing from the common way of the faithful in faith and morals, they will make them known to the bishop. The latter shall then call together before him those accused, who, if they do not purge themselves of the matter of which they are accused, or if after the rejection of their error they lapse into their former wickedness, shall be canonically punished. But if any of them by damnable obstinacy should disapprove of the oath and should perchance be unwilling to swear, from this very fact let them be regarded as heretics.

We wish, therefore, and in virtue of obedience strictly command, that to carry out these instructions effectively the bishops exercise throughout their dioceses a scrupulous vigilance if they wish to escape canonical punishment. If from sufficient evidence it is apparent that a bishop is negligent or remiss in cleansing his diocese of the ferment of heretical wickedness, let him be deposed from the episcopal office and let another, who will and can confound heretical depravity, be substituted. . . .

Canon 21

All the faithful of both sexes shall after they have reached the age of discretion faithfully confess all their sins at least once a year to their own (parish) priest and perform to the best of their ability the penance imposed, receiving reverently at least at Easter the sacrament of the Eucharist, unless perchance at the advice of their own priest they may for a good reason abstain for a time from its reception; otherwise they shall be cut off from the Church (excommunicated) during life and deprived of Christian burial in death. Wherefore, let this salutary decree be published frequently in the churches, that no one may find in the plea of ignorance a shadow of excuse. But if anyone for a good reason should wish to confess his sins to another priest, let him first seek and obtain permission from his own (parish) priest, since otherwise he (the other priest) cannot loose or bind him.

Let the priest be discreet and cautious that he may pour wine and oil into the wounds of the one injured after the manner of a skillful physician, carefully inquiring into the circumstances of the sinner and the sin, from the nature of which he may understand what kind of advice to give and what remedy to apply, making use of different experiments to heal the sick one. But let him exercise the greatest precaution that he does not in any degree by word, sign, or any other manner make known the sinner, but should he need more prudent counsel, let him seek it cautiously without any mention of the person. He who dares to reveal a sin confided to him in the tribunal of penance, we decree that he be not only deposed from the sacerdotal office but also relegated to a monastery of strict observance to do penance for the remainder of his life. . . .

Canon 22

Since bodily infirmity is sometimes caused by sin, the Lord saying to the sick man whom he had healed: "Go and sin no more, lest some worse thing happen to thee" (John 5: 14), we declare in the present decree and strictly command that when physicians of the body are called to the bedside of the sick, before all else they admonish them to call for the physician of souls, so that after spiritual health has been restored to them, the application of bodily medicine may be of greater benefit, for the cause being removed the effect will pass away. We publish this decree for the reason that some, when they are sick and are advised by the physician in the course of the sickness to attend to the salvation of their soul, give up all hope and yield more easily to the danger of death. If any physician shall transgress this decree after it has been published by the bishops, let him be cut off (*arceatur*) from the Church till he has made suitable satisfaction for his transgression. And since the soul is far more precious than the body, we forbid under penalty of anathema that a physician advise a patient to have recourse to sinful means for the recovery of bodily health.

Canon 68

In some provinces a difference of dress distinguishes the Jews and Saracens from the Christians, but in others confusion has developed to such a degree that no difference is discernible. Whence it happens sometimes through error that Christians mingle with the women of Jews and Saracens, and, on the other hand, Jews and Saracens mingle with those of the Christians. Therefore, that such ruinous commingling through error of this kind may not serve as a refuge for further excuse for excesses, we decree that such people of both sexes (that is, Jews and Saracens) in every Christian province and at all times be distinguished in public from other people by a difference of dress, since this was also enjoined on them by Moses. On the days of the Lamentations and on Passion Sunday they may not appear in public, because some of them, as we understand, on those days are not ashamed to show themselves more ornately attired and do not fear to amuse themselves at the expense of the Christians, who in memory of the sacred passion go about attired in robes of mourning. That we most strictly forbid, lest they should presume in some measure to burst forth suddenly in contempt of the Redeemer. And, since we ought not to be ashamed of Him who blotted out our offenses, we command that the secular princes restrain presumptuous persons of this kind by condign [deserved] punishment, lest they presume to blaspheme in some degree the One crucified for us.

Reprinted from *Disciplinary Decrees of the General Councils,* ed. and trans. H. J. Schroeder (St. Louis: B. Herder Book Co, 1937), pp. 237–39, 242–44, 259–60, 263, 290–91.

17.2 Franciscan Spirituality: Francis and Clare

Francis of Assisi (circa 1181–1226) and Clare of Assisi (1194–1253) both came from families of wealth in the prosperous urban environment of Italy, and both rejected these riches and status in favor of the spiritual values of poverty and humility. The Franciscan orders, including the Poor Clares, came out of the mendicant movement in the thirteenth century that sought new ways to express spirituality in an increasingly materialistic society.

Francis knew the life of a wealthy merchant through his upbringing, experimented with the life of chivalry as a knight, and then chose poverty. In 1206, adhering literally to Jesus's injunction to give away everything to follow him, Francis renounced his family's wealth and set himself to minister to the poorest, including lepers, as well as to restore dilapidated churches. Disciples began to gather, and Francis eventually developed a Rule and sought permission from the pope, Innocent III, to found an order. The order grew in size and complexity, modifying Francis's original ideals of simplicity. Those ideals are expressed in the following selection, the "Will of Francis."

Clare renounced her family and possessions in 1214, and followed Francis. Although Francis tonsured her, neither he nor the church authorities would allow women to wander begging, so he established Clare and her followers in a house, which became the foundation of the Order of Poor Clares. The Clares follow a monastic rule like Benedictines, but are much more severe in their asceticism. The Clares spread rapidly in the thirteenth century, indicating the popularity of Clare's vision of Lady Poverty. The excerpt below is from a letter of Clare's to Agnes, an aristocratic woman who has taken up the life of poverty.

Questions

1. What are the main ideals that Francis stresses in his will? Why are these important to him?
2. Why does Clare see the life of poverty as so blessed?
3. What seems to inspire both Francis and Clare to lead the lives they choose?

Will of Francis

God gave it to me, Brother Francis, to begin to do penance in the following manner: when I was yet in my sins it seemed to me too painful to look upon the lepers, but the Lord Himself led me among them, and I had compassion upon them. When I left them, that which had seemed to me bitter had become sweet and easy. A little while after, I left the world, and God gave me such faith that I would kneel down with simplicity in any of his churches, and I would say, "We adore thee, Lord Jesus Christ, here and in all thy churches which are in the world, and we bless thee that by Thy holy cross Thou hast ransomed the world."

Afterward the Lord gave me, and still gives me, so great a faith in priests who live according to the form of the holy Roman Church, because of their sacerdotal character, that even if they persecuted me I would have recourse to them, and even though I had all the wisdom of Solomon, if I should find poor secular priests, I would not preach in their parishes against their will. I desire to respect them like all the others, to love them and honour them as my lords. I will not consider their sins, for in them I see the Son of God, and they are my lords. I do this because here below I see nothing, I perceive nothing physically of the most high Son of God, except His most holy body and blood, which the priests receive and alone distribute to others.

I desire above all things to honour and venerate all these most holy mysteries and to keep them precious. Wherever I find the sacred name of Jesus or his words, in unsuitable places, I desire to take them away and put them in some decent place; and I pray that others may do the same. We ought to honour and revere all the theologians and those who preach the most holy word of God, as dispensing to us spirit and life.

When the Lord gave me the care of some brothers, no one showed me what I ought to do, but the Most High himself revealed to me that I ought to live according to the model of the holy gospel. I caused a short and simple formula to be written and the lord Pope confirmed it for me.

Those who volunteered to follow this kind of life distributed all they had to the poor. They contented themselves with one tunic, patched within and without, with the cord and breeches, and we desired to have nothing more. . . . We loved to live in poor and abandoned churches, and we were ignorant and were submissive to all. I worked with my hands and would still do so, and I firmly desire also that all the other brothers work, for this makes for goodness. Let those who know no trade learn one, not for the purpose of receiving wages for their toil, but for their good example and to escape idleness. And when we are not given the price of our work, let us resort to the table of the Lord, begging our bread from door to door. The Lord revealed to me the salutation which we ought to give: "God give you peace!"

Let the brothers take great care not to accept churches, dwellings, or any buildings erected for them, except as all is in accordance with the holy poverty which we have vowed in the Rule; and let them not live in them except as strangers and pilgrims. I absolutely forbid all the brothers, in whatsoever place they may be found, to ask any bull from the court of Rome, whether directly or indirectly, in the interest of church or convent, or under pretext of preaching, or even for the protection of their bodies. If they are not received anywhere, let them go of themselves elsewhere, thus doing penance with the benediction of God. . . .

And let the brothers not say, "This is a new Rule"; for this is only a reminder, a warning, an exhortation. It is my last will and testament, that I, little Brother Francis, make for you, my blessed brothers, in order that we may observe in a more Catholic way the Rule which we promised the Lord to keep.

Let the ministers-general, all the other ministers, and the custodians be held by obedience to add nothing to and take nothing away from these words. Let them always keep this writing near them beside the Rule; and in all the assemblies which shall be held, when the Rule is read, let these words be read also.

I absolutely forbid all the brothers, clerics and laymen, to introduce comments in the Rule, or in this Will, under pretext of explaining it. But since the Lord has given me to speak and to write the Rule and these words in a clear and simple manner, so do you understand them in the same way without commentary, and put them in practice until the end.

And whoever shall have observed these things, may he be crowned in heaven with the blessings of the heavenly Father, and on earth with those of his well-beloved Son and of the Holy Spirit, the Consoler, with the assistance of all the heavenly virtues and all the saints.

And I, little Brother Francis, your servant, confirm to you, so far as I am able, this most holy benediction. Amen.

From Ogg, pp. 376–79.

The Letter of Clare to the Blessed Agnes

To the esteemed and most holy virgin, the Lady Agnes, daughter of the most excellent and illustrious King of Bohemia:

Clare, an unworthy servant of Jesus Christ and *useless* handmaid (cf. Lk 17:10) of the Cloistered Ladies of the Monastery of San Damiano, her subject and servant in all things, presents herself totally with a special reverent [prayer] that she *attain the glory* of everlasting happiness (cf. Sir 50:5).

As I hear of the fame of Your holy conduct and irreproachable life, which is known not only to me but to the entire world as well, *I greatly rejoice and exult in the Lord* (Hab 3:18). I am not alone in rejoicing at such great news, but [I am joined by] all who serve and seek to serve Jesus Christ. For, though You, more than others, could have enjoyed the magnificence and honour and dignity of the world, and could have been married to the illustrious Caesar with splendor befitting You and His Excellency, You have rejected all these things and have chosen with Your whole heart and soul a life of holy poverty and destitution. Thus You took a spouse of a more noble lineage, Who will keep Your virginity ever unspotted and unsullied, the Lord Jesus Christ:

> When You have loved [Him], You shall be chaste; when
>   You have touched [Him], You shall become pure;
>   when you have accepted [Him], You shall be a virgin."
> Whose power is stronger,
> Whose generosity is more abundant,
> Whose appearance more beautiful,
> Whose love more tender,
> Whose courtesy more gracious.
> In Whose embrace You are already caught up;
> Who has adorned Your breast with precious stones
> And has placed priceless pearls in Your ears
> and has surrounded You with sparkling gems
> as though blossoms of springtime
> and placed on Your head *a golden crown*
> *as a sign [to all] of Your holiness.*

Therefore, most beloved sister, or should I say, Lady worthy of great respect: because You are *the spouse and the mother and the sister* of my Lord Jesus Christ (2 Cor 11:2; Mt 12:50), and have been adorned resplendently with the sign of inviolable virginity and most holy poverty: Be strengthened in the holy service which You have undertaken out of an ardent desire for the Poor Crucified, Who for the sake of all of us *took upon Himself* the Passion *of the Cross* (Heb 12:2) and delivered us from the power of the Prince *of Darkness* (Col 1:13) to whom we were enslaved because of the disobedience of our first parent, and so *reconciled us* to God the Father (2 Cor 5:18).

> O blessed poverty,
>> who bestows eternal riches on those who love
>> and embrace her!
> O holy poverty,
>> to those who possess and desire you
>> God promises *the kingdom of heaven*
>> and offers, indeed, eternal glory and blessed life!
> O God-centered poverty,
>> whom the Lord Jesus Christ
>> Who ruled and now rules heaven and earth,
>> Who spoke and things were made,
>> condescended to embrace before all else!

The foxes have dens, He says, *and the birds of the air have nests, but the Son of Man,* Christ, *has nowhere to lay His head* (Mt 8:20), but *bowing His head gave up His spirit* (Jn 19:30).

If so great and good a Lord, then, on coming into the Virgin's womb, chose to appear despised, needy, and *poor* in this world, so that people who were in utter poverty and want and in absolute need of heavenly nourishment might become *rich* (cf. 2 Cor 8:9) in Him by possessing the kingdom of heaven, then *rejoice and be glad* (Hab 3:18)! Be filled with a remarkable happiness and a spiritual joy! Contempt of the world has pleased You more than [its] honours, poverty more than earthly riches, and You have sought to store up greater *treasures in heaven* rather than on earth, *where rust does not consume nor moth destroy nor thieves break in and steal* (Mt 6:20). *Your reward,* then, *is very great in heaven* (Mt 5:12)! And You have truly merited to be called a *sister, spouse, and mother* (2 Cor 11:2; Mt 12:50) of the Son of the Father of the Most High and of the glorious Virgin.

You know, I am sure, that the kingdom of heaven is promised and given by the Lord only to the poor (cf. Mt 5:3): for he who loves temporal things loses the fruit of love. Such a person *cannot serve God and Mammon* [Wealth], for *either the one is loved and the other hated,* or *the one* is served *and the other despised* (Mt 6:24).

You also know that one who is clothed cannot fight with another who is naked, because he is more quickly thrown who gives his adversary a chance to get hold of him; and that one who lives in the glory of earth cannot rule with Christ in heaven.

Again, [you know] that it is easier for *a camel to pass through the eye of a needle than for a rich man to enter the kingdom of heaven* (Mt 19:24). Therefore, you have cast aside Your garments, that is, earthly riches, so that You might not be overcome by the one fighting against You, [and] that You might enter the kingdom of heaven *through the straight path and the narrow gate* (Mt 7: 13–14).

> What a great laudable exchange:
> to leave the things of time for those of eternity,
> to choose the things of heaven for the goods of earth,
> to *receive the hundred-fold* in place on one,
> and *to possess* a blessed and eternal *life*.

Because of this I have resolved, as best I can, to beg Your excellency and Your holiness by my humble prayers in the mercy of Christ, to be strengthened in His holy service, and to progress from good to better, *from virtue to virtue* (Ps 83:8), so that He Whom You serve with the total desire of Your soul may bestow on You the reward for which You long.

I also beg You in the Lord, as much as I can, to include in Your holy prayers me, Your servant, though unworthy, and the other sisters with me in the monastery, who are all devoted to You, so that by their help we may merit the mercy of Jesus Christ, and together with You may merit to enjoy the everlasting vision.

Farewell in the Lord. And pray for me.

From *Francis and Clare* by Regis J. Armstrong, EOF.M.CAP., and Ignatius C. Brady, O.F.M. © 1982 by the Missionary Society of St. Paul the Apostle in the State of New York (New York: Paulist Press, 1982), pp. 190–94. Used by permission of Paulist Press. Notes omitted.

17.3 Mendicant Scholarship: Bonaventure

Saint Bonaventure (1221–1274) was a Franciscan leader and scholar well known for his mystical theology. An Italian by birth, he studied in Paris and eventually rose to become minister-general of the Franciscan Order. He oversaw the reshaping of the order, steering it away from the extremes of the Spiritual Franciscans who wanted to return to the original simplicity of Francis as they saw it, and rejected scholarship (18.2).

Bonaventure was a brilliant scholar in the area of mysticism. Unlike his contemporary, the Dominican Thomas Aquinas (17.4), Bonaventure was not concerned with rational or intellectual apprehensions of God, but solely with the interior or spiritual knowledge of God, somewhat in the tradition of Bernard of Clairvaux (16.1). The excerpt below from the prologue and chapter headings of Bonaventure's work *The Soul's Journey into God* indicates this mystical approach to theology.

Questions

1. What does Bonaventure desire in his studies?
2. What path does he advocate in the quest for the knowledge of God?
3. In what ways is this an expression of Franciscan spirituality?

Mystical Theology: Bonaventure (1221–1274)

Prologue

1. In the beginning
I call upon the First Beginning,
from whom
all illuminations descend
as from the *Father of Lights,*
from whom
comes *every good and every perfect gift.*

I call upon the Eternal Father
through his Son, our Lord Jesus Christ,
that through the intercession of the most holy Virgin Mary,
the mother of the same God and Lord Jesus Christ,
and through the intercession of blessed Francis,
our leader and father,
he *may enlighten the eyes* of our soul
to guide our feet
in the way of that peace
which surpasses all understanding.

This is the peace
proclaimed and given to us
by our Lord Jesus Christ
and preached again and again
by our father Francis.

At the beginning and end of every sermon he announced
    peace;
in every greeting he wished for peace;
in every contemplation he sighed for ecstatic peace—
like a citizen of that Jerusalem of which
that Man of Peace says,
who *was peaceable with those who hated peace:*
Pray for the peace of Jerusalem.

For he knew that the throne of Solomon would not stand
except in peace,
since it is written:
In peace is his place and his abode in Sion.

2. Following the example of our most blessed father Francis, I was
seeking this peace with panting spirit—I a sinner and utterly unworthy who
after our blessed father's death had become the seventh Minister General of
the Friars. It happened that about the time of the thirty-third anniversary of
the Saint's death, under divine impulse, I withdrew to Mount La Verna,
seeking a place of quiet and desiring to find there peace of spirit. While I
was there reflecting on various ways by which the soul ascends into God,
there came to mind, among other things, the miracle which had occurred to
blessed Francis in this very place: the vision of a winged Seraph in the form
of the Crucified. While reflecting on this, I saw at once that this vision
represented our father's rapture in contemplation and the road by which this
rapture is reached.

3. The six wings of the Seraph can rightly be taken to symbolize the six
levels of illumination by which, as if by steps or stages, the soul can pass
over to peace through ecstatic elevations of Christian wisdom. There is no
other path but through the burning love of the Crucified, a love which so
transformed Paul into Christ when he *was carried up to the third heaven* (2
Cor. 12:2) that he could say: *With Christ I am nailed to the cross. I live,
now not I, but Christ lives in me* (Gal. 2:20). This love also so absorbed the
soul of Francis that his spirit shone through his flesh when for two years
before his death he carried in his body the sacred stigmata of the passion.
The six wings of the Seraph, therefore, symbolize the six steps of illumination that begin from creatures and lead up to God, whom no one rightly
enters except through the Crucified. For *he who enters not through the
door, but climbs up another way is a thief and a robber.* But *if anyone enter
through this door, he will go in and out and will find pastures* (John 10: 1,
9). Therefore John says in the Apocalypse: *Blessed are they who wash their*

robes in the blood of the Lamb that they may have a right to the tree of life and may enter the city through the gates (Apoc. 22:14). It is as if John were saying that no one can enter the heavenly Jerusalem by contemplation unless he enter through the blood of the Lamb as through a door. For no one is in any way disposed for divine contemplation that leads to mystical ecstasy unless like Daniel he is *a man of desires* (Dan. 9:23). Such desires are enkindled in us in two ways: by an outcry of prayer that makes us *call aloud in the groaning of our heart* (Ps. 37:9) and by the flash of insight by which the mind turns most directly and intently toward the rays of light.

> 4. First, therefore, I invite the reader
> to the groans of prayer
> through Christ crucified,
> through whose blood
> we are cleansed from the filth of vice—
> so that he not believe
> that reading is sufficient without unction,
> speculation without devotion,
> investigation without wonder,
> observation without joy,
> work without piety,
> knowledge without love,
> understanding without humility,
> endeavor without divine grace,
> reflection as a mirror without divinely inspired wisdom.
> To those, therefore, predisposed by divine grace,
> the humble and the pious,
> the contrite and the devout,
> those anointed with *the oil of gladness,*
> the lovers of divine wisdom, and
> those inflamed with a desire for it,
> to those wishing to give themselves
> to glorifying, wondering at and even savoring God,
> I propose the following considerations,
> suggesting that the mirror presented by the external world
> is of little or no value
> unless the mirror of our soul
> has been cleaned and polished.
>
> Therefore, man of God,
> first exercise yourself in remorse of conscience
> before you raise your eyes

to the rays of Wisdom reflected in its mirrors,
lest perhaps from gazing upon these rays
you fall into a deeper pit of darkness.

5. It seemed good to divide this work into seven chapters,
giving each a title for a better understanding of the
     contents.

I ask you, then,
to weigh the writer's intention rather than his work,
the meaning of his words rather than his uncultivated
     style,
truth rather than beauty,
the exercise of affection rather than erudition of the
     intellect.
To do this,
you should not run rapidly
over the development of these considerations,
but should mull them over slowly
with the greatest care.

HERE ENDS THE PROLOGUE

Chapter Headings

Chapter One: On the Stages of the Ascent into God and on Contemplating Him through His Vestiges in the Universe

Chapter Two: On Contemplating God in His Vestiges in the Sense World

Chapter Three: On Contemplating God through His Image Stamped upon our Natural Powers

Chapter Four: On Contemplating God in His Image Reformed by the Gifts of Grace

Chapter Five: On Contemplating the Divine Unity through Its Primary Name Which Is Being

Chapter Six: On Contemplating the Most Blessed Trinity in Its Name Which Is Good

Chapter Seven: On Spiritual and Mystical Ecstasy in Which Rest Is Given to Our Intellect When through Ecstasy Our Affection Passes Over Entirely into God

From Bonaventure, *The Soul's Journey into God,* by Ewert Cousins. © 1978 by The Missionary Society of St. Paul the Apostle in the State of New York (New York: Paulist Press, 1978), pp. 53–58. Used by permission of Paulist Press. Notes omitted.

17.4 Intellectual Synthesis: Thomas Aquinas

Thomas Aquinas (1225–1274) had the most profound impact on Catholic thought since Augustine of Hippo. Often in histories of medieval theology, authors refer to early medieval "Augustinian" thought as replaced by "Thomist." Thomist theology dominates Catholic doctrine from the thirteenth century down through the modern era.

Aquinas is another Italian, like Bonaventure, who was educated in Paris. Unlike the Franciscan Bonaventure, Aquinas was a Dominican, who remained a scholar in Paris and Italy for the rest of his life. His life's work was to demonstrate how Aristotelian thought could work with Christian theology. His synthesis was an effort to resolve the tension between extreme rationalists, Averröists (15.3), and their opponents, such as Bernard of Clairvaux (16.1), who feared that this humanist reasoning would destroy faith.

Aquinas used reason, then, to demonstrate the superiority of Christian belief over Judaism and Islam. In his massive *Summa Theologica,* which he started in 1266, Thomas assembled reasoned arguments on virtually every theological subject, integrating the ideas of Aristotle ("the Philosopher") and Christian thought. The excerpt below on the question of God's existence is comparable to the arguments of Anselm (15.1) and Moses Maimonides (15.4), and to the methods of Abelard (15.2) and Averröes (15.3).

Questions

1. What is Aquinas's purpose in writing, and how does that compare to Bonaventure's reasons for writing about God?

2. How does Aquinas show that the existence of God is a logical belief? How does that compare to Anselm's arguments?

3. How does Aquinas's method of argument work? How does it compare to the works of Abelard, Averröes, and Maimonides?

Thomas Aquinas, Summa Theologica

Prologue

Because the Doctor of catholic truth ought not only to teach the proficient, but also to instruct beginners (according to the Apostle: As unto little ones in Christ, I gave you milk to drink, not meat (1 Cor. 3:1–2), we purpose in this book to treat of whatever belongs to the Christian religion, in such a way as may tend to the instruction of beginners. We have considered that students in this doctrine have not seldom [i.e., frequently] been hampered by what they have found written by other authors, partly on account of the multiplication of useless questions, articles, and arguments, partly also because those things that are needful for them to know are not taught according to the order of the subject matter, but according as the plan of the book might require, or the occasion of the argument offer, partly, too, because frequent repetition brought weariness and confusion to the minds of readers. Endeavoring to avoid these and other like faults, we shall try, by God's help, to set forth whatever is included in this sacred doctrine as briefly and clearly as the matter itself may allow. . . .

First Part, Question 2: The Existence of God

Whether the Existence of God Is Self-Evident?

Objection 1. It seems that the existence of God is self-evident. Now those things are said to be self-evident to us the knowledge of which is naturally implanted in us, as we can see in regard to first principles. But as Damascene says (*De Fide Orth.* i, 1, 3), *the knowledge of God is naturally implanted in all.* Therefore the existence of God is self-evident.

Obj[ection] 2. Further, those things are said to be self-evident which are known as soon as the terms are known, which the Philosopher (1 *Poster.* iii) says is true of the first principles of demonstration. Thus, when the nature of a whole and of a part is known, it is at once recognized that every whole is greater than its part. But as soon as the signification of the word "God" is understood, it is at once seen that God exists. For by this word is signified that thing than which nothing greater can be conceived. But that which exists actually and mentally is greater than that which exists only mentally. Therefore, since as soon as the word "God" is understood it exists mentally, it also follows that it exists actually. Therefore the proposition "God exists" is self-evident.

Obj[ection] 3. Further, the existence of truth is self-evident. For whoever denies the existence of truth grants that truth does not exist: and, if truth does not exist, then the proposition "Truth does not exist" is true: and if there is anything true, there must be truth. But God is truth itself: *I am the way, the truth, and the life* (Jn. 14:6). Therefore "God exists" is self-evident.

On the contrary, No one can mentally admit the opposite of what is self-evident; as the Philosopher (*Metaph.* iv, lect. vi) states concerning the first principles of demonstration. But the opposite of the proposition "God is" can be mentally admitted: *The fool said in his heart, There is no God* (Ps. 52:1). Therefore, that God exists is not self-evident.

I answer that, A thing can be self-evident in either of two ways: on the one hand, self-evident in itself, though not to us; on the other, self-evident in itself, and to us. A proposition is self-evident because the predicate is included in the essence of the subject, as "Man is an animal," for animal is contained in the essence of man. If, therefore the essence of the predicate and subject be known to all, the proposition will be self-evident to all; as is clear with regard to the first principles of demonstration, the terms of which are common things that no one is ignorant of, such as being and non-being, whole and part, and such like. If, however, there are some to whom the essence of the predicate and subject is unknown, the proposition will be self-evident in itself, but not to those who do not know the meaning of the predicate and subject of the proposition. Therefore, it happens, as Boëthius says *(Hebdom., the title of which is: "Whether all that is, is good"),* "that there are some mental concepts self-evident only to the learned, as that incorporeal substances are not in space." Therefore I say that this proposition, "God exists," of itself is self-evident, for the predicate is the same as the subject; because God is His own existence as will be hereafter shown (Q.3, A.4). Now because we do not know the essence of God, the proposition is not self-evident to us; but needs to be demonstrated by things that are more known to us, though less known in their nature—namely, by effects.

Reply [to] Ob[jection] 1. To know that God exists in a general and confused way is implanted in us by nature, inasmuch as God is man's beatitude. For man naturally desires happiness, and what is naturally desired by man must be naturally known to him. This, however, is not to know absolutely that God exists; just as to know that someone is approaching is not the same as to know that Peter is approaching, even though it is Peter who is approaching; for many there are who imagine that man's perfect good which is happiness, consists in riches, and others in pleasures, and others in something else.

Reply [to] Obj[ection] 2. Perhaps not everyone who hears this word "God" understands it to signify something than which nothing greater can be thought, seeing that some have believed God to be a body. Yet, granted that everyone understands that by this word "God" is signified something than which nothing greater can be thought, nevertheless, it does not therefore follow that he understands that what the word signifies exists actually, but only that it exists mentally. Nor can it be argued that it actually exists, unless it be admitted that there actually exists something than which nothing greater can be thought; and this precisely is not admitted by those who hold that God does not exist.

Reply [to] Obj[ection] 3. The existence of truth in general is self-evident but the existence of a Primal Truth is not self-evident to us. . . .

Whether It Can Be Demonstrated That God Exists?

Objection 1. It seems that the existence of God cannot be demonstrated. For it is an article of faith that God exists. But what is of faith cannot be demonstrated, because a demonstration produces scientific knowledge; whereas faith is of the unseen (Heb. 11:1). Therefore it cannot be demonstrated that God exists.

Obj[ection] 2. Further, the essence is the middle term of demonstration. But we cannot know in what God's essence consists, but solely in what it does not consist; as Damascene says (*De Fide Orth.* i, 4). Therefore we cannot demonstrate that God exists.

Obj[ection] 3. Further, if the existence of God were demonstrated, this could only be from His effects. But His effects are not proportionate to Him, since He is infinite and His effects are finite; and between the finite and infinite there is no proportion. Therefore, since a cause cannot be demonstrated by an effect not proportionate to it, it seems that the existence of God cannot be demonstrated.

On the contrary, the Apostle says: *The invisible things of Him are clearly seen, being understood by the things that are made* (Rom. 1:20). But this would not be unless the existence of God could be demonstrated through the things that are made; for the first thing we must know of anything is, whether it exists.

I answer that, Demonstration can be made in two ways: One is through the cause, and is called *a priori,* and this is to argue from what is prior absolutely. The other is through the effect, and is called a demonstration *a posteriori;* this is to argue from what is prior relatively only to us. When an effect is better known to us than its cause, from the effect we proceed to the knowledge of the cause. And from every effect the existence of its proper cause can be demonstrated, so long as its effects are better known to us; because since every effect depends upon its cause, if the effect exists, the cause must pre-exist. Hence the existence of God, in so far as it is not self-evident to us, can be demonstrated from those of His effects which are known to us.

Reply [to] Obj[ection] 1. The existence of God and other like truths about God, which can be known by natural reason, are not articles of faith, but are preambles to the articles; for faith presupposes natural knowledge, even as grace presupposes nature, and perfection supposes something that can be perfected. Nevertheless, there is nothing to prevent a man, who cannot grasp a proof, accepting, as a matter of faith, something which in itself is capable of being scientifically known and demonstrated.

Reply [to] Obj[ection] 2. When the existence of a cause is demonstrated from an effect, this effect takes the place of the definition of the cause in proof of the cause's existence. This is especially the case in regard to God, because, in order to prove the existence of anything, it is necessary to accept as a middle term the meaning of the word, and not its essence, for the question of its essence follows on the question of its existence. Now the names given to God are derived from His effects; consequently, in demonstrating the existence of God from His effects, we may take for the middle term the meaning of the word "God."

Reply [to] Obj[ection] 3. From effects not proportionate to the cause no perfect knowledge of that cause can be obtained. Yet from every effect the existence of the cause can be clearly demonstrated, and so we can demonstrate the existence of God from His effects; though from them we cannot perfectly know God as He is in His essence. . . .

Whether God Exists?

Objection 1. It seems that God does not exist; because if one of two contraries be infinite, the other would be altogether destroyed. But the word "God" means that He is infinite goodness. If, therefore, God existed, there would be no evil discoverable; but there is evil in the world. Therefore God does not exist.

Obj[ection] 2. Further, it is superfluous to suppose that what can be accounted for by a few principles has been produced by many. But it seems that everything we see in the world can be accounted for by other principles, supposing God did not exist. For all natural things can be reduced to one principle which is nature; and all voluntary things can be reduced to one principle which is human reason, or will. Therefore there is no need to suppose God's existence.

On the contrary, It is said in the person of God: *I am Who am.* (Ex. 3:14).

I answer that, The existence of God can be proved in five ways.

The first and more manifest way is the argument from motion. It is certain, and evident to our senses, that in the world some things are in motion. Now whatever is in motion is put in motion by another, for nothing can be in motion except it is in potentiality to that towards which it is in motion; whereas a thing moves inasmuch as it is in act. For motion is nothing else than the reduction of something from potentiality to actuality. But nothing can be reduced from potentiality to actuality, except by something in a state of actuality. Thus that which is actually hot, as fire, makes wood, which is potentially hot, to be actually hot, and thereby moves and changes it. Now it is not possible that the same thing should be at once in actuality and potentiality in the same respect, but only in different respects. For what is actually hot cannot simultaneously be potentially hot; but it is simultaneously potentially cold. It is therefore impossible that in the same respect and in the same way a thing should be both mover and moved, *i.e.,* that it should move itself. Therefore, whatever is in motion must be put in motion by another. If that by which it is put in motion be itself put in motion, then this also must needs be put in motion by another, and that by another again. But this cannot go on to infinity, because then there would be no first mover, and, consequently, no other mover; seeing that subsequent movers move only inasmuch as they are put in motion by the first mover; as the staff moves only because it is put in motion by the hand. Therefore it is necessary to arrive at a first mover, put in motion by no other; and this everyone understands to be God.

The second way is from the nature of the efficient cause. In the world of sense we find there is an order of efficient causes. There is no case known (neither is it, indeed, possible) in which a thing is found to be the efficient cause of itself; for so it would be prior to itself, which is impossible. Now in efficient causes it is not possible to go on to infinity, because in all efficient causes following in order, the first is the cause of the intermediate cause, and the intermediate is the cause of the ultimate cause, whether the intermediate cause be several, or one only. Now to take away the cause is to take away the effect. Therefore, if there be no first cause among efficient causes, there will be no ultimate, nor any intermediate cause. But if in efficient causes it is possible to go on to infinity, there will be no first efficient cause, neither will there be an ultimate effect, nor any intermediate efficient causes; all of which is plainly false. Therefore it is necessary to admit a first efficient cause, to which everyone gives the name of God.

The third way is taken from possibility and necessity, and runs thus. We find in nature things that are possible to be and not to be, since they are found to be generated, and to corrupt, and consequently, they are possible to be and not to be. But it is impossible for these always to exist, for that which is possible not to be at some time is not. Therefore, if everything is possible not to be, then at one time there could have been nothing in existence. Now if this were true, even now there would be nothing in existence, because that which does not exist only begins to exist by something already existing. Therefore, if at one time nothing was in existence, it would have been impossible for anything to have begun to exist; and thus even now nothing would be in existence—which is absurd. Therefore, not all beings are merely possible, but there must exist something the existence of which is necessary. But every necessary thing either has its necessity caused by another, or not. Now it is impossible to go on to infinity in necessary things which have their necessity caused by another, as has been already proved in regard to efficient causes. Therefore we cannot but postulate the existence of some being having of itself its own necessity, and not receiving it from another, but rather causing in others their necessity. This all men speak of as God.

The fourth way is taken from the gradation to be found in things. Among beings there are some more and some less good, true, noble and the like. But "more" and "less" are predicated of different things, according as they resemble in their different ways something which is the maximum, as a thing is said to be hotter according as it more nearly resembles that which is hottest; so that there is something which is truest, something best, something noblest and, consequently, something which is uttermost being; for those things that are greatest in truth are greatest in being, as it is written in *Metaph.* ii [Aristotle's *Metaphysics*]. Now the maximum in any genus is the cause of all in that genus; as fire, which is the maximum of heat, is the cause of all hot things. Therefore there must also be something which is to all beings the cause of their being, goodness, and every other perfection; and this we call God.

The fifth way is taken from the governance of the world. We see that things which lack intelligence, such as natural bodies, act for an end, and this is evident from their acting always, or nearly always, in the same way, so as to obtain the best result. Hence it is plain that not fortuitously, but designedly, do they achieve their end. Now whatever lacks intelligence cannot move towards an end, unless it be directed by some being endowed with knowledge and intelligence; as the arrow is shot to its mark by the archer. Therefore some intelligent being exists by whom all natural things are directed to their end; and this being we call God.

Reply [to] Obj[ection] 1. As Augustine says *(Enchir.* xi) *[Enchiridion]: Since God is the highest good, He would not allow any evil to exist in His works, unless His omnipotence and goodness were such as to bring good even out of evil.* This is part of the infinite goodness of God, that He should allow evil to exist, and out of it produce good.

Reply [to] Obj[ection] 2. Since nature works for a determinate end under the direction of a higher agent, whatever is done by nature must needs be traced back to God, as to its first cause. So also whatever is done voluntarily must also be traced back to some higher cause other than human reason or will, since these can change and fail; for all things that are changeable and capable of defect must be traced back to an immovable and self-necessary first principle, as was shown in the body of the *Article*.

Reprinted with permission from Thomas Aquinas, *Summa Theologica,* trans. Fathers of the English Dominican Province (New York: Benzinger Brothers, 1947), pp. 11–14.

–18–

Over the Line

Heretics, Inquisitors, and Other Radicals

Efforts in the thirteenth century to define and defend a European Christian identity often collided and produced tension between the spirits of prophecy and order. In the spirit of prophecy, many groups sought to return to the radical spiritual values of the martyrs, hermits, mystics, monks, and ascetics found in church history. Others, in the spirit of order, attempted to define systems of authority that would be impervious to corruption or influence. As evident in Chapter 17, both the spirit of order and the spirit of prophecy could effect remarkable reform, often working together, as in Pope Innocent III's convening of the Fourth Lateran Council and his approval of the Franciscan movement. However, reform in the order or in the spirit of Christianity often came into conflict with one another, as this chapter demonstrates. In the same spirit of prophecy that produced the Franciscans, heretical groups focused on poverty and spirituality rejected the order and materialism of the church. In the same spirit of order as Innocent's claims to papal monarchy, subsequent pope's extended papal supremacy, only to be met with powerful kings and scholarly political theorists opposing interference in the establishment of royal sovereignty.

The first two selections in this chapter examine the prophetic voices of spiritual reform found in the Waldensian and Albigensian heresies (18.1), and the Spiritual Franciscans (18.2). The same forces that produced the mendicant movement, lay piety responding to urban materialism, also generated "heresies," groups whom the church authorities declared to be outside the bounds of orthodoxy. Heresy as such exists only in opposition to an authoritative orthodoxy: groups that reject the church's authority to determine what is right are consequently declared heretical by church authorities. The church condemned groups for two

412

broad, and interrelated, reasons: theologies that varied from what the church taught, and defiance of the authority of the clergy (priests, bishops, popes). The church's opposition to these heresies leads to the creation of the inquisition as a tool of papal authority in Europe.

The third selection (18.3) also involves heretical opinions threatening the order of the church, in the form of political theories of power. As papal claims to supremacy increased in stridency—as, for example, under Pope Boniface VIII—theorists such as Marsilius of Padua began to formulate secular political claims rooted in law. Marsilius' theories were condemned as heretical, but nonetheless reflected an increasing secular view of political life that would come to dominate in the Renaissance. In all three sections of this chapter, authority in relation to heresy is a dominant issue that bears examining.

18.1 Heresy and Inquisition: Waldensians and Albigensians

The Waldensians and the Albigensians are good examples of the nature of heresy and the way that it grew in response to the materialism of society and in reaction to the dominance of the clergy. Their heretical theologies differ, but both of these heresies challenged church authority. The two documents here are descriptions from outsiders: the chronicle describing Waldo is anonymous and somewhat neutral, while the inquisitor Bernard Gui's interest in the Albigensians is professional and hostile.

Waldo (d. circa 1216), founder of the Waldensians, is in some ways similar to Francis and Clare (17.2). A merchant of Lyons, Waldo gave all of his wealth away and adopted poverty as a lifestyle in imitation of the apostles (circa 1173). He and his followers requested permission from the church to preach, but were turned down as uneducated lay people, including women, unfit to teach in the eyes of the church. By continuing to preach and teach, the Waldensians defied church authority and were branded heretical. As they moved in this direction of defiance, the Waldensians increasingly questioned the role of the clergy as necessary mediators in the spiritual life of the believer. Even though Waldo's movement sprang from the same desires as Francis's, Waldo's developed into heresy as a reaction from orthodoxy. The excerpt below is from a chronicle describing Waldo's conversion and his practices.

The Albigensian, or Cathar, heresy also reacted to the dominance of the clergy and the wealth of the church, but deviated dramatically from orthodoxy in its theology. The *Cathari* (the "Pure") revived Gnostic dualism (3.1). They posited the existence of two deities, one good and one evil, locked in a battle (a view rooted in Persian Zoroastrianism). Like earlier Gnostics and the Manichean heresy of Augustine of Hippo's time, the Cathars believed matter was evil, created by the evil God shown in the Old Testament story of Genesis. Christ represents the good

God and is pure spirit. As a result, Cathars advocated a strict, ascetic life to escape the materiality of the body; the few who achieved this lifestyle were known as the *perfecti*. A wider group of followers supported the Albigensian rejection of church wealth, often advocating, and carrying out, the appropriation of church property. Southern France was a hotbed for the Albigensian heresy, breaking into outright rebellion. Such an open challenge to church authority was perceived as dangerous to all of Christendom. When more peaceful efforts at eradicating this heresy failed (such as the preaching endeavors of Saint Dominic), Pope Innocent III authorized force by summoning a crusade against the Albigensians, a bloody affair which lasted from 1208 to 1229.

The Albigensian Crusade was a success for the authorities involved: the French monarchy extended its dominance over the area, and the papacy established a central office of inquiry (inquisition) into heresy, rather than leaving the task up to local church authorities. The powers of the inquisitors, using for example torture and secret testimony, provoked local reactions to this assertion of centralized power over regional authorities such as local bishops and lords. Thus, the stamping out of heresy and the assertion of papal authority evident in such inquisitions is one marker of the growth of church centralization. The document below is from Bernard Gui, an inquisitor who kept excellent records of his investigations, including details of the objectionable practices of the Albigensians.

Questions

1. What motivates Waldo? Compare his ideals with those of Francis.
2. Why do people around Waldo, such as his wife and the church authorities, disagree with his mission?
3. What is objectionable to Bernard Gui in the Albigensian beliefs and practices, and why?

Description of Waldo from An Anonymous Chronicle of 1218

And during the same year, that is the 1173d since the Lord's Incarnation, there was at Lyons in France a certain citizen, Waldo by name, who had made himself much money by wicked usury. One Sunday, when he had joined a crowd which he saw gathered around a troubadour, he was smitten by his words and, taking him to his house, he took care to hear him at length. The passage he was reciting was how the holy Alexis died a blessed death in his father's house. When morning had come the prudent citizen hurried to the schools of theology to seek counsel for his soul, and when he was taught many ways of going to God, he asked the master what way was more certain and more perfect than all others. The master answered him with this text: "If thou wilt be perfect, go and sell all that thou hast," etc.

Then Waldo went to his wife and gave her the choice of keeping his personal property or his real estate, namely, what he had in ponds, groves and fields, houses, rents, vineyards, mills, and fishing rights. She was much displeased at having to make this choice, but she kept the real estate. From his personal property he made restitution to those whom he had treated unjustly; a great part of it he gave to his two little daughters, who, without their mother's knowledge, he placed in the convent of Font Evrard; but the greatest part of his money he spent for the poor. A very great famine was then oppressing France and Germany. The prudent citizen, Waldo, gave bread, with vegetables and meat, to every one who came to him for three days in every week from Pentecost to the feast of St. Peter's bonds.

At the Assumption of the blessed Virgin, casting some money among the village poor, he cried, "No man can serve two masters, God and mammon." Then his fellow-citizens ran up, thinking he had lost his mind. But going on to a higher place, he said: "My fellow-citizens and friends, I am not insane, as you think, but I am avenging myself on my enemies, who made me a slave, so that I was always more careful of money than of God, and served the creature rather than the Creator. I know that many will blame me that I act thus openly. But I do it both on my own account and on yours; on my own, so that those who see me henceforth possessing any money may say that I am mad, and on yours, that you may learn to place hope in God and not in riches."

On the next day, coming from the church, he asked a certain citizen, once his comrade, to give him something to eat, for God's sake. His friend, leading him to his house, said, "I will give you whatever you need as long as I live." When this came to the ears of his wife, she was not a little troubled, and as though she had lost her mind, she ran to the archbishop of the city and implored him not to let her husband beg bread from any one but her. This moved all present to tears.

[Waldo was accordingly conducted into the presence of the bishop.] And the woman, seizing her husband by the coat, said, "Is it not better, husband, that I should redeem my sins by giving you alms than that strangers should do so?" And from that time he was not allowed to take food from any one in that city except from his wife.

From Robinson, pp. 380–81.

Bernard Gui, *Inquisitor's Guide*, on the Albigensians

It would take too long to describe in detail the manner in which these same Manichaean heretics preach and teach their followers, but it must be briefly considered here.

In the first place, they usually say of themselves that they are good Christians, who do not swear, or lie, or speak evil of others; that they do not kill any man or animal, nor anything having the breath of life, and that they hold the faith of the Lord Jesus Christ and his gospel as Christ and his apostles taught. They assert that they occupy the place of the apostles, and that, on account of the above-mentioned things, they of the Roman Church, namely the prelates, clerks, and monks, and especially the inquisitors of heresy, persecute them and call them heretics, although they are good men and good Christians, and that they are persecuted just as Christ and his apostles were by the Pharisees.

Moreover they talk to the laity of the evil lives of the clerks and prelates of the Roman Church, pointing out and setting forth their pride, cupidity, avarice, and uncleanness of life, and such other evils as they know. They invoke, with their own interpretation and according to their abilities, the authority of the Gospels and the Epistles against the condition of the prelates, churchmen, and monks, whom they call Pharisees and false prophets, who say, but do not.

Then they attack and vituperate, in turn, all the sacraments of the Church, especially the sacrament of the eucharist, saying that it cannot contain the body of Christ, for had this been as great as the largest mountain Christians would have entirely consumed it before this. They assert that the host comes from straw, that it passes through the tails of horses, to wit, when the flour is cleaned by a sieve (of horse hair); that moreover, it passes through the body and comes to a vile end, which, they say, could not happen if God were it.

Of baptism, they assert that water is material and corruptible, and is therefore the creation of the evil power and cannot sanctify the soul, but that the churchmen sell this water out of avarice, just as they sell earth for the burial of the dead, and oil to the sick when they anoint them, and as they sell the confession of sins as made to the priests.

Hence they claim that confession made to the priests of the Roman Church is useless, and that, since the priests may be sinners, they cannot loose nor bind, and, being unclean themselves, cannot make others clean. They assert, moreover, that the cross of Christ should not be adored or venerated, because, as they urge, no one would venerate or adore the gallows upon which a father, relative, or friend had been hung. They urge, further, that they who adore the cross ought, for similar reasons, to worship all thorns and lances, because as Christ's body was on the cross during the passion, so was the crown of thorns on his head and the soldier's lance in his side. They proclaim many other scandalous things in regard to the sacraments.

Moreover they read from the Gospels and the Epistles in the vulgar tongue, applying and expounding them in their favor and against the condition of the Roman Church in a manner which it would take too long to describe in detail; but all that relates to this subject may be read more fully in the books they have written and infected, and may be learned from the confessions of such of their followers as have been converted.

From Robinson, pp. 381–83.

18.2 Spiritual Franciscans: Na Prous Boneta

The Franciscans and the Waldensians stand on either side of the line between orthodoxy and heresy. Francis's order was approved by the pope, Waldo's was not. While Waldo rejected the authority of the priesthood, Francis clearly acknowledged it in his will. The Waldensians remained a lay, grassroots organization operating independently; the Franciscans became a normative part of the church structure. In the opinion of some followers of Francis, the incorporation of the order under the church's authority, with the consequent growth in power and prestige and the decline in radical poverty, was a betrayal of Francis's ideals. The Spiritual Franciscans sought to restore this pristine ideal. They challenged the order of the church by asserting the supremacy of the voice of prophecy, and ended up being declared heretical.

Na Prous Boneta was a Spiritual Franciscan, follower of the charismatic leader Peter John Olivi, who preached an apocalyptic message and taught radical poverty. Na Prous was condemned and executed for heresy by the inquisition in 1325. Her beliefs, visions, and claims to authority are known only from the following inquisition record.

Questions

1. For what reasons would inquisitors find Na Prous guilty of heresy?

2. What does she have to say about the authority of the church, and what claims does she make about her own authority?

3. Compare Na Prous to other visionary women, such as Perpetua (4.1), Marie D'Oignies (13.4), and Hildegard of Bingen (16.4). In what ways is she speaking in the same vein? In what ways is she "over the line?"

The Confession of Na Prous Boneta

The Confession of Na Prous Boneta, Heretic and Heresiarch,
Carcassone, France, 6 August 1325

Na Prous (Lady Prous) Boneta, the daughter of Duradus Bonetus, of the parish of St. Michael de Cadyera, in the diocese of Nimes, who was an inhabitant of Montpellier from about the age of seven years, as she says, and who was arrested there, accused and suspected of the heresy of the burned Beguines, was brought to the city wall of Carcassone, so that her confession made in court might be established legitimately, and set down freely, willingly, and without interrogation. In the year of our Lord 1325, on the sixth of August, she said and claimed that on Good Friday four years ago from her confession made in court as written below, while she was in the church of the Franciscans in Montpellier where she was listening to the service with some other people, she adored the crucifix, as it is customary to do. When she had made her adoration in this way, and had returned to her seat, the office being completed and the church emptied of most of the people, the Lord Jesus Christ transported her in spirit, indeed in her soul, up to the first heaven. When she was there she saw Jesus Christ in the form of a man as well as in his divinity; he appeared to her who is speaking, and showed her his heart, perforated almost like the little openings in a small lantern. From this heart there went out solar rays, indeed, rays brighter than the sun, which shone all around her. All at once she saw, clearly and openly, the divinity of God, who in spirit gave her his heart.

She drew near to him, and put her head on the body of Christ, and she saw nothing but such great clarity as Christ gave to her in those rays. Then she was returned to the place where she first saw that clarity and looked on Christ himself, and thus gazing at the rays, little by little, that is *petit a petit,* they covered the whole of Christ's body. When this had been seen and done, Christ replaced her in her seat as she had been before. When she came to herself in the greatest tears and weeping, in great warmth and love toward God, she wanted her other women companions and people to know what had happened. She didn't move from there until her companions called her. Then she got up and went out of the church, and in the cemetery she saw for the second time the Man with whom she wanted to sojourn, and rays again surrounded her, like the first time.

When she was at home and at table with her companions, and they were talking about the sermon they'd heard, the rays again shone all about her, and because of them she was so kindled with fervor and love that she couldn't eat. Leaving the table, she went up to the solar and began to pray. Afterwards, they went to the Tenebrae service, and there, in the same church as before, she saw a certain lady who spoke to her and immediately vanished.

She also said and claimed that on the following Holy Saturday, when she was again there in the church for the service, at the time of the elevation of the Host or a little before, God the Father appeared to her. High contemplation was given to her by God, and the grace of contemplating heaven and of seeing our Lord Jesus Christ, as well as continuous prayer and a continual sensing of Our Lord. From then on, so she claims, very often our Lord God said to her, "I myself have given Him to you, as to the Virgin, and I have kept Him with me." She claims that she frequently saw the Lord God to face, and he came there in the form and species of a man. Afterwards there was preached an indulgence at Magalone, to which she wanted to go, but the Lord prevented her from going, and said to her who is telling this, "Do you remember I shall be the Lord of one soul?" God then added, "Saint John the Baptist was the herald of the advent of Jesus Christ's holy baptism, and you are the herald of the advent of the Holy Spirit."

After she heard this, she realized that the Lord was comparing her first to the Virgin and then to Blessed John the Baptist, and in her heart she thought that she was unworthy of being compared with the Virgin and of being called the handmaiden of Christ, and unworthy of being compared with St. John, a voice crying in the wilderness. So she replied to the Lord, "Lord, I am truly nothing, for I feel myself to be a sinner and sin is nothing." She gave herself to contemplation, and prayed God to give that grace to another.

At length the Lord responded, "Whether you are willing or unwilling, this shall be yours." And the Lord added, "I myself give Him to you, and I myself retain Him." But this time He didn't say "as to the virgin" as he had said above, but he said it as she said.

She also claimed that she was accustomed to say prayers: in a loud voice she cried out to God three times, "Friend, friend, friend," but God the Lord didn't reply until the third cry and then he showed himself in a cloud and said this:

"And you, what do you want?"

She answered, "Lord, may you have mercy on all the sins of the Jews, the Saracens, and all the peoples of the world. Lord, grant this to us by your great mercy, and by the merit of your good works, that we may always live faithfully in your trust. Also, Lord, may you have mercy on yours and your poor family. May honor and glory be granted unto you, Lord."

When this prayer was over, the Lord God replied, "I know whom I have chosen." And however many times she completed this prayer, she fell into ecstasy, so she said, for she desired so much that God be loved and honored, and she was so indebted that frequently she slipped away while still speaking. . . .

Shortly afterwards she saw two other persons like God himself, who were joined in order one after the other; one of them began to run, and on his way put himself on the neck of her who is telling this, and another placed himself on her right arm. From then on the three persons of the Trinity came to her, and she saw them; this seeing was spiritual and not corporeal, just as sometimes something is seen by one person mentally which is seen physically by another—but she saw only spiritually. She also claimed that God frequently said to her, "I go away totally and I return, for I have chosen and made my chamber in you."

Also one time the Lord leapt on her neck and fashioned a white horse with a man on it for her, saying, "See how this man controls this horse however he wishes. Thus am I above all nature, and I rule you as I will, and I am with you wherever you are."

She further claims that the divinity which God gave to her telling this formed for itself a body of more precious and more pure understanding than the one she had, and there was no angel nor archangel nor saint in paradise who might have administered or impeded this. She likewise claims that the spirit which God gave her at another time despoiled hell and repaired all human nature. Also that God said to her, "The Blessed Virgin Mary was the donatrix of the Son of God and you shall be the donatrix of the Holy Spirit."

When she who is telling this heard this, she grew afraid and prayed God, saying, "Lord God, guard me from that sin of pride through which the angel Lucifer fell from heaven."

And the Lord God replied, "I shall hear your prayer."

She also claimed that God told her that Christ had two natures, one human and the other divine, and that the Gospel being destroyed is against his human nature, and that the destruction of the writing of the Holy Spirit given to Friar Peter John is against His divine nature.

Also Christ told her that the pope preceding the present one was like that good man who placed the body of Christ crucified in the tomb, and that this present pope, John XXII, is like Caiaphas, who crucified Christ. The poor Beguines who were burned, and also the burned lepers, were like the innocents beheaded by the command of Herod; likewise, just as Herod procured the death of innocent boy children, thus this Herod, the devil, procured the death of these burned Beguines and lepers. Similarly she claimed that Christ told her that the sin of this pope is as great as the sin of Cain, and a fourth part of it is as great as the sin of Caiaphas, and a fifth part as great as was the sin of Simon Magus, and another part as great as was the sin of Herod.

Christ also told her, as she claims, that the sin of this pope, when he betrayed the Franciscan friars to death, was as great as the sin of Adam when he ate the apple. And that when he condemned the Gospel, the sin of this pope was as great as the sin of Adam when he tasted the apple and took it out of greed, perceiving that he sinned; for it was then that he ought to have sought mercy from the Lord God our God.

Also that the sin of this pope, when he condemned the writing of Friar Peter John, the holy father, was as great as the sin of Adam when he ate the apple and on account of that accused the woman Eve, imputing to Eve the blame for this—that he had eaten the apple offered to him by her, for he ought to have ruled her, when he is the head of the woman, and instead he accused her. This pope is similar, for as head of the holy church of God, he should have ruled the church according to the will of God, that is, the will of our Lord Jesus Christ. And in just the same way as Adam, on account of this sin, lost the grace earlier given to him by God, so this pope, on the account of his sin, lost the grace given to him by the Lord Jesus Christ, for the punishment is equal to the sin, and consequently the sacraments have lost their virtue. Also, just as Adam could never regain the grace which he had lost, so this pope shall never regain the grace he lost, that he had at first; for just as the whole human nature was dead spiritually on account of the said Adam, the first man, so Christianity as a whole is dead spiritually because of this pope's sin.

Since the pope destroyed the writing of Friar Peter John, written by the hand of divinity, the sacrament of the altar lost its virtue and power, which it shall never recover. For this reason God took away from the pope and all others the grace of the sacraments. Likewise Jesus Christ told her, as she claimed, that St. Peter had confessed that Jesus Christ was the true Son of the living God, and that this pope confessed Christ to be a sinner, in that he said that Christ owned things in common with others and personally for his own use.

Jesus Christ told her that St. Francis began his order in that same perfection and altitude as had Christ, when he began with his apostles to hold to poverty, in that same perfection and altitude St. Francis began to hold to poverty with his brothers.

Whatever men and women who had vowed virginity and chastity and afterwards were given husbands or wives were discarded and led to evil by the pope; this pope similarly carried away from Christ all those men and women who, on account of the fear of those works that are going on presently [that is, the Inquisition and persecution of the Spiritual Franciscans], are given over to doing evil and saying and swearing ignobly concerning God.

Jesus Christ told her, as she claimed, that since this pope had produced so much wind and stupidity, so much malice and evil, therefore, as Christ had at first given him a name more beautiful than all the men of this world, so Christ himself afterwards gave the same pope the name more horrifying than all the men of this world; for first he was called apostle or pope, and afterwards Christ gave him this more terrifying name, that is, Antichrist, which name Christ imposed on him, as she asserted, on the next to the last Friday before the feast of the Lord's Nativity just passed. . . .

Likewise that God, when he ordained the orders of St. Francis and St. Dominic, did a great work, as great as when he created the world.

Likewise that as many souls as he has saved from the creation of the world up to that time in which he established the two orders, so many souls will he save until the end of the world. Likewise that as many saints as there were up to the aforesaid time, so many and such great saints shall there be until the end of the world.

Likewise, that St. Francis is as great a saint in paradise as is Blessed John the Baptist, for just as Blessed John prepared the way before the Lord, so St. Francis prepared the way before the Holy Spirit. Likewise the Lord told her, as she claims, that as many graces and as much glory as the Lord gave to Brother Peter John, so much and so many he gave to the Son of God in person, that is, to the extent that he was man and not to the extent that he was God; and for this reason it will now be necessary to believe that the Lord God gave to the said Friar Peter John the spirit completely, for otherwise men and women would not be saved. For she claims accordingly that God told her that in the body of Jesus Christ and in the body of his Mother, that is, the Virgin Mary, there was not any mingling of natures, when the whole might be everywhere the same. Likewise between the spirit in the body of the said friar Peter John and the spirit in the body of the one speaking, Na Prous, there is no mingling, for the spirit of friar Peter John and the spirit of Na Prous are one and the same, since the whole descends from God, as she said.

Likewise the Lord told her that in the same way as he, God, ruled the Church through the two bodies of flesh, that is, the bodies of Christ and of his mother the Virgin Mary, so in the same way he rules from henceforth the church through the two bodies of the spirit given to the aforesaid friar Peter John and to her speaking, Na Prous, both of which spirits are one, as she said.

Likewise she claimed that the Lord told her that it is necessary that whoever wishes to save himself must believe the words of the writing of the said friar Peter John, when they are written by the virtue of the Holy Spirit, and likewise that one must believe the words of this Na Prous, when they are spoke by virtue of the Holy Spirit, as she said. Afterwards, when they shall have known these things, another man cannot be saved, and moreover, he who does not believe in the words of Na Prous shall die an eternal death.

Likewise, the Lord God shall give two things to every person who believes in the words of Na Prous; that is, he will forgive the sins of the believing person, and he will give him the Holy Spirit.

Likewise, he who created the world redeemed me, and shall renew it. Likewise God sent his Son to a virgin to redeem human nature, and the Son of God sent the Holy Spirit to another virgin for redeeming human nature;

saying that God gave her to understand clearly that she is the virgin to whom God sent the Holy Spirit to redeem human nature. . . .

Likewise she said that if this pope who now is, that is Pope John XXII, and the cardinals, prelates, and doctors of the sacred page should say to her and demonstrate by reasonings and by the authority of holy scripture that the aforesaid things, which she holds and claims herself to believe and hold, are erroneous and heretical, and if they were to warn her to revoke the aforesaid errors, she would neither believe nor obey them, for, as she said, the Lord Jesus Christ, who told her the aforesaid things, is more experienced and more prudent than all the men of the whole world.

Likewise she said that if the pope should excommunicate her on account of that disobedience, she would not think herself to be excommunicated nor would she even believe herself to be damned, if she were to die under the aforesaid excommunication, for God has made her certain in another way, as she said, claiming that whoever should condemn her and burn her on account of the foregoing, she would believe herself to be saved and a glorious martyr in paradise.

Likewise she said that it shall be necessary henceforth for whoever shall wish to save himself to believe in the works of the Holy Spirit given to Friar Peter John and to her speaking, indeed that he believe in the words that are in the writing of the said Friar Peter John and in the words that she herself said; which words are all the work of the Holy Spirit. She says that now she had great discomfort, for it was necessary to say such things about herself that would seem to be able to be said out of vainglory, for she would prefer, as she claims, to be torn in pieces with swords, or that lightning from heaven should fall upon her and lay her stretched out the ground, rather than to say such things about herself, and that she would rather speak about any other creature, but for this God wishes and commands her, as she claims, that whoever shall have believed the writings of the said Friar Peter John and the words of the same Na Prous, and shall have preserved his commands, shall be baptized in the Holy Spirit, and the Lord will forgive his sins. . . .

When asked if God told her those words which she had recited above, she said yes, but that she would not say them to anyone living except when she was compelled by God himself.

The aforesaid woman made her deposition and confessed freely and willingly, and as many times as her testimony was read to her in the vernacular, she confirmed and approved it. And having been warned, called, and urged many times in court and elsewhere, to revoke and objure all the aforesaid things as erroneous and heretical, she persevered in them, claiming that in the aforesaid, as in the truth, she wishes to live and die.

18.3 Political Challenges: Marsilius of Padua

In the thirteenth century, both secular and church governance were growing in sophistication and complexity, centralizing and codifying their rule through laws and administrative systems. At the same time, the tension between these two centers of authority continued, as each competed to be in authority, whether a king over his regnum or the pope over Christendom. During the on-and-off contests between king or emperor and pope throughout the eleventh, twelfth, and thirteenth centuries, political theory also developed, a response to both the intellectual environment of the universities and law schools and the need for arguments and rebuttals in the courts of kings or popes. Two extreme political theories concerning the nature of governance and the relationship of secular to religious authority emerged in the thirteenth century. The pro-papal monarch view is evident in the claims of Pope Boniface VIII (1294–1303), who issued the injunction *Clericis Laicos,* and then the bold *Unam Sanctam,* wherein he asserted that there was only one source of salvation, found in the one church, under one head, the pope, who was the supreme authority over all of Christendom.

In opposition to such claims to universal supremacy granted by divine agency, thinkers such as Marsilius of Padua (circa 1280–circa 1343) began formulating political theories supporting secular authority, based on natural law. Marsilius was a scholar in Padua and Paris, who wrote the controversial *Defensor Pacis* (1324). Using developments in law and scholasticism, Marsilius argued for a natural, rather than divine, basis for governance, asserting royal sovereignty even over the church and suggesting that the church centered in Rome be stripped of all political authority. The result would be national churches independent of a pan-European church. Although Marsilius work was condemned as heretical (1327), his theories clearly bore fruit in later centuries.

Questions

1. What is the role of law in Marsilius's arguments for secular sovereignty?

2. Compare Marsilius's position with the agendas of Gregory VII (13.1), Innocent III (17.1), and Boniface VIII (discussed above): what are the alternatives for the governance of Christian society?

Marsilius of Padua, Defensor Pacis 1324

Conclusion 1. The one divine canonical Scripture, the conclusions that necessarily follow from it, and the interpretation placed upon it by the common consent of Christians, are true, and belief in them is necessary to the salvation of those to whom they are made known.

2. The general council of Christians or its majority alone has the authority to define doubtful passages of the divine law, and to determine those that are to be regarded as articles of the Christian faith, belief in which is essential to salvation; and no partial council or single person of any position has the authority to decide these questions.

3. The gospels teach that no temporal punishment or penalty should be used to compel observance of divine commandments.

4. It is necessary to salvation to obey the commandments of the new divine law [the New Testament] and the conclusions that follow necessarily from it and the precepts of reason; but it is not necessary to salvation to obey all the commandments of the ancient law [the Old Testament].

5. No mortal has the right to dispense with the commands or prohibitions of the new divine law; but the general council and the Christian "legislator" alone have the right to prohibit things which are permitted by the new law, under penalties in this world or the next, and no partial council or single person of any position has that right. [Note: In regard to the "legislator," Marsilius cites Aristotle as follows: 'The legislator or the effective cause of the law is the people, the whole body of the citizens, or the majority of that body, expressing its will and choice in a general meeting of the citizens, and commanding or deciding that certain things shall be done or left undone, under threat of temporal penalty or punishment."]

6. The whole body of citizens or its majority alone is the human "legislator."

7. Decretals and decrees of the bishop of Rome, or of any other bishops or body of bishops, have no power to coerce anyone by secular penalties or punishments, except by the authorization of the human "legislator."

8. The "legislator" alone or the one who rules by its authority has the power to dispense with human laws.

9. The elective principality or other office derives its authority from the election of the body having the right to elect, and not from the confirmation or approval of any other power.

10. The election of any prince or other official, especially one who has the coercive power, is determined solely by the expressed will of the "legislator." [Note: "Coercive" or "coactive" power is the power, residing in the

ruler or the officials of the state and derived from the "legislator," to compel observance of the laws or decrees of the state by force or threat of penalty. A coercive judgment is a judgment given by an official who has the power to enforce his decisions. Marsilius maintains that coercive power and coercive judgments are the prerogatives of the state and cannot be exercised by the church.]

11. There can be only one supreme ruling power in a state or kingdom.

12. The number and the qualifications of persons who hold state offices and all civil matters are to be determined solely by the Christian ruler according to the law or approved custom [of the state].

13. No prince, still more, no partial council or single person of any position, has full authority and control over other persons, laymen or clergy, without the authorization of the "legislator."

14. No bishop or priest has coercive authority or jurisdiction over any layman or clergyman, even if he is a heretic.

15. The prince who rules by the authority of the "legislator" has jurisdiction over the persons and possessions of every single mortal of every station, whether lay or clerical, and over every body of laymen or clergy.

16. No bishop or priest or body of bishops or priests has the authority to excommunicate anyone or to interdict the performance of divine services, without the authorization of the "legislator."

17. All bishops derive their authority in equal measure immediately from Christ, and it cannot be proved from the divine law that one bishop should be over or under another, in temporal or spiritual matters.

18. The other bishops, singly or in a body, have the same right by divine authority to excommunicate or otherwise exercise authority over the bishop of Rome, having obtained the consent of the "legislator," as the bishop of Rome has to excommunicate or control them.

19. No mortal has the authority to permit marriages that are prohibited by the divine law, especially by the New Testament. The right to permit marriages which are prohibited by human law belongs solely to the "legislator" or to the one who rules by its authority.

20. The right to legitimatize children born of illegitimate union so that they may receive inheritances, or other civil or ecclesiastical offices or benefits, belongs solely to the "legislator."

21. The "legislator" alone has the right to promote to ecclesiastical orders, and to judge of the qualifications of persons for these offices, by a coercive decision, and no priest or bishop has the right to promote anyone without its authority.

22. The prince who rules by the authority of the laws of Christians, has

the right to determine the number of churches and temples, and the number of priests, deacons, and other clergy who shall serve in them.

23. "Separable" ecclesiastical offices may be conferred or taken away only by the authority of the "legislator"; the same is true of ecclesiastical benefices and other property devoted to pious purposes. [Note: "Separable" offices of the clergy, according to Marsilius, are those functions commonly exercised by the clergy, which are not essentially bound up with their spiritual character. The terms essential and non-essential are used as synonymous respectively with inseparable and separable. The essential or inseparable powers of the clergy are "the power to bless the bread and wine, and turn them into the blessed body and blood of Christ, to administer the other sacraments of the church, and to bind and to loose men from their sins." Non-essential or separable functions are the government or control of one priest over others (i.e., the offices of bishop, archbishop, etc.), the administration of the sacraments, etc., in a certain place and to a certain people, and the administration of temporal possessions of the church. In respect to their separable functions the clergy are under the control of the state.]

24. No bishop or body of bishops has the right to establish notaries or other civil officials.

25. No bishop or body of bishops may give permission to teach or practice in any profession or occupation, but this right belongs to the Christian "legislator" or to the one who rules by its authority.

26. In ecclesiastical offices and benefices those who have received consecration as deacons or priests, or have been otherwise irrevocably dedicated to God, should be preferred those who have not been thus consecrated.

27. The human "legislator" has the right to use ecclesiastical temporalities for the common public good and defense after the needs of the priests and clergy, the expenses of divine worship, and the necessities of the poor have been satisfied.

28. All properties established for pious purposes or for works of mercy, such as those that are left by will for the making of a crusade, the redeeming of captives, or the support of the poor, and similar purposes, may be disposed of by the prince alone according to the decision of the "legislator" and the purpose of the testator or giver.

29. The Christian "legislator" alone has the right to forbid or permit the establishment of religious orders or houses.

30. The prince alone, acting in accordance with the laws of the "legislator," has the authority to condemn heretics, delinquents, and all others who

should endure temporal punishment, to inflict bodily punishment upon them, and to exact fines from them.

31. No subject who is bound to another by a legal oath may be released from his obligation by any bishop or priest, unless the "legislator" has decided by a coercive decision that there is just cause for it.

32. The general council of all Christians alone has the authority to create a metropolitan bishop or church, and to reduce him or it from that position.

33. The Christian "legislator" or the one who rules by its authority over Christian states, alone has the right to convoke either a general or local council of priests, bishops, and other Christians, by coercive power; and no man may be compelled by threats of temporal or spiritual punishment to obey the decrees of a council convoked in any other way.

34. The general council of Christians or the Christian "legislator" alone has the authority to ordain fasts and other prohibitions of the use of food; the council or "legislator" alone may prohibit the practice of mechanical arts or teaching which divine law permits to be practiced on any day, and the "legislator" or the one who rules by its authority alone may constrain men to obey the prohibition by temporal penalties.

35. The general council of Christians alone has the authority to canonize anyone or to order anyone to be adored as a saint.

36. The general council of Christians alone has the authority to forbid the marriage of priests, bishops, and other clergy, and to make other laws concerning ecclesiastical discipline, and that council or the one to whom it delegates its authority alone may dispense with these laws.

37. It is always permitted to appeal to the "legislator" from a coercive decision rendered by a bishop or priest with the authorization of the "legislator."

38. Those who are pledged to observe complete poverty may not have in their possession any immovable property, unless it be with the fixed intention of selling it as soon as possible and giving the money to the poor; they may not have such rights in either movable or immovable property as would enable them, for example, to recover them by a coercive decision from any person who should take or try to take them away.

39. The people as a community and as individuals, according to their several means, are required by divine law to support the bishops and other clergy authorized by the gospel, so that they may have food and clothing and the other necessaries of life; but the people are not required to pay tithes or other taxes beyond the amount necessary for such support.

40. The Christian "legislator" or the one who rules by its authority has the right to compel bishops and other clergy who live in the province under

its control and whom it supplies with the necessities of life, to perform divine services and administer the sacrament.

41. The bishop of Rome and any other ecclesiastical or spiritual minister may be advanced to a "separable" ecclesiastical office only by the Christian "legislator" or the one who rules by its authority, or by the general council of Christians; and they may be suspended from or deprived of office by the same authority.

From Thatcher, pp. 318–23.

–19–
Popular Religion
Story and Poetry

Popular religion is not always easy to access because the mundane experiences of daily life are not often recorded. However, in the writings of churchmen who ministered in the everyday life of the church, we get some glimpses of religious practice and attitudes, if only from the point of view of someone trying to preach to the laity. Stories are particularly revealing because they represent a two-way transmission: storytellers draw on ideas, experiences, and anecdotes from the world around them, and in retelling them, they convey a moral to their audiences. Storytelling was one of the major forms of entertainment in the Middle Ages, so the proficiency developed by mendicant preachers (19.1) had to rival that of wandering minstrels and local comedians. Monasteries told tales to exemplify their ideals, often in ways that comment on human society and its weaknesses (19.2). National heroes and their legends could spawn an entire industry, evident in the cult of Thomas Becket (19.3). In addition, the music provided by the church drew on, adapted, and influenced secular music. So the great hymns of the church, as exemplified in the last selection (19.4), also reflect religious experience in the thirteenth century.

19.1 Preacher's Tales: Caesarius of Heisterbach, Jacques de Vitry, Etienne de Bourbon

These three stories illustrate popular religion as expressed by those who preached to the populace. By the thirteenth century, preaching to the laity, as well as to the regular clergy in monasteries, had become a major task of not only priests but also monastic and mendicant leaders. As indicated in Chapter 17, one impetus for the creation of the Dominican Order was to preach to the laity as a preventive against heresy. Consequently, a rich tradition of sermon manuals and exemplum developed as aids to preaching, many of them emphasizing respect for the authority of the church or the power of the priesthood. Three widely used collections are excerpted below, from three famous preachers: Caesarius of Heisterbach, Jacques de Vitry, and Etienne de Bourbon.

The monastic leader Caesarius of Heisterbach (circa 1180–1250) collected a massive number of stories organized around central monastic themes, such as conversion and contrition; the stories are told by a monk to a novice asking for definitions of these concepts. Although each story relates to the central moral, all are full of details of everyday life, attitudes, and beliefs, some of them shockingly anti-Semitic and harsh. These stories function like the parables of Jesus in that they convey a spiritual message about who gets into the kingdom of God; sometimes Caesarius's sense of spiritual justice defies worldly justice.

Jacques de Vitry (circa 1170–1240) was the bishop of Acre in the Holy Land and later a cardinal. Of a noble family, he pursued studies in Paris, where he came under the spiritual influence of Marie d'Oignies, whose biography he wrote (13.4). His preaching of the Albigensian Crusade, and then the Fifth Crusade, eventually led him to the Holy Land, and then back to Rome into the papal curia. Like Caesarius, Jacques de Vitry was concerned with monastic spiritual values and the role that monasteries play in upholding these values, even at the expense of worldly social mores.

The Dominican inquisitor and preacher Etienne de Bourbon (d. circa 1261) drew his tales from everyday life and experience, seeking to reach the hearts and minds of common lay people who were easily led astray into heresy. His task as an inquisitor brought him into contact with many strange local beliefs, some of which he felt were heretical. In particular, he sought to emphasize the authority of the holy church and her priests as preeminent over local practice.

In all three examples, the storyteller is asserting a certain set of church values while using tales of experience drawn from everyday life.

Questions

1. How does Caesarius's tale of the young Jewess who converts illustrate "contrition"?

2. What kinds of monastic values is Jacques de Vitry conveying, in opposition to the expected social norms?

3. What view of the Eucharist and its uses do you think Etienne de Bourbon is supporting, and why?

Caesarius of Heisterbach
Contrition: The Conversion of a Jewish Maiden

Monk: A little while ago, the daughter of a Jew at Louvain was converted to the faith in the following manner. A clerk named Rener, chaplain to the

Duke of Louvain, was in the habit of going to the house of this Jew to argue with him about the Christian faith. His daughter [Rachel], then a little girl, would often listen very eagerly to the discussion, and would weigh, as well as her intelligence allowed, both the arguments of the Jew her father, and those of his clerical opponent; and so, little by little, she became by the providence of God, imbued with the Christian faith. Being taught secretly also by the clerk, she became so far contrite as to say that she wished to be baptized. A woman was brought to her, who withdrew her secretly from her father's house; the clerk baptized and placed her in a convent of the Cistercian Order, called Parc-aux-Dames. When her conversion became known, the infidel father was much grieved, and offered the Duke a great sum of money to restore to him his daughter, who, he complained, had been taken by stealth from his house. Now the Duke was quite willing to restore the girl, though a Christian, to her father, though a Jew; but the clerk Rener resisted him saying: "Sir, if you commit this crime against God and His church, never can your soul be saved." Dom Walter, the abbot of Villiers, also opposed him. The Jew, seeing that he was disappointed of the hope he had cherished from the Duke, is said to have bribed Hugo, the bishop of Liège, who took the part of the Jew to such an extent that he sent letters to the convent of nuns at Parc-aux-Dames, ordering them to restore his daughter to him. But when the Jew, accompanied by his friends and relations reached the convent, the maiden, who was established there, though she knew nothing of his coming, began to perceive a very evil odour, so that she said openly: "I do not know whence it comes, but an odour as of Jews is troubling me." Meanwhile the Jews were knocking at the window; and the abbess, as I believe, said to the girl: "Daughter Catharine," for so she had been named at her baptism, "your parents wish to see you." She replied, "That explains the odour I perceived; I will not see them"; and she refused to leave the house. At the end of the year the bishop of Liège was accused of this action of his before Dom Engilbert Archbishop of Cologne, in the Synod held by him, and he was ordered never again to trouble the aforesaid convent with regard to this girl who had been baptized. He was silenced for a time, but not really obedient; for not long afterwards he sent a letter summoning the young woman, under pain of excommunication, to come to Liège to answer the objections raised by her father. She came but under good protection. It was alleged, on the part of the Jew, that she was carried away and baptized by force when under age; and it was said to the girl: "Catherine, we have been told that you would gladly go back to your father, if you were allowed." She replied: "Who told you this?" and they answered: "Your father himself." Then in a clear voice she uttered these words: "My father truly has lied in his beard." Now when the Jew's advocate [a Christian lawyer] continued to urge her, Dom Walter, the abbot of Villers was much moved and said to him: "Sir, you are speaking against God and against your own honour. Be sure of this, that if you say one single word more against the girl, I will do all I can with the lord Pope, that you may never be allowed to speak in any cause again." Then being frightened by this he said privately to the abbot: "My lord abbot, what harm does it do to you if I can manage to get money out of this Jew? I will say nothing that can possibly hurt the girl." But presently when he received his fees from the Jew, he said to him: "I do not dare to say another word in this case." At the end of the year, when Dom Wido, abbot of Clairvaux, was making his visitation in the diocese of Liège, he met the bishop, warned him, and begged him to have respect for God and his own honour, and to cease from harassing a maiden already dedicated to Christ. To whom the bishop replied: "My good lord abbot, what has this case to do with you?" The abbot answered: "It has a great deal to do with me, and for two reasons; first because I am a Christian, and next, because that convent in which she is living is of the lineage of Clairvaux;" and he added, "I shall place this girl and her case under the protection of the lord Pope, and shall ground my appeal upon the letters written by you against her." At the time of the General Chapter, he sent to the Prior of Parc, through our abbot, letters which he had obtained from the lord Pope against the bishop, so that, if by any chance the bishop should attempt to harass the convent further on this girl's account, he might defend himself by these letters.

Novice: Just as, a little while ago, I was edified by the pity of the English bishop, so am I now scandalized by the avarice of him of Liège.

Monk: His defenders say that his persistence in this affair was due, not to love of money, but to zeal for justice. But it is difficult to believe this, because if he had been actuated by the motive of justice, he would certainly not have tried to force a baptised girl, a virgin consecrated to Christ and a nun in a Christian convent, to return to Jewish infidelity.

Novice: Yes, I fully agree with that.

From H. von E. Scott and C. C. Swinton Bland, *The Dialogue on Miracles,* Vol. I (NY: Harcourt Brace, 1929), pp. 107–109.

Jacques de Vitry: A Miracle of the Virgin

A certain very religious man told me that this happened in a place where he had been living. A virtuous and pious matron came frequently to the church and served God most devoutly, day and night. Also a certain monk, the guardian and treasurer of the monastery, had a great reputation for piety, and truly he was devout. When, however, the two frequently conversed together in the church concerning religious matters, the devil, envying their virtue and fame, tempted them sorely so that the spiritual love was changed to carnal. Accordingly they made an agreement and fixed upon a night in which the monk was to leave his monastery, taking the treasures of the church, and the matron was to leave her home, with a sum of money which she should secretly steal from her husband.

After they had left and fled, the monks on rising in the morning saw that the receptacles were broken and the treasures of the church stolen; and not finding the monk, they quickly pursued him. Likewise the woman's husband, seeing his chest open and the money gone, pursued his wife. Seizing the monk and the woman with the treasure and money, they brought them back and threw them into prison. Moreover so great was the scandal through all that part of the country and so much were all religious persons reviled that the damage from the infamy and scandal was far greater than from the sin itself.

Then the monk restored to his senses, began with many tears to pray to the blessed Virgin, whom from infancy he had always served, and never before had any such misfortune happened to him. Likewise the matron began urgently to implore the aid of the blessed Virgin whom, frequently, day and night, she had been accustomed to salute and before whose image she had been wont to kneel in prayer. At length the blessed Virgin appeared before them in great anger and after she had upbraided them severely, she said, "I am able to obtain pardon for your sins from my son, but what can I do about such an awful scandal? For you have so befouled the name of religious persons before all the people, that in the future no one will trust them. This is an almost irremediable injury."

At length the pious Virgin, overcome by their prayers, summoned the demons who had caused the deed and enjoined upon them that, as they had caused the scandal to religion, they must bring the infamy to an end. Since, indeed, they were not able to resist her commands, after much anxiety and various conferences they found a way to remove the infamy. In the night they placed the monk in the church and repairing the broken receptacle as it had been before, they placed the treasure in it. Also they closed and locked the chest which the matron had opened and replaced the money in it. And they set the woman in her room and in the place where she was accustomed to pray by night.

When, moreover, the monks found the treasure of their house and the monk, who was praying to God just as he had been accustomed to do; and the husband found his wife and the treasure; and they found the money just as it had been before, they began to be amazed and to wonder. Rushing to the prison they saw the monk and the woman in fetters just as they had left them. For one of the demons was seen by them transformed into the figure of a monk and another into the shape of a woman. When the whole city had come together to see the miracle, the demons said in the hearing of all, "Let us go, for long enough have we deceived these people and caused ill to be thought of religious persons." And having said this they vanished. Moreover all fell down at the feet of the monk and of the woman and demanded pardon.

Behold how great infamy and scandal and how inestimable damage the devil would have wrought against religious persons, if the blessed Virgin had not aided them.

From *TROS,* Vol. 2, No. 4, pp. 2–4.

Etienne de Bourbon: A Miracle of the Eucharist

For I have heard that a certain rustic, wishing to become wealthy and having many hives of bees, asked certain evil men how he could get rich and increase the number of his bees. He was told by some one that if he should retain the sacred communion on Easter and place it in one of his hives, he would entice away all of his neighbor's bees, which leaving their own hives, would come to the place where the body of our Lord was and there would make honey. He did this.

Then all the bees came to the hive where the body of Christ was, and just as if they had felt compassion for the irreverence done to it, by their labor they began to construct a little church and to erect foundations and bases and columns and an altar with like labor, and with the greatest reverence they placed the body of our Lord upon the altar. And within that little bee-hive they formed that little church with wonderful and the most beautiful workmanship. The bees of the vicinity leaving their hives came together at that one; and over that structure they sang in their own manner certain wonderful melodies like hymns.

The rustic hearing this, wondered. But waiting until the fitting time for collecting the swarm of bees and the honey-comb, he found nothing in his hives in which the bees had been accustomed to make honey; finding himself impoverished through the means by which he had believed that he would be enriched, he went to that one where he had placed the host, where he saw the bees had come together. But when he approached, just as if they had wanted to vindicate the insult to our Savior, the bees rushed upon the rustic and stung him so severely that he escaped with difficulty, and suffering greatly. Going to the priest he related all that he had done and what the bees had done. The priest, by the advice of his bishop, collected his parishioners and went in procession to the place. Then the bees, leaving the hive, rose in the air, making sweet melody. Raising the hive they found within the noble structure of that little church and the body of our Lord placed upon the altar. Then returning thanks they bore to their own church that little church of the bees constructed with such skill and elegance and with praises placed it on the altar.

By this deed those who do not reverence but offer insult instead to the sacred body of Christ or the sacred place where it is, ought to be put to great confusion.

From *TROS,* Vol. 2, No. 4, pp. 19–20.

19.2 Monastic Simplicity: "Our Lady's Tumbler"

The monastic and mendicant orders emphasize simplicity and humility as the chief virtues to be imitated in the life of a Christian. Consequently, the poor or the ignorant—or at least the idea of such unfortunates—often serve as examples of piety in stories. Stories of role reversal, where the high and mighty get their comeuppance through the lowly, were common in sermons. Within the monastery, such tales served as a reminder that in the cloister, one's rank or class in the world is, literally, immaterial. All the brothers or sisters are equal in serving God with whatever gifts God gave them. The following popular tale, told like a saint's life, not only reveals the principle of "the first shall be last" but also unmasks some of the social pretensions both within and outside the monastery. This story is similar to the popular Christmas story of the Little Drummer Boy, but involves instead a court jester who, to the monastics, represents the worldliest and most frivolous of occupations.

This story, like Jacques de Vitry's above, also features the Virgin Mary, whose cult grew dramatically in popularity in the high Middle Ages. Mary became the mother figure representing God, protecting, advocating for, and consoling her suppliants. The tumbler in this story has a powerful, and popular, patron in the person of the Virgin Mary.

Questions

1. In what ways is the tumbler's story like that of a saint?
2. What kinds of problems exist in the monastery that this tale tries to correct?
3. What beliefs and values would the monastery seek to foster in telling and recording this story?

"Our Lady's Tumbler"

Amongst the lives of the ancient Fathers, wherein may be found much profitable matter, this story is told for a true ensample. I do not say that you may not often have heard a fairer story, but at least this is not to be despised, and is well worth the telling. Now therefore will I say and narrate what chanced to this minstrel.

He erred up and down, to and fro, so often and in so many places, that he took the whole world in despite, and sought rest in a certain Holy Order. Horses and raiment and money, yea, all that he had, he straightway put from him, and seeking shelter from the world, was firmly set never to put foot within it more. For this cause he took refuge in this Holy Order, amongst the monks of Clairvaux. Now, though this dancer was comely of face and shapely of person, yet when he had once entered the monastery he found that he was master of no craft practiced therein. In the world he had gained his bread by tumbling and dancing and feats of address. To leap, to spring, such matters he knew well, but of greater things he knew nothing, for he had never spelled from book—nor Paternoster, nor canticle, nor creed, nor Hail Mary, nor aught concerning his soul's salvation.

When the minstrel had joined himself to the Order he marked how the tonsured monks spoke amongst themselves by signs, no words coming from their lips, so he thought within himself that they were dumb. But when he learned that truly it was by way of penance that speech was forbidden to their mouths, and that for holy obedience were they silent, then considered he that silence became him also; and he refrained his tongue from words, so discreetly and for so long a space, that day in, day out, he spoke never, save by commandment; so that the cloister often rang with the brothers' mirth. The tumbler moved amongst his fellows like a man ashamed, for he had neither part nor lot in all the business of the monastery, and for this he was right sad and sorrowful. He saw the monks and the penitents about him, each serving God, in this place and that, according to his office and degree. He marked the priests at their ritual before the altars; the deacons at the gospels; the sub-deacons at the epistles; and the ministers about the vigils. This one repeats the introit; this other the lesson; cantors chant from the psalter; penitents spell out the Miserere—for thus are all things sweetly ordered—yea, and the most ignorant amongst them yet can pray his Paternoster. Wherever he went, here or there, in office or cloister, in every quiet corner and nook, there he found five, or three, or two, or at least one. He gazes earnestly, if so he is able, upon each. Such an one laments; this other is in tears; yet another grieves and sighs. He marvels at their sorrow. Then he said, "Holy Mary, what bitter grief have all these men that they smite the breast so grievously! Too sad of heart, meseems, are they who make such bitter dole together. Ah, St. Mary, alas, what words are these I say! These men are calling on the mercy of God, but I—what do I here! Here there is none so mean or vile but who serves God in his office and degree, save only me, for I work not, neither can I preach. Caitif [coward] and shamed was I when I thrust myself herein, seeing that I can do nothing well, either in labor or in prayer. I see my brothers upon their errands, one behind the other; but I do naught but fill my belly with the meat that they provide. If they perceive this thing, certainly shall I be in an evil case, for these will cast me out amongst the dogs, and none will take pity on the glutton and the idle man. Truly am I a caitif, set in a high place for a sign." Then he wept for very woe, and would that he was quiet in the grave. "Mary, Mother," quoth he, "pray now your Heavenly Father that He keep me in His pleasure, and give me such good counsel that I may truly serve both Him and you; yea, and may deserve that meat which now is bitter in my mouth."

Driven mad with thoughts such as these, he wandered about the abbey until he found himself within the crypt, and took sanctuary by the altar, crouching close as he was able. Above the altar was carved the statue of Madame St. Mary. Truly his steps had not erred when he sought that refuge; nay, but rather, God who knows His own had led him thither by the hand. When he heard the bells ring for Mass he sprang to his feet all dismayed. "Ha!" said he; "now am I betrayed. Each adds his mite to the great offering, save only me. Like a tethered ox, naught I do but chew the cud, and waste good victuals on a useless man. Shall I speak my thought? Shall I work my will? By the Mother of God, thus am I set to do. None is here to blame. I will do that which I can, and honour with my craft the Mother of God in her monastery. Since others honour her with chant, then I will serve with tumbling."

He takes off his cowl, and removes his garments, placing them near the altar, but so that his body be not naked he dons a tunic, very thin and fine, of scarce more substance than a shirt. So, light and comely of body, with gown girt closely about his loins, he comes before the Image right humbly. Then raising his eyes, "Lady," said he, "to your fair charge I give my body and my soul. Sweet Queen, sweet Lady, scorn not the thing I know, for with the help of God I will essay to serve you in good faith, even as I may. I cannot read your Hours nor chant your praise, but at the least I can set before you what art I have. Now will I be as the lamb that plays and skips before his mother. Oh, Lady, who art nowise bitter to those who serve you with a good intent, that which thy servant is, that he is for you."

Then commenced he his merry play, leaping low and small, tall and high, over and under. Then once more he knelt upon his knees before the statue, and meekly bowed his head. "Ha!" said he, "most gracious Queen, of your pity and your charity scorn not this my service." Again he leaped and played, and for holiday and festival, made the somersault of Metz. Again he bowed before the Image, did reverence, and paid it all the honour that he might. Afterwards he did the French vault, then the vault of Champagne, then the Spanish vault, then the vaults they love in Brittany, then the vault of Lorraine, and all these feats he did as best he was able. Afterwards he did the Roman vault, and then, with hands before his brow, danced daintily before the altar, gazing with a humble heart at the statue of God's Mother. "Lady," said he, "I set before you a fair play. This travail I do for you alone; so help me God; for you, Lady, and your Son. Think not I tumble for my own delight; but I serve you, and look for no other guerdon on my carpet. My brothers serve you, yea, and so do I. Lady, scorn not your villein, for he toils for your good pleasure; and, Lady, you are my delight and the sweetness of the world." Then he walked on his two hands, with his feet in the air, and his head near the ground. He twirled with his feet, and wept with his eyes. "Lady," said he, "I worship you with heart, with body, feet and hands, for this I can neither add to nor take away. Now am I your very minstrel. Others may chant your praises in the church, but here in the crypt will I tumble for your delight. Lady, lead me truly in your way, and for the love of God hold me not in utter despite." Then he smote upon his breast, he sighed and wept most tenderly, since he knew no better prayer than tears. Then he turned him about, and leaped once again. "Lady," said he, "as God is my Savior, never have I turned this somersault before. Never has tumbler done such a feat, and, certes, it is not bad. Lady, what delight is his who may harbor with you in your glorious manor. For God's love, Lady, grant me such fair hostelry, since I am yours, and am nothing of my own." Once again he did the vault of Metz; again he danced and tumbled. Then when the chants rose louder from the choir, he, too, forced the note, and put forward all his skill. So long as the priest was about that Mass, so long his flesh endured to dance, and leap and spring, till at the last, nigh fainting, he could stand no longer upon his feet, but fell for weariness on the ground. From head to heel sweat stood upon him, drop by drop, as blood falls from meat turning upon the hearth. "Lady," said he, "I can no more, but truly will I seek you again." Fire consumed him utterly. He took his habit once more, and when he was wrapped close therein, he rose to his feet, and bending low before the statue, went his way. "Farewell," said he, "gentlest Friend. For God's love take it not to heart, for so I may I will soon return. Not one Hour shall pass but that I will serve you with right good will, so I may come, and so my service is pleasing in your sight." Thus he went from the crypt, yet gazing on his Lady. "Lady," said he, "my heart is sore that I cannot read your Hours. How would I love them for love of you, most gentle Lady! Into your care I commend my soul and my body."

In this fashion passed many days, for at every Hour he sought the crypt to do service, and pay homage before the Image. His service was so much to his mind that never once was he too weary to set out his most cunning feats to distract the Mother of God, nor did he ever wish for other play than this. Now, doubtless, the monks knew well enough that day by day he sought the crypt, but not a man on earth—save God alone—was aware of aught that passed there; neither would he, for all the wealth of the world, have let his goings in be seen, save by the Lord his God alone. For truly he believed that were his secret once espied he would be hunted from the cloister, and flung once more into the foul, sinful world, and for his part he was more fain to fall on death than to suffer any taint of sin. But God considering his simplicity, his sorrow for all he had wrought amiss, and the love which moved him to this deed, would that this toil should be known; and the Lord willed that the work of His friend should be made plain to men, for the glory of the Mother whom he worshipped, and so that all men should know and hear, and receive that God refuses none who seeks His face in love, however low his degree, save only he love God and strive to do His will.

Now think you that the Lord would have accepted this service, had it not been done for love of Him? Verily and truly, no, however much this juggler tumbled; but God called him friend, because he loved Him much. Toil and labor, keep fast and vigil, sigh and weep, watch and pray, ply the sharp scourge, be diligent at Matins and at Mass, owe no man anything, give alms of all you have—and yet, if you love not God with all your heart, all these good deeds are so much loss—mark well my words—and profit you naught for the saving of your soul. Without charity and love, works avail a man nothing. God asks not gold, neither for silver, but only for love unfeigned in His people's hearts, and since the tumbler loved Him beyond measure, for this reason God was willing to accept his service.

Thus things went well with this good man for a great space. For more years than I know the count of, he lived greatly at his ease, but the time came when the good man was sorely vexed, for a certain monk thought upon him, and blamed him in his heart that he was never set in choir for Matins. The monk marvelled much at his absence, and said within himself that he would never rest till it was clear what manner of man this was, and how he spent the Hours, and for what service the convent gave him bread. So he spied and pried and followed, till he marked him plainly, sweating at his craft in just such fashion as you have heard. "By my faith," said he, "this is a merry jest, and a fairer festival than we observe altogether. Whilst others are at prayers, and about the business of the House this tumbler dances daintily, as though one had given him a hundred silver marks. He prides himself on being so nimble of foot, and thus he repays us what he owes. Truly it is this for that; we chant for him, and he tumbles for us. We throw him largess: he doles us alms. We weep his sins, and he dries our eyes. Would that the monastery could see him, as I do, with their very eyes; willingly therefore would I fast till Vespers. Not one could refrain from mirth at the sight of this simple fool doing himself to death with his tumbling, for on himself he has no pity. Since his folly is free from malice, may God grant it to him as penance. Certainly I will not impute it to him as sin, for in all simplicity and good faith, I firmly believe, he does this thing, so that he may deserve his bread." So the monk saw with his very eyes how the tumbler did service at all the Hours, without pause or rest, and he laughed with pure mirth and delight, for in his heart was joy and pity.

The monk went straight to the abbot and told him the thing from beginning to end, just as you have heard. The abbot got him on his feet, and said to the monk, "By holy obedience I bid you hold your peace, and tell not this tale abroad against your brother. I lay on you my strict command to speak of this matter to none, save me. Come now, we will go forthwith to see what this can be, and let us pray the Heavenly King, and His very sweet, dear Mother, so precious and so bright, that in her gentleness she will plead with her Son, her Father, and her Lord, that I may look on this work—if thus it pleases Him—so that the good man be not wrongly blamed, and that God may be the more beloved, yet so that thus is His good pleasure." Then they secretly sought the crypt, and found a privy place near the altar, where they could see, and yet not be seen. From there the abbot and his monk marked the business of the penitent. They saw the vaults he varied so cunningly, his nimble leaping and his dancing, his salutations of Our Lady, and his springing and his bounding, till he was nigh to faint. So weak was he that he sank on the ground, all outworn, and the sweat fell from his body upon the pavement of the crypt. But presently, in this his need, came she, his refuge, to his aid. Well she knew that guileless heart.

Whilst the abbot looked, forthwith there came down from the vault a Dame so glorious, that certainly no man had seen one so precious, nor so richly crowned. She was more beautiful than the daughters of men, and her vesture was heavy with gold and gleaming stones. In her train came the hosts of Heaven, angel and archangel also; and these pressed close about the minstrel, and solaced and refreshed him. When their shining ranks drew near, peace fell upon his heart; for they contended to do him service, and were the servants of the servitor of that Dame who is the rarest Jewel of God. Then the sweet and courteous Queen herself took a white napkin in her hand, and with it gently fanned her minstrel before the altar. Courteous and debonair, the Lady refreshed his neck, his body and his brow. Meekly she served him as a handmaid in his need. But these things were hidden from the good man, for he neither saw nor knew that about him stood so fair a company.

The holy angels honour him greatly, but they can no longer stay, for their Lady turns to go. She blesses her minstrel with the sign of God, and the holy angels throng about her, still gazing back with delight upon their companion, for they await the hour when God shall release him from the burden of the world, and they possess his soul.

This marvel the abbot and his monk saw at least four times, and thus at each Hour came the Mother of God with aid and succor for her man. Never does she fail her servants in their need. Great joy had the abbot that this thing was made plain to him. But the monk was filled with shame, since God had shown His pleasure in the service of His poor fool. His confusion burnt him like fire. "Dominus," said he to the abbot, "grant me grace. Certainly this is a holy man, and since I have judged him amiss, it is very right that my body should smart. Give me now fast or vigil or the scourge, for without question he is a saint. We are witnesses to the whole matter, nor is it possible that we can be deceived." But the abbot replied, "You speak truly, for God has made us to know that He has bound him with the cords of love. So I lay my commandment upon you, in virtue of obedience, and under pain of your person, that you tell no word to any man of that you have seen, save to God alone and me." "Lord," said he, "thus I will do." On these words they turned them, and hastened from the crypt; and the good man, having brought his tumbling to an end, presently clothed himself in his habit, and joyously went his way to the monastery.

Thus time went and returned, till it chanced that in a little while the abbot sent for him who was so filled with virtue. When he heard that he was bidden of the abbot, his heart was sore with grief for he could think of nothing profitable to say. "Alas!" said he, "I am undone; not a day of my days but I shall know misery and sorrow and shame, for well I trow that my service is not pleasing to God. Alas! plainly does He show that it displeases Him, since He causes the truth to be made clear. Could I believe that such work and play as mine could give delight to the mighty God! He had no pleasure therein, and all my toil was thrown away. Ah me, what shall I do? what shall I say? Fair, gentle God, what portion will be mine? Either shall I die in shame, or else shall I be banished from this place, and set up as a mark to the world and all the evil thereof. Sweet Lady, St. Mary, since I am all bewildered, and since there is none to give me counsel, Lady, come thou to my aid. Fair, gentle God, help me in my need. Stay not, neither tarry, but come quickly with Your Mother. For God's love, come not without her, but hasten both to me in my peril, for truly I know not what to plead. Before one word can pass my lips, surely will they bid me 'Begone.' Wretched that I am, what reply is he to make who has no advocate? Yet, why this dole, since go I must?" He came before the abbot, with the tears yet wet upon his cheeks, and he was still weeping when he knelt upon the ground. "Lord," prayed he, "for the love of God deal not harshly with me. Would you send me from your door? Tell me what you would have me do, and thus it shall be done." Then replied the abbot, "Answer me truly. Winter and summer have you lived here for a great space; now, tell me, what service have you given, and how have you deserved your bread?" "Alas!" said the tumbler, "well I knew that quickly I should be put upon the street when once this business was heard of you, and that you would keep me no more. Lord," said he, "I take my leave. Miserable I am, and miserable shall I ever be. Never yet have I made a penny for all my juggling." But the abbot answered, "Not so said I; but I ask and require of you—nay, more, by virtue of holy obedience I command you—to seek within your conscience and tell me truly by what craft you have furthered the business of our monastery." "Lord," cried he, "now have you slain me, for this commandment is a sword." Then he laid bare before the abbot the story of his days, from the first thing to the last, whatsoever pain it cost him; not a word did he leave out, but he told it all without a pause, just as I have told you the tale. He told it with clasped hands, and with tears, and at the close he kissed the abbot's feet, and sighed.

The holy abbot leaned above him, and, all in tears, raised him up, kissing both his eyes. "Brother," said he, "hold now your peace, for I make with you this true covenant, that you shall ever be of our monastery. God grant, rather, that we may be of yours, for all the worship you have brought to ours. I and you will call each other friend. Fair, sweet brother, pray you for me, and I for my part will pray for you. And now I pray you, my sweet friend, and lay this bidding upon you, without pretense, that you continue to do your service, even as you were wont heretofore—yea, and with greater craft yet, if so you may." "Lord," said he, "truly is this so?" "Yea," said the abbot, "and verily." So he charged him, under peril of discipline, to put all doubts from his mind; for which reason the good man rejoiced so greatly that, as tells the rhyme, he was all bemused, so that the blood left his cheeks, and his knees failed beneath him. When his courage came back, his very heart thrilled with joy; but so perilous was that quickening that therefrom he shortly died. But theretofore with a good heart he went about his service without rest, and Matins and Vespers, night and day, he missed no Hour till he became too sick to perform his office. So sore was his sickness upon him that he might not rise from his bed. Marvelous was the shame he proved when no more was he able to pay his rent. This was the grief that lay the heaviest upon him, for of his sickness he spoke never a word, but he feared greatly lest he should fall from grace since he travailed no longer at his craft. He reckoned himself an idle man, and prayed God to take him to Himself before the sluggard might come to blame. For it was bitter to him to consider that all about him knew his case, so bitter that the burden was heavier than his heart could bear, yet there without remedy he must lie. The holy abbot does him all honour; he and his monks chant the Hours about his bed; and in these praises of God he felt such delight that not for them would he have taken the province of Poitou, so great was his happiness therein. Fair and contrite was his confession, but still he was not at peace; yet why say more of this, for the hour had struck, and he must rise and go.

The abbot was in that cell with all his monks; there, too, was company of many a priest and many a canon. These all humbly watched the dying man, and saw with open eyes this wonder happen. Clear to their very sight, about that lowly bed, stood the Mother of God, with angel and archangel, to wait the passing of his soul. Over against them were set, like wild beasts, devils and the Adversary, so they might snatch his spirit. I speak not to you in parable. But little profit had they for all their coming, their waiting, and their straining on the leash. Never might they have part in such a soul as his. When the soul took leave of his body, it fell not in their hands at all, for the Mother of God gathered it to her bosom, and the holy angels thronging round, quired [sang] for joy, as the bright train swept to Heaven with its burden, according to the will of God. To these things the whole of the monastery was witness, besides such others as were there. So knew they and perceived that God sought no more to hide the love He bore to His poor servant, but rather would that his virtues should be plain to each man in that place; and very wonderful and joyful seemed this deed to them. Then with meet reverence they bore the body on its bier within the abbey church, and with high pomp commended their brother to the care of God; nor was there monk who did not chant or read his portion that day within the choir of the mighty church.

Thus with great honour they laid him to his rest, and kept his holy body amongst them as a relic. At that time spoke the abbot plainly to their ears, telling them the story of this tumbler and of all his life, just as you have heard, and of all that he himself beheld within the crypt. No brother but kept awake during that sermon. "Certes," said they, "easy is it to give credence to such a tale; nor should any doubt your words, seeing that the truth bears testimony to itself, and witness comes with need; yea, without any doubt have we full assurance that his discipline is done." Great joy amongst themselves have all within that place.

Thus ends the story of the minstrel. Fair was his tumbling, fair was his service, for thereby gained he such high honour as is above all earthly gain. So the holy Fathers narrate that in such fashion these things chanced to this minstrel. Now, therefore, let us pray to God—He Who is above all other— that He may grant us so to do such faithful service that we may win the guerdon of His love.

Here ends the Tumbler of Our Lady.

From Eugene Mason, *Aucassin and Nicolette and Other Mediaeval Romances and Legends* (London: J.M. Dent, 1910; NY: E.P. Dutton, 1910), pp. 53–66.

19.3 Popular Saints: The Golden Legend of Thomas Becket

The stories of saints continued to be a popular way to convey lessons to the populace. The examples of their lives and the power of their miracles reinforced spiritual values and supported the centrality and authority of the church that sponsored these saints. The collection known as the "Golden Legend" attributed to Jacob de Voraigne was widely disseminated in medieval Europe. It contains the story of the martyred Archbishop Thomas Becket of Canterbury, whose cult rose and spread rapidly after his death.

The career, actions, and death of Thomas Becket (1117–1170) stand at the center of a web of conflicting interests in medieval Europe, particularly the tension between royal and ecclesiastical governance. He rose through the usual means of education in Paris and ecclesiastical preferment to be an advisor and friend of King Henry II. However, upon his appointment by Henry as archbishop of Canterbury, he suddenly became an ardent supporter of the church's rights, in opposition to Henry's plan to keep the church in England under royal control. What followed was a bitter struggle, with Becket spending several years in exile on the continent. Becket's death at the hands of some of Henry's nobles, who thought they were doing the king a favor, had the opposite impact: it created a martyr and made the king look foolish. Henry's forced penitence and flogging by the monks of Canterbury temporarily put a damper on his efforts to elevate the royal position in the church.

Soon after Becket's death, miracles were reported at his tomb, and the monks of Canterbury turned these effectively into a cult. The pilgrimage to Canterbury to see Becket's tomb became one of the most popular in Europe, immortalized in Chaucer's *Canterbury Tales*.

Questions

1. What aspects of Thomas Becket's life are saintly, at least in the view of his hagiographer?

2. What does this story reveal about popular attitudes toward religion and politics in the relationship of king to archbishop?

3. Why do you think Becket was such a popular saint and his tomb a favorite pilgrimage center?

Saint Thomas of Canterbury

S[aint] Thomas the martyr was son to Gilbert Beckett, a burgess of the city of London, and was born in the place where now stands the church called S. Thomas of Acre. And this Gilbert was a good devout man, and took the cross upon him, and went on pilgrimage into the Holy Land, and had a servant with him. And when he had accomplished his pilgrimage, he was taken homeward by the heathen [Muslim] men and brought into the Amerant prison of a prince named Amurath, where long time he and his fellowship suffered much pain and sorrow. And the prince had great affection towards this Gilbert, and had often communication with him of the Christian faith, and of the realm of England, by which conversation it fortuned that the daughter of this prince had especial love unto this Gilbert, and was familiar with him. And on a time she disclosed her love to him, saying if he would promise to wed her she should forsake friends, heritage and country, for his love and become Christian, and after long communication between them he promised to wed her if she would become Christian, and told to her the place of his dwelling in England. And after, by the purveyance of God, the said Gilbert escaped and came home. And after this it fortuned so that this prince's daughter stole privily away, and passed many a wild place and great adventure, and by God's purveyance at last came to London demanding and crying 'Becket! Becket!' for more English could she not; wherefore the people drew about her, what for the strange array of her, as for that they understood her not, and many a shrewd boy. So long she went till she came before Gilbert's door, and as she stood there, the servant that had been with Gilbert in prison which was named Richard, saw her and knew that it was she, and went in to his master, and told him how that this maid stood at his door; and anon he went out to see her. And as soon as she saw him she fell in a swoon for joy, and Gilbert took her up, and comforted her, and brought her into his house, and then went to the bishops, which then were six at Paul's, and rehearsed all the matter, and after they christened her, and forthwith wedded her unto Gilbert Becket, and within time reasonable and accustomed was brought forth between them a fair son named Thomas. And after this, yet the said Gilbert went again to the Holy Land and was there three years ere he came again. And this child grew forth till he was set to school, and learned well and became virtuous, and when he was twenty-four years old his mother passed out of this world. And after this he served a merchant of London a while in keeping his charge and accounts, and from him he went to Stigand, archbishop of Canterbury, and he was in so great favor with him that he made him archdeacon and chief of his counsel, and well executed he his office in punishing the culpable and cherishing the good people. And divers times went to Rome for to support and help holy church. And after this Henry II that was the emperice's son was made king of England, and he ordained this Thomas his chancellor, and had great rule, and the land stood in prosperity. And S. Thomas stood so greatly in the king's favor that the king was content with all that he did; and when the king went into Normandy he betook the governance of his son and the realm into the rule of S. Thomas, which he wisely governed till his return again. And anon after died Theobald, the archbishop of Canterbury, and then the king gave his nomination to S. Thomas, and by the chapter was elected in the year of his age forty-four, and was full loth to take that great charge upon him. And so at last, his bulls [papal sanctions] had, he was sacred and stalled [anointed and installed] and became a holy man, suddenly changed into a new man, doing great penance, as in wearing hair with knots, and a breech of the same down to the knees. And on a Trinity Sunday received he his dignity, and there was at that time the king with many a great lord and sixteen bishops. And from thence was sent the abbot of Evesham to the pope with other clerks for the pall which he gave and brought to him, and he full meekly received it. And under his habit he wore the habit of a monk, and so was he under within forth a monk, and outward a clerk, and did great abstinence making his body lean and his soul fat. And he used to be well served at his table, and took but little refection thereof, and lived holily in giving good example.

After this, many times the king went over into Normandy, and in his absence always S. Thomas had the rule of his son and of the realm, which was governed so well that the king could give him great thanks, and then abode long in this realm. And when so it was that the king did any thing against the franchise and liberties of holy church, S. Thomas would ever withstand it to his power. And on a time when the sees [bishops's seats] of London and of Winchester were vacant and void, the king kept them both long in his hand for to have the profits of them; wherefore S. Thomas was heavy, and came to the king and desired him to give those two bishopricks to some virtuous men. And anon the king granted to him his desire and ordained one master Roger bishop of Winchester, and the Earl of Gloucester's son, named Sir Robert, bishop of London. And anon after S. Thomas hallowed the abbey of Reading, which the first Henry founded. And that same year he translated S. Edward, king and confessor at Westminster, where he was laid in a rich shrine. And some short time after, by the enticement of the devil, fell great debate, variance, and strife, between the king and S. Thomas, and the king sent for all the bishops to appear before him at Westminster at a certain day, at which day they assembled before him, whom he welcomed, and after said to them how that the archbishop would destroy his law and not suffer him to enjoy such things as his predecessors had used before him. Whereupon S. Thomas answered that he never intended to do anything that should displease the king as far as it touched not the franchise and liberties of holy church. Then the king rehearsed how he would not suffer clerks that were thieves to have the execution of the law; to which S. Thomas said, that he ought not to execute them, but they belong to the correction of holy church, and other divers points. To the which the king said: 'Now I see well that thou wouldest fordo the laws of this land which have been used in the days of my predecessors, but it shall not lie in thy power,' and so the king being wroth departed. Then the bishops all counseled S. Thomas to follow the king's intent, or else the land should be in great trouble; and in like wise the lords temporal that were his friends counseled him the same; and S. Thomas said: 'I take God to record it was never mine intent to displease the king, or to take any thing that belongs to his right or honor.' And then the lords were glad and brought him to the king to Oxenford, and the king deigned not to speak to him. And then the king called all the lords spiritual and temporal before him, and said he would have all the laws of his forefathers there new confirmed, and there they were confirmed by all the lords spiritual and temporal. And after this the king charged them for to come to him to Clarendon to his parliament at a certain day assigned, on pain to run in his indignation; and at that time so departed. And this parliament was held at Clarendon, the eleventh year of the king's reign, and the year of our Lord eleven hundred and sixty-four. At this parliament were many lords who all were against S. Thomas. And then the king sitting in his parliament, in the presence of all his lords, demanded them if they would abide and keep the laws that had been used in his forefathers' days. Then S. Thomas spoke for the part of holy church, and said: 'All old laws that be good and rightful, and not against our mother holy church, I grant with good will to keep them.' And then the king said that he would not leave one point of his law, and waxed wroth with S. Thomas. And then certain bishops required S. Thomas to obey to the king's desire and will, and S. Thomas desired respite to know the laws, and then to give him an answer. And when he understood them all, to some he consented, but many he denied and would never be agreeable to them, wherefore the king was wroth and said he would hold and keep them like as his predecessors had done before him, and would not diminish one point of them. Then S. Thomas said to the king with full great sorrow and heavy cheer, 'Now, my most dear lord and gracious king, have pity on us of holy church, your bedemen [men serving him through prayer], and give to us respite for a certain time.' And thus departed each man. And S. Thomas went to Winchester, and there prayed our Lord devoutly for holy church, and to give him aid and strength for to defend it, for utterly he determined to abide by the liberties and franchise; and fell down on his knees and said, full sore weeping: 'O good Lord, I acknowledge that I have offended, and for mine offense and trespass this trouble comes to holy church: I purpose, good Lord, to go to Rome for to be absolved of mine offenses'; and departed towards Canterbury. And anon the king sent his officers to his manors and despoiled them, because he would not obey the king's statutes. And the king commanded to seize all his lands and goods into his hands, and then his servants departed from him; and he went to the seaside for to have gone over sea, but the wind was against him, and so thrice he took his ship and might not pass. And then he knew that it was not our Lord's will that he should yet depart, and returned secretly to Canterbury, of whose coming his followers made great joy. And on the morn came the king's officers for to seize all his goods; for the noise was that S. Thomas had fled the land; wherefore they had despoiled all his manors and seized them into the king's hand. And when they came they found him at Canterbury, whereof they were sore abashed, and returned to the king informing him that he was yet at Canterbury, and anon after S. Thomas came to the king to Woodstock for to pray him to be better disposed towards holy church. And then said the king to him in scorn: 'May not we two dwell both in this land? Art thou so sturdy and hard of heart?' To whom S. Thomas answered: 'Sire, that was never my thought, but I would fain please you, and do all that you desire; so that ye hurt not the liberties of holy church; for them will I maintain while I live, ever to my power.' With which words the king was sore moved, and swore that he would have them kept, and especial if a clerk [clergyman] were a thief he should be judged and executed by the king's law, and by no spiritual law, and said he would never suffer a clerk to be his master in his own land, and charged S. Thomas to appear before him at Northampton, and to bring all the bishops of this land with him; and so departed. S. Thomas besought God of help and succor, for the bishops which ought to be with him were most against him. After this S. Thomas went to Northampton where the king had then his great council in the castle with all his lords, and when he came before the king he said: 'I am come to obey your commandment, but before this time was never bishop of Canterbury thus entreated, for I am head of the Church of England, and am to you, Sir King, your ghostly father, and it was never God's law that the son should destroy his father who has charge of his soul. And by your striving have you made all the bishops that should abide by the right of the church to be against holy church and me, and ye know well that I may not fight, but am ready to suffer death rather than I should consent to lose the right of holy church.' Then said the king: 'Thou speak as a proud clerk, but I shall abate thy pride ere I leave thee, for I must reckon with thee. Thou understand well that thou were my chancellor many years, and once I lent to thee £500 which thou never yet have repaid, which I will that thou pay me again or else incontinent thou shalt go to prison.' And then S. Thomas answered: 'Ye gave me that £500, and it is not fitting to demand that which ye have given.' Notwithstanding he found surety for the said £500 and departed for that day. And after this, the next day the king demanded £30,000 that he had surmised on him to have stolen, he being chancellor, whereupon he desired a day to answer; at which time he said that when he was archbishop he set him free therein without any claim or debt before good record, wherefore he ought not to answer unto that demand. And the bishops desired S. Thomas to obey the king; but in no wise he would not agree to such things as should touch against the liberties of the church. And then they came to the king, and forsook S. Thomas, and agreed to all the king's desire, and the proper servants of S. Thomas fled from him and forsook him, and then poor people came and accompanied him. And on the night came to him two lords and told to him that the king's followers had emprised to slay him. And the next night after he departed in the habit of a brother of Sempringham, and so chevissed that he went over sea.

And in the meanwhile certain bishops went to Rome for to complain about him to the pope, and the king sent letters to the king of France not to receive him. And King Louis said that, though a man were banished and had committed there trespasses, yet should he be free in France. And so after, when this holy S. Thomas came, he received him well, and gave him license to abide there and do what he would. In the meanwhile the king of England sent certain lords unto the pope complaining about the Archbishop Thomas, making grievous complaints, which when the pope had heard them, he would give no answer until he had heard the Archbishop Thomas speak, who would hastily come thither. But they would not abide his coming, but departed without speeding of their intents, and came into England again. And anon after, S. Thomas came to Rome on S. Mark's day at afternoon, and when his caterer should have bought fish for his dinner because it was fasting day, he could get none for no money, and came and told to his lord S. Thomas so, and he bade him buy such as he could get, and then he bought flesh and made it ready for their dinner. And S. Thomas was served with a capon roasted, and his followers with boiled meat. And so it was that the pope heard that he was come, and sent a cardinal to welcome him, and he found him at his dinner eating flesh, which anon returned and told to the pope how he was not so perfect a man as he had supposed, for contrary to the rule of the church he eats this day flesh. The pope would not believe him, but sent another cardinal who for more evidence took the leg of the capon in his kerchief and affirmed the same, and opened his kerchief before the pope, and he found the leg turned into a fish called a carp. And when the pope saw it, he said, they were not true men to say such things of this good bishop. They said faithfully that it was flesh that he ate. After this S. Thomas came to the pope and did his reverence and obedience, whom the pope welcomed, and after communication he demanded him what meat he had eaten, and he said: 'Flesh as ye have heard before, because he could find no fish and very need compelled him thereto.' Then the pope understood of the miracle that the capon's leg was turned into a carp, and of his goodness granted to him and to all them of the diocese of Canterbury license to eat flesh ever after on S. Mark's day when it falls on a fish day, and pardon withal; which is kept and accustomed unto this day. And then S. Thomas informed the pope how the king of England would have him consent to divers articles against the liberties of holy church, and what wrongs he did to the same, and that for to die he would never consent to them. And when the pope had heard him he wept for pity, and thanked God that he had such a bishop under him that had so well defended the liberties of holy church, and anon wrote out letters and bulls commanding all the bishops of Christendom to keep and observe the same. And then S. Thomas offered to the pope his bishopric up into the pope's hand, and his miter with the cross and ring, and the pope commanded him to keep it still, and said he knew no man more able than he was. And after S. Thomas said mass before the pope in a white chasuble; and after mass he said to the pope that he knew by revelation that he should suffer death for the right of holy church, and when it should fall that chasuble should be turned from white into red. And after he departed from the pope and came down into France unto the abbey of Pounteney; and there he had knowledge that when the lords spiritual and temporal which had been at Rome were come home and had told the king that they might in no wise have their intent, that the king was greatly wroth, and anon banished all the kinsmen that were belonging to S. Thomas that they should incontinent void his land, and made them swear that they should go to him and tell to him that for his sake they were exiled; and so they went over sea to him at Pounteney and he being there was full sorry for them. And after there was a great chapter in England of the monks of Cysteaus and there the king desired them to write to Pounteney that they should no longer keep nor sustain Thomas the

Archbishop, for if they did, he would destroy them of that order being in England. And, for fear thereof they wrote so over to Pounteney that he must depart thence with his kinsmen, and so he did, and was then full heavy, and remitted his cause to God. And anon after, the king of France sent to him that he should abide where it pleased him, and dwell in his realm, and he would pay for the costs of him and his kinsmen. And he departed and went to Sens, and the abbot brought him on the way. And S. Thomas told him how he knew by a vision that he should suffer death and martyrdom for the right of the church, and prayed him to keep it secret during his life. After this the king of England came into France, and there told the king how S. Thomas would destroy his realm, and then there told how he would foredo such laws as his elders had used before him, wherefore S. Thomas was sent for, and they were brought together. And the king of France labored sore for to set them at accord, but it would not be, for that one would not diminish his laws and customs, and S. Thomas would not grant that he should do contrary the liberties of holy church. And then the king of France held with the king of England against S. Thomas, and was wroth with him and commanded him to void his realm with all his kinsmen. And then S. Thomas did not know whither to go; but comforted his kinsmen as well as he might, and purposed to have gone in to Provence for to have begged his bread. And as he was going, the king of France sent for him again, and when he came he cried him mercy and said he had offended God and him, and bade him abide in his realm where he would, and he would pay for the expenses of him and his kin. And in the meanwhile the king of England ordained his son king, and made him to be crowned by the Archbishop of York and other bishops, which was against the statutes of the land, for the Archbishop of Canterbury should have consented and also have crowned him, wherefore S. Thomas gat a bull in order to accurse them that so did against him, and also on them that occupied the goods longing to him. And yet after this the [French] king labored so much that he brought accord between the king of England and S. Thomas; which accord endured not long, for the king varied from it afterward. But S. Thomas, upon this accord, came home to Canterbury, where he was received worshipfully, and sent for them that had trespassed against him, and by the authority of the pope's bull openly denounced them accursed unto the time they come to amendment. And when they knew this they came to him and would have made him to absolve them by force; and sent word over to the king what he had done, whereof the king was much wroth and said: 'If he had men in his land that loved him, they would not suffer such a traitor in his land alive.'

And forthwith four knights took their counsel together and thought they would do to the king a favor, and conspired to slay S. Thomas, and suddenly departed and took their shipping towards England. And when the king knew of their departing he was sorry and sent after them, but they were on the sea and departed ere the messengers came, wherefore the king was heavy and sorry.

These are the names of the four knights: Sir Reginald Fitzureson, Sir Hugh de Morville, Sir William de Tracy, Sir Richard le Brito. On Christmas day S. Thomas made a sermon at Canterbury in his own church, and weeping, prayed the people to pray for him, for he knew well his time was nigh.

And these four knights aforesaid came to Canterbury on the Tuesday in Christmas week about Evensong time, and came to S. Thomas and said that the king commanded him to make amends for the wrongs that he had done, and also that he should absolve all them that he had accursed anon, or else they should slay him. Then said Thomas: 'All that I ought to do by right, that will I with a good will do, but as to the sentence that is executed I may not undo, unless they will submit them to the correction of holy church; for it was done by our holy father the pope and not by me.' Then said Sir Reginald: 'But if thou assoil [absolve] the king and all other standing in the curse, it shall cost thee thy life.' And S. Thomas said: 'Thou know well enough that the king and I were accorded on Mary Magdalene day, and that this curse should go forth on them that had offended the church.'

Then one of the knights smote him as he kneeled before the altar on the head. And one Sir Edward Grim, that was his crozier, put forth his arm with the cross to bear off the stroke, and the stroke smote the cross asunder and his arm almost off; wherefore he fled for fear, and so did all the monks, that were that time at compline. And then smote each at him, that they smote off a great piece of the skull of his head, that his brain fell on the pavement. And so they slew and martyred him, and were so cruel that one of them brake the point of his sword against the pavement. And thus this holy and blessed Archbishop S. Thomas suffered death in his own church for the right of all holy church. And when he was dead they stirred his brain, and after went in to his chamber and took away his goods, and his horse out of his stable, and took away his bulls and writings, and delivered them to Sir Robert Broke to bear into France to the king. And as they searched his chamber they found in a chest two shirts of hair made full of great knots, and then they said: 'Certainly he was a good man'; and coming down into the churchyard they began to dread and fear that the ground would not have borne them, and were marvelously aghast, but they supposed that the earth would have swallowed them all quick. And then they knew that they had done amiss. And anon it was known all about how that he was martyred, and anon after took this holy body and unclothed him and found bishop's clothing above and the habit of a monk under. And next his flesh he wore hard hair, full of knots, which was his shirt. And he was thus martyred the year of our Lord one thousand one hundred and seventy-one, and was fifty-three years old. And soon after tidings came to the king how he was slain, wherefore the king took great sorrow, and sent to Rome for his absolution.

Now after that S. Thomas departed from the pope, the pope would daily look upon the white chasuble that S. Thomas had said mass in, and the same day that he was martyred he saw it turned into red, whereby he knew well that that same day he suffered martyrdom for the right of holy church, and commanded a mass of requiem solemnly to be sung for his soul. And when the choir began to sing requiem, an angel on high above began the office of a martyr: *Laetabitur justus,* and then all the choir followed singing forth the mass of the office of a martyr. And the pope thanked God that it pleased him to show such miracles for his holy martyr, at whose tomb by the merits and prayers of this holy martyr our blessed Lord has showed many miracles. The blind have recovered their sight, the dumb their speech, the deaf their hearing, the lame their limbs, and the dead their life. If I should here express all the miracles that it has pleased God to show for this holy saint it should contain a whole volume.

From *The Golden Legend: Lives of Saints,* trans. William Caxton from the Latin of Jacobus de Voraigne, selected and ed. by George V. O'Neill (Cambridge: Cambridge University Press, 1914), pp. 189–204.

19.4 Great Hymns of the Faith: *Veni Sancte Spiritus*

Music played a central role in the services of the church. Monks chanted the services of the Divine Office, with the Psalms as a central component. The mass and other liturgical services included psalms, chants, and antiphons, as well as hymns especially written for the service. One of the great Latin hymns used in the Roman Rite is *Veni Sancte Spiritus,* attributed to Stephen Langton (1150–1228), archbishop of Canterbury. Langton sent the hymn to Pope Innocent III, who sponsored its use in the church to such an extent that the pope is sometimes given credit for the hymn. This hymn is still used at Pentecost in Catholic churches, sung between the Gospel and Epistle readings, and is in use in English in many versions and musical adaptations. The Latin is reprinted below, with a parallel literal English translation.

All of these hymns were composed in Latin. Latin, like Greek, is an inflected language: it uses endings on words to indicate grammatical function (subject, direct object, indirect object) rather than position in the sentence, as with modern English (Man bites dog or Dog bites man?

It makes a big difference where you put the words). Consequently, Latin sentences are leaner and can get by with fewer prepositions (such as *by* and *with*). Latin poetry, then, has a clean simplicity in its appearance, in which each word bears a great deal of weight and often multiple meanings. Structurally the sentences are aesthetically satisfying and can serve to enhance meaning.

Although no translation does justice to another language, it is possible to examine the original side-by-side with a literal translation and see how the poetry works. No effort has been made in the translation on the right to invent English rhyming or meter. To hear the patterning of this poem, read the Latin on the left side. This hymn, as many other classic Latin hymns, is available in innumerable versions by later composers, including Bach and Mozart.

Questions

1. What do you notice about the Latin words on the left? What patterns do you see?
2. What sentiments are expressed in this hymn? What spiritual truths does it seek to convey?
3. Why do you think this hymn would remain popular in church services?

Veni Sancte Spiritus

Veni, Sancte Spiritus,	Come, Holy Spirit
Et emitte caelitus	and send down from heaven
Lucis tuae radium	the ray of your light.
Veni, pater pauperum,	Come, Father of the poor,
Veni, dator munerum,	Come, Giver of gifts,
Veni, lumen cordium.	Come, Light of [our] hearts.
Consolator optime,	Consoler the best,
Dulcis hospes animae,	Sweet Guest of the soul,
Dulce refrigerium;	Sweet Refreshment;
In labore requies,	In labor, Rest,
In aestu temperies,	In heat, Mildness,
In fletu solacium.	In weeping, Solace.
O lux beatissima,	O light most blessed,
Reple cordis intima	Fill the inmost hearts
Tuorum fidelium.	Of your faithful.
Sine tuo nomine	Without your name
Nihil est in homine,	Nothing is in humanity,
Nihil est innoxium.	Nothing is innocent.

Lava quod est sordidum,	Wash what is filthy,
Riga quod est aridum,	Water what is dry,
Sana quod est saucium;	Heal what is wounded;
Flecte quod est rigidum,	Bend what is rigid,
Fove quod est frigidum,	Warm what is cold,
Rege quod est devium.	Guide what is strayed.
Da tuis fidelibus	Grant to your faithful
In te confitentibus	Who trust in you
Sacrum septenarium;	Sacred sevenfold gifts;
Da virtutis meritum,	Grant the reward of virtue,
Da salutis exitum,	Grant a deathway to salvation,
Da perenne gaudium.	Grant everlasting joy.

Translated by Karen Louise Jolly from *A Primer of Medieval Latin: An Anthology of Prose and Poetry,* by Charles H. Beeson (Washington, DC: Catholic University Press of America, 1925), p. 360. Reprinted with permission. Notes omitted.

–20–

Cross-Cultural Exchange
Missions and Dialogue

Contact between Europeans and peoples to the east of them in the Eurasian continent increased over the course of the thirteenth century. The expansion of the Mongols under Genghis Khan and his heirs, the spread of Islam throughout the region, and the increasing prospect of eastern trade routes caused European eyes to turn eastward. In particular, European rulers, the pope most especially, sent messengers to investigate the Mongol threat and initiate diplomatic maneuvers in the hopes of subduing the Mongols under Christian rule before the reverse could happen, Mongol control of Europe. Other mendicant missionaries followed, moving into China and India where they recorded their observations and attempted to open dialogue with the diverse religions they found there in hopes of converting these peoples to Roman Christianity.

Many of these foreign courts where the missionaries attempted debate—such as Khanbaliq (modern Beijing)—were quite cosmopolitan, with a variety of scholars from various religious traditions resident. While John of Plano-Carpini (20.1) thought the religion in the Mongol homeland superstitious and incomprehensible, William of Ruysbruck (20.2) found Buddhists and Nestorian Christians at the Mongol court in China, as did John of Monte Corvino (20.3) in his missions to China and India. Already present in many of the Islamic courts were Jewish scholars engaged in comparative religious studies, examining, as ibn Kammûna does below (20.4), the three monotheistic traditions of Judaism, Islam, and Christianity.

20.1 Missions to the Mongols: John of Plano-Carpini

John of Plano Carpini (d. 1252) was an Italian friar of the Franciscan order ("minorite") who traveled as a papal messenger to the Mongols ("Tartars") in 1246, along with five other representatives of the church.

He was sent by Pope Innocent IV to investigate these destructive people who were moving westward toward Europe. The pope may have hoped to turn them in some other direction, pacify them, or convert them to Christianity. The friar kept a record of his travels, which have come down to us in this form.

Questions

1. What does John see as the aim of his mission? Does he think they can be converted?
2. What observations does he make about the Mongols?
3. How do you think Europeans would react to this description of a foreign people?

John of Plano Carpini, Report on the Mongols

I: Introductory Epistle by John de Plano Carpini

To all the faithful in Christ, to whom this writing may come, I friar John de Plano Carpini, of the order of minorites, legate and messenger from the Apostolic see to the Tartars and other nations of the east, wish the Grace of God in this life, and glory in the next, and perpetual triumph over all the enemies of the Lord. Having learnt the will of our lord the Pope, and the venerable Cardinals, and received the commands of the holy see, that we should go to the Tartars and other nations of the east, we determined to go in the first place to the Tartars; because we dreaded that the most imminent and nearest danger to the Church of God arose from them. And although we personally dreaded from these Tartars and other nations, that we might be slain or reduced to perpetual slavery, or should suffer hunger and thirst, the extremes of heat and cold, reproach, and excessive fatigue beyond our strength, all of which, except death and captivity, we have endured, even beyond our first fears, yet did we not spare ourselves, that we might obey the will of God, according to the orders of our lord the Pope, that we might be useful in any thing to the Christians, or at least, that the will and intention of these people might be assuredly known, and made manifest to Christendom, lest suddenly invading us, they might find us unprepared, and might make incredible slaughter of the Christian people. Hence, what we now write is for your advantage, that you may be on your guard, and more secure; being what we saw with our own eyes, while we sojourned with and among these people, during more than a year and four months, or which we have learnt from Christian captives residing among them, and whom we believe to be worthy of credit. We were likewise enjoined by the supreme pontiff, that we should examine and inquire into every thing very diligently; all of which, both myself and friar Benedict of the same order, my companion in affliction and interpreter, have carefully performed.

II: Of the First Mission of Friars Predicants and Minorites to the Tartars . . .

III: Of the Situation and Quality of the Land . . .

IV: Of the Appearance, Dress, and Manner of Living of the Tartars

The appearance of the Mongols or Tartars is quite different from all other nations, being much wider between the eyes and cheeks, and their cheeks are very prominent, with small flat noses, and small eyes, having the upper lids opened up to the eyebrows, and their crowns are shaven like priests on each side, leaving some long hair in the middle, the remainder being allowed to grow long like women, which they twist into two tails or locks, and bind behind their ears. The garments of the men and women are alike, using neither cloaks, hats, nor caps, but they wear strange tunics made of buckram, purple, or baldequin. Their gowns are made of skins, dressed in the hair, and open behind. They never wash their clothes, neither do they allow others to wash, especially in time of thunder, till that be over. Their houses are round, and artificially made like tents, of rods and twigs interwoven, having a round hole in the middle of the roof for the admission of light and the passage of smoke, the whole being covered with felt, of which likewise the doors are made. Some of these are easily taken to pieces or put together, and are carried on sumpter-cattle; while others are not capable of being taken to pieces, and are carried on carts. Wherever they go, whether to war, or only traveling to fresh pastures, these are carried with them. They have vast numbers of camels, oxen, sheep, and goats, and such prodigious multitudes of horses and mares, as are not to be found in all the rest of the world; but they have no swine. Their emperor, dukes, and other nobles, are extremely rich in gold and silver, silks, and gems. They eat of every thing that is eatable, and we have even seen them eat vermin. They drink milk in great quantity, and particularly prefer that of mares. But as in winter, none but the rich can have mares milk, they make a drink of millet boiled in water; every one drinking one or two cups in the morning, and sometimes having no other food all day; but in the evening, every one has a small quantity of flesh, and they drink the broth in which it was boiled. In summer, when they have abundance of mares milk, they eat little flesh, unless it is given them, or when they catch venison or birds.

V: Of their Good and Bad Customs

Some of their customs are commendable, and others execrable. They are more obedient to their lords than any other people, giving them vast reverence, and never deceiving them in word or action. They seldom quarrel; and brawls, wounds, or manslaughter hardly ever occur. Thieves and robbers are nowhere found, so that their houses and carts, in which all their treasure is kept, are never locked or barred. If any animal go astray, the finder either leaves it, or drives it to those who are appointed to seek for strays, and the owner gets it back without difficulty. They are very courteous, and though victuals are scarce among them, they communicate freely to each other. They are very patient under privations, and though they may have fasted for a day or two, will sing and make merry as if they were well satisfied. In journeying, they bear cold or heat with great fortitude. They never fall out, although often drunk, never quarrel in their cups. No one despises another, but every one assists his neighbor to the utmost. Their women are chaste, yet their conversation is frequently immodest. Towards other people they are exceedingly proud and overbearing, looking upon all other men with contempt, however noble. For we saw, in the emperor's court, the great duke of Russia, the son of the king of Georgia, and many sultans and other great men, who received no honor or respect; so that even the Tartars appointed to attend them, however low their condition, always went before them, and took the upper places, and even often obliged them to sit behind their backs. Thy are irritable and disdainful to other men, and beyond belief deceitful; speaking always fair at first, but afterwards stinging like scorpions. They are crafty and fraudulent, and cheat all men if they can. Whatever mischief they intend they carefully conceal, that no one may provide or find a remedy for their wickedness. They are filthy in their meat and drink, and in all their actions. Drunkenness is honorable among them; so that, when one has drank to excess and throws up, he begins again to drink. They are most importunate beggars, and covetous possessors, and most niggardly givers; and they consider the slaughter of other people as nothing. . . .

VI: Of the Laws and Customs of the Tartars . . .

VII: Of their Superstitious Traditions

In consequence of certain traditions, they consider many indifferent actions as criminal. One is, to thrust a knife into the fire, or any way to touch a fire with a knife, to take meat from the pot with a knife, or even to hew any thing with an axe near a fire; as they consider all these things as taking away the force of the fire. Another is, to lean upon a whip, for they use no spurs, or to touch arrows with their whip, to strike their horse with their bridle, to take or kill young birds, or to break one bone upon another. Likewise, to spill milk, or any drink, or food, on the ground, or to make water in a house; for the last offense, if intentional, a man is slain, or he must pay a heavy fine to the soothsayers to be purified; in which case, the house, and all that it contains, has to pass between two fires, before which ceremony no person must enter the house, nor must any thing be removed from it. If any one takes a bit of meat that he cannot swallow and spits it out, a hole is made in the floor in the house, through which he is dragged and put to death. If any one treads on the threshold of a house belonging to one of their dukes, he is put to death. Many such things they account high offenses. But to slay men, to invade the territories of others, to take away the goods of other people, and to act contrary to the commands of God, is no crime among them; and they know nothing of the life to come, or of eternal damnation. But they believe in a future life, in which they shall tend flocks, eat and drink, and do those very things which they do in this life. At new moon, or when the moon is full, they begin any new enterprise; they call the moon the great emperor, and they worship that luminary on their knees. All who dwell in their houses must they call the moon the great emperor, and they worship that luminary on their knees. All who dwell in their houses must undergo purification by fire, which is performed in this manner. Having kindled two fires at a convenient distance, they fix two spears in the earth, one near each fire, stretching a cord between the tops of these spears, and about the cord they hang some rags of buckram, under which cord, and between which fires, all the men, and beasts, and houses must pass; and all the while, a woman stands on each side, sprinkling water on the passengers, and reciting certain verses. If any one is killed by lightning, all that dwell in the same house with the dead person must be thus purified; otherwise, the house, beds, carts, felts, garments, and everything else would be abandoned as unclean. When any messengers, princes, or other persons arrive, they and their gifts must pass between two fires for purification, lest they should bring witchcraft, poison, or any other mischief.

From Robert Kerr, *A General History and Collection of Voyages and Travels,* Vol. I (Edinburgh: William Blackwood, 1811), pp. 125–61, selections.

20.2 Buddhist-Christian Debate: William of Ruysbruck

William of Ruysbruck (Rubruquis or Roebruck, circa 1253) was another Franciscan friar sent to investigate the Mongols, in this case by the

French king Louis IX. The aim of his diplomatic mission was apparently to open dialogue with the Mongol khan, in the hopes of converting them to Christianity. Conversion, in the European view, was a way of pacifying a godless violent people, in the same way that the Europeans' ancestors had been converted and civilized by the coming of Christianity according to their church histories. However, what William and other Europeans found in the East was a cosmopolitan, urban society replete with a variety of religions and ancient traditions. The size, magnificence, and complexity of the eastern courts overwhelmed any ideas of easily converting these people to Christianity.

The court of the khan in China contained Muslims, Buddhists, Confucianists, Taoists, Nestorian Christians, and a variety of indigenous belief systems such as ancestor worship. In the following selection from William's account, he attempts to engage the Buddhists in debate, while simultaneously trying to exclude the Nestorian Christians. The discussion bogs down right away over the issue of what subject to tackle first, each side having a different notion of what is essential.

Questions

1. What do the Buddhists think is the first thing to establish? And what does William as a Christian want to discuss first, and why?
2. What different views of divinity do they have and how does this affect the dialogue?
3. In order to communicate Christian belief to the Buddhists, what obstacles do you think William needs to overcome?

Travels of William de Rubruquis into Tartary, about the Year 1253

All things being arranged, we convened at our oratory, and Mangu-khan [the Khan] sent three of his secretaries, a Christian, a Saracen [Muslim], and a Tuinian [Buddhist], to be judges of the controversy. It was first proclaimed, "This is the order of Mangu-Khan [the Khan], and none dare say that the commandment of God is otherwise. Let none speak contentiously, or use injurious words to one another, or make any tumult whereby this business may be hindered, upon pain of death." There was a great assembly, as every party had convened the wisest of their sect, and many others came flocking around to listen; but all were silent. The [Nestorian] Christians set me in the middle, willing that I should contend with the Tuinians [Buddhists]; who murmured against Mangu-khan [the Khan], as no khan had ever thus endeavored to search into their secrets. . . . Then he [the Chinese speaker] demanded whether I would dispute as to how the world was made, or as to what became of the soul after death? For they were desirous to begin with these questions, as they held them for the strongest in their doctrines, all the Tuinians [Buddhists] following the heresy of the Manicheans, believing in a *good* and *bad* principle, and they all believe that souls pass from body to body. In confirmation of this, the goldsmith [his translator] told me they had brought a person from Kathay, who, by the size of his body, appeared to be only three years old, yet was capable of reasoning, and knew how to write, and who affirmed that he had passed through three several bodies. Even one of the wisest of the Nestorians demanded of me whether the souls of brutes could fly to any place after death where they should not be compelled to labor.

To the before-mentioned question of the [Chinese man], I answered: "Friend, this ought not to be the commencement of our conference. All things are of God, who is the fountain and head of us all; and therefore we ought first to speak concerning God, of whom you think otherwise than you ought, and Mangu [the Khan] desires to know which of us has the better belief." The arbitrators allowed this to be reasonable, and I proceeded: "We firmly believe there is but one God in perfect unity; what believe you?" He said, "Fools say there is but one God, but wise men say there are many. There are great lords in your country, and here is still a greater, even Mangu-khan [the Khan]. So it is of the Gods, as in divers countries there are divers gods." To this I answered: "You make a bad comparison between God and men; for in this way every mighty man might be called a God in his own country." And when I meant to have dissolved the similitude, he prevented me, by asking, "What manner of God is yours, who you say is but one?" I answered: "Our God, beside whom there is no other, is omnipotent, and therefore needs not the help of any other; whereas all have need of his help. It is not so with men, as no man can do all things; wherefore there must be many lords on earth, as no one can support all. God is omniscient, or knows all things; and therefore has no need of any counselor, for all wisdom is from him. God is perfectly good; and needs not therefore any good from us. In God we live and move and have our being. Such is our God, and you must not hold that there is any other." "It is not so," said he; "for there is one highest in heaven, whose origin or generation we know not, and there are ten under him, and on earth they are infinite in number." To this he would have added other fables. I asked him respecting the highest God, of whom he had spoken, whether he were omnipotent, or if any of the inferior Gods were so? And fearing to answer this, he demanded, "Why, since our God was perfectly good, he had made the half of all things evil?" To this I answered, that this was false; for whosoever makes any evil is no God, and all things whatsoever are good. At this all the Tuinians [Buddhists] were astonished, and set it down in writing as false or impossible. He then asked me, "Whence comes evil?" "You ask amiss," said I, "for you ought first to inquire what evil is, before you ask whence it comes: But let us return to the first question, whether do you believe that any God is omnipotent? and when that is discussed, I will answer whatever you may demand." On this he sat a long time without speaking, and the judges appointed by the khan commanded him to make answer. At length he said, that no God was omnipotent; on which all the Saracens [Muslims] broke out into great laughter. When silence was restored, I said, "None of your gods, therefore, can save you in all dangers, since chances may happen in which they have no power. Besides, no man can serve two masters; how, therefore, can you serve so many Gods in heaven and in earth?" The auditory decreed that he should make answer to this, but he held his peace.

When I was about to have propounded reasons to prove the truth of the divine essence, and to have explained the doctrine of the Trinity, the Nestorians alleged that I had said quite enough, and that now they meant to speak; so I gave place to them. When, therefore, they would have disputed with the Saracens [Muslims], these men said that they agreed to the truth of the law and the gospel of the Christians, and would not dispute with them in any thing. . . . There was among the idolaters a priest of the sect of the Jugurs, who believe in one God, and yet make idols. With this man the Nestorians talked much, showing all things till the coming of Christ to judgment, and explaining the Trinity to him and the Saracens [Muslims] by similitudes. All of them hearkened to their harangue without attempting to make any contradiction; yet none of them said that they believed and would become Christians. The conference was now broken up. The Nestorians and Saracens [Muslims] sang together with a loud voice, and the Tuinians [Buddhists] held their peace; and afterwards they all drank together most plentifully.

Reprinted from Robert Kerr, *A General History and Collection of Voyages and Travels,* Vol 1 (Edinburgh: Blackwood, 1811), pp. 242–45.

20.3 Missions to India and China: John of Monte Corvino

None of the attempts in the earlier part of the thirteenth century succeeded in converting many Mongols or Chinese, or in getting the Mongol rulers to recognize papal supremacy. Late in the thirteenth century, another Franciscan mission was dispatched in the hopes of establishing a solid Christian presence in China. John of Monte Corvino went in 1290 to India and China, and was made archbishop of Khanbaliq in 1307. He ruled over a small community of Christians mostly drawn from expatriates living in China, but continued to struggle with the Nestorian Christians, whom he blamed for impeding the work of conversion. After his death in 1328, other Franciscans continued the work into the fourteenth century, but Roman Christianity did not become firmly established among the native populations.

The excerpt below from John of Monte Corvino's report describes his successes and failures, along with some of his frustrations over the lack of resources and assistance.

Questions

1. What problems does John have with the Nestorians, and why do you think these problems arise?
2. In what ways is John's mission a success, at least in his own eyes?
3. What kinds of things does John see as essential for his mission and its success? What are his desires, as he expresses them?

Missions to India and China

I, Friar John of Monte Corvino, of the order of Minor Friars, departed from Tauris, a city of the Persians, in the year of the Lord 1291, and proceeded to India. And I remained in the country of India, wherein stands the church of St. Thomas the Apostle, for thirteen months, and in that region baptized in different places about one hundred persons. The companion of my journey was Friar Nicholas of Pistoia, of the order of Preachers, who died there, and was buried in the church aforesaid.

I proceeded on my further journey and made my way to Cathay, the realm of the Emperor of the Tartars who is called the Grand Cham. To him I presented the letter of our lord the Pope, and invited him to adopt the Catholic Faith of our Lord Jesus Christ, but he had grown too old in idolatry. However he bestows many kindnesses upon the Christians, and these two years past I am abiding with him.

The Nestorians, a certain body who profess to bear the christian name, but who deviate sadly from the christian religion, have grown so powerful in those parts that they will not allow a christian of another ritual to have ever so small a chapel, or to publish any doctrine different from their own.

To these regions there never came any one of the Apostles, nor yet of the Disciples. And so the Nestorians aforesaid, either directly or through others whom they bribed, have brought on me persecutions of the sharpest. For they got up stories that I was not sent by our lord the Pope, but was a great spy and impostor; and after a while they produced false witnesses who declared that there was indeed an envoy sent with presents of immense value for the emperor, but that I had murdered him in India, and stolen what he had in charge. And these intrigues and calumnies went on for some five years, And thus it came to pass that many a time I was dragged before the judgment seat with ignominy and threats of death. At last, by God's providence, the emperor, through the confessions of a certain individual, came to know my innocence and the malice of my adversaries; and he banished them with their wives and children.

In this mission I abode alone and without any associate for eleven years; but it is now going on for two years since I was joined by Friar Arnold, a German of the province of Cologne.

I have built a church in the city of Cambaliech, in which the king has his chief residence. This I completed six years ago; and I have built a bell-tower to it, and put three bells in it. I have baptized there, as well as I can estimate, up to this time some 6,000 persons; and if those charges against me of which I have spoken had not been made, I should have baptized more than 30,000. And I am often still engaged in baptizing.

Also I have gradually bought one hundred and fifty boys, the children of pagan parents, and of ages varying from seven to eleven, who had never learned any religion. These boys I have baptized, and I have taught them Greek and Latin after our manner. Also I have written out Psalters for them, with thirty Hymnaries and two Breviaries. By help of these, eleven of the boys already know our service, and form a choir and take their weekly turn of duty as they do in convents, whether I am there or not. Many of the boys are also employed in writing out Psalters and other things suitable. His Majesty the Emperor moreover delights much to hear them chanting. I have the bells rung at all the canonical hours, and with my congregation of babes and sucklings I perform divine service, and the chanting we do by ear because I have no service book with the notes.

A certain king of this part of the world, by name George, belonging to the sect of Nestorian christians, and of the illustrious family of that great king who was called Prester John of India, in the first year of my arrival here attached himself to me, and being converted by me to the truth of the Catholic faith, took the lesser orders, and when I celebrated mass he used to attend me wearing his royal robes. Certain others of the Nestorians on this account accused him of apostasy, but he brought over a great part of his people with him to the true Catholic faith, and built a church on a scale of royal magnificence in honor of our God, of the Holy Trinity, and of our lord the Pope. . . .

This King George six years ago departed to the Lord . . . And after King George's death his brothers, perfidious followers of the errors of Nestorius, perverted again all those whom he had brought over to the church, and carried them back to their original schismatical creed. And being all alone, and not able to leave his Majesty the Cham, I could not go to visit the church above-mentioned, which is twenty days' journey distant.

Yet, if I could but get some good fellow-workers to help me, I trust in God that all this might be retrieved, for I still possess the grant which was made in our favour by the late King George before mentioned. So I say again that if it had not been for the slanderous charges which I have spoken of, the harvest reaped by this time would have been great!

Indeed if I had had but two or three comrades to aid me 'tis possible that the Emperor Cham would have been baptized by this time! I ask then for such brethren to come, if any are willing to come, such I mean as will make it their great business to lead exemplary lives, and not to make broad their own phylacteries.

As for the road hither I may tell you that the way through the land of the Goths, subject to the Emperor of the Northern Tartars, is the shortest and safest; and by it the friars might come, along with the letter-carriers, in five or six months. The other route again is very long and very dangerous, involving two sea-voyages;. . . . But, on the other hand, the first-mentioned route has not been open for a considerable time, on account of wars that have been going on.

It is twelve years since I have had any news of the Papal court, or of our order, or of the state of affairs generally in the west. Two years ago indeed there came hither a certain Lombard leech and surgeon, who spread abroad in these parts the most incredible blasphemies about the court of Rome and our Order and the state of things in the west, and on this account I exceedingly desire to obtain true intelligence. I pray the brethren whom this letter may reach to do their possible to bring its contents to the knowledge of our lord the Pope, and the Cardinals, and the agents of the Order at the court of Rome.

I beg the Minister General of our Order to supply me with an Antiphon, with the Legends of the Saints, a Gradual, and a Psalter with the musical notes, as a copy; for I have nothing but a pocket Breviary with the short Lessons, and a little missal: if I had one for a copy, the boys of whom I have spoken could transcribe others from it. Just now I am engaged in building a second church, with the view of distributing the boys in more places than one.

I have myself grown old and gray, more with toil and trouble than with years; for I am not more than fifty-eight. I have got a competent knowledge of the language and character which is most generally used by the Tartars. And I have already translated into that language and character the New Testament and the Psalter, and have caused them to be written out in the fairest penmanship they have; and so by writing, reading, and preaching, I bear open and public testimony to the Law of Christ. . . .

As far as I ever saw or heard tell, I do not believe that any king or prince in the world can be compared to his majesty the Cham in respect of the extent of his dominions, the vastness of their population, or the amount of his wealth. Here I stop.

Dated at the city of Cambalec in the kingdom of Cathay, in the year of the Lord 1305, and on the 8th day of January.

Reprinted from *Cathay and the Way Thither,* trans. Henry Yule (London: Hakluyt Society, 1866), Vol. I, pp. 197–203 passim.

20.4 Dialogue: Ibn Kammûna

Ibn Kammûna was a Jewish writer and thinker in Baghdad who compared Judaism, Christianity, and Islam in the following Arabic treatise, written circa 1280. In this treatise, he backs the centrality of monotheism. He acknowledges the similarities in the three monotheistic faiths, and he tries to show that Zorastrian dualists are really monotheistic and that even idol-worshiping pagans are attempting to reach the one God through their idols. Despite his conciliatory tone in recognizing the prophets Jesus in Christianity and Muhammad in Islam, he finds errors in their beliefs. In the selection below, he discusses the main Christian tenets, the flaws he sees in them, imagines a Christian rebuttal, and then replies to those rebuttals. In using this scholarly dialogue format, he demonstrates a good grasp of Christian doctrine and highlights some of the most troublesome parts of Christian belief for Jews. In particular, the Incarnation and the Trinity seem at odds with the notion of an omnipotent monotheistic deity, and the veracity of the New Testament Scriptures is problematic. Ibn Kammûna's treatise is significant because it allows us to see Christianity from the perspective of someone outside of it who nonetheless understands it.

Questions

1. What in the nature and life of Christ as taught by Christians is disturbing to ibn Kammûna and why?
2. Why does he question the Christian Scriptures?
3. How do you think a European Christian scholar would respond to his arguments?

Ibn Kammûna's Examination of the Three Faiths

On the belief of the Christians in the Lord Jesus Christ, who is Jesus the son of Mary, peace be upon them; his message; in what manner he is, according to them, both prophet and deity; opinions and counter-opinions therewith connected.

The Christians teach the following:

We believe all that is in the Torah and in the records of the Israelites, records whose veracity is irrefutable because they are widely known and available to the masses. We believe that toward the very end of the [sacred] history of the Jews, Deity became incarnate and an embryo in the body of a virgin chosen from among the noblest of the women of the Israelites, the progeny of David. She gave birth to a being outwardly human, and essentially divine; who was outwardly sent forth as a prophet, and essentially sent forth as a deity; he was fully man and fully deity. This is Christ, called the Son of God. God is the Father, the Son, and the Holy Ghost.

They maintain:

We are truly monotheists, though we make mention of Trinity with our tongues. We believe in God and in His sojourn among the Israelites as a distinction to them, for the divine power never ceased to be attached to them until their people rebelled against our Messiah, and crucified Him. Then divine wrath became unremitting against their people, and divine favor was continuous toward the few followers of Christ—from among whom Christ elected twelve persons corresponding to the number of tribes of Israel—and later favor was extended toward the gentile nations following those few believers. We are [spiritually] of the Children of Israel although we are not of their progeny. We are the more worthy of being designated as Israelites because we follow the Messiah and his Apostles. Those few believers were followed by the many who became the leaven for the community of the Christians, and they merited the status of the Israelites. The Christians were successful, and spread into many lands and nations calling the people unto the Christian faith, urging its worship with respect to the cult of Christ and his Cross, and complying with His decrees and with the testaments of His Apostles, as well as with laws derived from the Torah which Christians read and which is irrefutably true and divine. Those who have faith in this call follow it obediently, voluntarily, and willingly without being compelled thereto by sword or coercion.

The Christians agreed upon this creed in a resolution by a council of 318 persons in the time of Constantine. . . . [Nicene Creed follows]

There are many discrepancies among the four gospels which the Christian scholars try in some way to harmonize. The gospels contain many parables and sermons. They contain the command of noble moral traits; for example:

> If you requite evil with evil you merit no reward from your Father in Heaven; if you forgive men their trespasses your Father in Heaven will forgive your trespasses, but if you forgive not neither will He forgive you.

There was among Christians much dissension about the creed. Thus, some maintain existence in time for the Son, or say that God created the Son and empowered him to create the World; while the others say that Christ was born of His Father before all the worlds were created and was not created in time, as also stated in the agreed-upon creed. They had numerous councils which attempted to eliminate internal strife, and at these some of the dissenters were excommunicated, which led to much bloodshed among them. This is known from their history books.

Such changes in the stipulations of the Torah as—for example, to make lawful [the consumption of] the flesh of swine, and the abandonment of circumcision and laving [of hands]—are told of the Apostles, not about Jesus Christ, for he adhered to the stipulations of the Torah until the Jews seized him. He would enjoin them to comply with those stipulations and He said: I am not come to destroy, but to fulfil [the law].

When the Jews blamed him for what they imagined to be neglect of some Torah stipulations, he explained to them that it was not neglect, and clarified this unto them in accord with their jurisprudence and law, as is mentioned in the Gospel. His disciples continued for a long time with this adherence to the Torah, before they began to break its laws and declared that the Torah was abrogated and had been obligatory only until the advent of Jesus Christ. Most of this goes back to the apostle Paul.

The opponents of Christianity may say:

If the hypostases [particular individuals] you mentioned suggest three entities existing independently, the principle of monotheism invalidates that inference, and it also contradicts your creed on the unity of God. But if you mean that the hypostases are attributes, or that one of them is essence, and the other two are attributes, then have you not turned the attribute of power into a fourth hypostasis, and similarly the other terms to describe God into hypostases? Should they say:

His power is His knowledge

we say: His life also is His knowledge and why have you separated it into a hypostasis?

The idea of the union is not intelligible, because two things that unite are either existent or nonexistent, or one of the two is existent, and the other nonexistent. If the two exist, there is no union because they are two, not one; if the two do not exist, they become not one, and a third element, also nonexistent, appears; if one is nonexistent and the other remains, then clearly there is no union. The monotheistic principle is contradicted if, supposing union to mean mixing, blending, or compounding, the Father and Son are two separate substances in which the Son merges with Christ, and the Father, in the sense mentioned above, does not. If again the Son is an attribute, it cannot be understood about the knowing essence that its being knowing becomes blended with some body without the essence. Just as it is beyond understanding that Zayd can be in Baghdad while his being knowing is in Khurasan. Further, the knowledge of everything by Him must necessarily include the knowledge of God and the knowledge of Christ simultaneously, so the same attribute actually has two carriers, which is absurd. If, again, God was not knowing at the moment of union, then his being knowing would be a vain assertion, thus he would need a specifier (to endow him with knowledge), and this precludes him from divinity. . . .

Furthermore, God is too exalted to be described as having dwelled in the uncleanness of the menstruating womb and in the confinement of the belly and darkness; or that bodily eyes looked at Him; or that He was affected by slumber or sleep; or that He excremented in his clothes and urinated in his bed; or that He wept or laughed; or that He was helpless against what He did not want; or that He was lost in thought, imprisoned, overcome with fear and desirous of human possession; or that He fled. God is too exalted for it to be said that He ate, drank, and behaved like earthly humans; or that He could not assert Himself while ruling the world until He descended upon earth to guide men and save them from Satan; or that He came to purify men of their sins and to guide them from going astray; or that the Jews maltreated, tortured, crucified, and humiliated Him; or that He spent three days in His grave.

What sin before or after Christ was greater, in your opinion, than the one committed in his time? And yet the Devil, just as he did before the advent of Christ, has continued to lead astray and harm men following Christ's advent. The devil split your religion into various sects and you testify about one another's heresies. In some countries the apostles were slain, humiliated, and tortured. Oppression, enmity, massacre, and unbelief are widespread among Christians and other nations to this day.

One may say to the Christians:

If Christ is considered a God because he is, in your view, without a parent, then Adam and Eve, along with every primeval beast God created, are more wondrous than he in this respect. The prophet Elijah was unaffected in his human existence by misfortune and, after working numerous miracles, was taken into heaven before Christ, if that is a requisite for being God. If worshiping a human being were permissible, Elijah would be more entitled to deification than he who was imprisoned, humiliated, tortured, and crucified. The angels, also are too exalted to be commanded to descend. Jesus is worshiped, let us say, because the Gospel called him the Son of God, but on the other hand, you avow that God called Israel "my first-born son," and that Jesus called the apostles his brothers. It also says in the Gospel, "Love them which love you," and so on, down to "you will be like my Father and your Father which is in Heaven;" also, "if you requite trespasses with trespasses, you have no reward from your Father;" and, "if you forgive men their trespasses, your [heavenly] Father will also forgive you." And, if his divinity is claimed because of his miracles, then, to repeat, other prophets, too, had wrought them. . . .

Furthermore, all the miracles and other phenomena reported about Christ are presented on the authority of individuals who were his companions, and are neither properly transmitted nor reliable. Even should the tradition be sound it is not rationally improbable that some illusion or collusion had a part in it.

But if the soundness of the Christians' tradition cannot be established, then nothing can be ascertained of their claim that they know clearly, on the authority of the apostles and Christ, that their religion is never to be abrogated.

This is what I see fit to mention of the arguments against the Christians. I now proffer the best of what they might say in answer to these points. . . .

[The Christians reply:] As for the list of descriptions of and utterances about the Messiah that contradict His divinity—for example, sleeping, eating, having pains, and so on—they refer to the human aspect in Him, not to the divine. That is why we say He is fully human and fully divine. . . .

As for the claim of His divinity, it stems not from a few circumstances of His life that might be compared with those of the prophets and others, but from the sum total of His circumstances. It is well known that this was unparalleled either before or after Him.

If somebody else is designated as God's son, it is a metaphor, as both protagonist and antagonist will agree, but in relation to Jesus the term is truth. Proof thereof is the authority of the apostles from whom the creed of the Christian faith was handed down.

Christ's words "I come not to destroy the law . . . but to fulfill it," mean that the Law contains the promise of the advent of the messiah, and that all its precepts are obligatory up to the time of His advent, not forever or to the day of resurrection. Since His appearance, the Law has been fulfilled (1) by the consummation of the promise of his advent, and (2) by the completion of its obligatoriness.

Also, Jesus violated none of the stipulations of the Torah, but instead, observed all of them to the end, as we explained, and in this sense, too, He is fulfilling them. . . .

[Rebuttal:] But the Jewish interpretations of these passages preclude those of the Christians. Many of the prophetic texts were distorted by the Christians in the process of translation from Hebrew into Greek and Syriac, and later into Arabic, resulting in a significant discrepancy in meaning, although only in a few words. The Christians, at least partly, recognize the discrepancy. This distortion may be the result of intent or negligence, as well as an insufficient knowledge of the language of the original.

I have adduced the evidences the Christians quote from the prophetic books in the manner that they have translated them, rather than as the Jews have them in Hebrew.

In reply to the opinion that the tradition of the miracles of Jesus and of his life rests on the authority of individuals and, therefore, is not authoritatively transmitted and authentic, Christians may say that those individuals, according to the indubitable report of a great mass of people, wrought more miracles than Christ; further, that these miracles not only indicate the veracity of the miracles of Jesus, but are in truth substantially his, and only accidentally their miracles, and it would be proper to attribute them to Jesus rather than to those individuals. Thus it is established that all that has been reported about him—the miracles and so on—is true, and it becomes manifest therefrom that the truth of the Christian religion will not be abrogated.

In fact, *we* do *not* concede that the reports of the miracles by the companions of Jesus constitute authoritative transmission that induces certainty, like the authoritative transmission about the *existence* of Jesus and the apostles, and his crucifixion; they are rather of the type of rumors that spread, come into vogue, and become quasi-transmitted without being truly transmitted.

With regard to the argument that reason does not preclude that the miracles of Jesus occurred through illusion or collusion, the Christians claim their conviction that no such illusion and collusion ever occurred, or could possibly occur; and they claim that there is no difference, in the matter of improbability of illusion between the miracles of Jesus and those of Moses, such as the separation of the sea, and the like. No doubt was entertained about the death and disease of those whom Jesus revived and cured; it may be argued for the veracity thereof that if anyone had had doubts it would have become known among his enemies, Jews and others, in his time, and if it had become known at that time it would have been reported. Doubts have not been reported and, although some ascribed the miracles to magic, or the devil's aid, or to Jesus having learned God's highest name, it is clear that his contemporaries were certain of the absence of illusion or collusion.

This is an argument of *the convinced,* not convincing of certainty, but perhaps it might confirm a prevailing notion once their transmitted tradition is accepted.

But if the argument is supported by viewing all the details of the life of Jesus and his companions—their asceticism, piety, and endurance of great suffering in establishing the church and organizing their religion so thoroughly—then from the totality of these concomitants it becomes clear that their cause depends on divine support and concern from on high.

Some of the other arguments of the antagonists mentioned above stem from sheer defamation and rejection, and others will be refuted by the intelligent reader with some effort but no difficulty.

I did not find most of these retorts in discussions by Christians; I supplied these retorts on behalf of the Christians, and in supplementation of the investigation into their belief.

Reprinted with permission from *Ibn Kammûna's Examination of the Three Faiths: A Thirteenth-Century Essay in the Comparative Study of Religion,* trans. Moshe Perlmann (Berkeley: University of California Press, 1971), excerpts from pp. 78–79, 82–84, 86–88, 93–95, 98–99. Copyright © 1971. Notes omitted.

Part 6

Change and Contact in the Late Middle Ages, circa 1300–1500

The period from circa 1300/1350 to 1500 is variously designated the Late Middle Ages or the Renaissance, depending upon what areas and subjects are of interest. The period is one of dislocation, with the Black Death, the Hundred Years War, and the papal schism playing a major role in characterizing this era as a period of decline for the medieval European world. And yet at the same time, the Renaissance, beginning in Italy and spreading northward, grows out of the medieval foundations and sets the conditions for the early modern world; likewise, the Reformation of the sixteenth century is a response to late medieval developments. Whether the fourteenth and fifteenth centuries are perceived as the decline of the medieval or the rise of the modern, this is a period of dynamic change.

Part Six examines the positive and negative features of this period, looking in particular at the ways in which fourteenth- and fifteenth-century Europeans coped with their changing world. Chapter 21 examines dissenting opinions on church authority and knowledge in direct challenge to the order of the church, while Chapter 22 turns to alternative views of life in the spirit of prophecy, expressed by mystics and social activists. Chapter 23 also looks at spirituality, but as part of the lay experience of the religion, in church rituals, drama, and story. Chapter 24 provides a fitting conclusion to the book by examining cross-cultural contact, and the ways in which Christian worldviews affected European understanding of the "other."

In all of these sections, notions of what it means to be European and what it means to be Christian as an individual and as a society are being challenged by changing economic, social, and political circumstances both within Europe and outside of it. Christianity, both in the formal church and in the everyday experience of the laity, played a role in the way that European cultures developed in these centuries, and set the preconditions for the Reformation and the early modern world.

475

–21–

Dissent and Reform in Late Medieval Christendom

This chapter looks at views dissenting from the orthodox or at odds with the institutional church. Two Italian figures of the fourteenth century, Dante and Petrarch, give their reactions to the perceived corruption of the papacy (21.1). Dante reacts to the pontificate of Boniface VIII, while Petrarch bemoans the so-called Babylonian captivity, the period circa 1348–1377 when the popes resided in Avignon, France, away from the political corruption of Rome but within the domain and influence of the French monarchy. The papal schism following the Avignon papacy, during which two, and then three, popes competed for primacy, highlights the problems of authority and governance in medieval Europe. This schism also generated new political theories for the election of the pope, evident in the conciliar movement (21.2). Others, operating in the spirit of prophecy, continued to question the authority of the priesthood, as Wickliff does by rejecting transubstantiation in the Eucharist (21.3). All of these "challenges" have their roots in the social, political, and intellectual developments of the previous century, but are stronger and more dangerous to the order of things in the increasingly unstable world of the fourteenth and fifteenth centuries.

21.1 Views of the Papacy: Dante and Petrarch

As evident in previous chapters, the papacy was frequently embroiled in political controversies with secular rulers. These political wranglings had their beginnings in the eleventh-century effort to reform the church by getting rid of secular influence and corruption, such as simony (Chapter 13). As the battles of the investiture contest became more heated, and as centralized monarchal governance became dominant, popes and papal theorists increasingly laid claim to supremacy as the ultimate means of separating the church from temporal control. These efforts reached a peak with Pope Innocent III (17.1), and went over the top with Boniface VIII (see 18.3). Throughout most of this growth in church prestige, wealth, and authority, the general lay populations of Europe respected the papal office as an idealized force for justice acting as a counterbalance to local, territorial control by the aristocracy. However, after Boniface VIII, and with the Avignon papacy and the papal schism, a broad spectrum of the laity, from intellectuals to common folk, turned against the perceived wealth, power, and corruption of the church and its churchmen. The church as represented in its rulers lost its moral authority as a force in late medieval Europe.

One hotbed of reaction to papal monarchy comes from Italy itself, where a great deal of the politicking occurred, and where the Renaissance, with its secular humanist thinkers, began questioning the way things were. One forerunner of these literary attacks on the social and political world of Italy and Europe as a whole is found in the *Divine Comedy* of Dante Alighieri (1265–1321). Dante's tripartite vision encompasses hell (*Inferno*), limbo (*Purgatorio*), and heaven (*Paradisio*), and comments on everything from sordid sin and political corruption to romantic love and sublime spirituality. The section below is from the *Inferno,* the pit where the simoniac popes and bishops are roasting their feet (upside down). Dante's attack on the papacy is quite specific: he cleverly places the not-yet-dead Boniface VIII in this ring of hell. Another Italian, Francesco Petrarch (1304–1374), was a Renaissance humanist famous for restoring classical style and literature. His commentary below on the papal court in Avignon, where he resided for a time, reflects his distaste for the political clutter of church life in this period, and his longing for a classical purity and apostolic spirituality.

Questions

1. Why does Dante condemn these men, and with what kinds of punishment?

2. Why is Petrarch unhappy in Avignon?

3. By what criteria do both Dante and Petrarch judge churchmen? Who or what should set the standard for appropriate behavior and lifestyle for prelates, in their view?

Dante: The Pope in Hell

O Simon Magus! O wretched followers of his and robbers
    ye, who prostitute the things of God, that should be
    wedded unto righteousness,

for gold and, silver! now must the trump sound for you:
　　for ye are in the third chasm.
Already we had mounted to the following grave, on that
　　part of the cliff which hangs right over the middle of
　　the fosse.
O Wisdom Supreme, what art thou showest in heaven, on
　　earth and in the evil world, and how justly thy Goodness
　　dispenses!
I saw the livid stone, on the sides and on the bottom, full
　　of holes, all of one breadth; and each was round.
Not less wide they seemed to me, nor larger, than those
　　that are in my beauteous San Giovanni made for stands to
　　the baptizers;
one of which, not many years ago, I broke to save one that
　　was drowning in it: and be this a seal to undeceive all men.
From the mouth of each emerged a sinner's feet, and legs
　　up to the calf; and the rest remained within.
The soles of all were both on fire: wherefore the joints
　　quivered so strongly, that they would have snapped in
　　pieces withes and grass-ropes.
As the flaming of things oiled moves only on their outer
　　surface: so was it there, from the heels to the points.
"Master! who is that who writhes himself, quivering more
　　than all his fellows," I said, "and sucked by ruddier
　　flame?"
And he to me: "If thou wilt have me carry thee down
　　there, by that lower bank, thou shalt learn from him about
　　himself and about his wrongs."
And I: "Whatever pleases thee, to me is grateful: thou art
　　my lord, and knowest that I depart not from thy will; also
　　thou knowest what is not spoken."
Then we came upon the fourth bulwark; we turned and
　　descended, on the left hand, down there into the
　　perforated and narrow bottom.
The kind Master did not yet depose me from his side, till
　　he brought me to the cleft of him who so lamented with
　　his legs.
"O whoe'er thou be that hast thy upper part beneath,
　　unhappy spirit, planted like a stake!" I began to say; "if
　　thou art able, speak."
I stood, like the friar who is confessing a treacherous

assassin that, after being fixed, recalls him and thus
delays the death;
and he cried: "Art thou there already standing, Boniface?
art thou there already standing? By several years the writ
has lied to me.
Art thou so quickly sated with that wealth, for which thou
didst not fear to seize the comely Lady by deceit, and
then make havoc of her?"
I became like those who stand as if bemocked, not
comprehending what is answered to them, and unable
to reply.
Then Virgil said: "Say to him quickly, 'I am not he, I am
not he whom thou thinkest.' " And I replied as was
enjoined me.
Whereat the spirit quite wrenched his feet; thereafter,
sighing and with voice of weeping, he said to me: "Then
what askest thou of me?
If to know who I am concerneth thee so much, that thou
hast therefore passed the bank, learn that I was clothed
with the Great Mantle;
and verily I was a son of the She-bear, so eager to
advance the Whelps, that I pursed wealth above, and here
myself.
Beneath my head are dragged the others who preceded me
in simony, cowering within the fissures of the stone.
I too shall fall down thither, when he comes for whom I
took thee when I put the sudden question.
But longer is the time already, that I have baked my feet
and stood inverted thus, than he shall stand planted with
glowing feet:
for after him, from westward, there shall come a lawless
Shepherd, of uglier deeds, fit to cover him and me.
A new Jason will it be, of whom we read in Maccabees;
and as to that high priest his king was pliant, so to this
shall be he who governs France."
I know not if here I was too hardy, for I answered him in
this strain: "Ah! now tell me how much treasure
Our Lord required of St. Peter, before he put the keys into
his keeping? Surely he demanded nought but 'Follow
me!' "
Nor did Peter, nor the others, ask of Matthias gold or

silver, when he was chosen for the office which the guilty
soul had lost.

Therefore stay thou here, for thou art justly punished; and
keep well the ill-got money, which against Charles made
thee be bold."

And were it not that reverence for the Great Keys thou
heldest in the glad life yet hinders me,

I should use still heavier words: for your avarice grieves
the world, trampling on the good, and raising up the
wicked.

Shepherds such as ye the Evangelist perceived, when she,
that sitteth on the waters, was seen by him committing
fornication with the kings;

she that was born with seven heads, and in her ten horns
had a witness so long as virtue pleased her spouse.

Ye have made you a god of gold and silver; and wherein
do ye differ from the idolater, save that he worships one,
and ye a hundred?

Ah Constantine! to how much ill gave birth, not thy
conversion, but that dower which the first rich Father took
from thee!"

And whilst I sung these notes to him, whether it was rage
or conscience gnawed him, he violently sprawled with
both his feet.

And indeed I think it pleased my Guide, with so satisfied
a look did he keep listening to the sound of the true words
uttered.

Therefore with both his arms he took me; and, when he
had me quite upon his breast, remounted by the path
where he had descended.

Nor did he weary in holding me clasped to him, till he
bore me away to the summit of the arch which is a
crossway from the fourth to the fifth rampart.

Here he placidly set down the burden, pleasing to him on
the rough steep cliff, which to the goats would be a
painful passage; thence another valley was discovered
to me.

Inferno Canto XIX from *The Divine Comedy of Dante Alighieri,* the Carlyle-Wicksteed translation (New York: Elsevier-Dutton, 1932), pp. 106–109.

Petrarch on the Papal Court at Avignon

I have a double Parnassus, one in Italy, the other in France, places of refuge, such as they are, for the exiled Muses. I was very happy in my Ausonian [Italian] Helicon. . . . But now I am living in France, in the Babylon of the West. The sun, in its travels sees nothing more hideous than this place on the shores of the wild Rhone, which suggests the hellish streams of Cocytus and Acheron. Here reign the successors of the poor fishermen of Galilee; they have strangely forgotten their origin. I am astounded, as I recall their predecessors, to see these men loaded with gold and clad in purple, boasting of the spoils of princes and nations; to see luxurious palaces and heights crowned with fortifications, instead of a boat turned downwards for shelter. We no longer find the simple nets which were once used to gain a frugal sustenance from the Lake of Galilee, and with which, having labored all night and caught nothing, they took, at day break, a multitude of fishes, in the name of Jesus. One is stupefied nowadays to hear the lying tongues, and to see worthless parchments, turned by a leaden seal, into nets which are used, in Christ's name, but by the arts of Belial, to catch hordes of unwary Christians. These fish, too, are dressed and laid on the burning coals of anxiety before they fill the insatiable maw of their captors. Instead of holy solitude we find a criminal host and crowds of the most infamous satellites; instead of soberness, licentious banquets; instead of pious pilgrimages, pre- ternatural and foul sloth; instead of the bare feet of the apostles, the snowy coursers of brigands fly past us, the horses decked in gold and fed on gold, soon to be shod with gold, if the Lord does not check this slavish luxury. In short, we seem to be among the kings of the Persians or Parthians, before whom we must fall down and worship, and who cannot be approached except presents be offered. O, ye unkempt and emaciated old men, is it for this you labored? Is it for this that you have sown the field of the Lord and watered it with your holy blood? But let us leave the subject.

Commiserate the cruel fate which holds your friend here. He may merit punishment, but certainly not one like this. Here I am, at a more advanced age, back in the haunts of my childhood, dragged again by fate among the disagree- able surroundings of my early days, when I thought I was freed from them. I have been so depressed and overcome that the heaviness of my soul has passed into bodily afflictions, so that I am really ill and can only give voice to sighs and groans. Although many things offer themselves which I wanted to commu- nicate to you, as both my stomachs are troubling me, you need look for nothing agreeable from me today. Sweet water cannot come from a bitter source. Nature has ordered that the sighs of an oppressed heart shall be distasteful, and the words of an injured soul, harsh.

From *TROS*, Vol. 3, No. 6, pp. 26–27.

21.2 Papal Schism: The Conciliar Movement

The schism had its immediate cause in the divide between an Avignon papacy and a return of the papacy to Rome, but the issue the schism raised was an old one: if the pope is the supreme authority, who has the authority to resolve a succession dispute over the papacy? Certainly secular rulers, particularly the Holy Roman Emperor, had claimed the right to intervene on various occasions, as when Emperor Henry III appointed the reformer Leo IX, initiating a series of reform popes who then sought to reverse that precedent (see 13.1); in this instance, no emperor was willing to forcibly intervene. Thus the current crisis brought forward an alternative, conciliarism, whereby a council would have authority to decide the next pope. The conciliar movement, and opposition to it, is represented here in three documents: The Council of Pisa efforts (1409), the Council of Constance assertions (1415), and Pope Pius II's rejection of conciliar authority (1459).

The immediate circumstances behind the schism are these: The Avignon papacy was brought to an end in 1376 by Pope Gregory XI when he tried returning to Rome, was gravely disappointed by the conditions, but died before returning to Avignon as he planned. Under pressure from the Roman populace, the cardinals (mostly French) elected a benign Italian as pope (Urban VI), thinking he would follow their plan to return to Avignon. Instead, he turned into an avid reformer bent on staying in Rome and reducing the influence of the cardinals. The French cardinals then rebelled against Urban and declared his a false election, claiming that the Roman mob had forced them into choosing the man; they then elected a new pope, Clement VII. The very cardinals charged with the succession produced two popes, and this dual papacy persisted, creating a quandary for all of Christendom for almost forty years: which pope was the divinely ordained one?

Various resolutions were attempted, some disastrous. The conciliar option was attempted at the Council of Pisa in 1409, even though such a maneuver had no precedent—normally only a pope could call a council and the two current popes denied that such a council had authority over them. So the Pisa council first established its legal authority in the excerpt below, and then proceeded to elect a third pope, with the aim of creating some reform measures thereafter to prevent such an incidence again (the oath, below). What they succeeded in doing was creating a three-way split, with three popes now competing. The situation became intolerable. The Council of Constance (1415–1418), called by the Holy Roman emperor, resolved the dispute by deposing two popes (the third resigned) and electing the conciliarist Martin V. In the process, the Council of Constance asserted conciliar authority both to end the immediate schism and as a permanent mechanism in the governance of the church, as the excerpts below indicate. The Council of Constance claims represent the high point of conciliar authority in the governance of the church; the popes, even Martin V, opposed the rights of councils to meet as an independent body, as Pius II does below in the bull *Execrabilis,* 1459.

Conciliarism, even though it ultimately failed, reflects the growing movement in secular governance toward constitutional governance, evident in Marsilius of Padua's treatise (18.3). By the mid-fifteenth century, the pope in Rome, claiming supreme authority and rejecting conciliar governance, was no longer an effective international authority, but was embroiled in the local political scene of Renaissance Italy. The worldly character of the late-fifteenth-century popes certainly contributed to the massive Reformation response in the sixteenth century.

Questions

1. What are all the possible sources of authority in Europe, and how could they resolve the papal schism?
2. What are the deeper issues that the Councils of Pisa and Constance try to resolve?
3. What fundamentally different views of authority are proposed by councils versus popes?

Council of Pisa, 1409

This holy and general council, representing the universal church, decrees and declares that the united college of cardinals was empowered to call the council, and that the power to call such a council belongs of right to the aforesaid holy college of cardinals, especially now when there is a detestable schism. The council further declared that this holy council, representing the universal church, caused both claimants of the papal throne to be cited in the gates and doors of the churches of Pisa to come and hear the final decision [in the matter of the schism] pronounced, or to give a good and sufficient reason why such sentence should not be rendered. . . .

Oath

We, each and all, bishops, priests, and deacons of the holy Roman church, congregated in the city of Pisa for the purpose of ending the schism and of restoring the unity of the church, on our word of honor promise God, the holy Roman church, and this council now collected here for the aforesaid purpose, that, if any one of us is elected pope, he shall continue the present council and not dissolve it, nor, so far as is in his power, permit it to be dissolved until, through it and with its advice, a proper, reasonable, and sufficient reformation of the universal church in its head and in its members shall have been accomplished.

From Thatcher, pp. 327–28.

Council of Constance

Sacrosancta (1415)

In the name of the Holy and Indivisible Trinity, of the Father, Son, and Holy Ghost. Amen.

This holy synod of Constance, constituting a general council for the extirpation of the present schism and the union and reformation of the Church of God in head and members, legitimately assembled in the Holy Ghost, to the praise of omnipotent God, in order that it may the more easily, safely, effectively, and freely bring about the union and reformation of the Church of God, hereby determines, decrees, ordains, and declares what follows:

It first declares that this same council, legitimately assembled in the Holy Ghost, forming a general council and representing the Catholic Church militant, has its power immediately from Christ, and every one, whatever his position or rank, even if it be the papal dignity itself, is bound to obey it in all those things which pertain to the faith, to the healing of the schism, and to the general reformation of the Church of God in head and members.

It further declares that any one, whatever his position, station, or rank, even if it be the papal, who shall contumaciously refuse to obey the mandates, decrees, ordinances, or instructions which have been, or shall be, issued by this holy council, or by any other general council legitimately summoned, which concern, or in any way relate to, the above mentioned objects, shall, unless he repudiate his conduct, be subjected to condign penance and be suitably punished, having recourse, if necessary, to the resources of the law. . . .

Frequens (1417)

A frequent celebration of general councils is an especial means for cultivating the field of the Lord and effecting the destruction of briars, thorns, and thistles, to wit, heresies, errors, and schism, and of bringing forth a most abundant harvest. The neglect to summon these fosters and develops all these evils, as may be plainly seen from a recollection of the past and a consideration of existing conditions. Therefore, by a perpetual edict, we sanction, decree, establish, and ordain that general councils shall be cele-brated in the following manner, so that the next one shall follow the close of this present council at the end of five years. The second shall follow the close of that, at the end of seven years, and councils shall thereafter be celebrated every ten years in such places as the pope shall be required to designate and assign, with the consent and approbation of the council, one month before the close of the council in question, or which, in his absence, the council itself shall designate. Thus, with a certain continuity, a council will always be either in session, or be expected at the expiration of a definite time.

This term may, however, be shortened on account of emergencies, by the supreme pontiff, with the counsel of his brethren, the cardinals of the holy Roman Church, but it may not be hereafter lengthened. The place, more-over, designated for the future council may not be altered without evident necessity. If, however, some complication shall arise, in view of which such a change shall seem necessary, as, for example, a state of siege, a war, a pest, or other obstacles, it shall be permissible for the supreme pontiff, with the consent and subscription of his said brethren, or two thirds of them (duarum partium), to select another appropriate place near the first, which must be within the same country, unless such obstacles, or similar ones, shall exist throughout the whole nation. In that case, the council may be summoned to some appropriate neighboring place, within the bounds of another nation. To this the prelates, and others, who are wont to be sum-moned to a council, must betake themselves as if that place had been designated from the first. Such change of place, or shortening of the period, the supreme pontiff is required legitimately and solemnly to publish and announce one year before the expiration of the term fixed, that the said persons may be able to come together, for the celebration of the council, within the term specified. . . .

From Robinson, pp. 511–13.

Pius II: The Decree Excecrabilis 1459

The execrable and hitherto unknown abuse has grown up in our day, that certain persons, imbued with the spirit of rebellion, and not from a desire to secure a better judgment, but to escape the punishment of some offense which they have committed, presume to appeal from the pope to a future council, in spite of the fact that the pope is the vicar of Jesus Christ and to him, in the person of St. Peter, the following was said: "Feed my sheep" [John 21:16] and "Whatsoever thou shalt bind on earth shall be bound in heaven" [Matt. 16:18]. Wishing therefore to expel this pestiferous poison from the church of Christ and to care for the salvation of the fold entrusted to us, and to remove every cause of offense from the fold of our Savior, with the advice and consent of our brothers, the cardinals of the holy Roman church, and of all the prelates, and of those who have been trained in the canon and civil law, who are at our court, and with our own sure knowledge, we condemn all such appeals and prohibit them as erroneous and detestable.

From Thatcher, p. 332.

21.3 A Lollard View of the Eucharist: Wickliff's Wicket

Popular, and budding nationalist, rejections of the international authority of the Roman Church lay the groundwork for the later Reformation, even though these attacks were forcefully stamped out in the fifteenth century. One example of the kind of movement that challenged the church on theological and national grounds were the English Lollards. The learned opinions of John Wickliff, arguing that human lordship is limited and can be removed from those of bad character, were picked up by less educated followers, the Lollards, as the basis for open rebellion against unjust authority.

John Wickliff (1328–84) was an Oxford Ph.D., who, failing to get an appointment from the pope, served the English king instead. He attacked both the pope during the period of the Avignon papacy, challenged the doctrine of transubstantiation in the Eucharist, and placed individual experience and interpretation of the Scripture above church councils or the pope. Like the Franciscans and other voices in the spirit of prophecy, Wickliff idealized poverty and condemned the wealth of the church; at the same time, like other political thinkers, he objected to the papacy's foreign interference in the affairs of the English nation. Protected from the death sentence by powerful friends, his works and ideas were nonetheless condemned as heretical, and his subsequent followers, the Lollards, were burned at the stake for heresy. One of his most extreme arguments, objectionable even to his friends, but picked up later in the Reformation, was his attack on transubstantiation, the doctrine of the Real Presence of Christ in the bread and wine of the Eucharist. This doctrine, implicit in early medieval practice and gradually articulated in the logical language of scholastic thought in the high Middle Ages, was illogical to the late medieval Wickliff. The excerpt below explains his reasoning.

Questions

1. What is the basis or source for Wickliff's arguments?
2. Why does he think transubstantiation is illogical?
3. What does he object to in the formal church of his day?

Wickliff's Wicket

A very brief definition of these words, hoc est corpus meum *(this is my body.)* . . .

And most of all they [the clergy] make us believe a false law that they have made upon the sacred host, for the most false belief is taught in it. For where find ye that ever Christ, or any of his disciples or apostles, taught any man to worship it? For in the mass creed it is said, I believe in one God only, our Lord Jesus Christ the Son of God, only begotten and born of the Father before all the world; he is God of God, Light of light, very God of very God, begotten and not made, and of substance even with the Father, by whom all things are made. And in the psalm Quicunque vult, it is said, The Father is God, The Son is God, The Holy Ghost is God. The Father is unmade, The Son is unmade, and The Holy Ghost is unmade. And you that are an earthly man, by what reason may you say that you make your Maker? Whether may the thing that is made say to the maker, Why have you made me thus? Or may it turn again and make him that made it? Surely not. Now answer you that say that every day you make of bread, the body of the Lord, flesh and blood of Jesus Christ, God and man. Forsooth you answer greatly against reason, by those words that Christ spoke at his supper on Serethursday [Thursday before Easter] at night, Matt. xxvi. Mark xiv. that Christ took bread and blessed it and broke it, and gave it to his disciples and apostles, and said, Take ye, and eat ye, this is my body which shall be given for you. And also he, taking the cup, gave thanks, and gave to them, and said, Drink ye all hereof, this is my blood of the new testament which shall be shed out for many to the remission of sins; as saith Luke, When Jesus had taken bread, he gave thanks and broke it to them and said, Take ye, eat ye, this my body that shall be given for you, do ye this in remembrance of me.

Now understand you the words of our Savior Christ, as he spoke them one after another—as Christ spoke them. For he took bread and blessed, and yet what blessed he? The scripture says not that Christ took bread and blessed it, or that he blessed the bread which he had taken. Therefore it seems more that he blessed his disciples and apostles, whom he had ordained witnesses of his passion; and in them he left his blessed word which is the bread of life, as it is written, Not only in bread lives man, but in every word that proceeds out of the mouth of God, Matt. iv. . . .

. . . We are sown in natural bodies, and shall rise again spiritual bodies. Then if Christ shall change thus our deadly bodies by death, and God the Father spared not his own Son, as it is written, but that death should reign in him as in us, and that he should be translated into a spiritual body, as the first again rising of dead men. Then how say the hypocrites that take on them to make our Lord's body? Make they the glorified body? Either make they again the spiritual body which is risen from death to life? or make they the fleshly body as it was before he suffered death? And if they say also that they make the spiritual body of Christ, it may not be so, for what Christ said and did, he did as he was at supper before he suffered his passion. . . . And if they say that they make Christ's body as it was before he had suffered his passion, then must they needs grant that Christ is to die yet. . . .

Furthermore, if they say that Christ made his body of bread, I ask, With what words made he it? Not with these words, *"Hoc est corpus meum;"* that is to say in English, "This is my body," for they are the words of giving, and not of making, which he said after that he broke the bread; then parting it among his disciples and apostles. . . . Where our clergy are guilty in this, judge you or they that know most, for they say that when you have said, *"Hoc est corpus meum,"* that is to say, "This is my body;" which you call the words of consecration, or else of making; and when they are said over the bread, you say, that there is left no bread, but it is the body of the Lord. But truly there is nothing but a heap of accidents, as witness ruggedness, roundness, savor, touching and tasting, and such other accidents. Then, if you say that the flesh and blood of Christ, that is to say, his manhood, is made more, or increased by so much as the ministration of bread and wine is, the which you minister—if you say it is so—then you must needs consent that the thing which is not God today shall be God tomorrow; yea, and that thing which is without spirit of life, but groweth in the field by kind, shall be God at another time. And we all ought to believe that he was without beginning, and without ending; and not made, for if the manhood of Christ were increased every day by so much as the bread and wine draws to that you minister, he should increase more in one day by cartloads than he did in thirty-two years when he was here in earth. . . .

Therefore all the sacraments that are left here in earth are but minds [reminders] of the body of Christ, for a sacrament is no more to say but a sign or mind of a thing passed, or a thing to come; for when Jesus spoke of the bread, and said to his disciples, Luke xxii. As you do this thing, do it in mind of me, it was set for a mind of good things passed of Christ's body. . . .

. . . And so the bread that Christ broke was left to us for mind of things passed for the body of Christ, that we should believe he was a very man in kind as we are, but as God in power, and that his manhood was sustained by food as ours. For St. Paul says he was very man, and in form he was found as man. And so we must believe that he was very God and very man together, and that he ascended up very God and very man to heaven, and that he shall be there till he come to doom the world. And we may not see him bodily, being in this life, as it is written Peter i. For he says, Whom you have not you love, into whom you now not seeing believe. And John says in the first chapter of his gospel, No man saw God; none but the only begotten Son that is in the bosom of the Father, he has told it out. And John says in his first epistle, the third chapter, Every man that sins sees not him, neither knows him. By what reason then say you that are sinners, that you make God? truly this must needs be the worst sin, to say that you make God, and it is the abomination of discomfort, that is said in Daniel the prophet to be standing in the holy place; he that reads let him understand. . . .

Now therefore pray we heartily to God, that this evil time may be made short for the chosen men, as he has promised in his blessed gospel, Matt. xxiv. And the large and broad way that leads to perdition may be stopped, and the strait and narrow way that leads to bliss may be made open by holy scriptures, that we may know which is the will of God, to serve him in truth and holiness in the dread of God, that we may find by him a way of bliss everlasting. So be it.

Reprinted from *Writings of The Reverend and Learned John Wickliff, D.D.* bound with *Writings and Examinations of Brute Thorpe, Cobham, Hilton, Pecock, Bilney and Others, with the Lantern of Light Written about A.D. 1400* (London: The Religious Tract Society, 1831), pp. 157–67; excerpts.

–22–

Diversity in Christianity
Late Medieval Spirituality

As the previous chapter indicates, the conditions for heterodoxy were growing in the fourteenth and fifteenth centuries, and the spirit of prophecy, evident in Wycliff's attacks, was increasingly hostile to the order of the church. This chapter focuses exclusively on the spirit of prophecy operating within the bounds of the order of the church, and in particular on the contemplative life. "Contemplatives" or the "contemplative life" refers to the practice of individual meditation for the purpose of drawing closer to God. Many adopted an ascetic lifestyle, some had visions, a few even had mystical experiences, but the goal of the contemplative was to focus on God through introspective prayer, meditation on divine revelation, and humility.

Such contemplatives played a role not only in spiritual matters but also in the social life of their communities. The Flemish mystic John of Ruysbroeck (22.1) and the Byzantine mystic Gregory of Palamas (22.4), are examples of the growing literature of mysticism in this period, a spirituality that provided an alternative view of life to the problematic temporal world. The English recluse Julian of Norwich (22.2) and the Italian activist Catherine of Siena (22.3) also had direct apprehensions of God through visions of Christ and his blood; these women served as spiritual advisors and social advocates for the poor and imprisoned.

22.1 Contemplative Practice: John of Ruysbroeck

While many mystics taught others by writing directly from their experiences, as does Julian of Norwich (22.2), others endeavored to instruct by explaining how contemplation leads to the experience of God, relying heavily on Neoplatonic philosophy in the tradition of Pseudo-Dionysius the Areopagite (5.3). The Flemish mystic John of Ruysbroeck (1273–1381) wrote several treatises on spiritual encounters with the divine that

491

remained steadfastly orthodox, directly opposing the heretical Free Spirit groups. The excerpts below are from his treatise *The Sparkling Stone,* in which he lays out the path of spiritual development in allegorically meaningful sets of threes, and then in the mystical meaning of the stone. The last section is concerned with making the distinction between God and man in the mystical union, in order to deny the heresy of the divinity of man prevalent in the Free Spirit heresy.

Questions

1. What is the path that John of Ruysbroeck lays out for those who want to contemplate God?

2. In what ways does he use a Neoplatonic worldview? Compare Ruysbroeck to Pseudo-Dionysius the Areopagite.

3. What orthodox doctrines does he insist on, and why?

Jan van Ruysbroeck, The Sparkling Stone

Prologue

The man who would live in the most perfect state of Holy Church must be a good and zealous man; an inward and ghostly man; an uplifted and God-seeing man; and an outflowing man to all in common. Whenever these four things are together in a man, then his state is perfect; and through the increase of grace he shall continually grow and progress in all virtues, and in the knowledge of truth, before God and before all men. . . .

Chapter 3: Through Three Things a Man Becomes God-Seeing

Further, you must know that if this ghostly man would now become a God-seeing man, he needs must have three other things. The first is the feeling that the foundation of his being is abysmal, and he should possess it in this manner; the second is that his inward exercise should be wayless; the third is that his indwelling should be a divine fruition.

Now understand, you who would live in the spirit, for I am speaking to no one else. The union with God which a spiritual man feels, when the union is revealed to the spirit as being abysmal—that is, measureless depth, measureless height, measureless length and measureless breadth—in this manifestation the spirit perceives that through love it has plunged itself into the depth and has ascended into the height and escaped into the length; and it feels itself to be wandering in the breadth, and to dwell in a knowledge which is ignorance. And through this intimate feeling of union, it feels itself to be melting into the Unity; and, through dying to all things, into the life of God. And there it feels itself to be one life with God. And this is the foundation, and the first point, of the God-seeing life.

And from this there arises the second point, which is an exercise above reason and without condition: for the Divine Unity, of which every God-seeing spirit has entered into possession in love, eternally draws and invites the Divine Persons and all loving spirits into its self. And this inward drawing is felt by each lover, more or less, according to the measure of his love and the manner of his exercise. And whosoever yields himself to this indrawing, and keeps himself therein, cannot fall into mortal sin. But the God-seeing man who has forsaken self and all things, and does not feel himself drawn away because he no longer possesses anything as his own, but stands empty of all, he can always enter, naked and unencumbered with images, into the inmost part of his spirit. There he finds revealed an Eternal Light, and in this light, he feels the eternal demand of the Divine Unity; and he feels himself to be an eternal fire of love, which craves above all else to be one with God. The more he yields to this indrawing or demand, the more he feels it. And the more he feels it, the more he craves to be one with God; for it urges him to pay the debt which is demanded of him by God. This eternal demand of the Divine Unity kindles within the spirit an eternal fire of love; and though the spirit incessantly pays the debt, an eternal burning continues within it. For, in the transformation within the Unity, all spirits fail in their own activity, and feel nothing else but a burning up of themselves in the simple Unity of God. This simple Unity of God none can feel or possess save he who maintains himself in the immeasurable radiance, and in the love which is above reason and wayless. In this transcendent state the spirit feels in itself the eternal fire of love; and in this fire of love it finds neither beginning nor end, and it feels itself one with this fire of love. The spirit for ever continues to burn in itself, for its love is eternal; and it feels itself ever more and more to be burnt up in love, for it is drawn and transformed into the Unity of God, where the spirit burns in love. If it observes itself, it finds a distinction and an otherness between itself and God; but where it is burnt up it is undifferentiated and without distinction, and therefore it feels nothing but unity; for the flame of the Love of God consumes and devours all that it can enfold in its Self.

And thus you may see that the indrawing Unity of God is nought else than the fathomless Love, which lovingly draws inward, in eternal fruition, the Father and the Son and all that lives in Them. And in this Love we shall burn and be burnt up without end, throughout eternity; for herein lies the blessedness of all spirits. And therefore we must all found our lives upon a fathomless abyss; that we may eternally plunge into Love, and sink down in the fathomless Depth. And with that same Love, we shall ascend, and transcend ourselves, in the incomprehensible Height. And in that Love which is wayless, we shall wander and stray, and it shall lead us and lose us in the immeasurable Breadth of the Love of God. And herein we shall flee forth and flee out of ourselves, into the unknown raptures of the Goodness and Riches of God. And therein we shall melt and be melted away, and shall eternally wander and sojourn within the Glory of God. Behold! by each of these images, I show forth to God-seeing men their being and their exercise, but none else can understand them. For the contemplative life cannot be taught. But where the Eternal Truth reveals Itself within the spirit all that is needful is taught and learnt.

Chapter 4: Of the Sparkling Stone, and of the New Name Written in the Book of the Secrets of God

And therefore the Spirit of our Lord speaks thus in the Book of the Secrets of God, which St John wrote down: TO HIM THAT OVERCOMES, He says, that is, to him who overcomes and conquers himself and all else, WILL I GIVE TO EAT OF THE HIDDEN MANNA, that is, an inward and hidden savor and celestial joy; AND WILL GIVE HIM A SPARKLING STONE, AND IN THE STONE A NEW NAME WRITTEN WHICH NO MAN KNOWS SAVING HE THAT RECEIVES IT. This stone is called a pebble, for it is so small that it does not hurt when one treads on it. This stone is shining white and red like a flame of fire; and it is small and round, and smooth all over, and very light. By this sparkling stone we mean our Lord Christ Jesus, for He is, according to His Godhead, a shining forth of the Eternal Light, and an irradiation of the glory of God, and a flawless mirror in which all things live. Now to him who overcomes and transcends all things, this sparkling stone is given; and with it he receives light and truth and life. This stone is also like to a fiery flame, for the fiery love of the Eternal Word has filled the whole world with love and wills that all loving spirits be burned up to nothingness in love. This stone is also so small that a man hardly feels it, even though he treads it underfoot. And that is why it is called CALCULUS, that is, "treadling." And this is made clear to us by St Paul, where he says that the Son of God EMPTIED HIMSELF, AND HUMBLED HIMSELF, AND TOOK UPON HIM THE FORM OF A SERVANT, AND BECAME OBEDIENT UNTO DEATH, EVEN THE DEATH OF THE CROSS. And He Himself spoke through the mouth of the Prophet, saying: I AM A WORM, AND NO MAN; A REPROACH OF MEN AND DESPISED OF THE PEOPLE. And He made Himself so small in time that the Jews trod Him under their feet. But they felt Him not; for, had they recognized the Son of God, they had not dared to crucify Him. He is still little and despised in all men's hearts that do not love Him well. This noble stone of which I speak is wholly round and smooth and even all over. That the stone is round teaches us that the Divine Truth has neither beginning nor end; that it is smooth and even all over teaches us that the Divine Truth shall weigh all things evenly, and shall give to each according to his merits; and that which he gives shall be with each throughout eternity. The last property of this stone of which I will speak is, that it is particularly light; for the Eternal Word of the Father has no weight, nevertheless It bears heaven and earth by Its strength. And It is equally near to all things; yet none can attain It, for It is set on high and goes before all creatures, and reveals Itself where It wills and when It wills; and, in Its lightness, our heavy human nature has climbed above all the heavens, and sits crowned at the right hand of the Father.

Behold, this is the sparkling stone which is given to the God-seeing man, and in this stone A NEW NAME IS WRITTEN, WHICH NO MAN KNOWS SAVING HE THAT RECEIVES IT. You should know that all spirits in their return towards God receive names; each one in particular, according to the nobleness of its service and the loftiness of its love. For only the first name of innocence, which we receive at baptism, is adorned with the merits of our Lord Jesus Christ. And when we have lost this name of innocence through sin, if we are willing still to follow God—especially in three works which He wishes to work in us—we are baptized once more in the Holy Ghost. And thereby we receive a new name which shall remain with us throughout eternity. . . .

Chapter 10: How We, Though One with God, Must Eternally Remain Other Than God

Though I have said before that we are one with God, and this is taught us by Holy Writ, yet now I will say that we must eternally remain other than God, and distinct from Him, and this too is taught us by Holy Writ. And we must understand and feel both within us, if all is to be right with us.

And therefore I say further: that from the Face of God, or from our highest feeling, a brightness shines upon the face of our inward being, which teaches us the truth of love and of all virtues: and especially are we taught in this brightness to feel God and ourselves in four ways. First, we feel God in His grace; and when we apprehend this, we cannot remain idle. For like as the sun, by its splendor and its heat, enlightens and gladdens and makes fruitful the whole world, so God does to us through His grace: He enlightens and gladdens and makes fruitful all men who desire to obey Him. If, however, we would feel God within us, and have the fire of His love ever more burning within us, we must, of our own free will, help to kindle it in four ways: We must abide within ourselves, united with the fire through inwardness. And we must go forth from ourselves towards all good men with loyalty and brotherly love. And we must go beneath ourselves in penance, betaking ourselves to all good works, and resisting our inordinate lusts. And we must ascend above ourselves with the flame of this fire, through devotion, and thanksgiving, and praise, and fervent prayer, and must ever cleave to God with an upright intention and with sensible love. And thereby God continues to dwell in us with His grace; for in these four ways is comprehended every exercise which we can do with the reason, and in some wise, but without this exercise no one can please God. And he who is most perfect in this exercise, is nearest to God. And therefore it is needful for all men; and above it none can rise save the contemplative men. And thus, in this first way, we feel God within us through His grace, if we wish to belong to Him.

Secondly: when we possess the God-seeing life, we feel ourselves to be living *in* God; and from out of that life in which we feel God in ourselves, there shines forth upon the face of our inward being a brightness which enlightens our reason, and is an intermediary between ourselves and God. And if we with our enlightened reason abide within ourselves in this brightness, we feel that our created life incessantly immerses itself in its eternal life. But when we follow the brightness above reason with a simple sight, and with a willing leaning out of ourselves, toward our highest life, there we experience the transformation of our whole selves in God; and thereby we feel ourselves to be wholly enwrapped in God.

And, after this, there follows the third way of feeling; namely, that we feel ourselves to be one *with* God; for, through the transformation in God, we feel ourselves to be swallowed up in the fathomless abyss of our eternal blessedness, wherein we can nevermore find any distinction between ourselves and God. And this is our highest feeling, which we cannot experience in any other way than in the immersion in love. And therefore, so soon as we are uplifted and drawn into our highest feeling, all our powers stand idle in an essential fruition; but our powers do not pass away into nothingness, for then we should lose our created being. And as long as we stand idle, with an inclined spirit, and with open eyes, but without reflection, so long we can contemplate and have fruition. But, at the very moment in which we seek to prove and to comprehend what it is that we feel, we fall back into reason, and there we find a distinction and an otherness between ourselves and God, and find God outside ourselves in incomprehensibility.

And hence the fourth way of distinction; which is, that we feel God *and* ourselves. Hereby we now find ourselves standing in the Presence of God; and the truth which we receive from the Face of God teaches us that God would be wholly ours and that He wills us to be wholly His. And in that same moment in which we feel that God would be wholly ours, there arises within us a gaping and eager craving which is so hungry and so deep and so empty that, even though God gave all that He could give, if he gave not Himself, we should not be appeased. For, whilst we feel that He has given Himself and yielded Himself to our untrammeled craving, that we may taste of Him in every way that we can desire—and of this we learn the truth in His sight—yet all that we taste, against all that we lack, is but like to a single drop of water against the whole sea: and this makes our spirit burst forth in fury and in the heat and the restlessness of love. For the more we taste, the greater our craving and our hunger; for the one is the cause of the other. And thus it comes about that we struggle in vain. For we feed upon His Immensity, which we cannot devour, and we yearn after His Infinity, which we cannot attain: and so we cannot enter into God nor can God enter into us, for in the untamed fury of love we are not able to renounce ourselves. And therefore the heat is so unmeasured that the exercise of love between ourselves and God flashes to and fro like the lightning in the sky; and yet we cannot be consumed in its ardor. And in this storm of love our activity is above reason and wayless; for love longs for that which is impossible to it, and reason teaches that love is in the right, but reason can neither counsel love nor dissuade her. For as long as we inwardly perceive that God would be ours, the goodness of God touches our eager craving: and therefrom springs the wildness of love, for the touch which pours forth from God stirs up this wildness, and demands our activity, that is, that we should love eternal love. But the inward-drawing touch draws us out of ourselves, and calls us to be melted and noughted [made nothing] in the Unity. And in this inward-drawing touch, we feel that God wills us to be His; and therefore, we must renounce ourselves and leave Him to work our blessedness. But where He touches us by the outpouring touch, He leaves us to ourselves, and makes us free, and sets us in His Presence, and teaches us to pray in the spirit and to ask in freedom, and shows us His incomprehensible riches in such manifold ways as we are able to grasp. For everything that we can conceive, wherein is consolation and joy, this we find in Him without measure. And therefore, when our feeling shows us that He with all these riches would be ours and dwell in us for ever more, then all the powers of the soul open themselves, and especially the desirous power; for all the rivers of the grace of God pour forth, and the more we taste of them, the more we long to taste; and the more we long to taste, the more deeply we press into contact with Him; and the more deeply we press into contact with God, the more the flood of His sweetness flows through us and over us; and the more we are thus drenched and flooded, the better we feel and know that the sweetness of God is incomprehensible and unfathomable.

And therefore the prophet says: O TASTE, AND SEE THAT THE LORD IS SWEET. But he does not say how sweet He is, for God's sweetness is without measure and therefore we can neither grasp it nor swallow it. And this is also testified by the bride of God in the Song of Songs, where she says: I SAT DOWN UNDER HIS SHADOW, WITH GREAT DELIGHT, AND HIS FRUIT WAS SWEET TO MY TASTE.

Reprinted from *John of Ruysbroeck, The Adornment of the Spiritual Marriage, The Sparkling Stone, The Book of Supreme Truth,* trans. C. A. Wynschenk Dom, ed. Evelyn Underhill (London: J.M. Dent & Sons, 1916), pp. 181, 184–89, 208–12.

22.2 Anchoress: Julian of Norwich

Anchoresses wanted to live secluded lives devoted to God in a way similar to the hermits of early Christianity (6.1). However, these women (and some male "anchorites") did not want to join the communal religious life of the monastery, nor did they want to retreat entirely from European society into some remote desert as the hermits did. Rather, they desired a spiritual retreat from material life while remaining physically in their communities. In some cases, these individuals simply walled themselves up in a single room in their homes, receiving physical sustenance from donations and spiritual sustenance through visits from the priest. Sometimes they communicated with the public through a window. Like mystics and strict monks, anchoresses lived ascetic lives, practicing abstinence and sometimes engaging in mortification of the body through hair shirts (prickly fur worn inside out, hidden under outer garments) or other physical punishments as a means of focusing on God instead of the body. In their love for God, they devoted most of their time to prayer and meditation. Anchorholds, the enclosed cells in which these individuals lived without ever leaving, often became attached to church buildings. People came to the anchoress as they might to a saint, seeking spiritual advice or comfort. The prominence of such women in the church indicates the strong leadership role that women exerted in medieval Christianity, outside or beside the male-dominated hierarchy of the priesthood.

Julian of Norwich (1343–1413) was a recluse enclosed at the Church of St. Julian in the English town of Norwich. She had mystical visions of great sensual power, which she recorded in detail and interpreted allegorically. On the basis of her experiences and her dedicated life in her enclosure, she was much sought after for advice and wisdom. Her book of *Showings,* both the earlier short text and the later long version, reveal her as a thoughtful, well-read orthodox Christian endeavoring to put into words the unspeakable mysteries of her visions, in which she sees

God directly and is utterly transformed by this contact. The visions are vivid in their materiality, conveyed in color, sensation, smell, and also emotion. The images she sees of Christ are often graphic in their description of his bleeding and dying body; she also employs maternal imagery for the Godhead more than any other medieval mystic.

The excerpts below from the long text of the *Showings* interpret her visions of the dying Christ, her reflections on her own sinfulness, and her views on the motherhood of God.

Questions

1. What vision of Christ does Julian have, and what does he mean to her?
2. How does she view herself in relation to God?
3. What sensory experiences embody spiritual meaning for Julian?

Julian of Norwich, Revelations of Divine Love

Chapter 27

After this the Lord brought to my mind the longing that I had to Him before. And I saw that nothing letted [hindered] me but sin. And so I looked, generally, upon us all, and methought: *If sin had not been, we should all have been clean and like to our Lord, as He made us.*

And thus, in my folly, before this time often I wondered why by the great foreseeing wisdom of God the beginning of sin was not letted: for then, methought, all should have been well. This stirring [of mind] was much to be forsaken, but nevertheless mourning and sorrow I made therefore, without reason and discretion.

But Jesus, who in this Vision informed me of all that is needful to me, answered by this word and said: *It behooved that there should be sin; but all shall be well, and all shall be well, and all manner of thing shall be well.*

In this naked word *sin,* our Lord brought to my mind, generally, *all that is not good,* and the shameful despite and the utter noughting [made nothing] that He bare for us in this life, and His dying; and all the pains and passions of all His creatures, ghostly and bodily; (for we be all partly noughted, and we shall be noughted following our Master, Jesus, till we be full purged, that is to say, till we be fully noughted of our deadly flesh and of all our inward affections which are not very good;) and the beholding of this, with all pains that ever were or ever shall be,—and with all these I understand the Passion of Christ for most pain, and overpassing. All this was shewed in a touch and quickly passed over into comfort: for our good Lord would not that the soul were affeared of this terrible sight.

But I saw not *sin:* for I believe it has no manner of substance nor no part of being, nor could it be known but by the pain it is cause of.

And thus pain, *it* is something, as to my sight, for a time; for it purgeth, and maketh us to know ourselves and to ask mercy. For the Passion of our Lord is comfort to us against all this, and so is His blessed will.

And for the tender love that our good Lord has to all that shall be saved, He comforteth readily and sweetly, signifying thus: *It is sooth that sin is cause of all this pain; but all shall be well, and all shall be well, and all manner [of] thing shall be well.*

These words were said full tenderly, showing no manner of blame to me nor to any that shall be saved. Then were it a great unkindness to blame or wonder on God for my sin, since He blameth not me for sin.

And in these words I saw a marvelous high mystery hid in God, which mystery He shall openly make known to us in Heaven: in which knowing we shall verily see the cause why He suffered sin to come. In which sight we shall endlessly joy in our Lord God.

Chapter 57

. . . For soothly I saw that we are that which He loveth, and do that which Him pleaseth, lastingly without any stinting: and [that by virtue] of the great riches and of the high noble virtues by measure come to our soul what time it is knit to our body: in which knitting we are made Sensual.

And thus in our Substance we are full, and in our Sense-soul we fail: which failing God will restore and fulfil by working of Mercy and Grace plenteously flowing into us out of His own Nature-Goodness. And thus His Nature-Goodness maketh that Mercy and Grace work in us, and the Nature-goodness that we have of Him enableth us to receive the working of Mercy and Grace.

I saw that our nature is in God whole: in which [whole nature of Manhood] He maketh diversities flowing out of Him to work His will: whom Nature keepeth, and Mercy and Grace restoreth and fulfilleth. And of these none shall perish: for our nature that is the higher part is knit to God, in the making; and God is knit to our nature that is the lower part, in our flesh-taking: and thus in Christ our two natures are oned. For the Trinity is comprehended in Christ, in whom our higher part is grounded and rooted; and our lower part the Second Person hath taken: which nature first to Him was made-ready. For I saw full surely that all the works that God hath done, or ever shall, were fully known to Him and aforeseen from without beginning. And for Love He made Mankind, and for the same Love would be Man.

The next Good that we receive is our Faith, in which our profiting beginneth. And it cometh [out] of the high riches of our nature-Substance into our Sensual soul, and it is grounded in us through the Nature-Goodness of God, by the working of Mercy and Grace. And thereof come all other goods by which we are led and saved. For the Commandments of God come therein: in which we ought to have two manners of understanding: [the one is that we ought to understand and know] which are His biddings, to love and to keep them; the other is that we ought to know His forbiddings, to hate and to refuse them. For in these two is all our working comprehended. Also in our faith come the Seven Sacraments, each following other in order as God hath ordained them to us: and all manner of virtues.

For the same virtues that we have received of our Substance, given to us in Nature by the Goodness of God,—the same virtues by the working of Mercy are given to us in Grace through the Holy Ghost, *renewed:* which virtues and gifts are treasured to us in Jesus Christ. For in that same time that God knitted Himself to our body in the Virgin's womb, He took our Sensual soul: in which taking He, us all having enclosed in Him, oned it to our Substance: in which oneing He was perfect Man. For Christ having knit in Him each man that shall be saved, is perfect Man. Thus our Lady is our Mother in whom we are all enclosed and of her born, in Christ: (for she that is Mother of our Saviour is Mother of all that shall be saved in our Saviour;) and our Saviour is our Very Mother in whom we be endlessly borne, and never shall come out of Him.

Plenteously and fully and sweetly was this shewed, and it is spoken of in the First, where it saith: *We are all in Him enclosed and He is enclosed in us.* And that [enclosing of Him in us] is spoken of in the Sixteenth Shewing where it saith: *He sitteth in our soul.*

For it is His good-pleasure to reign in our Understanding blissfully, and sit in our Soul restfully, and to dwell in our Soul endlessly, us all working into Him: in which working He willeth that we be His helpers, giving to Him all our attending, learning His lores, keeping His laws, desiring that all be done that He doeth; truly trusting in Him.

For soothly I saw that our Substance is in God.

From *Revelations of Divine Love, Recorded by Julian, Anchoress at Norwich, Anno Domini 1373,* a version from the ms. in the British Museum, ed. Grace Warrack (London: Methuen, 1901), pp. 55–57, 138–41.

22.3 Comforting the Condemned: Catherine of Siena

Saint Catherine of Siena (circa 1347–1380) was one of the preeminent voices of prophecy in her time, a contemplative who ministered to condemned prisoners and wrote visionary literature and letters to popes and emperors exhorting them to behave as God would have them. Like many mystics, her ascetic and contemplative life, her strength of character, and her wisdom were widely admired. She came from a humble family background, joined the Dominican Order, and then devoted her life to serving the poor and teaching. Catherine self-consciously lived in imitation of her namesake, the martyr Saint Katherine of Alexandria.

As a Dominican of the third order (lay), Catherine of Siena and her disciples traveled, preaching and supporting reform of the church. She also had numerous mystical experiences, and began writing letters, often describing these visions and explaining the theological truths she learned from them (her intellectual acumen was recognized in 1970 when, in a rare move, she was made a Doctor of the Church, in the same category with Augustine of Hippo and Thomas Aquinas). She also involved herself in church politics by urging the pope to return from Avignon to Rome, supporting and advising the Roman claimant during the schism (21.2). She died of a stroke at the age of thirty-three, the same age as Jesus, a parallel she herself recognized.

One of the most spectacular acts of charity in which Catherine engaged was the practice of the *conforteria,* the lay confraternity that worked in the prisons comforting those condemned to death. Members of these groups would counsel and comfort, placing the image of Christ before the prisoner so that in death the condemned could be identified with Christ, and vice-versa. The comforter remained with the prisoner all the way through the execution, even, as Catherine does, holding the man's severed head until the pulse stops. In the letter below to her spiritual director and friend, Friar Raimondo delle Vigne of Capua, Catherine describes her mystical experience of Christ's blood as she assists Niccolò di Toldo, a political prisoner, at his beheading.

Questions

1. How does Catherine bring comfort to Niccolò?
2. What does his death mean to her?
3. What experience of Christ does she have?

Catherine of Siena, Letter to Fra Raimondo of Capua, 1375

In the Name of Jesus Christ crucified and of sweet Mary:

Most beloved and dearest father and dear my son in Christ Jesus: I Catherine, servant and slave of the servants of Jesus Christ, write to you, commending myself to you in the precious Blood of the Son of God; with desire to see you inflamed and drowned in that His sweetest Blood, which is blended with the fire of His most ardent charity. This my soul desires, to see you therein, you and Nanni and Jacopo my son. I see no other remedy by which we may reach those chief virtues which are necessary to us. Sweetest father, your soul, which has made itself food for me—(and no moment of time passes that I do not receive this food at the table of the sweet Lamb slain with such ardent love)—your soul, I say, would not attain the little virtue, true humility, were it not drowned in the Blood. This virtue shall be born from hate, and hate from love. Thus the soul is born with very perfect purity, as iron issues purified from the furnace.

I will, then, that you lock you in the open side of the Son of God, which is an open treasure-house, full of fragrance, even so that sin itself there becomes fragrant. There rests the sweet Bride on the bed of fire and blood. There is seen and shown the secret of the heart of the Son of God. Oh, flowing Source, which givest to drink and excitest every loving desire, and givest gladness, and enlightenest every mind and fillest every memory which fixes itself thereon! so that naught else can be held or meant or loved, save this sweet and good Jesus! Blood and fire, immeasurable Love! Since my soul shall be blessed in seeing you thus drowned, I will that you do as he who draws up water with a bucket, and pours it over something else; thus do you pour the water of holy desire on the head of your brothers, who are our members, bound to us in the body of the sweet Bride. And beware, lest through illusion of the devils—who I know have given you trouble, and will give you—or through the saying of some fellow-creature, you should ever draw back: but persevere always in the hour when things look most cold, until we may see blood shed with sweet and enamoured desires.

Up, up, sweetest my father! and let us sleep no more! For I hear such news that I wish no more bed of repose or worldly state. I have just received a Head in my hands, which was to me of such sweetness as heart cannot think, nor tongue say, nor eye see, nor the ears hear. The will of God went on through the other mysteries wrought before; of which I do not tell, for it would be too long. I went to visit him whom you know: whence he received such comfort and consolation that he confessed, and prepared himself very well. And he made me promise by the love of God that when the time of the sentence should come, I would be with him. So I promised, and did. Then in the morning, before the bell rang, I went to him: and he received great consolation. I led him to hear Mass, and he received the Holy Communion, which he had never before received. His will was accorded and submitted to the will of God; and only one fear was left, that of not being strong at the moment. But the measureless and glowing goodness of God deceived him, creating in him such affection and love in the desire of God that he did not know how to abide without Him, and said: "Stay with me, and do not abandon me. So it shall not be otherwise than well with me. And I die content." And he held his head upon my breast. I heard then the rejoicing, and breathed the fragrance of his blood; and it was not without the fragrance of mine, which I desire to shed for the sweet Bridegroom Jesus. And, desire waxing in my soul, feeling his fear, I said: "Comfort thee, sweet my brother, since we shall soon arrive at the Wedding Feast. Thou shalt go there bathed in the sweet Blood of the Son of God, with the sweet Name of Jesus, which I will never to leave thy memory. And I await thee at the place of justice." Now think, father and son, his heart then lost all fear, and his face changed from sorrow to gladness; and he rejoiced, he exulted, and said: "Whence comes such grace to me, that the sweetness of my soul will await me at the holy place of justice?" See, that he had come to so much light that he called the place of justice holy! And he said: "I shall go wholly joyous, and strong, and it will seem to me a thousand years before I arrive, thinking that you are awaiting me there." And he said words so sweet as to break one's heart, of the goodness of God.

I waited for him then at the place of justice; and waited there with constant prayer, in the presence of Mary and of Catherine, Virgin and martyr. But before I attained, I prostrated me, and stretched my neck upon the block; but my desire did not come there, for I had too full consciousness of myself. Then up! I prayed, I constrained her, I cried "Mary!" for I wished this grace, that at the moment of death she should give him a light and a peace in his heart, and then I should see him reach his goal. Then my soul became so full that although a multitude of people were there, I could see no human creature, for the sweet promise made to me.

Then he came, like a gentle lamb; and seeing me, he began to smile, and wanted me to make the sign of the Cross. When he had received the sign, I said: "Down! To the Bridal, sweetest my brother! For soon shalt thou be in the enduring life." He prostrated him with great gentleness, and I stretched out his neck; and bowed me down, and recalled to him the Blood of the Lamb. His lips said naught save Jesus! and, Catherine! And so saying, I received his head in my hands, closing my eyes in the Divine Goodness, and saying, "I will!"

Then was seen God-and-Man, as might the clearness of the sun be seen. And He stood wounded, and received the blood; in that blood a fire of holy desire, given and hidden in the soul by grace. He received it in the fire of His divine charity. When He had received his blood and his desire, He also received his soul, which He put into the open treasure-house of His Side, full of mercy; the primal Truth showing that by grace and mercy alone He received it, and not for any other work. Oh, how sweet and unspeakable it was to see the goodness of God! with what sweetness and love He awaited that soul departed from the body! He turned the eye of mercy toward her, when she came to enter within His Side, bathed in blood which availed through the Blood of the Son of God. Thus received by God through power—powerful is He to do! the Son also, Wisdom the Word Incarnate, gave him and made him share the crucified love with which He received painful and shameful death through the obedience which he showed to the Father, for the good of the human race. And the hands of the Holy Spirit locked him within.

But he made a gesture sweet enough to draw a thousand hearts. And I do not wonder, for already he tasted the divine sweetness. He turned as does the Bride when she has reached the threshold of her bridegroom, who turns back her head and her look, bowing to those who have accompanied her, and with the gesture she gives signs of thanks.

When he was at rest, my soul rested in peace and in quiet, in so great fragrance of blood that I could not bear to remove the blood which had fallen on me from him.

Ah me, miserable! I will say no more. I stayed on the earth with the greatest envy. And it seems to me that the first new stone is already in place. Therefore do not wonder if I impose upon you nothing save to see yourselves drowned in the blood and flame poured from the side of the Son of God. Now then, no more negligence, sweetest my sons, since the blood is beginning to flow, and to receive the life. Sweet Jesus, Jesus Love.

Reprinted with permission from *Saint Catherine of Siena as Seen in Her Letters*, trans. Vida D. Scudder, 3rd ed. (London: Dent & Sons, 1926), pp. 110–14.

22.4 Divine Wisdom: Saint Gregory Palamas of Byzantium

Saint Gregory Palamas (d. 1359) was a Byzantine monk, mystical theologian, and archbishop of Thessalonica. He represents a school of thought about the contemplative life known as *hesychasm* that reinterprets the ideas of earlier Neoplatonic mystical writers, such as Pseudo-Dionysius the Areopagite (5.3). *Hesychia* means "stillness" or "quiet"; hesychasm teaches methods of meditation involving controlled breathing and posture as the monks gaze inward to achieve the vision of light (God). Palamas was a defender of this monastic practice against those who claimed that since God was ineffable he could not be directly known. While Palamas acknowledged, as all monotheists would, that God's essence is unknowable—a finite human cannot understand an infinite being—he argued that God is knowable through his "energy" in the form of light that can be apprehended by the finite human. What the monks experienced in their practice of contemplation was truly part of God, if not his total essence.

Hesychasm in the fourteenth century (sometimes called Palamism after its defender) became a volatile political issue. The Hesychast party, after great conflict, became dominant and hesychasm became the orthodox theological position for the Byzantine church. Because of the monastic base for this party, monasticism and monks dominated church positions thereafter. For example, Eastern Orthodox monastic bishops and patriarchs sponsored the spread of Orthodoxy into Slavic regions. Consequently, this theology of prayer directed at a mystical experience of God was widespread.

The following selections from Gregory's *The One Hundred Fifty Chapters* give some samples of his reasoning about the human understanding of God, comparing this way of knowing to that of the philosophers.

Questions

1. In what ways can a human being know God, according to Gregory?
2. What methods does Gregory use to argue his position?
3. Why do you think this view of God and humanity is so important to Gregory?

Gregory Palamas, The One Hundred and Fifty Chapters

1. That the world had a beginning both nature teaches and history confirms; the discovery of the arts, the introduction of laws and the governance of states also clearly affirm this. For we know the founders of almost all the arts, those who established the laws, and those who first administered the states. Furthermore, we see none of the first writers on any subject whatever surpassing the account of the beginning of the world and of time, as Moses recorded it. And Moses himself, who described the beginning of the generation of the world, provided irrefutable proofs of his veracity through such extraordinary words and deeds that he convinced virtually every race of men and persuaded them to deride the sophists who have argued the contrary. Since the nature of this world is such that it always requires a new cause in each instance and since without this cause it cannot exist at all, we have in these facts proof for an underived, self-existent primordial cause.

2. The nature of the contingent existence of realities in the world proves not only that the world has had a beginning but also that it will have an end, as it is continually coming to an end in part. Sure and irrefutable proof is also provided by the prophecy of Christ, God over all, and of other men inspired by God, whom not only the pious but also the impious must believe as truthful, when they see that they are right also in all the other things which they have predicted. From these men we can learn that this world

will not in its entirety return to utter non-being, but, like our bodies and in a manner that might be considered analogous, the world at the moment of its dissolution and transformation will be changed into something more divine by the power of the Spirit. . . .

25. Here and in such things lie the true wisdom and the saving knowledge which procure blessedness on high. What Euclid, what Marinos, what Ptolemy could understand? What Empedocleans, Socratics, Aristotelians or Platonists with their logical methods and mathematical proofs? Or rather, what sort of sense perception has grasped such things? What mind apprehended them? If the spiritual wisdom seemed earthbound to those natural philosophers and their followers, consequently the one who stands supereminently superior to it turns out also to be such. For almost as the irrational animals are related to the wisdom of those men (or, if you wish, like little children for whom the pancakes they have at hand would seem superior to the imperial crown, or even to everything known by those philosophers), just so are these philosophers to the most excellent wisdom and teaching of the Spirit.

26. Knowing God in truth to the extent that this is possible is not only incomparably better than Hellenic philosophy, but also, knowing what place man has before God, alone of itself, surpasses all their wisdom. For of all earthly and heavenly things man alone was created in the image of his Maker, so that he might look to him and love him, and that he might be an initiate and worshipper of God alone and might present his proper beauty by faith in him and inclination and disposition towards him, and that he might know that all other things which this heaven and earth bear are inferior to himself and completely devoid of intelligence. Since the Hellenic sages have not been able to understand this at all, they have dishonoured our own nature and acted impiously towards God; "They worshipped and served the creature rather than the Creator," endowing the sense-perceptible and insensate stars with intelligence, in each case proportionate in power and rank to its corporeal magnitude. And worshipping these in their sorry manner, they address them as superior and inferior gods and entrust them with dominion over the universe. On the basis of sensible things and philosophy on such have these men not inflicted shame, dishonour and the ultimate penury on their own souls, and also the verily intelligible darkness of punishment?

27. The knowledge that we are made in the image of the Creator does not permit us to deify even the intelligible world, for it is not the bodily constitution but the very nature of the mind which possesses this image and nothing in our nature is superior to the mind. If there were something superior, that is where the image would be. But since our superior part is the

mind—and even though this is in the divine image, it was nevertheless created by God—, why then is it difficult to understand, or rather, how can it not be self-evident that the maker of our intellectual being is also the maker of all intellectual being? Therefore, every intellectual nature is a fellow servant with us and is in the image of the Creator, even though they be more worthy of honour than we because they are without bodies and are nearer to the utterly incorporeal and uncreated nature. Or rather, those among them who kept to their proper rank and longed for the goal of their being, even though they are fellow servants, are honoured by us and because of their rank are much more worthy of honour than we are. But those who did not keep to their rank but rebelled and denied the goal of their being have become utterly alienated from those who are near God and they have fallen from honour. But if they try to draw us too towards a fall, they are not only worthless and without honour but also opposed to God and harmful and most hostile to our race.

28. But natural scientists, astronomers, and those who boast of knowing everything have been unable to understand any of the things just mentioned on the basis of their philosophy and have considered the ruler of the intelligible darkness and all the rebellious powers under him not only superior to themselves but even gods and they honoured them with temples, offered them sacrifices, and submitted themselves to their most destructive oracles by which they were fittingly much deluded through unholy holy things and defiling purifications, through those who inspire abominable presumption and through prophets and prophetesses who lead them very far astray from the real truth.

29. Not only are man's knowledge of God and his understanding of himself and his proper rank (which knowledge now belongs to those who are Christians, even those considered uneducated laymen) a more lofty knowledge than natural science and astronomy and any philosophy in these subjects, but also our mind's knowledge of its own weakness and the search for its healing would be incomparably superior by far to the investigation and knowledge of the magnitudes of the stars and the reasons for natural phenomena, the origins of things below and the circuits of things above, their changes and risings, their fixed positions and retrograde motions, their disjunctions and conjunctions, and, in general, the entire multiform relation that results from their considerable motion in that region. For the mind that realizes its own weakness has discovered whence it might enter upon salvation and draw near to the light of knowledge and receive true wisdom which does not pass away with this age. . . .

57. Now that the kingdom of heaven has drawn near to us through the condescension of God the Word unto us, let us not remove ourselves far

from it by living an unrepentant life. Rather, let us flee the wretchedness of "those who sit in darkness and the shadow of death." Let us acquire the works of repentance: a humble attitude, compunction and spiritual mourning, a gentle heart full of mercy, loving justice, striving for purity, peaceful, peacemaking, patient, glad to suffer persecutions, losses, disasters, slander and sufferings for the sake of truth and righteousness. For the kingdom of heaven, or rather, the King of heaven—O the unspeakable munificence!—is within us. To him we ought always to cling by works of repentance and perseverance, loving as much as possible him who loved us so much.

58. The absence of passions and the presence of virtues establish love of God, for hatred of evil things and the consequent absence of the passions introduce instead the desire for and the acquisition of good things. How could one who loves and possesses good things not love in a special way the master who is goodness itself and who alone is both provider and preserver of all good? In him he has his being in a singular manner and him he bears within himself through love, according to the one who said, "He who abides in love abides in God and God in him." You should know not only that love for God is based on the virtues, but also that the virtues are born of love. And so the Lord says at one point in the Gospel, "He who has my commandments and keeps them, he it is who loves me"; and on another occasion, "He who loves me will keep my commandments." But neither are the works of virtue praiseworthy and profitable for those who practise them without love, nor indeed is love without works. Paul at one time makes ample demonstration of this when he writes to the Corinthians, "If I do such and such but have not love, I gain nothing." And in turn, at another time, the disciple specially beloved by Christ does likewise when he says, "Let us not love in word or speech but in deed and in truth."

59. The supreme and worshipful Father is Father of Truth itself, namely, the Only-Begotten Son. And the Holy Spirit has a spirit of truth, just as the Word of Truth demonstrated previously. Therefore, those who worship the Father in spirit and truth and hold to this manner of belief also receive the energies through these. 'For the Spirit,' says the Apostle, 'is the one through whom we offer worship and through whom we pray'; and the Only-Begotten of God says, "No one comes to the Father except through me." Therefore, 'those who thus worship the supreme Father in spirit and truth are the true worshippers.'

Reprinted from *Saint Gregory Palamas: The One Hundred and Fifty Chapters*, ed. Robert E. Sinkewicz (Toronto: Pontifical Institute, 1988), pp. 83, 85, 109, 111, 113, 151, 153, by permission of the publisher. © 1988 by the Pontifical Institute of Mediaeval Studies, Toronto. Notes omitted.

–23–

Religious Expression
Ritual, Drama, and Story

This chapter follows the same trends of spirituality as Chapter 22, but in popular religion, as lay people sought meaningful spiritual experiences both within and outside of the official church. The church increasingly regularized the practice of Christianity, evident in the pope's explanation of the seven sacraments (23.1). However, most communities developed their own local pageants to celebrate in dramatic form the stories and lessons of the Bible, evident in the Chester Cycle of mystery plays (23.2). Stories of saints continued to play a role in communicating Christian values, evident in the Russian story of Great John (23.3).

23.1 Ritual: The Seven Sacraments Explained by Pope Eugene IV

For most Christians in Europe, religious experience was centered in the services of the church. Some heretical groups, such as the Lollards (21.3), denied that the priests possessed a special power to perform liturgical functions, such as the transformation of the Eucharist. But the majority of residents of Europe who saw themselves as Christians accepted the authority of the church and the power of the rituals performed there. These rituals, from the ancient rites of baptism and the Eucharist to healing ceremonies and ordination of priests, were gradually codified in the Middle Ages. At the council of Florence in 1438, seven were officially designated as the "sacraments," rituals holding a special power to confer blessing. The letter of Pope Eugene, below, explains the meaning of these seven sacraments to the churches in Armenia.

The ancient kingdom of Armenia, roughly between the Black Sea and the Caspian Sea, survived and developed under a number of cross-cultural influences, situated as it was in an area of heavy traffic. In late antiquity, the Armenians were under the dual influence of Byzantium and Persia; in the seventh century they felt the impact of the Arab conquests, yet maintained a Christian identity. Under the expansion and devastation of the Seljuk Turks in the twelfth century, Armenians moved westward into western Kurdistan; from there they assisted the Crusaders in establishing their kingdom at Edessa, allied themselves with the Holy Roman Empire, and came under western cultural influence. However, Armenia fell in 1375 to the Mamluks, Islamic Turkish mercenary forces who established a dynasty in the Middle East.

At the Council of Florence called in 1437, Pope Eugene IV and the besieged Byzantine emperor John VIII worked out an exchange ending the centuries-old divide between the eastern and western churches in the hopes of standing together against the Turkish threats in the Middle East, a union rejected by most Eastern Orthodox believers. Unfortunately, the European Crusade to assist the Byzantines failed, and, inevitably in any case, Constantinople fell to Turkish control (in 1453), ending the Byzantine Empire. Nonetheless, the Council of Florence initiated unions between the Latin or Roman Church of the west and several other eastern churches, including the Coptic Church in Egypt and the Armenian Church. The letter from Pope Eugene explaining the essential rituals of the western church to a distant cousin and former ally, now under Islamic rule, is part of an effort to reconnect and unite diverse Christian peoples.

Questions

1. What is the purpose of the sacraments as a whole?

2. Why are these seven, individually and collectively, significant for church life?

3. What impact would these sacraments have on the religious experience of an ordinary Christian?

Pope Eugene IV, An Account of the Seven Sacraments Written for the Armenians, 1438

We have drawn up in the briefest form a statement of the truth concerning the seven sacraments, so that the Armenians, now and in future generations, may more easily be instructed therein.

There are seven sacraments under the new law: that is to say, baptism, confirmation, the mass, penance, extreme unction, ordination, and matrimony. These differ essentially from the sacraments of the old law; for the latter do not confer grace, but only typify that grace which can be given by the passion of Christ alone. But these our sacraments both contain grace and confer it upon all who receive them worthily.

·The first five sacraments are intended to secure the spiritual perfection of every man individually; the two last are ordained for the governance and increase of the Church. For through baptism we are born again of the spirit; through confirmation we grow in grace and are strengthened in the faith; and when we have been born again and strengthened we are fed by the divine food of the mass; but if, through sin, we bring sickness upon our souls, we are made spiritually whole by penance; and by extreme unction we are healed, both spiritually and corporeally, according as our souls have need; by ordination the Church is governed and multiplied spiritually; by matrimony it is materially increased.

To effect these sacraments three things are necessary: the things [or symbols], that is, the "material"; the words, that is, the "form"; and the person of the "ministrant," who administers the sacrament with the intention of carrying out what the Church effects through him. If any of these things be lacking, the sacrament is not accomplished.

Three of these sacraments—baptism, confirmation, and ordination—impress indelibly upon the soul a character, a certain spiritual sign, distinct from all others; so they are not repeated for the same person. The other four do not imprint a character upon the soul, and admit of repetition.

Holy baptism holds the first place among all the sacraments because it is the gate of spiritual life; for by it we are made members of Christ and of the body of the Church. Since through the first man death entered into the world, unless we are born again of water, and of the spirit, we cannot, so says Truth, enter into the kingdom of heaven. The material of this sacrament is water, real and natural—it matters nothing whether it be cold or warm. Now the form is: "I baptize thee in the name of the Father, and of the Son, and of the Holy Ghost." . . .

The ministrant of this sacrament is the priest, for baptism belongs to his office. But in case of necessity not only a priest or deacon may baptize, but a layman or a woman—nay, even a pagan or a heretic, provided he use the form of the Church and intend to do what the Church effects. The efficacy of this sacrament is the remission of all sin, original sin and actual, and of all penalties incurred through this guilt. Therefore no satisfaction for past sin should be imposed on those who are baptized; but if they die before they commit any sin, they shall straightway attain the kingdom of heaven and the sight of God.

The second sacrament is confirmation. The material is the chrism made from oil, which signifies purity of conscience, and from balsam; which signifies the odor of fair fame; and it must be blessed by the bishop. The form is: "I sign thee with the sign of the cross and confirm thee with the chrism of salvation, in the name of the Father, and of the Son, and of the Holy Ghost." The proper ministrant of this sacrament is the bishop. While a simple priest avails to perform the other anointings, this one none can confer save the bishop only; for it is written of the apostles alone that by the laying on of hands they gave the Holy Ghost, and the bishops hold the office of the apostles. We read in the Acts of the Apostles, when the apostles who were at Jerusalem heard how Samaria had received the word of God, they sent to them Peter and John; who, when they were come, prayed that they might receive the Holy Ghost; for as yet it was fallen upon none of them—they were only baptized in the name of the Lord Jesus. Then they laid hands upon them and they received the Holy Ghost. Now, in place of this laying on of hands, confirmation is given in the Church. Yet we read that sometimes, for reasonable and urgent cause, by dispensation from the Holy See, a simple priest has been permitted to administer confirmation with a chrism prepared by a bishop.

In this sacrament the Holy Ghost is given to strengthen us, as it was given to the apostles on the day of Pentecost, that the Christian may confess boldly the name of Christ. And therefore he is confirmed upon the brow, the seat of shame, that he may never blush to confess the name of Christ and especially his cross, which is a stumbling-block to the Jews and foolishness to the Gentiles, according to the apostle. Therefore he is signed with the sign of the cross.

The third sacrament is the eucharist. The material is wheaten bread and wine of the grape, which before consecration should be mixed very sparingly with water; because, according to the testimony of the holy fathers and doctors of the Church set forth in former times in disputation, it is believed that the Lord himself instituted this sacrament with wine mixed with water, and also because this corresponds with the accounts of our Lord's passion. For the holy Pope Alexander, fifth from the blessed Peter, says, "In the offerings of sacred things made to God during the solemnization of the mass, only bread and wine mixed with water are offered up. Neither wine alone nor water alone may be offered up in the cup of the Lord, but both mixed, since it is written that both blood and water flowed from Christ's side."

Moreover the mixing of water with the wine fitly signifies the efficacy of this sacrament, namely, the union of Christian people with Christ, for water signifies "people," according to the passage in the Apocalypse which says, "many waters, many people." And Julius, second pope after the blessed Sylvester, says: "According to the provisions of the canons the cup of the Lord should be offered filled with wine mixed with water, because a people is signified by the water, and in the wine is manifested the blood of Christ. Therefore when the wine and water are mixed in the cup the people are joined to Christ, and the host of the faithful is united with him in whom they believe."

Since, therefore, the holy Roman Church, instructed by the most blessed apostles Peter and Paul, together with all the other churches of the Greeks and Latins in which glowed the light of sanctity and of doctrine, has from the beginning of the nascent Church observed this custom and still observes it, it is quite unseemly that any region whatever should depart from this universal and rational observance. We decree, therefore, that the Armenians likewise shall conform themselves with the whole Christian world, and that their priests shall mix a little water with the wine in the cup of oblation.

The form of this sacrament is furnished by the words of the Savior when he instituted it, and the priest, speaking in the person of Christ, consummates this sacrament. By virtue of these words, the substance of the bread is turned into the body of Christ and the substance of the wine into his blood. This is accomplished in such wise that the whole Christ is altogether present under the semblance of the bread and altogether under the semblance of the wine. Moreover, after the consecrated host and the consecrated wine have been divided, the whole Christ is present in any part of them. The benefit effected by this sacrament in the souls of those who receive it worthily is the union of man with Christ. And since, through grace, man is made one body with Christ and united in his members, it follows that through this sacrament grace is increased in those who partake of it worthily. Every effect of material food and drink upon the physical life, in nourishment, growth, and pleasure, is wrought by this sacrament for the spiritual life. By it we recall the beloved memory of our Savior; by it we are withheld from evil, and strengthened in good, and go forward to renewed growth in virtues and graces.

The fourth sacrament is penance. The material, as we may say, consists in the acts of penitence, which are divided into three parts. The first of these is contrition of the heart, wherein the sinner must grieve for the sins he has committed, with the resolve to commit no further sins. Second comes confession with the mouth, to which it pertains that the sinner should make confession to his priest of all the sins he holds in his memory. The third is satisfaction for sins according to the judgment of the priest, and this is made chiefly by prayer, fasting, and almsgiving. The form of this sacrament consists in the words of absolution which the priest speaks when he says, "I absolve thee," etc.; and the minister of this sacrament is the priest, who has authority to absolve either regularly or by the commission of a superior. The benefit of this sacrament is absolution from sins.

The fifth sacrament is extreme unction, and the material is oil of the olive, blessed by a bishop. This sacrament shall not be given to any except the sick who are in fear of death. They shall be anointed in the following places: the eyes on account of the sight, the ears on account of the hearing, the nostrils on account of smell, the mouth on account of taste and speech, the hands on account of touch, the feet on account of walking, and the loins as the seat of pleasure. The form of this sacrament is as follows: "Through this holy unction and his most tender compassion, the Lord grants thee forgiveness for whatever sins thou have committed by the sight,"—and in the same way for the other members. The minister of this sacrament is a priest. The benefit is even the healing of the mind and, so far as is expedient, of the body also. Of this sacrament the blessed apostle James says: "Is any sick among you? Let him call for the elders of the church and let them pray over him, anointing him with oil in the name of the Lord: and the prayer of faith shall save the sick, and the Lord shall raise him up; and if he have committed sins, they shall be forgiven him."

The sixth sacrament is ordination. The material for the priesthood is the cup with the wine and the paten with the bread; for the deaconate, the books of the Gospel; for the subdeaconate, an empty cup placed upon an empty paten; and in like manner, other offices are conferred by giving to the candidates those things which pertain to their secular ministrations. The form for priests is this: "Receive the power to offer sacrifice in the Church for the living and the dead, in the name of the Father, and of the Son, and of the Holy Ghost." And so for each order the proper form shall be used, as fully stated in the Roman pontifical. The regular minister of this sacrament is the bishop; the benefit, growth in grace, to the end that whosoever is ordained may be a worthy minister.

The seventh sacrament is matrimony, the type of the union of Christ and the Church, according to the apostle, who says, "This is a great mystery; but I speak concerning Christ and the church." The efficient cause of marriage is regularly the mutual consent uttered aloud on the spot. These advantages are to be ascribed to marriage: first, the begetting of children and their bringing up in the worship of the Lord; secondly, the fidelity that husband and wife should each maintain toward the other; thirdly, the indissoluble character of marriage, for this typifies the indissoluble union of Christ and the Church. Although for the cause of adultery separation is permissible, for no other cause may marriage be infringed, since the bond of marriage once legitimately contracted is perpetual.

From Robinson, pp. 348–54.

23.2 Drama: The Chester Cycle, The Last Judgement

Over the course of the Middle Ages, both churchmen and the laity recognized and exploited the dramatic potential of the rituals of the church and the stories of the Bible. Dramas and liturgical plays in monasteries became more elaborate; as urban lay piety expanded, townspeople and guilds took an interest in dramatizing religious stories. By the late Middle Ages, many communities were staging elaborate cycles of biblical plays in outdoor settings, often involving hundreds of people in an open field. These plays were quite inventive and elaborate, including music, comedy routines, local humor, and social commentary, as well as serious dramatization of religious ideals.

These documented "mystery" plays come in sets or cycles, covering a whole range of biblical stories from Creation to Last Judgment. The following selection is the last play in the Chester Cycle of sixteen plays. It covers the Last Judgment, visible in the carvings over the doorways of many churches, here set to life with Christ judging both the damned and those enduring purgatory, the place of cleansing prior to entering heaven.

Questions

1. What view of the spiritual dimension, of God, angels, and demons, is given in the play?

2. In the human dimension, why do you think these high-ranking people were chosen as representatives of human beings at judgment?

3. What religious, political, and social messages come out in this play?

The Chester Cycle, #16 The Last Judgement

GOD THE FATHER: I God, greatest of degree,
For whom no beginning could be,
The Master over land and sea
As clearly may be proved,
In my Godhead are persons three
All of us indivisible be
And that sovereign right that is in me
To others may be moved.
It is an age since I in my might
Did make a reckoning of the right.
Now to the doom I set my sight
That the dead shall truly dread.
Therefore, my angels, fair and bright
Look that you wake up each worldly wight [human]
That they may all come into my light,
All those for whom I bled.

1ST ANGEL: Lord, that madest through thy might,
Heaven and earth, day and night,
Without distance, swift as light
Your bidding shall be done.
Straight to awake each worldly wight
I shall be ready upon this height,
To show them forth into thy sight
And them you shall see soon.
(ANGELS *blow their trumpets*)

1ST POPE: While I lived in flesh and blood,
Thy great Godhead that is so good
I never knew although I should,
Thy worship to begin.
The wits, Lord, thou sent to me
I used to come to great degree;
The highest office under thee
On earth thou puttest me in.
When I on earth was at my own will
The world did blind and call me still,
But thy commandments to fulfil
I was full negligent.
But purged it is with pains ill
In Purgatory that sore can grill
Yet with thy grace here on this hill
I stand after great torment.

1ST EMPEROR: Ah, Lord and sovereign saviour
That placed me living in great honour
And made me king and emperor
Highest of kith and kin;
My flesh, lying fallen as the flower
Thou hast restored now by thy power
And with pains and great langour
Cleansed me of my sin.
In Purgatory my soul hath been
A thousand years in pain so keen
Till there is no sin upon me seen:
Purged to be one of thine.
Though I was for riches renowned
And all my days to sin was bound,

Yet at the last contrition me found
And now I stand in thy line.

1ST QUEEN: While I on earth all rich could go
I dressed in satin and silk also
And velvet too that brought me woe
With all such other weeds
That all might excite lechery;
Pearls and other jewellery
Against thy bidding used I,
And other wicked deeds.
Neither prayed I, nor ever fast;
Save alms deeds if any passed;
And great repentance at the last
Which has brought me to thy grace.
Now saved I hope for ever to be
For the cleansed sins that were in me.
Thy last judgement may I not flee
But come now before thy face. (*The Damned enter*)

2ND POPE: Alas, O woe is me, alas!
Now am I worse than ever I was;
My body has taken my soul, alas,
That long has been in hell.
Together they stay, I have no grace,
Defiled they look before my face,
And after my death here in this place
In pain for ever to dwell.
Now bootless it is to ask mercy
For, living, highest in earth was I
For my knowledge chosen in papacy
But covetousness did me tear.
Also silver and simony
Made me Pope full unworthy.
They burn me now full bitterly
For of bliss I am quite bare.
Of all souls in Christianity
That were damned while I held the See.
Now to give account behoveth me
Through my lapses forlorn.
Also damned now must I be,

Before I can elsewhere flee:
Make me dead I conjure thee,
As though I had never been born.

2ND EMPEROR: Alas, oh world, why went I there?
Alas, that ever my mother me bare.
Of all this woe I must work my share,
Escape can I not this chance.
Alas, do evil, who is there that dare?
We can protest no more against this care
For to feel pain we ordained are
For ever without deliverance.
Now is manslaughter upon me seen,
Now covetousness makes my pains more keen,
Now wrong-working, secret unseen,
All in the world have I wrought.
Misgotten money I revelled among
And now I am in the hellish throng
Hurt, burnt and whipped by the deadly thong.
In pain I for ever am caught.

2ND QUEEN: Alas, that I was woman wrought!
Alas, that God me out of naught
And with his precious blood me bought
To work against his will!
Lechery I never wrought
But ever to do that sin I sought
And of filth in deed and thought
I had never yet my fill.
Fie on pearls, fie on pride,
Fie on gowns! They may not abide.
Fie on beauty which quickly has died!
These have harrowed me in hell.
Against my lot I may not chide.
This bitter chance I must abide
Of woe and dread suffer the tide
Which no living tongue can tell.

(JESUS *descends:* ANGELS *bring the instruments of the Passion*)

JESUS: You good and evil, that here are sent;
Here you come to your judgement:

Now you will learn what is for you meant
And in what manner.
And all mine, on goodness bent,
Prophets, patriarchs here present
Must know my word with good intent
Therefore I am now here.

But you shall hear and see no less
That I give you all in righteousness;
Charitable deeds, both more and less
I will recall now here.
Of earth through me man made thou was
And put in place of great fineness,
From which straight through wickedness
Away thou hastened there.

After dying on the rood tree
And my blood shedding as thou mayst see
To deprive the devil of all ye
And win ye all away,
That selfsame blood, behold all ye,
Still remembered now it should be
For these good reasons that I offer ye
Of which I will now say.

One cause was this certainly
That to my Father almighty
At my ascension offer might I
This blood craving a boon:
That he of you should have mercy
And more gracious therafter be,
Though you had all sinned horribly
Not taking vengeance too soon.

1ST POPE: Ah, Lord, though I lived in sin
In Purgatory I have long been,
Suffering so long with fire and din
To bring me at last to bliss.

1ST EMPEROR: Yes, Lord, and therein have I be
More than three hundred years and three;

Now I am clean, forsake not me,
Although I did amiss.

1ST QUEEN: And I, Lord, to thee cry and call,
Thine own Christian now and thrall,
That of my sins am purged all,
Of thy joy I thee pray.

JESUS: Come hither to me, my darlings dear,
That blessed in the world always were;
Take my realm, all together
That for you ordained is.
For while I was on earth here
You gave Me meat in good manner,
Therefore in Heaven bliss clear
You shall forever have, I wis [know].
In thirst you gave me to drink,
When I was naked also clothing
And when I needed harbouring
You kept me out of the cold.
And other deeds to my liking
You did on earth while living;
Therefore you shall be quit your sin
And receive back a hundredfold.

Therefore, my angels, go you anon
And take my chosen, everyone
And show them where they shall be gone
To live for aye in bliss.
On my right hand they shall be set
For that of yore I promised
When they did as I to them said
And lived without amiss.

1ST ANGEL: Lord, we shall never cease,
Till we have brought them to their peace,
Those souls who have gained an eternal lease
In this land as they shall see.

2ND ANGEL: And I know them all, so good and fine
The bodies, Lord, that are all thine;

They shall have joy without repine
And that shall ne'er ended be.

(*They lead off the Saved Souls singing* "Salvator mundi
Domine")

1ST DEVIL: Ah, righteous Judge, with most of might
That are now set to doom aright,
Mercy thou hadst to those bright
To save those good men from repine.
Do as thou hast promised
With those sinful as thou hast said
To our kingdom let them be led
And name these men for mine.
Judge this Pope mine in this place
That is worthy for his great trespass;
Not to be thine through grace
But come through sin to be mine.
This Emperor and Queen would never know
Poor men, them alms to show.
Therefore put them in my row
Where fire shall burn them fine.

2ND DEVIL: Nay, I dispute with him in this
Though he sit as High Justice;
And if I see he is righteous
Soon I shall make assay.
These words, God, thou saidst express
As Matthew beareth witness,
That according as man's deed was,
Rewarded he should be.
And lest thou forget, good man,
I shall recall how the text ran
For speak Latin well I can
And that thou soon shalt see.
Therefore righteous if thou be
These men in this row belong to me;
For one good deed here before thee
They have not come to show.
If there be any, speak on, let us see;
If there be none, condemn them to me,

Or else thou art as false as we
And all men shall well know.

1ST DEVIL: Yea, this thou saidst in good intent
That when thou came to judgement
Thy angels from thee should be sent
To part the evil from the good,
And put them into great torment
Where moaning and groaning were fervent.
These words to clerks here present
I will repeat, by the rood:

"Sic erit in consummatione saeculi; exibunt angeli et
separabunt malos de medio justorum, et mittent eos in
caminum ignis, ubi erit fletus et stridor dentium." [Thus it
will be at the ending of the world; the angels will go forth
and separate the evil from the midst of the righteous, and
send them into the pit of fire, where there will be weeping
and gnashing of teeth.]

Therefore deliver these men
And as I once broke my head
I will make them grin
And ruthfully to cry.
And in as hot a chimney
As is ordained for me,
Baked all shall they be
And in bitter moan shall fry.
This proud Pope here present
For covetousness was always bent

This Emperor died without amendment
Therefore I hold them mine.
This Queen used man's heart to stir
She spared no sin in no manner,
Now she has lost all her allure
She too shall peak and pine.

JESUS: Lo, you men that wicked have been
What Satan sayeth you have heard and seen,
Rightful judgement this has been;

For grace is put away.
When time of grace was lasting
To seek it you had no liking;
Therefore must I in everything
Do righteousness today.
And though my sweet mother dear
And all the saints that ever were
Prayed for you right now here
All that were now too late.
No grace may come through their prayer,
Or righteousness has no power
Therefore go to the fire in fear
You gain no other grace.
When I was hungry and thirsty both
And naked was, you would not Me clothe
And sick and in great woe
You would not visit Me.
Nor yet in prison to come
Nor of your meat give Me some,
Nor shelter give me when I was numb.
Never kind to Me were ye.

2ND POPE: When wast thou naked or harbourless
Hungry, thirsty or in sickness?
Or ever in a prison. Never, I guess.
See this we never could.

2ND EMPEROR: Had we thee hungry or thirsty seen,
Naked, sick or in prison been,
Harbourless or cold by any mean,
Have helped you be sure we would.

JESUS: Nay, when you saw the least of mine
That on this earth were forced to pine
With riches ye never helped them to dine
To fulfil all my desire.
And since you would nothing incline
To help the poorest of mine
For me your love it was not fine,
Therefore go to the fire.

1ST DEVIL: Ah, Sir Judge, this goeth aright
By Mahound much of might,

You be mine, each wight
Ever to live in woe.
A doleful death for you, I say,
For such as you now I have my way.
Since you served me both night and day
You shall be rewarded so.
Go we forth to hell from high
Without end there shall ye lie
For you have lost just as did I
The bliss that lasteth ever.
Judged you be into Hell's belly
Where endless sorrow is nigh
And one thing I tell you truly;
Delivered will you be never. (DEVILS *take them away*)

(THE FOUR EVANGELISTS *enter*)

MATTHEW: I, Matthew, of this bear witness,
For in my gospel I writ express
This, that my Lord of His goodness
Has enacted here.
All by me were warned before,
To save their souls for evermore,
That through their lives are punished sore
And damned to fire in their fear.

MARK: I, Mark, now openly say,
That they were warned by many a way
How their living they should array
Heaven's bliss to recover.
So that excuse themselves they never may
For they are all worthy, in good fay,
To suffer the doom given this day
And damned to be for ever.

LUKE: And I, Luke, on earth living
My Lord's words in every thing
I wrote all, from my knowing,
That all men know might.
And therefore I say forsooth, I wis,
Excuse for this none there is;

Against my talking they did amiss
This doom it goeth aright.

JOHN: And I, John the Evangelist,
Bear witness of things that I wist
In which they might full well have trust
And not have done amiss.
And all that ever my Lord said here,
I wrote it all in my manner;
Therefore excuse you that stand damned here
I may not well, I wis.

(*If it is desired, the entire company can be introduced for this play and separated at the Judgement. All who remain after the devils have taken their protesting selection should join in singing a final Alleluia.*)

Reprinted with permission from Maurice Hussey, *The Chester Mystery Plays: Sixteen Pageant Plays from the Chester Craft Cycle* (London: William Heinemann, 1957), pp. 142–52.

23.3 Story: Great John in Russia

The story of Great John, archbishop of Novgorod, is a good example of a late medieval saint's life and of the values and beliefs of the Russian (Eastern Orthodox) Church. Russia was founded by East Slavs, with some Scandinavian influx in the ninth century, and Byzantine influence in the tenth century. Christianization thus came from the Eastern Orthodox Church of Byzantium. After the fall of Constantinople in 1453, Moscow became the Eastern Orthodox capital. Mongol incursions into Russia in the thirteenth century separated Russia from western contact; but the Christian rule centered in Moscow grew and created a centralized governance in the late fourteenth and fifteenth centuries, accompanied by a flowering of literature.

Archbishop John lived in the twelfth century, but stories of his life remained popular and underwent a renaissance in the fifteenth century, when Novgorod, his city, sought to assert its independent identity during the rise of the Muscovite realm. This story is probably from a collection edited by Pachomius the Serb after Bishop John's relics were rediscovered in 1439. Only a portion of the story is given here, written by Pachomius in a complex style called "weaving of words." The story eventually concludes with a procession of clergy and laity to the church, asking for Bishop John's forgiveness and his return.

Questions

1. What is saintly about Archbishop John? Compare this story to other saints stories you have read (6.2, 7.1, 8.4, 13.4, 19.3).
2. What is the nature of the demon, and what role does he play in the story?
3. What would the hearers of this story learn from it?

The Story of Great John, Archbishop of Novgorod the Great

FATHER, MAY YOUR BLESSING BE WITH US

This story should not lapse into oblivion, for God Almighty, who placed John in the bishopric, permits people to be overcome by temptation. He does this to sanctify and glorify them, testing their mettle as one might test gold. God has said: "I will glorify those who glorify me." Wondrous is God among the host of his saints, and God himself glorifies them.

And Christ said: "I give you power over evil spirits."

Once, in the evening, John, Archbishop of Great Novgorod, went to recite his evening prayers, as was his custom. At that time there was a vessel filled with water near his cell, and the Reverend Father used it for his ablutions. Suddenly he heard someone struggling in the water of this vessel. Coming closer to the vessel, and realizing that this was the design of the devil, he read a prayer so as to confine the demon in the vessel. The devil wished to frighten the holy father, but he was defeated in this purpose by the firm adamant [power of the cross]. The devil wanted to get out of the vessel, but could not overcome this power. A short time later, the demon could no longer endure and so began to shriek: "Oh, what a miserable plight! I am burned by fire and cannot resist any longer. Let me go at once, O servant of God."

The bishop answered: "And who are you? How did you get in this vessel?"

This devil answered: "I am an evil demon and came to this place so that I might corrupt you, hoping that you would become frightened and cease your praying. But you confined me so cruelly in this vessel, and here I am burned terribly by the fire. O woe is me, a cursed one! How could I become tempted? How could I get in this vessel? I am bewildered! Release me now, you servant of God. I shall not return to this place again!"

And the evil demon shrieked so, that finally the bishop spoke, saying: "For your daring I order that you this very night take me from Novgorod the Great to the city of Jerusalem. And place me before the church wherein is the Lord's Sepulcher. And this very night you must bring me back to my cell, which you have dared to enter. And only then shall I release you."

The demon promised to comply with the will of the bishop, and said: "Please, only release me from confinement, you servant of God."

Without releasing the demon from the power of the cross, the holy bishop let the devil out of the vessel and said to him: "Ready yourself and appear before me as a horse. Then I will mount you and you will fulfill my request."

The devil, like a cloud of darkness, left the vessel and appeared as a horse before the cell door. The bishop went from his cell and, having armed himself with the cross and Grace, mounted the demon and that very night arrived in the city of Jerusalem in which is located the Holy Sepulcher of the Lord and the Tree of Life. Retaining his power over the demon, the bishop forbade it to move from the spot where it stood. And the demon, remaining under the power of the cross, was unable to move away.

In the meantime the Reverend Father went to the Church of the Holy Resurrection and, standing before the door of this church, knelt and prayed. And the doors of the church opened of their own accord, while the tapers and censers of the Lord's Sepulcher began to burn. The bishop, shedding tears, thanked God. And he venerated and kissed the Holy Sepulcher and the Tree of Life and the other shrines. Then he left the church, having fulfilled his longing. And the church doors closed after him of their own accord.

The bishop found the demon standing in the form of a horse and in the same place, as he had been ordered. And mounting the demon, the bishop found himself that very night in his cell, in the city of Novgorod the Great.

Leaving the saint's cell, the devil said: "O John, you forced me to labor, carrying you in one night to Jerusalem and that very same night carrying you back to Novgorod the Great. I was bound to do so, by the power of the cross, as if I were bound by shackles. I had to undergo many calamities. Reveal to no one what has happened this night. If you do, I will lead you into temptation. You will be tried and sentenced for lechery, abused, and put on a raft in the river Volkhov [a common punishment for criminals]."

To prevent the abuse of the demon, Bishop John made the sign of the cross.

The bishop had the custom of discussing problems of the spirit with the honorable abbots, most learned priests, and God-abiding men, since he considered it a necessity that he share his wisdom with others and open to them the sublimity of the Holy Trinity. He never tired of teaching men, and he often told to them the occurrences of his own life, describing them as those of another man. "I know," he told them once, "a certain man who happened to go from Novgorod to the city of Jerusalem in one night, worshiped there at the Lord's Sepulcher, and returned that very night to Novgorod the Great." The abbots and the others were astounded.

But from that time on, and with the permission of God, the demon began to lead the bishop into temptation. The people had the vision many times of a harlot leaving the cell of the bishop. Many officials of the city, who used to come to the bishop's cell to receive his blessing, would see there a woman's necklace of coins and also a woman's robe and sandals. And they felt sore offended, and wondered what to say of this. But all this was the design of this demon who expected that the people would rise up against the bishop, would speak unjustly of him, and would drive him from their midst.

The people took council with the officials, and declared: "It is unjust for such a bishop, who is a whoremonger, to occupy the apostolic seat. Let us go and drive him from our midst, for about such people King David said: 'And words will pour forth from the mouth of the flatterer and they will speak of righteousness, lowliness, pride, and destruction. This they do for they worship the devil, even before the assembly of Jews.' "

But let us return to the narration. When the people came to the cell of the bishop, the demon walked among the people, and they saw him as a girl, leaving the cell of the saint. And the people began to exclaim that she should be seized, but they could not do so, although they followed her for a long time.

The bishop heard the cries of the people and came out to them and said: "What has happened, my children?" But the citizens paid no heed to these words, and told him what they had seen, condemned him as a whoremonger, abused him, and, after wondering what should be done with him, they decided: "Let us put him on a raft in the middle of the river Volkhov so that he may float down the river and away from our city."

And so they took the ascetic, holy, and great bishop of God, John, to the great bridge which spanned the river Volkhov, led him down to the river, and put him on a raft. And so the dream of the evil demon was fulfilled. However, God's Grace shone on the face of the bishop, and his prayers to God overcame the demon's design. The demon had begun to rejoice, but when John, the bishop of God, was put on the raft in the middle of the river Volkhov, the raft immediately began to move upstream, although it was not driven by anyone. The raft on which the bishop was sitting was pushed upstream from the great bridge to the Monastery of St. George, and against a strong current. The bishop was praying for the people on the raft, saying: "O Lord, forgive them this sin, for they know not what they do."

And seeing this, the demon was abashed, and began to weep.

The people of Novgorod, seeing this miracle, rent their garments, returned, and said: "We have sinned; we have committed an injustice to this father, and we have condemned our pastor. We now know that this has happened through the designs of a demon."

-24-

Cross-Cultural Contact

This last chapter concludes the book with an examination of what happens when European Christians travel abroad, and how they come to understand cultural differences. Social instability, such as occurred in the late medieval period, often breeds intolerance. With regard to the internal "foreigners" to Christian society—the Jews—the fourteenth and fifteenth centuries were ones of violent persecution as they became scapegoats for the Black Death (24.1). Even Christian travelers meeting other Christians in Europe had some interesting encounters, as happened to the Italian Quirini when he and his crew were shipwrecked in a remote part of Norway (24.2). Europeans' conceptions of peoples outside of Europe varied, and often relied on fanciful or fictional accounts. Yet these stories, such as Mandeville's Travels (24.3), reveal a great deal about the cross-cultural mentality of Europeans. These perceptions in turn affected the ways in which the first European explorers crossing the Atlantic understood the peoples they met, as Columbus's journal reveals (24.4).

24.1 The Black Death and Jews:
Jean de Venette and Jacob von Königshofen

The Black Death, or the plague that struck Europe in 1348–1350, was a cataclysmic event in the European mentality. The two variants of the plague—the bubonic and pneumonic—decimated Europe, killing by some estimates at least a third of the population. Some areas were lightly hit, while some towns and villages were completely wiped out. Although the main sweep of the disease lasted only two years, it continued to cycle throughout the fourteenth-century and remained endemic into the sixteenth century. The economic, social, and psychological impact of the fourteenth-century devastation lasted for generations.

Reactions to the death and disorder took on religious dimensions. The Flagellants, believing the plague was God's punishment for sin, went on penitential pilgrimages whipping themselves bloody. Others blamed the Jews, accusing them of poisoning the wells, and rioted through the Jewish quarter massacring the inhabitants. The church and secular authorities condemned such extremes to no avail. Popular fears spawned violence, either self-inflicted as with the Flagellants or the more devastating mob attacks on Jews.

The most vicious massacres of Jews occurred in Germany, as the two excerpts below describe. Jean de Venette was a French chronicler who records the devastation of the plague and reactions to it, including the attacks on Jews in Germany. Jacob von Königshofen (1346–1420) was a Strasbourg historian who studied the archives and used earlier materials to give a detailed account of the massacre of Jews in his city. Neither author seems to be in sympathy with these atrocities and both indicate that popular sentiment and mob action lay behind the events.

Questions

1. What various theories circulated concerning the plague, according to Jean de Venette?

2. What, according to Jacob von Königshofen, caused the massacre of the Jews in Strasbourg?

3. What does the violence against Jews that both authors describe reveal about popular culture and attitudes in the fourteenth century?

Jean de Venette, Chronicle 1348–1350

In A.D. 1348, the people of France and of almost the whole world were struck by a blow other than war. For in addition to the famine which I described in the beginning and to the wars which I described in the course of this narrative, pestilence and its attendant tribulations appeared again in various parts of the world. In the month of August, 1348, after Vespers when the sun was beginning to set, a big and very bright star appeared above Paris, toward the west. It did not seem, as stars usually do, to be very high above our hemisphere but rather very near. As the sun set and night came on, this star did not seem to me or to many other friars who were watching it to move from one place. At length, when night had come, this big star, to the amazement of all of us who were watching, broke into many different rays and, as it shed these rays over Paris toward the east, totally disappeared and was completely annihilated. Whether it was a comet or not, whether it was composed of airy exhalations and was finally resolved into vapor, I leave to the decision of astronomers. It is, however, possible that it was a presage of the amazing pestilence to come, which, in fact, followed very shortly in Paris and throughout France and elsewhere, as I shall tell. All this year and the next, the mortality of men and women, of the young even more than of the old, in Paris and in the kingdom of France, and also, it is said, in other parts of the world, was so great that it was almost impossible to bury the dead. People lay ill little more than two or three days and died suddenly, as it were in full health. He who was well one day was dead the next and being carried to his grave. Swellings appeared suddenly in the armpit or in the groin—in many cases both—and they were infallible signs of death. This sickness or pestilence was called an epidemic by the doctors. Nothing like the great numbers who died in the years 1348 and 1349 has been heard of or seen or read of in times past. This plague and disease came from *ymaginatione* or association and contagion, for if a well man visited the sick he only rarely evaded the risk of death. Wherefore in many towns timid priests withdrew, leaving the exercise of their ministry to such of the religious as were more daring. In many places not two out of twenty remained alive. So high was the mortality at the Hôtel-Dieu in Paris that for a long time, more than five hundred dead were carried daily with great devotion in carts to the cemetery of the Holy Innocents in Paris for burial. A very great number of the saintly sisters of the Hôtel-Dieu who, not fearing to die, nursed the sick in all sweetness and humility, with no thought of honor, a number too often renewed by death, rest in peace with Christ, as we may piously believe.

This plague, it is said, began among the unbelievers, came to Italy, and then crossing the Alps reached Avignon, where it attacked several cardinals and took from them their whole household. Then it spread, unforeseen, to France, through Gascony and Spain, little by little, from town to town, from village to village, from house to house, and finally from person to person. It even crossed over to Germany, though it was not so bad there as with us. During the epidemic, God of His accustomed goodness deigned to grant this grace, that however suddenly men died, almost all awaited death joyfully. Nor was there anyone who died without confessing his sins and receiving the holy viaticum. To the even greater benefit of the dying, Pope Clement VI through their confessors mercifully gave and granted absolution from penalty to the dying in many cities and fortified towns. Men died the more willingly for this and left many inheritances and temporal goods to churches and monastic orders, for in many cases they had seen their close heirs and children die before them.

Some said that this pestilence was caused by infection of the air and waters, since there was at this time no famine nor lack of food supplies, but on the contrary great abundance. As a result of this theory of infected water and air as the source of the plague the Jews were suddenly and violently charged with infecting wells and water and corrupting the air. The whole world rose up against them cruelly on this account. In Germany and other parts of the world where Jews lived, they were massacred and slaughtered by Christians, and many thousands were burned everywhere, indiscriminately. The unshaken, if fatuous, constancy of the men and their wives was remarkable. For mothers hurled their children first into the fire that they might not be baptized and then leaped in after them to burn with their husbands and children. It is said that many bad Christians were found who in a like manner put poison into wells. But in truth, such poisonings, granted that they actually were perpetrated, could not have caused so great a plague nor have infected so many people. There were other causes; for example, the will of God and the corrupt humors and evil inherent in air and earth. Perhaps the poisonings, if they actually took place in some localities, reinforced these causes. The plague lasted in France for the greater part of the years 1348 and 1349 and then ceased. Many country villages and many houses in good towns remained empty and deserted. Many houses, including some splendid dwellings, very soon fell into ruins. Even in Paris several houses were thus ruined, though fewer here than elsewhere.

After the cessation of the epidemic, pestilence, or plague, the men and women who survived married each other. There was no sterility among the women, but on the contrary fertility beyond the ordinary. Pregnant women were seen on every side. Many twins were born and even three children at once. But the most surprising fact is that children born after the plague, when they became of an age for teeth, had only twenty or twenty-two teeth, though before that time men commonly had thirty-two in their upper and lower jaws together. What this diminution in the number of teeth signified I wonder greatly, unless it be a new era resulting from the destruction of one human generation by the plague and its replacement by another. But woe is me! the world was not changed for the better but for the worse by this renewal of population. For men were more avaricious and grasping than before, even though they had far greater possessions. They were more covetous and disturbed each other more frequently with suits, brawls, disputes, and pleas. Nor by the mortality resulting from this terrible plague inflicted by God was peace between kings and lords established. On the contrary, the enemies of the king of France and of the church were stronger and wickeder than before and stirred up wars on sea and on land. Greater evils than before pullulated everywhere in the world. And this fact was very remarkable. Although there was an abundance of all goods, yet everything was twice as dear, whether it were utensils, victuals, or merchandise, hired helpers or peasants and serfs, except for some hereditary domains which remained abundantly stocked with everything. Charity began to cool, and iniquity with ignorance and sin to abound, for few could be found in the good towns and castles who knew how or were willing to instruct children in the rudiments of grammar.

In the same year, 1348, Blessed Yves Hellory of Brittany, priest and confessor of wonderful virtue and grace, was canonized by the church and Pope Clement VI. The following year his body was raised from the ground by the prelates and the clergy of Brittany, and many signs and wonders were then wrought through him and by God on his account. At that time also the church under his invocation in the street of Saint Jacques of Paris was first begun and the foundations laid. How his virtues and sanctity flourished is clearly declared in the church at Tréguier in Brittany, where his body rests.

In the year 1349, while the plague was still active and spreading from town to town, men in Germany, Flanders, Hainaut, and Lorraine uprose and began a new sect on their own authority. Stripped to the waist, they gathered in large groups and bands and marched in procession through the crossroads and squares of cities and good towns. There they formed circles and beat upon their backs with weighted scourges, rejoicing as they did so in loud voices and singing hymns suitable to their rite and newly composed for it. Thus for thirty-three days they marched through many towns doing their penance and affording a great spectacle to the wondering people. They flogged their shoulders and arms with scourges tipped with iron points so zealously as to draw blood. But they did not come to Paris nor to any part of France, for they were forbidden to do so by the king of France, who did not want them. He acted on the advice of the masters of theology of the University of Paris, who said that this new sect had been formed contrary to the will of God, to the rites of Holy Mother Church, and to the salvation of all their souls. That indeed this was and is true appeared shortly. For Pope Clement VI was fully informed concerning this fatuous new rite by the masters of Paris through emissaries reverently sent to him and, on the grounds that it had been damnably formed, contrary to law, he forbade the Flagellants under threat of anathema to practice in the future the public penance which they had so presumptuously undertaken. His prohibition was just, for the Flagellants, supported by certain fatuous priests and monks, were enunciating doctrines and opinions which were beyond measure evil, erroneous, and fallacious. For example, they said that their blood thus drawn by the scourge and poured out was mingled with the blood of Christ. Their many errors showed how little they knew of the Catholic faith. Wherefore, as they had begun fatuously of themselves and not of God, so in a short time they were reduced to nothing. On being warned, they desisted and humbly received absolution and penance at the hands of their prelates as the pope's representatives. Many honorable women and devout matrons, it must be added, had done this penance with scourges, marching and singing through towns and churches like the men, but after a little like the others they desisted. . . .

In the year A.D. 1350 Pope Clement VI, Desiring to procure the salvation of the souls of men, decided to reduce to fifty years the interval between the plenary indulgences which are granted in the holy city of Rome every hundred years after the Lord's Incarnation. For the life of men is perishable and transitory and the wickedness of men abounds in the world, woe is me! and increases. Therefore in the year 1350 he granted plenary indulgence to all who, truly penitent, would journey to visit the places sacred to the apostles Peter and Paul and to the other saints in the city of Rome. Great numbers of both sexes went on this pilgrimage throughout the year in spite of the recent plague, which was still active in certain parts of the world.

Jacob von Königshofen, The Cremation of Strasbourg Jewry St. Valentine's Day, February 14, 1349

About the Great Plague and the Burning of the Jews

In the year 1349 there occurred the greatest epidemic that ever happened. Death went from one end of the earth to the other, on that side and this side of the sea, and it was greater among the Saracens than among the Christians. In some lands everyone died so that no one was left. Ships were also found on the sea laden with wares; the crew had all died and no one guided the ship. The Bishop of Marseilles and priests and monks and more than half of all the people there died with them. In other kingdoms and cities so many people perished that it would be horrible to describe. The pope at Avignon stopped all sessions of court, locked himself in a room, allowed no one to approach him and had a fire burning before him all the time. [This last was probably intended as some sort of disinfectant.] And from what this epidemic came, all wise teachers and physicians could only say that it was God's will. And as the plague was now here, so was it in other places, and lasted more than a whole year. This epidemic also came to Strasbourg in the summer of the above mentioned year, and it is estimated that about sixteen thousand people died.

In the matter of this plague the Jews throughout the world were reviled and accused in all lands of having caused it through the poison which they are said to have put into the water and the wells—that is what they were accused of—and for this reason the Jews were burnt all the way from the Mediterranean into Germany, but not in Avignon, for the pope protected them there.

Nevertheless they tortured a number of Jews in Berne and Zofingen [Switzerland] who then admitted that they had put poison into many wells, and they also found the poison in the wells. Thereupon they burnt the Jews in many towns and wrote of this affair to Strasbourg, Freiburg, and Basel in order that they too should burn their Jews. But the leaders in these three cities in whose hands the government lay did not believe that anything ought to be done to the Jews. However in Basel the citizens marched to the city-hall and compelled the council to take an oath that they would burn the Jews, and that they would allow no Jew to enter the city for the next two hundred years. Thereupon the Jews were arrested in all these places and a conference was arranged to meet at Benfeld [Alsace, February 8, 1349]. The Bishop of Strasbourg [Berthold II], all the feudal lords of Alsace, and representatives of the three above mentioned cities came there. The deputies of the city of Strasbourg were asked what they were going to do with their Jews. They answered and said that they knew no evil of them. Then they asked the Strasbourgers why they had closed the wells and put away the buckets, and there was a great indignation and clamor against the deputies from Strasbourg. So finally the Bishop and the lords and the Imperial Cities agreed to do away with the Jews. The result was that they were burnt in many cities, and wherever they were expelled they were caught by the peasants and stabbed to death or drowned. . . .

[The town-council of Strasbourg which wanted to save the Jews was deposed on the 9th–10th of February, and the new council gave in to the mob, who then arrested the Jews on Friday, the 13th.]

The Jews Are Burnt

On Saturday—that was St. Valentine's Day—they burnt the Jews on a wooden platform in their cemetery. There were about two thousand people of them. Those who wanted to baptize themselves were spared. [Some say that about a thousand accepted baptism.] Many small children were taken out of the fire and baptized against the will of their fathers and mothers. And everything that was owed to the Jews was cancelled, and the Jews had to surrender all pledges and notes that they had taken for debts. The council, however, took the cash that the Jews possessed and divided it among the working-men proportionately. The money was indeed the thing that killed the Jews. If they had been poor and if the feudal lords had not been in debt to them, they would not have been burnt. After this wealth was divided among the artisans some gave their share to the Cathedral or to the church on the advice of their confessors.

Thus were the Jews burnt at Strasbourg, and in the same year in all the cities of the Rhine, whether Free Cities or Imperial Cities or cities belonging to the lords. In some towns they burnt the Jews after a trial, in others, without a trial. In some cities the Jews themselves set fire to their houses and cremated themselves.

The Jews Return to Strasbourg

It was decided in Strasbourg that no Jew should enter the city for a hundred years, but before twenty years had passed, the council and magistrates agreed that they ought to admit the Jews again into the city for twenty years. And so the Jews came back again to Strasbourg in the year 1368 after the birth of our Lord.

Reprinted with permission from Jacob R. Marcus, *The Jew in the Medieval World: A Source Book 315–1791* (Cincinnati: The Union of American Hebrew Congregations, 1938), pp. 45–47.

24.2 Meeting Other Christians: Travels of Quirini in Norway

In April of 1431, Pietro Quirini, a Venetian nobleman and merchant, went on a trading voyage from the Venetian-owned island of Crete to Flanders, carrying wine, Cyprus wood, pepper, and ginger. The trip, marred by contrary winds and overlays for repairs, turned into a disaster when, on November 5, they were unable to enter the English Channel and the winds carried them out into the Atlantic, where rudderless and eventually without a mast they were driven northward. On December 17, they abandoned the ship and embarked on two boats, one of which did not survive. The other, with Quirini and forty-seven others, traveled north-eastward, with many men dying of exposure and thirst. The remainder, sixteen survivors, eventually landed on a small rocky island off the coast of Norway on January 5. Of those, apparently eleven survived the harsh conditions and were rescued by some villagers from the nearby island of Rost, and eventually made their way home through Sweden. The following selection describes their rescue by the Rost villagers and how they were treated.

Questions

1. By what means are the shipwrecked men able to communicate and get along with the Norwegian villagers?

2. What did the Venetian travelers think of the culture of the villagers?

3. What does this selection show you about cultural differences within Christendom?

Travels of Quirini in Norway

[Quirini and his companions are shipwrecked on a small rocky island off the coast of Norway]

... Next day at dawn, sixteen weak, miserable and exhausted wretches, the sad remains of forty-seven who had originally taken refuge in the large boat, went on shore and laid themselves down in the snow. Hunger, however, soon obliged them to examine if there might not remain some of the provisions which they had brought with them from the ship: All they found was a very small ham, an inconsiderable remnant of cheese, and some biscuit dust in a bag, mixed with the dung of mice. These they warmed by means of a small fire, which they made of the boat seats, and in some measure appeased their hunger.... Despairing now of any relief, as they were utterly destitute of any means to repair their boat, they constructed two small tents of their oars and sails, to shelter themselves from the weather, and hewed the materials of their boat in pieces to make a fire to warm themselves. The only food they were able to procure consisted in a few muscles and other shell-fish, which they picked up along the shore. Thirteen of the company were lodged in one of the tents, and three in the other. The smoke of the wet wood caused their faces and eyes to swell so much that they were afraid of becoming totally blind; and, what added prodigiously to their sufferings, they were almost devoured by lice and maggots, which they threw by handfuls into the fire. The secretary of Quirini had the flesh on his neck eaten bare to the sinews by these vermin, and died in consequence; besides him, three Spaniards of a robust frame of body likewise died, who probably lost their lives in consequence of having drank sea water while in the boat; and so weak were the thirteen who still remained alive, that during three days they were unable to drag away the dead bodies from the fire side.

Eleven days after landing on this rock or uninhabited island, Quirini's servant, having extended his search for shellfish, their only food, quite to the farthest point of the island, found a small wooden house, both in and around which he observed some cow-dung. From this circumstance the forlorn people concluded that there were men and cattle at no great distance, which inspired them with fresh hopes of relief, and revived their drooping spirits. This house afforded them abundant room and good shelter; and all, except three or four, who were too weak to be able for the fatigue of removing to such a distance, changed their abode to this hut, crawling with great difficulty through the deep snow, the distance being about a mile and a half, and they took with them as much as they were able of the ruins of their boat, to serve them for fire-wood.... [2 days later they find a large

fish beached, on which they initially gorge themselves, and then feed off of
it for fourteen days.]

. . . About eight miles from the rock upon which they now were, which
Fioravente informs us was called *Santi,* or Sand-ey by the natives, there was
another isle named *Rustene,* which was inhabited by several families of
fishers. It happened that a man and two of his sons came over from Rost to
Sandey to look after some cattle which were missing. Observing the smoke
from the hut in which Quirini and his wretched companions had taken
shelter, curiosity led them to examine the hut. On their approach, their
voices were heard by the people within the hut; but they believed it to be
only the screaming of the sea-fowl who devoured the bodies of their deceased companions. Christopher Fioravente, however, went out to examine
whence the unusual sound proceeded; and espying the two youths, he ran
back in haste, calling aloud to his companions that two men were come to
seek them. Upon this the whole company ran out immediately to meet the
lads, who on their parts were terrified at the sight of so many poor famished
wretches. These latter debated for some time among themselves whether
they should not detain one of their visitors, with the view of making themselves more certain to procure assistance; but Quirini dissuaded them from
this projected violence. They all accompanied the youths to the boat, and
entreated the father and sons to take two of their people along with them to
their habitations, in order the sooner to procure them assistance from
thence. For this purpose they chose one Gerrard of Lyons, who had been
purser of the ship, and one Cola a mariner of Otranto, as these men could
speak French and a little German.

The boat with the fishermen, and the two men who had been deputed to
seek assistance, went over to Rostoe on Friday the 31st of January
1432. On their landing, the inhabitants were much astonished at their appearance, but were not able to understand them, though the strangers addressed them in different languages; till at last one of the strangers began to
speak a little German with a German priest of the order of friars predicant
[Dominicans] who lived there, and informed him who they were and
whence they came. On Sunday the 2d February, which happened to be the
festival of the purification of the blessed Virgin, the priest admonished all
the people of Rostoe to assist the unhappy strangers to the utmost of their
power, at the same time representing the hardships and dangers they had
undergone, and pointing to the two famished wretches then present. Many
of the congregation were softened even to tears at the recital, and a resolution was formed to bring away the miserable survivors as soon as possible,
which they accomplished the next day. In the mean time, those who remained behind at Sandey considered the absence of their companions as

extremely long; and what with hunger, cold and anxiety, they were almost dead. Their joy may be more easily conceived than expressed, when they perceived six boats approaching to their relief. On landing, the Dominican priest inquired which of them was the captain of the unhappy crew; and when Quirini made himself known as such, the priest presented him with some rye bread and some beer, which he looked upon as manna sent from heaven. After this the priest took him by the hand, and desired him to choose two of his companions to accompany him; and Quirini pitched upon Francis Quirini of Candia [Crete], and Christopher Fioravente a Venetian, all three embarking in the boat of the principal man of Rostoe along with the priest. The rest of the company were distributed in the other five boats; and these good Samaritans went even to the tents where these unfortunates had first dwelt, taking away with them the only survivor of the three men who had staid behind from weakness, and buried the other two; but the poor invalid died next day.

On the arrival of the boats at Rostoe, Quirini was quartered with the principal person of the island: This man's son led him to his father's dwelling, as his debility was so great he was unable to walk without assistance. The mistress of the house and her maid came forwards to meet him, when he would have fallen at her feet; but she would not permit him, and immediately got him a basin of milk from the house, to comfort him and restore his strength. During three months and a half that Quirini dwelt in this house, he experienced the greatest friendship and humanity from the owners; while in return he endeavored by complaisance to acquire the good will of his kind hosts, and to requite their benevolence. The other partners of his misfortunes were distributed among the other houses of the place, and were all taken good care of.... [there follows a description of Rostoe, how it barters its fish for goods from Germany, England, Scotland, and Prussia, sending it first 1000 miles to Bergen.]

The inhabitants of these rocks are a well-looking people, and of pure morals. Not being in the least afraid of robbery, they never lock up any thing, and their doors are always open. Their women also are not watched in the smallest degree; for the guests sleep in the same room with the husbands and their wives and daughters; who even stripped themselves quite naked in presence of the strangers before going to bed; and the beds allotted for the foreigners stood close to those in which their sons and daughters slept. Every other day the fathers and sons went out a fishing by day-break, and were absent for eight hours together, without being under the least anxiety for the honor and chastity of their wives and daughters. In the beginning of May, the women usually begin to bathe; and custom and purity of morals has made it a law among them, that they should first strip themselves quite naked at home, and they then go to the bath at the distance of a bow-shot from the house. In their right hands they carry a bundle of herbs to wipe the moisture from their backs, and extend their left hands before them, as if to cover the parts of shame, though they do no seem to take much pains about the matter. In the bath they are seen promiscuously with the men. They have no notion of fornication or adultery; neither do they marry from sensual motives, but merely to conform to the divine command. They also abstain from cursing and swearing. At the death of relations, they show the greatest resignation to the will of God, and even give thanks in the churches for having spared their friends so long, and in now calling them to be partakers of the bounty of heaven. They show so little extravagance of grief and lamentation on these occasions, that it appeared as if the deceased had only fallen into a sweet sleep. If the deceased was married, the widow prepares a sumptuous banquet for the neighbors on the day of burial; when she and her guests appear in their best attire, and she entreats her guests to eat heartily, and to drink to the memory of the deceased, and to his eternal repose and happiness. They went regularly to church, where they prayed very devoutly on their knees, and they kept the fast days with great strictness.

Their houses are built of wood, in a round form, having a hole in the middle of the roof for the admission of light; and which hole they cover over in winter with a transparent fish skin, on account of the severity of the cold. Their clothes are made of coarse cloth, manufactured at London, and elsewhere. They wore furs but seldom; and in order to inure themselves to the coldness of their climate, they expose their new born infants, the fourth day after birth, naked under the sky-light, which they then open to allow the snow to fall upon them; for it snowed almost continually during the whole winter that Quirini and his people were there, from the 5th of February to the 14th of May. In consequence of this treatment, the boys are so inured to the cold, and become so hardy, that they do not mind it in the least. . . .

In the month of May, the inhabitants of Rostoe began to prepare for their voyage to Bergen, and were willing also to take the strangers along with them. Some days before their departure, the intelligence of their being at Rostoe reached the wife of the governor over all these islands; and, her husband being absent, she sent her chaplain to Quirini with a present of sixty stockfish, three large flat loaves of rye-bread, and a cake: And at the same time desired him to be informed, that she was told the islanders had not used them well, and if he would say in what point they had been wronged, instant satisfaction should be afforded; it was also strongly recommended by that lady to the inhabitants, to give them good treatment, and to take them over to Bergen along with themselves. The strangers returned their sincere thanks to the lady for the interest she took in their welfare, and gave their full testimony, not only to the innocence of their hosts in regard to what had been alleged, but spoke of the kind reception they had experienced in the highest terms. As Quirini still had remaining a rosary of amber beads which he had brought from St. Jago in Gallicia, he took the liberty of sending them to this lady, and requested her to use them in praying to God for their safe return into their own country.

When the time of their departure was come, the people of Rostoe, by the advice of their priest, forced them to pay two crowns for each month of their residence, or seven crowns each; and as they had not sufficient cash for this purpose, they gave, besides money, six silver cups, six forks, and six spoons, with some other articles of small value, which they had saved from the wreck, as girdles and rings. The greater part of these things fell into the hands of the rascally priest; who, that nothing might be left to them of this unfortunate voyage, did not scruple to exact these as his due for having acted as their interpreter. On the day of their departure, all the inhabitants of Rostoe made them presents of fish; and on taking leave, both the inhabitants and the strangers shed tears. The priest, however, accompanied them to Bergen, to pay a visit to his archbishop, and to give him a part of the booty.

From Robert Kerr, *A General History and Collection of Voyages and Travels,* Vol. I (Edinburgh, 1811), pp. 490–98 passim.

24.3 The Imagined World: Mandeville's Travels, on Prester John

Sir John Mandeville is the fictitious name representing a late fourteenth-century Englishman who purportedly traveled widely in Europe and in the East; however, the book is a clever compilation of various sources and stories whose author(s), or even country of origin (possibly French), are debatable. However far the putative author may have actually traveled, a good deal of what he wrote is pure, delightful fiction (hence the popularity of his book among European readers). Despite its fanciful descriptions, the book had an impact on Europeans who later did travel. For that reason, and because it represents something of the European imagination of the "others" who lived outside their world, the book is an important historical resource.

The section below is from his description of Prester John, a legendary figure whom Europeans believed was a powerful Christian ruler in India. In this selection, the wonder of the eastern world felt by many Europeans is evident; the East is exotic, fantastic, and inhabits a realm akin to Paradise.

Questions

1. Why is Prester John so noteworthy to Mandeville?
2. What view of Christianity in the larger world outside Europe does Mandeville present?
3. What overall view of East and Southeast Asia comes through in Mandeville's description?

The Travels of Sir John Mandeville

Chapter XXX Of the Royal Estate of Prester John. And of a Rich Man That Made a Marvellous Castle and [Called] It Paradise and of His Subtlety

This emperor, Prester John, holds full great land, and hath many full noble cities and good towns in his realm and many great diverse isles and large. For all the country of Ind is devised in isles for the great floods that come from Paradise, that depart all the land in many parts. And also in the sea he hath full many isles. And the best city in the Isle of Pentexoire is Nyse, that is a full royal city and a noble, and full rich.

This Prester John hath under him many kings and many isles and many diverse folk of diverse conditions. And this land is full good and rich, but not so rich as is the land of the great Chan [Khan]. For the merchants come not thither so commonly for to buy merchandises, as they do in the land of the great Chan, for it is too far to travel to. And on that other part, in the Isle of Cathay [China], men find all manner thing that is need to man—cloths of gold, of silk, of spicery and all manner avoirdupois. And therefore, albeit that men have greater cheap in the Isle of Prester John, natheles, men dread the long way and the great perils in the sea in those parts.

For in many places of the sea be great rocks of stones of the adamant, that of his proper nature draweth iron to him. And therefore there pass no ships that have either bonds or nails of iron within them. And if there do, anon the rocks of the adamants draw them to them, that never they may go thence. I myself have seen afar in that sea, as though it had been a great isle full of trees and buscaylle, full of thorns and briars, great plenty. And the shipmen told us, that all that was of ships that were drawn thither by the adamants, for the iron that was in them. And of the rotten-ness, and other thing that was within the ships, grew such buscaylle, and thorns and briars and green grass, and such manner of thing; and of the masts and the sail-yards; it seemed a great wood or a grove. And such rocks be in many places thereabout. And therefore dare not the merchants pass there, but if they know well the passages, or else that they have good lodesmen.

And also they dread the long way. And therefore they go to Cathay, for it is more nigh. And yet it is not so nigh, but that men must be traveling by sea and land, eleven months or twelve, from Genoa or from Venice, or he come to Cathay. And yet is the land of Prester John more far by many dreadful journeys.

And the merchants pass by the kingdom of Persia, and go to a city that is called Hermes, for Hermes the philosopher founded it. And after that they pass an arm of the sea, and then they go to another city that is called Golbache. And there they find merchandises, and of popinjays, as great plenty as men find here of geese. And if they will pass further, they may go securely enough. In that country is but little wheat or barley, and therefore they eat rice and honey and milk and cheese and fruit.

This Emperor Prester John taketh always to his wife the daughter of the great Chan; and the great Chan also, in the same wise, the daughter of Prester John. For these two be the greatest lords under the firmament.

In the land of Prester John be many diverse things and many precious stones, so great and so large, that men make of them vessels, as platters, dishes and cups. And many other marvels be there, that it were too cumbrous and too long to put it in scripture of books; but of the principal isles and of his estate and of his law, I shall tell you some part.

This Emperor Prester John is Christian, and a great part of his country also. But yet, they have not all the articles of our faith as we have. They believe well in the Father, in the Son and in the Holy Ghost. And they be full devout and right true one to another. And they set not by no barretts, ne by cautels [beguilements], nor of no deceits.

And he hath under him seventy-two provinces, and in every province is a king. And these kings have kings under them, and all be tributaries to Prester John. And he hath in his lordships many great marvels.

For in his country is the sea that men call the Gravelly Sea, that is all gravel and sand, without any drop of water, and it ebbeth and floweth in great waves as other seas do, and it is never still ne in peace, in no manner season. And no man may pass that sea by navy, ne by no manner of craft, and therefore may no man know what land is beyond that sea. And albeit that it have no water, yet men find therein and on the banks full good fish of other manner of kind and shape, than men find in any other sea, and they be of right good taste and delicious to man's meat.

And a three journeys long from that sea be great mountains, out of the which goeth out a great flood that cometh out of Paradise. And it is full of precious stones, without any drop of water, and it runneth through the desert on that one side, so that it maketh the sea gravelly; and it beareth into that sea, and there it endeth. And that flume runneth, also, three days in the week and bringeth with him great stones and the rocks also therewith, and that great plenty. And anon, as they be entered into the Gravelly Sea, they be seen no more, but lost for evermore. And in those three days that that river runneth, no man dare enter into it; but in the other days men dare enter well enough.

Also beyond that flume, more upward to the deserts, is a great plain all gravelly, between the mountains. And in that plain, every day at the sun-rising, begin to grow small trees, and they grow till mid-day, bearing fruit; but no man dare take of that fruit, for it is a thing of faerie. And after mid-day, they decrease and enter again into the earth, so that at the going down of the sun they appear no more. And so they do, every day. And that is a great marvel.

In that desert be many wild men, that be hideous to look on; for they be horned, and they speak nought, but they grunt, as pigs. And there is also great plenty of wild hounds. And there be many popinjays, that they call psittakes in their language. And they speak of their proper nature, and salute men that go through the deserts, and speak to them as pertly as though it were a man. And they that speak well have a large tongue, and have five toes upon a foot. And there be also of another manner, that have but three toes upon a foot, and they speak not, or but little, for they can not but cry.

This Emperor Prester John when he goeth into battle against any other lord, he hath no banners borne before him; but he hath three crosses of gold, fine, great and high, full of precious stones, and every of those crosses be set in a chariot, full richly arrayed. And for to keep every cross, be ordained 10,000 men of arms and more than 100,000 men on foot, in manner as men would keep a standard in our countries, when that we be in land of war. And this number of folk is without the principal host and without wings ordained for the battle. And when he hath no war, but rideth with a privy meinie, then he hath borne before him but one cross of tree, without painting and without gold or silver or precious stones, in remembrance that Jesus Christ suffered death upon a cross of tree. And he hath borne before him also a platter of gold full of earth, in token that his noblesse and his might and his flesh shall turn to earth. And he hath borne before him also a vessel of silver, full of noble jewels of gold full rich and of precious stones, in token of his lordship and of his noblesse and of his might.

He dwelleth commonly in the city of Susa. And there is his principal palace, that is so rich and so noble, that no man will trow it by estimation, but he had seen it. And above the chief tower of the palace be two round pommels of gold, and in everywhich of them be two carbuncles great and large, that shine full bright upon the night. And the principal gates of his palace be of precious stone that men call sardonyx, and the border and the bars be of ivory. And the windows of the halls and chambers be of crystal.

And the tables whereon men eat, some be of emeralds, some of amethyst, and some of gold, full of precious stones; and the pillars that bear up the tables be of the same precious stones. And the degrees to go up to his throne, where he sitteth at the meat, one is of onyx, another is of crystal, and another of jasper green, another of amethyst, another of sardine, another of cornelian, and the seventh, that he setteth on his feet, is of chrysolite. And all these degrees be bordered with fine gold, with the other precious stones, set with great pearls orient. And the sides of the siege of his throne be of emeralds, and bordered with gold full nobly, and dubbed with other precious stones and great pearls. And all the pillars in his chamber be of fine gold with precious stones, and with many carbuncles, that give great light upon the night to all people. And albeit that the carbuncles give light right enough, natheles, at all times burneth a vessel of crystal full of balm, for to give good smell and odor to the emperor, and to void away all wicked airs and corruptions. And the form of his bed is of fine sapphires, bended with gold, for to make him sleep well and to refrain him from lechery; for he will not lie with his wives, but four sithes in the year, after the four seasons, and that is only for to engender children.

He hath also a full fair palace and a noble at the city of Nyse, where that he dwelleth, when him best liketh; but the air is not so attempre [temperate], as it is at the city of Susa.

And ye shall understand, that in all his country nor in the countries there all about, men eat not but once in the day, as they do in the court of the great Chan. And so they eat every day in his court, more than 30,000 persons, without goers and comers. But the 30,000 persons of his country, ne of the country of the great Chan, ne spend not so much good as do 12,000 of our country.

This Emperor Prester John hath evermore seven kings with him to serve him, and they depart their service by certain months. And with these kings serve always seventy-two dukes and three hundred and sixty earls. And all the days of the year, there eat in his household and in his court, twelve archbishops and twenty bishops. And the patriarch of Saint Thomas is there as is the pope here. And the archbishops and the bishops and the abbots in that country be all kings. And everyone of these great lords know well enough the attendance of their service. The one is master of his household, another is his chamberlain, another serveth him of a dish, another of the cup, another is steward, another is marshal, another is prince of his arms, and thus is he full nobly and royally served. And his land dureth in very breadth four months' journeys, and in length out of measure, that is to say, all the isles under earth that we suppose to be under us.

Beside the isle of Pentexoire, that is the land of Prester John, is a great isle, long and broad, that men called Mistorak; and it is in the lordship of Prester John. In that isle is great plenty of goods.

There was dwelling, sometime, a rich man; and it is not long since; and men called him Gatholonabes. And he was full of cautels [beguilements] and of subtle deceits. And he had a full fair castle and a strong[hold] in a mountain, so strong and so noble, that no man could devise a fairer ne stronger. And he had let mure all the mountain about with a strong wall and a fair. And within those walls he had the fairest garden that any man might behold. And therein were trees bearing all manner of fruits, that any man could devise. And therein were also all manner virtuous herbs of good smell, and all other herbs also that bear fair flowers. And he had also in that garden many fair wells; and beside those wells he had let make fair halls and fair chambers, depainted all with gold and azure; and there were in that place many diverse things, and many diverse stories: and of beasts, and of birds that sung full delectably and moved by craft, that it seemed that they were quick. And he had also in his garden all manner of fowls and of beasts that any man might think on, for to have play or sport to behold them.

And he had also, in that place, the fairest damsels that might be found, under the age of fifteen years, and the fairest young striplings that men might get, of that same age. And all they were clothed in cloths of gold, full richly. And he said that those were angels.

And he had also let make three wells, fair and noble, and all environed with stone of jasper, of crystal, diapered with gold, and set with precious stones and great orient pearls. And he had made a conduit under earth, so that the three wells, at his list, one should run milk, another wine and another honey. And that place he called Paradise.

And when that any good knight, that was hardy and noble, came to see this royalty, he would lead him into his paradise, and show him these wonderful things to his disport, and the marvelous and delicious song of diverse birds, and the fair damsels, and the fair wells of milk, of wine and of honey, plenteously running. And he would let make divers instruments of music to sound in an high tower, so merrily, that it was joy for to hear; and no man should see the craft thereof. And those, he said, were angels of God, and that place was Paradise, that God had behight to his friends, saying, *Dabo vobis terram fluentem lacte et melle* [I will give you a land flowing with milk and honey]. And then would he make them to drink of certain drink, whereof anon they should be drunk. And then would them think greater delight than they had before. And then would he say to them, that if they would die for him and for his love, that after their death they should come to his paradise; and they should be of the age of those damsels, and they should play with them, and yet be maidens. And after that yet should he put them in a fairer paradise, where that they should see God of nature visibly, in his majesty and in his bliss. And then would he show them his intent, and say them, that if they would go slay such a lord, or such a man that was his enemy or contrarious to his list, that they should not dread to do it and for to be slain therefore themselves. For after their death, he would put them into another paradise, that was an hundred-fold fairer than any of the other; and there should they dwell with the most fairest damsels that might be, and play with them ever-more.

And thus went many diverse lusty bachelors for to slay great lords in diverse countries, that were his enemies, and made themselves to be slain, in hope to have that paradise. And thus, often-time, he was revenged of his enemies by his subtle deceits and false cautels.

And when the worthy men of the country had perceived this subtle falsehood of this Gatholonabes, they assembled them with force, and assailed his castle, and slew him, and destroyed all the fair places and all the nobilities of that paradise. The place of the wells and of the walls and of many other things be yet pertly seen, but the riches is voided clean. And it is not long gone, since that place was destroyed.

The Travels of Sir John Mandeville (the version of the Cotton Manuscript in modern spelling). (London: Macmillan, 1900), pp. 178–85.

24.4 Classifying the Other: Columbus's Journal

In hindsight, the voyages of Christopher Columbus (1451–1506) mark a dramatic turning point in European history, with global implications. But Columbus's ventures not only introduce a new phase of cross-cultural contact for Europeans, but also carry with them the European past. Columbus was a product of medieval European history, and his attitudes and views were shaped by late medieval economic, political, and cultural conditions. Thus, his responses to native American groups reflect the understandings of a fifteenth-century, relatively pious, European layperson of the Catholic faith. What Columbus writes in his journal about the peoples he meets says a lot about the late medieval religious worldview regarding the human condition.

The following selections are from extracts of Columbus's journal that Bartolome de las Casas (1474–1566) incorporated into his *History of the Indies* (Columbus's original journal is lost). These particular excerpts highlight the religious elements in Columbus's reaction to native American groups.

Questions

1. How does Columbus classify the native American groups he meets? What labels does he use to describe them?
2. Why does he think that they will be easy to convert to Christianity?
3. What role does Christian belief play in this European conceptualization of new peoples?

The Journal of Christopher Columbus

Friday, 12th of October

. . . At two hours after midnight the land was sighted at a distance of two leagues. They shortened sail, and lay by under the mainsail without the bonnets. The vessels were hove to, waiting for daylight; and on Friday they arrived at a small island of the Lucayos, called, in the language of the Indians, *Guanahani* [Watling Island]. Presently they saw naked people. The Admiral went on shore in the armed boat, and Martin Alonso Pinzon, and Vicente Yañez, his brother, who was captain of the *Niña*. The Admiral took the royal standard, and the captains went with two banners of the green cross, which the Admiral took in all the ships as a sign, with an F and a Y [Fernando and Ysabel] and a crown over each letter, one on one side of the cross and the other on the other. Having landed, they saw trees very green, and much water, and fruits of diverse kinds. The Admiral called to the two captains, and to the others who leaped on shore, and to Rodrigo Escovedo, secretary of the whole fleet, and to Rodrigo Sanchez of Segovia, and said that they should bear faithful testimony that he, in presence of all, had taken, as he now took, possession of the said island for the King and for the Queen, his Lords making the declarations that are required, as is more largely set forth in the testimonies which were then made in writing.

Presently many inhabitants of the island assembled. What follows is in the actual words of the Admiral in his book of the first navigation and discovery of the Indies. "I," he says, "that we might form great friendship, for I knew that they were a people who could be more easily freed and converted to our holy faith by love than by force, gave to some of them red caps, and glass beads to put round their necks, and many other things of little value, which gave them great pleasure, and made them so much our friends that it was a marvel to see. They afterwards came to the ship's boats where we were, swimming and bringing us parrots, cotton threads in skeins, darts, and many other things; and we exchanged them for other things that we gave them, such as glass beads and small bells. In fine, they took all, and gave what they had with good will. It appeared to me to be a race of people very poor in everything. They go as naked as when their mothers bore them, and so do the women, although I did not see more than one young girl. All I saw were youths, none more than thirty years of age. They are very well made, with very handsome bodies, and very good countenances. Their hair is short and coarse, almost like the hairs of a horse's tail. They wear the hairs brought down to the eyebrows, except a few locks behind, which they wear long and never cut. They paint themselves black, and they are the color of the Canarians, neither black nor white. Some paint themselves white, others red, and others of what color they find. Some paint their faces, others the whole body, some only round the eyes, others only on the nose. They neither carry nor know anything of arms, for I showed them swords, and they took them by the blade and cut themselves through ignorance. They have no iron, their darts being wands without iron, some of them having a fish's tooth at the end, and others being pointed in various ways. They are all of fair stature and size, with good faces, and well made. I saw some with marks of wounds on their bodies, and I made signs to ask what it was, and they gave me to understand that people from other adjacent islands came with the intention of seizing them, and that they defended themselves. I believed, and still believe, that they come here from the mainland to take them prisoners. They should be good servants and intelligent, for I observed that they quickly took in what was said to them, and I believe that they would easily be made Christians, as it appeared to me that they had no religion. I, our Lord being pleased, will take hence, at the time of my departure, six natives for your Highnesses, that they may learn to speak. I saw no beast of any kind except parrots, on this island." The above is in the words of the Admiral. . . .

Thursday, November the 1st, [at "Rio de Mares"]

. . . "These people," says the Admiral, "are of the same appearance and have the same customs as those of the other islands, without any religion so far as I know, for up to this day I have never seen the Indians on board say any prayer; though they repeat the *Salve* and *Ave Maria* with their hands raised to heaven, and they make the sign of the cross. The language is also the same, and they are all friends; but I believe that all these islands are at war with the Gran Can, whom they called *Cavila,* and his province *Bafan.* They all go naked like the others." . . .

Tuesday, 6th of November

. . . "They are a people," says the Admiral, "guileless and unwarlike. Men and women go as naked as when their mothers bore them. It is true that the women wear a very small rag of cotton-cloth, and they are of very good appearance, not very dark, less so than the Canarians. I hold, most serene Princes, that if devout religious persons were here, knowing the language, they would all turn Christians. I trust in our Lord that your Highnesses will resolve upon this with much diligence, to bring so many great nations within the church, and to convert them; as you have destroyed those who would not confess the Father, the Son, and the Holy Ghost. And after your days, all of us being mortal, may your kingdoms remain in peace, and free from heresy and evil, and may you be well received before the eternal Creator, to whom I pray that you may have long life and great increase of kingdoms and lordships, with the will and disposition to increase the holy Christian religion as you have done hitherto. Amen!" . . .

Monday, 12th of November

. . . The Admiral says that, on the previous Sunday, the 11th of November, it seemed good to take some persons from amongst those at *Rio de Mares,* to bring to the Sovereigns, that they might learn our language, so as to be able to tell us what there is in their lands. Returning, they would be the mouthpieces of the Christians, and would adopt our customs and the things of the faith. "I saw and knew" (says the Admiral) "that these people are without any religion, not idolaters, but very gentle, not knowing what is evil, nor the sins of murder and theft, being without arms, and so timid that a hundred would fly before one Spaniard, although they joke with them. They, however, believe and know that there is a God in heaven, and say that we have come from heaven. At any prayer that we say, they repeat, and make the sign of the cross. Thus your Highnesses should resolve to make them Christians, for I believe that, if the work was begun, in a little time a multitude of nations would be converted to our faith, with the acquisition of great lordships, peoples, and riches for Spain. . . .

Tuesday, 27th of November

. . . The Admiral also says:—"How great the benefit that is to be derived from this country would be, I cannot say. It is certain that where there are such lands there must be an infinite number of things that would be profitable. But I did not remain long in one port, because I wished to see as much of the country as possible, in order to make a report upon it to your Highnesses; and besides, I do not know the language, and these people neither understand me nor any other in my company; while the Indians we have on board often misunderstand. Moreover, I have not been able to see much of the natives, because they often take to flight. But now, if our Lord pleases, I will see as much as possible, and will proceed by little and little, learning and comprehending; and I will make some of my followers learn the language. For I have perceived that there is only one language up to this point. After they understand the advantages, I shall labor to make all these people Christians. They will become so readily, because they have no religion nor idolatry, and your Highnesses will send orders to build a city and fortress, and to convert the people. I assure your Highnesses that it does not appear to me that there can be a more fertile country nor a better climate under the sun, with abundant supplies of water. This is not like the rivers of Guinea, which are all pestilential. I thank our Lord that, up to this time, there has not been a person of my company who has so much as had a headache, or been in bed from illness, except an old man who has suffered from the stone all his life, and he was well again in two days. I speak of all three vessels. If it will please God that your Highnesses should send learned men out here, they will see the truth of all I have said. I have related already how good a place *Rio de Mares* would be for a town and fortress, and this is perfectly true; but it bears no comparison with this place, nor with the *Mar de Nuestra Señora.* For here there must be a large population, and very valuable productions, which I hope to discover before I return to Castille. I say that if Christendom will find profit among these people, how much more will Spain, to whom the whole country should be subject. Your Highnesses ought not to consent that any stranger should trade here, or put his foot in the country, except Catholic Christians, for this was the beginning and end of the undertaking; namely, the increase and glory of the Christian religion, and that no one should come to these parts who was not a good Christian." . . .

Monday, 24th of December

. . . Here the Admiral addresses the following words to the Sovereigns: "Your Highnesses may believe that there is no better nor gentler people in the world. Your Highnesses ought to rejoice that they will soon become Christians, and that they will be taught the good customs of your kingdom. A better race there cannot be, and both the people and the lands are in such quantity that I know not how to write it. I have spoken in the superlative degree of the country and people of Juana, which they call Cuba, but there is as much difference between them and this island and people as between day and night. I believe that no one who should see them could say less than I have said, and I repeat that the things and the great villages of this island of Española, which they call *Bohio,* are wonderful. All here have a loving manner and gentle speech, unlike the others, who seem to be menacing when they speak. Both men and women are of good stature, and not black. It is true that they all paint, some with black, others with other colors, but most with red. I know that they are tanned by the sun, but this does not affect them much. The houses and villages are pretty, each with a chief, who acts as their judge, and who is obeyed by them. All these lords use few words, and have excellent manners. Most of their orders are given by a sign with the hand, which is understood with surprising quickness."

Reprinted from *The Journal of Christopher Columbus (During His First Voyage, 1492–93), and Documents Relating the Voyages of John Cabot and Gaspar Corte Real,* trans. Clements R. Markham (London: Printed for the Hakluyt Society, 1893), pp. 36–38, 65, 71–72, 73, 90–91, 131–32.

Recommended Readings

General and Reference

Barraclough, Geoffrey, ed. *The Christian World: A Social and Cultural History.* New York: Harry N. Abrams, 1980.

Boswell, John. *Christianity, Social Tolerance and Homosexuality.* Chicago: University of Chicago Press, 1980.

Brown, H. O. J. *Heresies: The Image of Christ in the Mirror of Heresy and Orthodoxy from the Apostles to the Present.* Garden City: Doubleday, 1984.

Brundage, James A. *Sex, Law and Marriage in the Middle Ages.* Brookfield, VT: Variorum, 1993.

Bullough, Vern L., and James Brundage. *Sexual Practices and the Medieval Church.* Buffalo, NY: Prometheus Books, 1982.

Bynum, Caroline Walker. *The Resurrection of the Body in Western Christianity, 200–1336.* New York: Columbia University Press, 1995.

Ferguson, Everett, ed. *Encyclopedia of Early Christianity.* New York: Garland, 1990.

Kieckhefer, Richard. *Magic in the Middle Ages.* Cambridge: Cambridge University Press, 1990.

Leff, Gordon. *Medieval Thought: St. Augustine to Ockham.* Baltimore: Penguin, 1958.

Manschreck, Clyde L. *A History of Christianity in the World,* 2nd ed. Englewood Cliffs, NJ: Prentice-Hall, 1985.

McGinn, Bernard. *Visions of the End: Apocalyptic Traditions in the Middle Ages.* New York: Columbia University Press, 1979.

McGinn, Bernard, John Meyendorff, and Jean LeClerq, eds. *Christian Spirituality: Origins to the Twelfth Century.* New York: Crossroad, 1985.

McManners, John, ed. *The Oxford Illustrated History of Christianity.* Oxford: Oxford University Press, 1992.

Murray, Alexander. *Reason and Society in the Middle Ages.* Oxford: Clarendon Press, 1978.

Pelikan, Jaroslav. *Jesus through the Centuries: His Place in the History of Culture.* New York: Harper & Row, 1985.

Russell, Jeffrey Burton. *A History of Medieval Christianity: Prophecy and Order.* Arlington Heights, IL: Harlan Davidson, 1968.

555

Smalley, Beryl. *The Study of the Bible in the Middle Ages.* Oxford: Basil Blackwell, 1952. Originally published 1953; repr. Notre Dame: University of Notre Dame, 1964.

Southern, Richard W. *Western Society and the Church in the Middle Ages.* Harmondsworth: Penguin, 1970.

Part 1 Orthodoxy and Heterodoxy

Bauer, Walter. *Orthodoxy and Heresy in Earliest Christianity.* Philadelphia: Forress, 1971.

Brown, Peter. *Power and Persuasion in Late Antiquity: Towards a Christian Empire.* Madison, WI: University of Wisconsin Press, 1992.

Clark, Gillian. *Women in Late Antiquity: Pagan and Christian Lifestyles.* Oxford: Clarendon Press, 1993.

Danielou, J., and H. Marrou. *The First Six Hundred Years.* New York: McGraw-Hill, 1964.

Frend, W. H. C. *The Early Church.* Philadelphia: Fortress Press, 1982.

Harnack, Adolf von. *The Mission and Expansion of Christianity in the First Three Centuries.* New York: Harper & Row, 1962.

Harris, Stephen L. *Understanding the Bible: A Reader's Guide and Reference.* Palo Alto, CA: Mayfield, 1980.

Jones, A. H. M. *Constantine and the Conversion of Europe.* Toronto: University of Toronto Press, 1978.

Ladner, Gerhart. *The Idea of Reform: Its Impact on Christian Thought and Action in the Age of the Fathers,* rev. ed. New York: Harper & Row, 1967.

MacMullen, Ramsay. *Christianizing the Roman Empire,* A.D. 100–400. New Haven: Yale University Press, 1984.

McNamara, Jo Ann. *A New Song: Celibate Women in the First Three Christian Centuries.* New York: Institute for Research in History and Haworth Press, 1983.

Momigliano, Arnaldo. *On Pagans, Jews and Christians.* Middletown, CT: Wesleyan University Press, 1987.

———. *The Conflict between Paganism and Christianity in the Fourth Century.* New York: Oxford University Press, 1963.

Part 2 Patterns of Accommodation in Late Antiquity

Brown, Peter. *Augustine of Hippo.* Berkeley: University of California Press, 1967.

———. *The Cult of the Saints: Its Rise and Function in Latin Christianity.* Chicago: University of Chicago Press, 1982.

Browning, Robert. *The Byzantine Empire,* 2nd ed. Washington, DC: Catholic University of America Press, 1992.

Goffart, Walter. *The Narrators of Barbarian History (AD 500–800): Jordanes, Gregory of Tours, Bede, and Paul the Deacon.* Princeton: Princeton University Press, 1988.

Herrin, Judith. *The Formation of Christendom.* Princeton: Princeton University Press, 1987.

Knowles, David. *Christian Monasticism.* New York: McGraw-Hill, 1969)

LeClerq, Jean. *The Love of Learning and the Desire for God,* 2nd ed. New York: Mentor-Omega, 1977.

Mayr-Harting, Henry. *The Coming of Christianity to Anglo-Saxon England,* 3rd ed. University Park, PA: Pennsylvania State University Press, 1991.

Nie, Giselle de. *Views from a Many-Windowed Tower: Studies of Imagination in the Works of Gregory of Tours.* Amsterdam: Rodopi, 1987.

Straw, Carol. *Gregory the Great: Perfection in Imperfection.* Berkeley: University of California Press, 1988.

Part 3 Christian Society in the Early Middle Ages

Bachrach, Bernard. *Early Medieval Jewish Policy in Western Europe.* Minneapolis: University of Minnesota Press, 1977.

Barlow, Frank. *The English Church 1000–1066,* 2nd ed. London: Longman, 1979.

Flint, Valerie. *The Rise of Magic in Early Medieval Europe.* Princeton: Princeton University Press, 1991.

Jolly, Karen Louise. *Popular Religion in Late Saxon England: Elf-Charms in Context.* Chapel Hill: University of North Carolina Press, 1996.

Marenbon, John. *Early Medieval Philosophy (480–1150),* rev. ed. London: Routledge, 1988.

Paxton, Frederick S. *Christianizing Death: The Creation of a Ritual Process in Early Medieval Europe.* Ithaca: Cornell University Press, 1990.

Richards, Jeffrey. *The Popes and the Papacy in the Early Middle Ages, 476–752.* London: Routledge, 1979.

Runciman, Steven. *The Byzantine Theocracy.* Cambridge: Cambridge University Press, 1977.

Russell, Jeffrey. *Dissent and Reform in the Early Middle Ages.* Berkeley: University of California Press, 1965.

Tellenbach, Gerd. *The Church in Western Europe from the Tenth to the Early Twelfth Century,* trans. Timothy Reuter. Cambridge: Cambridge University Press, 1993.

Wallace-Hadrill, J. M. *The Frankish Church.* Oxford: Clarendon Press, 1983.

Part 4 Order and Prophecy

Barraclough, Geoffrey. *The Medieval Papacy.* New York: Norton, 1968.

Brooke, Christopher. *The Twelfth-Century Renaissance.* New York: Harcourt, Brace, and World, 1969.

Bynum, Caroline Walker. *Jesus as Mother: Studies in the Spirituality of the High Middle Ages.* Berkeley: University of California Press, 1982.

Erickson, Carolly. *The Medieval Vision: Essays in History and Perception.* New York: Oxford University Press, 1976.

Geary, Patrick. *Furta Sacra: Thefts of Relics in the Central Middle Ages.* Princeton: Princeton University Press, 1978.

———. *Living with the Dead in the Middle Ages.* Ithaca: Cornell University Press, 1994.

Gilson, Etienne. *A History of Christian Philosophy in the Middle Ages.* New York: Random House, 1955.

———. *The Mystical Theology of Saint Bernard.* New York: Sheed & Ward, 1940.

Heffernan, T. J. *Sacred Biography: Saints and Their Biographers in the Middle Ages.* New York: Oxford University Press, 1988.

Kedar, Benjamin Z. *Crusade and Mission: European Approaches toward the Muslims.* Princeton: Princeton University Press, 1984.

Lawrence, C. H. *Medieval Monasticism: Forms of Religious Life in Western Europe in the Middle Ages.* London: Longman, 1989.

Moore, R. I. *The Formation of a Persecuting Society: Power and Deviance in Western Europe, 950–1250.* New York: Basil Blackwell, 1987.

Newman, Barbara. *Sister of Wisdom: St. Hildegard's Theology of the Feminine.* Berkeley: University of California Press, 1987.

Riley-Smith, Jonathan. *The Crusades: A Short History.* New Haven: Yale University Press, 1987.

Roth, Norman. *Jews, Visigoths and Muslims in Medieval Spain: Cooperation and Conflict.* Leiden: E.J. Brill, 1994.

Tellenbach, Gerd. *Church, State, and Christian Society at the Time of the Investiture Contest,* trans. R. F. Bennett. Oxford: Blackwell, 1959).

Ward, Benedicta. *Miracles and the Medieval Mind.* Philadelphia: University of Pennsylvania Press, 1982.

Part 5 New Paths of Order and Prophecy

Barlow, Frank. *Thomas Becket.* Berkeley: University of California Press, 1986.

Brooke, Rosalind. *The Coming of the Friars.* London: G. Allen & Unwin, 1975.

Brooke, Rosalind, and Christopher Brooke. *Popular Religion in the Middle Ages.* London: Thames & Hudson, 1985.

Chazan, Robert. *Daggers of Faith: Thirteenth-Century Christian Missionizing and Jewish Response.* Berkeley: University of California Press, 1989.

Hamilton, Bernard. *The Medieval Inquisition.* New York: Holmes & Meier, 1981.

Klaniczay, Gabor. *The Uses of Supernatural Power: The Transformation of Popular Religion in Medieval and Early-Modern Europe.* Princeton: Princeton University Press, 1990.

Lawrence, C. H. *The Friars: The Impact of the Early Mendicant Movement on Western Society.* London: Longman, 1994.

Peters, Edward. *Inquisition.* New York: Free Press, 1989.

Russell, Jeffrey B. *A History of Witchcraft, Sorcerers, Heretics, and Pagans.* London: Thames and Hudson, 1980.

Sayers, Jane. *Innocent III: Leader of Europe 1198–1216.* London: Longman, 1994.

Part 6 Change and Contact in the Late Middle Ages

Bynum, Caroline Walker. *Holy Feast and Holy Fast: The Religious Significance of Food to Medieval Women.* Berkeley: University of California Press, 1987.

Duffy, Eamon. *The Stripping of the Altars: Traditional Religion in England, 1400–1580.* New Haven, CT: Yale University Press, 1992.

Leff, Gordon. *Heresy in the later Middle Ages*. Manchester: Manchester University Press, 1967.

McFarlane, K. B. *The Origins of Religious Dissent in England*. New York: Collier, 1966.

Mollat, Guillaume. *The Popes at Avignon*. New York: Harper, 1965.

Oakley, Francis. *The Western Church in the Later Middle Ages*. Ithaca: Cornell University Press, 1979.

Tierney, Brian. *Foundations of the Conciliar Theory*. Cambridge: Cambridge University Press, 1955.

Ullmann, Walter. *The Origins of the Great Schism*. London: Burns, Oates, and Washbourne, 1948.

Index

Numbers in italics refer to readings in the text.

Aachen. *See* Aix-la-Chapelle
  See also Amma Syncletica
Abbesses (amma)
  Amma Syncletica, 130–131
  Hildegard, 369–370
  Leoba and Anglo-Saxon, 205
  Paula and Eustochium, 102
Abbots (abba), 215, 305
  individuals, 130–131, 135–136, 239,
    251, 256, 369–370
  Bernard, 369–370
Abelard, 351, 355–357, 358, 363,
    369–370, 376, 405
Abraham, 269–270, *11.4*
Abstinence. *See* Asceticism
Acts of the Apostles, 16, 19, 40, 115
Aedesius, 161
Africa and African, 28–29, 34, 53, 105,
    160–161, 165–166
  Egypt, *2.1*
  Ethiopia, *7.1*
  Nubia, *7.2, 14.4*
Afterlife. *See* Death; Resurrection
Agnes, 395
Aix-la-Chapelle (Aachen), 239
Albigensians (Cathars), 387–388,
    412–414, *18.1b*
Alcuin, *10.1*
Alexandria
  Alexandrian leaders and thinkers, 28–29,
    35, 53–54, 63–64, 66–67, 162
Alfred the Great, 216, 231–232, 238–239,
    248–249, 283–284
  Life of, *9.4, 12.1b*
  writings, *10.3*

Altar of Victory, dispute, *2.4*
Ambrose, 28, *2.4b*
Amma. *See* Abbesses
Anchoresses, anchorites, 498
Anglo-Saxons, 184–186, 194,
    231–232, 248–249,
    255–256, 263–264, 283–284,
    288–289
Anglo-Scandinavian, 284
Animism, 288
Anselm of Bec, 355, 358, 363, 405
  writings, *15.1*
Antioch, 29, 53, 66, 102
Antisemitism, 292
  See also Judaism
Anthony, Abba, 130–131, 135
Apostates, 29
Arab Islamic, 28–29, 219, 346, 511
  See also Islam
Arabia, South, 99–100, 160–161, 171
  martyrs, *7.3*
Arabic, 22, 28, 155, 171, 294, 468
Aragawi, 162
Archbishops, 248, 305, 351, 445–446,
    454, 464, 505, 526–527
Arianism (Arius), *3.3*
  spread, 13–14, 53, 162, 184, 189,
    218–219
Aristotle and Aristotelian thought, 34,
    350–351, 357–358, 363, 405
Armenians, 510–511
Asceticism, 35, 52, 54, 73, 84,
    101–102, 129–131, 135, 162,
    186, 304, 307, 322, 395,
    412–413, 491, 498, 502

Asia
  East, *7.4, 20.1, 20.2*
  South, *20.3, 24.3*
Asser, 232, 248–249, 284
  Life of Alfred, 9.4, 12.1b
Athanasius, patriarch of Alexandria, 64, 162
Augustine of Canterbury, 194
Augustine of Hippo, 101, 105–106, 215, 244, 405
  writings, *5.2*
Authority (issues and conflicts), *5.2, 9.1, 9.2, 9.3, 9.4, 13.1, 13.2, 16.1, 17.1, 18.3, 21.1, 21.2*
Averroës, 351, 363, 405
  writings, *15.3*
Averroists, 357–358
Avignon papacy, 477–478, 483, 487, 502
Axumite Kingdom, 161–162, 166, 171
  See also Africa, Ethiopia
Ælfric of Eynsham, 255–256
  sermon, *11.1*

Babylonian Captivity, 477
Baghdad, 294, 468
Baptism, 15–16, 22–23, 27, 260
  examples, *8.2, 8.3, 12.1, 19.1a, 20.3*
  rituals, *1.3, 23.1*
Bartolome de los Casas, 549
Basil of Caesarea, 84
Becket, Thomas, 445–446
  Life, 19.3
Bede, 194, 231, 239, 248
  Ecclesiastical History, 8.3
Beghards and Beguines, 321–322
Beijing. *See* Khanbaliq
Benedict of Nursia, 130, 135–136, 186
  Life, *6.2a*
Benedictines, 135–136, 370
  Rule, *6.2b*
Bernard of Clairvaux, 338, 347, 350, 369–370, 401, 405
  writings, *16.2, 16.4*
Bernard Gui, *18.1b*
Bethlehem, 102
Bible (Scripture), 13–17, 19, 34–35, 52, 58, 101–102, 239, 255–256, 375–376, 468, 487, 516
  excerpts, *1.1, 1.2*
Bishopric, 147, 306
Bishoprics, 205

Bishops
  individual, 22, 45, 64, 66, 84, 105, 147, 62, 166, 189, 205, 232, 308, 382, 431
  role, 53, 64, 162, 166, 184–185, 189, 215–216, 248, 305–308, 314–315, 506
  See also Archbishops; Partriarchs
Blessings, *11.2*
  See also Rituals
Boethius, 101, 115, 122, 239, 244
  Consolation of Philosophy, 5.4
Bonaventure, 387, 400–401, 405
  Mystical Theology, 17.3
Boneta, Na Prous, *Confession, 18.2*
Boniface, missionary to Germany, *8.4*
Boniface VIII, Pope, 413, 424, 477–478
Britain. *See* Anglo-Saxons; England
Brussels, 264
Buddhism, 178–179, 461–462
Burial. *See* Death
Byzantium, Byzantine, 13, 130, 135, 154–155, 160–161, 166, 171, 179, 215–216, 227–228, 283–284, 294, 334, 348, 490, 505–506, 510–511, 526
  See also Eastern Orthodoxy

Caesarius of Heisterbach, *19.1a*
Caliph Mahdi, *12.4*
Canossa, 308
Canterbury, 194, 317, 351, 445, 454
Cardinals, 315, 431, 483
Carolingian, 205, 227, 239, 244, 317
Catechumen, 22, 27
Cathars. *See* Albigensians
Cathedrals, 303, 369
Catherine of Siena, *22.3*
Catholicism (Roman), 13, 63–64, 154, 101, 184, 189, 215, 219, 385, 388, 405, 454, 549
Celibacy (Chastity), 73, 84, 256, 374
  See also Sexuality
Celts, 99, 184–186, 194, 231
Celtic Christianity, *8.1*
Chalcedon, Council of, 58, 66–67, 162, 166
  Creed, *3.4c*
Chants, 288, 382, 454
Charlemagne, 188, 205, 216, 227–228, 231–232, 238–240, 243, 248–249, 283–284

Charlemagne *(continued)*
  Coronation, *9.3*
  Letter, *10.1a*
Charms, 283–284, *12.2*
Chaucer, 317, 445
Chester Cycle, *23.2*
China, 13, 67, 99–100, 160–161, 178–179,
    213, 457, 462, 464–465
  See also Asia, East
Christmas, 228, 436
Circumcision, 19
Cistercian, 369
City of God, 105–106, *5.2b*
Clare of Assisi, *17.2b*
Clement of Alexandria, *2.2b,* 358, 376
Clement VII, Pope, 483
Clergy, 185, 238, 240, 243, 248, 256, 370,
    413, 430, 526
Clericis Laicos, 424
Clotilda (Clothilde), 188–189, 194
Clovis, 188–189, 194–195, 213, 215, 227
Cnut, King, 284
Columba, *8.1*
Columbus, *24.4*
Columcille, 186
Communion. *See* Eucharist
Conciliarism, 483–484
  See also Councils
Confession, 317
Confessions, 5.2a
Confucianism, 161, 178, 462
Constance Council, *21.2b*
Constantine, 28, 39–40, 45, 63–64, 185,
    189, 215–216, 218, 375
Constantinople, 29, 66, 216, 348, 511, 526
  Second Council of, 58, *3.3b*
Contemplative tradition, 84–85, 101–102,
    116, 122, 369–370, 375, 490–491,
    501–502, 505
Contrition, 431
Conversion, 14, 19, 22–23, 27, 34, 39–40,
    45, 100–101, 106, 115, 129, 147,
    161–162, 165–166, 171, 184–186,
    188–189, 194–195, 205, 213–216,
    219, 231, 238, 248, 256, 283–285,
    292, 413, 431, 457–458, 462,
    464–465, 550
  stories, *2.3, 7.2, 8.2, 8.3, 12.1*
  See also Missions
Coptic, 22, 28–29, 54, 131, 161, 166, 511
Cordoba, 357

Coronation of Charlemagne, *9.3*
Councils, 63–64, 67, 162, 189, 215–216,
    334, 388–389, 412, 52–53, 58,
    483–484, 487, 510, 511
Creatio ex nihilo, 58
Creeds, 52, 63–64, 66–67, 160, 184, *3.3,*
    3.4
Cross, 39–40, 96, 179, 263–264, *2.3,*
    11.3
Cross-cultural Interaction, *1.2, 2.4, 7.2,*
    12.1, 12.4, 14.1–4, 20.1–4, 23.1,
    24.1–4
Crusades, 303–304, 369–370, 431, 511
  accounts of, *14.1–4, 16.2*
  Albigensian, 388, 414, 431
Cyril of Alexandria, *3.4b*

Daniel, Bishop of Winchester, 205
  Letter to Boniface, 8.4a
Dante Alighieri, *21.2a*
Death and Illness, *4.1–3, 7.3, 11.2, 12.2,*
    13.4, 16.2, 19.3, 22.3, 23.2, 24.1
  See also Martyrdom
Decius, Emperor, 29, 58
Defensor Pacis, 18.3
Demons, 22, 131, 288, 516, 527
Devil, 22, 54, 131
Dhu-Nuwas, Yusuf, 171
Dialectics, 355
Dictatus Papae, 307
Dissent, 53, 475, 477
Divestment, 306, 315
Dionysius, Patriarch of Alexandria, *2.1*
Dominic and Dominicans, 386–387, 400,
    405, 414, 430–431, 502
Drama, 214, 255, 269–270, 475, 510,
    515–516
Dream of the Rood, 11.3
Dualism, 54, 413, 468
Dyophysitism, 66–67, 178–179, 294
  creed, *3.4a*

Eastern Orthodoxy (Byzantium and
    Russia), *6.4, 7.2, 9.1, 22.4, 23.3*
Ecclesiastical History, 8.3
Edwin, King of Northumbria, 194–195,
    205, 213, 215
  conversion, *8.3*
Egypt, 13, 29, 54, 63, 67, 131, 135,
    160–162, 165–166, 186, 363, 511
  See also Africa

Einhard, 232
Life of Charlemagne, 9.3a
Elves, 288–289
Emanationism, 58
England (English), 100, 184, 194, 205,
    216, 231, 239, 248–249, 255–256,
    283–284, 292, 351, 388, 445,
    454–455, 487, 490, 498, 538, 543
Ethelburga, Northumbrian queen, 194
    papal letter to, *8.3*
Ethiopia, 5, 13, 99–100, 161–162,
    165–166, 171
    See also Africa
Etienne de Bourbon, *19.1c*
Eucharist (the Mass), 15, 22, 260, 288,
    431, 454, 477–487, 510
Eucharius, hymn to, *16.5*
Eugene IV, Pope, 510–511
    Account of the Seven Sacraments, 23.1
Eugenius III, Pope, 375
Eusebius of Caesarea, 28, 39–40, 64
    Life of Constantine, 2.3
Eustochium, 102
Excommunication, 45, 308
Execrabilis decree, *21.2c*
Exile, 22, 351, 445
Exiled, 22
Exorcism, 22, 260–261, 288

Family, 28, 34, 45, 74, 84, 85, 102, 227,
    260, 261, 395, 431, 502
Fasting, 73, 131
    See also Asceticism
Felicitas, martyrdom, *4.1*
Flagellants, 531–532
Florence, Council of, 510–511
France (French), 188, 244, 283–285, 317,
    322, 334, 338, 388, 413–414, 477
Francis of Assisi, 387–388, 395–396, 400,
    413–414, 417
    will, *17.2a*
Franciscans, 322, 386–387, 395, 400–401,
    405, 412, 417, 457, 461, 464–465,
    487, 532, 543
Franco-Papal Alliance, 227
Franks, 147, 184–185, 188–189, 194, 205,
    213, 227–228, 231, 239, 243, 248,
    334, 284, 346–347
Friars, 457–458, 461, 502
    See also Dominicans; Francisicans;
        Mendicants

Frumentius, 162
Fulda, monastery, 205, 239

Galatians, 1.2
Gandersheim, 269
Garima, 162
Gelasius, Pope, *9.1a*
Gentiles, 14–16, 19, 27, 292
Germany (Germans), 184–185, 205, 269,
    306–308, 315, 322, 338, 370, 388,
    532
Ghenghis Khan, 457
Giles, Saint, 317
Gnosticism, 13–14, 52–54, 413
    writings, *3.1*
Gospel(s), 16, 19, 35, 54, 454
Gothic, 63, 184, 218, 303, 369
Goths, 218
Grammar, 239
Greek, 13, 15, 16, 22, 34–35, 54, 58,
    64, 66, 84, 101–102, 115, 122,
    155, 160, 171, 244, 348, 373,
    454
Gregory I (the Great), Pope, 58, 84, 85,
    122, 135–136, 147, 188, 189, 194,
    227, 239, 244, 248–249
    Life of Saint Benedict, 6.2a
Gregory VII, Pope, 306–308, 424
    Letter, *13.1*
Gregory XI, Pope, 483
Gregory of Nyssa, 58, 84, 122, 244
Gregory of Palamas, 491, 505–506
    writings, *22.4*
Gregory of Tours, 188–189, 227, 194
    History of the Franks, 8.2
Guthrum, 284

Healing, 16, 147, 260, 288, 317, 510
Heathens, 27, 256, 333
Heaven, 178, 478, 516
Hebrew, 15, 34, 35, 101–102, 129, 338,
    375
Helen, mother of Constantine, 39–40
Hell, 478
Henry IV, Emperor, 306–308
Henry V, Emperor, 314–315, 483
Henry II, King of England, 445
Herbs, 288, 373
Heresy, 13–14, 52–53, 412–414
    See also Heterodoxy
Hermann, Bishop of Metz, 308

Hermits, 99, 102, 129–131, 135, 185–186, 269, 370, 412, 498
Hessians, 205
Hesychasm, 505–506
Heterodoxy and Heresy, *3.1–4, 7.4, 9.2, 12.4, 17.1, 18.1–2, 21.3*
Hildegard of Bingen, 369–370, 417
  writings, *16.1, 16.3, 16.5*
Himyarites, 171
Hippolytus, 22, 260
  Baptismal Ceremony, *1.6*
Hrotsvit of Gandersheim, 269
  play *Abraham, 11.4*
Humility, 84, 115, 130, 395, 436, 490
Hungary, 338
Hymns, 430, 454, 455

Iberian Peninsula, 189, 218
  See also Spain
Iceland, 284
Icons and Iconoclasm, 129, 130, 154–155
Idols, 468
Incarnation, 35, 66, 67, 351, 468
India, 160–161, 294, 457, 464, 543
Indies, 549
Inferno, 21.1a
Innocent III, Pope, 387–388, 395, 412, 414, 424, 454, 478
  Letter, *17.1a*
Inquisition, 385, 412–414, 417, 431
Investiture, 305–308
Investiture Conflict (Papal-Imperial), *5.2, 9.1, 13.1–2, 18.3, 21.2*
Ireland. *See* Celts
Islam, *12.4, 14.3, 15.3, 20.4*
Israel, 131
Italy (Italian), 122, 189, 228, 308, 351, 395, 400, 405, 475, 477–478, 483–484, 490, 531

Jacob de Voraigne, 445
  Golden Legend, 19.3
Jacob von Königshofen, 531–532
  writings, *24.1*
Jacques de Vitry, 321–322, 430–431
  writings, *13.4, 19.1b*
James, Saint (Santiago), 317
Jarrow, 194, 205
Jean de Venette, 531–532
  writings, *24.1*

Jerome, 101–102
  Prefaces, *5.1*
Jerusalem, 29, 35, 155, 317, 334
Jews and Judaism, *1.1, 9.2, 12.3, 14.2, 15.4, 17.1, 19.1a, 20.4, 24.1*
John, 16, 17, 35, 58, 115, 130, 155, 165, 166, 239, 243, 244, 294, 375, 388, 417, 457, 458, 464, 465, 487, 490, 491, 510, 511, 526, 527, 543, 544
John's, 16, 155, 465, 526
John of Damascus, 130, 154–155, 294
  On the Divine Images, 6.4
John of Ephesus, *7.2*
John of Monte Corvino, *20.3*
John of Plano-Carpini, *20.1*
John of Ruysbroeck, *22.1*
John Scottus Eriugena, 58, 115, 239
  writings, *10.2*
Judaizers, 19
Julian (Julianus), missionary to Nubia, 166
Julian of Norwich, 490, 498–499
  Showings, 22.2
Justinian, 58, 165–166, 215–217
  Law Code, *9.1b*

Kammûna, ibn, *20.4*
Khan, 457, 462
Khanbaliq (Beijing), 457, 464
Kingship, 188, 213–219, 227–228, 231–232
  See also Monarchy, Royalty
Knighthood, 333–335, 372–373

Laity, 255, 303, 307, 317, 430, 475, 478, 515, 526
Lateran, IV Council, *17.1*, 412
Latin, 15, 22, 99, 101–102, 122, 239, 244, 248, 260–261, 348, 351, 357, 454–455, 511
Last Judgment, 58, 73, *23.2*
Law, 19, 53, 213–219, 387–389, 413, 424
Laws, 387, 424
Lay proprietorship of churches, 305
Leechbook, 12.2
Leo I, Pope, 228
Leo IX, Pope, 306–307, 483
Leo the Isaurian, Emperor, 155
Leoba, *8.4c*
Leofric Missal, 11.2b
Lepers, 322, 395
Lex Visigothorum, 9.2b

Lindisfarne, 205
Literature (Poetry, Drama, Fiction),
    11.3–4, 16.5, 19.4, 23.2, 24.3
Liturgy, 219, 260–261, 288–289, 338,
    454, 510–511, 516
    See also Ritual
Logos, 35, 66
Lollard, 487
Lollards, 487, 510
Lombards, 227, 228
Louis IX, 462

Macrina, 84–85, 122
    Life of, *4.2*
Mainz, 338
Mamluks, 511
Man-bearer, 67
Mandeville, 543–544
    Travels, 24.3
Manicheans, 413
Marie d'Oignies, 321–322, 417
    Life, 13.4
Marmoutier, 147
Marriage, 54, 84, 194, 285
Marsilius of Padua, 387, 413, 424–425,
    484
    Defensor Pacis, 18.3
Martin V, Pope, 484
Martin of Tours, Saint, 130, 147, 239, 317
    Martinellus, 6.3
Martyrdom (martyrs), 22, 28–29, 73–74,
    84, 129, 147, 161, 171–172, 317,
    412, 445, 502
Mary, Virgin, 66–67, 101
    miracles, *19.2b, 19.3*
Mass. *See* Eucharist
Materialism, 7, 54, 303, 315, 317, 387,
    395, 412–413, 499
Medicine, 260, 283–284, 357, 369–370,
    373
Meditation, 130, 147, 306, 382, 490, 498,
    505
Melkites, 294
Memorial of Symmachus, 2.4a
Mendicants (friars), 315, 385–388, 395,
    400, 412, 430, 436, 457
    See also Dominicans; Franciscans
Merovingians, 227
Messiah, 17
Military and militarism, 40, 189, 205, 232,
    333–334, 337, 346–347, 375

Milvian Bridge, Battle of, 40
Minorite (friar), 457
Minstrels, 430
Miracles, 6–7, 16, 74, 129, 147, 445
Missal, 260
Missions and missionaries, *7.1, 7.2, 7.4,
    8.3, 8.4, 20.1, 20.2, 20.3*
Monarchy, concept of, 385, 388, 412, 424,
    477–478
Monastic impulse, *6.1–2, 8.1, 13.4, 17.2,
    19.2, 22.3*
Monasticism, 84, 129–131, 135, 185–186,
    248, 370, 506
Mongols, 179, 457, 458, 461–462, 464,
    526
Monica, mother of Augustine of Hippo,
    106
Monophysitism, 66–67, 161–162, 166, 294
Monotheism, 45, 64, 161, 294, 457, 468,
    505
Montanists, 35
Moscow, 526
Moses Maimonides, 351, 363, 405
    Guide of the Perplexed, 15.4
Motherhood of God, 499
Muhammad, 294, 468
Music, 369–370, 382, 430, 454
Muslim, 155, 218, 284, 294, 304, 334,
    346, 357
Muslims, 284, 317, 333, 334, 338, 347,
    385, 462
Mysticism, 115, 303, 322, 400, 475, 491
Mysticism and Visionary Literature, *4.1,
    5.3, 11.3, 13.4, 16.4, 22.1–4*

Nag Hammadi, 54
Najarân, 171
Neoplatonism, 101, 115, 244, 363, 490,
    491, 505
Nestorianism. *See* Dyophysitism
Nestorius, 66–67
Nicea, Council of, 58, 63–64, 184, 189,
    215
Nicene Creed, 3.3b
Non-Chalcedon, 67, 166
    See Chalcedon, Council of
Normandy and Normans, 283, 284–285,
    308, 351
Northumbria, 194, 205, 239, 248
Norway, 531, 538
Novellae of Justinian, *9.1a*

Novgorod, 526
Nubia (Nubian), 161, 165–166, 348
Nuns, 130, 205, 269, 322, 374, 382

Origen, 52, 58–59, 73, 85, 96
  writings, *3.2*
Orthodoxy, defined, 13–14, 52–54,
  387–388, 412–413
Orthodoxy, Eastern. *See* Eastern
  Orthodoxy
Ostrogoths, 122
Otherworldly, 28–29, 34, 52–54, 84, 116,
  129–130
Our Lady's Tumbler, 19.2

Paganism, 27, 29, 35, 58, 97, 194, 205,
  288, 468
Palamism, 506
Palestine, 15, 17, 40, 160, 333, 338, 347
Pantaleon, 162
Papacy, 215–217, 305–315, 387–389,
  412–414, 477–478, 483–484
Papal theories, *9.1, 13.1–2, 16.1, 17.1,*
  18.3, 21.1
Paris, 400, 405, 424, 431, 483
Parousia, 28
Paschal II, Pope, *13.2*
Patriarch, 28, 29, 162,
Patriarchs, 28–29, 53, 162, 166, 216, 284,
  294, 506
Patrick, 185
Paul (Saul of Tarsus), 16, 19, 115, 218,
  292
  Letter to the Galatians, *1.2*
Paula, 102
Penance and penitence, 317, 445
Penitentials, 214, 531
Pentecost, 454
Pepin the Short, 205, 227–228
Perfecti, 413
Periphyseon, 10.2
Perpetua, 73–74, 84, 172, 186, 417
  Martyrdom, *4.1*
Persecution, 27–29, 39, 58, 67, 74, 84, 129,
  162, 171, 292, 338, 363, 370, 376, 531
Persia (Persian), 13, 161, 171, 178, 294,
  413, 511
Petrarch, *21.1b*
Philosophy, 35, 64, 122, 239, 244, 294,
  350–351, 355, 357–358, 363,
  369–370

Pietro Quirini, Travels, *24.2*
Pilgrimage and pilgrims, 130, 147,
  303, 304–307, 317, 333–334,
  337, 347–348, 372, 445, 446,
  531
Pilgrim's Guide to Santiago de
  Compostela, 13.3
See also Martin of Tours, *Martinellus*
Pisa, Council of, *21.2a*
Pius II, Pope, 483–484
  Decree *Execrabilis, 21.2c*
Plague, 531–532
Plato, 34, 84, 115–116, 129
Poetry, 122, 147, 186, 263–264, 269–270,
  338, 377, 382, 455
Polytheism, 27
Pope. *See* Papacy
Popular Religion, *6.3, 11.1–2, 12.2, 13.3,*
  19.1–3, 23.3
Poverty, 84, 130–131, 387, 395–396,
  412–414, 417, 487, 491, 502
Prayer, 131, 260–261, 491, 498, 506
Preachers and preaching, 256, 369–370,
  388, 413–414, 417, 430–431
Prester John, 543–544
Priests and priesthood, 215, 238–239,
  255–256, 260–261, 288, 305, 317,
  370, 388, 413, 417, 430–431, 477,
  498, 510
  individuals, 34, 63, 155
Prisons (jails), 58, 74–84, 122, 502
Prophecy and Order, 303–304
Prophetic, 74, 303, 304, 306, 370, 376,
  385, 386, 412
Prophets, 129, 375, 468
Proslogion, 15.1
Protestant (Reformation), 64, 105, 475,
  487
Pseudo-Dionysius the Areopagite, 101,
  115–116, 244, 490–491, 505
  writings, *5.3*
Purgatory, 516

Rabbi Ephraim, *14.2b*
Rationalism, 34–35, 105–106, 350–351,
  358, 363, 401, 405
Rationality, modes of, 6–7
Recared, Visigothic king, 219
Recluses. *See* Hermits
Reconquista, 317
Redemption, 269

Reform, 205, 248, 256, 303–307, 314–315, 317, 369–370, 385–388, 412, 475, 477, 483–484, 502

Reincarnation, 58

Reintegration, 58

Relics and reliquaries, 73, 99, 129–130, 147, 154, 317, 526

Renaissances, 84, 213, 238–240, 243–244, 248, 526
    Italian, 413, 475, 478, 484

Resurrection and the afterlife, 16, 58–59, 73–74, 84–85, 96–97, 130

Revelation, 16, 34–35, 54, 350, 490

Ritual, 4, 13, 14, 16, 22, 23, 54, 219, 260, 283, 284, 510

Rituals, *1.3, 11.2, 12.2, 19.4, 23.1*

Robert of Clari, *14.4*

Rollo, 285

Rome, 19, 22, 29, 39, 45, 102, 106, 161, 185, 189, 227, 228, 238, 305, 308, 317, 348, 424, 431, 477, 483, 484, 502

Royalty (kings and emperors), *9.1–4, 13.1–2, 18.3*

Russia (Russian), 510, 526
    See also Eastern Orthodoxy

Ruthwell cross, 264

Sacraments, 260, 510, 511

Saints' lives, *2.1, 4.1–2, 6.2–4, 7.1, 8.4, 13.3, 19.3, 23.3*

Salama, Abba, 162

Salvation, 19, 58, 269, 304, 424

Samaritan, 16–17

Santiago de Compostela, 317, 348
    Pilgrim's Guide, 13.3

Saxons, 184–185, 205

Scandinavians, 231, 255, 284, 526

Schism, 475, 477–478, 483–484, 502

Scholasticism, 303–304, 350–351, 375–376, 387, 424, 487

Scripture. *See* Bible

Sefer Zekhirah, 14.2b, 372

Sermons, 101, 155, 214, 255–256, 369–370, 376, 388–389, 430, 436

Severus el-Ashmunein, *2.1,* 166

Sexuality, 54, 84, 129, 131, 269, 374

Simeon of Beth Arsham, *7.3*

Simony, 305, 477–478

Sin and sinners, 22, 58, 260, 269, 478, 499, 531

Slavs (Slavic), 506, 526

Solomon bar Simson, *14.2a*

Song of Songs, 16.4

Soul and body, 54, 58, 73, 106, 130–131, 260, 317

Spain, 189, 218, 317, 334, 351, 357, 363

Sparkling Stone, 22.1

Spirituality, 28, 147, 269, 303, 305–307, 369–370, 375, 385, 395, 401, 412, 475, 478, 490, 510

Stephen Langton, 454

Summa Theologica, 17.4

Sweden, 538

Symmachus, *2.4*

Symphonia, 16.5

Synagogue, 283, 292

Syncletica, 130–131, 135

Syncretic, 27

Syria (Syrian, Syriac), 13, 22, 53–54, 67, 102, 135, 161–162, 171, 178, 269, 294

Taoism, 178, 462

Tauberbischofsheim, 205

Templars, 347,.369, 372

Temptations, 131

Tertullian, 28, 34–35, 376
    writings, *2.2*

Thalia of Arius, 3.3a

Theodora, Empress, 165–166

Theodoric, 122, 189

Theodosius, 45, 53, 216, 218

Theology, *2.2, 3.2, 5.1–2, 5.4, 10.1–3, 11.1, 15.1–4, 16.3–4, 17.3–4, 21.3*

Thomas Aquinas, 357, 387, 400
    writings, *17.4*

Timothy, Patriarch of the East Syrian Church, *12.4*

Tombs, 73, 96, 317, 445, 446

Towns, 303–306

Trade, 161, 171, 178, 284, 457, 538

Tradition and Diversity, 5, 13–14

Transubstantiation, 477, 487–488

Travel. *See* Cross-cultural Interaction

Treaties, 231, 284–285

Trinity, 63, 288, 294, 468

Turks, 333, 372, 511

Typological, 102, 256

Universe A and Universe B, 6–7

Universities, 350, 363, 375, 387, 424

Urban II, Pope, *14.1*
Urbanization, 303
Usama ibn Munqidh, *14.3*

Vernacular language, 239, 248
Vikings, 205, 231, 248, 283–285
Virginity, 269
Visigoths, 189, 215, 218–219
Visions, 74, 322, 370, 417, 490, 498–499,
    502
Vows, 307, 369, 370

Waldensians, 387, 412–413, 417
    Waldo, *18.1*
Warfare, 130, 334–335, 346, 372, 475
Wearmouth, 194, 205

Wessex, 231, 248
Wickliff, 477, 487–488, 490
Wickliff's Wicket, *21.3*
William of Ruysbruck, *20.2*
Willibald, 205
Women, *1.1, 2.3, 4.1–2, 6.1,
    7.2–3, 8.2–4, 11.4, 13.4,
    16.1, 16.3, 16.5, 17.2, 18.2,
    22.2–3*
Worldview, defined, 6
Worship, 22, 27, 96, 154, 155, 382

Yin and Yang, 178

Zachary, Pope, 228
Zoroastrianism, 413, 468

Dr. Karen Louise Jolly is Associate Professor of History at the University of Hawai'i at Mānoa, where she teaches medieval European history, the history of Christianity, and world history. She received her Ph.D. from the University of California at Santa Barbara, studying under both Jeffrey B. Russell and C. Warren Hollister. Her research specialities are in Anglo-Saxon history, popular religion, and magic. She has an earlier book, *Popular Religion in Late Saxon England: Elf Charms in Context* (Chapel Hill: University of North Carolina Press, 1996).